INDIA'S FOREIGN POLICY
MODI 2.0
Challenges and Opportunities

INDIA'S FOREIGN POLICY MODI 2.0
Challenges and Opportunities

Editor

Sudhir Singh

In Association with
SOCIETY FOR SOCIAL EMPOWERMENT, NEW DELHI

INDIA'S FOREIGN POLICY MODI 2.0: *Challenges and Opportunities*
Editor: *Sudhir Singh*

ISBN 978-81-942837-7-5

First Published in 2020

Copyright © SOCIETY FOR SOCIAL EMPOWERMENT, NEWDELHI

All rights reserved. No part of this publication may be reproduced, stored in a retrieval system, or transmitted in any form or by any means, electronic, mechanical, photocopying, recording or otherwise, without the prior written permission of the Publisher.

Disclaimer: The views and opinions expressed in the book are the individual assertion of the Authors. The Publisher does not take any responsibility for the same in any manner whatsoever. The same shall solely be the responsibility of the Authors.

Published by
PENTAGON PRESS LLP
206, Peacock Lane, Shahpur Jat,
New Delhi-110049
Phones: 011-64706243, 26491568
Telefax: 011-26490600
email: rajan@pentagonpress.in
website: www.pentagonpress.in

Printed at Aegean Offset Printers, Greater Noida, U.P.

CONTENTS

	Preface	ix
	About the Contributors	xxvii
1	Indo–Iran Relationship: Challenges and Opportunities in the Changing Context *Aaradhana Singh*	1
2	Changing Political Matrix in Nepal: India's Search for Continuity Amidst Change *Alok Kumar Gupta and Vandana Mishra*	16
3	A New Foreign Policy Agenda for Modi: "Look West" *Alokka Dutta*	32
4	Modi's Foreign Policy: A Changing Scenario on Indo-US Relations *Amulya K Tripathy and Roshni Kujur*	46
5	Indian Diaspora as a Factor in Indo–Gulf Relations *Anisur Rahman and Naziya Naweed*	62
6	The Growing Chinese Dominance Potential Security Concerns for India and the Region: With Special Reference to South China Sea *Chandra Mohan Upadhyay*	72
7	Modi Government's Afghan Policy *D. Gopal*	86
8	Russia's Role in Asia-Pacific *Deepak Yadav*	97
9	Revisiting Modi's "Act East Policy": The Case of South Korea *Geetha Govindasamy*	111

10	India's Participation in United Nations Police (UN Police) for Post-Conflict Reconstruction: A Critical Analysis *Jayshree Tandekar*	124
11	Narendra Modi: Reconstructing India's Foreign Policy Objectives *K. Jayaprasad*	141
12	India's Soft Power Approaches in Southeast Asia: Challenges and Expectations *Koushiki Dasgupta*	154
13	Strategic Convergence in Indo-Japan Relations: Emerging Trajectory in the 'Act East' Horizon *Mohor Chakraborty*	162
14	Rise of the 'Islamic State' and Its Implications *Nazmul Arifeen*	183
15	Great Game in Central Asia: Where Does India Stand? *Pramod Kumar Sharma*	203
16	Sino-India Bustle for Securing Hydrocarbons in Africa: Zero-Sum or Win-Win? *Pranav Kumar*	212
17	Tibetan Struggle for Right to Self-determination and India–China Relation: A National Security Perspective *Rakhee Viswambharan*	226
18	India and Australia: Closer and Closer *RFI Smith*	234
19	Maritime Dimensions of China's Maritime Silk Route and India's Act East Policy *R S Vasan*	252
20	India–Singapore Bilateral Relation *S. Manivasakan*	270
21	"Friends, Allies and Politics": Some Musings on India-Latin American Relations *Sabu Thomas*	282
22	Indian Diaspora: A Reckoning Force, A Lobby Group, and a Friend of NDA–II Government in Stabilizing Relations between India and other Nations *Salu Dsouza*	291

23	India-China-US Relations: Prospects for a Strategic Triangle *Shyna V V*	301
24	Indo-Pak Relations: Contemporary Challenges *Sudhir Singh*	319
25	India–Taiwan Relations: Looking towards the Future *Sumit Kumar*	333
26	The US Policy Towards Asia Pacific and India's Maritime Security *Suresh R.*	351
27	Contemporary Indo-Bhutanese Relations: Issues of Concern for the Modi Government *Unnikrishnan G.*	360
28	Sustainable India-Australia Partnership Calls for Rationalization of their Expectations vis-à-vis Preferences *Y. Yagama Reddy*	369
	Index	387

PREFACE

The birth of India took place after a long struggle against one of the most powerful colonial power of the contemporary world in 1947. The first Prime Minister of India, Jawaharlal Nehru had two options in the immediate aftermath of independence: first, to enter into an alliance with either of the two existing blocs namely Capitalist block led by the United States and the Communist bloc led by the USSR; second, to maintain neutrality. Nehru opted for neutrality. The prevailing global security architecture had presented an extremely complex situation in the wake of Cold War that was in its initial phase. Nehru's embrace of neutrality led to the emergence of Non-Aligned Movement (NAM). Although this decision has been under consistent attack and also has been criticized on various counts about its failures towards not serving the purpose particularly at several core national interests fronts. Nehru was abided by the Wilsonian idealism and kept the egalitarian agenda of national interests under the carpet.

It is evident with the fact that Tibet issue was taken up firstly in the United Nations by Pakistan because Nehru was apprehensive if India will raise it at international platforms than China will be upset.

In the 1950s Tibet was boiling and needed India's support but Nehru was optimistic enough to believe in goodwill and justice will prevail in Chinese leaders and Justice will be delivered to Tibetans. This was not only a Himalayan blunder and converted India into a weak nation for decades to come in the power architecture of Asia. Nehru avoided Patel's Kautilyan advice on Tibet. Few years before 1954 treaty in which Nehru surrendered Tibet to China, Sardar Patel advised Nehru not to believe China. Writing to Nehru on 7th November 1950, weeks before his death, Patel warned Nehru that

> "China is no longer divided. It is united and strong. Recent and bitter history also tells us that communism is no shield against imperialism and that the Communism are as good or as bad imperialists as any other. Chinese ambitions in this respect not only cover the Himalayan slopes on our side but also include parts of Assam.

... Chinese irredentism or imperialism are different from the expansionism or imperialism of the western powers. The former has a cloak of ideology which makes it ten times more dangerous. In the guise of ideological expansion lie concealed radical, national or historical claims."[1]

The Chinese attack of 1962 was an ample proof of the adverse impact of that policy, when India was face to face with the situation akin to the theory of Prison Dilemma in international politics; i.e. either to seek the support of USA or should it align with USSR.

India could not have a strong international personality despite the strong legacy of promoter of peace, non-violence, and international brotherhood at the global level. The collapse of the USSR provided the possibility to India to acquire a strong international personality. Consequently, from P.V. Narsimha Rao to Modi government every successive regime has kept the agenda of national interest above the egalitarian agenda of idealism in the realm of foreign policy. The process of globalization has also been a push factor in this regard in international politics. The Pokhran-II (May 1998) further emboldened the Indian might in the realm of international politics. The whole world was compelled to concede Indian might but not as the promoter of peace but also as a power to be reckoned with, which could assert itself if necessary, for protecting national interest and sustainable development.

However, the erstwhile dynamics of the international politics has taken a new turn after 11 September 2001 terrorist attack on World trade center, in the USA. This attack has changed the whole gamut of international politics and also proved that even the US is not safe vis-à-vis terrorist attacks. This also challenged the US claim as only hegemony in the world. The advent of multi-polarity in international politics has provided a new impetus to the emergence of India as one of the dominant poles. At the same time, it has left many challenges for the formulators of foreign policy to cope and respond adequately the changing circumstances.

Since its inception Indian foreign policy has been obsessed with Pakistan and China. We have fought three and half war with Pakistan by now and one war with China. It is also true that Pakistan has been partially successful towards making India bleed at thousand places since the defeat of 1971 war. Not only in Punjab, Kashmir but also throughout India they have been creating troubles. In the backdrop of NATO withdrawal from Afghanistan, the threat of terror has increased. Pulwama (2019) has proved this impending danger. In April 2019, many churches and hotels across Sri Lanka were attacked on the occasion of Easter and over 200 people were killed. This terror attack was owned by the ISIS.

Consequently, in contemporary world, Indian policy-makers have to achieve many important goals to transform India into a dominant power in the international system. All these development makes it imperative for Indian policy-makers to reformulate the contours of foreign policy. The first challenge before the policy-makers is to decentralize the focus (Pakistan and China) of erstwhile foreign policy and articulate the national interest in broader perspectives of changing international scenario. There are many arenas in the globe which has remained away from the radar of our foreign policy. Prime Minister Modi visited over 84 countries during his 1st term and covered many unattended countries and ensure our national interests. He has returned for the second term (2019-24) and this sustainability is bound to accelerate proactive foreign policy.

Right from its inception in 1991 not a single PM has visited all 5 countries of Central Asia which PM Modi has visited within a week together in July 2015. Central Asia is extremely important for the promotion of our national interests. In May 2019, PM Modi returned into power again for second term (2019-2024). President of Kyrgyzstan was present to witness his swearing in. He is additionally chairman of the regional organization SCO in which India has also been admitted as member. It vindicates the importance of Central Asia in PM Modi's foreign policy commitment.

Energy security is of utmost importance. Kazakhstan, Turkmenistan and Uzbekistan are endowed with enormous hydrocarbon reserves. Connectivity through the North-South Transport Corridor featured in Modi's speeches in both countries as much as the impending implementation of the two gas pipelines. These are implementable but hinges on the political situation in Pakistan and Afghanistan.[2] Iran could be important facilitator of our interests in Afghanistan and Central Asia. PM Modi had visited entire Central Asia in 2015 and pledged a lot, now it is the time to implement possible assurances to promote our national interests. In return many central Asian leaders paid the return visits to New Delhi and this process has accelerated our relations with this important region.

India had organized Africa Summit in New Delhi in October 2015; perhaps it is maiden largest gathering of African leaders in 21st century after March 1947 Afro-Asia summit at New Delhi. In the backdrop of growing importance of Africa due to abundance of natural resources and engagements of important global powers, it is a Himalayan step to engage Africa in a massive way. It is an open secret that energy security remains core of the saga of our growth and needless to say that Africa could be a good source of energy security in coming decades. It is our moral accountability to help Africa to follow the ideas mooted during our freedom struggle to cement South-South cooperation. Fortunately, India is positioned today by all counts to provide massive support to Africa in their quest for peace, stability and sustainable development.

Till the end of the cold war, our foreign policy formulators have been obsessed with Pakistan and later on China. These countries are important for us, but we must realize that we have already emerged as an important Asian power and emerging as a global power. For the realization of our global power aspirations we must decentralize our focal attention towards all regions of the globe. Modi government has understood this reality and acting with this vision. During his 1st term, Prime Minister Modi has already visited 84 countries. Senior & Junior foreign ministers have covered all continents. Many critics are viewing PM's visit to many countries in a negative way, but they must understand that India's expanding global profile demands more high-profile visits to facilitate our national interests.

Since the days of Kautilaya, maximization of national interest has remained the sole concern of bilateral relationship. There are no permanent friends or foes in international politics and the only permanent thing is commonality of interests.

Narasimha Rao government initiated "Look East Policy". India is well connected with its immediate neighbor Southeast Asia on various counts. Buddhism is one of the prominent religions of this region that has its origin in India. There are enough commonalities in the field of culture too. However, there remains a tremendous scope for more economic, technological and cultural cooperation between India and nation-states of Southeast Asia. Our relationship with ASEAN countries has huge imprint of our overall foreign policy. Modi government has converted 'Look East Policy' into 'Act East Policy' in 2014 and extended it from Myanmar to Australia.

China is concerned of India's look east policy and calls it as being borne out of a misguided "fear of China," reflecting "a lack of understanding of the (Peoples Liberation Army's) PLAs strategic ambitions."[3]

Compliance of the norms of international law has remained core concern of ASEAN & East Asian countries in South & East China Seas. China has declared both Sea's as their backyard lakes and unwilling to obey the norms on UNCLOS (1982). Despite high profile trade relations with China, ASEAN countries ($

587.87 billion dollor in 2018-19) are concerned very much for the compliance of international laws in this dispute. The Philippines is also a disputant country against China over South China Sea. Its President's concern about it is worth mentioning here:

> "The Philippines is one of the disputant countries against China over South China Sea. Philippines President Benigno S. Aquino III called for nations around the world to do more to support the Philippines in resisting China's assertive claims to the seas near his country, drawing a comparison to the West's failure to support Czechoslovakia against Hitler's demands for Czech land in 1938.
>
> Like Czechoslovakia, the Philippines face demands to surrender territory piecemeal to a much stronger foreign power and needs more robust foreign support for the rule of international law if it is to resist.
>
> If we say yes to something, we believe is wrong now, what guarantee is there that the wrong will not be further exacerbated down the line?"
>
> He said. "At what point do you say, 'Enough is enough'? Well, the world has to say it—remember that the Sudetenland was given in an attempt to appease Hitler to prevent World War II.[4]
>
> Tokyo and Manila are even more expressive about their willingness to uphold territorial claims, no matter the cost. On many occasions, Abe has vowed publicly that he will 'never make concessions' over the sovereignty of the Diaoyus/Sankakus and will defend 'Japanese territory at all costs."[5]

South China Sea has emerged as a bitter bone of flashpoint between China and the disputant countries of ASEAN. It has emerged as an important potential global flashpoint. The Nation of Bangkok warns in an editorial that:

> "If the current tension continues in South China Sea, especially between the Philippines and China, it could lead to an all-out war. This is not an alarmist's warning but a real concern. With poisonous rhetoric and growing tension, there is a possibility that conflicting parties would cross the line. This could be a result of miscalculation."[6]

Chinese behavior in the back drop of their acquisition of economic power has become unruly which is bound to create conflicts. China wanted to dominate Asia as America is dominating the globe but wanted multiple power structures at the global level. For Mearsheimer, 'rising powers tend to seek regional hegemony and China is heading in this direction'.[7] They are violating it in South and East China Sea. In the case of Tibet too, China has violated all norms of the international standards to respect human rights. The prevailing situation in the Asia-Pacific is vindication of this Chinese attitude which is not only detrimental for the stability and development of the region but a looming threat to global peace as well.

In the backdrop of changing security architecture in Asia, deepening Indo-Japan bonhomie is interesting. Indo-Japan relations have grown phenomenally since Pokhran-2 (1998) and due to convergences of interests have emerged as one of the strategic fulcrum of India's newly launched ' Act East Policy'. Modi government has upgraded zero sum game policy with China. For that purpose, Japan has emerged as a golden asset for India. In his August-September 2014 Japan visit, PM Modi and Japanese PM, Shinzo Abe proved that they have immense convergences and are bound to cooperate. PM Modi and PM Abe met more than 11 times during last five years. Japan, India and United States has given the nomenclature of JAI and holding trilateral meetings regularly. The triangle of Japan, United States and India has given uneasy momentum for the Chinese.

PM Abe has emerged as longest serving PM of Japan and has been in the helm of power since 2012. He has vowed to repeal 9th article of the Japanese constitution and if he will do that it will pave the way to ease Japan to take active participation in the strategic activities in Asia. According to Kenji Hiramatsu, Japan's Ambassador to India, "Our relationship is perhaps best in our history. Many things have happened in the investments, trade and business fields. But now I think security and strategic relations are rapidly catching up." PM Abe stated in October 2018 that a strong India is beneficial for Japan…security and strategic relations are rapidly catching up.[8] Chinese are extremely jealous from this deepening relationship.

The growing bonhomie between United States and India has created a situation akin of 'Prisoner's Dilemma' for China. It was vindicated with the Chinese consent of the designation of Masood Azhar as global terrorist by the United Nations in May 2019, which was blocked by China 4 times since 2009. China is willing to keep India neutral and does not wish her to go to close embrace of the United States.

In August 2019, Modi government scrapped special status of Kashmir but Chinese despite visits of high-profile Pakistani leaders were guarded when they suggested both to settle the problem on the basis of existing bilateral framework of resolving disputes.

After Pakistani foreign minister Beijing visit in August 2019 in the backdrop of scrapping of article 370, joint statement stressed "China recognises that the Kashmir dispute must be properly resolved "based on the UN Charter, relevant

UN Security Council resolutions and bilateral agreement".[9] China is willing to keep India neutral and does not wish her to go to close embrace of the United States.

According to eminent strategic thinker Pervez Hoodboy, Pakistan status at the global stage has reduced a lot:

> "Third, patrons have their own interests. To call a friendship higher than the Himalayas, deeper than the oceans, and stronger than steel may be good poetry. But patrons act after a cold calculation of losses and gains. China's silence on Kashmir and its climb-down in May at the United Nations on Masood Azhar's blacklisting shows just how carefully it weighs things. Saudi Arabia, on which Pakistan pins its hopes, went along with India."[10]

The editorial comment of the prestigious Pakistani daily 'Dawn' comments vindicated Pakistan's isolation on this issue.

"The crisis in India-held Kashmir could trigger global consequences, yet the world has not responded to Pakistan's urgent exhortations with the level of robustness the situation warrants. Instead of full-throated condemnation, there is language of equivocation.

Indeed, some countries, most notably the US and UAE, have even gone along with India's brazenly false assertion that stripping Kashmir, an internationally recognised disputed territory, of its special status is an "internal matter". Saudi Arabia's bland reaction thus far avoids expressing any opinion whatsoever."[11]

"It's a game-changer in Indian politics... It's not like a third party can get India to walk back its decision. The deed is done," says the usually strong India critic, Michael Kugelman, at the Asia Program in Woodrow Wilson Center in Washington DC.[12]

Despite Pakistan's all round efforts and British Member of Parliament protest, United Arab Emirates has conferred its highest national award to PM Modi. Pakistani diplomacy has been frustrated after it. Even Muslim world is not believing the Pakistani version about Kashmir. It is vindicated with the following statement of Pakistani foreign minister Shah Mehmood Qureshi:[13]

> "International relations are above religious sentiments. The UAE and India have a history of relations in connection with investment. However, I will soon have a meeting with the UAE foreign minister to inform him about the prevailing situation in India-held Kashmir," he said while responding to media queries regarding the grant of the UAE's highest civilian award to Indian Prime Minister Narendra Modi."

In April 2018 in the backdrop of Doklam (2017) crisis, Wuhan summit (April 2018) took place between PM Modi and the Chinese President Xi. It was reflected in this unusual summit between two durable rivals that Chinese are willing to keep India in loop despite widening trust deficit. In June 2019, both leaders met at Bishkek and pledged to meet for Wuhan kind of summit in India in later part of 2019 and it took place at Mahabalipuram near Chennai in October 2019. China has provided support to Pakistan in the backdrop of abrogation of article 370 but it was not taken seriously by the United Nations and larger international community.

During Cold War era India-United States relations were termed as 'Estranged Democracies' which has been converted as "Engaged Democracies' in 21st century. President George W. Bush (2000-2008) contributed immensely to cement these ties.

President Bush and his Indian interlocutors were careful not to define their relations in terms of opposition to China. Bush's surprising warmth to India, his willingness to invest huge political capital in transforming the bilateral relationship, and his courageous decision to facilitate nuclear energy trade with India were widely interpreted as driven by a desire to make India a counterweight to a rising China. While there were no official proclamations to this effect, a key architect of Bush's India policy, Robert Blackwill, would later reveal the centrality of the China factor. "President George W. Bush based his transformation of US-India Relations on the core strategic principle of democratic India as a key factor in balancing the rise of Chinese power", he noted. He made it clear that this was not based on the concept of 'containing' China. Nonetheless, Blackwill added, without this China factor at the fore 'the Bush Administration would not have negotiated the Civil Nuclear Agreement and the Congress would not have approved it.'[14]

During President Barrack Obama's tenure (2009-2016) the Bush era's warmth has declined a bit but again it had improved in the second half of his tenure. The warmth President Obama has shown during PM Modi's September 2014 United States visit was self-explanatory. China has been utmost jealous of this cooperation among democracies. President Obama became maiden US president to visit India twice and maiden to become chief guest for Republic Day functions in January 2015. President Donald Trump has taken over in January 2017 and despite many odds sustained the relationship. His administration has started 2+2 exclusive dialogue with India in September 2018. In the backdrop of prevailing full-blown trade war with China since July 2018, it is extremely important. US Secretary of state stressed that designation of Massod Azhar as global terrorist by the UN is the diplomatic victory of the United States. Given the level of bonhomie between Pakistan and the United States during the Cold War and even post-Cold War, it is unique. Even US supported Indian airstrike at Balakot, Pakistan in the backdrop of Pulwama terror attack by the JeM in February 2019. According to Munir Akram, Pakistan's representative at the UN,

> "Pakistan is near if not in the eye of the brewing Sino-US storm. Neutrality is not an option for Pakistan. The US has already chosen India as its strategic partner to counter China across the 'Indo-Pacific' and South Asia. The announced US South Asia policy is based on Indian domination of the subcontinent. Notwithstanding India's trade squabbles with Donald Trump, the US establishment is committed to building up India militarily to counter China.
>
> On the other hand, strategic partnership with China is the bedrock of Pakistan's security and foreign policy. The Indo-US alliance will compel further intensification of the Pakistan-China partnership. Pakistan is the biggest impediment to Indian hegemony over South Asia and the success of the Indo-US grand strategy. Ergo, they will try to remove or neutralise this 'impediment'."[15]

PM Modi met President Trump twice in the backdrop of abrogation of article 370 from Kashmir. PM Modi and President Trump jointly addressed rally of the people of the Indian origin in Houston (Texas) in September 2019. President Trump condemned terrorism in this rally and outlined on strengthening the bond among democratic countries. Democracy has become an instrument of fear for the Chinese especially after 1989 student movement in Beijing. Chinese have adopted Globalization in 1978 but forgotten that it has two components and without freedom it will not be sustainable for a longer period of time. Hong Kong has witnessed democratic movement in the middle of 2019. Chinese think otherwise and always apprehensive that success of democracy in their next door may facilitate the wind of democracy in China as well. Coincidently majority of ASEAN countries, United States, Japan, South Korea, Australia and India all have adopted democracy as a way of governance.

Global Times, the mouth piece of Chinese regime had expressed this frustration in December 2010. "'The title of "the biggest democratic nation" looks like a glass of red wine enjoyed together by India and the West. But it doesn't generate anything substantial that is of India's national interests. With a huge population and much work left to be done in developing the economy, perhaps India won't get too drunk to act superior in front of China, because such superiority will delight India much less than it delights the West.' See who wins the Dragon-elephant contention".[16]

Australia is also close to this region and the relations between India and Australia has been smooth so far, but scope is there for further deepening. PM Modi visited Australia in November 2014 after a gap of 28 years and this visit has further deepened the relationship. United States and Australia has been durable allies since decades and sustained it even today. The arc of democracy (United States, Japan, India and Australia) has emerged as a new realignment in Indo-Pacific. Despite high profile trade volume between China and ASEAN, basic reason of the formation of the ASEAN (1967) was containment of China and still it is prevailing reality. It could be felt in the prevailing trust deficit between disputant ASEAN countries and China over South China Sea issue. Australia is another important country in the Indo-Pacific region which wanted multipolar Asia. Australia-India relations has also improved particularly in the backdrop of November 2014. It was the maiden Indian PM's visits after three decades and has accelerated the pace of deepening of bilateral relationship. Australia is India's maritime neighbour and our deepening bonhomie has saddened China. India has been engaged in joint maritime exercises with coincidently democratic countries. (Japan, United States, Australia and many ASEAN countries). This has created apprehensions in Chinese strategist thinkers. China's naval watchers have in particular been suspicious of naval exercises involving India, Japan, Australia and the United States, ostensibly aimed at balancing Chinese maritime power in the Asian littorals.[17]

China has emerged a critical foreign policy challenges for India. Despite high profile trade at the volume of $ 87 billion in the FY 2018-19, trust deficit is prevailing heavily in favor of China. ($ 53 billion dollor in 2018)

In recent years China has clubbed its Pakistan policy with it India's policy. Since 2006 every South Asia visiting Chinese leader is compulsorily visiting[18] Islamabad. India demanded that China respect India's 'core national interests' in relation to its territorial integrity, in much the same way that Delhi does to Beijing on Tibet and Taiwan. This new equivalence between Tibet and Kashmir marks a new moment in the long-running territorial disputes between India and China.[19] Weeks before September 2014 Chinese President's India visit, former foreign minister, late Sushma Swaraj demanded that Beijing must respect Indian sensitiveness if it wishes that New Delhi will reciprocate. This was again retreated by India in August 2019 when India bifurcated Jammu & Kashmir and made Ladakh union territory.

General Zia-ul-Haq started to use terror as an instrument of Pakistan's foreign policy and till date it has remained sustainable. Right from the commencement (2001) of 'Operation Enduring Freedom' in Afghanistan, Pakistan has remained the recipient of largest largesse from the United States due to its participation in 'global war against terror'. Despite that it gave safe havens to Osama Bin Laden and Mullah Omar. More importantly, as the senior most US military officer in 2011, Admiral Mike Mullen, told the US Congress, the Haqqani network is a "veritable arm of the Pakistan's Inter-Services Intelligence Agency."[20] Pakistani military has sustained the unique Afghan policy since 1979 not to stabilize Afghanistan and use it as rear base. Pakistani army is the ultimate boss and has taken a policy decision that no truce will be with India. Military supported terror groups kept attacking important Indian targets since last two decades. According to Morell CIA former Deputy Director

> "What they don't realise is that it's impossible to keep those terrorist groups under control. And that eventually comes back to bite you. You know, I believe that Pakistan, at the end of the day, maybe the most dangerous country in the world."[21]

In December 2014, NATO forces have withdrawn from Afghanistan. Afghan President, Ashraf Ghani has taken some conciliatory steps to garner Pakistani support for peace but since 2009 every year more than 2500 innocent people have been killed, and Pakistani invisible hands are responsible for these deadly attacks. Combined right from 2009 till July 2015, 16,874 people have been killed in terror related violence. One estimate puts the number of conflict-related deaths at more than 40,000 this year (2018) almost equal to the combined total for Syria and Yemen—according to data compiled by the US-based Armed Conflict Location and Event Data Project.[22] President Ghani showed his will to cooperate with Pakistan but increasing number of casualties has forced him to change his mind. He lambasted Pakistan for insurgent attacks Ghani told a news conference.

"We hoped for peace, but we are receiving messages of war from Pakistan".[23] President Trump administration has therefore prevented security support to Pakistan and candidly admitted that Pakistan is part of Afghan problem and could not be part of solution. Pakistani PM Imran Khan visited Washington in July 2019 and had a meeting with US president Donald Trump. US led NATO forces is willing to eject from Afghanistan and president Trump wishes that it should be completed before US incoming presidential election in 2020. Imran Khan assured president Trump that he will prevail upon Afghan Taliban to adhere peaceful means but history of Pakistan-Afghan Taliban shows that never it became a reality. Just before the Afghan polls, President Trump declared that US-Taliban talk is dead now due to sustainability of Taliban in violence. However, Afghanistan remains one of the critical challenges for Modi-2 government because if Afghanistan will be relatively peaceful then only, we can successfully contain onslaught of terror and sustain our growth saga.

President Ghani is now aware about the core motives of Pakistan. Now India along with likeminded countries like Iran, Russia, United States, Central Asian Republics, China must take every possible step to stabilize Afghanistan.

Pakistan has always been a non-entity for India on almost all counts. Despite consistent Pakistani cross border support to all shades of anti-social activities in India through ISI nurtured non-state actors, India has revealed tremendous courage, patience and success towards managing the same and this vindicates the fact that Indian capability has enormously increased. In post-Pulwama through Balakot air surgical strike Modi government has dismantled many traditional myths about nuclear deterrence. Balakot is in deep Pakistan and parts of Pakistani province of Khyber-Pakhtunwah. This strike has dismantled the concept of nuclear deterrence and established Israeli model of retaliation after any terror attack for India. This move was decisive and vindicated will power of Modi government. It has also accelerated India's global standing and minus China entire global community stand with us.

Despite this important successful strategic move against Pakistan Modi government need to engage Pakistan at the low level even when it is an open secret that no tangible results are expected. It will promote India's global profile.

With China, which has remained India's second obsession, in spite of border problems both the countries have been converging towards building a positive relation and they are now engaged constructively in economic exchange. Despite the legacy of hatred, the Chinese have understood the basic fact that in post-9/11 world system the US is hell bent to encircle China and for that purpose India could be of immense importance. Given this reality in the changing parameters of the international system, the Chinese are quite intelligent to understand that they are required to keep India into good humor. During Kargil conflict (1999) both Prime Minister and Chief of Army Staff of Pakistan visited Beijing to garner Chinese support which they not only declined but even suggested Pakistan that they could enter dialogue with India for an ultimate solution of all outstanding issues including Kashmir. China adopted almost the same line in the backdrop of Pulwama and Balakot. In addition, China has already conceded that Sikkim is an integral part of India and established trade links with historic silk route passing through the Nathu La Pass and connecting Tibet. Manasarovar yatra has also been started from 2015 through Nathula in the backdrop of Prime Minister Modi's May 2015 Beijing visit. Bilateral trade between China and India increased from less than $ 3 billion in 2000 to $ 87 billion in 2018-19.[24]

Although huge trade balance in favor of China ($ 53 billion in 2018-19) has remained unpleasant for India. The Sino-Indian border problem remains unresolved. During PM Vajpayee's June 2003, Beijing visit it was agreed that national security adviser from both sides will lead their respective delegations to resolve thorny border dispute but till October 2019, despite 22 rounds of this high voltage talks, no progress has been made.

The evolution of post-9/11 world order has brought about tremendous changes in the international system which has necessitated an overhauling and reformulation of foreign policy of almost all-important countries of the world so that they can respond to emerging new challenges. In this rapidly changing international scenario, traditional geo-politics has given way to the logic of geo-economics. Every important nation is busy to improve upon their economic profile in spite of bickering in relations at the bilateral level. The US–China, China-Japan, ASEAN-China and Sino-Indian relations are classic examples of this argument. Both the US and China has variety of differences, but their economic relations are surging ahead. In recent years despite border disputes, India and China are also engaging and courting each other to enhance their geo-economic relations. There are some other important areas in this changing international scenario, which has led to certain changes in traditional contents of India's foreign policy.

First is the energy security. Currently India is the 5th largest consumer of energy. It has been estimated that India would be third global energy consumer by 2030 superseding Russia and Japan. This expanding economy needs more energy and therefore it needs to reformulate the whole energy policy keeping this reality in mind. We are geographically closer to the major sources of energy. Traditional means of transporting energy has given way to technology driven energy transfer where local, regional and international politics plays a greater role in the energy market. India requires rethinking in next 5 decades how it could ensure energy security for itself. Of course, India could develop its domestic means of energy, but it needs to exploit external alternative sources of energy and that requires fundamental reformulation into policies towards energy rich countries particularly Africa, Latin America and Central Asia. In the backdrop of prevailing turmoil in the Middle East, it is extremely required. Modi government has taken comprehensive steps in this direction. Modi government has adopted 'Look West Policy' which is intended to stress on Middle East. During post-Pulwama crisis, right from Saudi Arabia to Iran, major gulf countries supported India's stand and even allowed then Indian FM, late Sushma Swaraj to deliver pre-scheduled key note address in OIC despite Pakistan's boycott. PM Modi received highest civilian award from 'order of Zayed' by UAE in August 2019.

The award has earlier been bestowed on several world leaders, including Russian President Vladimir Putin, Queen Elizabeth II and Chinese President Xi Jinping. This award is significant because it had been given in the backdrop of Kashmir crisis.

Another important sector is Diaspora, which emerges as an important factor into post-Cold War international politics. We have around 30-35 million Indian Diaspora across the globe. Majority among them are settled into the powerhouse of the international system (western world) and emerged as an important determinant factor into the formulation of their respective countries foreign policies. The post-9/11 scenario has provided a new opportunity for India to exploit the situation. In financial year 2018-2019 our Diaspora has sent $ 80 billion as remittances pushing China into third place. At the same time, it is an open secret that we have not been adequately successful to safeguard the basic interests of our Diaspora, which we need to focus with our increasing profile into international system. Diaspora is not only contributing enormously into our sustainable sound financial health but additionally they are brilliant unpaid Ambassador of our interest situated at the powerhouse of the international system. We need to strengthen this component of our foreign policy.

Maritime security has emerged as an important fulcrum of strategic strength. Indian Ocean is an important ocean where over 55 per cent global trade is traversing. Our economy is expanding, and this sustainability needs more energy consumption and for that purpose we must ensure maritime security. It has been said that whosoever has dominated Indian Ocean has dominated Asia therefore we must take every possible step for the strengthening of our maritime security. China has launched $ 40 billion 'maritime silk route' policy. The basic intent of this policy has been to contain India in the Indian Ocean region. It is also following 'string of parleys' policy within South Asia against India. Modi-2 must allocate adequate resources to modernize our ailing fleet to cope up expanding challenges in the blue waters right from the Indian Ocean till Pacific Ocean. We must reformulate our policies to cope up these emerging situations. We have to allocate adequate resources to the navy to introduce new infrastructure to meet with the emergent situation.

Science & technology sector is an important sector in which India has done a marvelous progress. It has provided us scope to engage more and more countries. Right from poverty ridden African countries to many under developed third world countries, India has tremendous scope to support in their developmental work especially in the field of science and technology.

India has immense soft power leverage in Indo-Pacific in particular and rest of globe in general. Earlier we only had soft power, now we have adequate hard power at our disposal. With the cocktail of soft and hard power India could achieve unique position in Indo-Pacific which is all set to replace as the custodian of global power in coming decades.

Since its inception Indian foreign policy had been obsessed with idealism which into the realm of international politics was bound to fail. India needs to reformulate the whole contours of its foreign policy. We must not get obsessed with Pakistan and China and must decentralize our attention across the globe and every region of the planet must be under our focus. There is no permanence in international relations the only thing which is permanent is converges of interests. Nearly 2300 years ago, the seminal Indian strategic thinker, Kautilya insisted on this point in an excellent manner in his seminal book 'Arthshastra'. It is pertinent and relevant even today than his lifetime and we need to incorporate it as the main determinants of our foreign policy. Modi-1 has followed realism in its first term and expected to strengthen it in the second term as well.

Indian democracy has developed remarkably in comparison with democracies which came into being after the end of the Second World War. We have made tremendous progress at domestic level. But at the political level India has not made much progress as still for the electoral benefit, political parties keep opposing or supporting foreign policy issues as per their electoral interests. This is not a healthy trend. Political parties need to reformulate their behavior with the view that they have no difference on basic features of foreign policy and of course successive government needs to keep political parties more engaged in the process of the formulation of foreign policy. We must take some lesson from western democracies, where changing of governments has very miniscule impact on the priorities of their foreign policy. Fortunately, we have political consensus among major political parties on our 'Act East and China Policy' but we have to achieve consensus on other issues also.

In western world, the academic community has been an integral part of the formulation of foreign policy and we need to replicate it. The increasing profile of India at global level has also put us into delicate situation and to cope with the situation we need to engage this class also into the decision-making process. The intellectual communities are more aware about the nitty gritty of the foreign policy than the carrier diplomats and there is a strong need of their synergy for the protection and promotion of our interests.

Since independence Indian foreign policy has been guided by certain cardinal principles. Prime among them is 'third world unity'. This was one of the basic determinants of our foreign policy. Although in post-Cold War scenario, India has acquired enormous prestige at the international level. But with this ratio Indian engagement has not increased with the third world countries. We have been under various colonial regimes for centuries and they have exploited us blatantly and so is the case of majority of third world countries. Without empowering the suffering of humanities of those countries, we could not establish justice based new international economic order (NIEO). Fortunately, we have acquired tremendous competence in science and technology sector. We need to develop those hapless countries with our technological expertise and thus cement the basic unity among third world countries. This would be an important contribution towards the establishment of justice based international system and as well in the restoration of multi-polar Asian and global system.

Another important determinant of Indian foreign policy has been decentralization of power structure into the international bodies including the United Nations. In 1945 when the UN came into being, permanent membership was extended only to five countries. At the outset of 21st century the power dynamics of the international system has changed phenomenally. There is an urgent need to decentralize the UN system and the incorporation of five or ten more permanent members into the Security Council to ensure democracy within its structure. India's candidature to the Security Council as the permanent member is the strongest one. India needs to shape its UN policies to cope up these challenges.

The contemporary world is confronting many turbulent issues, which has posed severe challenges for the survival of humanity. Climate Change is one of the most serious among them. The developed countries have damaged the environment through their industrial waste and excessive luxurious life style, but they have not taken adequate measures for the safeguard of the same. Now the whole humanity is confronting the challenges posed by the climate change. It is estimated that if corrective measures are not taken with immediate effects, sea level will enhance from 2020, and all low lands will sub-merge. Additionally, this change will create many problems and could escalate conflicts therefore there is strong need to explore the matter seriously. Our foreign policy must take it as one of the immediate priorities because our neighborhood is going to be sub-merged. The developed countries that have contributed enormously to create this situation must contribute generously into the corrective measures. Likewise, eradication of poverty, removal of illiteracy and prevention of drug abuse and trafficking and HIV/AIDS are working as the push factor of conflicts throughout the world therefore international community must take it as serious challenges.

Modi led NDA government has taken gamut of positive and proactive steps to address gamut of concerns to ensure our national interests. Modi regime has finished its first term (2014-19) and during this stipulated time, India has been respected on international platforms. In post-Pulwama it was vindicated with the attitude of the major global powers. PM Modi has already returned into power in May 2019 for second term (2019-24) with enhanced majority. Modi government requires to consolidate the gains made during 1st term and take some exclusive steps to ensure our national interests during second term.

These are the broader issues that have been widely covered through different papers included in this book. This book is intended to provide an intellectual input to the formulators of the foreign policy to cope with the changing international system. We hope that this book will be of some use to all stake holders of the foreign policy and at least to the wider spectrum of the students of foreign policy.

Sudhir Singh

NOTES

1. Guha, Ramchandra, *India After Gandhi; the History of the World's Largest Democracy*, Macmillan, London, 2007, p. 169.
2. P.L. Dash, When Central Asia Calls, *The Indian Express*, New Delhi, July 27, 2015.
3. Dai Bing, "India and China's great game in full swing", China Internet Information Center, October 22, 2010. Stable URL http://www.china.org.cn/opinion/2010-10/22/content_21181802.htm Accessed on January 8, 2011.
4. Keith Bradsher, Philippine Leader Sounds Alarm on China, *New York Times*, New York, February 5, 2014.
5. Teddy Ng, 'Shinzo Abe Slams Beijing "Provocations" on Island Tour', *South China Morning Post*, Hong Kong, 18 July 2013.
6. "Temperatures Rising in the South China Sea", *The Nation*, Bangkok, 28 May 2012.

7. Mearsheimer, John J. China's Unpeaceful Rise, *Current History*, 2006, 105 (690), P-161.
8. *Times of India*, New Delhi, October 3, 2018
9. Naveed Siddiqui, China to 'Uphold justice for Pakistan on Kashmir Issue, *Dawn*, Karachi, August 9, 2019.
10. Pervez Hoodbhoy, Client and Patrons, *Dawn*, Karachi, July 6, 2019.
11. A Tepid Response, Editorial, *Dawn*, Karachi, August 9, 2019.
12. Manish Pandaya, Modi's 370 removal a game-changer, Pak isolated: U.S. experts, *Print*, New Delhi, August 11, 2019.
13. Shakeel Ahmed, FM moves to paper over UAE award for Modi, *Dawn*, Karachi, August 26, 2019.
14. Robert Blackwill, The Future of US-India Relations, Address to the Confederation of Indian Industry, New Delhi, May 5, 2009, available at http://www.stratpost.com/the-future-of-us-indiarelations- blackwill accessed on January 9, 2011.
15. Munir Akram, Pakistan and Sino-Us Cold War, *Dawn*, Karachi, June 9, 2019.
16. *Global Times*, December 16, 2010, available at http://opinion.globaltimes.cn/editorial/2010-12/602061.html accessed on January 10, 2011.
17. 'Australia woes India to Counter balance China', *The Global Times*, July 27, 2017.
18. Xinjiang has been boiling since last few years and emerged as bleeding grounds of China. It is an open secret that all Non State Actors of Pakistan has extended its support to this movement. Despite this serous factor since 2006 every Chinese leaders (President, PM) while visiting India visiting Pakistan also. In September 2014, Chinese President could not visit Islamabad due to ongoing unrest in Islamabad.
19. Pranab Dhal Samanta, India equates Jammu & Kashmir with Tibet, *The Indian Express*, November 15, 2010, available at http://www.indianexpress.com/news/india-equates-jammu-&-kashmir-withtibet/ 711151/ accessed on January 11, 2011.
20. C. Raja Mohan, After Mullah Omar, *The Indian Express,* New Delhi, August 4, 2015.
21. Pak uses terrorism as tool against India: Ex-US spymaster (Former Deputy Chief of the CIA), Rediffmail.com, May 3, 2019.
22. 2014 among deadliest years in AF with 10 k civilian casualties, *The Times of India*, New Delhi, August 9, 2015 and 'Worse every day; Afghans expect 2019 to be even deadlier', *AFP, Dawn*, Karachi, December 30, 2018.
23. Ashraf Ghani slams Pakistan over recent Kabul attacks, *Dawn*, Karachi, August 10, 2015.
24. *Global Times*, Beijing, April 11, 2019.

ABOUT THE CONTRIBUTORS

Ms. Aaradhana Singh is teaching in the Department of Political Science, Central University of Himachal Pradesh, Dharamshala.

Dr. Alok Gupta is teaching Political Science in Central University of Bihar, Gaya, Bihar.

Dr. Alokka Dutta is teaching Political Science, in Bhagini Nivedita College, University of Delhi.

Dr. Amulya Kr. Tripathi is teaching Political Science, in Behrampur University, Orrisa.

Prof. Anisur Rahman is Director, UGC-Human Resource Development Centre, Jamia Millia Islamia, New Delhi.

Dr. Chandra Mohan Upadhaya is teaching Political Science in Kisan P.G. College, Bahraich, Uttar Pradesh.

Dr. Deepak Yadav is teaching Political Science in Kalindi College, University of Delhi, New Delhi.

Prof. D. Gopal, School of Social Sciences, IGNOU, New Delhi.

Dr. Geetha Govindasamy is teaching in Faculty of Arts and Social Sciences, University of Malaya, Kuala Lumpur, Malaysia.

Dr Jayshree Tandekar is teaching Political Science in Gargi College, University of Delhi, New Delhi.

Prof. K. Jayprasad is Dean, School of Cultural Studies & Pro Vice-Chancellor, Central University of Kerala, Kasaragod.

Prof. Koushiki Das Gupta is teaching in the Department of History in Vidhyasagar University, West Bengal.

Dr. Mohar Chakravorty is teaching Political Science in South Calcutta Girls' College, Calcutta University, Kolkata.

Mr. Nazmul Arifeen is Research Officer at Bangladesh Institute of International and Strategic Studies (BIISS), Dhaka, Bangladesh.

Ms. Naziya is pursuing her PhD from Center of West Asian Studies, Jamia Millia Islamia, New Delhi.

Dr. Pranav Kumar, teaching Political Science in Central University of South Bihar, Gaya.

Dr. Pramod Kumar Sharma was ICSSR post-doctoral fellow and based in New Delhi.

Mrs. Rakhee Viswambharan, teaching Political Science & Head, Department of Political Science, Sree Narayana College, Chempazhanthy, Thiruvananthapuram, Kerala.

Prof. R.F.I. Smith, Adjunct Professor, School of Management, RMIT University, Melbourne, Australia.

Dr. Roshini Kujur is teaching Political Science in Behrampur University, Orrisa.

Dr. Sabu Thomas is teaching Political Science in Post Graduate Department of Political Science Government College Madappally, Calicut, Kerala.

Dr. Salu Dsouza, Assistant Professor, Symbiosis Law School, Symbiosis International (Deemed University), Wathoda, Nagpur.

Dr. Sayna, V.V. was Research Scholar, School of International Studies, Pondicherry Central University.

Dr. Sumit Kumar is Fellow, Maulana Abul Kalam Azad Institute of Asian Studies, Ministry of Culture, Govt. of India, Kolkata.

Prof. Suresh R, is teaching Political Science & Hon. Director, V K Krishna Menon Study Centre for International Relations, Department of Political Science, University of Kerala, Kariavattom, Thiruvananthapuram, Kerala.

Dr. Sudhir Singh is teaching Political Science, Dyal Singh College, University of Delhi, New Delhi.

Prof. S. Manivasakan is the Director, Centre for the South and Southeast Asian Studies, University of Madras, Chennai.

Mr. Unnikrishnan G, is Research Scholar, Department of Political Science, University of Kerala, Trivandrum.

Prof. Y. Yagama Reddy (Retd.), Former Director, Centre for Southeast Asian & Pacific Studies, Sri Venkateswara University, Tirupati.

Commodore RS Vasan Indian Navy (Retd), Director Chennai Centre for China Studies and Head Strategy and Security Studies, Center for Asia Studies, Chennai.

Ms. Vandana Mishra is Research Scholar in Central University of South Bihar, Gaya.

1

Indo–Iran Relationship:

Challenges and Opportunities in the Changing Context

Aaradhana Singh

> *"Among all the nations and races who have come in contact with India none of them has so everlasting influence on our culture and civilisation as that of Iranians."*
>
> *– Discovery of India by Pandit Jawahar Lal Nehru*

The ties between India and Iran date back to the Persian Empire of Cyrus the Great. The nations have long influenced each other in the fields of culture, art, architecture, and language, especially during 1526-1757 when the Mughals ruled India. India and Iran also shared a border until 1947. For many centuries, Persian remained the language of Indian judiciary. The first Persian newspaper "Mirat-ul-Akhbar" that was started by Raja Ram Mohan Roy, an Indian social reformer, tells us about the influence that Persian culture had on our history and society. However, after independence, particularly during Cold War era India's relation with Iran could not sustain the same warmth due to a gamut of prevailing compulsions. Iran, along with Pakistan and Turkey, joined the American-led capitalist block after the Second World War and in contrast India adopted the dogma of non-alignment and tilted towards the Soviet Union–led socialist block. Pakistan has remained a factor between India and Iran. But after the end of the Cold War, many changes have taken place at the bilateral as well multilateral level and these changes have brought India and Iran closer than ever despite many divergent interests and opinions. In the backdrop of the July 2015 nuclear deal with the Western world, Indo–Iran relationship was getting smoother but President

Donald Trump again clamped sanction against Iran and finally scrapped the nuclear deal. These prevailing aspects will be analysed within the ambit of this chapter.

India and Iran have a lot of issues of convergences and few points where they diverge. It must be mentioned that the Indo–Iran divergences are manageable; therefore, despite many odds India and Iran relations strengthened after the Cold War.

Kautilya had opined that convergences in interests are the basic formulators of the foreign policy. Growing India–Iran bonhomie has vindicated this fact. It has also rejected the traditional notion that religious synergy could be a common bond between co-religious countries. Saudi Arabia is the self-proclaimed harbinger of the global Islam and Iran also considers herself fit for the same role but both never had cordial relations particularly after the Cold War. So is the case with Pakistan and Iran. The fact remains that there are more convergences of interests between Saudi Arabia and Iran than between Iran and Pakistan. Saudi Arabia is a key ally of Pakistan and Iran-Pakistan has huge trust deficit. The systematic elimination of Shias started from General Zia-ul-Haq period and all anti-Shia sectarian militant groups have enjoyed tacit support of the military. This ongoing establishment (Pakistani military in Pakistani context) supported violence against the Shias and that has angered Iran. Pakistan and Saudi Arabia proximity has also accelerated the prevailing trust deficit between Pakistan and Iran.

Imran Khan–led PTI came into power in August 2018. Pakistan is facing unprecedented economic crisis. Saudi Arabia came forward to help and gave $3 billion support and oil of the same amount with late payment.

A major bone of contention between Saudi Arabia and Iran is treatment of Shia Muslims in Saudi Arabia and elsewhere. In the southern provinces of Saudi Arabia, which is the hub of oil reserves, Shias are in majority and additionally these areas are the important contributors of Saudi oil production. Shias are persecuted in Saudi Arabia because the ruling Saud family of Saudi is basically propagating Wahhabism as their ideology which is Sunni hyperviolent ideology with zero tolerance for the Shias. In the backdrop of Syria and Yemen crisis, sectarian angle is going to be significant within the Arabian world.

Besides, Saudi Arabia has propelled Wahhabism, which perpetuates intolerant Islam and even considers Shias as non-Muslim. Being the richest country of the Muslim world, Saudi Arabia has propagated this ideology of Wahhabism throughout the globe. Iran started protesting export of Wahhabism by Saudi Arabia particularly after 1979 revolution and since then has sustained its protest.

When we go and take a look at the history, General Zia-ul-Haq captured power after overthrowing an elected government led by Zulfikar Ali Bhutto (a Shia), in July 1977. And through implementation of Nizam-e-Mustafa in 1979 (Rule of the Prophet), Zia consolidated his position. Shias of Pakistan took this initiative as the beginning of their marginalization within Pakistani society as had been mooted against Ahmadis by declaring them as non-Islamic. Since then, more than 20,000 Shias have been killed in Pakistan in sectarian violence. Pakistan is a Sunni-majority country but Shias constitute around 20–25% of the overall population. They are educated, wealthy and possess big land holdings as well. There are ample evidences that Pakistani state and particularly army is nurturing Sunni sectarian groups to eliminate the sphere of influence of Shias. It is also due to the fact that Shias prefer to vote PPP, which is led by Bhutto family and has been harbinger of democratic movements. This has not gone well with the army and it has extended tacit support to the Sunni groups to eliminate Shias. 1979 Iranian Revolution has further boosted the moral of Pakistani Shias and they are hell bent to sustain their exclusive position in the power structure of Pakistan. This has accelerated the sectarian violence against the Shias and being the custodian of Shias across the globe, Iran remains upset with Pakistan.

Iran has proclaimed itself as the custodian of the Shias globally whereas Saudi Arabia has taken up the same role, but for the Sunnis. This bitter enmity between these both countries is accelerating violence within their territory where both sects are dominant by all counts. For the last three decades, Pakistan has become a battleground for them to propagate their interests. We are aware of the nexus between the Taliban and Al-Qaeda with Pakistan. The assassination of Osama Bin Laden in May 2011 at Abbottabad (Pakistan) has vindicated the fact that both have been working with tacit understanding. Interestingly, the Taliban and Al-Qaeda both are claiming themselves as the harbinger of global Islamic Ummah but they are killing Shias in Pakistan. Taliban ruled over Afghanistan from 1996 to 2001. During this period, they executed thousands of Shias and fiercely tried to divide the ethnic and sectarian mosaic of Afghanistan. In Mazar-e-Sharif, many officers of the Iranian consulates have been killed during the Taliban period (1996–2001) which brought both Afghanistan and Iran at the brink of a war. Due to the mediation by Prime Minister of Pakistan, Nawaz Sharif (1997–99), the tension subsided. Even at this juncture, Shias are under serious threat from the Taliban and their Sunni counterparts, and their sustainable elimination has been going on both in Pakistan and Afghanistan. We are aware that Saudi Arabia and Pakistan are two important countries out of three, who gave recognition to the Taliban government as required under the provisions of the international law. The third one was UAE.

Since March 2011, violence in Syria is taking place between the government and the opposition forces, and according to the United Nations and other global agencies, till December 2018 around 5,25,000 people have been killed. The Tehrik-e-Taliban Pakistan (a Sunni militant organisation) had declared in July 2013 that they had dispatched their fighters to wage Jihad against the government forces in Syria. One of the most important motivating factors behind this decision of the TTP is that the President Assad is Shia. Saudi Arabia along with their supporters is with the opposition forces and Iran along with China and Russia is supporting President Assad's government. It exposed the egalitarian claim of the Sunni militant groups that they are fighting for the cause of Islam.

Afghanistan is a matter of utmost concern both for India and Iran. During the Taliban regime, India and Iran along with Russia extended their support to Northern Alliance led by legendary leader Ahmed Shah Masood. By December 2014, NATO forces withdrew themselves from Afghanistan. Since 18 years, Karzai and Ghani regimes, an elected one is ruling the country and has tried to build the strength of Afghan National Army (ANA) but there are apprehensions that after the NATO withdrawal, the ANA would not be able to properly contain Taliban. In this prevailing situation, Taliban may take over and given its previous governance record, it could be detrimental for the national interests of both India and Iran. By the end of 2019, this apprehension rules the roost in Afghanistan. In this situation, they must forge a strong alliance to protect and promote their interests in Afghanistan. Needless to say that Pakistan will not allow this to happen; therefore, India and Iran must formulate a combined strategy to handle this situation. Saudi Arabia, the traditional arch rival of Iran, will also support Pakistani position to export its narrow version of Islam as it had already done during the previous Taliban regime. Needless to say that Taliban has been the harbinger of the conservative version of Islam in Afghanistan.

Iran is traditionally a peaceful country. Iran established a national army only recently, under the Pahlavi dynasty. The country has no martial tradition unlike its western neighbour Turkey. After Iraq war, Tehran has avoided direct military conflict, but its military expenditure is slightly higher than compared to those of smaller Gulf countries.[1] In the case of India and Iran, there are less divergences and more convergences of interests and that makes the case that they should cooperate. The changing security architecture of South and South West Asia has also pushed both countries on the same platform. There are many critical areas where the national interests of the two countries are converging.

Drug trafficking and terrorism is a major concern for both countries. Since the last three decades more than 5,000 Iranian border guards have been killed while containing drug trafficking. Iran shares a large portion of its border with Afghanistan and Pakistan and therefore is being used as a convenient route by drug traffickers to export drugs to Europe. There are strong inter-linkages between drug trafficking and terror network and India and Iran are the worst affected nations from this menace. Pakistan and Afghanistan are the dens of global drug trafficking and terror network. To prevent these situations from having a spillover effect on India and Iran, they must come together and take adequate steps to cope with the future challenges.

Since independence, Pakistan sees India as its mortal enemy. During Cold War, Iran and Pakistan shared a cordial relation. Iran extended its adequate support to Pakistan during 1965 war. In 1979, the monarchy of Iran was thrown out by an Islamic revolution led by Ayatollah Khomeini. He was considered one of the leading Islamic ideologues along with Maulana Maududi of Pakistan and Sayyid Qutb of Egypt. Iran has been supportive to the right to self-determination of Kashmiri Muslims particularly during the cold war.

Iran–India relationships have grown manifolds due to many compulsions brought by the end of the Cold War. Many converging interests have been the real cementing force of the Indian foreign policy, as was aptly stated by Kautilya. Three Indian Prime Ministers have visited Iran since the end of the Cold War. In 1993, Prime Minister Narsimha Rao visited Tehran and opened new vistas of a deepening relationship. In 2001, Prime Minister, Atal Bihari Vajpayee visited Tehran. This visit was unique because it initiated cooperation in many areas that were unexplored previously—Central Asia, energy and military matters, cooperation in Afghanistan that began along with strategic security. Iranian leaders had reciprocated these top visits. Many other dignitaries from both countries also visited each other. In 2003, Iranian president visited India and was honoured as the Chief Guest for the Republic Day of India, a very special invitation only reserved for the closest Indian friends. In August 2012, Prime Minister Dr. Manmohan Singh visited Iran to participate in the 16th Summit of the NAM. During this visit, many rounds of negotiations were held with notable delegations. It was agreed that along with Afghanistan, India and Iran must work together on the areas of common benefits. PM Modi also visited Iran in 2016. PM Modi met

Iranian leaders many a times on other platforms as well; the last time they met was during SCO summit in Bishkek in June 2019.

In April 2013, Foreign Minister Salman Khurshid visited Tehran and it was agreed that Chabahar port facility will be expanded. India and Iran have already connected Central Asia through this port while making Delaram Zaranj highway in western Afghanistan. It has also reduced Afghanistan's dependence over Karachi port for trade and other necessities. During this visit, many bilateral agreements were inked ranging from energy supply to defense cooperation. India by all available calculations will become world's third largest energy consumer by 2020. In April 2015, transport minister Nitin Gadkari visited Tehran and pledged the connectivity of Central Asia and Afghanistan through newly developed Chabahar port jointly built by India and Iran. Iranian President Hassan Rouhani and Indian PM Modi met in Ufa (Russia) in July 2015 and had a 90-minute bilateral talk. During this meeting, it was pledged that India and Iran will accelerate their bilateral relations. In July 2015, Iran and the Western world signed a nuclear deal and now gradually, the decade-long sanctions imposed against Iran were supposed to be lifted. In August 2015, Iranian Foreign Minister, Javad Zarif, had visited New Delhi and met PM and other ministers. Again it was pledged that cooperation on all fronts will be accelerated. During a one-day visit of Mr. Zarif issues, related to Islamic State threat, energy investments, Afghanistan and development of Chabahar port were discussed. He also stated that India is an important player in West Asia and can play a leading role in the region. PM Modi conveyed India's commitment to work with Iran for development of the Chabahar port that would have far-reaching benefits, not only for the people of India and Iran, but also for Afghanistan and the entire Central Asian region. Mr. Zarif acknowledged India's support during turbulent times. PM Modi visited Iran in May 2016. His delegation included many top brasses including Surface and Shipping Transport Minister, Nitin Gadkari. Many agreements were inked during this visit.[2] Iran has enormous energy reserves and India is today the 5th global energy consumer and by 2025 will be 3rd largest energy consumer after pushing Japan and Russia. It is also opined by the global economic pundits that India will be representing 23% of global GDP by 2050. For the sustainability of India's growth saga, sustainable and diverse supply of energy is must.

India has more than double the Muslim population of Iran and one fourth among them are Shias. They are peaceful, stay away from any anti-state activities and are contributing enormously in the national development. It is also a big state of satisfaction for Iran because almost all countries where Shias are under suppression are Islamic countries, but despite the majority of Hindus, Shias are comfortable in India.

The United States and India share a good relationship since the last two decades. The nuclear agreement inked in 2008 and the deepening bonhomie is the testimony. Dr. Manmohan Singh visited Tehran despite a huge protest by U.S.-led block. Tension still prevails between Iran and the Western countries over the nuclear issue despite truce made by President Obama and President Rouhani after their telephonic conversation in the latter part of 2013. In the backdrop of this tension, Dr. Singh's visit was path breaking. Many bilateral treaties were inked during the visit. This visit gave renewed hope to Iran and negated the notion that it has been isolated at the international level. President Donald Trump has discarded previous agreement inked by President Obama with Iran and imposed gamut of sanctions despite the opposition of their NATO allies.

Afghanistan remains a top agenda between India and Iran because of convergence of interests. Iran never supported Taliban and forged a Northern Alliance along with Russia and India. During its five years (1996–2001) of rule, the Taliban executed thousands of Shias in Afghanistan. Being the only Shia-majority country on the globe and an immediate neighbour of Afghanistan, it was a matter of serious concern for Iran. In the recent decades, Iran was compelled to understand that Saudi Arabia has started sharing a much deeper relationship with Pakistan; therefore, it has set a new tone for its relationship with India. Under the Imran Khan–led PTI government which came into power in August 2018, the bonhomie between Saudi and Pakistan has further emboldened.

Kautilya had said that an enemy's enemy is a friend and trust deficit between Iran and Pakistan has provided India an opportunity to cooperate with Iran on a variety of issues. Iran has cooperated with several other regional countries, notably India and Russia, to gain influence in any post-American Afghanistan. During the Afghan civil war in the post-Soviet period, these three countries constituted the bloc that supported the Northern Alliance in opposition to the Pakistani and Saudi-supported Taliban forces.

Strategic Imperatives for the Development of Chabahar for India and Iran

In order to address its need to secure energy routes, and to contain the growing Chinese influence in the Arabian Sea, Persian Gulf, and the Indian Ocean, India brought Iran into an economic and strategic alliance. India invested huge resources for the construction of Iranian Port of Chabahar. It will be easily accessible for Indian imports and exports through road and rail links to Afghanistan and Central Asia. In the last week of February 2019, a Himalayan step was taken in this direction when maiden Afghan goods were uploaded on ships at Chabahar port which is jointly developed by Iran and India.

According to Afghan officials, 23 trucks carrying 57 tonnes of dried fruits, textiles, carpets and mineral products were dispatched from western Afghan city of Zaranj to Iran's Chabahar port. The consignment will be shipped to the Indian city of Mumbai. At the inauguration of the new export route, President Ashraf Ghani said Afghanistan was slowly improving its exports in a bid to reduce its trade deficit. "Chabahar port is the result of healthy cooperation between India, Iran and Afghanistan this will ensure economic growth".[3] Chabahar has provided an easy access to a port to Afghanistan and has ended Afghani dependence over Karachi port of Pakistan for export/import activities. Chabahar port has enabled both countries to engage in trade by passing Pakistan.

Chabahar's geo-strategic location plays an important role in connecting India to Afghanistan and Central Asia both militarily and economically. India perceives Central Asia, Iran, and Afghanistan situated at the crossroads of overland trading routes as a potential consumer market for Indian products. Similarly, Iran wants to get India's cost-effective source of high-technology inputs.[4] India's ultimate objective is to bypass Pakistan, and also cooperate with Iran on a highway and rail system that leads from Chabahar port into Afghanistan and Central Asia. Highway connecting Afghanistan and Central Asia has been in order for many years. Rail system has to be restored. Modi government has inaugurated 1st phase of the port and it became operational and has also secured its exemption from the American sanctions against Iran. The first meeting of the follow-up committee for implementation of the trilateral Chabahar agreement between India-Afghanistan and Iran was held in the port city of Chabahar on 21 December 2018 to finalise trade and transit corridors. They agreed on the routes for the trade and transit corridors between the three countries. India Ports Global Limited had opened an office in the port city and taken over operations of the port.

The Chabahar port in the Sistan-Balochistan province on the energy-rich nation's southern coast is easily accessible from India's western coast and is increasingly seen as a counter to Pakistan's Gwadar port, which is being developed with Chinese investment under the ambit of CPEC and is located just 80 km east from Chabahar.[5]

On the other hand, there is active Chinese cooperation in the Port of Gwadar, since it is the only port which can serve the best interests of both China and Pakistan in the region. The Port will, therefore, enable China to keep a strict watch on India's growing influence in the Indian Ocean, the Arabian Sea, and Persian Gulf. Hence, the possibility of any future economic and military collaboration between India and the US in the region can be effectively dealt with. Another geographical advantage of the port is that it will reduce the distance for energy imports from Persian Gulf to China. Gwadar also holds a geo-strategic significance for China because of its proximity with the sea lanes between West Asia and China. It is vital for oil trade. As a gateway to the Indian Ocean, Gwadar will provide Beijing with a listening base from where the Chinese may exert surveillance on hyper-strategic sea links. The military activities of the Indian and American navies in the region can also be closely watched by the Chinese. Gwadar port will also provide a strong base for Chinese ships and submarines. Since Gwadar Port can fulfil its political, security and commercial objectives vis-à-vis India, China has spent a huge amount on its construction. It is one of most significant signature projects of the Chinese President Xi Jinping. The port will also help both China and Pakistan to promote trade with Gulf States possessing 63% of world's oil reserves.[6]

China has acknowledged the strategic significance of Gwadar no less than that of the Karakoram Highway.[7] This will further strengthen the relations between China and Pakistan. China is also interested to turn Gwadar into an energy-transport hub by building an oil pipeline from Gwadar into Chinese Province of Xinjiang. The proposed pipeline will carry crude oil from Arab and African states. Gwadar's strategic advantage to China is due to its close proximity with the Strait of Hormuz. The presence of the US forces in the region poses not only a threat to Chinese navy but, also to its commercial interest. Gwadar provides China with a strong base where it can monitor US naval activity in the Persian Gulf and Indian activities in the Arabian Sea. China has already set up electronic posts at Gwadar for monitoring maritime traffic through the Strait of Hormuz and the Arabian Sea. It seems like a historical irony that Gwadar, which used to belong to the Omani sultan, was offered to India in the 1950s under Nehru. At the time, India refused on the grounds that it would not be able to defend it from Pakistan.[8]

Chabahar is a part of the Indian grand design to apparently develop transportation infrastructure. It is however viewed with suspicion to sabotage Pakistan's future strategy of expanding its influence in Central Asia and beyond. Chabahar provides India easy access to Afghanistan and Central Asia through

Indian Ocean. India's ultimate desire is to connect Chabahar with Central Asian republics through roads and a network of railway system to bypass Pakistan, and to reduce the dependency of Central Asian countries on the Pakistani port of Gwadar. Iran is already enjoying close socio-cultural and economic relations with the Central Asian republics. Iran is working on several projects in Tajikistan including the Anzob tunnel, and has constructed a bridge over the Amu Darya (Oxus River) that connects Chabahar with the Khojent route. In addition, the construction of 218-km-long Zaranj–Delaram highway that now links Afghanistan to the Iranian port of Chabahar and also connects Herat and Kabul via Mazar-e-Sharif in the north and Kandhar in the south—thereby providing easier inroads in Afghanistan and possibly even further, to Central Asia via Iran.[9]

Owing to the fact that Central Asian countries are land-locked, they depend on Iranian ports, especially on Chabahar for trade and commercial relations with the rest of the world. Moreover, Afghanistan is more friendly and close to India than Pakistan. In this regard, with its eco-strategic positioning in Iran, India gets opportunity to have an access to warm waters through this region. The creation of North–South Corridor is the best prospect for Iran to expand its transit corridor to India. The idea of North–South Corridor has multiple purposes and is, therefore, seen as an opening to bypass East–West Silk Road Project.[10]

Thus, India gains more security, political, economic and strategic advantages from Iran, Afghanistan and Central Asia as compared to China. Iran is more stable than Pakistan. It has better relations with Afghanistan and the Central Asian states. Bordering Azerbaijan and Turkmenistan, Iran has a natural geographical advantage by providing access to Sea for the Central Asian States. However, intensifying competition between India and China in Arabian Sea and Central Asia, and the growing US concerns about China's offensive capabilities made the global and regional security environment more complex and sensitive.

For India and Iran, the stability of Afghanistan, containment of terrorism, containment of drug trafficking, integration of Central Asia with larger world, energy security, pipeline issues and development of commerce and cooperation in energy sector are some of the important cementing factors of their bilateral relationship. The nuclear issue and Western sanctions on Iran and Kashmir issues are issues of contention between both countries.

There are a range of divergences between India and Iran. These divergences need to be narrowed down. The first and most important among them is nuclear issue. Due to the 2008 nuclear treaty, India and United States have been converted from being Cold War–era Estranged Allies to Engaged Allies in the 21st century. This development maintains Kautilya's theory that convergences of interests play a decisive role in the realm of international relations. Islamic State has become a serious cause of concern for the countries in the Middle East. Iran is the only country within this region that has shown its willingness to contain Islamic State. The United States is also concerned to contain Islamic State. This is equally true to contain the resurgent Taliban in Afghanistan. The resurgent Taliban and the Islamic State is also a serious security threat for India, Russia and China. This prevailing security architecture in the Middle East and South West Asia has pushed India and Iran to deepen their relationship.

This cooperation will bring durable peace and cooperation in the most volatile part of the globe. India, today, is perhaps the only capable country to convince both of them on this issue. Bringing United States and Iran closer on the same page on diverse conflicting issues is in the larger national interest of India and of regional peace also. It will also provide stability to the security of South West Asia. India must convey to the United States that Iran is mutually beneficial for us. India must also advice Iran that instead of confronting the US, it must cooperate with the Western world to protect Shia Muslims on humanitarian grounds. Iran was trying to free Shia places of worships in Iraq but it yielded no adequate results since it was not vacated due to American military operation. After the death of Saddam Hussain in 2003, global community got to know that two of the most sacred places of Shia worship, Najaf and Karbala are in Iraq and not in Iran. Iran must also shed its mindset of opposition for the sake of opposition to the United States. It is also equally applicable for the United States. India is better positioned today to mediate between two bitter rivals probably first time after the end of the Second World War.

Second most important irritant between India and Iran is the Kashmir issue. Recently, Iran has not extended its support to the cause but previously it had extended its support to independence of Kashmir. Iran must understand with its experience in Iraq war that religion cannot be a promoter of national interests. Since many decades, Iran is competing with Saudi Arabia on a number of issues. Both are harbingers of Islam, so then a question that arises is why are they fighting against each other? Only convergences of interests are the cementing factor in foreign policy. It is an open secret that India and Iran's interests converge on several grounds; therefore, they are cooperating not only for the protection and promotion of their national interests but also for peace and stability in the region.

Iran is yet another point of contention between India and the United States although recently India has been motivated by the US to participate in UN-led Western sanctions against Iran. Global concern over Iran's nuclear weapons development program, and the potential for subsequent proliferation has driven US efforts to coordinate a coercive international sanctions regime. India, however, has a long historical and mutually beneficial relationship with Iran centred on trade, commerce, and cultural diffusion, with India currently importing significant amounts of oil from and facilitating the financing of Iranian energy companies—the targets of Western sanctions. India and Iran are two important old civilizations and have been connected to each other since millennia.

After the end of the Cold War, there has been a shift in the global distribution of power from the West to the East. While the political system globally can still be described as unipolar, Asia is characterized by multipolarity. The powers of Asia compete for power, influence and resources. India is amongst the great powers on the rise. India is the seventh largest country in the world, the second most populous and the world's largest democracy.[11] It is one of the world's most powerful economies and has highly professional armed forces, which have made India emerge as an entity that can help shift the global balance of power.

In this changing political environment, India has struggled to define itself and comprehend its power capabilities as well as the possibilities and limitations of that power. Indian global thinking is characterized by a lack of consensus on a strategic framework that can structure its foreign relations.[12] India could change the game while invoking real spirit of NAM in the context of Iran. Given the pressure by the United States on India in this context, we must take a principle stand and advise both to settle their thorny issues through amicable means of settling disputes. Fortunately, the situation is emerging to help India's ideal line on Iran.

Concluding Observations

What complicates India's Iran policy is that the US and Iran are adversaries. The US wants to isolate Iran, partly through imposing strict economic sanctions on the country, and it wants its other ally countries, including India, to follow this suit. Under President Donald Trump's administration, this prevailing issue has been further complicated. This forces India to engage in a delicate act of balance between, on the one hand, pursuing its regional goals and beneficial policies towards Iran, and on the other hand ensuring that the relationship with the US does not suffer. The question is how big a part the United States' policy has played on the Indian foreign policy's decisions that concern Iran. Since President Rouhani's rule, Tehran has perhaps understood realist aspects of the delicacy of its diplomacy particularly towards the West led by the United States.

It is a compulsion also of both the parties to resolve the crisis. Things are going on positively at least till date and one must hope that a win-win situation will be achieved by both the parties. At the outset of 21st century, the contours of international system have changed radically. It has provided an opportunity for both the countries. India is growing rapidly and all set to become third global energy consumer by 2022. The sustainable growth of India could not be ensured till the ensuring of energy security. Iran is one of the top five global energy-producing countries and its geographical location also gives India an advantage. Iran could be an excellent energy security guarantor to India. In contrast, it can also provide a sustainable energy consumer to Iran. In Central Asia too, Iran and India have several convergences. They wish to connect Central Asia with the Iranian port of Chabahar. It will give an impetus not only to Central Asian Republics but also to India and Iran. Iran is an energy-producing country and its sustainable growth depends on the sale of its precious natural resource. Due to its growing energy requirements, India is and will be an important buyer of Iranian energy products.

Eminent Indian security analyst, Raja Mohan has rightly stated in November 2013, "Any nuclear deal between Washington and Tehran will immediately bring down oil prices, relieve the current macroeconomic pressures on India, and improve Delhi's energy security calculus over the longer term. US–Iran rapprochement will help to strengthen Afghanistan against the Taliban and Pakistan and expand India's room for regional maneuver after 2014."[13] The deal between Washington and Tehran has already been concluded but new regime of President Trump has changed the contours of United States–Iran relations. President Trump administration is tilted towards Saudi Arabia and set to dent Iran. New sanctions have been clamped against Iran by Trump administration and the United States is expecting that India should do away with oil imports from Iran. United States has deployed its all-powerful navy in the Strait of Hormuz and it is going to be stationed there till 2020 US presidential election.

India–United States bilateral relations have deepened since last two decades. In September 2018, United States gave 2+2 dialogue status to India where foreign and defence secretary came together and had a summit level talk with their Indian counterparts. India has to convince United States that Iran has been a stabilizing factor in Afghanistan and Central Asia. Iraq and Syria conflict could not be resolved without Iranian cooperation. Iran is an important player and it had been part and parcel of Indian efforts along with Russia and Central Asian Republics to contain Taliban and formation of the Northern Alliance during Taliban rule over Afghanistan (1996-2001). In the backdrop of NATO withdrawal from Afghanistan, this proximity is utmost required and the US interest is also served. Containment of the Islamic State has remained a serious concern for the Western block, Iran, India, Russia and China. The way Islamic State has been executing its captives, it reminds us of the medieval barbarism and through these heinous acts, it has emerged as a threat to global humanity. Iran could be pivotal to contain Islamic State because one of the undeclared objectives of the Islamic State has been to weaken Iranian influence in the Middle East.

India will extremely benefit with its growing bilateral relationship with Iran and vice versa. Both countries have come together on a wide range of interests—be it economic, strategic, or others; therefore, they must minimize the divergences. In August 2013, Vice President of India was present in the swearing-in ceremony of new Iranian President Rouhani. It was an excellent goodwill gesture. Both countries are availing good relationships but to cope up with the emerging challenges, they urgently need to enhance it.

Iranian President Hassan Rouhani visited New Delhi in February 2018. President Rouhani and PM Modi had extensive talks and inked nine agreements. It includes easing visa rules and cooperation on medical sector apart from a maritime agreement on Chabahar port development.[14] Trade, investment and regional connectivity between India and Iran received a boost from this visit. Deepening India–Iran bonhomie is quite important for the peace and stability in Southwest Asia. One of the most important obligations for a country is to provide basic human rights and security to its people. Both India and Iran could do it successfully through a deepened relationship. It is of utmost importance to both the countries to promote their bilateral relationship. Modi government has adopted 'Look West Policy'. The mandate of this policy has been to engage countries which are situated west to India. Iran is one of the fulcrums of India's Look West Policy due to its energy reserves and geo-strategic location. Modi government has taken many pro-active steps to accelerate Indo-Iran relationship despite many prevailing issues. The prevailing trust deficit between Iran and the United States has complicated India's option for energy security. India imports 12% of its energy demand from Iran. Due to the US sanctions, India is compelled to stop the imports. If tension between the US and Iran will aggravate further, global oil prices will go up and that could be detrimental for Indian surging economy because India imports over 90% of its energy requirements. Modi-II government is expected to forward its previous NDA policies led by PM Vajpayee with the timely modifications in the context of Indo–Iran relationship.

NOTES

1. Shahram Chubin, "Is Iran a Military Threat", *Survival,* Vol-56, No-2, April-May 2014, p. 66.
2. "Can't forget support India gave us during difficult times, Iran", *The Times of India,* New Delhi, August 15, 2015 & India TV, May 2016.
3. Afghanistan launches new export route to India through Iran, *Reuters,* February 26, 2019.
4. Juli A. MacDonald, "Rethinking India and Pakistan's Regional Intend", *The National Bureau of Asian Research Analysis,* 14:4: 2009: 5-26.
5. India, Af and Iran discuss Chabahar port operations, *Times of India,* New Delhi, December 25, 2018.
6. Rajeev Ranjan Chaturvedy, *Interpreting China's Grand Strategy at Gwadar,* Institute of Peace and Conflict Studies, 14 February 2006.
7. *Dawn,* Karachi, *July 4, 2006.*
8. Source: Indrani Bagchi, Access to Omani port to help India Check China at Gwadar, Delhi Extends Its Strategic Reach to West, *Times of India,* New Delhi, February 14, 2018.
9. *Tehran Times (Tehran)* November 28, 2011.
10. Mohammad Arifeen, "Chahbahar Port: Its Importance for India", *The News International (Rawalpindi),* November 22, 2011.
11. Brzezinski, Zbigniew. 2012. *Strategic Vision.* New York: Basic Books, pp. 20, 162.
12. Pant, Harsh V. 2008. *Contemporary debates in Indian foreign and security policy: India negotiates its rise in the international system,* UK: Palgrave Macmillan, p. 1.
13. C. Raja Mohan, "The Great Game Folio", *The Indian Express,* New Delhi, 20 November 2013.
14. India-Iran sign 9 agreements, Focus on Chabahar port, *NDTV,* New Delhi, February 17, 2018.

2

Changing Political Matrix in Nepal:
India's Search for Continuity Amidst Change

Alok Kumar Gupta and Vandana Mishra

Indian Prime Minister Narendra Modi visited Nepal four times in his first four years of tenure. He went to Nepal twice on a state visit and once as an attendee to the 18th South Asian Association for Regional Cooperation Conference in Kathmandu. His third visit was on May 11-12, 2018, which followed his two telephonic conversations with Nepal's Prime Minster K.P. Oli and the then Union External Affairs Minister Late Sushma Swaraj's visit to Nepal in February 2018, subsequent to which Oli had come to India on a three-day visit in April 2018.[1] His fourth visit was to attend the 4th BIMSTEC (Bay of Bengal Initiative for Multi-Sectoral Technical and Economic Cooperation) on August 30-31, 2018. I.K. Gujral as Prime Minster was the last to make a bilateral visit to Nepal in June 1997. The visit was in view of the changing matrix in the neighbourhood of India. According to some experts, India faces the danger of losing its grip on Bhutan and the Maldives alongside Nepal. Therefore, Modi needs to do a lot more to prove he is serious about his 'Neighbourhood First' policy. Undoubtedly, the change in the political contours of Nepal necessitated hectic and engaging diplomatic activity on parts of India not only in Nepal but in the entire neighbourhood as well. It has also started showing results in Maldives, Bangladesh, Sri Lanka, Afghanistan and Nepal barring strains in bilateral relations with Pakistan. Here is an account of development in Nepal and imperatives for India.

The year 2017[2] has been historical for Nepal for the sole reason that it took a strong leap forward towards entrenching its hard-earned democracy. Elections were held in Nepal for all the three tiers of government, i.e. federal, provincial and local. It was for the first time in the history of Nepal that all the elections were organised in the same calendar year after the promulgation of the new constitution of Nepal in September 2015. Nepal indeed has come a long way from the quagmire of the first conflict between monarchy and its supporters on the one hand and pro-democracy forces on the other; second, the prolonged struggle of the two successive constituent assemblies towards generating consensus over a number of issues to redesign power arrangements in Nepal by way of hammering out a constitution for itself; third, on account of unstable coalition governments, which have been the norm since multi-party democracy was established in 1990. The scale of victory that the Left Alliance has achieved has been expected by most experts to bring political stability in the otherwise politically volatile country thus far.[3] However, such expectations are the consequences of long tumultuous Nepal that has led to a deep sense of frustration within the common man and the political leadership alike. Therefore, it is quite premature to predict about the scale of stability in Nepal in the aftermath of the New Government in accordance with the provisions of the New Constitution.

Nepal has been shattered in the recent past on account of natural and political earthquakes. The natural earthquake jolted Nepal in April 2015 killing over 8000 people and displacing lakhs of others. Nearly 600,000 houses were damaged with schools and hospitals incurring massive damages. Nearly 25,000 classrooms were reduced to rubble in the devastating earthquake.[4] The political earthquake has been striking Nepal for over two to three decades making it politically volatile and unstable. Monarchy stands abolished but a multi-party parliamentary democracy is yet to consolidate.

Economically, Nepal stands a shattered country by now on account of several pitfalls. Last three decades have been politically turbulent for Nepal which also witnessed a violent insurgency movement for about ten years. The insurgency alongside the 2015 earthquakes is increasingly responsible for breaking the backbone of its economy. Political stability of course contributed towards policy paralysis and Nepal's politics was neck-deep in power struggle rather than being able and committed to plan its development and work on its plan subsequently. Consequently, Nepal continued to be in dire need for employment for its people, health facilities, safe drinking water, education, road networks and other basic amenities. According to government data, over 2 million Nepalis were working abroad in 2011, as they could not find employment at home.[5] Therefore, one can only imagine the kind of economic development that Nepal badly needs to provide its citizens a decent life where they are able to meet their daily needs.

Nepal is a natural buffer between China and India. The present ruling Nepali Congress (NC) is considered pro-India and the Left Alliance is seen closer to China. K.P. Oli as leader of the Left Alliance is all set to become the Prime Minister of Nepal. He will be forced to be pragmatic in maintaining a geopolitical balance with both India and China. The simple reason is that Nepal cannot ignore India and engage with China at the cost of its relations with India which is its natural ally. Therefore, diplomatically Nepal is again in a complex situation and how it will adjust its relations with both its giant neighbours shall be interesting to watch for journalists, academicians and policy-analysts alike. Given the post-election political scenario, it makes it imperative to explore the subsequent development and analyse it in the context of its impact on Indo-Nepal relations. This chapter is an attempt to understand as to whether winning of Nepal's Left Alliance is India's diplomatic failure or it has strengthened its policy of mutual non-interference in internal affairs of its neighbours.

Elections in Nepal[6]: An Overview

The current Legislature, i.e. Parliament's mandate was expiring on 21st January 2018; therefore, by this time the elections were needed to be completed. Nepal was already late for the same as the Local and Federal provincial elections had to be held latest by May 2017, but there were a number of impending issues still existing like agreement on a number of provinces and their boundaries.[7] Yet Nepal organised elections from May through December 2017 in five separate stages for all the three levels of government, i.e. local, provincial, and national. The election witnessed shifting alliance between and among different political parties. Most important alliance was Nepal's largest communist parties: the Communist Party of Nepal (Maoist Centre) and the Communist Party of Nepal (Unified Marxist-Leninist; CPN-UML), the former being led by Pushp Kamal Dahal (Prachanda) and the latter by K.P. Sharma Oli. Both these parties had been bitter rivals, and they announced plans to run together for the provincial and national polls and merged into a single, unified party following the elections. Unity enabled them to win a majority and turn the table on NC, erstwhile dominant political party of Nepal. The leaders of Left Alliance in Nepal claimed to bring 'prosperity through stability' during their election campaign.[8]

The Left Alliance came out victorious in the elections at all three levels of government. In the national parliament, the Left Alliance has achieved a majority which is little short of the two-thirds majority needed to make any changes to the Nepal's Constitution. NC, the ruling party of Nepal, suffered serious reverses and secured less than a quarter of seats in parliament.[9] The Left Alliance secured overwhelming majorities in both the federal bicameral legislature (the House of Representatives and National Assembly) and the provincial assemblies. The alliance formed the governments in six out of seven provinces. The Left Alliance combined to secure 70 percent of the first-past-the-post seats. Out of 165 total FPTP constituencies, CPN-UML won 80 seats; the CPN (Maoist Centre) won 36 seats. The centrist NC, which suffered a serious setback, received only 23 seats, under 14 percent of the total available. Two Madhes-based parties, the Rashtriya Janata Party–Nepal (RJPN) and the Sanghiya Samajbadi Forum (SSF), combined to secure 21 seats; other fringe parties won the remaining five seats.[10]

The parallel elections of Nepal also include the elections for the proportional-representation (PR) seats. In this election, the voters indicate their support for a party rather than a candidate and seats are distributed accordingly. Elections for the PR seats are organised through a closed-party list ballot system. Accordingly, CPN-UML and NC were almost even. UML secured 33.25 percent of votes, NC 32.78 percent, and CPN (Maoist Centre) 13.66 percent. The two Madhes-based parties each secured just under 5 percent. Only five parties—the CPN-UML, NC, CPN (Maoist Centre), SSF, and RJPN—won enough of the vote to secure seats under the PR category.[11] Out of 275 seats in the House of Representatives, the left alliance holds 174 (121 for the CPN-UML, and 53 for Maoists), the NC 63, the RJPN 17, and the SSF 16.[12]

As far as the governments in seven provinces are concerned, the left alliance formed government in six provinces out of seven. Province No. 2, bordering India, is the only exception in which a non-left government could become a possibility. As Nepal's upper house, the National Assembly, saw most seats elected by the provinces, the election results effectively had the Left Alliance control of both houses of the Nepali Federal Parliament because in out of seven provinces, Left Alliance has majority in six.

Nepal's first successful local elections were concluded in September 2017. Nepalis elected over 35,000 representatives to run 753 local governments. CPN-UML won control of 296 out of total 753 local bodies, and CPN (Maoist Centre) won another 106 in these local-level elections. Of the 35,000 elected representatives, nearly 14,000 are women, which has changed their numerical presence in local bodies. All told, the parties that later formed the Left Alliance won control for 402 local bodies, which is a clear majority. The NC that emerged as the largest party after the elections held in 2013 fell to the second largest party in the local-level polls. In the latest elections, there were no considerable changes in these voting patterns.[13] The majority of these newly elected representatives do not have previous experience in government. Many have backgrounds in the private sector, including as real estate agents, contractors, and middlemen with known track records of voraciously serving their own private interests and their patrons in political parties.[14] How they will govern in the public interest should be of greater concern than their background. It becomes obvious from the personal profile of these elected representatives that given their ignorance about process of governance on the one hand and their economic well-being on the other will be enough to create a mess. This may contribute towards political instability at the local level. Nepal suffered badly on account of Maoist insurgency during 1996-2006 and it gripped the countryside badly. Consequently, the local elections were called off in 2002 amid security concerns and most of the villages were being administered by centrally appointed bureaucrats. Even during the days of drafting the Constitution for Nepal the Constituent Assembly put off the local bodies elections.[15] Accordingly, the local bodies had a long spell of absence of governance which again will amount to incapacity. The new found power may reach to the head of these representatives and their actions may be detrimental to their locality in particular and the polity of Nepal in general.

However, the successful completion of election ensured for Nepal a new political course. By February of 2018,[16] one federal government, seven provincial governments, and 753 municipal governments, were in place with co-equal standing under the new Constitution. The anxieties of those who stand to lose power and the eagerness of those with newfound power must be tempered by the existential challenges that lie immediately ahead of the new republic under the new Constitution:[17]

> Newly elected leadership had to focus on accommodating the three nested power centres and their distinct preferences, needs, and interests. Working out the jurisdiction, authority, and resources for each will require time as well as a nuanced approach—deploying peaceful negotiation, dignified compromise, and lawful challenge in court.[18] Prima facie it seems that Nepal's political leadership is not yet mature to that extent to give a positive direction to these future challenges. Aspirations and expectations of both the leaders and the lead were high but with restraints and constraints, and patience was needed at all the levels to give Nepal's polity a gradual stability with consequent development. A considerable period of time is over by now and it seems Nepal

is on the right course with political stability defying the forecasts of instability of most pundits.

The tortuous transition toward democratic consolidation in a federal structure and the building up of new institutions must be understood as deep deficits that need to be addressed in both politics and the rule of law. Political leadership will have to develop a high level of political maturity and raise themselves above power-politics to execute this onerous task which Oli thus far has successfully executed.

Elections to the National Assembly (Upper House) of the Federal Parliament were scheduled to take place on February 8, 2018. This was decided after President Bidya Devi Bhandari approved the National Assembly Act to pave the way for holding the elections. The National Assembly will have a total of 59 members. Of these, 56 were to be elected by an electoral college comprising assembly members of the seven provinces and chiefs and deputy chiefs of municipalities and rural municipalities. Rest of the three were to be nominated by the President as per the recommendation of the government.[19] Given the majority of Left Alliance at most levels of the electoral-college, the Left Alliance continued to have majority in the National Assembly, the Upper House of Nepal Parliament as well. At present, the Left Alliance has 41 seats, NC has 13 seats, Samajbadi Party Nepal has two seats and RJPN has two seats. Thus, a new Nepal has born under the leadership of Prime Minister K.P. Oli.

Elections in Nepal: Indo-China Concerns

Elections in Nepal were being monitored closely by both the South Asian rivals India and China. Main concern was related to the curiosity as to who will form the government: the Left Alliance of the Communist Party of Nepal (Unified Marxist-Leninist) and CPN (Maoist Centre) or the democratic block led by the centrist NC party. Hence, both India and China were concerned about the results of the election as both have been competing covertly and overtly to curve out a larger share of influence within Nepal. There are several reasons behind their competition and wish to enlarge their influence in Nepal.

Though the winning left coalitions of Nepal were harping that it would follow a balanced foreign policy, yet the indications were not in that direction. Khadga Prasad (KP) Sharma Oli has a strange way of demonstrating this. Oli visited the border with China in Rasuwagadhi after the elections and declared that Rasuwagadhi-Kerung border point, the only trade and transit point between Nepal and China, would be upgraded to international standards.[20] Therefore, even before taking the oath of Office of Prime Minister, Oli has demonstrated his allegiance and tilt towards China.

China's major security interests in Nepal include its border with the Tibet autonomous region, a potential hotbed of domestic instability over questions of sovereignty to Tibetans. China also has been pursuing a policy of encirclement of India by cultivating India's neighbours. China has been successful in its endeavours one after the other: first, through interference in internal political affairs of these countries and making all efforts to install either a left or a pro-left government which has greater sense of allegiance towards China, and secondly, through investing in these countries in building their infrastructure for which China is economically competent. Nepal has been no exception to this trap of China's foreign policy choice. However, this has serious strategic implications for India.

Firstly, by all probabilities the new government that has come to power in Nepal will sustain for its full term of five years as it is an alliance on the same side of ideological spectrum and with a comfortable majority. Nepal has largely been politically unstable on account of lack of majority in the past. This has created problems for both India and China as far as their developmental works in Nepal are concerned. A politically stable government in Nepal would facilitate both the countries towards conducting a long-term sustained diplomacy to bag developmental projects and execute the same in due time. India will continue to be at a loss as it has a bad impression of talking more and delivering less on the ground. China has an excellent record of executing most and that too before time. China also has advantage in terms of its deep pocket compared to India.

Secondly, the blockade along Indo-Nepal border, during the crisis that occurred on account of Madhesi protest against September 2015 Nepal's Constitution, angered a large part of the Nepalese population, allowing China to step in as an alternative to India by providing internet access as well as alternative trade routes through which goods and other relevant services were supplied to Nepal. There is no doubt that transiting goods and services through China is costlier than through India for Nepal, yet Nepal wants to open a viable route through China to reduce its over-dependence on India. This will have long-term implications for India in terms of mitigating its leverage over Nepal, thereby undermining its influence over Nepal. Last election results have made it more obvious that India is seriously bound to lose on several counts with a pro-China government coming into existence in Nepal.

Thirdly, Nepal's economy has been ailing since the earthquake of 2015 as its reliance on aid and remittances remains at an all-time high. China's attraction under such circumstances is quite natural. China has pledged $8.3 billion to build roads and hydropower plants, even as Indian commitments remain in the realm of $317 million.[21] It makes it obvious that China has a fat purse over India and that too with an added advantage of a pro-China government in the seat of authority in Nepal. China thus has all reasons to be happy about the last election results. India has to be worried about the same though India has no choice but to keep repeating the oft-quoted phrase that we have enough space in the South Asian region to keep operating and engaging with our neighbours alongside China.

Fourthly, as part of its "One Belt, One Road" (OBOR) initiative China is looking into the possibility of connecting Kathmandu to Lhasa in Tibet via railways at an estimated cost of $8 billion. China's activities have been steadily expanding in Nepal after its support for OBOR materialized. This development took place in spite of India's stiff resistance to OBOR.[22] Given the fact that India is deadly opposed to China's OBOR, it would be tremendous loss to India that its trusted neighbours are falling to China's project one after the other. It is indeed a serious policy-failure on part of India that it has failed to cajole its neighbours to maintain their loyalty towards India. India is bound to lose tremendously if its neighbours are integrated more with China than India. The loss will be strategic which would further undermine its security.

Fifthly, the Deuba government had decided to cancel a major $2.5 billion hydroelectric project awarded to Chinese state company China Gezhouba Group in November 2017 much to the annoyance of Chinese political leadership. The new Oli government by all means will reverse the decision. He earlier also warned, "The issue here is about foreign investment and such investment and such decisions cannot be taken on a whim."[23] Once again India, which has enough enterprising experience and expertise in hydroelectricity will lose a project to China with the advent of the new government in Nepal and the same would be imitated in other areas as well. However, with the signing of Arun-III, India seems to have compensated the loss and is aggressive towards its Nepal policy.

Sixthly, China has donated over 32,000 solar power-generating systems to Nepal to enhance its domestic capacity and to provide electricity to communities that have been without power since the 2015 earthquake. The donated items included 32,000 sets of household solar power generation systems and 325 sets of solar power generation systems.[24] India too has been working hard and expanding its expertise in solar power generation since last one decade. Indian business communities could have opportunities in Nepal on this count. However, their prospects would be lessened or may be diminished to zero with a left pro-China government in Nepal and China taking lead in this area too.

Last but more important is that China has been investing heavily in Nepal as it seeks to expand its influence in the land-locked country which is heavily dependent on supplies of essential goods from India. Oli during his brief stint in power in 2015-16 signed the Transit Transport Agreement (TTA) with China to improve the connectivity between Nepal and Tibet in a bid to end decades-old dependency on India for daily supplies. China in a strategic move agreed to extend the train link in Tibet to Nepal to improve the connectivity by road and rail. China has also been instrumental towards addressing environmental problems and climate change, which will benefit Nepali people from the perspective of health and time.[25] Therefore, it is obvious that given a left dispensation in Nepal with a pro-China profile, Nepal is bound to have greater integration and engagement with China which India needs to be cautious about. The last two visits of Modi might have been able to restrain China in Nepal to an extent.

India's Recalibrating its Relation with Nepal: Search for Continuity Amidst Change

India's responses to Nepal and its demands were given a strong boost when Narendra Modi took the reins in his hands as Prime Minister of India. His proactive outreach, however, suffered a setback first due to the Madhesi crisis, and second due to Oli's allegations that India was responsible for triggering and engineering the downfall of his government. India seems to have made renewed efforts to cement the cracking ties with Nepal. However, the country was too busy in the then ongoing elections in Gujarat and Himachal Pradesh. Gujarat being the home-state of Prime Minister Narendra Modi, the entire political leadership was busy in the management of Gujarat and was left with hardly any time and spirit to manage the elections in Nepal. Therefore, Modi may have managed to minimise his loss in Gujarat but ignored to manage the same in Nepal. It cannot even be said that India mismanaged its relations with Nepal or elections in Nepal; rather India and Indian leadership ignored the mega-event taking place in Nepal, which is right under its nose.

India thus has paid the price for the same and is allowing China to step into the vacuum created on the turf left by India. China was pro-active since the pre-election days and was able to achieve notable diplomatic success by helping the Left Alliance win elections in Nepal. China undoubtedly has caused an irreparable loss to India which cannot be easily replenished. India thus suffered diplomatic loss in Nepal because of taking things lightly and ignoring the same.

Winning of Left Alliance in Nepal was certainly not a welcome sign for India under any circumstances and will have tremendous implications in future for Indo-Nepal relations. One may even go to the extent of saying that with this, Indo-Nepal relations have entered into a new phase. NC, which is considered to be a pro-Indian party, stands routed in the elections with almost blunted teeth in Nepal politics and will be of no help to India.

The Indian Ministry of External Affairs had welcomed the outcome of Nepali elections as it has no choice but to do so as diplomatic etiquette. In its official statement, it said,

> We congratulate the government and the people of Nepal. India has age old unique, time tested ties of friendship with the country. We look forward to working with the next democratically elected government in Nepal to advance our close and multifaceted partnership across all sectors and to support Nepal in its pursuit of peace, stability, economic prosperity and all round development.[26]

The then Indian External Affairs Minister Late Ms. Sushma Swaraj also visited Nepal marking the beginning of an engagement with the CPN-UML leader and Prime Minister-elect K.P. Sharma Oli. She met a wide cross-section of political leadership of Nepal to avoid embarrassment. Her visit also coincided with the announcement of Rs. 650 crore for Nepal in the Union Budget of India.[27] The visit was indeed a damage control exercise on part of Indian political dispensation.

India took a further stride in its bilateral relations when Indian Prime Minster Modi visited Nepal for the third time on May 11-12, 2014. High-level visits at a bilateral level undoubtedly carry loads of political significance. Narendra Modi compensated the diplomatic loss during his third visit and re-established his lost ground in terms of allegations that he was responsible towards bringing down of earlier Oli's government in Nepal. It will also help India entrench its sphere of influence in Nepal. India though late but has started its endeavours to cultivate positive relations with the new Government of Nepal as an effort to keep continuity in its Nepal policy amidst change in Nepal.

Modi started his third visit from Janakpur, the heartland of Madhes or the southern planes whose residents are ethnically and socially close to Indians across the border. His desire to start his visit from Janakpur in the Madhesi-majority Terai region had two motivating elements: first, the government of Nepal had cancelled his visit to Janakpur and the Muktinath temple in northern Nepal during his second visit in 2014; second, Janakpur is both putative birthplace of Sita and, as the temporary capital of Province 2,[28] important to the Madhesi plains people's longstanding demand for proportional representation in the Nepalese parliament through a constitution amendment, which India has pushed through diplomatic pressure and direct economic interference.[29] However, a section of the experts also mentions about the wariness of Madhes about Modi as all hills-people and some plains-people see stereotyping of the Nepalese as sub-continental subordinates like Gurkhas, Sherpas and migrant workers to India, and of the country as a political satellite and a religious cash cow. However, during this visit, this notion stood refuted as Nepal allowed Modi to not only visit both these venues but also use them to attempt to endear himself to this Hindu-majority country riven by anti-India and especially anti-Modi protests.[30] Thus, Modi killed two birds with one stone by commencing his visit from Janakpur in Province 2, especially with the message that India stood with their demand for the constitutional amendment. He advised the Madhesis to unite and consolidate power, and assured them of Indian support for an amendment to the Nepalese constitution. However, he refrained from commenting on matters related to Madhes, especially the demand that Sunsari, Moran and Jhapa be joined with Province 2 and Kailali and Kanchanpur with Province 5.[31]

Modi also inaugurated the construction of a mega hydropower plant during his visit as part of his government's move to counter Chinese influence in its backyard. He with Oli laid the foundation stone of the $1.4 billion India-backed Arun-III hydropower plant,[32] a long-mooted project that could be a game-changer for energy-starved Nepal. It will also generate employment opportunities as well as create commercial and economic opportunities in Nepal.[33] Plant is the first of five mega hydropower projects, two of which are backed by Chinese companies, to begin construction, which marks a diplomatic win for India.[34] Modi thus through his visit has tried to ensure that as part of his 'neighbourhood first' policy, India can also deliver on big-ticket infrastructure promises. Nepal has enough water to be a hydro powerhouse, but it has so far harnessed less than 2 percent of that potential according to different estimates. India thus has tremendous opportunity in this field which it seems to have understood well under Modi's leadership.

Modi visited Nepal for the fourth time during August 30-31, 2018 to attend the 4th BIMSTEC[35] meeting and further deepened the India-Nepal friendship alongside holding a series of bilateral meetings with regional leaders.[36] The two-day summit led to the Kathmandu Declaration which deplored the terror attacks in all parts of the world including in BIMSTEC countries and stressed that there can be no justification whatsoever for any act of terrorism. Modi met with Oli once again on the sidelines of this Summit and held a detailed review on all aspects of the bilateral relationship including ways to further deepen economic and trade ties. He did the same review exercise with Thailand counterpart Chan-o-cha, Myanmar's President Win Myint, Bangladesh's PM Sheikh Hasina, and Sri Lanka's President Maithripala Sirisena. This further reiterated his commitment to his 'neighbourhood first' policy.

During his earlier visit while he addressed the Nepalese Parliament, he had announced Rs.10,000 crore as concessional line of credit to Nepal. He had also proposed HIT formula for the development of Nepal which is endowed with rich hydropower potential. By HIT he meant, H for Highways; I for I-ways; and T for Transways, and had said these three combined together would pave the way for rapid development of the country and India wants to give this gift to Nepal at earliest.[37] On his third visit, Modi inaugurated the "Ramayana Circuit" in which India will run the Janakpur-to-Ayodhya bus service. The trip is aimed at developing 15 destinations in India under the Ramayana Circuit: Ayodhya, Nandigram, Shringverpur in Uttar Pradesh, Chitrakoot in Madhya Pradesh, Sitamarhi, Buxar and Darbhanga in Bihar, Mahendragiri in Odisha, Jagdalpur in Chhattisgarh, Nashik and Nagpur in Maharashtra, Bhadrachalam in Telangana, Hampi in Karnataka, and Rameshwaram in Tamil Nadu.[38] Thus, Modi has also been working on expanding India's connectivity with Nepal to extend India's cultural outreach. A number of agreements were also inked during Oli's April 2018 visit to India. Oli's major takeaway from India included the construction of an India-funded railway line connecting Raxaul in Bihar with Kathmandu, the laying of the Motihari-Amlekhgunj cross-border petroleum product pipeline, and the inauguration of the Integrated Check Post at Birgunj in Nepal.[39] Thus, with these visits and countervisits, Indo-Nepal bilateral ties seem to have been put on the right course with correction in foreign policy.

Nepal's New Leverage

Nepal with the announcement of election results and winning of Left Alliance has acquired greater room for manoeuvrability now between China and India. Nepal knows it well that India will try to prevent Nepal from developing closer links with China and could thus blackmail India to serve its national interests. India, therefore, must not prevent Nepal from developing closer links with China so long as Nepal is able to and is protecting India's interests. Nepali political leadership also understands that the links with India are natural and are rooted in history, culture and geography which cannot be severed so easily. India may be apprehensive about Oli's Nepal using China card against India but at the same time India should know that all governments in Nepal have been doing the same so far. Therefore, India must not be wary of Nepal's newfound friend in India's competitor in the region, and rather adopt an aggressive Nepal policy in which it must have devoted officials working round the clock to enhance engagement at all levels with Nepal. Modi for now seems to have been doing so and Indo-Nepal bilateral ties are on the right path.

Nepal's Prime Minister after the election results made a remark that his party was eager to work in collaboration with neighbouring countries and would forge a partnership with India to move towards the path of economic prosperity.[40] As discussed above, Nepal is in serious need for economic development with varied requirements. India thus needs to explore its complementarity with Nepal in the changing world and circumstances and try forging an alliance for the same. Leaving the Nepal's turf wide open for China will be another policy blunder on part of India. India needs to think positively that with a new political dispensation in Nepal, the country has acquired a new leverage where it can make India to work hard to deliver fast and concretely on the ground, rather than talk rhetoric without matching the same on the ground. Modi has perfectly taken it as an opportunity.

Nepal no doubt has acquired a new leverage which it will use against India in furtherance of its national interests. Yet it needs to use it cautiously and judiciously without annoying the other and maintaining the same in the long run. Nepal under Oli will have to strike a delicate balance between his two giant neighbours India and China. Oli will have to adjust his image between anti-India and pro-China stand. Oli is not the sole political actor in Nepal and India too has its clout within Nepali leadership though outside power. Nepal needs to take care of the same and make efforts not to earn the wrath of them. Nepal's leverage must not turn out to be a battle-turf for the two big competitors of the region, i.e. China and India.

Conclusion

Both Oli's visit to India in April 2018 and Modi's visit to Nepal in May and August 2018 were landmark in the sense of providing a strong boost to Indo-Nepal bilateral ties and India's 'neighbourhood first' policy. India must understand that Nepal is geo-strategically and traditionally too important for it. Hence, India cannot afford to lose Nepal to China. India thus will have to deal with Nepal irrespective of the kind of political set up that exists there. Hopefully, Nepal after the restoration of democracy in real sense of the term will be able to mitigate the partisan politics both within and without and focus on development as there is no major political agenda for parties than the development of Nepal and its people. Nepal may finally embark on a journey of peace and economic development. Nepal requires stability, good governance and economic development all in one go. Onus lies on Nepal as to how it uses both its giant neighbours reaping maximum benefit from both in furtherance of its national interests, rather than pitting one against the other with a view to blackmail each of them.

The contrary views are already being advanced that Nepal's political instability is far from over. The instability and lack of ownership of the Constitution is largely due to the denial of space to traditional political forces, a factor that external actors including India refuse to acknowledge. During the past 13 years, India and other external actors aligned with forces that raised arms against the state to push for a radical change in politics in preference to an evolutionary process accepted in other democracies. Nepal's new political dispensation thus needs to be magnanimous enough to appreciate the demands being articulated by Madhesis and such forces for their due rehabilitation by way of making adequate arrangements in the Constitution as they are their own citizens, though of different origin. Fact remains that they are by now completely assimilated in Nepali population and are very much like indigenous communities. Such an act will certainly bring greater political cohesion within Nepal's polity and would also make its federal structure increasingly meaningful.

The massive victory of Left Alliance in Nepal may sound like waning of the influence of traditional forces. However, the rise of communists is only natural and not phenomenal, something that Left force in Nepal needs to know and understand. Their political future would stabilise only when they are able to perform and stand on the aspirations of voters. Accordingly, Nepal's new political dispensation needs to comprehend the complex challenges at local, regional and international levels and formulate adequate and apt responses to meet and mitigate those challenges on the ground.

India may have suffered a diplomatic setback for a while which is on account of its own engagement at sub-national politics. However, it needs to realise that all is not lost and must work hard to compensate the diplomatic loss that it has caused to itself. Therefore, India under Modi seems to have accepted the mandate of the Nepalese people and has started dealing in the right direction with the left leadership from the day new dispensation took oath in Nepal. The changing approach in Indian leadership could be an assurance of tremendous positive development in Indo-Nepal ties in near future.

NOTES

1. Pramod Jaiswal, "Modi's historic Nepal visit was aimed more at his Indian constituency than bilateral ties", *Scroll*, May 18, 2018, www.scroll.in
2. Year 2074 in the lunar calendar.
3. Nepal adopted a multi-party parliamentary democracy in 1990. However, all early parliaments were dissolved before they completed their five-year term. This led to political instability in Nepal. The parliamentary system adopted after 1990 also reported number of anomalies and aberrations like corruption, and horse-trading. In 1999, the parliamentary elections were held for the last time which was later dissolved in 2001 and a state of emergency was declared. Nepal underwent a long spell of absence of any elected body which sabotaged its governance system. The first Constituent Assembly (CA) was elected in 2008 after a peace deal was struck with Maoists in 2006. The first CA could not complete the task of Constitution writing, so again it was elected in 2013 which subsequently promulgated its Constitution in September 2015. Both the CAs included more than 30 parties, which was the main cause of government instability.
4. PTI, "China donates over 32,000 solar power generators to Nepal", *Indian Express*, January 22, 2018.
5. Kamal Dev Bhattarai, "What Caused the Left Alliance's Landslide Victory in Nepal?", December 19, 2017, *The Diplomat*, www.thediplomat.com
6. There are three types of elections in Nepal as per the newly promulgated constitution. They are elections to the Federal Parliament, elections to the State Assemblies and elections to the local government. Two electoral systems are used: parallel voting for House of Representatives and Provincial Assemblies, and first past the post is used for local elections.
7. *Nepal Times*, Editorial, January 21, 2018, www.nepaltimes.com
8. Peter Gill, "The Rise of Nepal's Left Alliance", January 29, 2018, *The Diplomat*, www.thediplomat.com
9. Nepali Congress, the country's oldest political party and one that favours close ties with India had won 105 out of 240 directly elected seats in the CA elections of 2013. The CPN-UML came second with 91 seats and UCPN-Maoists had only 26 seats then which was the dominant party in the 2008 CA elections. See Gardiner Harris, "Election Results in Nepal Signal a Political Right Turn", November 25, 2013, www.nytimes.com
10. Ibid., No. 5.
11. Ibid.
12. Ibid.
13. Ibid.
14. George Varughese, "Nepal Embarks on New Political Course", *Nepal Times*, November 29, 2017.
15. Peter Gill, "Nepal: Elections at the Epicenter", May 19, 2017, *The Diplomat*, www.thediplomat.com
16. K.P. Oli was sworn in as First Prime Minister under the new constitution on 15 February 2018 and he won 208 votes in Motion of Confidence.

17 Ibid., No. 14.
18 Ibid., No. 14.
19 "Nepal to Hold National Assembly Elections on Feb 8", January 06, 2018, www.theshillongtimes.com
20 Harsh V Pant, "China's Moment in Nepal: Implications for India", December 27, 2017, *The Diplomat*, www.thediplomat.com
21 Ibid., No. 20.
22 Ibid.
23 Ibid.
24 Ibid., No. 4.
25 Ibid.
26 As quoted in Pant, ibid., No. 20.
27 Kallol Bhattacherjee, "India will work with Oli government, says Sushma", *The Hindu*, February 02, 2018.
28 Province 2 is area-wise the smallest, second-most populous and most densely populated province of Nepal. It also has the country's most thriving business community. But among this pro-India section that comprises more than a fifth of Nepal's population, Madhesi here hold the opinion that Modi did not push hard enough for a constitutional amendment that would topographically and politically empower them. However, the two Madhes-based parties in Nepal's parliament, the Rashtriya Janata Party–Nepal and Federal Socialist Forum Nepal, supported Oli's government during the March 2018 vote of confidence. As mentioned in Pramod Jaiswal, "Modi's historic Nepal visit was aimed more at his Indian constituency than bilateral ties", *Scroll*, May 18, 2018, www.scroll.in
29 As alleged, India had actively backed the 135-day blockade that had frozen essential cross-border trade from September 2015 to February 2016, a week after the constitution was promulgated. For details, see Jaiswal, ibid.
30 Ibid., No. 1.
31 Ibid., No. 1.
32 Arun-III is located near Num, a remote village in the Sankhuwasabha district in northeastern Nepal. The cost of the project escalated from Rs. 5,700 crore to an estimated Rs. 7000 crore as of April 2018.
33 "Narendra Modi visits Nepal in a bid to counter China influence", *The Times of India*, May 12, 2018, www.timesofindia.indiatimes.com
34 Chinese firms pledged more than $8.3 billion in investment in 2017, dwarfing Indian commitments of $317 million. Nepal also signed up to China's OBOR infrastructure initiative in 2017, which is an irritant to India. See Ibid., No. 33.
35 The Bay of Bengal Initiative for Multi-Sectoral Technical and Economic Cooperation (BIMSTEC) is a regional grouping comprising India, Bangladesh, Myanmar, Sri Lanka, Thailand, Bhutan and Nepal.
36 PTI, "PM Modi wraps up Nepal visit after attending BIMSTEC Summit", August 31, 2018, www.moneycontrol.com
37 From www.narendramodi.in
38 Ibid., No. 1.
39 Ibid., No. 1.
40 PTI, "In a bid to mend ties, Sushma Swaraj assures Nepal support for political stability", *The Indian Express*, February 02, 2018, www.theindianexpress.com

3

A New Foreign Policy Agenda for Modi:
"Look West"

Alokka Dutta

India has seen the West Asia almost entirely through the prism of commercial interests, namely imports of energy and exports of migrant labour. This is understandable given these two factors have supported poverty reduction, a central policy priority. Now, however geopolitical winds are shifting as West Asia is rapidly becoming more strategically important to India. This is due in part to the anticipated decline, relative to other powers, of Washington's interest and influence in the region, creating room for newcomers. China's growing involvement further increases the stakes, as does India's ambitions for a sphere of influence encompassing the Western Indian Ocean. In responding to both opportunities and threats, Delhi should adopt a long-term vision, targeting states and actors most important for India's strategic ascendance and increasing engagement commensurately. A 'Look West Policy' (LWP) like India's famed 'Look East Policy' has often been spoken about, but there has not been a formal institutionalisation of the same. This will need a concentrated focus—like the LEP—for the region, to formulate effective policies. While trade is a significant component of this relationship, the essence of the LWP will be the multi-dimensionality of its character. As much as India trades with the region, also important are the issues of security, culture, people linkages and those of wider geopolitical and geostrategic linkages.

It is also true that India has always been supportive of Arab cause, especially Palestinians since India's independence. The great leaders like Mahatma Gandhi and Pandit Jawaharlal Nehru strongly supported the rights of Arabs. They felt that the socio-economic and political problems of West Asian people were not 'different from those of Indians. The both leaders had the same view on the issue of Palestine and other West Asian in the same sense that England belongs to the English or France to the French.[1] India had in fact, supported the cause of Palestine in every UN and other international forums. She extended all possible material and moral support to Palestinian people.

It is however witnessed since the early 1990s that India's West Asian policy began to shift from its earlier policy. The proactive policy towards West Asia has continued under the new government of Prime Minister Narendra Modi who has given India's Foreign policy the much needed boost. It is now debated whether India's changing West Asian policy is in favour of India's national interest or not? This could be understood by considering some factors which are vital in explaining India's interest in West Asian countries.

Economic Factors

No doubt political and diplomatic factors based on national interest, are important. But at the same time, economic interest is one the most crucial factors that should be given priority, while formulating foreign policy. Taking this factor in to consideration, India is having a good relation with the West Asian countries since ancient times. The trade relation between the two traced back to the early part of the 20th century. Geographical proximity and economic interdependence are perhaps responsible factors for having greater interaction between, two regions which leads to mutual benets. There have been substantial commitments of investments by way of joint ventures from both sides. Many agreements were signed between India and these countries in order to promote trade and investment in their countries. It is noted that Indian imports from the region were estimated at more than $3 billion, while exports were estimated at less than $ 2 billion in 1991. These values increased to more than $ 8 billion of imports and less than $ 4.5 billion of exports to this region in 2000.[2] It is thus observed that bilateral trade got impetus on account of economic liberalisation taking place in India and the West Asian countries. The total valtie of trade with this region was more than $ 5 billion in 1991 than $ 12 billion in 2000. This would be expected go upto $ 130 billion by 2013-14 which was around $100 billion 2009-10.

It we look in terms of country wise, Saudi Arabia is one of the most important trading partners in the Gulf region. It is the 14th largest market for India and accounts for 7 percent of India total exports[3]. On the other hand, India is the fifth largest market for Saudi Arabia contributing about 4.5 percent of its total exports. Thus on the trade front, India has to explore opportunities-to add more items to its export basket. Currently India's export to Saudi Arabia mainly constitutes cereals, man-made filament, apparels & clothing, Iron and Steel[4]. The country has to focus more and more on value added industrial products and services. It is moving steadily towards a free market economy with gradual decontrolling of many important sectors of the economy. The service sector that offers potential of greater employment opportunities has been identified as one of the major focal areas. This offers an excellent opportunity to Indian industry to forge partnership with its counterparts in the Kingdom to build strong and vibrant economic relations between the two countries.

UAE is another major trading partner of India in the Gulf region. It is in fact India's biggest market in this region. India's exports to the UAE are diversified and contain a large basket of goods. Thus the significance of the UAE. For India is not only for imports but also for exports. This is so because U A13 has emerged as the topmost trading partner in the region. The UAE alone represents 70 per cent of India's exports to the GCC Countries[5]. Exports to the UAE comprise 6 percent of India's global exports. The major items of exports from India are gems and jewellery, textiles, manufactures of metals, machinery and instruments, plastic and linoleum, tea, Basmati rice, drugs, pharmaceuticals and chemicals primary and semi-finished iron and steel. Apart from this, information and news exports are emerging as a new area. On the other hand, India's main imports from the UAE are petroleum crude and products, pearls, precious and semi-precious stones, gold metaliferious ores and scrap, fertilisers and organic and inorganic chemicals.

There are many advantages to have good trading relations with the UAE. As it is the nearest destination and Dubai has emerged as the major trade centre and a gateway to entire Arab world. Almost 95 percent of trade to the GCC and 85 percent to the WANA region transits through Dubai. It is noted that many Indian companies are setting up their centre in Dubai and Sharjah and bidding for many ventures into the world market. Thus we can say that UAE is an important trading partner in this exports[7]. Narendra Modi became the first Prime minister to visit UAE after 34 years. After a successful two day visit to the UAE in August 2015 both states came down heavily on countries sponsoring terrorism against other states. The two sides decided to elevate India-UAE relationship to a comprehensive strategic partnership and chart out a new course for cooperation in key areas like trade and investment, defence, security, maritime security and intelligence sharing.

There is substantial trade to Qatar via Dubai. A number of consumer goods from India are available and popular in Qatar. There are good prospects for diversification and expansion due to the low level of customs duties in Qatar (4%), which is close to the proposed common GCC external tariff of 5%. India's export basket is fairly diversified and includes foodstuffs, spices, tea, coffee, textiles, ready-made-garments, jewellery, light engineering goods, basic chemicals, steel pipes, and consumer electronics. As the Qatari market is competitive and highly quality conscious, There is a room for expanding our exports further in areas where we are globally competitive.

India's imports from Qatar consist largely of urea, ammonia, sulphur, ethylene and polyethylene. India has substantial dealings with the Qatar Fertiliser Company (QAFCO) and the Qatar Petrochemical Company (QAPCO). India has not been a major customer for Qatari crude oil/products. However, it is set to emerge as one of Qatar's most important customers for LNG. With the third largest gas reserves in the world, Qatar is poised to emerge as a significant international supplier of energy for many decades to come. The Government of Qatar has made large investments in the development of its two LNG projects and port at Ras Laifan. With its large, expanding and long term requirements of natural gas, India is naturally keen to take advantage of the existence of a reliable and virtually inexhaustible source of natural gas situated so close to its own consuming centres.' This is the biggest agreement of this type in the world and will significantly raise the economic and commercial profile of India in Qatar, and of Qatar in India. This will also make India the biggest buyer of natural gas from Qatar. Within a week of the Prime Minister Modi's government assuming office, South Block hosted two important events: the foreign minister of Oman visited the new Indian minister of external affairs, and a ministerial delegation from Qatar followed shortly after, to hold foreign office consultations with their Indian counterparts. The timing of these visits is significant. It indicates more seriousness among the Indian leadership towards deepening New Delhi's engagement with West Asia.

India and Bahrain enjoys a trouble free and close political relationship. They also have a mutually beneficial bilateral economic cooperation. Bahrain is a small country but important one. Both these countries are very close to each other in many respects. India also exports a comparatively large amount of goods and services to Bahrain. Since most of Bahrain's needs are met through imports. There exists a good potential for enhanced exports from India. The Indian private sector could play a more active role in this area; Participation in exhibitions, bilateral business visits and consistency in quality and supply schedules can go a long way in promoting Indian exports. The policy of Bahrain Government joint ventures especially in the small and medium industries[8]. India can take a lead in this field in order to enhance exports to Bahrain.

There are mainly five items of exports from India to Bahrain. These are textile, wood, vegetables, meat and rice. Moreover, there are good prospects for export of Indian products, particularly agricultural products, sanitary fixtures, drugs & pharmaceuticals', plywood, ceramic tiles, power generation and transmission equipment, light engineering goods, leather products, textiles and related products. Information technology is the new emerging field of India's efforts. There is a large number of NRI business communities in Bahrain, which is engaged primarily in trading activity. They have invested in their business establishment in Bahrain. "These establishments include agencies for Titan and IHMT watches, India televisions, etc.

Our relations with Oman are historical There is evidence of people-to-people contacts dating back to the seventh century. In olden days, there was constant sea trade between the two countries. An Indo-Oman Treaty of Friendship, Navigation and Commerce was signed by Sultan Said and the President of India in 1953[9]. It was probably one of the first agreements to be signed between India and any Arub country. The umbrella agreement for cooperation in the hydrocarbon field was at breakthrough in exploiting the potential for economic competition with Gulf States. The economic content was further concretized with the signature of the Agreement on Economic, Trade and Technical Cooperation which aimed at strengthening cooperation in the economic, commercial, industrial, tourist and technical fields. There was also the setting up of a Joint Commission to meet annually to follow up and to review developments.

The recognition of Oman's strategic significance was further highlighted by the demonstration of a new political will and new economic initiatives. India's need for energy sources particularly for the Southern Grid and the possibility of supply of gas through a submarine pipeline heightened the awareness on both sides of the existence of common strategic interests. This has become explicit in Oman's proposal to develop a 'Strategic Trade Alliance'. It is interesting to note that Oman is the only country in the region where India has the surplus balance of trade.[10]

The cooperation between India and Kuwait has increased in the field of science and technology. A number of visits have taken place between the two countries especially between the two apex bodies in the field of science and technology

Kuwait Institute of Scientific Research (KISR) and Council of Scientific and Industrial Research (CSIR). A number of Indian Scientists/Researchers are with KISR and other such organizations to develop cooperation for mutual benets.

The trade relations between India and Iran continued to register growth. The new economic policies followed both by India and Iran provided new opportunities for economic cooperation. This is of course in the field of energy sector oil and gas. The other fields where cooperation is required are in the field of textile machinery, bio-technology, power generation, agro-processing. Apart from this, Iran could play a very important role in providing India and commercial linkages with the central Asian countries. They are emerging as big markets for Indian goods.

India and Iraq have traditionally been very close to each other. Iraq was one of the major sources of India's oil imports and also was good markets for Indian goods. But after the Gulf crisis in 1990-91 and in 2001, its economic activities were badly disturbed. Iraq is fighting its own battle to get rid of foreign powers such as the US and the UK. They have undemocratically invaded Iraq and are still occupying it, taking the pretext of bringing democracy there. As far as the relation with Israel is concerned, it must be taken into consideration of the national interest in mind. Israel can not be more important than these Gulf countries from any point of view. The previous NDA government was misled and adopted the policy which favoured Israel rather than Gulf countries. It is noted that as soon as this current regime came to power, it is realised by the government and there is a correction in its foreign policy towards the Gulf. India accords high priority to its relations with Iran, Prime Minister Naredra Modi told visiting Iranian Foreign Minister Javad Zarif when the latter visited him in August 2015. Prime Minister Modi's upcoming visit to Iran will be a milestone in bilateral relations of the two countries.

We further see that India's economic relations with Yemen has the positive sign after the first meeting of Indo-Yemen joint committee which cooperation such as trade and investment, small scale industry, telecommunication, hydrocarbons, civil aviation, construction, science and technology, health and education, etc.

Relative importance of the Gulf in comparison to Israel. It is noted that there is a flourishing mutually beneficial economic connection with the Gulf region for India. India's crude oil import from the Gulf is worth $17 to $18 billion annually, India's annual trade with Arab countries is about $10 billion. Whereas,

Israel's annual trade with India is only about $ 1.2 billion. Thus we can argue that the Gulf countries are vital destination not only for trade and investment but also for energy supply to India.

Energy Factor

The energy factor must be taken into account, while deciding West Asian policy. This is so because the Gulf energy is not only important to the Indian economy but also to the world economy. It is considered to be the integral part of the global economy because of its one third share of world oil production. The Gulf has well over half of the world's proven oil reserves. Most of the supply required to meet growing world demand is expected to come from OPEC especially from the region. It is expected that production would rise to 60 mbd by 2020 from 28 mbd in 1998. Virtually all this increase would come from this region[11]. Thus, the Persian Gulf region remains the largest depository of oil reserves and the major source of hydrocarbons. OPEC estimates are that oil reserves are over one trillion barrels, which can meet the requirement for more than 40 years. This was all due to the new discoveries which added the net 415 billion barrels to the World reserves.

The global proven natural gas reserves are put around 15.9 trillion cubic meters which is 38% increase over the 1988 estimates. Despite all, this cannot be ignored the pace of energy consumption which is so high that can upset current supply of energy. It is also obvious that hydrocarbons are non-renewable source of energy. So, their life span is bound to be limited. But this is also true that threat is not so imminent as far as physical reserves are concerned. Definitely, it is going to continue a longer period of time. It is also possible that by that time, there may be more new discovery of oil and gas in this region.

Thus, the Gulf holds an indispensable position in terms of energy stock for most of the countries like India. The region holds 63 percent of total world oil reserves and 34 percent of the world proven natural gas.

Additional advantage to the Gulf. Thus it is now clear that the Gulf is enormously important to India simply because it meets the bulk of our energy needs and having a large number of Indians in the Gulf. India must adopt a policy which can promote mutual understanding the economic cooperation. India has to play proactive role in order to maintain its interest in the region. If India wants to maintain its growth of 7-8 percent in GDP. It is also clear that Gulf is strategically the most important to India mainly due to its close proximity geographically. Hence, importing oil from this region is economically most viable[12]. Thus having a cordial, strong and good relation with West Asian is crucial for India.

According to the Vision Document, the share of oil and gas in the total energy will be 45 percent by the year 2025. India's oil consumption has exceeded 100 million tones of which 33 million tones are indigenous. While remaining 77 million tones comes from other countries. The demand for crude oil and petroleum products is expected to grow to 190 million tones in 2012, and 364 million tones in 2025. On the other hand, it is noted that domestic production has been declining. Indian oil reserves would dry up even if only 30 percent of its demand were met from domestic production. The demand is growing at the rate of 5.77 percent to meet this growing demand. There are five countries that provide bulk of it. These countries are Saudi Arabia, UAE, Kuwait, Iran and Nigeria accounting for more than 75% of oil. This clearly indicates the importance of these countries as far as the case of India's imports is concerned.

It is also observed that Saudi Arabia is the leading country that account for nearly 20% of total imports. The GCC countries such as Saudi Arabia, UAE, Kuwait, Qatar and Bahrain account for more than fifty percent. The Persian Gulf which include Iraq and Iran constitutes around 60 percent of import[13]. Thus, India is presently importing 70 percent of hydrocarbon which is expected to grow in future, since the consumption of energy is rapidly increasing in India owing to development taking place in different sectors of the economy. It is evident that there is a dominance of the GCC countries in terms of oil supply to India.

Just like food and defense, energy security challenges is one of the most important concerns for India in the age of globalization and liberalization. So, it has been realized that it now is strategically important for India to have strong economic linkage with the Gulf countries in order to meet energy security challenges. This is so because India still imports more than 60 percent of its oil from the Gulf countries and this percentage is expected to rise further. Presently India ranks sixth in the world in terms of energy consumption. The US, China, Russia, Japan and Germany comes before India in this respect. India is amongst those countries which imports over 70 percent of petroleum requirements from outside the country. Moreover, it is important to note that out of the total petroleum imports, more than 60 percent comes from the Gulf which constitutes six Gulf Cooperation Council countries such as Bahrain, Kuwait, Qatar, Saudi Arabia, United Arab Emirates and two more countries, Iran and Iraq. These countries are crucial countries for oil importer like India and China which has also recently become a net importer of oil. Hence, we can say that Gulf has immense significance for India not only for trade and energy but also for employment opportunities available in this region and remittances sending home.

Employment Factor

The Gulf countries are not only important from trade and investment, oil and natural gas point of view, but they are equally crucial for India in terms of employment to Indians in their respective countries. It is reported that at least 5 million Indians are employed in this region. These expatriate Indians remit more than $10 billion dollars to India every year[14]. Prior to the mid-1970s, there were mainly Arabs such as Egyptians, Yemenis, Palestinians, Lebanese and Sudanese in this region. It was noted that the Gulf monarchies grew increasingly worried about the possible political repercussions in the 1970s. Palestinians were viewed as politically subversive, Yemenis were involved in various anti regime activities. As a result, the Gulf countries started to opt of workers from South and South East Asia who were seen as less likely to get involved in host countries politics.

After the oil boom of 1973, the Gulf countries recruited foreign workers from both Arab and Asian countries for construction and industrialization. Indians also benefited from it. These were about 2.5 lakh Indian expatriates in 1975. This number rose to over 1.5 million in 1991. In the year 1999, there were 3 million Indian nationals gainfully employed in the Gulf. The number of Indian workers in the Gulf reached over 3.6 million in 2004. Of this, Saudi Arabia alone had 1.5 millions Indians and UAE had 1 million Indians. Qatar and Bahrain had more than 1,00,000 Indian each. There were about 4.5 lakh Indian expatriates each in Kuwait and Oman.

It is also true that Saudi Arabia and the United Arab Emirates import the maximum number of Indian labour in their respective countries followed by other GCC countries. This is evident that there is a shortage of manpower in these, countries which is supplied by surplus manpower countries like India. The Indian government is now changing its migration policy in order to promote manpower employment in these countries. This is important because the manpower contributes significantly in the development of 'country where they are employed as well the country—wherefrom they come. Hence, we can say that this expatriate Indian labour force is the real asset to India and to the host countries as well. This is so because both India and host countries are beneficiaries on accounts of the contribution made by these-expatriates.

Moreover, it also noted that all the Gulf States have launched many developmental programmes and schemes for overall development of their countries. They need highly qualified and trained personnel who can work in their developmental-project. Hence, they will have to rely on skilled expatriate workers. It is here suggested that Indian government must act in this direction in order— to enhance the prospect of Indian workers in this region. Since India has vast reservoir of well trained technical manpower in all-disciplines such as Engineering, Medical, Management, Computer Sciences, etc. It is desirable that a large number of Indians may be able to find lucrative job abroad, especially in the Gulf. This can be made possible if we have strong and friendly relations with West Asian countries as we have had in the past.

Remittance Factor

It is proved beyond, doubt that Gulf remittances brought by the Indian expatriates help in the foreign exchange earnings to a great extent. It was fully realized by the Indian government at the time of the Gulf crisis which took place in 1990. Before the Gulf war, the annual remittances were more than $2 billion. By 1994-95, it amounted to $ 6.2 billion. At the turn of the century, this amount went up to $ 12 billion in 2000-01. By 2003-04, it amounted approximately $ 14 billion a year which was a major asset to the country. In 2005, India's remittances reached $ 21.7 billion that replaced China whose remittances were $21.3 billion. Of India's $ 21.7 billion, $ 16 billion came from the Gulf countries[15]. In 2010, the World Bank reported" that India had received $ 55 billion from abroad". It was estimated that during the last 5 years the remittances have been more than double and India continues to retain its position in the World. It is interesting" to note that the major chunk of remittance is still coming from the Gulf. Thus the Gulf region is very important for India in this respect. This huge amount definitely strengthens India's balance of payment. Kerala is one of the Indian states whose economy is largely based on the Gulf remittances. There are many other such states like Andhra Pradesh, Tamil Nadu; Punjab, Bihar, etc., where a huge amount of remittances are coming. These remittances' are used for economic development by migrants households in India. PM Modi from his recent visit to UAE is looking to lift bilateral trade that currently stands at $59 billion, attract investment into infrastructure projects at home and connect with the large Indian community that makes up nearly 30% of U.A.E.'s population and sends millions of dollars back in remittances each year.

Social and Cultural Factor

Education and health which are in fact the crucial factors for human resource development is identified as a major sector for future cooperation between India and the Gulf countries. Many agreements were signed between the two sides to promote—cooperation in the field of education and arts. Two important languages Arabic and Persian of this region have been taught in India for a long time. In the same way, "Urdu and Hindustani are spoken and understood the people in the Gulf region. Bollywood film stars are very popular in the Gulf for their performance. They frequently visit Dubai, Muscat and many other Gulf cities on their popular demand by people. This all clearly indicates the significance of common culture prevailing in the Gulf and India. Not only this, there are over 60 Indian schools which have been established in the Gulf countries. All schools follow CBSE pattern, except one which is affiliated to the KSB (Kerala State Board)". Indian Ambassador is the patron of all the Indian schools in the country. The control of the Indian schools has under the Board of Directors who is appointed by the Ambassador from among permanent members of the Indian community. The Board coordinates the functioning of management committees of all Indian schools.

There are more than 30 Indian schools in the UAE. They are doing well and are catering the needs of Indian children and Emiratis to the Central Board of Secondary Education. They are all well established and are serving the needs of the large Indian community residing in Kuwait and the Kuwaitis alike. It is noted that there are four major Indian schools such as Indian school, Muscat: Indian schools, Al Ghubia Indian school, Wadi Kabir and Indian school, Dar Sait that are located in Muscat (Oman). Recently an Indian school of Seeb an adjacent township has started functioning. The oldest school is Indian school Muscat initially known as Arya Kelavani Mandal which was founded in 2nd July 1939. Hindu Maliajan Association took the responsibility of managing the school. Thus, the presence of 15 Indian schools in various pans of Oman indicates that Indian community attaches a great deal of importance to education for its coming generation. For higher and technical education, their wards generally come to India.

There is an educational prospects in both sides. Indian IT companies have been actively involved in setting up an IT park in Muscat & Knowledge Oasis in Muscat (KOM). Both the IT colleges have an Indian connection. One is in affiliation with Manipal Academy of Higher Education while other is a joint venture with Birla Institute of Technology Ranchi.[18] Both are doing very well there.

Omani companies also have several Joint ventures m India. Oman Computer Services International develops Computer Software at Bangalore. Shantha Bio-techniques, Hyderabad is one of India's most well-known bio-technology company. Nisma Airocon International, Chennai manufactures heat pump air conditioners. The Zubair group has setup a furniture manufacturing unit in Tamilnadu in collaboration with Balaji group of Chennai. Bahwan Cybertec have an IT training company in Chennai and regularly send trainees from Oman to India. These trainees go back to Oman with great satisfaction.

Sultan Qaboos university in Muscat is the only university which is well reputed and most important institution of higher learning in Oman. It was found that many Omanis have studied in India and they still keep coming in large number to Indian universities and institution of higher education especially in technical subject such as engineering, IT and medicine. Bangalore, Pune, and Chennai are the major cities where they prefer to come for education. It is presently estimated that there are over 1500 Omanis who pursue higher education. It was also found that every year a number of Qmani officials co me to India to acquire training in different fields under the ITEC programme of the government or India. There were about 53 Omani officials will come to India in 2004 for number of training courses in different fields such as IT, audit, pharmaceuticals, Entrepreneurship, language Agriculture and rural development Accounts and Finance, Educational Planning and Administration, etc. This sector in fact needs to be addressed more seriously for mutual benefits. More and more Gulf students should be attracted to pursue their higher education in India.

As far as the socio-cultural factor is concerned, it is witnessed that a large number Indian Muslims go to two holy places (Mecca and Madinah) for pilgrimage every year on the occasion of Eid-Adha. This pilgrimage provides enough opportunities for cultural interaction between Indians and West Asian people. This cultural interaction strengthens our overall relations for our mutual benefit.

Conclusion

While there was a general consensus among the scholars on the need for greater Indian involvement as our interest are manifold in this region but the actualization of this involvement remains a significant challenge. That West Asia is currently in turmoil is an understatement. There are a number of challenges that plague the region and have caused significant upheaval in recent years. First, the horrific rise of the Islamic State (IS) and the spread of its extremist ideology in Iraq and Syria. The spill-over effects of IS to other countries in the region and the spread of extremism to other parts of the world are also of grave concern. Second, the repercussions of the Arab Spring are still being felt in the region with Syria and Yemen on the brink of civil war. Military intervention by other Arab states in these conflicts and the rapidly intensifying humanitarian crises that these conflicts have created are serious causes of concern for the region. Third, the Arab states are greatly wary of Iran's nuclear aspirations and its increasing involvement in the Arab world's conflicts through Finally, America's waning interest and involvement in the Middle East has created a future of uncertainty for regional security.

India has traditionally followed a 'hands-off' approach toward West Asian countries and consequently enjoyed good relations with them... West Asia has always been of strategic importance to India with roughly seven million Indians residing in the region and the Gulf supplying nearly two-thirds of India's oil and gas. A pro-active Indian approach to West Asia and its problems would also ensure greater visibility for India vis-à-vis the rising influence of China. In recent years, China has signalled its geo-political and economic ambitions by signing multi-billion dollar investment deals and defense agreements with West Asian states. India on the other hand has shied away from pursuing stronger bilateral defense and security relationships for various ideological and geopolitical reasons, with the notable exception of Israel. It is argued that Prime Minister Modi's impending visit to Israel might raise concerns with the Arab states regarding Indian intentions in the region. However, India has long shared a close relationship with Israel, albeit a closeted one, and should not be a cause for any apparent concern now. There is a sense that Israel and Arab states can both enjoy a stronger relationship with India based on mutual interests. Nevertheless, foreign policy has been prominent during the Modi government's first year in office. Even as West Asia is roiled by a range of conflicts, the government has successfully managed the mounting rescue missions for Indians living in trouble spots of this region. India needs to position itself as a force for stability in the region, which in turn will require enormous diplomatic engagement.

NOTES

1 A.K. Ramakrishnan, "Mahatma Gandhi Rejected Zionism," Released August 15, 2001, The Wisdom Fund, P.O. Box 2723, Arlington, VA 22202 website : http://www.twf.org
2 Bansidhar Pradhan, "Changing Dynamics of India's West Asian Policy", International Studies, Vol. 40, No. 1, 2004, p. 4.

3. Anisur Rahman, Indo-Saudi Relations: A Need for Coming Closer, Strategic Bulletin, Vol. IV, Nos. 2&3, May-Sep 1999, p. 20.
4. Jaideep Singh and Tersest Schaffer, Overview South Asia Monitor, CSIS, vol.9, Issue#2, Thursday 29, 2004 (accessed through Internet).
5. Shivaji Sarkar, "Tapping Alternative Market", Special Gulf News (accessed through internet) published on 14/8/2004.
6. Ibid.
7. Govt. of India, Annual Report, 2000-2001, The Gulf, West Asia & North Africa, p., 38 (accessed through Internet)
8. Indian Embassy (Bahrain) Indo-Bahrain Relations (accessed through Internet) http://indianembassy-bah.com
9. Embassy of India (Muscat), Indo-Oman Relations (accessed through Internet) http://www.indemb-oman.org/india-oman-relation.html
10. Muhammad Azhar, Gulf Economies and Indo-Gulf Relations, (Delhi: New Horizon Publishers, 1999).
11. Anisur Rahman, "Gulf a Crucial Factor in India's Energy Requirements for Development" in S.N. Malakar (ed) Book on India's Energy Security and the Gulf, (New Delhi, Academic Excellence 2006), p. 28.
12. Ibid.
13. Girijest Pant, India's Energy Security: The Gulf Factor, Occasional Paper Series: CWAAS/SIS, JNU, GSP 2002.
14. Anisur Rahman, Indian Labour Migration to the Gulf: A Socio-Economic Analysis (New Delhi: Rajat Publications, 2001), p. 34.
15. The Times of India, New Delhi, Friday, November 18, 2005.
16. Ministry of Overseas Indian Affairs, Government of India, Annual Report 2010-11.
17. P.C. Jain, Indian in Oman, GSP Occasional paper, Series (CWAAS/SIS/JNU New Delhi).
18. Embassy of India, (Muscat). Into-Oman Relations, (accessed through internet) http://indemb.oman.org/commercial-services-eco relations.html

4

Modi's Foreign Policy:
A Changing Scenario on Indo-US Relations

Amulya K Tripathy and Roshni Kujur

U.S.-India Relations from Cold War to Post-Cold War
After India achieved independence in 1947, in this period the US viewed South Asia as a region largely peripheral to its central strategic needs. Though the decade of 1950s was endorsed in poverty and underdevelopment, as a weak and a divided nation was staggeringly picking up its broken bits, the policy of Non-Alignment, had polarized into two blocs. The decision of the US to sell arms to Pakistan further distanced the two countries and India felt alienated from America. India's strong socialist leanings and growing closeness with the Soviet Union further strained the relations further. The reign of John F Kennedy (1961-1963), saw India as a partner against the rising power of communist China. During the 1962 Sino-Indian war, the US publicly supported India's interpretation of its border with China in the eastern Himalayas and even ferried military equipment to India.[1] (Neville 146)

However, despite its potential importance and occasional periods of Indo-U.S. cooperation, India refused to serve US as an active ally in the battle against global communism. For its part, India refused to join either the American or the Soviet side in the Cold War conflict and instead charted its own "non-aligned" policy.

The collapse of Communism, American interests and outlook towards the international order gradually changed. Meanwhile its continued help to Pakistan kept India estranged from it. However, the 1980s saw some sunshine and the bilateral relations began to improve due to numerous high level visits and inking of several economic, military and cultural agreements.

"The key of American perspective vis-à-vis India during the Cold War had been the strategic importance of its military ally namely, Pakistan, to whom it had funnelled some $650 million under Military Assistance Programme (MAP) alone between 1950 and 1980. In fact, Pakistan had become the second largest recipient of MAP aid (after Iran) and that this assistance had been provided as part of a general "Northern Tier" strategy to limit Soviet expansion into the middle East, South Asia and the Indian ocean".[2]

Indira Gandhi's visit to the US in 1982 resulted in the latter agreeing to supply fuel and spare parts for the nuclear power plant at Tarapur. Rajiv Gandhi's visit to the US in 1985 was a great success on a bilateral agreement on scientific and technological exchanges which followed with the Indo-US Bilateral tax treaty in 1988.

U.S.–India Perceptions in post-9/11

The 9/11 attack on America in 2001 became a new parameter that began to influence politics world over including the Indo-US relations. Stephen P. Cohen said, no part of the world has more been affected by the terrorists' attack of September 11, 2001, than South Asia.[3] Terrorism, nuclear proliferation, rise of China and economic and environmental concerns became major factors determining the ties between the two states at the dawn of the new millennium. While the terror attack on Pentagon and World Trade Centre created suspicions against Pakistan, China's rapid rise became a major cause of concern for the US as it turned towards India as the safety valve in South Asia. Bill Clinton's love for India catapulted the position of a 'strategic partner'. There were a number of factors which made South Asia a central point in US war against terrorism. Also, American foreign policy began to develop a feeling of threat from the Islamic revivalism after the end of the Cold War as Afghanistan and Pakistan shared the regime of Taliban. As the United State prepared to launch its global war it put a tough choice before the states that "Either you are with us or against us". This indicated a decisive message with regard to the future course of relationship between US and Pakistan? Thereby in 2000, India and the USA agreed to establish a Joint Working Group on Counter-Terrorism. In the same year Bill Clinton's visit to India changed the equations between the top leaderships of the two countries. In 2001, Bush lifted post-Pokharan II sanctions imposed on India. In 2002, the

Indo-US High Technology Cooperation Group came into being. In 2005 an Open Skies Agreement was signed between the two countries. In the same year Manmohan Singh visited America and many agreements, including the civil nuclear deal, were inked. In the 21st century, the US has become India's largest investment partner with American direct investment of $9 billion accounting for 9% of total foreign investment into India. The end of the Cold War freed India-U.S relations from the constraints of global bipolarity, but interactions continued for a decade to be affected by the burden of history, most notably the longstanding India–Pakistan rivalry and nuclear weapons proliferation in the region. Recent years, however, have witnessed a sea change in bilateral relations, with more positive interactions, as President Bush calls India a "natural partner" of the United States and his Administration seeks to assist India's rise as a major power in the new century.

What factors will create certain challenges for the United States and India under Modi? As the United States and India built a new relationship over the past 15 years, one of the claims for the relationship concerns the shared values of the two multi-ethnic, multi-religious, secular democracies. While he has been legally cleared in India, Modi has never formally apologized for the riots. Many Indians and some Americans worry that his background in the RSS and his views of India as a homeland for Hindus may portend a Hindu-first approach—creating a chilling effect for India's minorities, and moving India away from the celebration of diversity.

NDA II: Modi's Foreign Policy

After a historic election victory, Narendra Modi was sworn in as India's 15th prime minister on Monday, May 26, ending two terms of rule by the Nehru–Gandhi dynasty. Modi's political vehicle, the Bharatiya Janata Party (BJP), advocates a strong India that can resist pressure from world powers or regional rivals. Indeed, when in power previously, it was a BJP-led government under Atal Bihari Vajpayee that made India into a nuclear power and underlined its independence by refusing to sign the Nuclear Non-Profileration Treaty.

But Modi—equipped with the strongest mandate to rule in a generation—is not expected to pursue a Hindu nationalist policy. Modi "may have started his career on the extreme right, but he's coming more toward the centre now. And he will have to," says Sreeram Chaulia, a political analyst of the Jindal School of International Affairs in Delhi. This also applies to foreign policy where Modi has little experience, says Professor C.S.R. Murthy of Jawaharlal Nehru University in the Indian capital: "In my assessment he is not sophisticated enough to understand the nuances of foreign policy and conduct the course of negotiations. It will take time. He will require some proper advice." According to this school of thought, Modi will first have to deliver on his election pledge to get the country's faltering economy back on its feet. With an average growth rate of around 5 per cent over the last two years, the economy has not been expanding fast enough to provide jobs for the 13 million young Indians flooding onto the job market every year. Moreover, the manufacturing sector only accounts for 15 per cent of the economy compared to 31 per cent in China. This is where Modi's expertise—on display for 12 years in Gujarat—in attracting domestic and foreign investment, creating jobs and a building a modern infrastructure could come into play.

After being sworn in as India's prime minister, speculation is mounting about what impact Narendra Modi's brand of Hindu nationalism will have on his country's foreign policy. India's foreign policy has long been determined by a triple bottom line—interests, values and public opinion. All three are relatively impervious to changes of government. Each BJP policy will adhere to at least one of those drivers, and the degree of change from previous policy will be determined by how the government interprets each driver and how readily changes can be pushed through a strong-willed foreign service. PM Narendra Modi began his tenure with a diplomatic coup of sorts, securing the attendance of all South Asian Association for Regional Cooperation (SAARC) heads of states and Mauritius at his swearing-in ceremony. One guest who stood apart from all was the Pakistani Prime Minister Nawaz Sharif.

The Indian PM inviting Pakistan for his big day was meant to be a chance to reset ties. But three months after this historic event, there was a definite freeze in the India-Pakistan relationship.

India decided to call off the Foreign Secretary level talks with Pakistan, that were to set the agenda for the two prime ministers after the Pakistani High Commissioner met Kashmiri separatist leaders in the capital. The Modi government dubbed the meeting as interference in its internal affairs, setting a new 'Lakshman Rekha' in Indo-Pak ties.

Modi and Indo-US Relations: An Expectations Policy Agenda

Observing the Modi's US visit, a leading authority on Indo-US relations, Ashley J Tellis said, "It is important that both sides have an honest conversation about the kind of relationship they seek."

Indian Prime Minister Narendra Modi's forthcoming visit to Washington will provide India and the United States with a golden opportunity to repair their faltering partnership. Bilateral relations have deteriorated in recent years because of poor policy choices in India on nuclear liability, taxation, and trade. Moreover, India's recent political paralysis and crumbling economic growth have suppressed the opportunities for more robust commercial ties. In these circumstances, the latter-day approach to India pursued by the administration of US President Barack Obama has not helped. By permitting sectoral interests to define the content of US engagement with India, Washington has allowed a pernicious transactionalism to gradually replace the strategic vision that previously guided the evolution of bilateral relations. This mistake was compounded by the obsessive complaints of senior US government officials about India's economic policies. If Modi's private remarks to visiting American officials recently are any indication, the Indian prime minister seeks to end this stagnation. But his approach, which seemingly centres on soliciting huge international investments for important, high-profile projects at home, offers poor prospects for any deep US involvement that would quickly resuscitate joint cooperation between the two countries.[4]

At the moment, these concerns remain speculative. Modi's national campaign focused on growth and governance. He has publicly denounced extreme anti-Muslim statements proffered by some of his supporters. And the last period of BJP governance at the federal level, from 1998–2004, offers an instructive precedent. Though the BJP established them as a national force in the early 1990s through appeals to religion—such as a truck kitted out like a chariot of a Hindu god for a campaign about temple-building—their term in government was marked by a different ethos. Under Prime Minister Atal Behari Vajpayee, the BJP moderated its most extreme wing, further liberalized the Indian economy, and transformed relations with the United States.

This may become Modi's legacy as well, should he rein in the religious nationalists and keep his own sights focused on his campaign promises of economic growth and surajya, or "good governance". And this is where Washington can best meet Modi—on the pragmatic common ground important to his Administration, and to the United States.

Getting the Economics Right

Modi seeks to right the wrongs which have slowed India's growth and kept India near the bottom of the World Bank's Doing Business index in 2013, India ranked 134 out of 189, below Yemen. The BJP platform focuses on infrastructure, foreign direct investment, intellectual property rights, manufacturing, and restoring India to its pre-modern-era primacy as a centre of global trade. This trade-led political slate represents the best opening in some years to expand economic ties. New Delhi sees the United States developing trade deals across Asia and Europe, and wonders where it fits. Signalling these paths to broadened economic ties will restore confidence in India that the United States has a strategic goal in sight. Getting India on a path towards the hugely important TPP will underscore the priority Americans place on ties with India, on track to become the world's third-largest economy by 2025. It will also create a more constructive atmosphere in which both governments can continue working on current market-access frictions.

Filling the Void in Afghanistan

The US and NATO troop drawdowns in late 2014 created great uncertainty for India. New Delhi fears that once the international presence departs from Afghanistan, the Taliban and related groups—like the Haqqani network or the Lashkar-e-Taiba, both designated terrorist organizations under UN and the US authorities—will refocus more forcefully on Indian targets. India has played a critical role providing development and humanitarian assistance to Afghanistan since the turn of the century, emerging as its fifth-largest bilateral donor. It is also the region's dominant economic power, with companies willing and able to explore opportunities in Afghanistan, and the business knowledge networks to provide trade linkages for a country that desperately needs to develop its own sustainable economy. India stands out as the country most capable of providing ongoing assistance, development partnership, technology transfer, education, and business connectivity appropriate for Afghanistan's greatest needs. It has also, in response to requests from Kabul, begun to provide security sector assistance such as training, and funding Afghan equipment purchases from Russia.

The United States should begin to consult much more intensively with New Delhi as the drawdown continues, pulling India into conversations akin to those of a close NATO partner. Washington should also focus urgently on the unresolved problem of Pakistan as a terrorist safe haven, including the egregious example of Lashkar-e-Taiba Chief Hafiz Saeed—on whom the United States in 2012 authorized an award of up to $10 million for information leading to his arrest—openly holding rallies across Pakistan.

Visa Issue

Visas have emerged as a central friction in the US–India relationship, because

New Delhi and the Indian IT services sector sees them as a market access barrier in the United States. This is a shame, because the growth in people-to-people contact has been one of the most successful aspects of the changed relationship between New Delhi and Washington. To keep up with the visa demand over the past decade, the United States has invested more than $100 million into building larger consulate facilities across India. Of all the H-1B visas (for highly skilled temporary workers) issued worldwide, 64 per cent go to Indian citizens; China is second, with a mere 8 per cent. From Washington's perspective, it's hard to see how Indians could perceive such a dominant position as constrained by barriers. But it's also true that the total number of H-1B visas available has shrunk since its high point at the end of the Clinton administration.

As the new Indian government settles into New Delhi, this pragmatic agenda, building on campaign promises critical to India and the United States will reinforce the larger strategic importance of a strong US—India relationship. While the jury may be out for some time on how Modi will govern India, the urgent need to regain a collaborative spirit on the economic front should be at the top of Washington's inbox. As US withdrawal from Afghanistan proceeds, India should be at the forefront of US consultation to ensure sustainable stability for the region.

Finally, given the difficulties advancing comprehensive immigration reform in Congress, there are some concrete steps the Obama administration can take to alleviate several frictions related to visa issues. Each of these would result in meaningful progress for both sides, and would advance US national interests.

Modi's Mission in United States: A New Agenda

On the final day of Prime Minister Narendra Modi's visit to the US, Defence Cooperation Agreement was extended with India by another 10 years. The pact, which was to expire in June next year, will now be in force till 2025.

The development follows India's decision to increase the foreign direct investment (FDI) cap for the defence sector from 26 per cent to 49 per cent. The issue was taken up at Modi's extensive meeting with US Defense Secretary Chuck Hagel, before the prime minister's summit-level talks with President Obama at the Oval Room of the White House.

The pact, New Framework for the US-India Defence Relationship, was signed in June 28, 2005, by then defence minister (now President) Pranab Mukherjee and his American counterpart Donald Rumsfeld.

The Indian Cabinet is yet to approve Rs 15,000 crore worth of US defence deals, including one for sale of 22 AH-64E Apache attack choppers, 15 Chinook heavylift helicopters and the Javelin anti-tank guided missiles. American defence equipment makers like General Electric and Boeing had met Modi a day earlier and expressed their desire to expand operations in India.

Civil Nuclear Agreement

On the civil nuclear agreement between the two countries, an India-US group is to address all implementation issues for speeding up deployment of American nuclear reactors in India. The agreement on this had hit a roadblock in 2010, when India rolled out a nuclear liability law. For his summit talks with Obama, Modi drove straight from Blair House, where he was lodged, to the famous West Wing of the White House. The talks were first in a restrictive format and later at a delegation level.

At his joint media briefing with Obama after the meeting, Modi said both sides were "committed to taking forward the civil nuclear partnership agreement. We are serious about resolving at the earliest the issues related to civil nuclear energy cooperation. This is important for India to meet its energy security needs."

This was Modi's second meeting with the US President since taking charge as India's prime minister. On Monday, the two leaders had discussed bilateral issues over a private dinner in an informal setting. The body language of both leaders looked relaxed after delegation-level talks, with Obama sipping a drink occasionally and Modi wearing a constant wide grin. After this meeting, Modi took everyone by surprise by addressing the media, jointly with Obama, in Hindi. During his visit to the US, the prime minister had earlier addressed the United Nations General Assembly (UNGA) in Hindi. On economic ties, Modi hinted that the government was going for further economic and policy reforms that would help in "rapid growth" of bilateral trade and investment partnership. Both sides discussed the recent standoff over the World Trade Organization's (WTO's) trade facilitation agreement (TFA). Modi revealed he had frank discussions with Obama and expected US support in addressing India's concerns over public stockholding for food security. In a definitive step, Modi also sought easy access for Indian services firms in the American market. At the time of going to press, Modi and Obama were expected to issue a joint statement on strategic ties between their two countries. Later in the day, Modi was scheduled to address the US-India Business Council.

Obama's visit as Chief Guest for the Indian Republic Day showed a new venture of Modi's foreign policy with United States. It is beyond expectations, in spite of past embarrassed relations of Modi with the US. The same day after accepting India's invitation Obama administration informed it's old ally Pakistan that Obama will visit Pakistan too. It shows Obama administration's weakness with Pakistan.

Obama Visit, a Sign of Progress

US President Barack Obama recently said that the United States could be India's "best partner", as he wrapped up a three-day visit to New Delhi by highlighting the shared values of the world's biggest democracies. Speaking to an audience of young people, the US president reiterated that the relationship between Washington and New Delhi "can be one of the defining partnerships of this century."[5] Relations between the two countries haven't always been smooth.

Another reason this visit was significant is that it symbolized a rapid improvement in the US-India ties, which were nearly undone at the end of 2013 over a row involving Devyani Khobragade, India's deputy consul general in New York. Accused of visa fraud and underpaying her house-keeper, she was arrested and strip-searched by the US law enforcement wing, sparking angry protests and diplomatic retaliations from India.

It appeared unlikely that Obama's visit would result in major policy breakthroughs on the issues that will dominate his agenda with Modi. But the mere fact that the talks were happening was being viewed as a sign of progress given the recent tensions that have marred relations between the US and India. The relationship hit rock bottom in 2013 when Indian Deputy Consul General Devyani Khobragade was arrested and strip-searched in New York over allegations that she lied on visa forms to bring her maid to the US while paying her a pittance. Her treatment caused outrage in New Delhi and India retaliated against US diplomats.

Ties between the US and India have been steadily improving since Modi took office last May. He and Obama met for the first time late last year in Washington, and officials from both countries say they quickly developed an easy chemistry. That came as something of a surprise to regional analysts given Modi's difficult history with the US. He was denied a visa to the US in 2005, three years after religious riots killed more than 1,000 Muslims in the Indian state where he was the top elected official.[6] On the White House Blog on Obama's visit it is said, The President and Prime Minister Modi pledged to enhance US–Indian cooperation on our mutual climate and clean energy goals. From our highly successful US-India Partnership to Advance Clean Energy (PACE) umbrella program to technical work on emerging technologies, the US and India made important progress on combating climate change.

The agreements include:

- Enhancing bilateral climate change cooperation to achieve a successful and ambition agreement in Paris this year.
- Cooperating on Hydroflurocarbons to make concrete progress in the Montreal Protocol this year.
- Expanding PACE-R, the US-India Joint Clean Energy Research and Development Center, to extend funding for research on solar energy, energy efficiency, and advanced biofuels.
- Launching air quality cooperation to help urban residents reduce their exposure to harmful levels of air pollution.

Further the U.S. and India agreed on to combat climate change here.

True Global Partners: Incentivizing Trade and Investment

Under President Obama, trade between the two countries has increased by about 60 per cent to nearly $100 billion a year—a record high. But that's still hundreds of billions less than the trade we do with China. "We've got to do better," the President said, speaking at a U.S.-India Business Council Summit in New Delhi. So, the US President announced a series of additional steps that will generate more than $4 billion in trade and investment with India while supporting thousands of jobs in both countries:

> The Export-Import Bank will commit up to $1 billion in financing to support "Made-in-America" exports to India. OPIC will support lending to small and medium businesses across India that will result in more than $1 billion in loans in underserved rural and urban markets. The US Trade and Development Agency will aim to leverage nearly $2 billion in investments in renewable energy in India.[7]

The Obama Visit: A Sign of Development?

The US President Barack Obama's two-day visit to India can be summarised through meaningful issues that dampened trade, investment and strategic relations between the world's largest democracies. In this flash, we look beyond the much publicised 'bear-hug' to list four positive areas from the Obama visit and their economic implications for India.

Civil Nuclear Deal: A 'break-through' but yet to workout

The two nations resolved a longstanding deadlock on the implementation of a 2008 civil nuclear deal, which was hamstrung by India's enactment of a liability law that exposed US nuclear plant vendors to excessive legal proceedings. Under the new arrangement, suppliers would be indemnified against unlimited liability through an insurance pool. If successfully implemented, renewed investments by US vendors would help in reducing India's widening energy deficit and aid infrastructure growth.

Cooperation towards Strengthening India's Defence Capabilities

The two leaders endorsed efforts to enhance collaboration in defence technology transfer and co-development. India still imports an unreasonably high share (70%) of its defence equipment needs, a bulk of which (76%) comes from Russia followed by the US (7%). Thus, steps to upgrade India's domestic defence industry are imperative. In this context, policy efforts, including recent lifting of foreign investment limits in defence (49% from 26%) and deeper Indo-US defence ties bode well for India's domestic defence sector and the economy in general.

Commitment to invest USD 4 billion in India—a focus on renewable energy sector. The pledge includes:

(1) USD 1 billion in financing by the US Export-Import Bank to export 'Made in America' products,
(2) USD 1 bn to be lent by US Overseas Private Investment Corporation to small and medium enterprises in rural India, and
(3) USD 2 bn committed by US Trade and Development Agency for renewable energy.

Meeting unmet demand for electricity in rural India, which constitutes 47% of 1.2 billion population, through renewable sources can greatly reduce India's kerosene subsidy bill and minimize resource intensity of the economy. Share of renewable energy in India's total installed power capacity has jumped from just 2% in 2002 to 13% currently. While greater foreign investments would help boost India's renewable energy sector further, it needs to be complemented by government efforts to tackle regulatory barriers, resolve land acquisition issues, ease infrastructure constraints and mitigate storage and distribution losses. India has other options beyond cooperation with China.

Diplomatic interpretations of Mr. Obama's visit centred on US efforts to make India its South Asian anchor and a strategic counter weight to China in its 'pivot Asia' strategy. This notwithstanding, we expect Stronger links with the US—the only bright spot in the developed world today—to help India improve its trade balance at least bilaterally. This would contrast with its rapidly deteriorating trade deficit with China, which recorded a huge USD 31 bn in 2013.

Trump and Modi: A New Phase

At the beginning, Trump's election brought uncertainties for India. Given the investment it has made in the U.S. relationship, the Modi government reached out swiftly to the president-elect and his transition team. It has since kept up that outreach, including with three phone calls between Modi and Trump. On visits to the United States, the Indian finance minister, petroleum and natural gas minister, national security advisor, and foreign and commerce secretaries have met their counterparts, as well as the secretaries of commerce, defence, homeland security, and state. U.S. national security advisor H.R. McMaster, in turn, has travelled to India. Working-level cooperation has continued in a number of spheres. When the country has been in the American spotlight, the attention has been of the unwanted kind: related to attacks against Indians, criticism from Trump himself over climate issues, or reports on the president's businesses in India. There has been some sense of relief that the country has been missing from presidential tweets, but being missing from the priority list is problematic.

On the bilateral front, the Indian government has to adapt to President Trump's more transactional approach, rather than the more strategic one that prevailed towards India in previous administrations. On economic issues, there continue to be differences on trade, investment, and immigration policies. The Trump administration has highlighted concerns over the trade deficit with India (which, at $30.8 billion is a tenth that with China, but nonetheless is under administration review), tariffs (referring to a country with a 100 percent tariff on motorcycle imports), intellectual property concerns, and market access for American companies. Complaints on these fronts have also come from some members of Congress and the private sector. India, in turn, is concerned about standards and technical regulations that affect its exports to the United States, and potential changes to the high-skilled visa programs (particularly, but not only, H-1Bs). The safety of Indians and, to some extent, Indian Americans in the United States has also been an issue, particularly after the killing of an Indian engineer in Kansas. On the regional front: To its west, India has been following the administration's review of Afghanistan policy. Delhi is concerned about the security situation there, the Ghani government's stability, and what it sees as a China-Pakistan-Russia-

Iran tactical tag-team, particularly vis-à-vis the Taliban. It wants to see Washington remain engaged in Afghanistan, but will also be wary if this means a carrots-heavy approach toward Pakistan.

The second term of Modi in 2019 had hope of development of relations under Trumph. So, observed as enthusiastic. But in US Trumph is facing quite oppositions from his Republic Party even.

Howdy Modi-Trumph Show

In Houston, America, a grand spectacle was created with Narendra Modi in presence of Donald Trump. The massive rally of nearly 50000 people cheered both the leaders. Both these leaders praised each other and criticized 'Islamic Terrorism' and Pakistan. It is true that the South Asia, West Asia have been suffering the cancer of terror, what is forgotten in the hysteria created in the name of 'Islamic terrorism' is the fact that the seeds of this terrorism were sown by the American policy, which not only had designed the syllabus for brain washing of Muslim youth, using the retrograde version of Islam, the whole exercise was funded by America to the tune of 8000 million dollars and seven thousand tons of armaments. The dreaded activity was programmed to fight the Russian army which was occupying Afghanistan. America in a shrewd manner deployed the products of terror training to its benefit and now is trying to wash its hands off the whole thing. As Hillary Clinton had pointed out "let them come from Saudi Arabia and other countries, importing their Wahabi brand of Islam so that we can go beat the Soviet Union."[8]

There are many sidelights of the gala event. The media is full of the massive response to the Modi event, while what was equally important and has been hidden. The protests by different groups, protests against policies of Modi in India have been ignored by media. In America while a substantial number of those from Indian origin are supporters of Hindu nationalism and many are *Modi Bhakts* too, there is a good number of those who are concerned about the state of human rights and health of democracy back home. Right from America, Bernie Sanders, the Democrat leader tweeted about Trump endorsing Modi overlooking the violation of the norms of freedom of religion and violation of human rights here in India. Sanders in a tweet said, "When Donald Trump stays silent in the face of religious persecution, repression and brutality, the dangerous message this sends to autocratic leaders around the world is: "Go ahead, you can get away with it." In his long speech the central point of what Modi said was that 'all is well' in India.

Modi can say so despite the gross violation of basic citizen's rights of large number of Indians, including those in Kashmir. His primary constituency is away from the 'last man', to focus on whom 'father of our nation' Gandhi had suggested for us. While the large section in the audience lapped everything which Modi said, large number of protesters outside the stadium did drew attention to the reality of Indian situation under Modi rule.

From among the protestors the most apt comment came from the Coalition of groups 'Alliance for Justice and Accountability'. Sunita Vishwanathan, part of the alliance and member of 'Hindus for Human Rights', hit the nail on the head, when she stated "We are horrified that our religion, which teaches *Vasudaiva Kutumbakam* (whole World is my family) is being hijacked by extremists and nationalists who are lynching Muslims, trampling democracy and law and order and arresting, if not murdering, those who are speaking out,... We are especially appalled by the most recent nightmare of the Kashmiri people and the situation of 1.9 million people in India who are rendered stateless due to the imposition of the travesty called the National Register of Citizens."[9]

One is at loss to understand the direction which India as a nation is taking at present, more so from last few years. While our Prime Minister is celebrating and addressing the rallies in America the Indian economy is taking a nose dive.

The central focus of the policy making and concerns of the ruling Government has seen a drastic change. In the initial years of republic, solid foundations of industries, Universities and irrigation system were laid. The idea was this is what the nation needs; focus on issues related to livelihood. There were many weaknesses in the planning and implementation of these policies, but the direction was right. This did lead to improvement in levels of literacy, health related indices, economic growth, agricultural production, milk production to list the few.

Conclusion

US President's short visit to India certainly has long-term positive implications for India, especially so given that the Modi government has kept up the tempo on wide ranging reforms since its landslide victory last May. With that said, most reforms have been enacted through executive action while legislation remains a significant obstacle for the new Government given its lack of majority in the upper house of Indian parliament. This would weigh on India's ability to push through difficult structural reforms across land acquisition, labour, mining and taxation, which require legislative approval.

"I think Modi surprised everyone by, with very little hesitation, embracing the United States," said Milan Vaishnav, a South Asia expert at the Carnegie Endowment for International Peace. "To give credit where credit is due, the Obama administration stepped in very quickly after his election to signal that he was willing to do business."

Obama also had a good rapport with former Indian Prime Minister Manmohan Singh. However, US officials expressed some frustration that their personal warmth never translated into policy breakthroughs.

Though in NDA-II rule Modi has started the US policy in a new look, but all UPA policies are being followed. In spite of that, Modi is keen to progress on every aspect of Indo-US relations. From Obama's visit too it is evidenced a secular India can serve better in domestic as well international affairs.

This is also apparent from the visit of both leaders to each other's country and signed agreement for a steady progress in relations. Apart from international and regional compulsion, both leaders came in close ties leaving the past behind.

In last September Modi's visit to US further boost the relations. After the meeting, PM Modi had said US and India shares an "uncompromising commitment" on climate change and thanked President Obama for supporting "India's permanent membership in a reformed United Nations Security Council.[10]

"I am encouraged by India's commitment to clean energy. Its leadership on climate change will set tone for decades," President Obama said after the meeting.[11]

Recently Modi's approach towards South Asian countries has witnessed a new era. What constrained Modi is the Chinese's huge support to Pakistan on supply of military equipment and openly vetoed in UN against India, in support of Pakistan. Here India's role should be very cautious. Of course, it is to Chinese interest to be with India for its economic interest. Furthermore, Modi should seriously think over Obama's advice on secularism in India. India's secular foundation has been internationally known and it should be maintained. Under Modi India is taking her US policy in a different way, which is quite confusing. Particularly relations with US under Trumph. It is quite risky.

NOTES

1. Maxwell, Neville, *India's China War*. Dehra Dun: Natraj Publishers, 1970, pp. 146, 270–71, 364, 378, 385.
2. Tripathy, Amulya K and Tripathy, Rabi Narayan (2008), *US Policy Towards India A Post Cold War Study*, New Delhi, Reference Press, p. 2.

3   Cohen, Stephen P. *India Emerging Power*, Washington, DC: The Brooking Institute Press, 2002, p. 13.
4   http://www.dw.com/en/narendra-modis-foreign-policy-challenges/a-17662599
5   Tellis, Ashley J. *What Modi must do in the US to reset the relationship*, Washington DC September 27, 2014 Last Updated at 00:24 IST
6   Obama, Barack, President, US and India Can be best Partner, Times of India, New Delhi, Jan 27th, *Time Magazine*, 23 Jan 2015
7   White House Blog, Jan, 26, 2015)
8   NDTV, September 29, 2015
9   TOI, Sep 28, 2015, 10.23
10 Ram Punyani, Howdy Modi: Bypassing Travails Being Faced by India, Secular Perspective, Sept, 24, 2019.
11 Ibid

5

Indian Diaspora as a Factor in Indo–Gulf Relations

Anisur Rahman and Naziya Naweed

Introduction

Relations between India and the Arab world date back to the dawn of the civilization. Extensive seafaring marked an essential step in establishing strong cultural ties between the two regions. In addition, continued commercial interactions played a crucial role in influencing each other's language and culture. People-to-people contact started between the two landmasses when Indian scholars and scientist move to the Arab world while the study of mathematics and science brought Arab scholars to India (Ahmad, 2011). Consequently, this trend becomes the foundation on which their present-day relation exists.

Within a very short span of time, it was witnessed that the Indo Arab relation reached its peak with the emergence of two great political leaders Jawaharlal Nehru and Gamal Abdel Naseer in Indian and Egypt (Heptulla, 1991). Subsequently, the Indian government institutionalised its friendship with the Arab world. India, since independence, championed the cause of Palestinian people for their separate homeland. Nehru, along with other Congressman, provided consistent support to the Arab cause. Besides, the then government viewed Egypt (Cairo) as an essential key to the success of India's policy in the Arab World. Later, the shared voice against the anti-colonialism also become the basis for forging their ties, which is itself evident in the Arab world joining the Non-Aligned Movement.

It is a well-known fact that the relations between India and GCC economies are significant in terms of trade. Moreover, migrant remittance also becomes a notable factor which makes their relationship unique. But any comprehensive understanding of the recent trends in Indo-Gulf relations calls for taking the interest of both sides into consideration since the two regions are dependent on each other for the development of their respective economies. For India, on the one hand, the remittance its Diaspora sends back to the country of origin is an essential factor for economic development. On the other hand, for the Gulf economies, too, Indian Human Resource is the vital source for the diversification of its economies. Not only the pattern has generated interdependency but also now their relationship has gone much beyond the ambit of energy, trade, and commerce to the vibrant presence of Diaspora in the region. As a result, this significant pool of human resource has made India an important country for the Gulf. Therefore, it would not be wrong to say that Indian Diaspora is becoming an essential bridging link between the two regions.

India's Foreign Policy

Foreign policy can be defined as a tool in the hand of the state that determines its relationship with other countries keeping in mind their national interests. Concerning India's foreign policy per se, cultural legacy, historical linkages, geography, and economic considerations are the underlying determinants that shape its primary objectives and principles.

The development of India's Foreign Policy towards the West Asian region in general and to the Gulf, in particular, is determined by its strategic, geopolitical concerns and economic factor, particularly energy and oil. Apart from it, the intricate underpinnings of Shia-Sunni divide, the role of ISIS, geostrategic environment, have also a role to play in formulating a robust policy in the region. The rise of Israel on the world stage and growing proximity between India and Israel, accounting for more than $4 billion trade, marks an essential source of fraction for the Arab world. The renewed interest of India in Israel comes at the expense of the Palestinian rights to which it stands. More so, it could work against the prospects of establishing peace in the region.

India cannot overlook the region which is rich in oil and the large chunk of migrants who play an essential role in economic development in the region. There are about 9 million Indians who are working in the Gulf region. It is in this context that one cannot sideline the importance of Diaspora. Therefore, it is crucial on the part of the policymakers to make Indian Diaspora a reference point in formulating India's Foreign Policy as they are a vital contributor to our economy.

On the other hand, Saudi Arabia and UAE are in search of investment partners, so maintaining cordial relations with the region becomes an utmost important for both (Joshi, 2017).

Let us now discuss the presence of Indian Diaspora in the region.

The Presence of Indian Diaspora

The modern Indian Diaspora is about 200 years old, which is, in fact, the creation of British colonialism. Demographically, the Indian Diaspora is the second largest in the world after the Chinese Diaspora. Currently, the total number of overseas Indians is exceeding 17 million (Business Standard, 2018), settled in more than 110 countries, including US, Canada, UK, European countries, Australia, West Asian Countries, Southeast, and Far Eastern countries. In the context of West Asia, the oil boom of 1973, led the massive influx of both skilled and semi-skilled workers from Asian countries particularly from India, to the Gulf countries (Rana, 2011, p. 98). Taking India as a reference point, dispersion of population globally was the result of the migration process that aimed at achieving better jobs and decent standards of living. The move not only led to the unprecedented economic advancement of the region but also attracted a large number of human resources resource from abroad to meet the growing labour requirement. Mostly, Indian labour belonging to Kerala, Tamil Nadu, and Uttar Pradesh migrated to the economies of GCC.

Diaspora has achieved salience in recent times as an essential factor for strengthening relations between the home and the host countries. According to Mark Leonard, "The untapped potential in the global Diaspora could, with sustained involvement, yield several advantages to policymakers" (Leonard, 2002). To channelize the affairs of Indians abroad, Ministry of overseas Indian Affairs, was created in 2004. Since then, this ministry is working in order to address the issues pertaining to the Diaspora community. One of the other functions of it was to engage them for their mutual benefit and interests. Now, the ministry has merged with the Ministry of External Affairs. With the repeated incidences of Human rights abuses abroad, it is the imperative of the government to protect their right so that they could become economically, socially, and strategically, crucial for both (home and host) countries. The Diasporas provide essential links and contact points between home and host societies. They build transnational networks which transact not only emotional and familial bonds but also cultural, social, and economic interests.

Growing Volume and Composition of Diaspora in the Gulf

The foreign population has been increasing speedily for the last few decades in the Gulf countries. The number of Indians has consistently grown, as clearly shown in table 1. The size of Indian migrants was 1.5 million that had risen to 8.7 million in 2017. During the last 25 years, the number of Indians has increased more than five times in the Gulf countries and it is expected to grow as they are preferred by the gulf employer.

Table 1: Size of Indian Workers in the Gulf Countries 1991–2017

Countries	1991	1999	2004	2008	2012	2017
Bahrain	100,000	1,50000	100,000	233,955	350,000	316,175
Kuwait	88,000	2,00000	450,000	5,11,161	579,390	919,354
Oman	220,000	4,50,000	450,000	4,32,000	718,642	783,959
Qatar	75,000	100000	1,00,000	239,000	5,00,000	697,500
Saudi Arabia	6,00,000	12,00000	1,500,000	13,50,652	1,789,000	3,255,864
UAE	400,000	7,50,000	1,000,000	14,11,000	1,750,000	2,803,751
Others	22,000	1,50,000	NA	NA	NA	NA
Total	1,505,000	8,764,829	3,600,000	41,77,768	5,687,032	8,776,603

Source: Prakash C. Jain and Kundan Kumar(eds), *Indian Labour Diaspora in the Gulf: An Overview in Indian Trade Diaspora in the Arabian Peninsula*, New Academic Publishers, New Delhi 2012, p 328; Annual Report Ministry of External Affairs http://mea.gov.in/images/attach/NRIs-and-PIOs_1.pdf

In the Indian context, it is clear that Uttar Pradesh, Andhra Pradesh, Bihar, Kerala, Punjab, West Bengal, and Rajasthan were the states that sent the highest number of Indian immigrants to the Gulf countries. Uttar Pradesh sends the most significant number of labour to Gulf Countries, as shown in table 2. In the year 2017, Uttar Pradesh sends 86,173 labour to the Gulf, Bihar sent 68,295, Tamil Nadu the figures are 38,341. In the January-June period of the year 2017, Bihar emerged as the state to have sent the maximum number of migrants to the Gulf countries. The other states of India only constitute 109,560 immigrates.

Reliance on foreign labour has resulted in expatriates currently constituting 88 percent of the workforce in the UAE, 83 percent in Qatar, 81 percent in Kuwait, 72 percent in Saudi Arabia, 55 percent in Bahrain, and 54 percent in Oman. However, the composition of expatriate workers has changed periodically. If the current trend continues, the number of migrant workers will grow by another 1 million. It is equally likely that the number of non-Gulf Arab workers in the GCC states will diminish, and the presence of Asian workers would likely to grow further. During the last four decades, the proportion of non-citizens in the Gulf has steadily increased, which is contrary to the plans and desires of the Gulf

Table 2: Top 10 labour-sending Indian states during 2010-17

State	2010	2011	2012	2013	2014	2015	2016	2017
AndhraPradesh	43131	43052	49782	59789	52121	44644	26574	11138
Uttar Pradesh	136542	156023	189002	214712	226798	234958	141482	86173
Kerala	102886	87404	97244	84970	65475	42755	24962	16337
Bihar	58746	70932	82759	94609	97359	106719	75480	68295
Punjab	28599	31537	36547	46977	45079	44381	30762	26449
Rajasthan	46844	42745	49935	50617	47767	45925	35029	31914
West Bengal	26938	28474	34670	39419	49048	62343	51247	33955
Gujarat	8091	8403	6871	8418	7743	6795	4496	4194
Maharashtra	17729	16721	19059	19383	18976	15217	10363	7687
Karnataka	16955	15582	17819	17670	14953	11867	6423	5144
Total	486461	500873	583688	636564	625319	615604	406818	291286

Source: Annual Report, MOIA, GOI, 2008-2017 https://emigrate.gov.in/ext/home.action (accessed on 15/01/2018)

countries. The data reveals that the percentage of non-nationals vary from country to country, ranging from 32.0 percent in Saudi Arabia to 88.5 percent in the United Arab Emirates (Fargues and Brouwer, 2012). The percentage of expatriate workers in the GCC countries grew from 22.9 percent in 1975 to 38.5 percent in 2002 and then to 48.1 percent of the total population of 48.1 million GCC residents (Fargue & Brouwer, 2012). Now, the overall percentage share of foreign nationals in the GCC countries accounts for 51 percent (Gulf Labour Markets and Migration, 2016).

Economic and Social Benefit of Diaspora

The flow of funds from migrant workers back to their families in their home country is an essential source of income in many developing economies. Not only has it contributed significantly in foreign exchange earnings and GDP growth of nations but has also enhanced the economic betterment of migrants' families. India is one of the world's largest remittance recipient country with $79 billion in 2018, followed by China, Mexico, the Philippines, and Egypt. According to the World Bank, global annual remittance accounts for $529 billion in 2018, and it is expected to reach a target of $550 in 2019 (World Bank, 2018). With regards to the GCC, the total share of remittance from Saudi Arabia is $11.2 billion, Kuwait $4.6 billion, Qatar $4.1 billion, Oman $3.3 billion and UAE $13.8 billion (The Economic Times, 2018). In total, the total remittance from the GCC coming to India is estimated to be more than $37 billion.

In present times, Indian communities living in Gulf region have become an asset to Indian foreign policy not only in terms of the development of our economy through remittances but also working as a soft power tool in diplomacy. The basis of India's soft power is visible in terms of culture, language, skills, Bollywood, food, yoga, its democratic character, neutrality, and non-interference. Indian Diasporas are not only economically beneficial to India but also projecting the country's image abroad. They are similarly making their food and culture accessible in terms of attracting tourism to the home country. In addition to economic remittances, they also bring social remittance to the homeland. There is a visible change in their attitude towards education and social mobility. The most significant advantage is that it has also led to social acceptance of the migrants in the home country.

Diaspora Linkages with India's Foreign Policy

The Indian government was unable to realise the potential of Indian Diaspora in the early years of independence. Thus, India's Diaspora policy has evolved over times, from disengagement to active engagement in contemporary times. Events like 1970's global financial disruption and balance of payment crisis not only compelled India to alter its policy but also to ease restriction on financial inflows from its expatriates living abroad. Ever since then, India has understood the importance of its Diaspora, and their active involvement can reap several benefits for the labour sending country.

Post-independence Indian foreign policy mainly paid heed to non-alignment and anti-imperialism. Nehru believed that those "ethnic Indians who stayed for so long in the host country should consider themselves as part of that country, and they should integrate themselves into their culture and tradition" (Mahalingam, GRFDT). The year 1970 saw a paradigm shift, and the presence of its diasporic population abroad achieved salience over the years. This changed stand in the foreign policy discourse towards its migrant population is noticeable by each successive government. Various initiatives, like the celebration of Pravasi Bharatiya Divas (9th January) by Atal Bihari Vajpayee, PIO card scheme, National Pension Scheme, were undertaken. In 2004, the Ministry of Overseas Affairs came into effect as a way forward for the more active involvement of its Diaspora.

Under PM Manmohan Singh, Indian American communities were a guiding factor in the conclusion of the civil nuclear deal. Similarly, the current PM Narendra Modi has continuously focused on Diaspora as an essential asset in branding new India apart from the repeated call for democracy, demography, and demand. The PM not only visited UAE, where he addressed 50000 expat population working but also visited migrant's camps and expressed grave concerns for their situation. Moreover, the construction of a temple in the region signifies the importance accorded to Indian Diaspora.

Recently only, a landmark bill has been passed by the Indian Parliament that expands "proxy voting" facility to the overseas Indian. The Bill will permit the NRIs to appoint proxy voters to cast their vote. Hence, according to the law Minister Ravi Shankar Prasad, the move will allow the overseas Indians to actively participate in the electoral process of their homeland (The Economic Times, 2018). Furthermore, it will provide social protection and fundamental 'right to vote' to the overseas Indians. The new policy is looking at the Indian Diaspora from a new perspective. One cannot sideline that their contribution to the Indian economy and society in terms of time, expertise, and investment in all the sectors is crucial for India.

India's Policy Initiative

Concerning significant involvement with the region, one could argue that Indian Diaspora in the gulf has received low priority. The trend is evident from the limited number of ministerial visits to the region. Indian subcontinent in the year 1990 restricted their interactions to just the immediate neighbourhood 'South Asia' (G. Parthasarathy, 2018). It is only recently that renewed interest in the Indian living abroad has received considerable attention.

The change stance has been due to a massive influx of labour from India to the GGC economies. More than 9 million migrants are contributing to the development of the economies of both region. Since 2015, the Indian government has successfully concluded MoUs with Bahrain (2014), Kuwait (2007) Oman (2008), Qatar (1985), and UAE (2006). The nature of these MoUs ranges from concerns for Indian Expatriate to labour, employment, and human resources developments. Recently, more MoUs between Oman and UAE have been signed following the visit by PM. Out of the total, one was related to its Diaspora. Lately, the present-day government initiative by celebrating world Yoga day has added to its advantage, and now it is working as a soft power tool. This stance too got support from Qatar by observing international yoga day on 21st June.

In terms of building strong bilateral relations, several memorandums of understanding (MoUs) have been signed between Indian and the host countries since the 1980s pertaining especially for the protection of migrant workers. In one such MoU signed with UAE, the Ministry of Overseas Indian Affairs in the year 2011 highlighted five concerns (Ministry of Overseas Indian Affairs, Government of India, n.d.).

They were:

- Declaration of mutual intent to enhance employment opportunities and bilateral cooperation in the protection and welfare of workers.
- Host country to take measures for the protection and welfare of the workers in the organised sector.
- Statement of the broad procedures that foreign employers shall follow to recruit Indian workers.
- The recruitment and terms of employment to conform with the laws for both the countries.
- A Joint Working Group (JWG) to be constituted to ensure implementation of the MoU and to find solutions to bilateral labour problems (Ministry of Overseas Indian Affairs, Government of India, n.d.).

In spite of these MoUs signed, one cannot neglect the violations of Human rights of the migrant workers that surface the group. The workers employed in the destination countries were subject to abuse and exploitation, long, tedious working hours, delays in payment, to name a few.

Besides, some critical policies have been formulated by the Government of India for harnessing the potential of Indian Diaspora. They are as follows:

- Pravasi Bharatiya Divas (PBD)
- Indian Community Welfare Fund (ICWF)
- India Development Foundation of Overseas Indian (IDF-OI)
- India Centre for Migration (ICM)
- Registration portal for overseas Indians
- Scholarship program for Diaspora Children
- Global Indian Network of Knowledge (GLOBAL-INK)

The Gulf economies of Saudi Arabia, Kuwait, Oman, UAE, Bahrain, and Qatar are among the most extensive labour importing countries. It is not wrong to say that their presence even outnumbered the local population. Cheap labour from Egypt and Yemen were pulled to meet the requirements in the 1970s for construction work. In addition to this, for the nationals, public sector jobs were reserved, and for the migrants, private-sector jobs were open who come under the system of Kafala. Kafala or sponsorship is an 'employment framework in the Gulf' whereby national employee sponsors a migrant. They, in turn, exercise full control over him, for example, in seeking permission to leave the job or to return. Human rights activist have criticised this framework as it leads to exploitation of the migrant worker in the host land by the hands of the employee (Kane-Hartnett, 2018).

The Gulf States are motivated to hire foreign nationals for their infrastructural development. But due to Indian emigration policy and minimum referral wage (MRW), job priorities in the region have changed. So, they began to attract labours from Bangladesh and Pakistan (Asif Nawaaz, 2017). Within no time, the percentage share of the workforce increased from 2 percent in 2014 to 17 percent in 2016, particularly in Saudi Arabia. Some similar sort of figures is also found for Pakistani workforce. In the Indian context, the return migration from the Gulf region is emerging as a crucial challenge. Not only it raises concerns on 'how to rehabilitate the returnee' (Challagalla, 2018), but also requires policy framework so that they again become an asset to the Indian economy and society.

Conclusion

The Indian Diaspora has existed for much longer and has contributed to the growth story in two ways. Firstly, they have been able to make lifestyle changes and per capita changes in the home country. It is also witnessed that India gets economic and strategic benefits due to the enormous presence of its diaspora worldwide. Secondly, as Human resource development, they are equally beneficial to the host countries economy. Though, the Indian government has realised the significance of the remittance for country development. They have been taking steps towards channelising the potential of the Indian diaspora by making them invest in schemes back home that are mutually beneficial, still more steps need to be taken to safeguard the economic position as well as basic rights of the Indian diaspora abroad.

REFERENCES

Ahmad, A. (2011), Continuity and Change In Indo-Arab Cultural Relations: A Survey with Special Reference to Oman, 25.

Ahn, P (ed.). (2004). Migrant Workers and Human Rights: Out -Migration from South Asia, ILO, Subregional Office for South Asia, New Delhi.

As India becomes wealthier, 17 mn leave the country to settle abroad. *Business Standard.* (2018). https://www.business-standard.com/article/current-affairs/as-india-becomes-wealthier-17-mn-leave-the-country-to-settle-abroad-118112100113_1.html

Bill to allow proxy voting by NRIs passed by Lok Sabha. (2018). *The Economic Times.* // economictimes.indiatimes.com/articleshow/65343623.cms?utm_source= contentofinterest& utm _medium=text&utm_campaign=cppst

Challagalla, S. (2018). The diaspora and India's growth story. Retrieved March 31, 2019, from ORF website: https://www.orfonline.org/research/the-diaspora-and-indias-growth-story/

Fargues P. and I. Brouwer. 2012). GCC Demography and Immigration: Challenges and Policies., in *National Employment, Migration and Education in the GCC*, ed. S. Hertog, Cambridge: Gerlach Press.

G. Parthasarathy. (2018, September 27). Beyond South Asia -Indian Foreign Policy 3.0. Retrieved March 31, 2019, from https://www.livemint.com website: https://www.livemint.com/Politics/84BXShkr42gSNnFiV4yqcK/Beyond-South-Asia-Indian-foreign-policy-30.html

Government of India, Ministry of Overseas Indian Affairs, Annual Reports. (2014). http://moia.gov.in/writereaddata/pdf/Annual_Report_2014-15.pdf

Government of India, Report of the High Level Committee on Indian Diaspora. (2001). http://moia.gov.in/services.aspx?ID1=63&id=m10&idp=59&mainid=23

Gulf Labour Markets and Migration (GLMM) programme. Most recent national data. Data available at gulfmigration.eu.

Heptulla, N. (1991). Indo-West Asian Relations: The Nehru Era. Allied Publishers.

How the matrix of remittances is changing for Indians. *The Economic Times*. (2018). // economictimes.indiatimes.com/articleshow/64809196.cms?utm_source= contentofinterest &utm_medium=text&utm_campaign=cppst

India's Diaspora Policy and Foreign Policy: An Overview. (n.d.). Retrieved February 27, 2019, from http://www.grfdt.com/PublicationDetails.aspx?Type=Articles&TabId=30

India-Arab League Relations. Embassy of India, Cairo, Egypt. https://www.eoicairo.gov.in/eoi.php?id=Arab

Joshi, M. (2017). India and the world: Foreign policy in the age of Modi. Retrieved March 31, 2019, from ORF website: https://www.orfonline.org/research/india-and-the-world-foreign-policy-in-the-age-of-modi/

Kane-Hartnett | 2018, L. (2018, April 17). Kafala System: A Gateway to Slavery, Human Trafficking Search. Retrieved March 30, 2019, from Human Trafficking Search website: http://humantraffickingsearch.org/kafala-system/

Leonard, M. (2002). Diplomacy by Other Means. *Foreign policy*. https://foreignpolicy.com/2009/11/09/diplomacy-by-other-means/

Mahalingam, M. (2013). India's Diaspora Policy and Foreign Policy: An Overview. Global Research Forum on Diaspora and Transnationalism, Transnationalism.http://www.grfdt.com/PublicationDetails.aspx?Type=Articles&TabId=30

Nawaaz Asif. (2017). How India's Recent Migrant Policies Helped Bangladesh and Pakistan Eat into Our GDP. https://www.outlookindia.com/website/story/how-indias-recent-migrant-policies-helped-bangladesh-and-pakistan-eat-into-our-g/298076

Press Release, Record High Remittances Sent Globally in 2018 (n.d.). World Bank. https://www.worldbank.org/en/news/press-release/2019/04/08/record-high-remittances-sent-globally-in-2018

Rahman, A. (2001). Indian Labour Migration to the Gulf: A Socio-economic Analysis, New Delhi: Rajat Publications, New Delhi.

Rana, K.S. (2011). 21st-Century Diplomacy: A Practitioner's Guide. Bloomsbury Publishing USA.

Supporting Indian Workers in the Gulf: What Delhi Can Do. (n.d.). Accessed March 30, 2019. https://www.brookings.edu/research/supporting-indian-workers-in-the-gulf-what-delhi-can-do/.

The International Political Economy of Gulf Migration. (n.d). Middle East Institute. Accessed March 30, 2019. https://www.mei.edu/publications/international-political-economy-gulf-migration.

Weiner, M. (1982) International Migration and Development: Indians in the Pakistan Gulf, *Population and Development Review*, 9(1): 1-36.

6

The Growing Chinese Dominance Potential Security Concerns for India and the Region:
With Special Reference to South China Sea

Chandra Mohan Upadhyay

The growing dominance of the so called rising China, has every potential for global instability in the 21st century. The hypothesis treads cautiously on the premise that China is emerging as a revisionist power. It has got security implications and complications for the regional states in particular and the world in general. Any hypothesis to be sound should be tested on the basis of facts and not on fancies. Let us put the hypothesis to test, and leaving the judgement to the reader. By challenging the might of America in South-East Asia, China has given the first major hint of its intentions to dominate the region. China's growing economic and military power has encouraged its initiation of military conflicts. However, the liberalist view leads us to expect that China's growth will deepen Asia's economic interdependence, thereby increasing international stability and regional integration. According to this perspective, we should be worrying not about China's rise but about fear of the rise. Given that China is expected to continue growing and eventually equal the United States in terms of the size of its economy. Are we going to see China becoming more aggressive? Some scholars have compared the Chinese growth and aggression and have found that China has become more hostile to its opponents in territorial disputes. As China gains greater economic capability, it has become more hostile to its opponents. "To test the above hypotheses, we examine China's practice of initiating militarized conflicts with Asian states and major powers after the death of Mao Zedong, when it began to re-emerge... Using the Militarized Interstate Disputes dataset, which provides information on four types of military action (military threat, military display, use of force, and war, we measure the dependent variable: China's first military action against a particular state in a given year... The dataset contains 55 initiations of militarized conflict by China against Asian and major countries: 22 from 1976 to 1989 and 33 from 1990 to 2001.[1]

China's greater power has made the country more assertive, rather than cooperative, toward Asian states and major powers. This hypothesis that China will maintain its current uncompromising and adamant position in the South and East China Seas and elsewhere. Renouncing its earlier charade of peaceful rise, China is now asking others to 'get used to its muscle flexing'. China has searched strategic opportunities everywhere in the world. Now it is time for China to reap the rich dividends and South-China Sea provides ample opportunities for the realization of its great game ambitions. Belying any reference to history, China claims almost the entire South China Sea, through which about $5 trillion worth of trade passes each year. The littoral and regional countries along with United States have unequivocally criticized Beijing's build-up of military facilities in the sea and expressed concerns they could be used to restrict free movement. China has shown a great deal of disdain towards its neighbouring countries. The claims and counter-claims of territories in South-China Sea continue to fester. China's island-building, construction of facilities, and militarization of features in the area proceed unabated.

The rise of China is not disturbing the least because we once fought a war and lost but the implications of resultant dominance is spreading far and wide. It is appropriate to understand the mindset of China, before our painstaking.

Noted Scholar Lucian Pye points out a strange uniqueness of China, which still remains a "civilization pretending to be a nation-state."[2] The legendary, former US Secretary of State, Henry Kissinger aptly describes this situation, "The extent and variety of territory bolsters the sense that China is a world unto itself, and its rulers presiding over *tian xia*, or All under Heaven". For China, this is essential for a harmonious world order, where harmony emanates, to quote **Confucius** "from knowing your rightful place in the hierarchy".[3]

The multi-polarity of the 21st century is incompatible with this *tian xia* approach. It seems quite plausible that behind all the plans to integrate the world, there is a hidden agenda somewhere down the line to rediscover and regain that utopian centrality, lost long ago in the vicissitudes of time.

China has initiated a multifarious project, with a pious declaration of connecting the world economy, popularly known as 'One Belt, One Road' or OBOR. The OBOR, is basically a smoke-screen to hide the real ambitions of ruling the world. It is part of their cultural front to believe that, "China is a world into itself. China wants to integrate Eurasia through trillion Dollars of infrastructure. It has rightly been termed by critics As China's New **Marshall Plan**. In a world of competing economic and trade alliances OBOR needs to be compared with its contemporaries, the most famous European union has got just 27-members, OPEC has 13, the organization of Islamic States (OIC) has 57. OBOR surpasses all with its 60 members."[4]

The initiative has since been widely discussed between policy makers and academics both inside and outside China. Many questions have been asked, like why did China come up with such a strategy at this point of time, when it is already slowing down or what are the real intentions behind it? Is it not the Pax-China in disguise? To put it simply, this is a long-cherished dream of Middle-Kingdom or '*zhongguo*' by another name.

India decided not to participate. India was invited to the Beijing conclave. India has got a number of reasons for staying away. None of them was more important than the question of India's sovereignty over Pak-occupied Kashmir (POK), through which an important part of China's OBOR runs. The foreign office in Delhi affirmed that "No country can accept a project that ignores its core concerns on sovereignty and territorial integrity. International isolation is not India's biggest problem... India is too large an economy and political entity to be isolated by another power, occupying a vertical Geographical location, India can contribute to the success of China's belt and Road initiative or create needless complications. India's real challenge is to match its claim on territorial sovereignty with effective action on the ground."[5]

It is not India alone but the world community at large is quite concerned with the magnitude of initiatives around the globe. One of the most venerated scholars of international politics, Joseph S. Nye makes a stinging observation, "Marco Polo would be proud. And if China chooses to use its surplus financial reserves to create important infrastructure that helps poor countries...China's motives are not purely philanthropic"[6]

As the *Financial Times* puts it, BRI "unfortunately is no more a practical plan for investment than a broad political vision".[7]

The financial part of the plan is exposed more than ever. Many countries who earlier enthusiastically participated like Pakistan and Sri Lanka, are now reeling under the debt burden. Speaking at Shangri-La in Singapore Prime Minister Modi also underlined the deliberate debt-trap in the name of connectivity, "We understand the benefits of connectivity. There are many connectivity initiatives in the region. If these are to succeed, we must not only build infrastructure; we must also build bridges of trust. And for that, these initiatives must be based on respect for sovereignty and territorial integrity, consultation, good governance, transparency, viability and sustainability. They must empower nations, not place them under an impossible debt burden."[8]

Finally, all of this is possible if we do not return to the age of great-power rivalries. I have said this before: an Asia of rivalry will hold us all back; an Asia of cooperation will shape this century. So, each nation must ask itself, "Are its choices building a more united world, or forcing new divisions? It is a responsibility that both existing and rising powers have. Competition is normal, but contests must not turn into conflicts; differences must not be allowed to become disputes".[9]

Asian and particularly South-Asian countries have tried to balance the overbearing presence of China but in the absence of a strong US backing, these countries would fall back on China, as rightly maintained by Samuel P. Huntington "a band-wagoning propensity is likely to exist among Asian powers, which would preclude any US effort at secondary balancing".[10]

America is aware of this propensity and therefore it is ready with a strategy. American defence secretary James Mattis elaborated it at the 17th Asian Security Summit, Shangri-La, "America's Indo-Pacific strategy is a subset of our broader security strategy, codifying our principles as America continues to 'look west'. In it we see deepening alliances and partnerships as a priority; ASEAN's centrality remains vital; and cooperation with China is welcome wherever possible."[11]

India and the US both stressed that no one nation can or should dominate the Indo-Pacific. The maritime commons, is a global good, and sea lanes of communication are the arteries of economic vitality for all. It is in the best interest of the region to preserve that vitality. The US promised to help the regional players to build up naval and law-enforcement capabilities and capacities to improve monitoring and protection of maritime borders and interests. So long as littoral nations pool their resources to be a force multiplier for peace, no miracle is going to happen. Therefore, the regional states need to ensure that their military can more easily integrate with others. The strategy is to include Australia and New Zealand also in the ambit of Indo-Pacific security cooperation. The US values the role India can play in regional and global security and views the US–India relationship as a natural partnership between the world's two largest democracies based on a convergence of strategic interests, shared values and respect for a rules-based international order.

Considering the enormity of the challenge from China, Americans are invoking the cooperation from other Pacific allies, such as the United Kingdom, France and Canada to build a strong and lasting alternative. China on its part has promised several times to play by rules but never shied away from overt to covert arm-twisting of the regional countries. China's militarisation of artificial features in the South China Sea includes the deployment of anti-ship missiles, surface-to-air missiles, electronic jammers and, more recently, the landing of bomber aircraft at Woody Island. Despite China's claims to the contrary, the placement of these weapons systems is tied directly to military use for the purposes of intimidation and coercion. China's militarisation of the Spratlys is also in direct contradiction to President Xi's public assurances. Given the precarious nature of America leadership, India should take a lead. We must seriously invest in several groupings which are lying dormant like Indian Ocean Rim countries (IORC), & BIMSTEC, BBIN and Mekong-Ganga Cooperation (GMC), which was conceived more than a decade (year 2000) ago. Our record of translating conceptions into creations is dismal. It is here that our real test lies. It is in this regard a significant development is worth mentioning. India and Japan have launched a vision document for Asia-Africa Growth Corridor (AAGC). The AAGC initiative is part of Indo-Pacific freedom corridor being put in place by India and Japan with an eye on counterbalancing the Chinese OBOR. It aims for Indo-Japanese collaboration to develop quality infrastructure in Africa, complemented by digital connectivity. Let us examine the ground zero.

China's Domineering Behaviour with Philippines and other Regional Countries

China claims particularly on Scarborough Shoal in the Spratly Islands have been rejected by the International Tribunal of the Permanent Court of Arbitration (PCA) at the Hague. The PCA at Hague handed down its historic and sweeping award on maritime entitlements in South China Sea, overwhelmingly favouring the Philippines over China. The ruling was a major victory for the Philippines, particularly the tribunal's decision on China's "nine-dash line," through which Beijing attempts to lay claim to vast areas of the South China Sea. As expected, Beijing refused to accept the PCA ruling, hardened its legal and diplomatic positions, and within hours of the ruling, at least 68 national and local government websites in the Philippines were knocked offline in a massive Distributed Denial of Service (DDOS) attack. The crippling DDOS attacks against Filipino government networks continued over several days and targeted key government agencies, to include the Department of Foreign Affairs, the Department of National Defence, and the Central Bank. Within few months after the award, under the huge pressure from China, Philippines issued a conciliatory statement even as energy official announced that Manila would soon offer investors new oil and gas blocks at Reed Bank, off the Philippine coast but within the nine-dash line.[12]

Beijing, for its part, has always made clear that it regards the tribunal's decision as "null and void" and of no binding force.' Statements from Association of Southeast Asian Nations (ASEAN) states in the wake of the decision were muted. None urged China to adhere to the ruling; the strongest merely called for respecting international law. The real significance of the tribunal's decision was to clarify resource rights. Its main findings were twofold. "First, it ruled that China cannot claim historic rights to resources in the waters within the nine-dash line if those waters are within the EEZs of other coastal states. Such rights were extinguished when China ratified the UN Convention on the Law of the Sea in 1996. Second, the tribunal ruled that none of the features in the Spratlys is entitled to a 200-nautical-mile EEZ. Like Scarborough Shoal, all of the Spratly features are at most rocks entitled to 12-nautical-mile territorial seas."[13]

Although technically binding only on parties to the arbitration, the tribunal's decision has bolstered the position of ASEAN littoral states in the South China Sea. It has clarified that the EEZ entitlements of the Philippines, as well as Brunei, Indonesia, Malaysia, and Vietnam, are unencumbered by China's nine-dash line or any claimed EEZ from features in the Spratlys. Areas of overlap in the Spratlys are now limited to a 12-nautical-mile ring around rock features. Beyond these areas, China has no claim recognized under international law to fish or to extract oil or gas in the EEZs of other states outside the EEZ generated from China's mainland.

In assessing the impact of the award, what China and ASEAN states do is at least as important as what they say. In official statements issued on the day of and after the judgment, Beijing appeared to expressly assert, for the first time, that China's maritime claims in the South China Sea include "historic rights." It did not specify what it means by this. China is a country whose history is best known to it. It has claims over almost all the neighbouring countries. From centuries

Tibet had been an autonomous region, paying tributes to Chinese and adjoining Indian kingdoms. Suddenly China discovered its forgotten history only to capture the Tibet. It has still remnant claims over India after illegally capturing 24000 sq km of our motherland. It claims are wide ranging covering not only the landmasses but sea areas also. The South-China controversy is nothing but the same kind of historical claim over a number of countries. However, if Beijing is claiming historic rights to resources within the entirety of the nine-dash line (rather than historic fishing rights within territorial seas), its assertion flies in the face of the judgment. In May 2018, Beijing also imposed an annual fishing ban, which overlapped with the EEZs of the Philippines and Vietnam but excluded the Spratlys. The Philippines has been a key ally of the United States and a territorial rival of Beijing in the South China Sea. The impact of Beijing's action could be assessed by the fact that within a few days of this orchestrated drama the President of Philippines Duterte announced during a visit to China, his "separation" from Washington and realignment with Beijing. This is another form of bandwagoning.

India and South China Sea

Indian trade and economic linkages in the Pacific are becoming stronger and deeper. Not only are ASEAN and the far-eastern Pacific key target areas of the "Act East" policy, Asia's Eastern commons are increasingly a vital facilitator of India's economic development. With growing dependence on the Malacca Strait for the flow of goods and services, economics is increasingly a factor in India's Pacific policy. China must know that territorial conflicts in the SCS threaten the future trajectory of India's economic development, creating an unacceptable hindrance for regional trade and commerce. India believes that the disputes in the Southeast Asian littorals are a litmus test for international maritime law. In the aftermath of The Hague, tribunal's verdict on the South China Sea, New Delhi feels obligated to take a principled stand on the issue of freedom of navigation and commercial access as enshrined in the UNCLOS. "Beijing must know that regardless of the guarantees it seeks from India about staying neutral on the SCS, New Delhi cannot be seen to be condoning the aggression of armed Chinese naval ships, aircraft and submarines in the region."[14]

Beijing must know that New Delhi recognizes the threat that Chinese aggression poses for the wider Asian commons—in particular, the exacerbation of existing power asymmetries. In order to contribute to a fair and equitable regional maritime order, New Delhi must take a stand that restores strategic balance in maritime-Asia.

New Delhi's inability or rather the old habit of suppression of information and sometimes denial makes Indian positions unsustainable. Renowned scholar and journalist Arun Shourie has correctly summed up our position, "Wishful construction...paste a motive, fling a doubt at the messenger, discredit him...minimize what the adversary has done...manufacture explanations and at each turn summarily pronounce "But what else could we have been done".[15]

For instance, correlation the Indian maritime analysts discern between aggressive Chinese patrolling in the SCS and its growing deployments in the Indian Ocean Region; or the suspicion in Indian strategic circles that China might use its SCS bases as a springboard for active projection of power in the Indian Ocean and nevertheless keeping studied silence. So is the case of India's aggressive encirclement by China, its permanent presence in POK, its calculated incursions in Uttarakhand. Everywhere our response is not only inadequate but at best reactive. New Delhi should really worry about China's reclamation and militarization of features in its possession—particularly the deployment of missiles, fighters and surveillance equipment in its Spratly group of islands, allowing the PLAN (PLA Navy) effective control over the entire range of maritime operations in the SCS. New developments in China's military strategy are also notable. "Recently, Beijing has strengthened its anti-access/area denial (A2/AD) strategy in order to protect its core interests, including Taiwan, from interference by external forces, such as the United States. More specically, the A2/AD entails changes in military plans and strategies for air, maritime, submarine, space, and cyber warfare. For example, the People's Liberation Army Air Force (PLAAF) has decided to develop long-range mission capabilities and high-tech equipment, such as anti-satellite weapons".[16]

The People's Liberation Army Navy (PLAN) aims to expand its scope of influence from the first island chain, connecting Okinawa, Taiwan, and the Philippines, to the second island chain, connecting Guam and Saipan. In this regard, PLAN has declared a territorial sea baseline and air defence identification zone (ADIZ), has conducted regular patrols of the Diaoyu/Senkaku Islands, and has constructed artificial islands in the South China Sea, among other activities. Such military expansions present challenges to the US-led regional order that has existed in Asia since the end of World War II. Indian experts should also recognize the important role Beijing's militia forces play in achieving its regional objectives. India knows well that the main threat to maritime security in Asia isn't so much from the PLA Navy, but China's irregular forces. Chinese surveillance ships, coast-guard vessels and fishing fleets are the real force behind Beijing's dominance of the littoral spaces. "With the expansion of Chinese maritime activities in the IOR, New Delhi fears a rise in non-grey hull presence in the Eastern Indian Ocean. Already, China's distant water fishing fleet is now the world's largest, and is a heavily subsidized maritime commercial entity. While an increase in the presence of such ships doesn't always pose a security threat, India remains wary of Chinese non-military maritime activity in the Eastern Indian Ocean".[17]

Beijing's blueprint for maritime operations in the Indian Ocean involves the construction of multiple logistical facilities. China's 10-year agreement with Djibouti in 2015 for the setting up of a naval replenishment facility in the northern O bock region is widely seen as proof of the PLA Navy's strategic ambitions in the IOR. And this anticipation has proven right.

Djibouti is a resource-poor nation in the Horn of Africa. Its location also matters greatly to global commerce and energy, due to its vicinity to the Mandeb strait and the Suez-Aden canal, which sees 10 percent of oil and 20 percent of commercial exports annually. "The greatest worry is America's diminishing military footprints. It has begun to affect the calculation of allies and rivals alike".[18]

The US has tried to address this fear also. In his brilliant speech at Shangri-La Dialogue on June 2, 2018, James Mattis was quite forthcoming, "So make no mistakes, America is in the Indo-Pacific to stay. This is our priority theatre. Our interests and the regions, are inextricably intertwined.[19]

In fact, US and China are actually playing the role of the history. The United States embodies what Huntington considered 'Western civilization'. And tensions between American and Chinese values, traditions, and philosophies will aggravate the fundamental structural stresses that occur whenever a rising power, such as China, threatens to displace an established power, such as the United States. A conflicting situation is ensued, in the words of famous Historian Graham Allison, this is **Thucydides'** *trap*. According to Thucydides, "It was the rise of Athens, and the fear that this instilled in Sparta, that made war inevitable." Rising powers understandably feel a growing sense of entitlement and demand greater influence and respect. Established powers, faced with challengers, tend to become fearful, insecure, and defensive.[20]

With its new-found self-confidence, China is building military bases next door to the US AFRICOM in Djibouti. India must learn right lessons from several such episodes. China is just not any other strong nation being satisfied by playing a second fiddle. It has its global ambitions and it is unabashed about it. No victim card will fetch security and dignity to India. Long ago Thucydides reminded the succeeding generations through his 'Melian Dialogue' that, "Standard of justice depends on the equality of power to compel and in fact the strong do what they have the power to do and the weak accept what they have to accept."[21]

Our preparedness is not up to the mark and the kind of policy paralysis is visible even today. This is disappointing for a country which harbours the ambitions of attaining great power status. Indian leaders have not articulated the full extent of their anxieties over Chinese maritime operations in Asia. Regardless of the concessions on offer to New Delhi, Beijing must know that India will not agree to a compromise deal with China on the South China Sea.

It is in the light of this situation and Chinese overall aggressive posture in South China Sea that Indian Prime Minister Narendra Modi's visit to Vietnam in September 2016 and his Japan visit in the second week of November marked an important step forward in their ties. The fact that the PM chose to drop by Vietnam, on his way to the G20 Summit in Hangzhou, China, would not be lost on observers and must have ruffled quite a few feathers in Beijing. It also comes in the wake of July 12 awards handed down by the Permanent Court of Arbitration. Despite the open suggestion to India by China during the recent visit to Japan, Prime Minister Modi went on to stress, "India supports freedom of navigation and overflight, unimpeded commerce, based on the principles of international law, as reflected notably in the UNCLOS."[22]

In an age when geopolitics in the region is in a state of flux, it is essential for India to stand by our friends. Just as China has been wading into India's neighbourhood, there is no reason why India should shy away from doing the same in China's extended neighbourhood. With its soft power and of late hard power in full flow in Vietnam and Japan, New Delhi must be careful not to squander the new opportunities.

The Policy Alternative before India and the Region

For China, order is the highest value, and harmony results from a hierarchy. In some ways, Chinese exceptionalism is more sweeping than its American counterpart. The [Chinese] empire saw itself as the centre of the civilized universe. This notion is buttressed when we come across such kind of assertions, from no less a person than President himself. Xi claimed in his book that, "China's continuous civilization is not equal to anything on earth, but a unique achievement in world history".[23]

China's treatment of its own citizens provides the script for its relations with weaker neighbours abroad. During a meeting of the Association of Southeast Asian Nations, then Chinese Foreign Minister Yang Jiechi responded to complaints about Chinese assertiveness in the South China Sea by telling his regional counterparts and U.S. Secretary of State Hillary Clinton that, "China is a big country and other countries are small countries, and that's just a fact."[24]

China enters the global arena for *shi* or relative advantage. It is against the backdrop of hegemonic behaviour of China that Japan took the initiative. One of the interesting features of Japan's latest plan to revive the Indo-Pacific quadrilateral dialogue (Quad), is the move to associate the European powers with it. For Prime Minister of Japan, Shinzo Abe, who first discussed the idea of a quad a little over a decade ago, the four-nation forum is, in essence, a coalition of "maritime democracies". Abe argued that the maritime democracies have a stake in securing a rules-based global order, liberal trading system and freedom of navigation. "As a realist Abe is conscious of the fact that the growing power imbalance in Asia amidst the rapid rise of China can't be addressed by America's Asian alliance system alone. Abe has consciously courted special relationships with India, Australia and other regional powers. He also sees the need to keep the **quad** an open-ended organisation that can also benefit from the partnership with European powers."[25]

More than 70 per cent of European trade passes through Indo-Pacific. Both France and Britain have military presence and security arrangements in the Indian Ocean. France has many military facilities in the Indo-Pacific, including those in Reunion, Djibouti and the United Arab Emirates. Britain continues to control Diego Garcia. It also leads the Five Power Defence Arrangement (involving Singapore, Malaysia, Australia and New Zealand) set up in 1971. France has a variety of coordination mechanisms in the Pacific with the United States, Japan, Australia and New Zealand. As India is concerned about the strategic implications of China's port building in Gwadar (Pakistan), and Hambantota (Sri-Lanka), Canberra too is concerned about Chinese push for militarization of Vanuatu islands. Similarly, Japan has also burnt its fingers at Senkaku/Diaoyu islands. Therefore, this convergence of maritime democracies is not coincidental, but rather it is of late recognition of a common threat. India already has a strong bilateral security engagement with countries like France and Britain. Issues relating to maritime security have been at the top of the agenda. As Delhi prepares to cope with China's rapid naval advances in the Indian Ocean and deploys its ships far from the Indian shores, it needs to bring together its bilateral cooperation with individual European countries into a comprehensive strategic framework. Japan's plans to bring France and Britain on board the **QUAD** can only reinforce India's maritime partnerships with Europe.

Freedom of navigation, is one of the most essential aspects of maritime cooperation. No wonder, Prime Minister Narendra Modi found time during the busy election season to travel all the way south to Male, the capital of the Maldives. Modi's presence at the swearing-in of the new president of the Maldives, Ibrahim Mohamed Solih, underlined the renewed warmth in the relations between the two countries. Under Solih's predecessor, Abdulla Yameen, India's relations with the Maldives rapidly deteriorated even as China's influence began to rise. The intersection of Sino-Indian rivalry with domestic politics has also come to the fore in neighbouring Sri Lanka. India supported Prime Minister Ranil Wickremesinghe, while China openly sided with the former president Mahinda Rajapaksa. During Rajapaksa's decade-long rule of Sri Lanka (2004-15), Colombo seemed to steadily drift into China's orbit. Symbolising China's new influence in Lanka were the strategic contracts it won to build the Colombo port city and the construction of a new port at Hambantota in the southern part of the island. India, in turn, appeared to lose its historic primacy in the island state. Now we have regained our balance in Sri-Lanka also.

Like India in the Indian Ocean, Australia and New Zealand had underestimated the scale and speed of China's power projection into their South Pacific neighbourhood. So, did the US, which failed to react in time to China's push to gain control of the small rocks and islands of the South China Sea at the beginning of this decade. We cannot allow the historic opportunity, which has come to us in the name of Indo-Pacific, to be squandered, this time. To be sure, the novelty of the Indo-Pacific lies in recognising the growing strategic and economic interdependence of the Pacific and Indian Ocean littorals that we saw as separate theatres until recently. Noted strategic thinker C Raja Mohan is quite categorical here, "Indo-Pacific is also a sum of its many sub-regions that include the East China Sea, South-China Sea and South-Pacific to the east of the Malacca Straits as well as the Bay of Bengal, Arabian Sea and the waters of Africa to the west. What India does in these sub-region is far more important than the abstract debates on the Indo-Pacific. One such sub-region, the Andaman Sea—is likely to preoccupy India in the coming years."[26]

The Andaman Sea is flanked by the Andaman and Nicobar chain of islands in the West, Myanmar to the north, the Thai-Malay peninsula to the east, and the Sumatra island to the south. It funnels into the Straits of Malacca that connects the Indian and Pacific Oceans. The large amount of shipping that enters the Andaman Sea from the east heads to Singapore, from where it turns into the Pacific Ocean. After the Second World War, the partition of India and the Cold War between America and Russia, the Andamans became marginal to the new geopolitics. The rise of China and its projection of naval power way beyond its home waters is beginning to put the Andaman Sea back in play. Beijing has signed an agreement with Naypyidaw on building a deep-water port at Kyaukpyu on Myanmar's Arakan coast in the Bay of Bengal. The port will form an important part of the China-Myanmar Economic Corridor, which would connect Kyaukpyu to the Yunnan province in southwestern China via rail and highways. China is already assessing the cost of building Kra-canal to link the Andaman-Sea to the gulf of Thailand. China is also enhancing its military profile by selling nuclear Submarines to Bangladesh and Thailand, and conducting military exercises with Thailand and Malaysia.

For India, Andaman sea has assumed a new significance. As a sequel to our Look-East Policy, we have conducted largest ever naval exercise with Singapore, aptly called 'Simbex', in Andaman Sea. These exercises began 25-years ago. Prime Minister Modi's visited and renamed three islands; on the occasion of the 75th anniversary of Subhas Chandra Bose flying the tricolour in Port Blair has helped highlight the role of Andaman and Nicobar Islands in India's freedom struggle. New Delhi has decided to end the isolation of the island chain and promoting economic development, tighter integration with the mainland, strengthening military infrastructure, regional connectivity and international collaboration. It is in this regard that we can also connect our efforts out of Malabar exercises. The 22nd rendition of the Malabar naval exercise, held for the first time in waters off the coast of Guam and involving aircraft and ships from Indian Navy, the US Navy, and the Japan Maritime Self Défense Force (JMSDF), officially came to an end on June 16, 2018. The Malabar naval exercise began as a joint Indo-U.S. naval exercise in 1992. Japan became a permanent participant in 2015. This year, India once again refused Australia's bid to take part in the 2018 iteration of the exercise. This is very disappointing, given our penchant, particularly for cooperation among maritime democracies. It is again inhibiting to the evolution of **quad**. India does not need to be a scared partner of China's bandwagon. We are not supporting confrontationist India. We have to search every possible opportunity to work and collaborate with China. India has shown enough maturity and courage by joining Shanghai Cooperation Organization (SCO) which is also a brain child of China. What we want is a dignified presence at decision making table. We want respect for our unity, integrity and of course the security of our land, air and territorial waters along with the freedom of navigation across various sea-routes. The overbearing presence and the domineering behaviour of China has really created a disequilibrium. We have to address this imbalance in the right earnest, lest we should fall prey to another deceptive design of the devouring Dragon.

NOTES

1. Sung C. Jung and Kihyun Lee: The offensive realists are not wrong, Pacific Focus, Inha Journal of International studies, 2017
2. Pye Lucian: 1992, Social Science Theories in search of Chinese realities, China-Quarterly, 132
3. Kissinger Henry: 2011, On China, Delhi, Allen Lane, p. 7.
4. Indian Express 16 May 2017.
5. Mohan C Raja: May 2017, The Politics of Territory, Carnegie Foundation.
6. Nye Joseph: June 12, 2017, XI Jinping Marcopolo strategy, Project Syndicate.com.
7. Financial Times: May 12, 2017
8. Speech of Prime Minister Modi, at Shangri-La Dialogue, June 01, 2018, Online sources.
9. Ibid
10. Huntington S.P.: 1997, The Clash of Civilizations and The Remaking of World Order, Penguin Books India, p.233.
11. James Mattis: Speech at Shangri-La June 2, 2018
12. Foreign Affairs: July 2017.
13. ibid
14. Abhijit Singh: IDSA, New Delhi, August 2016.
15. Arun Shourie: 2013 'Self-Deception', Harper Collins, New Delhi, pp. 7,8.
16. Sung C. Jung and Kihyun Lee:2017, 'The offensive realists are not wrong', Pacific Focus, Inha Journal of International Studies (Abhijit 2016): IDSA New Delhi August, 2016)
17. Abhijit: 2016 August, IDSA, New Delhi
18. Joseph Braude and Tyler Jiang: Huffington post, online retrieved.
19. Indian Express: June 03, 2018
20. Graham Allison: 2017, Foreign Affairs.
21. The Globalization of World Politics: 2008, Oxford University Press, USA, p. 97.
22. Indian Express: July 13, 2017
23. Xi:2014, Governance of China, Foreign Language Press, p. 11.
24. Indian Express, June 05, 2010
25. C. Raja Mohan October 31, 2017, Indian Express.
26. C. Raja Mohan, Carnegie, November 13, 2018.

7

Modi Government's Afghan Policy

D. Gopal

United States led NATO forces have already withdrawn in December 2014. Now the entire security of Afghanistan is in the hands of the Afghan National Army (ANA) and Afghan police. In the backdrop of this much awaited withdrawal of NATO forces, it is opined by a gamut of pundits of Afghan affairs that things will be chaotic in the coming days. This withdrawal has also put the ANA under acid test because after 'Operation Enduring Freedom', it's the first time that Afghan security has been managed by their own developed security forces. Of course, NATO had given them due training but now in real terms they are on practical test.

It is stated that Afghanistan is a graveyard of empires. Since December 1979, when Soviet Union entered in Afghan theatre, Pakistan has been working on a unique Afghan policy and that is to maintain 'strategic depth' over India in Afghanistan. Pakistan is much concerned with the possibility of any emergence of a stable Afghanistan. Before 1979, Afghanistan was a relatively stable country. During those times, Afghan government was sustainable to raise the demand of Pakhtunistan. Afghanistan never accepted 'Durand Line' demarcated by the Britishers in 1893. Afghanistan has been arguing that the demarcation of this line was accepted by them under duress and according to international law any treaty inked under duress is unlawful. Due to sustainable anarchy since 1979 till date, Pakistan has been able to prevent Afghanistan to raise 'Pakhtunistan' issue. But despite prevailing 'Hobbesian nature of State' this issue still remains relevant. Even Taliban, which is considered an illegitimate child of Pakistan never accepted

'Durand Line', but on some other plea, a Muslim does not require visa to visit another Muslim country.

In the backdrop of NATO withdrawal, the security situation is getting grim. Afghan intervention in Afghanistan was one of the prominent reasons of the downfall of Soviet Union. United States has also started negotiating with the Taliban since October 2018 to withdraw before 2020 US presidential election.

Islamic State Looming Threat

From Afghanistan's perspective, failure of the Afghan government and security forces to effectively respond to the threat, or an escalation of conflict in the country, could allow the IS-inspired militants operating in Afghanistan to forge alliances and try to capture some area and announce a 'caliphate'. If Kabul achieves some sort of reconciliation with the Afghan Taliban.—Currently efforts are under way for this purpose—hard-line factions or commanders among the Afghan Taliban, who do not believe in political reconciliation could support the IS, strengthening the IS-inspired groups already operating in the country.[1]

At the same time, the Afghan Taliban may not be able to grab hold of the reins of power but by following the IS model; in case they do not achieve reconciliation with the government in Kabul, they could carve out a part of Afghan territory and proclaim an Islamic 'caliphate'. The ongoing dialogue between the Taliban and the United States which has been facilitated by Pakistan could provide immediate relief to the violent torn Afghanistan but it still depends on many factors.

After the partition of the sub-continent, Pakistan emerged as a new entity. But Pakistan and Afghanistan have had bitter relationship till December 1979 Soviet intervention. In 1989 the Soviets withdrew and a vacuum was created which was filled by the growth of the Taliban, which finally captured power in 1996. Taliban was illegitimately nurtured by Pakistan to pursue its goal to maintain its strategic depth over India. Since then terror remained an instrument of Pakistan's foreign policy. Afghan Jihad was consolidated by the US-led forces during Soviet intervention but later on emerged as an independent global movement led by Osama Bin Laden. After Operation Enduring Freedom (2001) he took shelter in Pakistan and finally was killed by US commandos in May 2011 at Abbotabad. His elimination has vindicated the nexus between the Jihad factory and Pakistan.

During the period of the Taliban rule in Afghanistan (1996–2001), India's internal security was badly hit due to sustainable cross-border support.

In 1999 an Indian Airlines plane was highjacked from Kathmandu and eventually taken to Kandahar. This incident dramatically underscores why New Delhi cannot take its eyes off Afghanistan and the Taliban. JM quickly became one of the most vicious terrorist groups operating in India that has long ties with Afghanistan and the Taliban (it has also enjoyed support from the ISI), threatening vital Indian national security interests.[2]

India's engagement with Afghanistan advances its position as an important power beyond South Asia, other interests in Afghanistan specifically advance regional security concerns localized in Afghanistan and Pakistan. Many of these are tied to the proliferating Islamist militant groups which have terrorized India. Virtually every Islamist militant group operating in and against India (e.g. HUJI, Lashkar-e-Taiba (LeT), and Harkat-ul-Mujahideen/Harkat-ul-Ansar among others) trained in Afghanistan and Pakistan.

Since 2001 India has upgraded its presence in Afghanistan particularly in reconstruction efforts and built many infrastructure assets. This has enraged Pakistan because it perceives that Afghanistan is their strategic backyard and Indian presence is a hurdle to sustain it. Pakistan provided tacit support to the attacks on Indian Embassy in Kabul and other personnel working across Afghanistan.

Since the last two decades, hundreds of terrorist attacks involving LeT and other terror groups based in Pakistan have occurred throughout India. Former Pakistani President, Asif Ali Zardari termed them 'Non-State Actors' but the open secret is that these elements have come into India from the Pakistani soil. train bombings in Mumbai, November 2008 Mumbai carnage, Pune in 2013, Jammu in 2014, 2015 and July 2015 in Punjab and latest in Kashmir in Feb. 2019.

Right from the commencement of 'Operation Enduring Freedom' Pakistan has remained the recipient of largesse from the United States due to its participation in 'global war against terror'. Despite that it gave safe havens to Osama Bin Laden and Mullah Omar. More importantly, as the senior most US military officer in 2011, Admiral Mike Mullen, told the US Congress, the Haqqani network is a "veritable arm of the Pakistan's Inter Services Intelligence Agency."[3] Pakistani military has sustained the unique Afghan policy since 1979 not to stabilize Afghanistan and use it as rear base. In December 2014, NATO forces have withdrawn from Afghanistan. The new Afghan President, Ashraf Ghani, has taken some conciliatory steps to garner Pakistani support for peace but since 2009 every year more than 2500 innocent people have been killed and Pakistani invisible hands are responsible for these deadly attacks. Right from 2009 till July 2015,

16,874 people have been killed in terror related violence;[4] from January 2015 to July 2015 alone 4,921 people have been killed which is self-explanatory. President Ghani showed his will to cooperate with Pakistan but increasing number of casualties has forced him to change his mind. Afghan President Ashraf Ghani lambasted Pakistan over a recent wave of insurgent attacks in the capital Kabul that killed at least 56 people. "The last few days have shown that suicide bomber training camps and bomb-producing factories, which are killing our people are as active as before in Pakistan," Ghani told a news conference.

"We hoped for peace but we are receiving messages of war from Pakistan."[5] President Ghani is now aware about the core motives of Pakistan.

It is crystal clear from the above indications that Pakistan is not going to permit and any real stabilization in Afghanistan and perceives it detrimental to its interests. Although it is doing lip services for peace building but has maintained tacit understanding with the terror groups accountable for acceleration of violence in Afghanistan, including Taliban and Haqqani. This situation is creating a dangerous situation for Indian security. As I have already insisted that sustainability of 'Hobbesian State of Nature' in Afghanistan had proved negative for our security in the past, it may replicate in future as well if Pakistan-fostered terror groups will have control over power in Kabul. According to Michael Kugelman, Deputy Director, Asia Programme, and South Asia Senior Associate at the Woodrow Wilson Centre in Washington, DC, and a leading specialist on India, Pakistan, Afghanistan and their relationship with the United States, "India is a perfect security ally for the US—and an Afghan political settlement that leaves the Taliban in a position of power would be a blow to Indian strategic interests. But it would not necessarily pose as grave a security threat for India as some commentators may fear."[6]

In this situation billion dollar question remains that how India will cope up with the situation. It is a wider question because if Afghanistan will destabilize further it will put black clouds over the security challenges in South, South West, Central Asia in particular but in the whole globe in general as well. Modi government has to face one of the most difficult security challenges once Taliban led government will be taking control of power in Kabul. Diplomacy has however been an art to make impossible things possible. Even in this hypothetical scenario, India will use diplomacy to convince Taliban that its support will be good for larger interest of the country then it can moderate the looming security threat.

Policy Options for India

But given the prevailing situation in the power corridor in Islamabad at the outset of 2015 it is clear that Islamabad has not learnt any lessons from its past mistakes. Islamabad is still hell-bent to use terror as an instrument of its foreign policy. On 26 January 2014, an outlawed militant group, the Jaish-e-Muhammad (JeM) hold a rally of the militants at Muzaffarabad.

Maulana Masood Azhar, commander of the JeM declared, "Kashmir is part of Pakistan and unless Kashmiri Muslims get their rights, there cannot be any friendship with India."[7] On May 26, 2014, under the leadership of Narendra Modi new government called PM Nawaz Sharif but he was warned by Hafiz Saeed.

In September 2019, Presidential elections is scheduled in Afghanistan. In the wake of this crucial election the Taliban has stepped up its attacks. President Ghani has pointed his accusations on Pakistan directly as the sponsor of these attacks. Pakistan is dedicated to bleed India too at thousand places. It has been revealed by Riyaz Bhatkal that Pakistan's ISI has given Rs. 26 crore to Indian Mujahideen in the last three years for anti-India operations.[9] On 23 May 2014, Indian consulate in Herat was attacked and again the needle of suspicion tilted towards military–Jehadi nexus in Pakistan. It is opined that this attack was an attempt to derail the goodwill created by the invitation of Indian PM designate Narendra Modi to Pakistan PM, Nawaz Sharif.[10] PM Sharif finally attended the swearing-in ceremony and had a meeting with the new Indian PM, Modi. In this prevailing situation the demand of the time is that India must prepare herself to contain propelling incidents of cross-border terror. We have to face this situation as an essential reality. At the same time, we must sustain our efforts to ensure peace and development in Afghanistan. Afghanistan of 2015 is different and people of Afghanistan are hell-bent to sustain peace. Since the last one decade they have experienced relative peace. Over 70 per cent voting in the Presidential election despite all-round violent threat by the Taliban in 2014 has vindicated the courage and dedication of Afghan people and their urge to bring back peace and participatory democracy. India must ensure close cooperation with Iran, Russia and Central Asian Republics as they had during the Taliban rule in Afghanistan.

Eminent Indian security analyst, Raja Mohan had rightly stated in November 2013, "Any nuclear deal between Washington and Tehran will immediately bring down oil prices, relieve the current macroeconomic pressures on India, and improve Delhi's energy security calculus over the longer term. US–Iran rapprochement will help to strengthen Afghanistan against the Taliban and Pakistan and expand India's room for regional maneuer after 2014."[11] The interim deal between Washington and Tehran has already been concluded and finally will be inked by June 2015, and it is time when Indian diplomacy must act and bring Iran and United States on the same page to ensure peace and stability in Afghanistan. Iran is an important player and it had been part and parcel of Indian efforts along with Russia and Central Asian Republics to contain Taliban and formation of the Northern Alliance during its rule over Afghanistan. (1996-2001). In July 2015, Iran and the Western world has signed a nuclear deal and now gradually the various decade-long sanctions imposed against Iran will be lifted. In August 2015, Iranian Foreign Minister, Javad Zarif had visited New Delhi and met PM and other ministers. Again, it was pledged that cooperation on all fronts will be accelerated. During a one-day visit of Mr. Zarif issue related to Islamic State threat, energy investments, Afghanistan and development of Chabahar port were discussed. He also stated that India is an important player in West Asia and can play a leading role in the region. PM Modi conveyed India's commitment to work with Iran for development of the Chabahar port that would have far reaching benefit, not only for the people of India and Iran, but also for Afghanistan and the entire Central Asian region. Mr. Zarif acknowledged India's support during turbulent times. PM Modi has visited Tehran in 2016.[12] Iran-US trust deficit has increased a lot under president Donald Trump administration and that has put some strain on India's joint efforts in Afghanistan along with Iran but India has garnered waiver from the United States despite their turbulent relations with Iran to develop Chabahar port. President Donald Trump has moderated his Iran policies while declared that he is open for meeting with Iran's president. He made this deceleration in the joint press conference at G-7 Summit held at Paris on 24-26 August 2019.[13]

China is also concerned for Afghanistan. Chinese have anticipated that worsening of Afghan situation may propel terror-related violence in its western turbulent province of Xingjiang. China has already appointed special representatives for Afghanistan. Along with China, we have to solicit the support of Russia and Central Asian Republics.

President Ghani's visited Islamabad in September 2014 and convinced Pakistan's security 'establishment' to change its strategic approach to Afghanistan. Far from a regime entrenched in hostility and resentment towards Pakistan, Islamabad found a leader who acknowledged the vital and symbiotic nature of Pakistan-Afghan relations and understood Pakistan's concerns regarding India's role in Afghanistan. All the doors of economic and security cooperation between the two countries have been opened. Most significantly, Kabul has extended active cooperation to combat the Tehreek-i-Taliban Pakistan and Islamabad has committed to preventing cross-border attacks against Afghanistan and promoting reconciliation with the Taliban.

Kabul's posture towards the US is also visibly different. During his US visits, Ghani was effusive in his gratitude for America's military support and sacrifices and insistent in requesting its continued security and economic support. The US has consequently agreed to keep just under 10,000 troops and two military bases in Afghanistan in place for the present and continue its financial support to Kabul.

President Ghani has shown some flexibility towards Pakistan in comparison to his predecessor, President Karzai, and after December 2014 Peshawar school attack, both countries have pledged to work together. Speaking at the Council of Foreign Relations in New York on 26 March, he said he thought "Pakistan is integral to peace efforts with the Taliban."[14] However, in the veiled attack on Pakistan he stated that both countries were working to end 18 years of hostilities, and believes that improved relations with Pakistan are key to denying support for Afghan Taliban insurgents.

"Without sanctuary, a long-term rebellion is impossible. When sanctuaries end, peace breaks out. That is what happened in Central America and Latin America, that is what has happened in Africa," he said.[15]

In contrast historically, Afghanistan–India relations have been cordial. Due to its dual policy, Pakistan has become extremely unpopular and due to its huge investment of over $2 billion, India is well-respected among all sections of Afghans. According to former Pakistani NSA, Mahmud Ali Durrani, "Hamid Karzai mistrusted us, I blame Pervez Musharraf also, Once I told Musharraf, you should invite him here, but he disagreed. He said he is a third class chap. The Afghan people, by and large, have far greater respect for India than they have for us."[16]

Pakistan has assured United States that it will facilitate Afghan peace process. PM Imran Khan has assured it during his July 2019 Washington visit. In August 2019, Modi government scrapped special status of Kashmir but Chinese despite visits of high-profile Pakistani leaders were guarded when they suggested both to settle the problem on the basis of existing bilateral framework of resolving disputes.

After Pakistani foreign minister Beijing visit in August 2019 in the backdrop of scrapping of article 370, joint statement stressed "China recognises that the Kashmir dispute must be properly resolved "based on the UN Charter, relevant

UN Security Council resolutions and bilateral agreement"[17] Pakistan is willing to connect Afghanistan to Kashmir and that could be detrimental for recent peace building process in Afghanistan. Pakistan has been isolated on Kashmir issue despite its all-round efforts of internationalisation. The editorial comment of the prestigious Pakistani daily 'Dawn' comments vindicated Pakistan's isolation on this issue.

"The crisis in India-held Kashmir could trigger global consequences, yet the world has not responded to Pakistan's urgent exhortations with the level of robustness the situation warrants. Instead of full-throated condemnation, there is language of equivocation.

Indeed, some countries, most notably the US and UAE, have even gone along with India's brazenly false assertion that stripping Kashmir, an internationally recognised disputed territory, of its special status is an "internal matter". Saudi Arabia's bland reaction thus far avoids expressing any opinion whatsoever."[18]

"It's a game-changer in Indian politics... It's not like a third party can get India to walk back its decision. The deed is done," says the usually strong India critic, Michael Kugelman, at the Asia Program in Woodrow Wilson Center in Washington DC.[19]

In the last five days, Pakistan Prime Minister Imran Khan has lost the "Great Game on Kashmir". As the *NYT* wrote in a column on Friday, "Pakistan runs out of options on Kashmir".[20]

NDA-2 government has multiple challenges on this front. We have witnessed since 1999 till date that whenever we are proposing high profile peace talks with Pakistan it has been reciprocated by Kargil/Mumbai/Jammu/ Pathankot/ Pulwama, etc. Pakistan is still trying its level best to keep Kashmir bleeding and February 2019 Pulwama attack was the one of the most deadly efforts in this direction. Pakistani military has always linked Kashmir with Afghanistan and after the Soviet withdrawal in 1989 they started Jihad operation in Kashmir. It could be one of the serious challenges for Modi government. In the backdrop of abrogation of article 370 and the extension of another tenure to Pakistani army chief General Bajwa, it will be more serious.

The civil-political relations in Pakistan have been always tilted towards the army. Former PM, Yousuf Raza Gillani, had stated in 2012 while he was the PM that "Pakistani military is not within the Pakistani state but Pakistani state is within the Pakistani army."[21] It is important to mention here that he was leading the Pakistan People's Party coalition, his assertion was self-contradictory and proves that military is all powerful in Pakistan. But it possesses only veto when the issues related to India, Afghanistan and nuclear aspect arise. Pakistani army has portrayed India as the permanent foe and has nursed certain terror outfits to sustain its anti-India megalomania. When Benazir Bhutto took oath as the first woman PM of Pakistan in 1988, then Chief of Army Staff, General Aslam Beg took three assurances from her that she will not intervene in India, Afghanistan and Nuclear issue, and decisions will be formulated by the army on these affairs. The evidence is that she sustained the General Zia era foreign minister, Shebzada Yakub Khan as her FM also. Here it is significant to mention that Khan fought 1988 election on IJI ticket and got elected against Benazir's PPP.[22] In recent history in February 1999, PM Vajpayee rides a bus to Lahore and inked historical 'Lahore Declaration'. It was reciprocated by the army and its terror stooge through Kargil. PM Manmohan Singh had started engaging Pakistan in his first term but that was reciprocated by Mumbai terror attack in 2008. PM Modi called all SAARC leaders including Pakistani PM to be witness in his swearing in ceremony. This gesture was also reciprocated by March 2015 Jammu attack. Former Pakistani NSA stressed that "The political classes, by and large, want peace. Where the difference comes in is the religious political classes. But the biggest monster is the army. The army has always felt that India is a very serious threat to us. Every military of the world has to have an enemy, a threat to point their guns at."[23] In December 2015, PM Modi landed Lahore without prior announcement and attended PM Nawaz Sharif's granddaughter marriage but this gesture was reciprocated with January 2016 Pathankot air base attack.

Pakistani army is formulating and implementing Pakistan's Unique Afghan policy since 1979. It seems that it has not changed it even today. Pakistan despite global persuasion is not going to abandon its old Afghan policy. Civilian regime is ruling elite since 2008 till date but it has no teeth in case of foreign policy particularly on Afghan and India front and it is likely to be sustainable in foreseeable future. Needless to say that situation in Afghanistan will determine security architecture of India and will make an imprint on global peace as well. India must take all possible steps to ensure peace and stability with the tacit understanding with like-minded countries in Afghanistan.

Concluding Remarks

When Taliban was ruling over Afghanistan only 1 million children were attending school. By 2019, more than 9 million Afghan children are attending school. India has contributed into the creation of basic infrastructure in Afghanistan including much needed schools and hospitals. In the backdrop of abrogation of article 370 from Kashmir, Pakistani army will try to accelerate the pace of terror activities in Kashmir. Durability of peace and stability is in larger Pakistani national interests. Pakistan could not utilize its excellent geo-strategic location since pace will not ensure in Afghanistan. United States under Donald Trump administration is more than willing to withdraw its army from Afghanistan before 2020 US presidential election. Pakistani army has played double game with the United States on Afghan front previously and all indications are very much visible that they will do the same once US led NATO army will be entirely withdrawn. Pakistani army has played double game in Afghanistan since 1979 red army entry into the country. It believes that a weaker Afghanistan suits it better to sustain 'Strategic Depth' against India. It is part of the problem and could not be part of Afghan solution. The US should sustain and ensure peace deal with Afghanistan but must keep its army. PM Modi has returned into power with bigger majority in May 2019 election and will be facing difficult strategic situation over Afghan issue. After four decades of sustainable violence and chaos, however, contemporary Afghanistan is more than fit to embrace peace and stability. India has to play unique role in its realisation. It must accelerate its much praised reconstruing process. It is not only in larger interests of peace and stability in Afghanistan but will be helpful for better security architecture in South and South West Asia. It could also be facilitator of sustainable economic growth of India and at the larger extent will contribute to better global security.

NOTES

1. Muhhammad Amir Rana, Accessing the IS Threat, *Dawn*, Karachi, August 23, 2015.
2. Praveen Swami, "Terrorism in Jammu and Kashmir in theory and practice," *India Review*, 2, No. 3 (July 2003): pp. 55-88.
3. C. Raja Mohan, After Mullah Omar, *The Indian Express*, New Delhi, August 4, 2015.
4. 2014 among deadliest years in AF with 10 k civilian casualties, *The Times of India*, New Delhi, August 9, 2015.
5. Ashraf Ghani slams Pakistan over recent Kabul attacks, *Dawn*, Karachi, August 10, 2015.
6. 'There's a lot for India to be worried about', *Rediffmail.com*, New Delhi, August 19, 2019.
7. Tariq, Banned group holds rally in Muzaffarabad, *Dawn*, January 27, 2014.
8. Neeraj Chauhan, ISI gave Rs. 26 crore for anti-India ops, *The Times of India*, New Delhi, March 31, 2014.
9. *Jansatta*, New Delhi, 7 March 2019.
10. C. Raja Mohan, The Great Game Folio, *The Indian Express*, New Delhi, November 20, 2013.
11. Can't forget support India gave us during difficult times; Iran, *The Times of India*, New Delhi, August 15, 2015.
12. *BBC Hindi*, August 27, 2019.

13. Can't forget support India gave us during difficult times; Iran, *The Times of India*, New Delhi, August 15, 2015.
14. Ibid
15. Idea Exchange, Mahmud Ali Durrani, *The Indian Express,* March 22, 2015, p. 12.
16. Naveed Siddiqui, China to 'Uphold justice for Pakistan on Kashmir Issue, *Dawn*, Karachi, August 9, 2019.
17. A Tepid Response, Editorial, *Dawn*, Karachi, August 9, 2019.
18. Manish Pandaya, Modi's 370 removal a game-changer, Pak isolated: U.S. experts, *Print*, New Delhi, August 11, 2019.
19. Singh, Sudhir, Limits of Electoral Mandate in Pakistan, *Politico,* Vol. 1, No. 1, 2013, p. 37.
20. Ibid.
21. Rizvi, Hasan Aksari, *Military, State & Society in Pakistan,* St Martin Press, London, 2000, p. 43.
22. Ibid.

8

Russia's Role in Asia-Pacific

Deepak Yadav

One of the most important current questions faced by Russia with regards to Southeast Asia is how Moscow can become involved in relations within the region. Russia could keep its current policy of practical, neutral position, slowly but surely becoming more influential in the Southeast Asia's landscape due to trade and diplomacy. The best strategy would be to engage in "deep dialogue" with Southeast Asia's countries., in turn, would undoubtedly increase Russia's dynamics of cooperation with multilateral institutions and a broad range of regional countries.

Russia's key objectives include promoting economic cooperation. Russia will use its economic strength oil and gas, military hardware, nuclear energy to carve out a niche for itself in the region. Over half of ASEAN's members have bought military equipment from Russia's defense industry and sought its expertise in the energy sector. Moscow is quite pragmatic, showing that economic considerations play a crucial role in defining Moscow's aims in Southeast Asia, which is mainly considered as a marketplace for Russian weapons.

The Asia-Pacific region has been identified as the world's new center of gravity. The emerging new architecture revolving around Asian powers has given rise to questions about Russia's role in the region, given that the Eurasian giant has an Asian presence in the Far East. The mutual threat perceptions between Russia and other Asian nations have altered over the course of 20 years since the collapse of communism. Russia is now recognized as a non-threatening great power with global significance. The Asia-Pacific has always been a region of great importance for super powers throughout Cold War and after due to its unique geo-political and geo-economic importance. Both USA and USSR were engaged in a great ideological battle to get hold on this region and this is still continuing even after the end of Cold War. Russia has a long and varied history as a serious strategic player in Asia. It is only recently that it has been completely written off by the end of the Cold War and its attendant beliefs in the end of geopolitics. The mutual threat perceptions between Russia and other Asian nations have certainly altered over the course of 20 years since the collapse of communism, and Russia is now widely recognized as a nonthreatening great power with global significance. However, regional analysts are still skeptical over the degree to which Russia's vested interests lie in Asia, and whether these interests are compatible with those of other regional players.

Russia is distinctly interested in Asia-Pacific affairs because more than two-thirds of its territory is situated in this region. Development of the rich natural resources of Siberia and the Far East will be of exceptional importance for the future progress of Russia and the many states of the Asia-Pacific. The population of these areas is small compared to the total population of Russia. This makes it even more important to ensure transparency, predictability, stability, and security along the vast perimeter of Russia's eastern boundaries. On the whole, inter-state relations in the Asia-Pacific region and the trajectories of their evolution are favorable and meet the fundamental interests of Russia. The developments in the Asia-Pacific deeply affect the political and economic climate worldwide. During recent decades, the economic center of the world has been moving gradually toward the Asia-Pacific, and the international relations in the region are becoming more and more important in global affairs.

Russia consistently supports the establishment of a just and democratic world order based on strict observance of the international legal norms, goals, and principles of the UN Charter and on comprehensive security, sovereign equality, and mutual respect for the legitimate interests of all states. The fact that the vast majority of the Asia-Pacific states share this approach seems to explain why peace and stability prevail in the region. Since the Cold War ended, the political situation in the Asia-Pacific has been relatively stable and predictable. Many Asia-Pacific states have mutual territorial claims, and sometimes these contradictory claims can lead to drastic and even dangerous conflicts. However, these states have practical experience in solving such problems, which helps to avoid military action, material damage, and loss of human life. The agreements on the mutually acceptable demarcation of a huge part of the border between China, on the one hand, and

Russia, Kazakhstan, Kyrgyzstan, and Tajikistan, on the other hand, are a good example of this problem-solving skill. India and China also have good prospects for settling their border claims.

Although the Southeast Asian countries and China have not agreed on the ownership of the Spratly and Paracel Islands, they have elaborated a Code of Conduct in the South China Sea and are looking forward to arrangements for joint exploitation of the areas in dispute. Russia welcomes the commitment of the countries participating in developing the Code of Conduct because it is an important step in resolving the territorial dispute. Rather than resuming their confrontation over two islands near the east coast of Kalimantan, Malaysia and Indonesia opted to settle their dispute through the International Court of Justice.[1] From time to time, the dispute over the Senkaku Islands ignites, but in words rather than military actions. Today, when inter-state relations in Asia have a relatively low conflict potential, it is unlikely that territorial disputes could generate a serious challenge to regional security and stability.

The growing interest of Russian military-industrial and energy companies in Southeast Asia will give Russia cause to become increasingly interested in the security and stability of vital water corridors in the waters of East Asia. Despite protests from Beijing, Russia is intensifying its connections with Vietnam, arranging for joint oil and gas exploration and signing military contracts, including the sale of six submarines in 2009. Thailand, Indonesia, Laos and Malaysia are among other potential targets for Russia's armament deals. Most of those countries are America's partners in the "hub and spokes" cooperative security system and their close relations with Russia will only prove beneficial for the US, as Moscow would be more inclined to engage in conflict resolution that might erupt between China and them. Another area of joint interest is North Korea and nuclear non-proliferation. As stated in the Russian Foreign Policy Concept, political stability in Asia is crucial to Russia foreign policy priorities, especially on the question of non-proliferation. The readiness to participate in Korean talks and enforce a peaceful resolution is even more evident when placed in the context of Moscow's ambition to build a Trans-Korean railroad and a direct pipeline from the Russian Far East to the Korean market.[2]

The USSR was feared until the late 1980s for its bold force projection into the South Pacific and Indian Ocean. Some, such as Richard Herr, openly worried that the US and Australian policy of "strategic denial" vis-à-vis the USSR in the South Pacific had failed, and that regional governments had better acquaint themselves with this new reality. Canberra and Washington even worried that, in a nuclear war with the Soviet Union, the Naval Communications "North West Cape" facility would be a tempting first target either by a nuclear strike or Special Forces raid to prevent an American retaliation from the nuclear submarines which the base commanded. In fact, the Soviets, according to one among their ranks, carried out some of their training in the deserts of Kazakhstan to mimic the arid conditions of the Australian desert in the event of a future raid. Since the 1990s, many have perceived Russia as a feeble giant with clay feet. This soundly demonstrates the current dismissive consensus around Russia's role in Asia. This default position made sense when Russia was indeed riddled by chronic internal ills, violent conflicts, economic misery, separatism, a public health collapse, and the largest peace-time depopulation in recorded history. But it no longer makes sense today.

Russia–China Strategic Co-operation and the Geopolitics of Asia-Pacific

Russia being the largest country and China being the most populous country on the planet, both collectively are undoubtedly the two major powers of the international system. Russia being the successor of erstwhile Soviet Union wishes to regain the role once Soviet Union enjoyed whereas China being a communist country is also showing signs of new ambitions based on its history, population and military power and also its emergence as an important international economic actor. Relations between Moscow and Beijing have gone full circle in the past half century, from alliance to containment and now to strategic partnership.

To understand the ebbs and flows in Moscow's China policy, it is necessary to look into the Soviet history. History which is characterized as chronicle of the past provides the solid base for building up future relationships. In International Relations, there is no permanent 'friend or foe', as today's bitter enemy can become tomorrow's staunchest ally. It is interest which runs supreme, and Russia and China are not exceptions to it. Despite being communist countries, both Soviet Union and China counted each other as enemy number one and targeted each other with their nuclear weapons. But today Russia and China no longer consider each other as enemy and both countries have developed 'very deep' relations in the strategic field.

China has the largest population in the world, while Russia is the largest nation in terms of territory. Both are permanent members of the United Nations Security Council. Obviously, the significance of Sino-Russian relations extends far beyond the interests of the two nations. It also affects the stability of Asia and the world at large.

Soviet-China relations before the disintegration of USSR were characterized by a number of ups and downs. In February 1950, just four months after establishment of the PRC, the two countries signed the treaty of Friendship, Alliance and Mutual Cooperation. The first half of the 1950s was the honeymoon period. However, by the late 1950s differences in national interest and ideology emerged leading to serious disputes in early 1960s which developed into acute conflict and border clashes in 1969. Hence in the late 1960s and 1970s, the USSR regarded China as one of its main rivals and stationed approximately one million troops and one third of its SS-20 intermediate-range ballistic missile along the Sino-Soviet border, threatening to make a 'surgical' first strike on China's nuclear bases. Under serious threat, China had to prepare for a military intrusion from north. However, in 1980s two countries came to realization that these were not in the interests of either side and they made effort to alleviate the situation. These efforts resulted in the normalization of the relations during a state visit to Beijing by the then Soviet President Mikhail Gorbachev in May 1989 (Qimao, 1999: 206-207).[3] In the words of Gorbachev, 'New Thinking' stood for

> We need normal international conditions for our internal progress. But we want a world free of war, without arms races, nuclear weapons and violence, not only because this is an optimal condition for our internal development. (Gorbachev, 1987: 10-12)[4]

On 15 September 1992, President Yeltsin signed the "Order of Russian Federation's Relations with China" and reaffirmed that

(a) there is only one China;
(b) the PRC government is the sole legal representative of China;
(c) Taiwan is the part of China; and
(d) Russia will never establish official relation with Taiwan.[5]

Both Russia and China are opposed to US hegemonic policies and favour a multipolar world order with different power centers. In April 1997, Chinese president Zemin paid another visit to Moscow on April 23 and the two countries issued a joint statement on the multipolarisation of the world and establishment of a new international order. The statement rejected hegemony and power politics, and stated that the 'Cold War' mentality must also be abandoned and bloc politics opposed. They called for preservation of the Anti Ballistic Missile (ABM) Treaty of 1972 between Soviet Union and USA and supported lifting the UN Security Council sanctions against Saddam Hussain regime in Iraq.

On 24 November 1998, when Jiang Zemin paid another crucial visit to Russia, the Russian side reaffirmed its 'four no's position, the basic thrust of which was no support for any conception of 'Taiwan's independence'; no acceptance of the position of 'two Chinas' or 'one China and one Taiwan'; no support for Taiwan's participation in the UNO or other international organizations in which only sovereign states participated; and no sales of weapon to Taiwan.[6]

NATO bombing on Yugoslavia from March end to mid-June 1999 without getting any authorization from the UN Security Council sent shock waves in both Russia and China and tended to bring together the two in joint opposition of NATO action. NATO's intervention on 'humanitarian ground' was an ominous development. Being multi-ethnic and multi-religious states, both Russia and China have their own separatist movements, Russia in Chechnya and China in Taiwan, Tibet and Xinjiang province. Being a Slav country, Yugoslavia was traditionally a friend of Russia, and attack on it aroused Russian sentiments in the form of massive protests in Moscow.[7]

Both Russia and China have greater common ground to chalk out their strategy to deal with the outside world compare to the issues on which they are at odds. Russo-Chinese link is built on a number of shared concerns which includes

- The struggle against US led unipolar hegemonism;
- Unilateral humanitarian interventionism by passing UN;
- Islamic extremism and secessionism;
- Opposition to NATO enlargement and inter-reference in the internal matters;
- Opposition to NMD (National Missile Defense) and TMD (Theatre Missile Defense);
- Opposition to US withdrawal from ABM Treaty of 1972;
- Restructuring of UN;
- Opposition to US-led NATO forces to stay longer in the Central Asian region;
- Near mutual acceptance of Russia's hegemony as a guarantor of order in Eurasia;
- Strengthening the SCO;
- Working together in the multilateral forums like WTO etc.;
- Strengthening multilateralism by promoting BRICS.

The declaration of 'New World Order in 21st Century' confirms that the relation between 'two-headed eagle' and 'dragon' has reached its height. Both countries have gone very far and deep in their defense translations and no longer count each other as enemies. Their defense personnel, scientists, students are getting training in each other's establishments. Russia is building up nuclear reactors in China and has offered partnership in the state in the state-owned space agency GLONASS which itself indicates the comfort level in their ever flourishing bilateral relations.

One of the prime reasons for developing close ties between Moscow and Beijing is the US factor, the common cause of concern for the both countries. US's continuous military and economic support to Taiwan and its huge military presence poses grave threat to the Chinese sovereignty. USA has also agreed to deploy TMD technology to Taiwan, which may virtually neutralize Chinese missile capabilities and would disturb the strategic balance in the region.

Russia is consistently under immense pressure from western human rights groups and media on the issue of human rights violations in the Chechnya war. These groups had virtually shut their eyes on Moscow Theatre tragedy and Beslan School crisis in which hundreds of Russian people lost their lives. It shows as if these human rights groups and media people are acting at the behest of their respective governments to settle their political goals with Moscow. When the issue of human rights violations by US forces comes from Iraq or Afghanistan, these groups keep their mouth shut.

To neutralize these double standards on terrorism, both Russia and China call for implementation of UN charter and International Laws globally without any fear or favour. The most frequent violator of international laws, Israel always goes unpunished due to overt and covert support from the USA but a single incidence of Tianmen Square in China made it virtually untouchable in the international politics.

Initially there was some opposition within the Russian establishment to the entry of the US troops in Central Asia, an area of traditional Russian influence. However, subsequently, Moscow decided to allow air corridors, the use of its bases for the search and secure operations as well as sharing of intelligence regarding the terrorist networks operating in Afghanistan. Uzbekistan offered its airspace and bases to the US troops ahead of other CARs, whereas Moscow preferred to maintain the façade of coordinated stand of all the CIS states. Kyrgyzstan claimed that the granting of Manas air base was coordinated in advance with its partners in the CIS Collective Security Treaty.

Manas airbase of Kyrgyzstan is just 200 miles away from Chinese territory from where US troops can keep their eye on Chinese troop movements. Presence of US troops so close to the Chinese border made security experts in Beijing uncomfortable. Besides military bases in Pakistan and Kyrgyzstan, US acquired military bases in Baghram and Kandahar in Afghanistan and bases of Khanabad in Uzbekistan.

Development of closer ties between Russia and US, especially after coming of Obama regime, is causing concerns in Beijing. Before Obama regime, Bush administration worked closely with Russia especially after September 2001 terrorist attack.

After the September 11, 2001, attacks on New York and Washington and subsequent military action taken by US and NATO against Al-Qaeda and Taliban have radically altered the geopolitical situation in Central Asian Region. Russia and Central Asian republics acquired a prominence place in the US military strategy in Afghanistan military bases in Baghram and Kandahar in Afghanistan and the bases of Khanabad in Uzbekistan. It is believed that these facilities helped US military to quickly establish air superiority throughout Central Asia and even to the Middle East. It is believed that in offering bases to the USA, the Central Asian States sought security against the threat of terrorist attacks as well as gain maneuvering space vis-à-vis Russia and China. CARs hoped to gain financially from the US presence.

The impact of post–September 11 developments on China has been the mixed one. China gained in so far as combating international terrorism became the number one task of the US policy. Prior to it, economically and militarily growing China was increasingly being projected as emerging strategic rival of the sole super power. China reluctantly joined the international community in supporting the US war against terror but with certain conditions. China wanted UNSC to play a central role in the war against terrorism as a guarantee against the US unilaterism. In fact China insisted that struggle against terrorism also includes the 'East Turkistan' terrorist forces or the Uighur separatist movement in Xinjiang province.[8]

There is no doubt that the prospects of a prolonged US military presence in the Central Asian region are not welcome to either Russia or China. Post–September 11 developments in the region seem as a setback to SCO, because SCO was created to forge Russia–China partnership in the Central Asia for jointly maintaining peace, stability and economic cooperation in the region and keep a check on the Western influence in the region.

Russian and Chinese interests also converge on the issue of eastward expansion of NATO. For the first time ever, NATO crossed the border of a non-NATO member country, i.e. Afghanistan, in the name of fight against terrorism. Both Russia and China opposed the bombing on Belgrade, the capital of Yugoslavia in 1999. Also the US B-2 bombers dropped bomb on Chinese embassy in Belgrade causing many casualties. These incidences proved beyond doubt that US-led NATO forces are crossing their granted mandate in the name of fight against terrorism and in the name of humanitarian intervention. Russia and China have their own set of problems in Chechnya and Xinjiang, respectively.

At the time when NATO bombing was on, the 50th anniversary celebrations of the founding of NATO took place in Washington in which all the former Soviet republics with the exception of Russia participated. What aroused Russian and Chinese concern further and even the concern in countries like India was the enunciation of new strategies' doctrine of NATO that permitted use of force by it in regions beyond the areas of its traditional responsibility comprising the territories of its member states. So, now NATO forces could be used anywhere.

Against such unilateral hegemonism of the US and NATO, Russia–China want a multipolar world with many power centers. The declaration between Yeltsin and Jiang Zemin in 1997 openly talked about establishment of a multipolar world based on principles of Panchsheel. Both call for respect of State sovereignty, equality of states, eschewing of pursuit of hegemony, non-interference in internal affairs of other states, an equitable and just economic order, and the strengthening of UN. Both Russia and China also seek to work closely with NAM and champion the cause of third world.

The major bone of contention in the smooth relation was border dispute which is now solved. China has not only settled in border dispute with Russia but also with the Central Asian Republics in a peaceful manner. With the border dispute gone, there is no any serious issue left between Russia and China to doubt each other's intention.

Peaceful solution of Korean Peninsula problem is also in the priority list of Russia and China. The proposed NMD system of the USA is expressly aimed at providing defense against the 'rogue' states like Iran, Iraq and North Korea etc. The launch of Pyongyang's rocket over Japan in 1998 provided justification to US for such apprehensions. Russia and China, therefore, have sought to minimize the perception of North-Korean threat. They favour a rapprochement between North and South Korea and one between US and North Korea.

To counter the eastward expansion of NATO and withdrawal of US from ABM Treaty of 1972, President Putin made an overture to European Union and

NATO to reach some compromise solution. He called upon to EU and NATO to join forces with Moscow and set up a joint anti-missile shield during his visit to Rome on 5 June 2000. He said that such a system will avoid creating problems linked to an imbalance in the equilibrium of forces and will ensure 100 percent security to European countries.[9]

As far as economic ties between Russia and China are concerned, they lag behind political, diplomatic, strategic and military ties. It is apparent that the two countries are also to create economic interdependence. The economies of the two countries are mutually complementary. Russia is the major producer and supplier of energy while China is energy hungry and its needs are growing. Russia's main exports apart from defense equipments include fertilizer, steel, timber and machinery, while its main imports are consumer goods and food items.

There are some major pre-requisites for further growth in the scale and diversifications of Russo-Chinese economic collaboration. These are implementing joint programmes in the fuel and energy sector; stepping up cooperation in the field of investment; involving Russian companies in the strategy of accelerated development of China's western region; expanding cooperation between the two countries' border region and cooperation in the manufacturing sector and joint mastering of high technologies.

By strengthening trade with China, Russia will try to reduce its shortage of light industrial goods and electronics, and create an economic infrastructure using cheap Chinese labour in the less developed areas of Russian Far East. Russia will also be able to reduce the financial crunch of its arms manufacturing units by selling weapons to China which includes more than $2 billion every year. Russia can also benefit by sending part of its well-educated labour force to China to help create high-technology industries and reduce the chronic unemployment among highly educated youths.[10]

On the other hand, China will get benefitted by sending a certain amount of its unskilled labour force to Russia to work in the unstaffed industries. The excess of labour force available in China is about 200 million. This arrangement will reduce some burden of unemployment among Chinese people. In addition, China will have a chance to participate in the economic opening of oil fields resources in Russian Far East and Siberia.[11]

When Dragon Embraces Bear

Russian President Vladimir Putin had a fabulous APEC. After his country and

China clinched a massive $400 billion natural gas deal in May round the Power of Siberia pipeline, whose construction began this year they added a second agreement worth $325 billion around the Altai pipeline originating in western Siberia.

These two mega-energy deals don't mean that Beijing will become Moscow-dependent when it comes to energy, though it's estimated that Moscow will provide 17% of China's natural gas needs by 2020. (Gas, however, makes up only 10% of China's energy mix at present.) But these deals signal where the wind is blowing in the heart of Eurasia. Though Chinese banks can't replace those affected by Washington and EU sanctions against Russia, they are offering Moscow, battered by recent plummeting oil prices, some relief in the form of access to Chinese credit.

On the military front, Russia and China are now committed to large-scale joint military exercises, while Russia's advanced S-400 air defense missile system will soon enough be heading for Beijing. In addition, for the first time in the post-Cold War era, Putin recently raised the old Soviet-era doctrine of "collective security" in Asia as a possible pillar for a new Sino-Russian strategic partnership.

Chinese President Xi has taken to calling all this the "evergreen tree of Chinese-Russian friendship" or you could think of it as Putin's strategic "pivot" to China. In either case, Washington is not exactly thrilled to see Russia and China beginning to mesh their strengths: Russian excellence in aerospace, defense technology, and heavy equipment manufacturing matching Chinese excellence in agriculture, light industry, and information technology.

It's also been clear for years that, across Eurasia, Russian, not Western, pipelines are likely to prevail. The latest spectacular Pipeline opera Gazprom's cancellation of the prospective South Stream pipeline that was to bring yet more Russian natural gas to Europe will, in the end, only guarantee an even greater energy integration of both Turkey and Russia into the new Eurasia.

Seventh Meeting of BRICS at Ufa, Russia

The joint BRICS and SCO summit in Ufa has been organized by Moscow as the simultaneous holder of both the rotating chairmanships of the BRICS and the SCO. It is no coincidence, however, that the Seventh BRICS and Fifteenth SCO summits have been amalgamated as one large international summit. The Kremlin has used the opportunity to bring Russia's partners together. This is part of the integration process of the Silk World Order. There will be joint BRICS and SCO sessions and many important exchanges and discussions about a new archetype for the world.

The US is clearly worried about the Silk World Order that is emerging. It has begun to pull out all the stops, from courting Brazil on the eve of the summit in Ufa to calls for the European Union to not join China's banking project. The Pentagon's 2015 Military Strategy that addresses the possibility of confrontation with an updated "Axis of Evil" composed of China, Russia, Iran, and North Korea is catered to Washington's proclivity to confront the countries that are challenging a US-dominated international order.

The BRICS New Development Bank (NDB), the first institution of the BRICS, is being launched by Brazil, China, India, Russia, and South Africa. It is joined by the SCO Development Bank and by the recently launched Asian Infrastructure Investment Bank (AIIB) in the assault on Bretton Woods. Gone are the days of unchallenged US domination. The architecture of the post-Second World War or post-1945 global order is now in its death bed and finished. With or without Washington, a Silk World is emerging and its coming is being trumpeted from Ufa as the SCO strengthens and the BRICS institutionalizes itself as the cornerstone of a new multipolar world order.[12]

Conclusion

Given the contours of the Sino-Russian strategic partnership and its likely durability, what should be the US response? Perceiving this partnership as a full-fledged alliance, directed across the board against U.S. interests, is a mistake. The common rhetoric is easy to sustain, but what will happen if the United States negotiates with Russia in earnest on an antiballistic missile compromise? Would Chinese opposition to changes in the regime really block a bilateral deal? Are China's interests really engaged in NATO enlargement?

Sino-Russian cooperation will not markedly change questions on issues such as Taiwan or NATO enlargement. These issues remain bilateral or regional; the outside partner has little standing. Moreover, issues such as these remain subject to a dynamic outside the control of the distant partner. Russia will act in its own interests in Europe, and China in Asia. For example,

China remains comfortable with a framework in Korea that excludes Russia and Japan. Russia's European interests could well lead it much closer to Europe and the European Union in the years ahead. Chinese analysts cannot confidently exclude the European turn they feared in the early 1990s. Chinese economic interests place the United States, Japan, and a wide variety of Asian countries far ahead of Russia.

Although Sino-Russian economic ties have expanded, they have not reached the levels outside the arms trade that many in Moscow expected or hoped for. Sino-Russian cooperation at the UN could make future peacekeeping operations more difficult to negotiate (e.g., Macedonia) or make vetoes more likely as both countries now hold leverage over this body. Although current US-Russian differences are serious, US-Russian strategic talks on missile defense could yield a satisfactory outcome for Moscow that would complicate the situation in Beijing. Moreover, serious challenges have not yet arisen in Central Asia, though the next decade will bring changes of leadership, regional instability, and other problems there. If sustained Chinese migration pressure appears in the Russian Far East, the current strategic partnership will be difficult to maintain. Washington still controls many levers of influence, and the most ambitious bilateral expressions of solidarity and cooperation have yet to be tested.

The most important near-term consequence of Sino-Russian partnership is a negative one: the Russian contribution to Chinese military modernization. For the foreseeable future, China will have an enduring need for Russian military technology and systems, while Russia will have a variety of reasons to sell. Official statements from senior Russian defense officials indicate that they believe Russia has a long lead on China in key military capabilities and thus current sales do not create a military threat to Russia itself. Russia's own economic problems and the ideological motivations of some in the Russian foreign policy community create incentives for sales, not restraint. These sales—and the broader defense and technology cooperation that is linked to them—could in time alter regional military balances in areas of vital US interest in East and Southeast Asia or the Taiwan Strait. China does not need to match the military of the United States and its allies to affect this alteration. It need only develop capabilities that substantially raise the cost of US intervention in the region. At the very least, the upgrading of key Chinese military capabilities places an added burden on the United States and its regional allies in future crises.

The lure of economic integration makes Southeast Asia one of the most promising markets for foreign expansion in terms of both consumer markets and production sites. Southeast Asia is often regarded as a motor of growth and investment for Asia.[13] Economic considerations play a crucial role in defining Moscow's geopolitical postures drawing closer to Southeast Asia's countries. Russia's asset is having no territorial claims in Southeast Asia, and avoiding taking sides in the Asian Pacific regional disputes. Due to this condition, Southeast Asia's countries have tended to see Russia as a counterweight to both China and the United States.

NOTES

1. Rouben Azizian and Boris Reznik, "*Russia, America, and Security in the Asia-Pacific*" (2006), Asia-Pacific Center for Securities Studies, Honolulu, pp. 23-33.
2. Anton Barbashin, "A Pacific Vision for Russia and USA", *The Diplomat*, December 6, 2013.
3. Qimao, Chen (1999), "Sino-Russian Relationship after the Break Up of the Soviet Union" in Chaufrin Gennady (ed.), *Russia and Asia: Emerging Security Agenda*, New York: SIPRA, OUP.
4. Gorbachev, Mikhail (1987), "*Perestroika: New Thinking for our Country and the World*", London: Collins, pp. 123-128.
5. Chufrin, G. (1999), "*Russia and Asia: The emerging Security Agenda*", New York: Sipri Oxford University Press, pp. 292-296.
6. Jingjie, L. (2000), "Pillars of the Sino-Russian Partnership", *Orbis*, 44(4): 527-539.
7. Saiget, Robert J. (2000), "*China, Russia beef up cooperation on Ethnic Separatism, Taiwan, Terrorism*", Hong Kong: AFP, pp. 102-110.
8. Moltz, Clay (1995), "Regional Tensions in Russo-China Rapprochement", *Asian Survey*, 35(36): pp.23-54.
9. Menon, Rajan and Charles E. Ziegler (2002), "The Balance of Power and US Foreign Policy Interest in the Russian Far East" in Thorton J and Ziegler E.C. (eds.), *Russia's Far East a region at risk*, London: University of Washington Press, pp. 17-23.
10. Shaumian, T.L. (2003), "Geopolitical Changes in Central Asia and Positions of Russia, China and India", *China Report*, 38(3): 361-363.
11. Mikhail Alexseev, "'The Chinese Are Coming': Public Opinion and Threat Perception in the Russian Far East," *Program on New Approaches to Russian Security: Policy Memo 184* (Washington, D.C.: Council on Foreign Relations, January 2001).
12. Aliaksandr Kudrytski, "China Builds EU Beachhead with $5 Billion City in Belarus," *Bloomberg*, May 26, 2013.
13. Tomasz Burdzik, "Slowly but Surely: Russia's Foreign Policy in Southeast Asia", *Russian International Affairs Council*, April 22, 2019.

9

Revisiting Modi's "Act East Policy":
The Case of South Korea

Geetha Govindasamy

Modi's "Act East Policy"

India's foreign policy in the last decade has gone through a rebranding, especially the "Look East Policy" which was started by Prime Minister PV Narasimha Rao in the early 1990s. Indian leaders like Atal Bihari Vajpayee and Manmohan Singh expanded the policy attempting to make Southeast Asia and later, Northeast Asia a priority in Indian foreign policy. Like other Indian leaders, Prime Minister Narendra Modi who came into power in 2014 saw the benefits of having closer relations with dynamic economies of China, Japan and South Korea. There was a need to rejuvenate the economy as Modi was faced with high inflation, revenue and fiscal deficit coupled with delayed projects.[1] Hence, foreign investments were key in improving the infrastructure and expanding the country's balance of payment situation. Seen in this context, Modi's main aim has always been to attract investments and investors to set up industries in India. Forming "partnerships, technology and funds" with outside partners to make India a global manufacturing hub through the flagship "Make in India" initiative became a major goal in the Modi government.[2] The initiative aimed at drawing global investments into India so that the country could develop into a manufacturing powerhouse like China.[3] Primarily, the need to create a manufacturing hub corresponds with creating employment and for sustaining a balance in exports and imports.[4] When introducing his vision in 2014, with the slogan of "Sell

Anywhere but Make in India," Modi urged potential investors to set up their manufacturing facilities in India in sectors that included electronics, chemicals, pharmaceuticals, satellite and submarine.[5]

Since the Indian government has limited fiscal capacity to carry out large-scale investments and public-private partnerships (PPP) are still at a nascent state, foreign funding is key in developing the economy. Stronger strategic ties with Northeast Asian countries and better assimilation into the Asia-Pacific economy were deemed crucial for India given its developmental requirements. East Asian countries like China, Japan and Korea have foreign exchange reserves that India desperately needs for the success of its "Make in India" project. Simultaneously, it is reasonable to argue that these countries themselves are looking for investment destinations. For example, Japan's manufacturers prefer to invest overseas in fast-growing Asian economies due to decreasing labour force, high costs and regulatory barriers in their country.[6] Overall, Northeast Asian countries are attracted to India for its lower labour costs as well as a range of investment privileges and tax exemptions. In addition, India's large market and abundant source of raw materials are equally appealing to foreign investors. According to Samir Saran of the Observer Research Foundation,

> ...China has become the biggest provider of energy-generation equipment to India and wants to build high-speed trains here. It is why South Korea wants to build nuclear reactors and ports in India. And it is why the Japanese want to set up industrial corridors in India. Asia is also the source of most of the energy needs that are indispensable to this national project.[7]

Hence, it is not surprising that Modi rebranded the "Look East Policy" into an "Act East Policy" in November 2014 during an ASEAN meet in Myanmar's capital Naypyidaw. It can be perceived that the term "Act East" reflects an urgency in wanting to expand and secure ties not only with Southeast Asian nations but also Northeast Asian countries. Modi expects the "Act East Policy" to become a catalyst in reviving the Indian economy through proactive engagement with the economically vibrant Asia Pacific region. While attracting investments into the country, the policy also aims at assisting Indian businesses to link up with the markets of the Asia Pacific region. The "Act East Policy" remains a work in progress. Thus far, the Indian government has successfully managed to strengthen its relations with Japan and China. For example, Japan was India's third largest source of foreign direct investments between April 2000 and June 2018.[8] Japanese companies are involved in prominent infrastructure projects like that of the construction of the Ahmedabad-Mumbai bullet train service and the Delhi-

Mumbai Industrial Corridor which involves constructing cities, industrial parks and a range of transportation networks.[9] While Japan is involved predominantly in infrastructure projects, Chinese companies seem to prefer investing in Indian digital startups. In 2017, around US $2 billion from China was invested solely in Indian startups.[10] Some of the Chinese companies that are involved in Indian startups are Beijing Miteno Communication Technology (Media.net), Alibaba (Pay.tm), Alibaba with Foxconn Technology and Softbank (Snapdeal), Ctrip (MakeMyTrip), Tencent (Hike and Practo) and ByteDance (Dailyhunt).[11]

This chapter discusses Modi's "Act East Policy" in the context of "Make in India" initiative and South Korea–India bilateral relations. In addition, it highlights the challenges faced by foreigners in doing business in India. While China and Japan are very significant in ensuring the "Make in India" initiative succeed, this chapter stresses that South Korea which has been slow in entering the Indian market is equally worth exploring for many reasons. Given that Korea has made tremendous progress in infrastructure, technology and has an export-driven economy, there is scope for greater cooperation between India and Delhi.

In the past, Seoul has relied heavily on the Chinese market. According to the World Trade Organization data, 26.1 percent of South Korea's exports went to China in 2014.[12] In 2017, Beijing-Seoul relations worsened due to the diplomatic row over the deployment of a US-backed anti-missile system known as the Terminal High Altitude Area Defense (THAAD) in South Korea. After Beijing deemed THAAD as a threat to its national security, China-South Korea bilateral trade volume dropped 8.4 percent, compared to 2016, and South Korean investments in China significantly decreased to 22.3 percent in 2017.[13] Although relations have improved, South Korea has decided to reduce its dependence on China and concentrate investing more in ASEAN and India. South Korean Trade Minister Kim Hyun Chong observes,

> India is a country that has no sensitive issues with us geopolitically, so has little risk of its economic cooperation wavering due to external factors. China, for example, created serious problems for our country over the THAAD issue, but with India there are no such variables.[14]

As a result, South Korean President Moon Jae-In implemented the "New Southern Policy" in 2017, to expand investments into Southeast and South Asia.[15] The policy makes ASEAN and India as strategic partners, equal to that of South Korea's long-established diplomatic partners—the United States, China, Japan and Russia.[16] In Seoul's strategic calculations, the "New Southern Policy" is crucial for safeguarding the Korean economy and its strategic interests. Moon and Modi have also taken note of Washington's declining global influence and Beijing's rising influence. In the event of a trade war between China and the United States, South Korean exporters who depend heavily on China will be hugely affected. Moreover, a trade war will slow down Chinese economy which in turn has the capacity to affect South Korean exports to China.[17] Consequently, Modi's "Make in India" initiative is indeed a timely opportunity for South Korean investors.

South Korean small and medium enterprises are constantly looking to diversify investment destinations that will yield better profit margins and at the same time reduce the cost of manufacturing. At the same time, conglomerates like Samsung and Daewoo Motors invest overseas in order to expand their export markets. As South Korea has come to realize that it does not want to depend too much on China, the "Make in India" initiative which caters to both types of investments has become an appealing policy. In promoting the "New Southern Policy", South Korea perceives India will be capable of fulfilling a variety of Korea's needs as it has a relatively stable economic growth, a rising middle class, growing youth demographic, cost competitiveness of setting up businesses and huge numbers of educated as well as skilled workers. In other words, the objectives of the "New Southern Policy" coincides with the "Make in India" initiative in allowing Korean businesses greater market access and opportunities to expand in India.

Equally, India looks forward to working with South Korea under the context of the "New Southern Policy" in tandem with the "Act East Policy." From his days as the Chief Minister of Gujarat, Modi has always regarded South Korea as a role model for India, especially in developing its economy.[18] He understands that collaborating with middle powers like South Korea is vital if India aims to revive its economy and consolidate its position in a changing international scenario, more so in an environment where the United States and China are at loggerheads.

Bilateral Economic Ties

Diplomatic ties between India and Republic of Korea (ROK) were formally established in 1973. Bilateral trade relations have gathered momentum in recent years due to changes in the domestic and international environments of both countries. According to the Korea International Trade Association (KITA), bilateral trade between South Korea and India are shown in Table 1.

Trade imbalances have become an issue in bilateral relations. Table 1 shows while India imported goods worth $15,056 million from South Korea in 2017, its exports to Seoul were only $4,949 million. In order to boost exports and address the widening trade deficit with South Korea, the Indian government has taken a number of initiatives to identify specific products with export potential. The government seems to be seeking greater market access for Indian products related to information technology (IT), generic medicine and textiles.[20] Though India is a little cagey as its trade deficit with South Korean is quite considerable, Modi wants to increase bilateral trade to $50 billion by 2030.[21]

Table 1: South Korea–India Bilateral Trade between 2007 and March 2018
(Amount in million US$)

Year	Total trade	Growth (%)	Indian exports to ROK	Growth (%)	ROK Export to India	Growth (%)
2007	11,224	22.35	4,624	27.03	6,600	19.3
2008	15,558	39.00	6,581	42.32	8,977	36
2009	12,155	-21.88	4,142	-37.06	8,013	-10.7
2010	17,109	40.76	5,674	36.98	11,435	42.7
2011	20,548	20.10	7,894	39	12,654	10.7
2012	18,843	-8.30	6,921	-12.3	11,922	-5.8
2013	17,568	-0.07	6,183	-10.7	11,385	-4.5
2014	18,060	2.8	5,275	-14.6	12,785	12.4
2015	16,271	-9.9	4,241	-19.6	12,030	-5.9
2016	15,785	-2.9	4,189	-1.2	11,596	-3.6
2017	20,005	26.7	4,949	18.1	15,056	29.8
2018 (as of March)	4,964	2.9	1,365	11.8	3,599	-0.1

Source: Korea International Trade Association (KITA)[19]

South Korea's investment history in India is quite impressive. South Korean companies began increasing their investments into India when it liberalized its economy in 1991.[22] Samsung, LG and Hyundai Motors are some of the prominent Korean companies operating in India which continue to expand under the "Make in India" initiative.

Manufacturing sector dominates the investment sector. As an example, Table 2 indicates that Korean manufacturing investments into India increased compared to China between 2016 and 2017. Clearly, the shift is a response to Korean firms being the subject of boycotts in 2016 after Seoul announced the deployment of THAAD.

Small and medium Korean enterprises feature significantly in manufacturing investments. Some of these companies are part of the supply chain for bigger conglomerates like Samsung, Lucky Goldstar and Hyundai Motor. Major centres of Korean investment are Delhi, Noida, Gurgaon, Chennai, and Mumbai. For bigger Korean companies, India has become a manufacturing centre for domestic as well as overseas markets. As the second largest carmaker in India, Hyundai Motor's manufactured cars from the Chennai plant are exported to 123 countries globally.[24] Recently, Hyundai Motor announced that it will invest US $1 billion to expand facilities, manufacture new car models and electric cars in Tamil Nadu.[25]

Table 2: Korean Manufacturing Investment Destinations
(in millions of dollars % change from 2016-2017)

Country	2013	2014	2015	2016	2017	%age
China	4463	2576	2378	2452	2135	-12.90
Vietnam	782	1025	1146	1767	1393	-21.20
USA	759	718	838	847	741	-12.50
India	296	305	273	267	416	55.80
Mexico	55	236	903	414	365	-12.00
Malaysia	184	108	40	166	279	67.60
Hong Kong	246	205	125	374	218	-41.80
Singapore	29	176	77	84	202	142.10

Source: Export-import Bank Korea.[23]

Samsung, on the other hand, has two factories, in Noida and Sriperumbudur, near Chennai.[26] In July 2018, Samsung opened the world's largest mobile factory in Noida. According to Samsung India CEO HC Hong, the factory is a "symbol of Samsung's strong commitment to India and a shining example of the success of the government's 'Make in India' program."[27] Despite these developments, South Korea has made far less investments in India than China or Japan. Though India and South Korea are the world's seventh and 11th largest economies, bilateral trade was only worth $20 billion in 2017.[28]

In 2009, India and South Korea concluded a free trade agreement known as the Comprehensive Economic Partnership Agreement (CEPA). Under the CEPA, South Korea firms are allowed to own stakes of up to 65 percent in Indian firms.[29] According to the Korea Trade Investment Promotion Agency (KOTRA), Korean subsidiaries established in India are either wholly owned or have joint ventures with Indian companies. Due to difficulties in the 1990s, in trying to penetrate the market through joint ventures with Indian companies, 88% of Korean companies are wholly owned. Wholly owned subsidiaries are preferred as it allows Koreans to operate on economies of scale, have greater leverage in negotiating with local governments as well as initiate brand recognition more effectively.[30]

From the beginning of his administration, Modi has been targeting enhancing economic relations with South Korea. During his visit to Seoul in May 2015, Modi looked to secure promises of bigger Korean investments. Modi met with business tycoons from South Korea's largest conglomerates, including Samsung Electronics president Park Sangjin, LG Electronics president Kim Jin Hong, Hyundai Motor Company president Chung Jinhaeng and Hyundai Heavy Industries' Chief Executive Officer Choi Gil-sun.[31] Modi was hoping to obtain up to $10 billion in South Korean soft loans to fund infrastructure projects like the construction of smart cities and creation of Digital India initiatives that would improve connectivity throughout India. It was reported that US $10 billion will be sponsored by the Korean government and the Export-Import Bank of Korea for Indian infrastructure projects under certain conditions. The loan was to be used for creating 100 smart cities and building a high-speed railway as well as improving existing railroads.[32] The multi-billion dollar loan required detailed business plans and feasibility studies conducted by the Korean side. The extent to which Modi was able to obtain financial assistance for his projects is still unclear. According to 'India Briefing', the Export-Import Bank of Korea is still very much interested in supporting the US$10 billion plan to support infrastructure development throughout India.[33]

Despite the uncertainly, Modi has taken concrete steps to promote a conducive environment for Korean companies to invest in India. In January 2016, 'Korea Plus' was launched as a one-stop agency to facilitate Korean investments into India. A Memorandum of Understanding was signed between the Ministry of Trade, Industry and Energy, Republic of Korea and Invest India, the National Investment Promotion and Facilitation agency, to set up Korea Plus. The Korea Plus agency works closely with the embassies, central and local governments, associations and corporate sector to execute Korean investments in India. Since South Korea's manufacturing companies are eager to expand their business overseas, Korea Plus has become a key agency in attracting investments into India.[34]

Furthermore, Modi and Moon discussed the upgrading of the 2009 CEPA during Moon Jae-in's first visit to India in July 2018. As a result, an 'early harvest' package was agreed upon to look into goods, services, and investments in bilateral trade.[35] Both leaders also agreed to establish the Korea-India Future Strategy Group and the India-Korea Centre for Research and Innovation Cooperation (IKCRI) to promote future-oriented cooperation based on research, innovation and entrepreneurship.[36]

Moon's visit also brought about the awareness that Korea Trade Promotion-Investment Agency (KOTRA) which has five offices in India including New Delhi, Chennai, Bengaluru, Mumbai and Kolkata needs to expand its presence in India.

KOTRA then signed a Memorandum of Understanding with the Gujarat government and opened an office in Ahmedabad in 2018 to boost Korean trade in the state.[37]

Ease of Doing Business in India

To a large extent, foreign direct investment flows are determined by government actions in promoting a business-friendly environment. While Modi wants to attract investments, the reality is that there are numerous challenges in conducting business in India. India currently ranks 77 out of 190 countries according to the latest World Bank annual ratings. The index takes into account characteristics such as starting a business, securing electricity, obtaining construction permits, access to credit, taxation and trading across borders.[38] Due to the positive reforms undertaken by the Modi government, it is predicted that investors who make cross-border investment decisions will find India a more attractive investment destination than before. In the coming years, it will be critical for India to build on this momentum and make the country one of the most attractive places to run a business. There is a lot of room for improvements in indicators such as starting a business, enforcing contracts, registering property, paying taxes and resolving insolvency.[39] Some Korean investors are critical about capital availability and complications regarding the Goods and Services Tax (GST). Investors find that their local partners have difficulties in obtaining loans from Indian banks, and that the new GST structure is too complicated with six types of taxation.[40]

The overall question is how fast businesses can be conducted in India. While some reforms are making solid headway, the fact is that manufacturers still face significant challenges in India. While it only takes one day to register a piece of property in New Zealand, it takes 69 days to do the same in India. In terms of paying taxes, a Mumbai firm makes 13 payments a year while a Hong Kong businessmen makes just 3 payments in the same duration.[41] Generally, it can be concluded that India continues to be trapped in complicated procedures and challenges. The question remains how much of Modi's reforms have been successful at the lower levels of bureaucracy. Is there bipartisanship in wanting to implement Modi's "Make in India initiative"? It would also be helpful if India looks into collectively working together to enhance coordination within various ministries and government agencies, between state and central governments as well as both government and industry.

For the most part, it seems South Koreans are still wary of doing business in India. Korean companies have had their share of problems in building businesses in India. In July 2013, Posco, the world's sixth-largest steelmaker by revenue, halted plans to build a steel plant in Karnataka because of delays in obtaining land leases and mining permits.[42] Much earlier, in 2005, Posco agreed to invest US $12 billion in a steel plant in Odisha. However, Posco encountered a series of delays. Posco found it hard to procure land, mining leases and obtain environmental clearance against the backdrop of opposition from local tribal groups and environmental activists. Protests even extended to kidnapping Posco staff by activists. Ultimately, Posco failed to secure all of the 4,000 acres needed across three panchayats of Dhinkia, Nuagaon and Gadakujang in Jagatsinghapur district. Moreover, the central government decided that it will auction all mineral resources and no entity will be given a preferential treatment. This included iron ore, a key steelmaking raw material.[43]

As a result of the new policy, Posco had to incur higher costs due to the bidding process for securing iron ore blocks and getting a new captive mining license.[44] The Odisha government initially promised Posco that the license would be obtained without any extra cost. As a result, Posco's CEO Kwon Oh Joon, concluded,

> business conditions at home and abroad have changed due to a drop in global steel demand, growing deficit of subsidiaries.... Until Indian Prime Minister Narendra Modi offers better deals, Posco won't resume and for now will head to the west and do more downstream work.[45]

Posco's decision to hold back on building the steel plant was a major setback for Modi's manufacturing ambitions. Unpredictable policy changes are another cause of concern for South Korean investors. In March 2013, a Memorandum of Understanding was signed between Rajasthan State Industrial Development and Investment Corporation (RIICO) and South Korean Trade Promotion Agency to set up a South Korean investment zone in Ghilot. Unfortunately, South Korean companies decided to abandon the Ghilot industrial zone. Part of the reason was due to leasing conditions not being favourable to the Korean counterparts. South Korean companies found land prices to be high. More importantly, they preferred owning the land instead of opting out for a 99-year lease.[46] Had the project been a success, Rajasthan would have become the only Indian state to host two manufacturing zones, one Korean and the other Japanese.[47]

Concluding Remarks

While there are some apprehensions on the Korean side, analysts argue that Modi's ongoing economic development strategies will facilitate and strengthen Korea's investment relations with India. Since Korea and India have economic growth potential and complementary trade structures, such synergy is expected to create a win-win partnership. Continued potential Korean investments from bigger companies or chaebols suggest that there is great interest in tapping the Indian market. If these projects can succeed, then Korean small and medium companies will be part of the supply chain for the bigger companies. Investors clearly have shown support for Modi's economic reforms aimed at making India a more reliable and transparent place to invest. Reflecting on reforms in India's business environment, Song Song Yi, a researcher at KITA's Institute for International Trade is confident that,

> As long as the 'Modi-nomics' policies are well maintained and implemented until his term ends in 2019, the Indian market will grow into an attractive place to do business.[48]

In conclusion, Modi has already started the momentum in transforming India into a manufacturing hub by unlocking its full growth potential. Since Korean conglomerates and businesses are keen to tap new markets, India has the capability to serve as a base for exporting Korean products to Asia, Middle East, Africa and Europe.[49] Likewise, South Korea is crucial in Modi-nomics as it is viewed as a market, source of investment and funding for realizing the "Make in India" initiative. For now, it is estimated that more than 600 Korean companies of various sizes are present in India.[50]

To maximize the potentials, India and Korea need to revitalize and upgrade the CEPA. Further, the stalled US $10 billion agreed loan package from South Korea should be provided to India as soon as possible so that projects can be identified and started. The sustainability of the "Make in India" initiative remains a question in the context of how long Modi's government will last. Whatever the future outcome, the time has come for Indian leaders to extract economic opportunities which are accessible in the intersecting of the "Act East Policy" with the "New Southern Policy".

NOTES

1. "Narendra Modi on Indian economy: The 'elephant' is running on the right path", *LiveMint*, 12 August 2018, https://www.livemint.com/Politics/ZBenJvJBQHcIQwLbIHSfZL/Narendra-Modi-on-Indian-economy-The-elephant-is-running-o.html. Retrieved 1 February 2019.
2. Samir Saran, "Why the 'Asian Century' Might Actually Belong to India, Not China", *The World Post*, 6 February, 2015, http://www.huffingtonpost.com/samir-saran/asian-century-india-china_b_7496170.html. Retrieved 2 August 2015.

3   Anant Vijay Kala, "5 Things that Show Modi's Make in India Campaign is Working", *The Wall Street Journal*, 12 August 2015, http://blogs.wsj.com/briefly/2015/08/12/five-things-that-show-modis-make-in-india-campaign-is-working/. Retrieved 22 August 2015.
4   "PM to Investors: Sell Anywhere but 'Make in India,'" Rediff.com, 15 August 2015, http://www.rediff.com/business/report/come-make-in-india-modi-tells-global-investors/20140815.htm. Retrieved 12 August 2015.
5   Saran, op. cit.
6   "Abenomics encourages Japanese firms to invest – abroad," *South China Morning Post*, 26 September 2013, https://www.scmp.com/business/economy/article/1318151/abenomics-encourages-japanese-firms-invest-abroad. Retrieved 2 February 2019.
7   Saran, op. cit.
8   Sangeeta Mahapatra, "India and Japan Boost Relations With High-Tech Focus," *The Diplomat*, 2 November, 2018, https://thediplomat.com/2018/11/india-and-japan-boost-relations-with-high-tech-focus/. Retrieved 4 February 2019.
9   Mahapatra, ibid.
10 "Chinese companies invest $2bn in Indian startups: Report," *Hindustan Times*, 13 November 2018, https://www.hindustantimes.com/world-news/chinese-companies-invest-2bn-in-indian-startups/story-i3nLFPbudAxnfrLSidO4bM.html. Retrieved 2 February 2019.
11 Ibid.
12 Steven Denney, "South Korea's Economic Dependence on China", *The Diplomat*, 4 September 2015, http://thediplomat.com/2015/09/south-koreas-economic-dependence-on-china/. Retrieved 28 August 2015.
13 Dong Xiangrong, "China-South Korea ties poised to shake off past gloom," *Global Times*, 3 December 2018, http://www.globaltimes.cn/content/1130075.shtml. Retrieved 2 February 2019.
14 "Moon's trip seeks to turn India into 'next China' for S. Korea: Official," *Yonhap News*, 9 July, 2018, http://english.yonhapnews.co.kr/news/2018/07/09/0200000000AEN20180709000300315.html. Retrieved 3 February 2019.
15 Xiangrong, op. cit.
16 Sungil Kwak, "Korea's New Southern Policy: Vision and Challenges," *KIEP Opinions*, 12 November 2018, https://think-asia.org/bitstream/handle/11540/9407/KIEPopinions_no146.pdf?sequence=1. Retrieved 1 February 2019.
17 "South Korea will be one of 'hardest hit economies' if trade war breaks out," *South China Morning Post*, 4 July 2018, https://www.scmp.com/news/china/diplomacy-defence/article/2153645/south-korean-firms-may-get-caught-crossfire-us-trade. Retrieved 1 February 2019.
18 "I have always held Korea as a role model for economic growth: Modi," *United News of India*, 21 February, 2019. http://www.uniindia.com/-i-have-always-held-korea-as-a-role-model-for-economic-growth-modi/world/news/1506803.html. Retrieved 12 September 2019.
19 Embassy of India, Seoul, South Korea, "Brief on India-Korea Economic and Commercial Relations, http://www.indembassyseoul.gov.in/page/india-rok-trade-and-economic-relations/. Retrieved 2 February 2019.
20 "South Korea is looking to correct trade imbalance with India: Envoy," *Business Standard*, 31 August 2014, http://www.business-standard.com/article/news-ians/south-korea-looking-to-correct-trade-imbalance-with-india-envoy-114083100128_1.html. Retrieved 2 August 2015.
21 "India, S. Korea set sights on $50-billion trade," *The Hindu*, 10 July 2018, https://

www.thehindubusinessline.com/news/world/india-s-korea-set-sights-on-50-billion-trade/article24382091.ece. Retrieved 3 February 2019.

22. Soyen Park, "India-South Korea Relations Under the New Modi Government", *The Diplomat*, 13 August 2014, http://thediplomat.com/2014/08/india-south-korea-relations-under-the-new-modi-government/. Retrieved 3 August 2015.

23. Andrew Salmon, "South Korea expands its investment destinations," *Asia Times*, 18 October 2018, http://www.atimes.com/article/south-korea-expands-its-investment-destinations/. Retrieved 1 February 2019.

24. Tina Edwin, "We Need Make in India, Korean Style", DailyO, 18 May 2015, http://www.dailyo.in/business/make-in-india-south-korea-modi-korea-eximbank-Posco-soonki-kang-dipp-amitabh-kant-sagarmala-doosan-heavy-industry-hyundai-daewoo-lg/story/1/3777.html. Retrieved 3 August 2015.

25. D. Govardan, "Hyundai to put $1 billion more for expanding manufacturing," *The Times of India*, 13 November 2018, https://timesofindia.indiatimes.com/business/india-business/hyundai-to-put-1-billion-more-for-expanding-manufacturing/articleshow/66601065.cms. Retrieved 3 February 2019.

26. "Samsung Inaugurates World's Largest Mobile Factory in India; Honourable Prime Minister Shri Narendra Modi Flags-off 'Make for the World'," *Samsung Newsroom*, 9 July 2018, https://news.samsung.com/in/samsung-inaugurates-worlds-largest-mobile-factory-in-india. Retrieved 3 February 2019.

27. Rishi Iyengar, "Samsung goes big in India with 'world's largest mobile factory'," *CNN Business*, 17 July 2018, https://money.cnn.com/2018/07/09/technology/samsung-india-biggest-factory-noida-smartphone/index.html. Retrieved 3 February 2019.

28. "Moon, Modi to hold summit today," *The Korea Times*, 10 July 2018, http://www.indembassyseoul.gov.in/page/india-rok-trade-and-economic-relations/ https://www.koreatimes.co.kr/www/nation/2018/07/356_251990.html http://www.indembassyseoul.gov.in/page/india-rok-trade-and-economic-relations/. Retrieved 3 February 2019.

29. Ankit Panda, "South Korean President Park Geun-hye Visits India", *The Diplomat*, 16 January 2014, http://thediplomat.com/2014/01/south-korean-president-park-geun-hye-visits-india/. Retrieved 23 August 2015.

30. Embassy of India, Seoul, South Korea, "Brief on India-Korea Economic and Commercial Relations", http://www.indembassyseoul.gov.in/page/india-rok-trade-and-economic-relations/. Retrieved 22 August 2019.

31. "PM Modi meets CEOs of top South Korean companies", *Asian News International*, 19 May 2015, https://in.news.yahoo.com/pm-modi-meets-ceos-top-south-korean-companies-050804262.html. Retrieved 20 August 2015.

32. "Korea, India to Work Closer Together", *Chosun Ilbo*, 19 May 2015, http://english.chosun.com/site/data/html_dir/2015/05/19/2015051901182.html. Retrieved 20 August 2015.

33. "India, South Korea Trade and Investment Ties: Focus on CEPA, Make in India," *India Briefing*, 8 August 2018, https://www.india-briefing.com/news/india-south-korea-cepa-investment-electronics-infrastructure-17425.html/. Retrieved 2 February 2019.

34. "KOREA PLUS – 'The Gateway for Korean Investors in India'," *Invest India*, 12 December 2018, https://www.investindia.gov.in/team-india-blogs/korea-plus-gateway-korean-investors-india. Retrieved 4 February 2019.

35. Jyoti Mukul, "India-Korea CEPA: Harvest deal by 2019 even as two nations stick to guns," *Business Standard*, 10 July 2018, https://www.business-standard.com/article/economy-policy/india-korea-cepa-harvest-deal-by-2019-even-as-two-nations-stick-to-guns-118071001401_1.html. Retrieved 1 February 2019.
36. Ministry of External Affairs, India, "India and Republic of Korea: A Vision for People, Prosperity, Peace and our Future," 10 July 2018, https://mea.gov.in/bilateral-documents.htm?dtl/30041/India+and+Republic+of+Korea+A+Vision+for+People+Prosperity+Peace+and+our+Future. Retrieved 4 February 2019.
37. "KOTRA to open sixth office in India," *Yonhap News*, 17 January 2019, https://en.yna.co.kr/view/AEN20190117003100320. Retrieved 3 February 2019.
38. Kritika Suneja, "Ease of Doing Business: India jumps 23 notches, now at rank 77," *The Economic Times*, 1 November 2018, https://economictimes.indiatimes.com/news/economy/indicators/ease-of-doing-business-india-jumps-23-notches-now-at-rank-77/articleshow/66445814.cms. Retrieved 2 February 2019.
39. Asit Ranjan Mishra, "What India can do to better its ease of doing business rank," *LiveMint*, 2, November 2018, https://www.livemint.com/. Retrieved 2 February 2019.
40. "India and Korea: Increasing the opportunities for strong bilateral trade," *Electronics2b.com*, 11 April 2018, https://www.electronicsb2b.com/industry-buzz/india-korea-increasing-opportunities-strong-bilateral-trade/. Retrieved 2 February 2019.
41. Aarati Krishnan, "Behind India's leap in ease of doing business," *The Hindu*, 11 November 2018, https://www.thehindu.com/business/Economy/behind-indias-leap-in-ease-of-doing-business/article25469900.ece. Retrieved 2 February 2019.
42. "Posco Said to Be Backing Away from $12 Billion India Project", *Bloomberg Business*, 27 March 2015, http://www.bloomberg.com/news/articles/2015-03-27/Posco-said-to-be-backing-away-from-12-billion-india-project. Retrieved 15 September 2015.
43. Ibid.
44. Ibid.
45. Bhaskar Parichha, "Posco: The Cunning Businessman," *The Economy Lead*, 19 July 2015, http://www.economylead.com/blog/bhaskar-parichha/Posco-the-cunning-businessman-82362. Retrieved 20 September 2015.
46. Neha, "South Korean Industrial Zone May Soon be Established in Ghilot," *News of Rajasthan*, 28 September 2017, http://newsofrajasthan.com/south-korean-industrial-zone-may-soon-established-ghilot/. Retrieved 2 February 2019.
47. See Invest Rajasthan, http://www.investrajasthan.com/latest_news_details.php?id=34. Retrieved 18 August 2015.
48. "Please 'Make in India,' Modi urges Korean firms", *JoongAng Daily*, 19 May 2015, http://koreajoongangdaily.joins.com/news/article/Article.aspx?aid=3004351. Retrieved 20 September 2015.
49. Joel Lee, "Indian officials take 'Miracle on the Han' Cruise", *Korea Herald*, 28 June 2015, http://www.koreaherald.com/view.php?ud=20150628000146. Retrieved 3 September 2015.
50. "The Korean Connection," *Make in India*, date unavailable, http://www.makeinindia.com/the-korean-connection. Retrieved 1 February 2019.

10

India's Participation in United Nations Police (UN Police) for Post-Conflict Reconstruction:
A Critical Analysis

Jayshree Tandekar

> Post-conflict reconstruction is carried out in societies affected by intra-state conflicts. The United Nations has used its peacekeeping mechanism to carry out post-conflict reconstruction as this mechanism has already acquired legitimacy and credibility in international relations. As part of UN peacekeeping operations, the UN Police are assigned a number of functions in post-conflict reconstruction. India has emerged as one of the major police contributors. The Indian police officers are regularly deployed as UN Police to carry out post-conflict reconstruction. The objective of this article is to analyze India's participation in UN Police for post-conflict reconstruction. It aims to highlight the challenges faced and contributions made by the Indian police officers in post-conflict reconstruction. This article seeks to find answers to the following questions: How have the Indian police officers carried out post-conflict reconstruction? What are the challenges confronted by the Indian police officers in post-conflict reconstruction? To what extent the Indian police officers have been successful? What lessons can be drawn from the Indian police experience as UN Police for the Narendra Modi led NDA-II Government? These and related issues are the subject matter of this article.

India is one of the founding members of the United Nations. It joined the United Nations at a time when it was still a British colony. Over the years, India has emerged as a strong supporter of the United Nations in its peacekeeping efforts. The Indian participation in UN peacekeeping began in late 1940s when it served as a member on the United Nations Special Committee on Palestine (UNSCOP) from May to August 1947. This fact-finding committee was part of the preparatory stage for organizing the United Nations Truce Supervision Organization (UNTSO;

Krishnasamy 2001: 56). Till date, India has participated in 45 out of the total 71 UN peacekeeping operations (UN website a). According to latest figures, India has seconded 6,445 personnel to 10 UN peacekeeping operations out of the total 89,846 personnel deployed in mission areas in December 2018. Out of the total 6,445 personnel, India has sent 5,861 contingent troops personnel, 416 members of formed police units, 14 individual police officers, and 49 experts. Based on this contribution, India ranks fourth after Ethiopia, Bangladesh and Rwanda amongst the 123 contributing countries (UN website c). India has also suffered casualty of 164 personnel in UN peacekeeping operations, which is the highest amongst all the contributing countries (UN website f). There are certain principles that have shaped the Indian contribution to UN peacekeeping operations. For example, India believes that peacekeeping efforts should be undertaken only with the consent of conflicting parties and that too with the support and guidance of the United Nations. Moreover, India emphasizes that the differences between peacekeeping and peace enforcement should not be blurred (Krishnasamy 2010: 228). These are also the principles that have influenced India's participation in UN Police for post-conflict reconstruction.

This article is an attempt to present a general understanding of the Indian participation in UN Police for post-conflict reconstruction. It starts by describing the role of UN peacekeeping operations in post-conflict reconstruction and the functions that are assigned to UN Police as part of it. It then provides an overview of the Indian contribution to the UN Police. The central focus of this article is to analyze the various tasks that are mandated to the Indian police officers in post-conflict reconstruction and the challenges encountered. The article ends with the lessons that can be drawn from the Indian police experience as UN Police for the Narendra Modiled NDA-II Government.

Post-Conflict Reconstruction and United Nations Police (UN Police)

Post-conflict reconstruction is carried out in those societies that are affected by intra-state conflicts. Intra-state conflicts result from the inabilities and weaknesses of states to meet the demands of its citizens. Sometimes, they also occur due to the atrocities inflicted by states against their own people or the lack of central authority. In such situations, the individuals are the worst sufferers as their survival and security become difficult due to the chaos and lawlessness (Doyle and Sambanis 2006: 3-4). To redress the grievances of individuals and to ensure that they do not go through the ordeal of another intra-state conflict, the international community engages in post-conflict reconstruction. In particular, the United Nations has used its peacekeeping mechanism to carry out post-conflict reconstruction as this mechanism has an accepted standing in international relations (Dziedzic 1998: 6). As part of post-conflict reconstruction, the UN peacekeeping operations are given multiple civilian tasks not only to contain violence but also to establish durable peace. These tasks comprise of not only assuring that warring parties in intra-state conflicts obey ceasefires but also stabilizing law and order situation; disarmament, demobilization and reintegration of various factions; supplying humanitarian aid to the aggrieved people; setting up of government structures; re-establishing social and economic institutions; supporting the organization of elections; clearing of mines; defending and promoting human rights and strengthening rule of law (UNDPKO/DFS 2008: 26-28).

The military personnel are the first to be sent after the setting up of UN peacekeeping operations in conflict affected societies. But they cannot be expected to participate in post-conflict reconstruction as they do not have the requisite skills and training. Thus, the United Nations deploys international civilian personnel who have the skills and expertise to carry out post-conflict reconstruction. Usually, these international civilian personnel are administrators, economists, police, de-miners, electoral observers, human rights monitors, civil affairs and governance specialists, humanitarian workers, communication and public information experts, judicial and correction officers, and gender specialists (UN website a). The UN Police have become one of the most critical aspects of UN peacekeeping operations amongst all these international civilian personnel.

The UN Police are the unarmed police personnel sent by police contributing countries (PCCs). They are mandated to assist local authorities in and sometimes they are directly responsible for maintaining law and order in post-conflict societies or failed states. There are three different types of UN Police that are deployed in the mission areas: individual police officers (IPOs), formed police units (FPUs) and standing police capacity (SPC) experts. Of these, the IPOs are primarily responsible for post-conflict reconstruction. The IPOs have been regularly deployed in UN peacekeeping operations for carrying out post-conflict reconstruction. Currently, they are involved in post-conflict reconstruction in 10 out of the 14 UN peacekeeping operations (UN website a). As part of post-conflict reconstruction, the IPOs are required to build the capacity of local police. This is because in conflict-ridden societies, the local police personnel either lack motivation or are unable to execute policing duties (Schmidl 1998: 23). The incompetence of local police in maintaining law and order not only threatens the survival of local people but it also becomes difficult for the United Nations to carry out other reconstruction activities. Also, a stable law and order situation is essential for sustainable peace and development in a post-conflict society (Day and Freeman 2005: 141). Thus, it becomes essential to equip local police personnel with skills and resources in such a manner that they are able and willing to uphold law and order even after the withdrawal of IPOs. In order to build the capacity of local police, the IPOs perform number of functions such as demobilization, recruitment, vetting and certification, and training (each of these functions have been discussed in subsequent sections).

Indian Police and UN Peacekeeping Operations

India is one of the founding members of the United Nations. India has a long tradition of contributing to the UN efforts in peacekeeping. The Indian participation in UN peacekeeping began in late 1940s when it served as a member on the UNSCOP from May to August 1947. This factfinding committee was part of the preparatory stage for organizing the UNTSO (Krishnasamy 2001: 56). Till date, India has participated in 46 out of the total 71 UN peacekeeping operations (UN website a). The Indian contribution to UN peacekeeping operations includes not only military troops but also air force, navy, police and civilian personnel. It is no hidden fact that India is one of the top troop contributors to UN peacekeeping operations. But what is not widely known is that over the years, India has emerged amongst the top police contributors as well. Graph 1 depicts the Indian contribution to UN Police over the years.

Graph 1: Indian Contribution to UN Police (1992-2018)

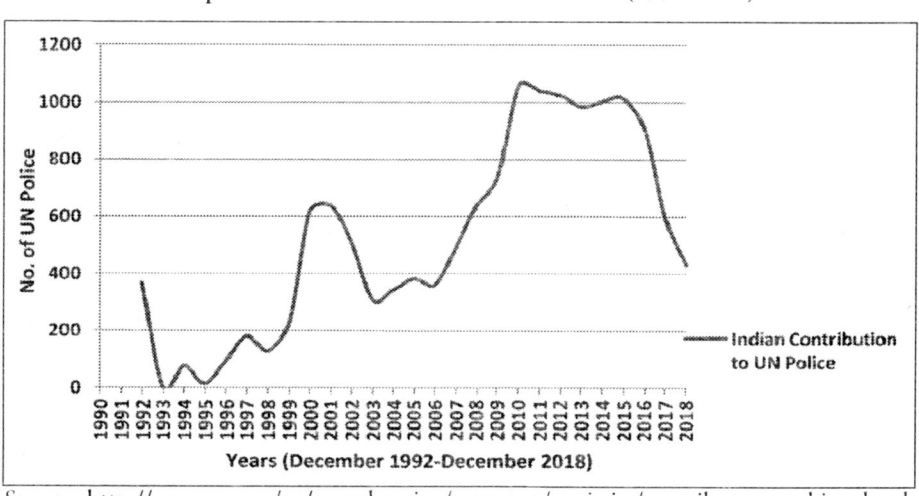

Source: http://www.un.org/en/peacekeeping/resources/statistics/contributors_archive.shtml. Accessed on 1 February 2019.

India contributed to the UN Police for the first time when it sent eight police officers for the United Nations Transitional Authority in Cambodia (UNTAC) in March 1992 and by October 1992, its contribution to UN Police in the UNTAC increased to 366 (UN website b). Since then, India has regularly seconded its police personnel to UN peacekeeping operations. Like in the case of military, India's contribution to UN Police has been largely influenced by its national interests of assuming a role in shaping the future of international system, and the desire of acquiring a permanent seat in the Security Council. In consequence of the pursuit of its national interests, India has sent its police personnel to about 24 UN peacekeeping operations (UN websites b and c).

Table 1 shows the list of UN peacekeeping operations in which India has contributed its police personnel. India has, on several occasions, made a much larger police contribution than the permanent members of the Security Council and the traditional peacekeepers. According to the latest figures, the Indian share in total 10,447 UN Police personnel deployed in December 2018 is 4.11% which is not only higher than the share of the permanent members of the Security Council (China 0.17%, United States 0.03%, France 0.24%, Russia 0.37% and United Kingdom that did not contributed any police personnel), but also more than the share of its neighbouring state Pakistan (1.34%) (UN website c). Of all the permanent members, the share of Russia is the highest. Even the share of the traditional peacekeeping countries such as Canada (0.18%) and the Scandinavian countries such as Sweden (0.49%), Norway (0.22%) and Finland (0.14%) is less than the Indian share (UN website c).

Table 1: List of UN Peacekeeping Operations in which India has sent its Police Personnel

1.	UN Peacekeeping Force in Cyprus (UNFICYP) (March 1964 – Present)
2.	UN Mission for the Referendum in Western Sahara (MINURSO) (April 1991 – Present)
3.	UN Angola Verification Mission II (UNAVEM II) (May 1991 – February 1995)
4.	UN Transitional Authority in Cambodia (UNTAC) (March 1992 – September 1993)
5.	UN Operation in Mozambique (ONUMOZ) (December 1992 – December 1994)
6.	UN Observer Mission in Georgia (UNOMIG) (August 1993 – June 2009)
7.	UN Angola Verification Mission III (UNAVEM III) (February 1995 – June 1997)
8.	UN Mission in Bosnia-Herzegovina (UNMIBH) (December 1995 – December 2002)
9.	UN Support Mission in Haiti (UNSMIH) (July 1996 – July 1997)
10.	UN Observer Mission in Angola (MONUA) (June 1997 – February 1999)
11.	UN Transition Mission in Haiti (UNTMIH) (August 1997 – December 1997)
12.	UN Civilian Police Mission in Haiti (MIPONUH) (December 1997 – March 2000)
13.	UN Observer Mission in Sierra Leone (UNOMSIL) (July 1998 – October 1999)
14.	UN Interim Administration in Kosovo (UNMIK) (June 1999 – Present)
15.	UN Mission in Sierra Leone (UNAMSIL) (October 1999 – December 2005)

16. UN Organization Mission in the Democratic Republic of the Congo (MONUC) (November 1999 – June 2010)
17. UN Mission in Liberia (UNMIL) (September 2003 – Present)
18. UN Operation in Cote d'Ivoire (UNOCI) (April 2004 – Present)
19. UN Mission in the Sudan (UNMIS) (March 2005 – July 2011)
20. UN Integrated Mission in Timor-Leste (UNMIT) (August 2006 – December 2012)
21. UN Stabilization Mission in Haiti (MINUSTAH) (June 2004 – Present)
22. UN Organization Stabilization Mission in the Democratic Republic of Congo (MONUSCO) (July 2010 – Present)
23. UN Mission in South Sudan (UNMISS) (July 2011 – Present)
24. UN Mission for Justice Support in Haiti (MINUJUSTH) (October 2017-Present)

Source: http://www.un.org/en/peacekeeping/resources/statistics/contributors_archive.shtml. Accessed on 1 February 2019.

Since December 2009, India had consistently emerged amongst the top five PCCs in the world. However, since December 2017, the Indian contribution to UN Police has declined. In December 2018, India ranked eighth as it contributed 430 police personnel to 4 out of the 10 UN peacekeeping operations with UN Police (UN website c). Table 2 shows the present mission-wise contribution of India to UN Police (in terms of IPOs as well as FPUs).

Table 2: Mission-wise Contribution of India to UN Police (December 2018)

Mission Name	Individual Police Officers		Formed Police Unit	
	Male	Female	Male	Female
MINUJUSTH	0	0	140	0
MONUSCO	0	0	272	4
UNFICYP	2	1	0	0
UNMISS	8	3	0	0

Source: www.un.org/en/peacekeeping/resources/statistics/contributors.shtml. Accessed on 3 February 2019.

The IPOs and FPUs sent by India have played a significant part in helping the local law enforcement agencies maintain law and order, and from time to time these police personnel have been honoured for their contribution. The biggest recognition of the Indian contribution to UN Police came in October 2014 when the Indian police officer Shakti Devi working with the United Nations Assistance Mission in Afghanistan (UNAMA) was awarded the International Female Policekeeper Award (Khajuria 2014: 1). This award is given by the Police Division of the UN Headquarters in New York to a female policekeeper in recognition of her work in UN peacekeeping. Further, on some occasions, the Indian police personnel have been given the opportunity to head the UN Police components in the mission areas. For instance, Mr. Sudesh Kumar (November 2007 – December

2009) and Mr. Rajesh Dewan (February 2009 – February 2011) were appointed as the UN Police Commissioners of the United Nations Organization Mission in the Democratic Republic of Congo (MONUC) and the United Nations Mission in Sudan (UNMIS) respectively (UN websites d and e), while Mr. Gautam Sawang and Mr. Sanjay Kundu were appointed as the UN Police Deputy Commissioners of the United Nations Mission in Liberia (UNMIL) and the United Nations Mission in South Sudan (UNMISS), respectively. The appointment of the Indian police personnel to lead UN Police components in mission areas is an indication of the growing reputation of India in UN peacekeeping. Similarly, the Indian FPUs have been appreciated for their contribution to maintaining stability and order in conflict-ridden societies. For instance, the 135-personnel Indian FPU-2 deployed in the Democratic Republic of Congo was awarded the UN Peacekeeping Medal in May 2013 for its 'high-level commitment' in fighting criminals and maintaining peace in Goma/North Kivu (Padovan 2013). Also, India is one of the first PCCs to send all-female FPU to UN peacekeeping operations. India deployed two successive all-female FPUs in Liberia in 2007 and 2008 to mentor unarmed local Liberian police personnel. These all-female FPUs were even awarded the UN Peacekeeping Medal for their contribution to peace process in Liberia (UNDPI 2008).

Apart from deploying its police personnel to field missions, India has seconded its police personnel to the Police Division as well which is the nodal point of the UN Headquarters in New York responsible for the UN Police-related matters. In particular, India has the distinction of having sent two Police Advisers to the Police Division: Mr. Om Prakash Rathore (1995-1997) and Dr. Kiran Bedi (2003-2005) (Nambiar 2014). Further, there are some Indian police personnel who have served in different capacities in the Police Division. For instance, one of the former chiefs of the Mission Management and Support Section (one of the sections of the Police Division) was Mr. Ajay Kashyap of Delhi Police. The appointment of the Indian police personnel to high-level posts in the Police Division not only adds to the Indian prestige but it also gives India greater opportunities to influence the UN peacekeeping decision making. However, such appointments of the Indian police personnel to the Police Division have been occasional.

Indian Police's Participation in Post-Conflict Reconstruction and Challenges Confronted

India has deployed its police officers for post-conflict reconstruction in UN peacekeeping operations set up in Bosnia-Herzegovina, Haiti, Sierra Leone,

Kosovo, Congo, Liberia, Sudan, Timor-Leste, Côté d'Ivoire and South Sudan. The objective of the Indian police in post-conflict reconstruction is to build the capacity of local police so that the latter can carry out policing duties effectively. By doing so, the local police personnel can provide safe and secure environment wherein people can live their lives normally and peacefully. Thus, in this way, the local police will also be able to win the trust and confidence of local population (Groenewald and Peake 2004: 15). Currently, there are 14 Indian police officers (ten male and four female police personnel) who have been mandated to carry out post-conflict reconstruction in four UN peacekeeping operations (UN website c). As part of post-conflict reconstruction, the Indian police officers are assigned number of functions such as demobilization, recruitment, vetting and certification, and training. Each of these functions has been discussed in the following sections.

Demobilization

During intra-state conflicts, sometimes the strength of local police exceeds the requisite numbers. This is because at times military personnel are integrated in local police so that the latter can robustly enforce law and order in the face of civil unrest, even if it means violating the rights of people. At other times, warring factions maintain their respective police forces that are operated by separate laws, organizational structures, and command and control. Apart from the swelling numbers, occasionally the local police are characterized by the presence of such personnel who work to serve the interests of political authorities and not of local people (Celador 2005: 370).

When the Indian police officers are deployed in such situations, they are first of all required to demobilize local police. Demobilization means dismissing military personnel from local police, dismantling police forces maintained by different warring factions, and weeding out those police personnel who are politically biased. This is because these personnel have not been recruited according to merit, and also they do not have the capacity to protect public interests. The demobilization also involves stripping these personnel of their equipment, uniforms and identity cards. By demobilization, local police personnel are freed from undue pressure of serving particular interests and they are reoriented to become true servants of public. For instance, at the time of signing of the Dayton Agreement, the Serbian, Croatian, and Muslim factions in Bosnia-Herzegovina maintained their own distinct police. As a result, there were 44,750 police personnel on duty in Bosnia-Herzegovina: 29,750 in Muslim-controlled areas, 3,000 in Croat-controlled areas, and 12,000 in the Republic of Srpska. As part of the United Nations Mission in

Bosnia-Herzegovina (UNMIBH), the Indian police officers removed and reduced the size of local police from 44,000 personnel to 17,000 (Smith et al. 2007: 21).

However, the Indian police officers have faced many difficulties in demobilizing local police. The major amongst them is the reality that not all demobilized personnel find employment despite participating in the reintegration programmes. Hence with no other alternative, these demobilized personnel have often engaged in criminal activities which in turn have contributed to the destabilization of internal law and order in post-conflict societies (Neild 2001: 25). Also, sometimes these demobilized personnel are integrated in local police in an attempt to portray the success of reintegration programmes (Stodiek and Zellner 2007: 8). However, this defeats the objective of demobilization. This is because there is always a possibility that these demobilized personnel can revert to their old ways, and hence hamper the security and confidence of local people.

Recruitment

Usually post-conflict societies are characterized by dwindling numbers in local police. Two reasons can be identified for this. Sometimes during conflicts, local police personnel are either killed or they leave their jobs and flee. Hence, there are not enough police personnel available to maintain law and order in post-conflict societies. At other times, it may so happen that after demobilization, the strength of local police may decline. In both these situations, it becomes necessary to recruit new personnel so that the local police can be brought to the pre-conflict size. At the same time, it is necessary to ensure that the local police system represents its society. Thus, recruitment in local police is carried out on the basis of ethnicity, gender and tribe. Generally, as part of the recruitment policy, quotas are determined for minority communities. Quota-based recruitment is particularly important in those societies where ethnic or sectarian differences have driven past conflicts. Such recruitment enhances the professional conduct of local police, while maximizing their ability to develop good relations with local communities (Celador 2005: 366). For example, in the United Nations Interim Administration in Kosovo (UNMIK), the recruitment of minorities in local police was a major goal of the Indian police officers (Smith et al. 2007: 19). In recent years, the emphasis has been placed on recruiting more women in local police in order to ensure that the women and girls who have gone through the trauma are able to express themselves freely before the female police personnel. As part of recruitment, the Indian police officers have assisted local governments in advertising posts, holding exams and conducting interviews of candidates.

However, the Indian police officers have faced several hurdles in recruiting candidates in local police. For one, quota-based recruitment can undermine the establishment of efficient local police as it often prevents the recruitment of meritorious personnel. In addition, there is a possibility that the quality of personnel recruited in local police may not be up to the mark. For instance, in an effort to meet the gender targets, the Indian police officers in Liberia (UNMIL) lowered the educational standards so much for female recruits that some were incapable of performing basic police functions even after training (Durch et al. 2012: 38-39). Apart from this, sometimes inappropriate personnel are recruited in local police so as to meet the requirements of local authorities. Also, there is always a possibility that despite being recruited in local police, the personnel belonging to different communities continue to report and receive orders from their respective community leaders. Thus, their loyalty to police service becomes questionable (Stodiek and Zellner 2007: 4). Moreover, given the paucity of time, occasionally demobilized personnel are recruited in local police. Such recruitment erodes the public legitimacy and credibility of local police. Also, there are chances that this recruitment results in the continuation of old "inappropriate institutional practices and the bureaucratic culture of former security forces" (Neild 2001: 25).

Vetting and Certification

Another essential function that the Indian police officers are authorized to carry out in post-conflict reconstruction is vetting and certification. The primary objective of vetting and certification is to screen and identify all those police personnel who are fit and capable of maintaining law and order. In order to accomplish this, the Indian police officers usually set certain criteria such as educational background, training and absence of any criminal conviction. This process of screening is known as vetting. Vetting involves carrying out investigation of all the existing as well as new recruits in local police. With the help of local authorities, the names of police personnel are advertised in local newspapers so that the people can provide all the necessary information about the police personnel's past. The old police records are also checked and verified. Those found guilty are generally dismissed or suspended by local authorities (Celador 2005: 370-371). Those police personnel whose records are clean are certified and allowed to continue in the police service. Thus, vetting helps to identify and bring to account all those police personnel who have violated laws during and after intra-state conflicts. It also cements the accountability of local police as the "neutral guarantor of rights" (Neild 2001: 27). For example, in the United Nations Mission in Timor-Leste (UNMIT), the Indian police officers were involved in vetting of 900 personnel of the Polisia Nasional de Timor-Leste (PNTL) (Lemay-Hébert 2009: 400).

But the Indian police officers have confronted some challenges during the vetting and certification of local police. For instance, the Indian police officers have to deal with the indifferences of local police authorities to the investigations carried out by them. Even after vetting, local police authorities do not dismiss those police personnel who are found unfit for policing or such personnel are let off after minor punishment. This was witnessed in Timor-Leste (UNMIT) when the higher policing authorities sent back most of the files for further investigation though the files had been submitted after vetting (Lemay-Hébert 2009: 400). It means that even after found guilty, such personnel continue to serve in the police. This not only nullifies the efforts and resources invested by the Indian police officers but it also undermines the confidence of people in local police. At other times, the database (records) of local police personnel is either absent as it has been destroyed during intra-state conflicts or it is outdated. As a result, it becomes difficult for Indian police officers to conduct investigations and secure testimonies of witnesses as the former do not have suitable records to rely on.

Training

Training is one of the most important functions that are assigned to the Indian police officers in post-conflict reconstruction. Training of local police is essential as it aims at transferring skills and knowledge to them, and it ensures that local police personnel acquire necessary experience to carry out their policing duties professionally. Generally, the Indian police officers provide training to different kinds of personnel in local police such as new recruits, current serving members, middle and senior management officers, and local police trainers. As part of training, these police personnel are taught a number of topics such as crime, traffic, border, conflict resolution and mediation, forensics, crowd control, anti-terrorism, information technology, democratic policing, community policing, human rights, finance, equipment maintenance and asset management (UNDPKO 2000: 61-66).

The Indian police officers usually impart three types of training to local police: classroom training, field training, and training of the trainers. The classroom training aims at providing theoretical understanding of various policing issues and the challenges that can be confronted by local police in implementing their duties. On the other hand, in field training, the local police are given practical knowledge of the topics covered in classroom training. For instance, as part of the United Nations Operation in Côte d'Ivoire (UNOCI), the Indian police officers delivered field training on fingerprinting techniques, judicial photography (descriptive images and crime scene) and criminal investigations (methodology of criminal investigation) to 70 Ivorian police officers (UNDPKO 2012: 6). The field training helps local police in developing and enhancing their basic skills such as response time, crime scene preservation, identifying and interviewing witnesses, and obtaining and safeguarding physical evidence. Sometimes, the Indian police officers impart training to the local police trainers so that the latter can train their fellow police personnel. The training of the trainers not only saves time and money but it also has a snowball effect. For example, the Indian police officers of the United Nations Stabilization Mission in Haiti (MINUSTAH) trained Haitian National Police (HNP) trainers in 'First Aid Instructor Training Programme' so that these local trainers could train other local police personnel in basic life saving techniques (UNDPKO 2012: 10). In some cases, Indian police officers have also helped local police authorities formulate training curricula on a number of issues such as gender and human rights.

However, occasionally it becomes difficult for the Indian police officers to train local police. Several reasons can be identified for this. The chief amongst them is the unwillingness of local police personnel to train under the Indian police officers. This is because sometimes local police consider the UN Police as outsiders who have little or no knowledge of the former's culture and society. Thus to avoid training, local police personnel put forward such conditions that cannot be met by the UN Police. Such situations were experienced by the Indian police officers of the UNMISS. Also, given the emphasis on early exit strategy, training of local police is often limited to short periods. Consequently, it becomes difficult for the Indian police officers to cover all the topics and address individual concerns of all participants at the same time. Moreover, training can be undermined by the absence of requisite infrastructure and resources. For example in Sierra Leone, the three regional police training centres at the provincial capitals of Bo, Kenema and Makeni were destroyed during conflict, and the police training school at Benguema could accommodate only 200 trainees per intake. The lack of adequate building infrastructure made it impossible for the Indian police officers of the United Nations Mission in Sierra Leone (UNAMSIL) to train more police personnel at one time and it also resulted in the reduction of classroom training duration from 6 months to 12 weeks (Meek 2003: 108).

Conclusion

India has emerged as one of the largest contributors of police to UN peacekeeping operations. India has deployed significant number of IPOs for post-conflict reconstruction. But these police officers have faced several problems while performing the tasks of demobilization, recruitment, vetting and certification, and training. Also, as is evident from Table 3, the Indian contribution to IPOs for post-conflict reconstruction has declined since 2010.

Table 3: Indian Contribution to Individual Police Officers (2009-2018)

	Individual Police Officers		
	Male	Female	Total
December 2009	96	7	103
December 2010	99	5	104
December 2011	65	4	69
December 2012	44	5	49
December 2013	26	8	34
December 2014	64	5	69
December 2015	62	4	66
December 2016	54	6	60
December 2017	23	7	30
December 2018	10	4	14

Source: http://www.un.org/en/peacekeeping/resources/statistics/contributors_archive.shtml. Accessed on 1 February 2019.

Based on the Indian police experience as UN Police, one of the first lessons that can be drawn for the Narendra Modi-led NDA-II Government is that despite the challenges confronted by the Indian police officers in post-conflict reconstruction, India cannot afford to decrease its contribution to the UN Police. Two reasons can be identified for this. For one, India faces stiff competition from its neighbouring countries in terms of the contribution to the UN Police. As can be seen from Table 4, Bangladesh and Nepal have emerged amongst the largest police contributors to UN peacekeeping operations. In particular, Bangladesh and Nepal have consistently ranked amongst the top six PCCs since December 2005. In fact, since December 2005, Bangladesh has seconded more police personnel than India. If India has to maintain its leverage in the developing world, it has to not only increase its deployment of IPOs but also contribute more than Bangladesh. At the same time, India has to understand that its contribution to UN Police in peacekeeping operations not only helps it to shape its image positively as a 'good international citizen' that is committed to global responsibilities but it also provides an opportunity for India to increase its presence within the United

Nations. Given the vast reservoir of the UN Police experience, India can stake claims in the important decision-making posts in the Police Division at the UN Headquarters in New York.

Table 4: Ranking of India and its Neighbouring Countries amongst Police Contributing Countries (2000-2018)

	India	Nepal	Bangladesh	Pakistan
December 2000	2	17	10	6
December 2001	3	19	14	6
December 2002	2	18	13	5
December 2003	4	10	13	9
December 2004	5	3	17	2
December 2005	6	3	2	5
December 2006	7	4	2	3
December 2007	8	5	1	3
December 2008	6	5	1	4
December 2009	5	4	1	3
December 2010	3	5	2	4
December 2011	3	6	1	4
December 2012	3	5	1	6
December 2013	4	5	1	6
December 2014	4	5	2	7
December 2015	4	5	3	7
December 2016	5	6	2	14
December 2017	7	6	4	20
December 2018	8	5	6	19

Source: http://www.un.org/en/peacekeeping/resources/statistics/contributors_archive.shtml. Accessed on 1 February 2019.

As far as the challenges are concerned, India can take several steps to ensure that its police officers do not face the same problems again and again in post-conflict reconstruction. India can begin by establishing a post of the Police Adviser in its permanent mission to the United Nations. Like in the case of many other UN member states, the police-related matters in the Indian permanent mission are dealt with by the Military Adviser. It is not reasonable to expect the Military Adviser to understand the difficulties that are faced by the Indian police officers. This is because military and police are two separate security institutions that have their own distinct identity, culture, doctrine, and command and control structures. Further, it would be useful if the Indian police officers are deployed for longer durations in the mission areas. This would enable them to build good relations with local authorities and local police personnel which in turn would help them to carry out their tasks more effectively. Also, a system of debriefing should be established wherein those Indian police officers who have already served in UN peacekeeping operations are able to record their experiences. Such a system would facilitate the identification of lessons learnt and the consequent formulation of policies by the Indian government.

Moreover, India should learn something from its neighbouring countries as well. China, one of its neighbours, has established the Peacekeeping CIVPOL (Civilian Police) Training Centre in Lanfang City. This is significant because the Chinese contribution to UN Police has been minimal. According to latest figures, in December 2018, China sent only 18 police personnel, which is twenty times less than the Indian contribution. The establishment of this training centre signifies the Chinese determination to second competent police personnel to UN peacekeeping operations (Choedon 2013: 220). Also, it reflects the Chinese resolve to increase its clout in the United Nations and its decision-making procedures. In the context of ambiguous Sino-India relations and given the Indian contribution to UN Police, it would only be better if India could set up a training institute that is dedicated entirely to cater to the needs of its potential UN Police personnel. This centre would teach and train the Indian police officers in tackling some of the challenges that are confronted by them in post-conflict reconstruction and hence improve their performance in the field. Such a development in turn would not only help enhance the image of India and add value to its participation in the UN decision making but also strengthen its position to counter the Chinese influence in the United Nations.

REFERENCES

Celador, Gemma Collantes (2005), "Police Reform: Peacebuilding Through 'Democratic Policing'?", *International Peacekeeping*, 12. 3: pp. 366; 370-371.

Choedon, Yeshi (2013), "India and Chinese Engagement in UN Complex Peacekeeping Operations: A Comparative Perspective", *China Report*, 49. 2: p. 220.

Day, Graham and Christopher Freeman (2005), "Operationalising the Responsibility to Protect The Policekeeping Approach", *Global Governance*, 11. 2: pp. 141.

Doyle, Michael W. and Nicholas Sambanis (2006), "Introduction: War-Making, Peacebuilding and the United Nations", in *Making War and Building Peace – United Nations Peace Operations*, Princeton: Princeton University Press, pp. 3-4.

Dziedzic, Michael J. (1998), "Introduction" in Oakley, Robert B., Michael J. Dziedzic and Eliot M. Goldberg (Ed.) *Policing the New World Disorder – Peace Operations and Public Security*, Washington D.C.: National Defense University Press, p. 6.

Durch, William J., Madeline L. England and Fiona B. Mangan with Michelle Ker (2012), *Understanding Impact of Police, Justice, and Corrections Components in UN Peace Operations*, Future of Peace Operations Program, Washington D.C.: The Henry L. Stimson Center, pp. 38-39.

Groenewald, Hesta and Gordon Peake (2004), *Police Reform Through Community-Based Policing –*

Philosophy and Guidelines for Implementation, New York: International Peace Academy, p. 15.

Khajuria, Sanjay (15 October 2014), "UN Peacekeeper Award for J&K Woman Cop in Afghanistan", *The Times of India*, p. 1.

Krishnasamy, Kabilan (2001), "'Recognition' for Third World Peacekeepers: India and Pakistan", *International Peacekeeping*, 8. 4: p. 56.

Krishnasamy, Kabilan (2010), "A Case for India's Leadership in United Nations Peacekeeping", *International Studies*, 47. 2-4: p. 228.

Lemay-Hébert, Nicolas (2009), "UNPOL and Police Reform in Timor-Leste: Accomplishments and Setbacks", *International Peacekeeping*, 16. 3: p. 400.

Meek, Sarah (2003), "Policing Sierra Leone", in Malan, Mark, Sarah Meek, Thokozani Thusi, Jeremy Ginifer, and Patrick Coker (Ed.) *Sierra Leone: Building Road to Recovery*, Pretoria, South Africa: Institute for Security Studies (ISS), p. 108.

Nambiar, Satish (26 January 2014), "India and United Nations Peacekeeping Operations", mea.gov.in, 1 February 2019, http://mea.gov.in/articles-in-indian-media.htm?dtl/22776/India+and+United+Nations+Peacekeeping+Operations.

Neild, Rachel (2001), "Democratic Police Reforms in War-Torn Societies", *Conflict, Security and Development*, 1. 1: pp. 25, 27.

Padovan, Clara (15 May 2013), "Indian Formed Police Unit-2 honoured with the UN Peace Medal in Goma", monusco.unmissions.org, 27 January 2019, http://monusco.unmissions.org/Default.aspx?tabid=10662&ctl=Details&mid=14594&ItemID=19806&language=en-US.

Schmidl, Erwin A. (1998), "Police Functions in Peace Operations: An Historical Overview", in Oakley, Robert B., Michael J. Dziedzic and Eliot M. Goldberg (Ed.) *Policing the New World Disorder – Peace Operations and Public Security*, Washington D.C.: National Defense University Press, p. 23.

Smith, Joshua G., Victoria K. Holt and William J. Durch (2007), *Enhancing United Nations Capacity to Support Post-Conflict Policing and Rule of Law*, Stimson Center Report No. 63, Report from the Project on Rule of Law in Post-Conflict Settings – Future of Peace Operations Program, Washington D.C.: The Henry L. Stimson Center, pp. 19; 21.

Stodiek, Thorsten and Wolfgang Zellner (2007), "The Creation of Multi-Ethnic Police Services in the Western Balkans: A Record of Mixed Success", www.ssoar.info, 2 February 2019, http://nbn-resolving.de/urn:nbn:de:0168-ssoar-260323.

United Nations (website a), https://peacekeeping.un.org/sites/default/files/unpeacekeeping-operationlist_1.pdf, 5 February 2019.

United Nations (website b), https://peacekeeping.un.org/en/troop-and-police-contributors, 1 February 2019.

United Nations (website c), https://peacekeeping.un.org/sites/default/files/1_summary_of_contributions_12.pdf, 3 February 2019.

United Nations (website d), http://www.un.org/en/peacekeeping/missions/past/monuc/leadership.shtml, 7 February 2019.

United Nations (website e), http://www.un.org/en/peacekeeping/missions/past/unmis/leadership.shtml, 5 February 2019.

United Nations (website f), https://peacekeeping.un.org/en/fatalities, 8 February 2019.

*UN Department of Peacekeeping Operations (2000), *United Nations Civilian Police Principles and Guidelines*, New York: United Nations, pp. 61-66.

UN Department of Peacekeeping Operations (2012), *UN Police Magazine*, January 2012 (8th edition),

New York: United Nations, pp. 6, 10.
*UN Department of Peacekeeping Operations and Department of Field Support (2008), *United Nations Peacekeeping Operations: Principles and Guidelines*, New York: United Nations, pp. 26-28.
UN Department of Public Information (14 November 2008), "Indian Female Police officers inspire women to join Liberian Police to support Rule of Law", UNIC/Press Release/171-2008, www.unic.org, 23 November 2014, http://www.unic.org.in/display.php?E=1178&K=India.

11

Narendra Modi:
Reconstructing India's Foreign Policy Objectives

K. Jayaprasad

Indian politics witnessed a fundamental change under Prime Minister Narendra Modi, who assumed power on 26th May 2014. After thirty years, a single party got absolute majority in the parliament and the BJP-led NDA Government redrafted India's domestic as well as foreign policy initiatives. Dynamic, positive and development-oriented programmes of Modi Government changed the political climate. As far as India's Foreign Policy is concerned, the 'Modi Doctrine' reshaped the Foreign Policy objectives. Rejecting the idealism of Nehruvian School, Modi opted a vibrant policy strictly concerned with national interest. National security and economic growth became the fundamental objectives. Within five years (2014-2019), Narendra Modi made an imprint as a statesman and elevated to the status of a world leader. Narendra Modi, being a realist, followed the Legacy of Prime Minister Vajpayee (1998-2004), with new vigour and dynamism, and also committed to protect India's economic, scientific, cultural, political, security and strategic interests. Narendra Modi re-drafted the relations with the neighbours and major powers of the world. Within a short span of five years, the Nation's Will asserted its dignity, self-respect, strength and gave the message of friendship and co-operation. He initiated a positive and confident Foreign Policy and succeeded in participating bilateral and multi-lateral summits. No previous Indian Prime Ministers had set such a record while in Office.

As Prime Minister Atal Bihari Vajpayee did in 1998, Narendra Modi took the mantle in 2014, from a weak Government at Home and its feeble and confused Foreign Policy record. For example, from 1989 to 1998, India had a succession of weak Governments and during this period the country witnessed six Prime Ministers. The collapse of the USSR in 1991 further confused the leadership. But, in 1998 Vajpayee changed the Foreign Policy by asserting India's prestige, power and national interest. He had contributed much to raise India's national self-confidence both in internal and external affairs. He reverted the Nehruvian Foreign Policy and dogmatic orientations and placed pragmatic Foreign Policy. He took a realistic approach and a strategy of peace through strength. As a result, India declared herself as a nuclear weapon state. Even though the USA and its allies imposed sanctions against India, within two years they were compelled to accept the nuclear policy of India. India received much recognition from the Super Powers only after changing the label of a 'soft State'. The NDA Government under Vajpayee changed the traditional Foreign Policy objectives of India and asserted security, economic development and peaceful world order. Discarding idealism, Vajpayee government followed a foreign policy that restored India's national self-confidence and power.

From 2004 to 2014 India witnessed a week foreign policy under UPA government headed by Dr. Manmohan Singh. The lack of leadership, dynamism, vision, confidence etc. was very much evident in Manmohan Singh's Foreign Policy. The dual leadership of UPA system further confused the matter. A vibrant Foreign Policy can sustain only on the foundation of a strong domestic policy. As the Prime Minister, Dr. Manmohan Singh had no command in the ruling UPA but the Chairperson Mrs. Sonia Gandhi controlled the power. Thus India lost ten years because of inaction, confusions and compromise policy both internally and externally. Prime Minister Manmohan Singh's two terms can be called as the 'lost decade' for India strategically. Despite economic growth the nations opted weakness and inability. This shows that, the GDP growth cannot translate into strong Foreign Policy in the absence of dynamic, forward-looking leadership and strategic goals. The UPA under Manmohan Singh and Sonia Gandhi failed to protect the national interest and national prestige. Hence, the Prime Minister, Narendra Modi had a huge task to reassert the Indian interest. On the lines of Vajpayee, he asserted national interest. Vajpayee Government initially faced the sanctions of the super powers including USA, but Narendra Modi has been welcomed by all. The world endorsed the new leadership of India. Every country's Foreign Policy had elements of continuity and change following a change in government. India's Foreign Policy under BJP Government led by Narendra Modi is not different. It is interesting that, immediately after the elections to the parliament in 2014, many experts were not confident on Narendra Modi's Foreign Policy initiatives. They looked through the 'prism' of political colour and predicted a dark picture of future foreign policy. Also Narendra Modi faced the visa denial from USA for 10 years. They believed that domestic priorities would dominate the scene. But within a short span of time, Narendra Modi succeeded in building the foundation of a strong domestic policy and a vibrant, progressive foreign policy with strong commitments to the protection of national interests.

It is to be noted that the swearing-in ceremony of Narendra Modi as Prime Minister itself was a diplomatic success and all the Chiefs of eight neighbouring SAARC countries along with Mauritius represented the function. The "neighbourhood first policy" of Narendra Modi changed the outlook of neighbours towards India. As a gesture to Modi's invitation to the swearing-in ceremony, both Pakistan and Sri Lanka released hundreds of Indian fishermen who were in their jails for a long period.

Ever since the Modi government came to power in 2014, there has been a serious debate on Modi Doctrine. It is a fact that Modi altered the foreign policy objectives drastically. National interest with more focus on National Security is the major concern of Modi's foreign policy. He declared zero tolerance to terror and warned Pakistan, but gave more thrust to improve relations with China. Modi succeeded in opening new chapters in both Indo-US and Indo-Russian relations. Sometimes, more importance was given to Japan, France, Germany, China, Israel, Australia, Brazil, South Africa etc. Act East Policy and strengthening the BRICS became core foreign policy initiatives. Modi's stand against cross-border terrorism has been revealed after Uri and Pulwama terrorist attacks in 2016 and 2019 respectively. He used air strikes to target terror camps in Pakistan. It was the first such act by India after the 1971 war with Pakistan. He altered India's Pakistan policy and also rejected the myth of Pakistan's nuclear capability.

Modi was aware of China's growing regional might and assertiveness. In a significant shift in its policy, India has entered into logistical bilateral and multilateral agreements in Indian Ocean and Indo-Pacific regions to ensure peace, stability and international sea routes safe and unhindered. On 27th November 2017, the USA, Japan, Australia and India started Quadrilateral Security Dialogue or Quad. On 10th March 2018, India and France entered into a far-reaching Logistics Support Agreement, which seeks to extend logistical support on reciprocal access to respective facilities for Indian and French armed forces. It would facilitate India's pressure in the pacific especially the French naval bases in French Polynesia and New Caledonia in the Southern Pacific. Strengthening India's presence in the Indian Ocean Regions, Modi signed agreements with Mauritius in March 2015, Iran in May 2016, Oman in February 2018, Mozambique in 2015, Seychelles in 2015 and Communications Compatibility and Security Agreement (COMCASA) with USA on 7th September 2018.

Modi opened a new era in Japan-India relations. Prime Minister Modi and Japan Prime Minister Shinzo Abe met in Tokyo in September 2014, and agreed that Japan-India relationship was upgraded to special strategic and global partnership. It arrived for long-term political, economic and strategic goals. They announced Japan and India Vision 2025 Special Strategic and Global Partnership working together for peace and prosperity of the Indo-Pacific Region and the world. Two agreements, related with Security, namely security measures for the protection of classified military information (2015) and Agreement for Co-operation in the peaceful uses of Nuclear Energy and Agreement for Transfer of Defence Equipment and Technology (2015) needs special mention. Under Modi, a new phase started in India-Israel relation. He was the first Indian Prime Minister, who visited Israel. With Modi's visit to Israel on July 2017, India's traditional approach towards Israel came to an end. He succeeded in improving relations with Islamic world especially with Saudi Arabia, UAE, Oman and Iran. Indo-Russian relations also entered into a warm one in spite of US reservations and sanctions on Russia.

Changes in Foreign Policy Objectives

In 2014, the BJP manifesto stated that equations will be mended through pragmatism and a doctrine of mutually beneficial and interlocking relationship based on enlightened national interest. Hence, immediately after assuming power, Narendra Modi re-constructed India's traditional foreign policy and opted for a vibrant policy initiative. Through his bilateral and multi-lateral engagements, Modi emerged as a world leader. Within five years of his Office, he made 41 foreign trips to six continents and visited 59 countries. India's relations with super powers improved and Prime Minister's multi-lateral and strategic engagements were a great success. India's fight against terrorism was endorsed by all super powers. As a result, no nation condemned India's air strike on terrorist camps in Balakot in Pakistan on 26th February 2019 as the retaliation to the terrorist attack on 14th February in Kashmir by Pakistan-based terrorist group Jaish-e-Mohammed. On this background, the Foreign Policy of the NDA Government (2014-2019) or the Modi Doctrine needs further analysis.

The fundamental changes initiated by Modi Doctrine are the following:

(i) Changes in Economic Objectives

Narendra Modi declared economic and technological objectives of his foreign policy. His motto was 'India First' and India first means that, India's requirement, when it comes to various areas like basic sanitations, food security, employment generation, defence and space technology, will be expressed with greater clarity and specificity to other countries. On 25th September, 2014, Modi government launched "Make in India" movement. As a strategy, it is the mission to respond to global and local challenges through preparations for a world-class manufacturing status and knowledge infrastructure that should create further knowledge for stepping on to global competitiveness. As a result, India emerged in 2015, as the top destination globally for Foreign Direct Investment (FDI), surpassing the USA and China. As per the current policy, 100% FDI is permitted in all 25 sectors, except for Space Industry, Defence Industry and media. This policy transformed India into a global design and manufacturing hub.

Drawing Business Report (DBR - 2019) acknowledges India's jump of 23 positions against its rank of 100 in 2017 to be placed now at 77th rank among 190 countries. As per the Reserve Bank of India Report, FDI in 2013-14 was 16,054 million dollars. In 2014-15, it was 24,748 million dollars and in 2015-16 it increased to 26,068 million dollars. In 2017-18, it further increased to 37,366 million dollars. All these figures show that there was a greater link between domestic and foreign policy objectives. Make in India is not a mere slogan, but it reveals the economic orientation of India's foreign policy. According to Modi, the domestic policy and interest should be represented in nation's foreign policy.

(ii) Greater Emphasis on National Power

The recognition of economic power and military power was the hallmark of Modi's foreign policy. Modi's Doctrine fundamentally changed the foreign policy objectives. He has imbibed Indian Foreign Policy with certain amount of risk taking unlike the risk aversion of the past. India is now taking a larger role as a global player. India is also one of the fastest growing economies in the world, and is considered as a major power and a potential super power. It is India's growing international influence that gives it a prominent voice in global affairs.

(iii) Concern with Border

Modi was against compromises on border and that message has already been given to both Pakistan and China. His government has put on priority both terrorism and border security by adopting zero tolerance policy. Troops of India and China were locked in a 75-day-long stand-off in Doklam, the tri-junction of India, Bhutan and China since 16th June 2017. India never compromised and the Indian Army prevented the Chinese road construction in Doklam. Finally, China agreed not to build the road further in the Doklam area and withdraw its troops from Doklam. Indian Army's tough stand in the stand-off also helped in putting pressure on China, which was made to understand that India will not back off, so easily without its demands being accepted, and thus China was compelled to withdraw their troops from Doklam. This was a major victory of Modi's national security policy and his military diplomacy.

(iv) Projecting a "Lakshman Rekha" in Indo-Pak Relations

India needs friendship with all its neighbours including Pakistan. But, Modi's concern was not limited to Pakistan and it is not the sole enemy. India offered friendships without compromises. For the first time under Prime Minister Modi, India asserted the "Lakshman Rekha" in relation with Pakistan. He stated that "building trust between the two nations is pre-requisite to any further meaningful moment on the relations". Hence, the Pak Officials' meeting with Kashmir separatists in India was the violation of 'Lakshman Rekha' and thus a trust breaking step. Therefore, Modi suspended all dialogues with Pakistan.

In many occasions, India reminded Pakistan of its responsibility. Immediately after the terrorist attack on Indian Army Camp in Uri on 18th September 2016, Prime Minister Modi assured the nation that those behind this despicable attack would not go unpunished. On 29th September 2016, Indian Army conducted surgical strikes against suspected militants in Pak-Occupied Kashmir. Also, India cancelled 19th SAARC Summit in Islamabad. Afghanistan, Bhutan and Bangladesh also stood with India. In the same way, the terrorist attack on the military convoy in Pulwama and killing of 42 Indian soldiers in Kashmir on 14th February 2019 was revenged with Air Strike by Indian Air Force on 26th February 2019 on the terrorist camp at Balakot in Pakistan. These military strikes carried out by the Indian Army along the Line of Control focussed only the terrorist camps and not Pak military or civilian centres. It will not be a solution, but it sends a strong message that India will not tolerate any violence sponsored by Pakistan or Pak-based terrorist groups. "Fight the terrorists in their own land" is the policy of Modi. It should be remembered that there was no adverse response from International Community against India in this regard. This is the victory of Modi's Foreign Policy. From the very beginning, Modi asserted India's right to protect its borders and zero tolerance towards terrorism.

(v) Non-Alignment to Re-alignment

Modi doctrine rejected non-alignment, but decided to be close to all countries and going beyond the spirit of Non-Aligned Movement. Prime Minister Modi was firm about taking independent decisions on India's national interest. This could be measured from India's association with France in Rafael Aircraft Deal and Logistic Support Agreement, defence ties with Russia, growing role of India in ASEAN, defence agreements with Japan, defence and security agreement with USA, Indian participation in Quadrilateral Security Dialogue with Japan, USA and Australia, defence procumbent ties with Israel etc. India's Foreign Policy is now not based on any dogmas, but on country's interest and development. Discarding the non-alignment here means projecting the national interest. Non-aligned India until the collapse of USSR played second fiddle to the ideological goal. Thus, the Nehruvian idealism in foreign policy has been totally rejected by Modi Doctrine.

(vi) Economic Relationship with Potential Adversaries

India's economic relationship, especially with China, is independent of its security relationship. Modi has already met Chinese President Xi-Jinping at many occasions, both in India and abroad. But no compromise can be expected on India's stand in border conflict and India's strategic partnership with Japan and India's participation in Quadrilateral Security Dialogue with USA, Australia and Japan. At the East Asia Summit in November 2014, Modi called for new norms aiming China's aggressive role in South China Sea. Since Modi took Office, there has been considerable progress in Sino-Indian relations. But Doklam incident created some hurdles.

Under its 'String of Pearls' policy, China has long been trying to ring-fence India by building strategic and economic bases in smaller countries like Sri Lanka, Bangladesh, Myanmar, Maldives etc. However, Prime Minister Modi has been pursuing an aggressive policy to contain China in India's backyard. India's best hope is that the neighbouring countries grow doubtful about China's infrastructure funding. No doubt, Modi's 'Neighbourhood First Policy' has been aggressively working, though it has some limitations.

(vii) Relationship with one country will not constrain with others

There are serious efforts for strategic partnership with Japan, US and Australia. India-Russia relations improved and also the Indo-US relations entered into a new peak. The USA also agreed to grant India a waiver from Iran sanctions, which would allow Indian Oil companies to continue to import from Iran. Though India's relations with USA improved under Modi, he also decided to purchase the five-billion-dollar Russian S-400 missile defence system in 2018. In West Asia, India has good relations with Israel, Saudi Arabia, UAE, Oman and Iran. In the current multi-polar world order, Narendra Modi followed a policy of multi-alignment rather than a policy of non-alignment. It is to be noted that for the first time the American President became the Chief Guest in the Republic Day Celebrations on 26th January 2015. Modi made the Republic Day Celebrations of 2018 a historical one by inviting all the heads of 10 ASEAN countries namely, Brunei, Cambodia, Indonesia, Laos, Malaysia, Myanmar, Philippines, Singapore, Thailand and Vietnam.

(viii) Participation of NRIs towards the Development of India
From the very beginning, Modi gave importance to the Indian diaspora and asked for their participation in the country's economic development. In his visits from USA to Australia, he addressed Indian diaspora. Engagement with non-resident Indians (NRIs) became an integral component of Modi's domestic and foreign policies. Modi believes that the 25-million-member overseas community is a potent untapped force and hence he wants to give them a major role in the economic growth of the country. To him, the NRIs are India's brand ambassadors and they are the symbols of the country's capabilities and strength. He gave greater emphasis on 'soft power' and inspired them to contribute to country's economic and technological development. He declared that the Overseas Indian Community can play a role in shaping start-ups in the country and also announced that NRI mentors will be brought on the same platform as Indian start-ups. He organized the 15th Pravasi Bharatiya Divas Convention in Varanasi on 21-22 January 2019 that was attended by around 5000 overseas Indian participants from 85 countries.

(ix) Look East Policy to Act East Policy
From the very beginning, Narendra Modi asserted that India should focus on improving relations with ASEAN and other East Asian Countries. Within a short period, Indian Foreign Minister Sushma Swaraj visited East Asian Counties. The East Asian Summit held on November 2014 in Myanmar opened a new avenue for Prime Minister Modi. He reassured the East Asian Leaders about investment-friendly climate of India and offered changes in policies to do business in India. In this summit, Modi launched Act East Policy. The policy seeks to revive India's relations with not only ASEAN countries but also included Koreas in the North to Australia and New Zealand in the South and from Bangladesh in the West to

Fiji and Pacific Island countries in the East. Act East Policy also aimed at promoting economic revival through implementation of India-ASEAN Free Trade areas in services and investment and strategic co-operation to fight terrorism, freedom of navigation, maritime security and defence co-operation. Modi also gave importance to soft powers such as Buddhism, tourism, people-to-people contacts and cultural and historical ties with this region.

(x) Neighbourhood Concern is a Priority in Modi's Foreign Policy

One of the major policy initiatives taken by Modi Government was its focus on its immediate neighbours in South Asia. Even before becoming the Prime Minister, Modi pointed out that his foreign policy would actively focus on improving ties with immediate neighbours, being termed as neighbourhood first policy. As noted above, he invited all Heads of States of SAARC countries and Mauritius in his oath-taking ceremony and on his second day in Office, he held bilateral talks with all heads of South Asian countries. His first foreign visit was to Bhutan. Modi held multilateral talks with neighbours during the SAARC Summit on November 26-27 2014 at Kathmandu in Nepal. Except with Pakistan, relations with all SAARC countries improved in this period. During the UPA rule (2004-2014), India's neighbourhood relations were very poor and China occupied its role in the region in that period. Unfortunately, due to the policy lapses of the UPA rule, China dominated the entire South Asia, not only economically and militarily but also strategically. But Modi succeeded in improving the relations with all of India's neighbours except Pakistan. Confidence-building measures of Modi succeeded in this region. For example, Bhutan stood with India during the Doklam standoff with China. On the Eastern border, India and Myanmar are the leading members of the BIMSTEC—Bay of Bengal Initiative for Multi-Sectoral Technical and Economic Co-Operation (Bangladesh, India, Myanmar, Sri Lanka, Thailand, Nepal and Bhutan) and the Mekong-Ganga Co-operation. On 4th June 2015, Naga terrorists killed 18 Indian soldiers. On 10th June, India conducted surgical strikes against insurgent camps along the India-Myanmar border and inflicted significant casualties. This military strike was endorsed by Myanmar Government. This was the first cross-border military intervention by India in the Eastern border after the Bangladesh War in 1971. Also, it is a fact that India-Bangladesh relations have been on an upward trajectory in the last five years under Modi.

Though China made inroads in Sri Lanka, India-Sri Lanka relations improved under Modi government. Modi visited Sri Lanka in 2015 and it should be noted that after a gap of 28 years, an Indian Prime Minister visited Sri Lanka. He was also the first Indian Prime Minister to reach out to 30,000 Indian Tamils in the central tea plantations. Later, he visited Sri Lanka for the second time in May 2017 to attend the International Day of Vesak celebrations in Sri Lanka.

India's relation with Nepal and Maldives also improved under Modi government. During the UPA rule, except Bhutan and Afghanistan, relations with all other SAARC countries worsened. But to an extent, Modi succeeded in improving relations with SAARC neighbours. Since Pakistan is continuing as the epicentre of terrorist groups and because of its failure to control cross-border terrorism towards India, there are limitations in the improvement of bi-lateral relations. The Indian surgical strikes in 2016 and Air strikes in February 2019 in Pakistan show that the hostility between the two countries will not end in near future.

(xi) Indo-US Relations Developed into a Global Strategic Partnership

The relationship between India and the USA, the two great democracies in the world flourished well under Prime Minister Modi. American President Obama congratulated Narendra Modi immediately after the elections in 2014 and invited Prime Minister Modi to USA. US Secretary of State John Kerry visited New Delhi on 1st August 2014 to prepare the grounds of Modi's first ever US visit as Prime Minister. He visited US from 27th to 30th September, 2014, beginning with his first address in the UN General Assembly followed by attending public reception by Indian American Community in Network's Madison Square Garden before the bilateral meeting with President Obama. This was followed by President Obama's visit to India and he became the first US President to grace Republic Day Celebrations as Chief Guest on 26 January 2015.

After President Donald Trump assumed power in USA, the bilateral relations improved much. Emergence of China and its imperialistic ambitions necessitated new strategic relation with USA. But the priorities were economic growth and meeting energy needs. At the same time India never compromised in WTO Trade Facilitation Agreement. In WTO, India asserted its plight of food security. The USA was also compelled to accept the Indian Stand. In 2016, India and United States signed the Logistic Exchange Memorandum of agreement and India was declared as a Major Defence Partner of the US. In 2018, India and US singed the long-pending COMCASA (Communications Compatibility and Security Agreement), agreement that would open the way for sales of more sensitive US military equipment to India.

India's strategic partnership with USA and its emergence as a leading global power was on display during other high-level gatherings in 2018 including two meetings of the Quadrilateral Partners (Australia, India, Japan and USA) and at the India-Japan-US trilateral meeting at the G-20 Summit in November 2018. In short, Narendra Modi opened a new era of friendship and co-operation with USA and gave more thrust to strategic partnership. It is to be noted that Modi succeeded in improving the relations with USA without affecting the warm relationship of India with Russia.

(xii) Narendra Modi's Multi-lateral Engagements Set a New Positive Record
Within six months after assuming office of the Prime Minister, Narendra Modi participated in five major multi-lateral engagement including summits like BRICS, ASEAN, East-Asian summit, SAARC, G-20 and UN General Assembly. In all these summits, he has been well received and also got elevated to the status of a World leader. Modi proposed the idea of International Day of Yoga in his first speech at the UN General Assembly on 27th September 2014. Later on 11th December 2014, the General Assembly unanimously endorsed the declaration of International Yoga Day and also accepted the 21st June as the date proposed by Prime Minister Modi. His all multi-lateral summits like G-20, WTO, UNO, ASEAN, BRICS, APEC, Commonwealth of Nations, Shanghai Co-operation Organization, Indian Ocean Rim Association, IBSA Dialogue Forum, Mekong-Ganga Co-operation, BIMSTEC etc. Modi emerged into a great Statesman. It was a fact that at the G-20 summit at Brisbane in Australia in 2014, Modi emerged as the tallest world leader. Commenting on Modi's popularity in Brisbane, the *Guardian* called Modi as the "G-20's Political Rock Star." The issue of black or unaccounted money kept in tax heavens (countries that allow foreigners to dump huge unaccounted money) abroad was also raised by Modi and was endorsed by G-20.

As the Prime Minister of India and as a Statesman, Narendra Modi's made remarkable contributions in reshaping India's foreign policy objectives. His foreign visits were highly required for India to make its presence felt as an emerging economic power in the international system. Pakistan's approach to cross-border terrorism was the major block to improve relations with that country. India's relations with China have shown much improvement. India decided not to be a part of 'One Belt One Road' project of China, because China-Pakistan Economic Corridor passes through Pak-Occupied Kashmir. Modi's contribution to improve the relation with Russia has been well received by that country and in April 2019,

Russia conferred its highest state honour to Narendra Modi. At the same time, relations with Islamic World also improved much for the first time in spite of Pakistan's objections. India was invited to OIC meeting in February 2019. Saudi Arabia, Afghanistan, UAE, Palestine etc. awarded their highest Civil honors to Narendra Modi. India's engagement with East Asian Nations, South America and European Union also improved much.

Conclusion

Modi Doctrine basically rejected the idealist dreams of Nehruvian foreign policy. Though he rejected ideology, he was full of pragmatic ideas. Prime Minister Modi highlighted the Indian values in international politics. He projected "Vasudhaiva Kutumbakam" in the BRICS summit in Brazil. As noted above, Modi succeeded in the declarations of International Yoga Day and now yoga has been well received by the world community, especially by more than 180 nations. At the UN speech, he stood for "G All" instead of varying global groupings. During his Japan visit, he projected the idea of "Vikasvad" i.e. development and rejected "Vistarvad" (Chinese ambitions in the region). At the East Asia summit, he demanded for new maritime norms to constrain China's claim in South China Sea. Also in G-20 summit in Australia, he sought the help of member states in getting black money information regarding money transfer. It is a fact that Narendra Modi's foreign policy appears geared to re-invent India as a more competitive, confident and secure country (*The Hindu*, 4 December 2014). It is the result of a strong domestic policy and concerned with national interest. As a realist, the focus is on economic development, but the final goal is a developed peaceful world. India stands for peace but does not reject the role of strength for maintaining that peace. As pointed out above, Narendra Modi followed the legacy of Prime Minister Vajpayee with a new vigour and dynamism and definitely discarding the Nehruvian foreign policy model. Since a portion of Indian land has been occupied by China and Pakistan, the diplomatic channels had their own limitations. It seems that Narendra Modi is not ready to compromise on border issues and also cross-border terrorism. Doklam and surgical strikes were warning signals to hostile neighbours. It is an accepted fact that under Narendra Modi there is a decisive shift in India's foreign policy. India has been elevated to the position of a global leader and now it has a definite role to define the priorities in the international system.

REFERENCES

Anirban Ganguly (ed), 'The Modi Doctrine: New paradigms in India's Foreign Policy ', Wisdom Tree, New Delhi, 2017.

Aparna Pande, 'From Chanakya to Modi', Harpercollins, 1st Edition – 2017.
M.K. Singh, 'Secrets of Modi's Foreign Policy', Surendra Publications, New Delhi, 2016.
Reeta Choudhari Tremblay, Asok Kapur, 'Modi's Foreign Policy', Sage Publications, New Delhi – 2017.
Siva Sankar Menon, 'Choices: Inside the making of Indi's Foreign Policy', Penguin, 2018.
Sreeram Chauria, 'Modi Doctrine: The Foreign Policy of India's Prime Minister', Bloomsbury, 2016.
Sunderpal Singh (ed), 'Modi World, Reconstructing Indian Foreign Policy', World Scientific Publishing Co.
The Times of India, 1st June, 2015.
The Hindu, 17th November, 2018.
Indian Express, 23rd February, 2019.
The Diplomat, 17th November, 2014.
Indian Today, 12th July, 2015.
The Economic Times, 15th November, 2014.
The Pioneer, 19th August, 2014.
Hindustan Times, 17th July, 2018.

12

India's Soft Power Approaches in Southeast Asia:
Challenges and Expectations

Koushiki Dasgupta

The question of soft power is one of the reinvented issues rising into the foreign policy debates in India. Traditionally power in global politics has always been focused in terms of military politics or economic strategies, but the idea of soft power has evolved as one of the most visible components of foreign policy strategy of many nations including India.

The concept was originally given by Joseph S Nye Jr and it was used to describe the potentials of American influence beyond the spell of its military and allied dominance. Nye's idea of soft power could be traced from his major works like, Bound to Lead (1990), The Paradox of American Power (2002), Soft Power (2004), Power in Global Information Age (2004) and the Future of Power (2011). According to him power could be executed either by coercion (sticks), inducement (carrots) or by attraction (soft power). If one is able to attract others, he can economies on the sticks and the carrots. Therefore, soft power is 'the ability to get preferred outcomes through the cooperative means of agenda setting, persuasion and attraction.[1]

A variety of agents like the NGOs, cooperative institutions, transnational and individual actors could become useful in creating the atmosphere of trust and credibility. However, the agents need to show some special attribute to attract others. Benignity, competence, and beauty are the three pillars of soft power capabilities and in case of the states; the choice of agents is itself very much important.[2]

Culture, political values and foreign policies are thee sources of soft power, however, all have their own limitations. While his initial thesis on soft power was published in 1990, later Nye brought a series of schemes which might be worth mentioning in case of India.[3]

Nature and modalities of soft power in India might be discussed under the following heads: (i) Soft Power is Cultural Power; (ii) Economic Strength is Soft Power; (iii) 'Soft Power is more humane than hard Power; (iv) Hard Power Can be measured, and Soft Power Cannot; (v) Soft Power is difficult to use; and (vi) Soft Power is irrelevant to the current terrorist threat.[4]

Whatever the modern propositions of soft power, the concept is not new in India. As are as South and South East Asia is concerned, since ancient times Hinduism touched all parts of the region except a few places. Interestingly the influence of Indic civilization of these parts of the region was not conditioned by dominance, coercion or violence rather the Indian priestly class, the navigators and the merchants introduced India to this region in forms of religion, culture, art, architecture script and others. It was the instance of India's natural spread of soft power over this region. It included giving attention and active support to the aspects of Indian society and culture that the world would find attractive. Definitely the advent of Islam in northern India and the subsequent era of cultural stagnation had left some depressing impact on the execution of soft power, south Indian rulers did not misuse the time and kept on exporting Indianans to the region. But in modern period, particularly the transitions of international politics changed and snapped the cultural linkages between India and Southeast Asia. In post-cold war period India took a serious note on the Look East policy and turned towards her southeast Asian neighbors but her fundamental interests on economic imperatives somehow cornered India's soft power approach in this region. However, no one can ignore the fact that soft power could have been useful only when backed by hard power strategies and in post 1990s decade expectations began to rise on the ground of India's growing economy and lucrative markets. New developments were adopted in the Look East policy, however these were far less than the actual prerequisite for soft power strategies specially when China has already grown as a leader in soft power mechanisms in that region. China's involvement into the regional affairs of the SAARC as well its growing soft power foreign policy bought some moments of discomfort too. It is to be mentioned here that Chinese soft power had been functioning under the purview of the state and it was backed by the economic achievements of Chain, while India's soft power was mostly steered up by its cultural and cultural agencies.[5]

India's soft power was looking more defensive without having any seeds of progressive transformations. It is not the case that India was not aware of China's trading and economic dominance over south and south east Asian region and India also took several steps on number of matters like bilateral trade, financial assistance, abolition of terrorism between the South Asian regional states but in a broader South Asian context such steps were not enough to meet the needs. One question remains pertinent here. In the Indian case what should be the actual relation between hard power and soft power? Does India needs both the power simultaneously to attain the status of a big power, do the one partly cover the other in certain situations? How the rise of liberal economic growth after 1990s in India complemented India's budding needs of soft power mechanisms? Discussing on the relationship between soft power and hard power considerations, former Union Minister of State of External Affair Shashi Tharoor argued that, 'soft power is one arrow in a nations security quiver, it is not an all-purpose panacea. And we have to accept that those who have suggested that our sot power can solve all our security challenges are wrong. When we seek of leveraging our soft power, we must ensure that we do enough to keep our people healthy, well-fed and secured not just form jihadi terrorism but the daily terror of poverty, hunger and ill health. At the same time it is not enough just to take care of basic needs. We have to preserve the precious pluralism that is such a civilizational asset. Our democracy, thriving free media, contentious NGOs, energetic human rights groups, and the repeated spectacle of our remarkable general elections—all these have made India a rare example of the successful management of diversity in the developing world'.[6]

According to him it has already become a belief that India had tried to concentrate more on soft power to get a majority status in her sphere of influence. In case of military strength and economic dominance India was lagging behind her nearest competitors like China in a case but India has the potential to tell the 'better story' in the language of Bollywood films, yoga, ayurveda, social diversity and a tradition of liberal thinking through the ages. "...India must remain the land of the better story.... India has an extraordinary ability to tell stories that are more persuasive and more attractive than those of its rivals Now this is not about propaganda. Indeed it will not work if it is directed from above, least of all by the government but its impact, through intangible, is enormous."[7]

No doubt, the task of telling the 'better story' could not be completed out of the preview of the government. The government must have a clear view on what to tell and how. The mechanisms and resources of soft power cannot be measured in a way hard powers are measured. For example no one can compare how India and China represented their civilizational values in the world and in the South East Asian region. To what extent it is possible to measure the influence on Indian culture and values on a country and if any, how the concerned country had executed its adherence and love for India on foreign policy mechanisms. No doubt such a measurement is tough to define but a basic outline of soft power qualities could be drawn to make India more familiar and appealing to others.

In post-1990s decade the government of India took major steps in this regard, particularly in 2007 the India-ASEAN Students Exchange programmes were introduced to build mutual understanding between the two regions covering all aspects of history, culture, economy, politics and other. It became a window of the Southeast Asian students to know India better and such visits no doubt strengthened the bonds of trust and accountability. Apart from this, in the ASEAN-India Commonwealth Summit held in December 2012, two events were organized in this respect. The Shipping Expedition of INS Sudarshini to ASEAN countries and the ASEAN India Car Rally. The shipping expedition was carried through the ancient trade route along the monsoon winds and spotted India's old and new maritime linkages with South East Asia. It also acknowledged the inter-linkages between the two regions in terms of trade, culture and intellectualism.

The ASEAN-India Car Rally was started from Yogyakarta, Indonesia and traversed through 8 of the 10 ASEAN nations and came to an end at New Delhi. The Car Rally was organised to show India's proximity to the ASEAN. It also wanted to promote tourism and public awareness on both o the regions. On June 21, 2013, the ASEAN-India Centre (AIC) was inaugurated. The Centre was envisaged in the ASEAN-India Vision Statement, adopted at the ASEAN-India Commemorative Summit on December 20, 2012 and the Government of India took multiple steps towards linking Indian higher education institutions with the ASEAN higher education system. Research initiatives were taken in the area o in biotechnology, information technology and bio medics as well as exchange of scholars and students in social sciences and economics. In this regard the Indian Council for Cultural Relations (ICCR) done well too. It has marked a print on Indian soft power in nurturing mutual understanding on the ethos of culture. But in an overall analysis it has become prominent that India exhibited limited success in projecting its soft power when comparing it with China. If the economists talked about the strategic failure of India in projecting its cultural capabilities along security lines, others hold the view that India has not yet resolved its national identity questions and hence failed to show its soft power resources on virtue of her national identity. Critics may well acquainted of the limitations of India's hard power strategies as a cause of her lack of enthusiasm in soft power approaches, no one can ignore that India is lagging behind far from China in using her democratic strengths as the most potential sot power recourse. Even though there seems to be little room for expectations on India's success in Southeast Asia, it remains a truth that if soft power is the ability of a nation to structure a situation so that other nations develop preferences or define their interests in ways consistent with one's nation, India had been successful and could score more success again. The tradition of India's public democracy, pluralism all had created a space for others living peacefully and in this respect India's slow but steady steps towards Southeast Asian region would not pose a cultural treat to others and it would not go or any civilizational clash with China in respect of soft power.

In recent times Prime Minister Narendra Modi put forward a comprehensive network of foreign policies and the basic mode of principles were reflected already in his party's election manifesto in 2014. One of the most striking features of his new policy was to build-up regional forums and how India could be linked up with it. The BJP adopted more or less similar agendas even in its last election manifesto, but in that case specific policies were highlighted in case of selected countries. In the new policy framework, Prime Minister Modi has elaborately stressed on a numbers of points like development of interlocking relationship on the basis of India's national interest; taking up uniform judgments on the internal issues lie terrorism and global warming; strengthing of regional forums like SAARC and ASEAN and to make ways of interactive dialogues between the global forums like BRICS, G20, SCO or others. Infact India's new soft power strategies took up a balanced attitude towards the states in terms of her own interest and not for any big powers interest. Accordingly steps were taken in favour of putting together the soft power avenues into external affairs through the selective modes of spiritual, cultural and philosophical magnitudes. Soft power is inherent in the history, culture and polices of a country and regional organisation could best be evolved as a source of consolidating the soft power by providing assistance to the states which are eager to make them attractive.

India's new foreign policy evolved as a proactive foreign policy which tried to drive events as opposed to just reacting to them and started looking more active rather than being neutral only. It seems to handle multiple relations at one time and keen to leave an impact on the world. This new policy is opposed to the stand of taking a lower profile and maintaining a balanced and indirect approach.

The new foreign policy under Narendra Modi picked up soft power as one of the prime components of foreign policy building as seen in case of the celebration of World Yoga Day and promotion of India's culture and heritage worldwide. Already the Indian film industry had evolved as the largest and arrest reaching medium of Indian culture and Indian soap operas have reached a growing global audience that has become increasingly familiar with Indian society and culture. Other than the electronic medium, Indian spices, cuisine and cricket diplomacy also came out as the mediums of soft power. But it's a question that how these elements of India's soft power could best be utilised to fulfil its foreign policy objectives in the coming decades in Southeast Asian region because references to Indian culture, to its Diaspora, to its socio-political values and to its economic development have been used as the rhetoric for image-polishing since a last few decades.

During the Prime Ministership of Narendra Modi, expectations of change stared gathering momentum over a few subjects. One such subject of soft power is eventually Buddhism. It must not be viewed as the new wine in an old bottle rather a definite shift in India's Look East policy is going on with an extra emphasis on what is called Buddha diplomacy. Commenting on P.M. Modi's three day visit to China in May 2015, South China Morning Post expressed, ' Buddhism and Yoga will form part of Indian Prime Minister Narendra Modi's soft power diplomacy as he visits China...and tries to increase his nations influence on the world's second largest economy. With a vast population o Buddhists in east and Southeast Asia, India is seeking help or the revival of Buddhist sites and is also helping to revive ancient temples in South and Southeast Asia including the Angkor Vat and Ta Prohm temples in Siem Reap in Cambodia, Vat Phou temple in Laos, Ananda temple in Myanmar and others. India has a plan to rope in the Mahayana Buddhists from China, South Korea, Japan, Taiwan, Singapore and Vietnam; Theravada Buddhists from Cambodia, Thailand, Laos, Myanmar and others. Buddha diplomacy thus, has emerged as a tool of soft power of India in South and Southeast Asian region.[8]

In order to espouse a strong networks of cultural connectivity with the region India established a separate Mission to ASEAN in April 2015 and India and ASEAN observed silver jubilee of their Dialogue Partnership, fifteen years of Summit Level interaction and five years of Strategic Partnership throughout 2017. Series of activities were promoted throughout the years and ultimately one ASEAN-India Commemorative Summit was held on the theme "Shared Values, Common Destiny" in 2018 at New Delhi. The official records on the commemorative activities have highlighted the following: (i) an ASEAN-India Regional Diaspora

Summit, (ii) a Youth Summit, (iii) a Music Festival, (iv) a Workshop on Blue Economy, (v) a Connectivity Summit, (vi) a Dharma-Dhamma Conference, (vii) a Hackathon and Startup Festival, (viii) a Global SME Summit, (ix) a Business and Investment Meet and Expo, (x) a Textiles Event, (xi) an ICT Expo, (xii) a Business Council Meeting, (xiii) a Ramayana Festival, (xiv) a Film Festival, and (xv) the inauguration of an India-ASEAN Friendship Park at New Delhi. Side by side the ASEAN-India Commemorative Summit had shown its strong commitments for the cause of mutual cooperation in the Maritime Domain. All these initiatives should be viewed as part of the friendship so far has been blossomed on grounds of mutual respect and strategic partnership. [9]

Approaches leading to cultural exchanges between these two regions are meant to be working in factor of a people to people contact. It covered the initiatives of inviting ASEAN students to India each year under Students Exchange Programme, special training course for ASEAN diplomats, exchange of parliamentarians, participation of ASEAN students in the National Children's Science Congress, ASEAN-India Network of Think Tanks, ASEAN-India Eminent Persons Lecture Series and others. These knowledge exchange projects were supported by diplomatic gestures by both of the regions simultaneously. For instance leaders of ASEAN countries were invited to grace the 69th Republic Day Parade as India's Guest of Honor and the second edition of the ASEAN-India Workshop on Blue Economy was jointly hosted with the Socialist Republic of Viet Nam in 2018 at New Delhi. Soft power when interpreted in terms of a cultural influence, if not hegemony, by one region to the other, should keep a tract on the projects aiming at India-ASEAN integration through CLMV (Cambodia Laos Myanmar and Vietnam) countries. It included training of English language for law enforcement officers and training of professionals dealing with capital markets in CLMV by National Institute of Securities Management Mumbai, scholarships for ASEAN students for higher education at Nalanda University, training of ASEAN Civil Servants in drought management, disaster risk management, sustainable ground water management etc.[10]

One should not become over apprehensive on these soft power visions of the Narendra Modi government in last five years. He/she should rather be far more engaging in the debates of how soft power has emerged to be an active element of Indian foreign policy so far.. India has already understood the realities of soft power dimensions in the Southeast Asian region that cultural exchange programme would bring out the best possible results only if India wins over the issues of economic despondency internally and externally as long as she aspires to continue her partnership with the ASEAN in a fruitful manner.

NOTES

1. Joseph S. Nye, Jr. The Future of Power. New York: Public Affairs 2011, p. 16.
2. Ibid
3. Joseph Nye, 'Soft Power', Foreign Policy, No. 80, Twentieth Anniversary (Autumn, 1990), pp.153-171.
4. Joseph Nye, 'Think Again: Soft Power', Yale Global Online, foreignpolicy.com/2006/02/23/think-again-soft-power. Last downloaded on 25 April, 2015.
5. Suzuki, Shogo, ed. The Myth and Reality of China's Soft Power. Edited by Inderjeet Parmar and Michael Cox, Soft Power and US Foreign Policy: Theoretical, Historical and Contemporary Perspectives London: Routledge, 2010, pp. 200-201.
6. Shashi Tharoor, 'India as a Soft Power', India International Centre Quarterly Weekly, Vol. 38, No.3/4: The Golden Thread; Essays in Honour of C.D Deshmukh, Winter 2011-Spring 2012, pp. 330-343.
7. Ibid.
8. www.globalresearch.ca/india-and-eas-asia by Ashok Sharma, Global Research, November 5, 2014.
9. For details see, https://mea.gov.in/aseanindia/20-years.htm, retrieved on 9 May 2019
10. Ibid.

REFERENCES

Garver, John W., ed. China's Influence in Central and South Asia: Is It Increasing? Edited by David Shambaugh, Power Shift: China and Asia's New DynamicsBerkeley: University of California Press, 2005

Joseph S. Nye, Jr. Bound to Lead. New York: Basic Books, 1990. Joseph S. Nye, Jr. The Paradox of American Power. New York: Oxford University Press, 2002.

Joseph S. Nye, Jr. Soft Power—the Means to Success in World Politics. New York: Public Affairs, 2004.

Joseph S. Nye, Jr. Power in a Global Information Age. London: Routledge, 2004.

Joseph S. Nye, Jr. The Future of Power. New York: Public Affairs 2011.

Raghavan, V. R. "Soft Power in the Asia-Pacific." In After the Unipolar Moment: Asiaand Regional Global Order. Singapore: IISS London and The Stanley Foundation US, 31 May 2007.

Suzuki, Shogo, ed. The Myth and Reality of China's Soft Power. Edited by Inderjeet Parmar and Michael Cox, Soft Power and US Foreign Policy: Theoretical, Historical and Contemporary Perspectives London: Routledge, 2010.

Wagner, Christian. "India's Soft Power: Prospects and Limitations." India Quarterly: A Journal of International Affairs 66, No. 4 (2010).

13

Strategic Convergence in Indo-Japan Relations:
Emerging Trajectory in the 'Act East' Horizon

Mohor Chakraborty

The saga of Indo-Japan relations, firmly rooted in history and shared common values, has carved a niche in the domain of India's foreign policy in general and 'Act East' policy in particular. The significance of the deepening bilateral strategic ties may be viewed in the context of the emergence of the Indo-Pacific region as a theatre of competition and cooperation—the twin facets of a pulsating sinusoid in international relations. While the competitive dimension finds reflection in a host of issues like the volatility and militarisation of the South China Sea, claimed by Beijing as a "core interest" area in relation to sovereignty, territorial integrity and national security, Sino-Japan tensions in the East China Sea or the nuclear ambitions of North Korea, the cooperative trend is demonstrated in the increasing strategic concurrence of major regional players—both at the bilateral and multilateral planes—like India, Japan, Vietnam and Australia, in consonance with the United States' (US) National Security Strategy unveiled by the Donald Trump administration and revival of the Quadrilateral Alliance (QUAD 2.0), with impetus on the Indo-Pacific, to primarily balance Sino-centrism in the region. On a bilateral pedestal, the burgeoning strategic cooperation between India and Japan assumes a pride of place, with the Indian Prime Minister, Narendra Modi exhorting Tokyo's 'Look at India' policy (Prime Minister, Narendra Modi's Remarks at the Indian Community Reception 2014)—a much-deserved 'quid pro quo' for New Delhi's 'Look East' and 'Act East' outlook. The burgeoning importance of the bilateral ties was aptly envisioned in the 'Vision Statement' released in course of the India-Japan Annual Summit in October 2018—an annual pedestal of interaction and deliberations between the two Prime Ministers—which not only acknowledged the transformation of relations "into a partnership with great substance and purpose", put forth as a "corner stone of India's Act East Policy", but also advanced the "new era in India-Japan relations" (Indo-Japan Joint Statement 2018) so as to further cooperate for peace, stability, inclusiveness and prosperity of Indo-Pacific.

The rationale guiding this evolving trajectory of Indo-Japan strategic collaboration was aptly highlighted by Kenji Hiramatsu, the Japanese Ambassador to India, when he elaborated almost two years ago:

> Japan and India have become true partners and that our relationship has entered a new stage. What is most important in our relationship is that we share strategic values and interests. We observe a shift in the global power balance and we are facing more complicated and globalized strategic situation especially in Asia. Japan needs a strategic partner for our deterrence and self-protection. ("Challenges and Prospects of Japan's Diplomacy—in the Context of India-Japan Relationship" 2016)

Extending this logic to the domain of the "multilateral", the crux of the matter was put across candidly by Admiral Harris Jr. (US Pacific Command) when he urged "like-minded" US partners, India, Japan and Australia to be "ambitious together" in providing a cooperative response to challenges to regional peace and security ("Let's Be Ambitious Together" 2016). The evolving strategic dynamics in the region attest to the inevitability of greater convergence among regional and extra-regional players, both on the bilateral and multilateral pedestal. In this backdrop, the National Democratic Alliance (NDA-II) government's impetus on Japan, within the broader framework of 'Act East', has emerged as a 'sine qua non' for responding to the evolving strategic paradigm in the Indo-Pacific region. Incidentally, Narendra Modi's selection of Japan as his first port of call (31 August – 3 September 2014) outside the immediate neighbourhood (South Asia) was not only concomitant with the strategic underpinnings of 'Act East', but also reflected "the high priority that Japan receives in our foreign and economic policies" and "Japan's paramount importance in my vision for development and prosperity in India and in peace, stability and prosperity in Asia at large" (Prime Minister of India's Departure Statement Ahead of his Visit to Japan 2014).

The Japanese Prime Minister, Shinzo Abe's reciprocation of this visit to India in December 2015, in a little more than a year's interval bears testimony to the increasing convergence of interests and mutual salience, anchored on India's 'Act East' Policy. Since then as noted above, the Prime Ministerial meetings have continued, with Modi and Abe making it an annual exercise. Given this premise, the chapter will highlight and analyse the following:

- The rationale guiding India's enhanced focus on Japan;
- Impulses conditioning this focus; and
- The dynamics of strategic cooperation and challenges on the pathway.

Contours of Indo-Japan Strategic Convergence: A Major Pillar of 'Act East'

The principal logic guiding the NDA-II administration's strategic focus on Japan within the 'Act East' domain is to balance China's assertive ascendance in the Indo-Pacific region, referred to by Modi, in no uncertain terms, as an "expansionist" approach, "encroaching on the land and in the waters of other nations" (Prime Minister of India's Keynote Address at the Luncheon Hosted by Nippon Kiedanren 2014). The buttressing of Chinese territorial claims by building artificial islands, runways and radar facilities in the South China Sea and related activism pertaining to the militarization of the South and East China Seas, its recalcitrance vis-à-vis the Permanent Court of Arbitration's ruling on the South China Sea (July 2016), the declaration of an Air-Defence Identification Zone (ADIZ) extending towards the Senkaku Islands, new fishing rules implemented on the Hainan coast and the People's Liberation Army (PLA)-Navy's shadowing of passing vessels not only disrupt the pre-existing order in Asia, but also significantly raise the possibilities of a military confrontation (Panneerselvam 2016). Furthermore, China's fielding of a series of interrelated missile, sensor guidance and other technologies designed to challenge and deny freedom of movement to other powers in the Asia-Pacific region, known as the Anti-access, area denial (A2/AD) programme, has been expanding its military outreach. It is believed that, this A2/AD capability will eventually be highly effective in extending a zone of exclusion out to or beyond the "Second Island Chain"—a line that connects Japan, Guam and Papua New Guinea posing a major challenge to regional stability (Biddle and Oelrich 2016: 7).

Given the backdrop of regional vitiation, Japan's *"Discovery of India"*, implying the rediscovery of India as a partner armed with the ability—and the responsibility—to "nurture and enrich these seas (the Indian and Pacific Oceans) to become seas of clearest transparency", sharing with it the values and interests of working "to enrich the seas of freedom and prosperity, which will be open and transparent to all" (Speech by Shinzo Abe 2007) makes Indo-Japan strategic partnership "indispensable" for ensuring peace and prosperity in the interconnected Asia, Pacific and Indian Ocean regions. Furthermore, India-Japan Special Strategic and Global Partnership, firmly rooted in history and based on common values, is the mainspring for promoting and safeguarding shared strategic objectives.

Secondly, the rhetorical component of Abe's vision of "discovering" India as a partner armed with the ability and responsibility of safeguarding the waterways has been complemented with Credit Suisse's September 2015 Military Strength Indicator, which has placed Japan (military strength score 0.72) and India (0.69) as the fourth and fifth strongest military powers in the world, respectively, trailing US (0.94) and China (0.79) at the first and third positions, respectively ("The End of Globalization or a More Multipolar World?" 2015: 41). In 2018, India sustained its position, trailing US and China as well (2018 Military Ranking Strength 2018). Among the Indian Ocean navies, the Indian Navy is the largest, operating two carriers 'INS Viraat' and 'INS Vikramaditya', while the third carrier 'INS Vikrant' will be inducted in 2020. The Indian Navy also has plans to build another aircraft carrier which may be nuclear propelled, upping the ante for the Navy to evolve as a three-carrier force by 2030. Besides, India is the only country in the Indian Ocean which operates a nuclear submarine 'INS Chakra', in addition to the indigenous nuclear-powered submarine, 'INS Arihant' ready for operations, thereby providing the third leg of the nuclear triad (Sakhuja 2016: 60-62). The Indian Navy has set the target of having 212 ships in its fleet by 2027. In 2018, the Government of India approved the indigenous manufacture of six new SSNs (nuclear attack submarines; Pubby, 2018: 3).

The growing prowess of the Indian Navy was demonstrated at the International Fleet Review held in Vishakhapatnam (4-8 February 2016), where Japan was represented by 'JS Matsuyuki'—a general purpose guided missile destroyer primarily in an Anti Submarine Warfare (ASW) role. In course of this grand show of naval power and sophistication, Narendra Modi acknowledged that the Indo-Pacific region remains the nation's priority, since it serves "as a strategic bridge with the nations in our immediate and extended maritime neighbourhood". Emphasizing the need for a "modern and multi-dimensional navy", Modi further asserted that India would continue to actively pursue and promote its geopolitical, strategic and economic interests on the seas, particularly in this region (United Through Oceans—International Fleet Review 2016: Introduction, 126). Therefore, the repertoire of India's steadily improving naval sinews serves as another important logic of its strategic convergence with Japan. The Indian Navy will be holding the next edition of IFR along with the navies of more than 46 nations, in February 2019.

Thirdly, to balance China's 21st-century Maritime Silk Road (MSR) project—the maritime component of China's ambitiously grand One Belt and One Road Initiative—complemented by its over-land counterpart, the Silk Road Economic Belt (SREB) envisioned to be established along the Eurasian land corridor from the Pacific coast to the Baltic Sea. The extensive domain of the "belt and road" architecture runs through the continents of Asia, Europe and Africa, connecting the vibrant East Asian economic circle at one end and the developed European economic circle at the other. While the SREB focuses on bringing together China, Central Asia, Russia and Europe (the Baltic), linking China with the Persian Gulf and the Mediterranean Sea through Central Asia and West Asia and connecting China with Southeast Asia, South Asia and the Indian Ocean, the MSR is designed to take off from China's coast to Europe through the South China Sea and the Indian Ocean in one route, and from China's coast through the South China Sea to the South Pacific in the other. The initiative poses a direct challenge to India's stature as a 'security provider' in the Indian Ocean, particularly with China's aim of making a "benevolent entry" through its spree of building infrastructure, ports, deep water ports and container terminals, which it hopes to connect with the mainland through a string of road and railway corridors, logistical stations, storage facilities and free-trade zones in India's "primary area of interest." Although the Chinese posture has been intent on allaying India's concerns with respect to the massive outreach and implications of MSR, calling upon its neighbour to join the effort with a "friendly, open, cooperative attitude", New Delhi has naturally been cautious and calculative in making headway on the issue. In response, the maritime guidance document, christened *Ensuring Secure Seas: Indian Maritime Security Strategy (IMSS-2015)* in October 2015, in order to bolster the Navy's operational sphere and influence in the Indian Ocean Region (IOR), justifies the significance of the Indian Navy as the primary instrument to secure the oceanic neighbourhood for economic purposes, given India's centrality in the IOR. Towards this end, the IMSS-2015 has recommended a four-pronged approach for the Indian Navy under the present and emerging circumstances: first, it has advocated steady increase in the Indian Navy's operational footprints across its areas of maritime interest, with a growing cooperative framework and contributions as a 'net security provider' in the neighbourhood, as maintaining the state of actual security available in an area, upon balancing prevailing threats, inherent risks and rising challenges in the maritime environment, against the ability to monitor, contain and counter all of these, including deployments for anti-piracy, maritime security, Non-combatant Evacuation Operations (NEO) and Humanitarian Assistance and Disaster Relief (HADR) operations; secondly, an expansion in maritime operational engagements, with increased number and complexity of exercises with foreign navies, coordinated mechanisms for maritime security operations, and enhanced training, technical and hydrographic cooperation with friendly maritime forces; thirdly, continued development of regional cooperative approaches for enhancing maritime security in the IOR, including operational interactions such as 'MILAN', Indian Ocean Naval Symposium (IONS) and emergence of maritime security cooperation as a priority area for the Indian Ocean Regional Association (IORA); and fourthly, the growth and development of the Indian Navy's force levels and maritime capabilities, with steady focus on indigenization (Ensuring Secure Seas: Indian Maritime Security Strategy 2015: 11-12). In keeping with this new maritime vision, India's burgeoning collaboration with Japan may be viewed from its perspective of expanding its web of alliances vis-à-vis China. This should be read in the context of the Indian Defence Minister, Manohar Parrikar's visit to Japan in March 2015, when he sought enhanced cooperation with India in the defence and security sector including maritime security and even called for exploring the possibility of conducting joint air exercises, representing a more active and assertive posture. Furthermore, the importance that Japan attaches to defence ties with India was attested to by the Japanese Ambassador to India, Takeshi Yagi's acknowledgement that the addition of two more defence attaches—one each from the Air Force and Coast Guard to the Embassy in 2015—has catapulted India within the elite club of only four other countries to which Japan sends its defence attaches from the three services and the Coast Guard (Economic Times 2015: 3).

Fourthly, India's rationale of greater strategic coordination with Japan received impetus with the Obama Doctrine (Pivot to Asia Policy), and the successive administration's focus on Indo-Pacific as part of the National Security Strategy, which identified India and Japan as solid pillars of its strategic pivot in the Indo-Pacific, while trying to undertake more concrete and decisive efforts at "constraining" China by a burgeoning counter-alliance. As part of its anti-China "pivot," Washington has been pushing for increased cooperation with India and Japan, as the Trilateral Dialogue (2015), the subsequent induction of Japan as a permanent participant in the 'Malabar' exercises and revival of QUAD 2.0 indicate. This collaboration is in addition to the Japan-India Maritime Exercise (JIMEX) held annually between the two countries since January 2012.

Fifthly, the Government of India's 'Make in India' initiative, particularly its defence manufacturing component, has opened greater avenues of collaboration between India and Japan with respect to joint development and production of defence equipment. The 'Make in India' dream project provides Japan investment opportunities in sectors like defence products manufacturing, supply chain sourcing and defence offsets—legal trade practices in the aerospace and military industries and arrangements in which the seller of a defence product or service agrees to buy products or services from its client as an inducement. The offsets policy was made part of the Defence Procurement Procedure (DPP) in 2005 for the first time and has seen several changes since then (Defence Manufacturing— Make in India 2015). The amended DPP announced in March 2016 was aimed at boosting the 'Make in India' policy, besides creation of major domestic defence industry to cater to its own needs as well as exports. New Delhi's decision to allow defence Foreign Direct Investment (FDI) up to 100% with a rider that the project should involve "modern technology" has enthused the Japanese defence industry with respect to its investment prospects, facilitated by Tokyo's relaxation of rules on export of defence equipment and technology (in April 2014), which hitherto concentrated exclusively on the domestic market in order to demonstrate its commitment to peace. With Japan's Shin Maywa Industries—manufacturer of US-2 search and rescue amphibious aircraft—betting big on the 'Make in India' plank, had offered to set up a plant in New Delhi (under the 30% offset clause) to cater to international demands (Economic Times 2016: 3). Over the last three years, several initiatives have been undertaken to promote greater participation and investment in the defence sector, facilitated by the revisions in the Defence Procurement Procedures, within the 'Make in India' framework, particularly with the introduction of Strategic Partnership Model, increase in FDI through automatic route to 49%, restricting licensing requirements for critical items, de-notifying several items previously produced only by Ordnance Factory Boards, etc.

Finally, as India strives to meet its escalating energy demands, the signing of a Memorandum of Understanding (MoU) on the Peaceful Use of Nuclear Energy in course of Japanese Premier, Shinzo Abe's visit to India in December 2015 has been a crucial development in this sphere. The India-Japan Agreement for Cooperation in the Peaceful Uses of Nuclear Energy entered into force on 20 July 2017, following its signature in November 2016, which not only reflected the depth of the bilateral strategic partnership, but also paved the way for enhanced cooperation in energy security and clean energy. The above-mentioned rationale has logically catapulted India and Japan as protagonists in their respective foreign policy domains, besides placing Japan at the heart of India's 'Act East' Policy.

Factors Responsible for Facilitating India's Japan Focus

The underlying rationale anchoring the evolving trajectory of Indo-Japan strategic ties offers credence to the transformation of India's policy from "looking" to "acting" East, and the course has been facilitated by the following initiatives and impulses.

First, demonstrating a marked departure from Japan's post-Second World War pacifism, on 18 September 2015, the Japanese Parliament (Diet) enacted two security laws, removing some of the key legal restrictions that the war-renouncing Constitution hitherto imposed on the Self-Defence Forces (SDF) during overseas missions, including the long-standing ban on collective self-defence enshrined in Article 9, and creating a new permanent law that allows Japan to deploy the SDF overseas for providing logistic support for United Nations-authorized military operations involving a foreign or multinational force. Under the new laws, Japan will theoretically be allowed to use collective self-defence to come to the aid of an ally under three conditions: if Japan's "survival" is at stake, there is no alternative, and the use of force is kept to the "minimum necessary" (Yoshida and Aoki 2015). Therefore, though the new security legislations are not country-specific, in the event of a regional conflict, India being Japan's "strategic partner" will certainly benefit from its provisions. Prime Minister Abe's success in passing these legislations amid large-scale resistance both within the Parliament and on the streets may be assessed in the wider ambit of its efforts to strengthen its role in the alliance with the United States, the surge of Chinese military muscles, made all the more volatile with Beijing's reclamation of land in contested areas in the South China Sea and the show of North Korean nuclear sinews in the Asia-Pacific region. Besides, Japan's decision to exercise the right of Collective Self-Defence, when 'people's right to life, liberty and the pursuit of happiness is fundamentally undermined', is a bold and commendable move as it will help arrest the rising anxieties in the region. Since both India and Japan depend on sea lanes of communication (SLOCs) for their trade and resource supplies through the Malacca Straits and the Indian Ocean, any impediment in the freedom of navigation by state or non-state actors may undermine their economic interests as maritime security is directly linked to economic security (Mishra and Khan 2015).

Secondly, Japan's new security legislations, in consonance with the "National

Defence Programme Guidelines for Financial Year/FY 2014 and Beyond", offer immense opportunities for realizing the optimum level of maritime strategic cooperation with India. While paving the way for the two countries to complement each other in the maritime security domain, the Guidelines recognize India's ascendance among the regional players, noting that "Japan will strengthen its relationship with India in a broad range of fields, including maritime security, through joint training and exercises as well as joint implementation of international peace cooperation activities" (National Defense Programme Guidelines for FY 2014 and Beyond, 2013: 2).

Thirdly, closely related to the first development, the Japanese Cabinet has approved a defence budget allocating 5.05 trillion Yen (US$ 42.1 billion) in December 2015 for FY 2016-2017 in the backdrop of the Japanese Self-Defence Force's preparation for assuming an expanded role and greater collaboration with other powers under the new security legislation. This may be viewed in conjunction with Japan's urge to steadily improve its defence capabilities during FY 2016, as the third fiscal year of this effort to develop a dynamic Joint Defence Force according to the National Defense Programme Guidelines (Medium Term Defense Programme for FY 2014-FY 2018, 2013: 1-2). The bolstering initiatives will focus on the enhancement of joint functions to seamlessly and dynamically fulfill its defence responsibilities including providing an effective deterrence and response to a variety of security situations, supporting stability in the Asia-Pacific Region. As the latest reports indicate, Japan's Defence Ministry looks towards US$ 65 billion for defence expenditure for the next fiscal year from April 2019, which happens to be the seventh straight annual increase and 2.1% more than 2018 (Straits Times 2018). Under the given circumstances, this escalated defence budget allocation would augur well for Japan's strategic cooperation and congruence with India and 'Make in India'.

Fourthly, within the scaffold of the 'Make in India' campaign, the Government of India, in its pursuit of attaining greater self-sufficiency in the realm of defence equipment, has prioritized military modernization, increasing stakes that foreign defence contractors were allowed to hold in joint defence ventures from 26% to 49%. Furthermore, India is expected to spend US$ 100 billion over the next decade on a defence upgrade programme, thus expanding the horizon of both indigenous initiative and foreign collaboration in this sphere. As a matter of fact, since during the period October 2014 to September 2015, the defence component of 'Make in India' received a lacklustre response of foreign investments (Rs. 56 lakh), New Delhi has announced encouraging changes in November 2015 in the sphere of attracting FDI in defence. Among these, the principal modifications include the option for investing in FDI up to 49% through automatic route and beyond 49% through the Foreign Investment Promotion Board (FIPB); allowing flexibility to vendors in offset contracts by amending offset policies (*Economic Times,* January 2016: 5), further supplemented by the introduction of some new rules in the Defence Procurement Procedure (DPP) in March 2016 by the Defence Ministry. The most important clauses of the revised DPP are the increase in the offset baseline from Rs 300 crore to Rs 2,000 crore; fast-track acquisitions by eliminating repetitive procedures; transparency; allowing procurements in case of single vendor situations with "proper justifications" etc. (Defence Procurement Procedure, 2016: 2-4). Furthermore, in DPP 2016, the Ministry of Defence has introduced a new category for acquisition—Indigenously Designed Developed and Manufactured (IDDM), which, along with the Buy and Make Indian categories will help global Original Equipment Manufacturers and Indian companies forge partnership for co-development and co-production (Basu 2016: 4). Incidentally, the DPP outlines are in sync with Japan's launching of the guidelines of the Ministry of Defence's Acquisition, Technology and Logistics Agency (ATLA) in October 2015, aimed at managing efficiently defence equipment acquisition, promoting defence equipment cooperation with its allies, and thus boosting Japan's involvement in international development programmes. The rationale of placing the growth of the Japanese defence industry at the core of the national defence strategy has not only been a valuable incentive to strengthen its industrial base, but also a key element in a new strategic approach to counter Beijing's regional influence by strategically coordinating with other countries (Japan Times 2015; Grevatt 2015). Furthermore, the latest Defence Production Policy 2018 of the Government of India attempts to further build on these initiatives and provide a focused, structured and significant thrust to development of defence design and production capabilities in the country. Its ambitious target of achieving a turnover of US$ 26 billion in defence goods and services by 2025 (Draft Defence Production Policy, 2018) is indeed an attractive proposition for emerging partners like Japan.

In addition, the inaugural India-Japan-US Foreign Ministerial level (trilateral) meeting on 29 September 2015 in New York has been a significant factor as well. Represented by the Indian Minister of External Affairs, Sushma Swaraj, Japan's Minister for Foreign Affairs, Fumio Kishida and the US Secretary of State, John Kerry, the three leaders, in course of this meeting, minced no words in articulating the increasing economic and strategic convergence in the "sea lanes of communication" in the lifeline of trade and commercial externalities. The Statement issued by the three Foreign Ministries at the conclusion of this meeting underscored "the importance of international law and peaceful settlement of disputes; freedom of navigation and over-flight; and unimpeded lawful commerce, including in the South China Sea" (George 2015: 10) and demonstrated their common stride against aggressive Chinese forays in the regional littorals. This may also be viewed in the context of India's moves towards attaining a more significant role in the Indo-Pacific region, with its potential of emerging as an "anchor of stability and security", thus providing ample opportunities for buttressing the dimensions of trilateral cooperation among India, Japan and US, as indicated by President Obama when he recently acknowledged:

> "We have elevated our trilateral cooperation with Japan. And we very much welcome India's increased ties with the region. It's clear that India can be an anchor of stability and security in the Asia Pacific and Indian Ocean region, and the United States looks forward to the work we can do together."

Furthermore, he expressed his resolve of expanding the scope of military exercises and maritime cooperation, such that the forces become interoperable in the region, where India's 'Act East' policy has demonstrated efforts at bolstering security partnerships (*Statesman*, 2016: 9). The above-mentioned Trilateral Dialogue was preceded by the inaugural Indo-Japan-Australia Trilateral Dialogue in June 2015 in New Delhi. In course of this dialogue, the three neighbours on the "same page" with regard to China's "aggressive bid" in the region expressed their collective willingness to play a greater role in Asia–Pacific maritime security matters, besides mulling the possibility of a joint naval exercise among the three nations (Pubby 2015: 5).

Also, in keeping with the decision embarked upon in the Trilateral meeting, Japan was inducted as a permanent member of the 'Malabar' Exercise in its 19th edition, held in the Bay of Bengal, during 14-19 October 2015. It may be recalled that 'Malabar', initiated as an India-US bilateral naval exercise in 1992, had been witness to Japan's participation as a non-permanent participant in 2007 and its subsequent editions in 2009, 2011 and 2014, much to China's chagrin. The discomfort index of China with respect to such joint naval maneuvers in the Indo-Pacific region, with India at the fulcrum, is definitely soaring. More recently, the 20th edition of the exercise, 'Ex Malabar-16' was conducted from 10 to 17 June 2016 in which the Japanese Maritime Self Defense Force was represented by the 'JS Hyuga' helicopter carrier, with SH 60 K integral helicopters and long-range maritime patrol aircraft, along with other assets. It demonstrated an impressive kaleidoscope of fleet strength, interoperability, coordination and development of common understanding of procedures for Maritime Security Operations among the Indian, Japanese and US Navies, through professional interactions in harbour, a diverse range of activities at sea, including complex surface, sub-surface and air operations. The exercise bore testimony to US' avowed policy of rebalance in the Asia-Pacific region, including (along with India's) sending out signals to China on issues of freedom of navigation in international waters, made all the more pertinent by Japan's aggressive voicing of its concerns about China's enlarging footprints in the South and East China Seas (Exercise Malabar 2016: Press Release).

Finally, the Japanese Premier, Shinzo Abe's visit to India (11-13 December 2015) demonstrated a new high in the strategic contours of bilateral cooperation. The highlights of this visit included the announcement of a series of military and defence-related agreements, in an endeavour to "transform the India-Japan Special Strategic and Global Partnership, a key relationship with the largest potential for growth, into a deep, broad-based and action-oriented partnership, which reflects a broad convergence of their long-term political, economic and strategic goals" (Joint Statement on India and Japan Vision 2025: Special Strategic and Global Partnership Working Together for Peace and Prosperity of the Indo-Pacific Region and the World 2015: Clause 2). It may be recalled that the establishment of the "Special Strategic and Global Partnership" has been preceded by the "Global Partnership between Japan and India" (August 2000), "Global and Strategic Partnership" (December 2006), further elevated to "Special Strategic and Global Partnership" in course of Narendra Modi's visit to Japan in September 2014. In course of Abe's visit, the two most significant agreements signed were the Agreement concerning the Transfer of the Defence Equipment and Technology, providing a framework to enhance defence and security cooperation by making available to each other, defence equipment and technology necessary to implement joint research, development and/or production projects or projects; and the Agreement concerning Security Measures for the Protection of Classified Military Information, which obligates both countries to protect classified military information exchanged, thereby facilitating more robust intelligence exchanges between their Forces (List of Documents Exchanged During the Visit of Prime Minister Shinzo Abe of Japan to India in New Delhi 2015). The unwavering commitment of Shinzo Abe and his Indian counterpart, Narendra Modi in realizing "a peaceful, open, equitable, stable and rule-based order in the Indo-Pacific region and beyond", while upholding "the principles of sovereignty and territorial integrity; peaceful settlement of disputes; democracy, human rights and the rule of law; open global trade regime; and freedom of navigation and over-flight", not only bolstered the foundation for their cooperation in working for "peace, security and development of the Indo-Pacific region" (Joint Statement on India and Japan Vision 2025: Clause 4) but also sent a clear message to China that its belligerent overtures in the regional waters would not go unchallenged. Towards this end, their mutual desire to further develop dialogue and exchanges in the security and defence fields, including through the full utilization of "2 plus 2" Dialogue, Defence Policy Dialogue, Military-to-Military Talks and Coast Guard–to–Coast Guard cooperation and the decision to inaugurate Air Force–to–Air Force staff Talks (Ibid., Clause 10) provided an architecture for advancing strategic cooperation between the two countries.

Challenges on the Trajectory: Way Ahead

The present trajectory of Indo-Japan strategic relations is not bereft of its challenges and the boulders on its path merit highlight and analysis. As of now, the US$ 1.3 billion Indo-Japan defence deal to procure 12 US-2i Shin Maywa amphibious search-and-rescue (SAR) aircrafts for the Indian Navy hit the roadblock over the pricing issue as the Indian Ministry of Defence found its hands tied with a narrow budget and senior officials of the Indian Navy are believed to have opposed to the deal. If implemented, the deal would be a part of Japan's first military equipment sale to India under the 'Make in India' initiative. The deal, talks for which have been going on since 2011, almost reached a conclusion when Narendra Modi visited Japan in 2014, and further strengthened with the Japanese Prime Minister's visit to India in December 2015. In course of Abe's visit, the 'Joint Statement on India and Japan Vision 2025' committed to deepening bilateral defence cooperation "including through two-way collaboration and technology cooperation, co-development and co-production", in addition to clearly expressing "their intention to explore potential future projects on defence equipment and technology cooperation such as US-2 amphibian aircraft" (Ibid., Clause 9). Besides the pricing issue, serious differences over the technological level that can account for surveillance and combat mission as well have mired the issue (Basu July 2016: 6). Furthermore, the deal was accorded minimum significance even during the meeting between the Defence Ministers (Parikkar and Gen. Nakatani) in New Delhi in July 2016. Evidently, Japan has been miffed about the delay in the aircraft deal since it was supposed to have opened up the defence market for commerce, facilitating its position as a leading defence exporter in Asia. As latest reports from the Defence Ministry suggest, India and Japan have moved closer toward concluding the first-ever bilateral defence deal, following agreement on price for the 12 SAR aircrafts. With Japan offering ShinMaywa US-2i amphibious aircrafts at a price concession of more than 10% per aircraft from $133 million per aircraft to around US$ 113 million, the deal is in the concluding stages of finalization. However, the deal is far from done yet, as the Japanese Ministry of Defence is intent on India establishing its procurement policy at the earliest, succeeding which Japan would flexibly respond to Indian requests for cooperation. Given its present status, though the agreement cannot be relegated to the graveyard, the existing challenges in finalising it do not augur well for the future of the 'Make in India' project.

Notwithstanding this major blemish in the visage of Indo-Japan strategic relations as discussed above, it is worth reckoning that the convergence of interests and opportunities to be explored far outweighs the challenge. In this context, the dovetailing of India's 'Act East' policy with Japan's "proactive contribution to peace", premised on the belief that as a "proactive contributor to peace", it needs to contribute more actively to the peace and stability of the region and the international community, while coordinating with other countries (Defense of Japan 2013), provides a plethora of opportunities for both the regional protagonists to coordinate towards facilitating and ensuring peace and stability of the Asia-Pacific region. Whether in supporting India's recent bid to a niche in the elite Nuclear Suppliers Group (NSG) or speaking in unison with New Delhi with respect to freedom of navigation and over-flight in the volatile South China Sea littorals, India and Japan have explicitly demonstrated their strategic alignment vis-à-vis China. For instance, Japan has been extremely forthcoming in garnering support for India's proposed membership from other members of the 48-member NSG, ahead of its crucial plenary meeting in Seoul in June 2016. Although China had maintained that the issue of the candidature of non-NPT signatories like India would be excluded from the Seoul agenda, Japan had not only led the way by first raising India's case at the plenary, but also "welcomed" its application, strongly recommending it to be considered (Hindustan Times 2016). Besides, vehemently criticising Beijing's rejection of the verdict of the Permanent Court of Arbitration (PCA) on the South China Sea (of July 2016), the Joint Statement released at the end of the Indo-Japanese Defence Ministerial Meeting on 14 July 2016 urged parties to "show utmost respect for the UNCLOS" (United Nations Convention on the Law of the Sea) by "ensuring freedom and safety of navigation and over-flight as well as unimpeded lawful commerce in international waters" and expressed "concern over recent developments" (referring to Chinese actions such as the landing of planes on artificial islands and the tirade against the tribunal judges; Joint Statement after the meeting Between Raksha Mantri and Japanese Defence Minister 2016: Clause 4). The Statement almost reiterated the concerns expressed in the Prime Ministerial Joint Statements issued during the exchange of their visits, wherein, noting the developments in the South China Sea, the two leaders "called upon all States to avoid unilateral actions that could lead to tensions in the region." The two leaders' vision for the Indo-Pacific is based on a rules-based order that respects sovereignty and territorial integrity of nations, ensures freedom of navigation and overflight as well as unimpeded lawful commerce, and seeks peaceful resolution of disputes with full respect for legal and diplomatic processes in accordance with the universally recognised principles of international law, including those reflected in the UNCLOS, without resorting to threat or use of force (Indo-Japan Joint Statement 2018).

Furthermore, they have expressed the view that "full and effective implementation of the 2002 Declaration on the Conduct of Parties in the South China Sea and early conclusion of the negotiations to establish a Code of Conduct in the South China Sea by consensus will contribute to peace and stability of the region" (Joint Statement on India and Japan Vision 2025: Clause 36). Finally, New Delhi has been riding the wave of Tokyo's enthusiasm in nurturing the flagship 'Make in India' campaign, acknowledging it as a "friend" that would matter the most in realizing India's economic and strategic dream. Within the broader pedestal of the 'Act East' policy, the synergistic trends between 'Make in India' and Japan's 'Partnership for Quality Infrastructure' (major component of Japan Revitalization Strategy) launched in May 2013 for promoting "quality infrastructure investment" in collaboration with other countries and international organizations (Announcement of "Partnership for Quality Infrastructure: Investment for Asia's Future" 2013) would also facilitate the development and strengthening of sustainable and resilient infrastructure, pivotal to augmenting mutual connectivity. The Japan-India partnership assumes a pride of place among the core relationships identified by Premier Abe in his "Diamond Concept" (*daiyamondo kousou*), where he envisioned that the United States, Japan, Australia, and India would form a virtual security "diamond" and work together to maintain the peace and stability of the Indo-Pacific region. Although challenges exist in the Indo-Japan strategic firmament, it is judicious on the part of both countries to exercise greater political will and diplomatic acumen in emphasising, sustaining and building on the expansive sea of opportunities.

REFERENCES

Prime Minister, Narendra Modi's Remarks at the Indian Community Reception, Tokyo (2 September 2014), http://www.narendramodi.in/pms-remarks-at-the-indian-community-reception-in-tokyo-6539 (accessed on 1 November 2018)

Indo-Japan Joint Statement (29 October 2018), Ministry of External Affairs, Government of India, https://www.mea.gov.in/outgoing-visit-detail.htm?30543/IndiaJapan+Vision+Statement (accessed on 28 November 2018)

"Challenges and Prospects of Japan's Diplomacy – in the Context of India-Japan Relationship", Japanese Ambassador to India, Kenji Hiramatsu's Address at Observer Research Foundation, New Delhi, (7 June 2016), http://www.in.emb-japan.go.jp/itpr_en/00_000057.html (accessed on 1 November 2018)

"Let's Be Ambitious Together", Raisina Dialogue Remarks by Admiral Harry B. Harris, Jr., New Delhi (2 March 2016), http://www.pacom.mil/Media/Speeches-Testimony/Article/683842/raisina-dialogue-remarks-lets-be-ambitious-together/ (accessed on 2 November 2018)

Prime Minister of India's Departure Statement ahead of his visit to Japan, New Delhi (29 August 2014), Press Information Bureau, Prime Minister's Office, Government of India, http://pib.nic.in/newsite/PrintRelease.aspx?relid=109178 (accessed on 2 November 2018)

Prime Minister of India's Keynote Address at the Luncheon Hosted by Nippon Kiedanren – Japanese Chamber of Commerce and Industry and the Japan-India Business Cooperation Committee, Tokyo (1 September 2014), narendramodi.in, http://www.narendramodi.in/pms-keynote-address-at-the-luncheon-hosted-by-nippon-kiedanren-the-japanese-chamber-of-commerce-and-industry-and-the-japan-india-business-cooperation-committee (accessed on 2 November 2018)

Panneerselvam, Prakash (August 2016), "Advancing India's relationship with Japan and South Korea: quest for Middle Power cooperation", Institute of Peace and Conflict Studies, Issue Brief No. 262, http://www.ipcs.org/issue-brief/india-the-world/advancing-india39s-relationship-with-japan-and-south-korea-quest-for-262.html (accessed on 2 November 2018)

Biddle, Stephen and Ivan Oelrich (Summer 2016), "Future warfare in the Western Pacific: Chinese antiaccess/area denial, U.S. Air Sea battle, and command of the commons in East Asia", *International Security*, 41 (1): p. 7

"Confluence of the Two Seas", Speech by Shinzo Abe, Parliament of India, New Delhi (22 August 2007), Ministry of Foreign Affairs, Japan, http://www.mofa.go.jp/region/asia-paci/pmv0708/speech-2.html (accessed on 5 November 2018)

"The end of globalization or a more multipolar world?" (September 2015), Credit Suisse Research Institute, p. 41, http://publications.credit-suisse.com/tasks/render/file/index.cfm?fileid=EE7A6A5D-D9D5-6204-E9E6BB426B47D054 (accessed on 5 November 2018)

Military Ranking Strength (2018), Global Firepower, https://www.globalfirepower.com/countries-listing.asp (accessed on 5 November 2018)

Sakhuja, Vijay (2016), "Indian Ocean politics and security", Institute of Peace and Conflict Studies Forecast, pp. 60-62, http://www.ipcs.org/special-report/india/ipcs-forecast-2016-182.html (accessed on 5 November 2018)

Pubby, M. (14 July 2018), "Indian Navy aiming at 200-ship fleet by 2027", *Economic Times*, p. 3

United Through Oceans – International Fleet Review 2016 (2016), Integrated Headquarters of the Ministry of Defence (Navy), New Delhi, p. Introduction, 126

Ensuring Secure Seas: Indian Maritime Security Strategy (October 2015), Directorate of Strategy,

Concepts and Transformation, Integrated Headquarters, Ministry of Defence (Navy), New Delhi, pp. 11-12, http://indiannavy.nic.in/sites/default/files/Indian_Maritime_Security_Strategy_ Document_25Jan16.pdf (accessed on 6 November 2018)

"India-Japan defence ties set to grow stronger", *Economic Times*, p. 3 (26 July 2015).

"Defence Manufacturing – Make in India" (2015). http://www.makeinindia.com/sector/defence-manufacturing (accessed on 6 November 2018)

"'Make in India' boost: Japan offers to set up plant in India for US-2 Amphibious Aircraft", *Economic Times*, p. 3, (1 February 2016).

Yoshida, Reiji and Mizuho Aoki (19 September 2015), "Diet enacts security laws, marking Japan's departure from pacifism", *Japan Times*, http://www.japantimes.co.jp/news/2015/09/19/national/politics-diplomacy/diet-enacts-security-laws-marking-japans-departure-from-pacifism-2/#.VqY9CPl97IV (accessed on 6 November 2018)

Mishra, Rahul and Shamsad A. Khan (11 December 2015), "How Shinzo Abe's visit will strengthen India's ties with Japan", dnaindia.com, http://www.dnaindia.com/analysis/standpoint-how-shinzo-abe-s-visit-will-strengthen-india-s-ties-with-japan-2154332 (accessed on 6 November 2018)

National Defense Programme Guidelines for FY 2014 and Beyond (2013), Ministry of Defense, Japan, http://www.mod.go.jp/j/approach/agenda/guideline/2014/pdf/20131217_e2.pdf, p. 2 (accessed on 10 November 2018)

Medium Term Defense Programme for FY 2014-FY 2018 (2013), Ministry of Defense, Japan, http://www.mod.go.jp/j/approach/agenda/guideline/2014/pdf/Defence_Programme.pdf, pp. 1-2 (accessed on 10 November 2018)

"Japan eyes record 65 billion defence budget amid North Korea, China threats", (31 August, 2018), https://www.straitstimes.com/asia/east-asia/japan-eyes-record-65-billion-defence-budget-amid-north-korea-china-threats (accessed on 26 November 2018)

"A mixed year for defence FDI and 'Make in India'", *Economic Times*, p. 5, (1 January 2016).

Defence Procurement Procedure 2016: Backgrounder (2016), Ministry of Defence, Government of India, http://www.mod.nic.in/writereaddata/Background.pdf, pp. 2-4 (accessed on 10 November 2018)

Basu, Nayanima (29 March 2016), "Defence procurement policy pushes 'Make in India'", *Hindu Business Line*, p. 4

Draft Defence Production Policy (2018), Ministry of Defence, Government of India, https://ddpmod.gov.in/sites/default/files/Draft%20Defence%20Production%20Policy%202018%20-%20for%20website.pdf (accessed on 26 November 2018)

"Defense Ministry launches new equipment management agency", *Japan Times*, (1 October 2015), http://www.japantimes.co.jp/news/2015/10/01/national/politics-diplomacy/defense-ministry-launches-new-equipment-management-agency/#.V7ZgRZh97IU (accessed on 10 November 2018)

Grevatt, John (2 October 2015), "Japan launches new procurement agency", *IHS Jane's Defence Industry*, http://www.janes.com/article/54984/japan-launches-new-procurement-agency (accessed on 10 November 2018)

George, Varghese K. (1 October 2015), "India, U.S., Japan say interests in Indo-Pacific converge", *The Hindu*, p. 10

US President Barack Obama's Interview with PTI, *The Statesman*, p. 9, (25 January 2016),

Pubby, M., (8 June 2015), "India kicks off trilateral talks with Japan and Australia; joint training,

naval exercises on agenda", *Economic Times*, p. 5.
"Exercise Malabar 2016" (2016), Press Release, Ministry of Defence (Navy), Government of India, http://indiannavy.nic.in/content/exercise-malabar-2016 (accessed on 10 November 2018)
Joint Statement on India and Japan Vision 2025: Special Strategic and Global Partnership Working Together for Peace and Prosperity of the Indo-Pacific Region and the World 2015, New Delhi (12 December 2015), Clause 2, Ministry of External Affairs, Government of India, http://www.mea.gov.in/incoming-visit-detail.htm?26176/Joint+Statement+on+India+and+Japan+Vision+2025+ Special+Strategic+and+Global+Partnership+Working+Together+for+Peace+and+Prosperity+of+the+IndoPacific+Region+and+the+WorldDecember+12+2015 (accessed on 15 November 2018)
List of Documents Exchanged During the Visit of Prime Minister Shinzo Abe of Japan to India, New Delhi (12 December 2015), Ministry of External Affairs, Government of India, http://www.mea.gov.in/incoming-visit-detail.htm?26177/List+of+documents+exchanged+ during+the+visit+of+Prime+Minister+Shinzo+Abe+of+Japan+to+India+in+New+Delhi+December+12+2015 (accessed on 15 November 2018)
Basu, Nayanima (14 July 2016), "India-Japan $1.3 bi defence deal fails to make headway", *Hindu Business Line*, p. 6
Defense of Japan - Annual White Paper (17 December 2013), Ministry of Defense, Japan, http://www.mod.go.jp/e/publ/w_paper/2013.html (accessed on 25 August 2016)
Pal Chaudhuri, Pramit and Jayanth Jacob (24 June 2016), "India bags all but China's vote, decision on NSG bid likely today", *Hindustan Times*, http://www.hindustantimes.com/india-news/india-bags-all-but-china-s-vote-decision-on-nsg-bid-likely-on-friday/story-8ZZdZHRnEyPtxgleWsjTOI.html (accessed on 25 November 2018)
Joint Statement after the Meeting Between Raksha Mantri and Japanese Defence Minister, New Delhi (14 July 2016), Clause 4, Press Information Bureau, Ministry of Defence, Government of India, http://pib.nic.in/newsite/PrintRelease.aspx?relid=147097 (accessed on 26 November 2018)
Announcement of "Partnership for Quality Infrastructure: Investment for Asia's Future" (21 May 2013), Ministry of Foreign Affairs, Japan, http://www.mofa.go.jp/policy/oda/page18_000076.html (accessed on 26 November 2018)

Bibliography
Official Documents and Reports
"Challenges and Prospects of Japan's Diplomacy – in the Context of India-Japan Relationship", Japanese Ambassador to India, Kenji Hiramatsu's Address at Observer Research Foundation, New Delhi (7 June 2016), http://www.in.emb-japan.go.jp/itpr_en/00_000057.html
"Confluence of the Two Seas", Speech by Shinzo Abe, Parliament of India, New Delhi (22 August 2007), Ministry of Foreign Affairs, Japan, http://www.mofa.go.jp/region/asia-paci/pmv0708/speech-2.html
"Defence Manufacturing – Make in India" (2015) http://www.makeinindia.com/sector/defence-manufacturing (accessed on 6 August 2016)
"Exercise Malabar 2016" (2016), Press Release, Ministry of Defence (Navy), Government of India, http://indiannavy.nic.in/content/exercise-malabar-2016
"Let's Be Ambitious Together", Raisina Dialogue Remarks by Admiral Harry B. Harris, Jr., New Delhi (2 March 2016), http://www.pacom.mil/Media/Speeches-Testimony/Article/683842/raisina-dialogue-remarks-lets-be-ambitious-together/

"The end of globalization or a more multipolar world?" (September 2015), Credit Suisse Research Institute, http://publications.credit-suisse.com/tasks/render/file/index.cfm?fileid=EE7A6A5D-D9D5-6204-E9E6BB426B47D054

2018 Military Ranking Strength (2018), Global Firepower, https://www.globalfirepower.com/countries-listing.asp

Announcement of "Partnership for Quality Infrastructure: Investment for Asia's Future" (21 May 2013), Ministry of Foreign Affairs, Japan, http://www.mofa.go.jp/policy/oda/page18_000076.html (accessed on 25 August 2016)

Defence Procurement Procedure 2016: Backgrounder (2016), Ministry of Defence, Government of India, http://www.mod.nic.in/writereaddata/Background.pdf

Defense of Japan - Annual White Paper (17 December 2013), Ministry of Defense, Japan, http://www.mod.go.jp/e/publ/w_paper/2013.html

Draft Defence Production Policy (2018), Ministry of Defence, Government of India, https://ddpmod.gov.in/sites/default/files/Draft%20Defence%20Production%20Policy%202018%20-%20for%20website.pdf

Ensuring Secure Seas: Indian Maritime Security Strategy (October 2015), Directorate of Strategy, Concepts and Transformation, Integrated Headquarters, Ministry of Defence (Navy), New Delhi, http://indiannavy.nic.in/sites/default/files/Indian_Maritime_ Security_ Strategy_ Document_ 25Jan16.pdf

Grevatt, John (2 October 2015), "Japan launches new procurement agency", IHS Jane's Defence Industry, http://www.janes.com/article/54984/japan-launches-new-procurement-agency

Indo-Japan Joint Statement (29 October 2018), Ministry of External Affairs, Government of India, https://www.mea.gov.in/outoging-visit-detail.htm?30543/IndiaJapan+Vision+Statement

Joint Statement after the Meeting Between Raksha Mantri and Japanese Defence Minister (14 July 2016), New Delhi, http://pib.nic.in/newsite/PrintRelease.aspx?relid=147097

Joint Statement on India and Japan Vision 2025: Special Strategic and Global Partnership Working Together for Peace and Prosperity of the Indo-Pacific Region and the World 2015 (12 December 2015), Ministry of External Affairs, Government of India, http://www.mea.gov.in/incoming-visit-detail.htm?26176/Joint+Statement+on+India+and+Japan+Vision+2025+Special+Strategic+ and+ Global+ Partnership+Working+ Together+for+Peace+and+ Prosperity+of+ the+ IndoPacific+ Region+and+the+WorldDecember+12+2015

List of Documents Exchanged During the Visit of Prime Minister Shinzo Abe of Japan to India (12 December 2015), Ministry of External Affairs, Government of India, http://www.mea.gov.in/incoming-visit-detail.htm?26177/List+of+documents+exchanged+during+the+visit+of+Prime+Minister+Shinzo+Abe+of+Japan+to+India+in+New+Delhi+December+12+2015

Medium Term Defense Programme for FY 2014-FY 2018 (2013), Ministry of Defense, Japan, http://www.mod.go.jp/j/approach/agenda/guideline/2014/pdf/Defence_Programme.pdf

National Defense Programme Guidelines for FY 2014 and Beyond Ministry of Defence (2013), Ministry of Defense, Japan, http://www.mod.go.jp/j/approach/agenda/guideline/2014/pdf/20131217_e2.pdf

Prime Minister of India's Departure Statement ahead of his visit to Japan, New Delhi (29 August 2014), Press Information Bureau, Prime Minister's Office, Government of India, http://pib.nic.in/newsite/PrintRelease.aspx?relid=109178

Prime Minister of India's Keynote Address at the Luncheon Hosted by Nippon Kiedanren - Japanese Chamber of Commerce and Industry and the Japan-India Business Cooperation Committee,

Tokyo (1 September 2014), http://www.narendramodi.in/pms-keynote-address-at-the-luncheon-hosted-by-nippon-kiedanren-the-japanese-chamber-of-commerce-and-industry-and-the-japan-india-business-cooperation-committee

Prime Minister, Narendra Modi's Remarks at the Indian Community Reception, Tokyo (2 September 2014), http://www.narendramodi.in/pms-remarks-at-the-indian-community-reception-in-tokyo-6539

Sakhuja, Vijay (2016), "Indian Ocean politics and security", Institute of Peace and Conflict Studies Forecast, http://www.ipcs.org/special-report/india/ipcs-forecast-2016-182.html

United Through Oceans – International Fleet Review 2016 (2016), Integrated Headquarters of the Ministry of Defence (Navy), New Delhi

Article in Journal

Biddle, Stephen and Ivan Oelrich (Summer 2016), "Future warfare in the Western Pacific: Chinese antiaccess/area denial, U.S. AirSea battle, and command of the commons in East Asia", *International Security*, 41 (1)

Articles in Websites

Mishra, Rahul and Shamsad A. Khan (11 December 2015), "How Shinzo Abe's visit will strengthen India's ties with Japan", dnaindia.com, http://www.dnaindia.com/analysis/standpoint-how-shinzo-abe-s-visit-will-strengthen-india-s-ties-with-japan-2154332

Panneerselvam, Prakash (August 2016), "Advancing India's relationship with Japan and South Korea: quest for Middle Power cooperation", Institute of Peace and Conflict Studies, Issue Brief No. 262, http://www.ipcs.org/issue-brief/india-the-world/advancing-india39s-relationship-with-japan-and-south-korea-quest-for-262.html

Newspapers
Economic Times
Hindu
Hindu Business Line
Hindustan Times
Japan Times
Statesman
Straits Times

Websites

http://www.dnaindia.com/analysis/standpoint-how-shinzo-abe-s-visit-will-strengthen-india-s-ties-with-japan-2154332

https://www.ddpmod.gov.in/sites/default/files/Draft%20Defence%20Production%20Policy%202018%20-%20for%20website.pdf

https://www.globalfirepower.com/countries-listing.asp

http://www.hindustantimes.com

http://www.in.emb-japan.go.jp/itpr_en/00_000057.html

http://www.indiannavy.nic.in

http://www.ipcs.org/issue-brief/india-the-world/advancing-india39s-relationship-with-japan-and-south-korea-quest-for-262.html

http://www.ipcs.org/special-report/india/ipcs-forecast-2016-182.html

http://www.janes.com/article/54984/japan-launches-new-procurement-agency

http://www.japantimes.co.jp
http://www.makeinindia.com/sector/defence-manufacturing
http://www.mea.gov.in
http://www.mod.go.jp
http://www.mod.nic.in
http://www.mofa.go.jp
http://www.narendramodi.in
http://www.pacom.mil/Media/Speeches-Testimony/Article/683842/raisina-dialogue-remarks-lets-be-ambitious-together
http://www.pib.nic.in/newsite/PrintRelease.aspx?relid=109178
http://www.publications.credit-suisse.com/tasks/render/file/index.cfm?fileid=EE7A6A5D-D9D5-6204-E9E6BB426B47D054
http://www.straitstimes.com
http://www.thehindubusinessline.com

14

Rise of the 'Islamic State' and Its Implications

Nazmul Arifeen

Introduction

Following the decapitation of its top leaders and battered by persistent attacks in Iraq and Afghanistan-Pakistan border, Al-Qaeda's activity was largely confined to merely producing video messages of its leaders and intimidating with threats of further attacks. Some analysts reckoned that terrorist organisations' ability to orchestrate further major attacks and inflict considerable damage on the West would significantly wane.[1] But in recent times, the withdrawal of multinational forces from Iraq witnessed the rise of another terrorist organisation, forked out of Al-Qaeda, which is known as the Islamic State in Iraq and al-Sham (ISIS) in the political landscape of the Middle East. The emergence of ISIS and its recent coming to prominence have questioned how analysts and policy-makers previously predicted the gravity of threats emanating from international terrorism.[2]

Not only has the emergence of ISIS caused bewilderment among political regimes in its Arab and non-Arab neighbourhoods, the terrorist organisation has also taken control over swathes of territories and declared a state in the domains under its control. The relative pace of its rise is, to some extent, unprecedented and unforeseen. No one could imagine that a non-state actor could quickly swept across vast areas transcending borders and pose existential threats to nation-states by redrawing boundaries, triggering mass influx of refugees and causing internal displacement of people.

The rise of ISIS has, therefore, garnered the interests of policy-makers as well as academicians at different levels. While the adversary has caused serious concerns for the countries in the region and beyond, analysts are preoccupied with explaining its rise and governments how to confront the new threat. One particular conundrum is that ISIS has blurred the difference drawn between what constitutes a traditional threat and what falls within the ambit of non-traditional threats. With formidable forces, which continue to pose serious security challenge to neighbouring countries and other extra-territorial actors like the coalition forces, it commands band of militia and territories governed by itself. Whether it is to be considered a traditional threat or a non-traditional threat also requires understanding how it capitalised on the political situation, sectarian divide and its "military" clout. Since understanding a threat is *sine qua non* for military actions or otherwise, defining ISIS and understanding its far-reaching implications have become important in order to effectively address the challenge.

Some analyses did predict a distant possibility of terrorist organisations becoming state actors viz. taking control of territorial states,[3] but these predictions failed in explaining the rise of ISIS in two ways. First, the terrorist organisation[4] rose to prominence sooner than anticipated. Second, the same group of analysts also believed that the centre of such events would likely to be Afghanistan-Pakistan border.[5] Therefore, there are some pertinent questions that deserve explanation. What conditions preceded such prompt ascendance of a terrorist group? What factors best explain the ascendance of ISIS that its predecessor Al-Qaeda could not materialise? What implications do these developments herald for regional politics in particular and international politics in general? These are the questions that have been analysed here.

This chapter seeks answers to a few questions as to what are the causes of rise of ISIS and to look at its various possible implications. It might be easier to analyse the causes of an ongoing crisis, but reaching a conclusion about the far-reaching implications is difficult as new developments unfold every day. These issues have been addressed in five sections. Following an introduction, the genesis of ISIS has been examined. The causes that gave rise to ISIS have been analysed next. The third section puts forward some arguments as to the possible implications of its rise. And finally, concluding remarks have been drawn based on the preceding discussions.

A Background of ISIS

The parent organisation of ISIS was Jamaat al-Tawhid wal-Jihad, founded by a Jordanian national Abu Musab al-Zarqawi, which operated in Jordan and Iraq.

After the attack of multinational forces in Iraq in March 2003, al-Zarqawi pledged allegiance to Osama bin Laden and changed the organisation's name to Tanzim Qaidat al-Jihad fi Bilad al-Rafidayn, which translates into Al-Qaeda in the Land of Two Rivers.[6] It was popularly called Al-Qaeda in Iraq (AQI) and Al-Zarqawi was its Emir. His organisation merged with six other terrorist outfits with similar agenda in 2006 for a brief period into Majlis Shura al-Mujahedin (MSM) until he was killed in June 2006. After his demise, Abu Ayyub al-Masri, taking the helm of MSM, disbanded and renamed the organisation as Islamic State in Iraq (ISI) in October 2006. After he was killed in a raid in April 2010 along with Abu Omar al-Baghdadi, Abu Bakr al-Baghdadi rose to the power of ISI in May 2010. He was not a leader of AQI to begin with, but of a smaller faction which joined Majlis Shura al-Mujahedin.[7] It is interesting to note that none of its leaders is known by their actual names; rather it has become customary among ISIS leadership to assume *nom de guerre* or "war names".

Nomenclatural Complexities Revolving the Notion of 'Islamic State'

Since its birth, as discussed earlier, the entity which is popularly known as ISIS has assumed a number of names and changed when necessary and as it grew in strength. This was because the names did not adequately embody its objectives of the time being. When it flexed its muscle into neighbouring states, the name Islamic State in Iraq confined its scope to move beyond Iraqi territorial boundaries. Therefore, the name was expanded to incorporate the Levant region.[8] However, as it continues to capture new provinces and its ambitions become inflated, ISIS has dropped the Levant region from its name in June 2014 and calls itself only 'Islamic State (IS)' that is much broader in sense and not confined by geographical terrain.

Table 1: A History of ISIS Names

Group Name	Years in Use
Jamaat al-Tawhid wal-Jihad (JTJ)	1999–2004
Al-Qaeda in the Land of Two Rivers (more popularly known as Al-Qaeda in Iraq, or AQI)	2004–2006
Majlis Shura al-Mujahedin (MSM)	2006
Islamic State of Iraq (ISI)	2006–2013
Islamic State of Iraq and al-Sham or the Levant (ISIS/ISIL)	2013–June 2014
Islamic State (IS)	June 2014–present

Source: The table is modified and updated by the author, from Aaron Y. Zelin, "The War between ISIS and al-Qaeda for Supremacy of the Global Jihadist Movement", The Washington Institute for Near East Policy Research Notes, No. 20, June 2014.

There is considerable debate over the use of its newly assumed name "Islamic State" as it is subject to various political as well as religious interpretations. ISIS has also exhibited state-like characteristics and performs governance activities in the region under its control. This also causes a theoretical problem whether this "state" would require assimilation into the international system. This political question also entails the boundaries and territorial limits of the so-called Islamic State. On the other hand, the religious conundrum of calling it the "Islamic State" or "Caliphate" as it calls itself begins with the question whether it should have the religious authority of Caliphate that Islam had during the seventh century onwards. The question on authority over all Muslims of the world had caused conflicts between ISIS and Al-Qaeda as well.

Owing to the same reason, international community never acknowledged its new name. Officially, the Western countries call it ISIL or ISIS. A United Nations (UN) resolution passed condemning the brutalities of ISIS described the entity as ISIL.[9] This chapter, however, uses the name ISIS which is widely used by international media.

Ideological Predilection of ISIS

Any academic discussion about ISIS also requires understanding of ideologies that the organisation adheres to. More so, because despite the fact that it was previously known as Al-Qaeda in Iraq, it recently has severed ties with Al-Qaeda Central. Its ideological basis requires scrutiny and, as the following discussions will further explore, estrangement with Al-Qaeda owing to ideological disagreements also benefitted ISIS in Iraq and Syria. It should be noted here that there is a tendency even among scholars to confuse between Wahhabism and Salafism that some scholars also called neo-Wahhabism.[10] John Esposito argues that the notions of Wahhabism and Salafism have often been inaccurately used as "a blanket term for Islamic fundamentalism, religious extremism, and radicalism".[11] However, some Salafists believe that "Wahhabism was not sufficiently rigorous in adhering to the Prophet's example".[12] ISIS adheres to Salafism ideology which is, therefore, more puritan than Wahhabism. It should be noted here that not all Salafists or Wahhabists are terrorists; rather, there are certain elements among those who believe in those ideologies, who resort to violent means to attain their political objectives.

The Causes of Rapid Rise of ISIS

The sudden emergence of hitherto unknown ISIS in political scenario of the Middle East has stirred considerable interest and uneasiness in the region and beyond. Although the name ISIS was barely heard before the departure of the multinational forces in Iraq, its origin dates back to more than a decade as briefly discussed earlier. The reason it was unheard of is because it originated as an independent entity, not directly linked with Al-Qaeda. Later, after the multinational forces' attack on Afghanistan, Al-Zarqawi pledged allegiance to bin Laden and changed its name to AQI. The US has targeted AQI and regularly decapitated its leadership in the past. It gained considerable attention from the international community because of its brutal killings, beheading of foreign nationals, sudden capture of lands and finally declaring a state out of nowhere. There are various reasons behind this rather confounding triumph of ISIS.

The rise of ISIS can be attributable to two different causes. There are certain "root causes" that built on over a long period of time and finally exploded. The rest of the causes can be identified as the "triggering causes" that immediately led to its recent upheaval that include the withdrawal of coalition forces from Iraq and subsequent political vacuum. While the root cause seeks to theoretically explain its causes of ascendance, the triggering causes explain how the recent development in the Middle East politics added momentum to ISIS objectives.

Favoured by Changing Strategic Landscape

The rise of ISIS is a simultaneous coincidence of two developments of international politics, namely the "Arab Spring" and the withdrawal of multinational forces from Iraq while the democratic institutions in the country were still very weak and political stability was not attained. Arab Spring gave rise to several democratic forces in the Middle East; among them was Free Syrian Army (FSA) supported by Western countries to fight against the Assad regime.[13] FSA was greatly empowered by the supply of weapons. This has made it a formidable adversary against the Assad regime. However, it did not have the capacity to retain and run functions of a state in the territories it previously captured. FSA could not continue to hold the control over the large cities it captured in Syria.

Western countries were convinced that democracy promotion was one of the most effective ways to counter radicalisation. For example, Michael Boyle explained why two successive US governments have taken the policy of democracy promotion as a remedy for terrorism.[14] As a continuation of such policies, the West has overtly or sometimes covertly supported the popular uprisings in the Middle East during the Arab Spring. However, by linking democracy promotion and fighting terrorism resulting in the policy of "regime change", the traditional autocratic governments were weakened in some countries leading to an internal political vacuum in the region.

Situation already deteriorated in Iraq because of the sectarian and ethnic divide. The coalition forces' withdrawal from Iraq created a vacuum in that country that ISIS did not waste time to take advantage of. The Iraqi provinces of Mosul and Diyala, which were once the epitome of the multinational forces' presence, have fallen to ISIS. The widely known Abu Gharib prison was attacked by ISIS fighters to help several hundred war prisoners escape. These incidents changed the landscape ensuing the departure of coalition forces. Lakhdar Brahimi noted that the West's top priority in the region had been to defeat ISIS, shifting away from toppling Assad regime.[15] Nevertheless, Western countries appear to be reluctant to commit to another bout of prolonged conflict in the region.

Neighbouring countries including Turkey, Iran, Saudi Arabia and others also have contradicting objectives, priorities and diverging national interests in these areas. For example, threats emanating from ISIS are not considered "immediate" by Turkey which is claimed to have negotiated with the terrorist group to free its diplomats.[16] International state-actors were also caught in the dilemma of arming the Syrian rebels or discontinuing it, as it turned out to be benefitting ISIS. Weakening Assad regime, which can be a major force to mount considerable opposition to ISIS, will embolden the latter. In addition, in the recent months, several factions from Syrian rebels joined ISIS along with the weapons supplied to them by the West. On the flipside, Western countries cannot 'ethically' arm Assad regime. This dilemma and the lack of decisive policy to collectively face a common enemy like the ISIS have actually emboldened it further.

There have also been policy shifts of major Western countries regarding the regions where the Global War on Terror (GWoT) should be fought. Explaining US President Obama's intention to pull out force from Iraq, Trevor McCrisken noted that his administration believed the "real war on terror" should not be pursued in Iraq, but rather in Afghanistan and Pakistan border.[17] Moving away from what Obama called a 'distraction' in the war on terrorism, the US decided to leave the Iraq theatre, while at the same time, sponsoring democracy promotion in the region by international community. The political vacuum that was created in the process was filled up by other non-state actors within the country.

Apart from these international political calculations, there are internal strategic considerations that greatly favoured ISIS. Many battered political forces have supported the ISIS not because of ideological predilection but tactical reasons that can be summed up in Kautilyan dictum "my enemy's enemy is my friend." It is understandable as to why top leaders of the ISIL military leadership come from the former Ba'athist army of Saddam Hussein. Saddam Hussein's daughter living-in-exile in Jordan also supported the cause of ISIS mainly because she holds personal vendetta against the current regime in Iraq. These developments, certainly along with many others, factored in the rapid rise of ISIS in the region.

Materialisation of 'Caliphate Dream'

Another important factor that gave impetus to the sudden rise of ISIS is its ability to deliver on its promises. Some analysts claim that ISIS is more successful than Al-Qaeda.[18] Indeed, favoured by the political situation and circumstances, as well as a power vacuum created by the outgoing coalition forces in the region, ISIS captured swathes of lands including important border crossings and strategic cities declaring itself the so-called Islamic State. In June 2014, the ISIS leader Abu Bakr al-Baghdadi declared himself the Caliph of the 'Islamic State' assuming the title Caliph Ibrahim-II. For many global jihadists[19] who were disillusioned by the failure of their ideological cause in such areas as Chechnya and Afghanistan, the victory of ISIS is a dream coming true. For them, no other organisation has been able to deliver so much in the name of "Jihad", let alone capturing foreign lands with foreign fighters. Although the Taliban came close to that level, but at its inception, the Taliban was mainly an internal political force within Afghanistan. During the Taliban takeover of Afghanistan in the late 1990s, despite question of their political legitimacy, they were not a terrorist organisation *per se*. Later, the group's intimacy with the Al-Qaeda and harbouring Osama bin Laden led to the invasion of Afghanistan by NATO forces in 2003.

Such claim of Caliphate also increased the appeal of ISIS. Even its parent organisation Al-Qaeda feels uneasy with the notion of "Islamic State". In recent months, cleavage between Al-Qaeda and ISIS became public when ISIS claimed authority over al-Nusra Front which, according to ISIS claims, was sent by al-Baghdadi to open battle front in Syria. In an audio message, al-Baghdadi declared that al-Nusra Front would merge with ISIS which was soon opposed by both Ayman al-Zawahiri, the current leader of Al-Qaeda Central, and Abu Musab al-Zawlani, the leader of al-Nusra Front.

Apparently, 'internationalisation' of terrorist agenda also helped ISIS attract more foreign fighters. Many foreign fighters who joined the "Syrian jihad" with al-Nusra Front are foreign terrorists who travelled to the country to fight Assad regime. Laurent Vinatier argued that Al-Nusra Front's reluctance to join ISIS going beyond Syrian territories apparently disgruntled foreign fighters who were deserting the Front to join ISIS because of its global agenda.[20]

The tangible success, perceived by radical ideologues of Salafism and Wahhabism, of establishing the so-called Caliphate has, therefore, made certain appeal to terrorists from all over the world. Foreign fighters swarmed in the domain controlled by ISIS on an unprecedented scale. One estimate suggests that currently there are 12,000 foreign fighters from as many as 81 countries including the US, Britain, France and Australia in the West and Malaysia, Indonesia, Pakistan and India from the East.[21] What is more interesting is the fact that amongst the foreign fighters, there are also women who travelled mainly from Western countries to join the battle.[22] One estimate suggests that approximately 60 women joined from Britain alone.[23] While there may be various motivations, at the same time, it depicts the degree of appeal that ISIS has been able to create.

Political Economy of ISIS Rise

Financing terrorist activities and control over interrupted flow of monetary supply have always been the lifeline of Al-Qaeda and the likes. Al-Qaeda was severely crippled by the stringent financial regulations put in place to deprive it of outside financial assistance. It has been argued that terrorist organisations benefitted from extortion, trade in narcotics, illicit arms deals as well as endowments received from sympathisers. But ISIS has been successful in breaking away from that tradition by diversifying its sources of finance. Not only does it sustain the economic burden of running an organisation like itself, analysts also claim that ISIS regularly pays its militia.[24]

Capturing major oil fields and selling antiques and precious metals immensely helped ISIS rise.[25] Evidence shows that ISIS income generated from oil revenue alone is approximately US$2 million a day.[26] However, there is debate over what parties this oil is being sold to. Apart from oil, there are other sources of income from extortion, robbery of banks and other financial institutions and endowments from its sympathisers. This implies that while Al-Qaeda was mainly financed by its patrons in the Gulf States, ISIS on the other hand, is largely autonomous. No terrorist organisations in the recent decades have known to have so much resource.

Despite this, the sustainability of such economic activity remains under question. The Middle Eastern countries adjacent to ISIS territories are already oil rich. This implies that there is no market for ISIS-produced oil in the vicinity. The government and the opposition in Syria blame each other for buying oil from ISIS. Despite the fierce animosity between Assad regime and ISIS, the two belligerent parties continued to benefit from each others in economic terms. As Valérie Marcel argues, ISIS sells its oil to Syrian regime "in exchange for immunity against air strikes".[27] Some claim that Turkey is one of the state buyers of ISIS oil.[28] Nevertheless, ISIS' capacity to refine oil is very limited. It mostly sells oil in the local market for electricity production and majority of its oil is sold through black market. Lack of formal trading mechanism will reduce the possibility of ISIS to continuously depend on oil revenue. This limited opportunity will not allow it to grow further economically.

Identity Politics in the Middle East

Identity politics is another root cause of the emergence of ISIS which was fanned deliberately during the Iraq war by different groups. The coalition forces attempted to empower minority groups and communities that were marginalised during the previous regime. To a great extent, therefore, the emergence of ISIS is the result of identity politics in the Middle East. It was also a historical phenomenon that was engrained during the partition of these countries that cut across tribes erecting virtual state-boundaries between and among different ethnic groups and sects, while at the same time depriving large groups like the Kurds of statehood. In the recent past, its rise is also attributable to the Western policies that Sunni population, who once enjoyed political power during the regime of Saddam Hussein, feel alienated and marginalised. It is, thus, also a result of political exclusion of the Sunni population from the power of Iraq.[29] There is certainly a sectarian element in the ongoing battle between ISIS and its adversaries most of whom are Shi'ites. However, trying to view the problem through only sectarian lens would result in oversimplification of the problem.[30] In this particular case in Iraq and Syria, sectarian identities have been used for political ends.

After the defeat of Saddam Hussein, the multinational forces instated the government of Nouri al-Maliki, a Shi'ite political leader, and Jalal Talabani, an ethnic Kurd, in the political power of Iraq. Both Shi'ites and Kurds were subjected to state repression during the Saddam Hussein era. As such, the new government took policies that deprived the previous political elites from the amenities that they once enjoyed. These reversals make a large number of the Sunni population feel alienated.[31] ISIS has taken advantage of this sense of alienation among the Sunni population. At the same time, while both Al-Qaeda and ISIS are terrorist organisations, the fundamental difference between the two is that the latter has a clear identity-based agenda. Fareed Zakaria noted that Al-Qaeda had a pan-Islamic approach and its goal was "to rally the entire Muslim world to jihad against the West". On the contrary, the terrorist elements that later emerged as ISIS deliberately adopted an anti-Shi'ite stance because of existing resentment between the two groups.³² It was also conducive to attract Sunni support. Therefore, ISIS politicised sectarian identity so as to achieve its political goals.

Apart from the Shi'ite-Sunni divide, Muslims are also divided in ideological line as well, namely Salafism and Wahhabism. Although not all Wahhabists and Salafists are terrorists, at least, some of those who subscribe to these beliefs are radical extremists. The ideology of ISIS is also responsible for deliberate fanning of sectarian violence. As mentioned before, ISIS believes in Salafist ideology which is more puritan than Wahhabism. Both Salafism and Wahhabism are of Sunni ideology but their beliefs are not exactly the same. Al-Qaeda is mainly a Wahhabi organisation; on the contrary, ISIS is mostly a Salafist one which is also known as neo-Wahhabism. Coupled with increasing hatred against Shi'ite population caused by change in the political landscape, ISIS has found a safe haven in Iraq.

Intensifying Recruitment in Cyberspace through Social Media

One striking feature of ISIS was the relatively fast pace of its membership growth. Experts have previously showed how terrorist organisations like Al-Qaeda made extensive use of internet and social media.³³ But as it appears, ISIS has taken that to a whole new level. This can be attributable to innovative ways ISIS has taken advantage of newer media and social communications. While Al-Qaeda was dependent on clandestine website requiring passing security checks, ISIS has utilised online communication and social media to reach to its recruits. It maintains a Twitter account, developed an Android application that allows users to remain constantly updated and always connected with the upper chain of command. While Al-Qaeda communication medium was limited to producing audio/video messages once in a while, ISIS has frequently released videos. It regularly publishes an e-magazine called *Dabiq*³⁴ and relays its messages through this. The online activity campaign has also paid off as foreign terrorists are moving into the battlefield to join the ISIS.

Confronted by Weaker Adversaries in Iraq and Syria

Another reason that explains the relatively unchallenged rise of ISIS is the existence of weak Iraqi national forces left alone by the multinational forces' withdrawal and battered foes like Assad regime, which already lost control of many strategic areas. Iraqi cities like Mosul, Falluja, Tikrit and in Syria, Raqqa and Aleppo fell.³⁵ The newly formed Iraqi army severely lacks both training and capacity to wage a war against such an organised and experienced "militia" as ISIS. When Syrian rebels already took control of major cities in Syria supported by multinational forces' airstrikes, it was relatively easier on part of ISIS to drive away Syrian rebels from those territories.

The battle is being waged on several fronts in Syria as well: between Assad regime and the rest of the oppositions including Free Syrian Army, between Free Syrian Army and Al-Qaeda elements like al-Nusra Front and finally between ISIS and al-Nusra Front. Opening up a number of fronts in the battle has weakened all parties concerned and caused mutual destruction. However, ISIS remained comparatively less battered and became victorious in the multifrontal battle. As previously mentioned, estrangement with al-Nusra Front, the Al-Qaeda affiliate in Syria, has also helped ISIS. The reason behind the animosity was the former's reluctance to internationalise its battle agenda beyond the Syrian theatre. But the Front was already supported by foreign fighters who migrated from faraway lands to join the battle and as such already had a global approach to jihad. When these groups left al-Nusra Front for ISIS, they brought in arms and ammunition supplied by the West and other regional actors.

The preceding analyses do not presume that the rise of ISIS can only be explained through the above-mentioned causes. Certainly, there were other factors involved. However, a deeper analysis reveals that these factors could better explain the relative rapidity of ascendance of ISIS in Iraq and Syria.

Implications of Rise of the 'Islamic State'

The rapid rise of ISIS also heralds multifarious ramifications for global and regional politics. Needless to say, the heat of its growing influence is being felt in the neighbourhood of ISIS-controlled territories. Apart from Iraq and Syria where ISIS currently operates, Turkey, Jordan, Yemen and Saudi Arabia are likely to be among the first nations to take the blow. In the longer term, however, its impact will spread. Gradually, its impact will reach faraway places from the epicentre of the crisis as the following sections argue.

Will There Be a Domino Effect?

One possible outcome of the rise of ISIS in the neighbouring countries can be explained through the 'domino effect'. In international relations context, domino theory[36] denotes that the success of an actor in a given region may trigger chain reaction, *e.g.* encourage others in its vicinity to do the same. For example, the civil uprisings dubbed as the 'Arab Spring' itself triggered a domino effect in the region.[37] The chain reaction of what started as a street protest in Tunisia soon swept across the Arab world including Egypt, Libya, Yemen, Bahrain and Syria, either leading to change of regime or being forcefully quelled. Therefore, instability can sometimes be contagious in international politics. Likewise, originating in Iraq, the ISIS crisis already spilled over to Syria. Just the way Arab Spring spread over to neighbouring countries, inspired by the success in Iraq, ISIS leadership ordered its comrades to cross over to Syria and recruit forces which soon became a formidable threat in that country.

Nevertheless, this will be a sheer exaggeration to suggest that mass people of the Middle East are likely to follow the path of ISIS by extending their support for it. Rather, in this particular case, what is more important is the likelihood of other terrorist organisations joining ISIS. As Jack Snyder noted, intrinsically connected with the domino effect is the concept of 'bandwagon' which implies an actor's alignment with stronger forces in international politics. An actor's triumph often encourages other actors with similar agenda to jump on the former's bandwagon.[38] By the same token, emboldened by the success of ISIS, terrorist organisations elsewhere may be encouraged to follow suit, extend support or even merge with ISIS. There are already evidences of such developments. Nigeria-based terrorist organisation Boko Haram—which previously supported the ideological cause of ISIS—recently captured a town called Gwoza in Borno State of Nigeria and declared it a new "part of the Islamic Caliphate".[39] In South Asia, two terrorist organisations including the Pakistani Taliban (also known as Tehrik-e-Taliban or TTP) pledged allegiance to ISIS.[40] Such actions can be interpreted as similar to bandwagoning. Further bandwagoning with ISIS might be observed in the days ahead.

But given the inherent dearth of accommodative attitude in ISIS, it remains to be seen whether it will able to bring considerable number of such terrorist groups under its umbrella. Of late, ISIS has fallen out with its parent organisation Al-Qaeda and has engaged in fratricidal brutalities by killing fellow comrades of other terrorist organisations including al-Nusra Front. This also casts doubt on the possibility that ISIS will be able to sustain its appeal to other terrorist organisations.

New Polarisation in the Region

The emergence of the force within a relatively short period of time has brought to the forefront the question of reordering current polarisation in the region, because what is alarming for regional as well as global politics is that ISIS is not a conventional terrorist organisation; rather it has an expansionist agenda that seeks to carve out a "Caliphate" in the region undermining status quo and altering long-demarcated geographical boundaries. And given its recent success and resources at its disposal, it would be difficult for any country in that region to face the challenges singlehandedly. Therefore, analysts talked about changing the balance of power by creating new security architecture that accommodated regional powers to fight the common enemy.[41]

It is true that there has been no significant sign of shift in existing balance of power in the region so far, but latest developments in the regional politics of the Middle East would make new polarisation inevitable. First, Western countries appear to be hesitant over the decision to arm the Syrian rebels, as it was previously revealed that weapons—intended for Kurdish *peshmerga* fighters to fight against ISIS—had ended up in the hands of ISIS.[42] Its previous policies of weakening Assad regime had actually benefited ISIS. Scholars also argued that arming Syrian rebels would not actually prevent ISIS' rise either.[43] As a result, the West has moved away from its previous priority of toppling Assad regime in the short term.[44] Assad regime, therefore, is no longer the arch-enemy of the West in Syria; rather it can be an effective tool in neutralising the threats of ISIS. Such temporary shift in the Western countries' policies has created new polarisation in the region.

Second, another notable indicator of change in the regional political alignment is faster sign of rapprochement between Iran and the West.[45] Iran is perhaps the only country that is not likely to side with ISIS, because the country is an antithesis to what ISIS stands for. Iran is the only Shi'ite country in the region with considerable clout as well as interest in defeating the ISIS. It is true that after the departure of Mahmood Ahmadinejad, the former Iranian President, from the political scene of the country, the present regime showed interest to recommence negotiation with the West. Nevertheless, now there is another reason, viz. the common threat of ISIS for the West and Iran to forget their differences and focus on one common enemy. Whatever the case, as long as the threat of ISIS persists, the West will avoid any direct confrontation with Iran.

Although there is no valid reason to believe that there will be any dramatic shift of power in regional politics of the Middle East, but as this paper discussed, there would be new political polarisation and realignment within the regional theatre of the Middle East. Indeed, it is difficult to predict how long this emerging status quo will last. After the Cold War, Western countries barely needed to align with a country that was previously considered the "axis of evil". The second sign in new polarisation, albeit for a short-to-medium term, would be cooperating with the Assad regime in Syria. Despite Syrian support for groups like Hezbollah, it is also true that Assad's regime, albeit autocratic, is a secular force. Recent images and videos shown by ISIS indicate that weapons supplied to Free Syrian Army fell into the wrong hands of ISIS. For greater strategic interest, it has become imperative for the international community to cooperate with the current Syrian regime.

However, it can be argued that disintegration of the courtiers like Iraq and Syria would serve greater purpose of securing the interest of the West's most important ally in the region—Israel. But in order to do so, no party would be willing to empower a Frankenstein like ISIS. These calculations would lead to a shift in the existing alignment and polarisation in the Middle East and move a step back from the Arab Spring.

Terrorists' Homecoming

One of possibly devastating impacts of the ISIS, both within the region and globally, would be managing the returnees from the battlefields. As seen in the previous case in "Afghan Jihad" against the former Soviet Union, when the "mujahideens" returned to their homeland, they played an active role in spreading extremist ideologies in their localities. The first leader of ISIS, Abu Musab al-Zarqawi himself was a returnee of Afghan war.[46] In the case of ISIS, the fallout will be much more dreadful as the foreign fighters will bring with them the battlefield experience of fighting trained armies, not to mention the connection with the global terrorist network. They would be far more seasoned and efficient in spreading the ideology, organising like-minded radicals and orchestrating attacks compared to home-grown terrorists.

Previously, it was revealed that the proliferation of terrorist organisations in South Asia, to a great extent, was caused by Afghan war veterans who fought alongside the Mujahideens during the Soviet invasion of Afghanistan. But the problems would be more difficult to manage this time as discussed before. While the Afghan war veterans in South Asia were mostly confined within the walls of *madrasas*;[47] however, the trends of the foreign fighters who have joined ISIS fight show that they belong to upper-middle class of the population and to diaspora population abroad. Unlike the madrasa returnees with little knowledge and assimilation with the mainstream society in the previous cases, these new returnees would be more assimilated with the mainstream society and having the means and knowledge to spread the ideology through social and other online media. That alone may spread these ideas in South Asia. The second important threat to watch out for is the backward linkage or family ties of diaspora who keep active connections with distant family members back home. Scholars have claimed that "twenty-seven of the fifty most active contemporary terrorist organizations are either part of a diaspora or are supported by one".[48] This may also increase the chance of further indoctrination of terrorists elsewhere.

Influx of Refugees into Neighbouring Countries
Following the crisis, people—especially minorities belonging to Kurd, Yazidi, Druze and other populations—left the conflict zone *en masse* and took shelter in neighbouring countries. Even Muslim Shi'ites who are not-so-minority in Iraq and Syria also fled the areas. One estimate suggests the figure of refugees fleeing into Turkey from Syria is about 130,000 in recent days.[49] However, according to the European Commission, 10.8 million people have been affected by the ISIS rise; among them 4.7 million are in areas that are difficult to reach.[50]

The influx of refugees has multiple implications. To begin with, it will put enormous pressure on the economies of the host countries. The question of who will share the burden is yet to be sorted out by the international community. Despite sympathies for fellow Arabs, no Arab country would be willing to permanently take the refugees as their citizens. A country like Turkey that is not an Arab nation has valid reasons to be worried, as allowing refugees to stay for long term will adversely affect its demography because of interracial marriage. In addition, as it has been observed elsewhere in the world, refugee camps are fertile grounds for terrorist recruitment.[51]

Safety of Migrant Workers
Another important consequence of the crisis could be reduced safety of migrant workers. It should be mentioned here that the Middle East, in general, is dependent on migrant workers from Asian countries and poorer Arab nations of the region.[52] In some cases, migrant workers outnumber indigenous population.[53] During battle between groups, migrant workers were caught in line of fire in Iraq and Syria. According to one report, many migrant workers are stranded in the zone unable to get out of the country.[54] Despite several South Asian nations' diplomatic maneuver to bring back their migrant workers from conflict-prone Iraq, many remain in that country. It is also difficult to assess the exact number of migrant population in Iraq as there are various channels of migration and it is difficult to keep track of temporary incoming workers. Many people have crossed over to that country from other countries. While evacuating a large number of foreign migrant workers will be a challenge for sending countries, there are also other

aspects of the problem. Workers from poorer countries living in conflict zones are reluctant to come back because they are still able to earn and remit money to their families. Second, any international migration incurs huge economic cost. Leaving those countries would imply irrecoverable economic loss for people who migrated there for a better life.

Nevertheless, since the inception of Iraq war, the number of South Asians, for example, in that country greatly reduced as home countries took evacuation measures. If the crisis continues, economies of other gulf countries will take the blow resulting in short-to-medium term economic stagnation. This, coupled with security concerns, is likely to lead to further reduction of migrants in those countries. South Asian countries have dependence on money remitted by their diasporas all over the world. It is not that only migrant workers of Iraq and Syria will dwindle because of the crisis. It has been predicted that as the ISIS crisis turns into a protracted conflict, international business is likely to reduce investments in crisis zones in the Middle East. Thus, the economies of neighbouring states will be affected in the medium term, if not immediately. Therefore, should the crisis persist, remittance flow from the Middle Eastern countries will reduce drastically.

Conclusion

As the chapter shows, certain political developments in the region created conducive space for the rise of ISIS. Owing to multinational forces' departure from Iraq, there was no strong opponent in Iraq to counter its burgeoning influence. This has emboldened ISIS to continue its spread across the country. Weakened political regimes in Syria and elsewhere were by-products of Arab Spring and, in the process, caused a political vacuum. This also catalysed its rise. The imminent crisis may threaten countries in the neighbourhood; nevertheless, there is a lack of urgency among abutting states to confront an enemy that would require attacks in other sovereign states. Therefore, ISIS faced little resistance from international community barring a few air strikes. Its apparent success in materialising what it calls the "Caliphate" by capturing lands bred further success as terrorists from other countries keep joining its bandwagon. Its state-of-the-art tactics on cyberspace also allowed it to reach more audience and recruit globally. Finally, diversification of financial resources by capturing oil fields gave it the required capital to run an organisation like itself.

This chapter also argues that the rise of ISIS would encourage other like-minded terrorist organisations to join hands with ISIS and is likely to further revitalise international terrorism. If it continues to increase in power, this may lead to a "domino effect" in the region as other terrorist organisations would rally behind it. In case of its demise caused either by leadership decapitation or collective military action by other state actors in the region, those who joined ISIS and became a part of a larger terrorist network would return to their home countries and may spread terrorist ideology or even orchestrate further attacks elsewhere. ISIS has weakened in 2019 in comparison with their hold in 2015. In South Asia, it is active and has recruited local volunteers as militants, and they are willing to fight for their parochial cause. It is also active in Afghanistan and has some regions fighting against the Taliban to ensure their hold. India has taken many bold steps in the form of surgical strikes in PoK and even at Balakot in the backdrop of Pulwama terror attack (2019). Bangladesh has also taken comprehensive steps under the able leadership of PM Sheikh Hasina. Sri Lanka's serial blasts in April 2019 have vindicated that it is also not away from the ambit of global terror outfits. But Pakistan is not eager to take any comprehensive steps and only taken cosmetic steps to contain terror. For the larger peace and stability within South Asia, all countries must adopt zero tolerance against terrorists.

NOTES

1. Fawaz A. Gerges, *The Rise and Fall of Al-Qaeda*, New York: Oxford University Press, 2011.
2. International terrorism or transnational terrorism is acts of terrorist violence that has implications for more than one country and, therefore, requires international cooperation to be addressed. See, B. Peter Rosendorff and Todd Sandler, "The Political Economy of Transnational Terrorism", *Journal of Conflict Resolution*, Vol. 49, No. 2, 2005, pp. 171-182.
3. Rick Nelson *et. al.*, "Confronting an Uncertain Threat: The Future of Al-Qaeda and Associated Movements", Center for Strategic and International Studies (CSIS), September 2011.
4. There are considerable debates among scholars as to what constitutes a terrorist organisation. This chapter uses the definition provided by Colin Wight that stipulates that terrorism is "form of violent political" expression and that violence "illegitimate"; it involves "deliberate targeting of non-state actors and institutions" despite the fact that the "victims are not the intended recipients of the political message". See Colin Wight, "Theorising Terrorism: The State, Structure and History", *International Relations*, Vol. 23, March 2009, pp. 99-106.
5. Rick Nelson, *op. cit.*
6. Gordon Corera, "Unraveling Zarqawi's al-Qaeda Connection", *Terrorism Monitor*, Vol. 2, No. 24, 2005.
7. Peter Beaumont, "Abu Bakr al-Baghdadi: The ISIS chief with the Ambition to Overtake al-Qaida", *The Guardian*, 12 June 2014.
8. The Levant (or al-Sham in Arabic and widely used in Islamic texts) is a biblical name of a region that once comprised present-day Syria, Lebanon, Jordan, Palestine, Israel and Southern Turkey.
9. United Nations Security Council Resolution No. S/RES/2170 (2014), adopted by the Security

Council at its 7242nd meeting, 15 August 2014.
10. Wight, *op. cit.*
11. John L. Esposito, *Unholy War: Terror in the Name of Islam*, New York: Oxford University Press, 2002, pp. 105-106.
12. David Commins, *The Wahhabi Mission and Saudi Arabia*, New York: I.B. Tauris, 2006, p. 173.
13. Zeke J Miller, "Congress Votes to Arm Syrian Rebels", *Time*, 18 September 2014.
14. Michael J. Boyle, "Between Freedom and Fear: Explaining the Consensus on Terrorism and Democracy in US Foreign Policy", *International Politics*, Vol. 48, No. 2/3, 2011, pp. 412–433.
15. Paper presented by Lakhdar Brahimi, Former UN and Arab League Special Envoy to Syria, on "Syria's Conflict and the Impact on its Neighbours: The Long View" in The Royal Institute of International Affairs, 14 October 2014.
16. Alessandria Masi, "Turkey Freed 46 Turkish Hostages From ISIS Using 'Diplomatic And Political Negotiations'", *International Business Times*, 22 September 2014.
17. Trevor McCrisken, "Ten Years On: Obama's War on Terrorism in Rhetoric and Practice", *International Affairs*, Vol. 87, No. 4, 2011, pp. 782-783.
18. See, Jay Sekulow, *Rise of ISIS: A Threat We Can't Ignore*, New York: Howard Books, 2014.
19. The Arabic word *jihad* can have several meanings with religious connotations as described in Islamic scriptures or without. Transnational terrorist groups have often used the word to justify their violent political means. For a detailed discussion on *jihad* and its various connotations, see, Richard Bonney, *Jihad: From Qur'an to bin Laden*, New York: Palgrave Macmillan, 2004.
20. Laurent Vinatier, "Foreign Jihadism in Syria: The Islamic State of Iraq and al-Sham", Security Assessment in North Africa, *SANA Dispatch*, No. 4, April 2014.
21. Abdul Basit, "Foreign Fighters in Iraq and Syria – Why So Many?" *Counter Terrorism Trends and Analysis*, Vol. 6, No. 9, 2014, pp. 4-8.
22. Richard Barrett, "Foreign Fighters in Syria", The Soufan Group, June 2014, available at http://soufangroup.com/wp-content/uploads/2014/06/TSG-Foreign-Fighters-in-Syria.pdf, accessed on 07 September 2014.
23. Basit, *op. cit.*
24. Michael Jonsson, "Following the Money: Financing the Territorial Expansion of Islamist Insurgents in Syria", Swedish Defence Research Agency, *FOI Memo*, No. 4947, 23 May 2014, available at http://foi.se/Global/V%C3%A5r%20kunskap/S%C3%A4kerhetspolitiska %20studier/Asien/Rapporter_och_memon/FOI%20Memo%204947.pdf, accessed on 15 August 2014.
25. Jay Sekulow, *op. cit.*
26. David Sanger and Julie Davis, "Struggling to Starve ISIS of Oil Revenue, U.S. Seeks Assistance from Turkey", *The New York Times*, 13 September 2014.
27. Valérie Marcel, "ISIS and the Dangers of Black Market Oil", Royal Institute of International Affairs, 21 July 2014, available at http://www.chathamhouse.org/expert/comment/15203, accessed on 02 September 2014.
28. *Ibid.*
29. Andrew Phillips, "The Islamic State's Challenge to International Order", *Australian Journal of International Affairs*, Vol. 68, No. 5, 2014, pp. 495-498.
30. F. Gregory Gause, "Beyond Sectarianism: The New Middle East Cold War", Brookings Doha

Center Analysis Paper, No. 11, July 2014.
31 Michael Lipka, "The Sunni-Shia Divide: Where They Live, What They Believe and How They View Each Other", Pew Research Center, 18 June 2014, available at http://www.pewresearch.org/fact-tank/2014/06/18/the-sunni-shia-divide-where-they-live-what-they-believe-and-how-they-view-each-other/, accessed on 27 September 2014.
32 Fareed Zakaria, *The Post-American World*, New York: W. W. Norton & Company Ltd, 2008, pp. 11-12.
33 Brian Michael Jenkins, "Is Al Qaeda's Internet Strategy Working?", RAND Corporation, 06 December 2011, available at http://homeland.house.gov/sites/homeland.house.gov/files/Testimony%20Jenkins%20.pdf, accessed on 15 August 2014.
34 "The Islamic State's (ISIS, ISIL) Magazine", The Clarion Project, 10 September 2014, available at http://www.clarionproject.org/news/islamic-state-isis-isil-propaganda-magazine-dabiq, accessed on 17 September 2014.
35 "Areas Under ISIS Control", *The New York Times*, 12 June 2014.
36 Domino theory also guided many US policies during the Cold War era. In simplest terms, the theory suggested that if one country fell to communism, adjacent nations would follow suit. For further discussion on 'domino effect' in international relations, see, Jerome Slater, "The Domino Theory and International Politics: The Case of Vietnam", *Security Studies*, Vol. 3, No. 2, 1993-94, pp. 186-224.
37 Parag Khanna, "The Domino Effect of Arab Unrest", *CNN*, 02 February 2011, available at http://edition.cnn.com/2011/OPINION/02/01/roundup.jordan.egypt/, accessed on 01 September 2014.
38 Jack Snyder, "Introduction", in Robert Jervis and Jack Snyder (eds.), *Dominoes and Bandwagons: Strategic Beliefs and Great Power Competition in the Eurasian Rimland*, New York: Oxford University Press, 1991.
39 Cahal Milmo and Tom Witherow, "Boko Haram Closes in on its Dream of an African Caliphate – and ISIS Gives its Blessing, and Advice on Strategy", *The Independent*, 08 September 2014.
40 Najib Sharifi, "ISIS Makes Inroads in Afghanistan, Pakistan", *Foreign Policy*, 30 September 2014.
41 Marco Vicenzino, "Confronting ISIS through a New Balance of Power in Middle East", *The Huffington Post*, 11 September 2014, available at http://www.huffingtonpost.com/marco-vicenzino/confronting-isis-through-_b_5804618.html, accessed on 22 September 2014.
42 Ted Thornhill, "ISIS Arming Themselves with US-Made Military Hardware to Wage Jihad across the Middle East after Seizing Weapons from Syrian Rebels and Iraqi Soldiers", *The Daily Mail*, 09 September 2014.
43 Marc Lynch, "Would Arming Syria's Rebels Have Stopped the Islamic State?", *The Washington Post*, 11 August 2014.
44 David Ignatius, "Obama Wants Assad to Go, But Not Too Soon", *The Washington Post*, 19 June 2013.
45 David Usborne and Nigel Morris, "Iraq Crisis Prompts Reconciliation between Iran and the West: From Great Satan to the Great Rapprochement", *The Independent*, 16 June 2014.
46 Corera, *op. cit.*
47 Taj Hashmi, "Islamic Resurgence in Bangladesh: Genesis, Dynamics and Implications", in Satu Limaye, Robert Wirsing, and Mohan Malik (eds.), *Religious Radicalism and Security in South Asia*, Hawaii: Asia-Pacific Center for Security Studies (APCSS), 2004, pp. 40-41.

48 Louise Richardson, "The Roots of Terrorism: An Overview", in Louise Richardson (ed.), *The Roots of Terrorism*, London: Routledge, 2006, p. 6.
49 Ben Hubbard, "Raids by ISIS Push Flood of Refugees Into Turkey", *The New York Times*, 22 September 2014.
50 European Commission, *ECHO Fact Sheet*, October 2014, available at http://ec.europa.eu/echo/files/aid/countries/factsheets/thematic/civil_protection_en.pdf, accessed on 23 October 2014.
51 Gabriel Sheffer, "Diasporas and Terrorism", in Richardson, *op. cit.*, pp. 120-121.
52 Toby Shelley, *Exploited: Migrant Labour in the New Global Economy*, London: ZED Books, 2007, pp. 01-10.
53 *Ibid.*
54 Syed Zain Al-Mahmood, "South Asian Migrant Workers Stuck in Wartorn Iraq", *The Wall Street Journal*, 02 July 2014.

15

Great Game in Central Asia:
Where Does India Stand?

Pramod Kumar Sharma

In July 2015, Prime Minister Narendra Modi became the maiden Indian Prime Minister to visit all the five Republics of Central Asia since their inception, giving a clear indication that India under the Modi Government is determined to develop a new bond of ties with the countries of Central Asia. Needless to add, these countries have assumed huge significance for India for various reasons, one being the fact that they can prove to be instrument in meeting India's growing energy requirement in the coming years. The CAR region has also risen to prominence in the backdrop of "Operation Enduring Freedom" launched in 2001 as far as the global efforts against counter-terrorism are concerned. It is in this context that this chapter attempts to understand the significance of Central Asia for India and to examine as to what extent India and the Countries of Central Asia have been able to deepen and expand their relations.

II

India has emerged as one of the fastest growing global economy. India is the 5th largest global energy consumer and will become the 3rd largest country by 2022. The prevailing anarchy in the Middle East, which has remained an important source of natural oil and gas for us, has caused concerns for India. At the same time, containing terror and drug trafficking has emerged as another area common interest between CAS and India. Nursing the ambitions of emerging global power, it is our moral duty to ensure peace and stability in this extended neighborhood.

The Central Asian republics of Kazakhstan, Kyrgyzstan, Tajikistan, Turkmenistan and Uzbekistan became independent in the 1990s. Since then, these countries have remained diplomatically engaged with India. In fact, New Delhi has developed strategic partnership with three of the five republics. In 2012, India announced the 'Connect Central Asia' policy and also announced to hold an India-Central Asia Dialogue at Track II annually in one of the republics. These measures have indeed contributed significantly in strengthening India's bilateral relations with the countries of Central Asia. For instance, the inauguration of Kazakhstan-Turkmenistan-Iran railway line has given the region a short and easy access to the Indian Ocean. India, on the other hand, has been making investment in Iran's Chabahar port and it has become operational in 2018. This alternative route has eased the business connectivity between the outside world and this region. This route has provided an alternative route to Afghanistan and reduced its dependence over Pakistan (Karachi port). Central Asia has already been connected by Zarnej–Delaram road constructed by India in Afghanistan and linked to Chabahar port. PM Modi attended SCO summit in Bishkek, Kyrgyzstan in June 2019 and expressed hope that this new route will accelerate all-round cooperation with Central Asian Republics. PM Modi explained that "connectivity plays an important role for ease of trade between the two countries and Iran's Chabahar port has emerged as a new route between India and Afghanistan. 2021 will be observed as a year of friendship between India and Kyrgyzstan. India will hold 'Namaskar Eurasia' trade show in Bishkek. PM Modi urged Indian companies and investors to explore areas such as medicine, textiles, railway, hydro power, mining, minerals and tourism in Kyrgyzstan."[1]

Newly appointed External Affairs Minister S. Jaishankar participated in the 5th CICA Summit in Dushanbe. In his address, he stated that "globalisation is under stress due to new and emerging geo-political and geo-economic fault lines. India supports a rule-based order in Asia, and rest of the world."[2]

III

From the onset of the Cold War till the disintegration of the USSR, the Countries of Central Asia remained under the control of the Soviet bloc. However, the collapse of the Soviet Union freed these countries to choose a new path for their future. In addition, Central Asia's stature further got scaled up in the international era, given the fact that other countries view this part of the world very crucial in securing access oil and gas. In fact, since the late 1990s, the International Energy Agency has viewed Central Asia as one of the largest undeveloped energy reserves in the world, especially for the production of oil and natural gas.³ Given increasingly pressing problems with energy supply and its sequential impact on the global economy as we enter the 21st century, Central Asia has become a more significant region for energy studies. The five Central Asian nations of Kazakhstan, Kyrgyzstan, Tajikistan, Uzbekistan and Turkmenistan have emerged firmly onto the global energy stage.⁴ Since the end of the last century, Barry Buzan, who co-worked with Wæver and de Wilde, has suggested five distinct sectors of security concern in the contemporary era: military, political, economic, environment and societal. "Economic" security naturally includes the securing of natural resources.⁵

To facilitate energy competition in the region, the major powers have found it increasingly necessary to rationalize their ambitions ideologically. The United States works from a platform of liberal democracy and "human rights above sovereignty", Russia offers its own idea of "sovereign democracy" to the Central Asians, and China portrays itself as a non-interventionist "responsible state" in the region. As one of the powers in the region, India lacks a unique ideology to increase its influence in Central Asia. However, India may play the cocktail of soft and hard power and under the dynamic leadership of Prime Minister Modi, India can effectively exercise the amalgam of soft and hard power in Central Asia in order to serve its national interests.

From the perspective of nation-states, interests always transcend ideologies because blindly following ideologies could result in deviation from national interests. If the two are in conflict, excessively fanatical ideological pursuit would be discouraged, and reporting of the regime's sacrificing the mere pursuit of ideologies would be toned down. Ideological energy diplomacy has to retain flexibility for the regimes: that is the general acceptance in the home countries housing the energy resources. Without showing concern for the actual situation, fanatically following ideologies can go against the national interest, just as an authentic follower of Marxism can go against the perceived national interests of a Marxist government.⁶ In statist regimes, excessively fanatical ideological pursuit would be discouraged; in less state-centric regimes, reports of the regimes sacrificing the ideological pursuit would also be toned down. In other words, without the energy concerns, it is difficult to preach these ideologies with any sincerity on their own and once their dogmatic interpretations no longer serve state interests, they are effectively redundant.

IV

Scholarly interest in Central Asia, which is commonly perceived as "landlocked, poor, peripheral, fearful, defenseless, Muslim, and undemocratic", has become widespread since the five republics gained independence.[7] There are many aspects to the importance of the region. Some scholars stress the significance of its Islamic religion while discussing security issues in Central Asia.[8] For some, geopolitics plays a greater role in the region, which has been described as the "second Persian Gulf", the new "grand chessboard", the "heartland of the heartland" or the "Great Game II".[9] The Cold War complex also haunts the republics. Despite this unease, energy politics seems to be of the greatest concern on this grand chessboard. Of the global powers that have prime energy interests in the region, the US, Russia and China are the leading competing forces, although nations such as Japan and India also have their sights on the region.[10] Various studies on energy encroachment in Central Asia share two common assumptions: the stakeholders are rationalist-based, and realist- or neo-realist-orientated.[11] Although early scholars and realist practitioners may not have obviously included economic concerns in their works, latecomers have started featuring energy resources in the political realist analysis of international relations.

Gilpin regards Thucydides' work on the History of the Peloponnesian War to be partially driven by energy competition; at that time, it was wheat to fuel human bodies.[12] In the contemporary world, natural oil and gas has become the lifeline of energy and India is growing rapidly. Thus, it is an important challenge before Modi government to ensure uninterrupted energy supply to accelerate India's economic growth in coming decades. In the last term (2014-19), Modi government has worked hard on this plank. Central Asia has remained an important instrument to this particular dynamics of Modi's foreign policy.

Given the policies used by the US, Russia and China, one may well question whether another great power candidate adjacent to Central Asia, i.e. India, could apply the same strategy. Undoubtedly, India also has strong interests in Central Asia. As the second largest growing economy in the world, India relies heavily on energy imports to sustain its domestic economic expansion. According to the International Energy Outlook, India was the fifth largest oil consumer in 2007 and its demand grew to almost 3 million barrels per day (bbl/d) in 2008.[13] In 2009, 68 percent of its oil was imported, and its dependency on oil imports is expected to increase to 92 percent by 2020.[14] In this context, considerable progress by India to obtaining Central Asian resources has been made. For instance, since 2004, India has invested US$3 billion in the Sakhalin-3 oil field and the joint

Russian-Kazakh Kurmangazy oil field in Central Asia. India also signed an agreement with Uzbekistan to launch a US$60 million joint venture for India's state-owned gas utility.[15]

The countries of Central Asia are endowed with significant hydrocarbon and mineral resources and are close to India geographically. Kazakhstan is the largest producer of uranium and has huge gas and oil reserves as well. Similarly, Uzbekistan is also rich in gas, and is an important regional producer of gold along with Kyrgyzstan. Tajikistan has vast hydropower potential besides oil deposits, and Turkmenistan has the fourth largest gas reserves of the world. Geographically, the strategic location of these countries makes them a bridge between different regions of Asia and between Europe and Asia. Although the significance of the region in India's economic and energy security is clear, lack of direct surface connectivity has been affecting the economic engagement. However, the recent inauguration of Kazakhstan-Turkmenistan-Iran railway line has given the region a short access to the Indian Ocean. India, on the other hand, has been making investment in Iran's Chabahar port. This alternative route has eased the business connectivity of the outside world with the region.[16]

India and Iran have already got connected in Central Asia through this port while construction of the Delaram-Jarnej road in western Afghanistan has further improved connectivity between India and Central Asia. In fact, in April 2015, India's Surface Transport Minister Nitin Gadkari during his visit to Iran stressed on the point that the newly developed Chabahar port jointly built by India and Iran can prove to be instrumental in cementing relations between India and Central Asian countries. Prime Minister Modi's visit to this part of the world further witnessed many bilateral agreements ranging from energy supply to defense cooperation. Iranian President Rouhani and Indian Prime Minister Modi met in Ufa (Russia) in July 2015 and had a 90-minutes bilateral talk. During this meeting, it was pledged that India and Iran will accelerate their bilateral relations. In July 2015, Iran and the western world had signed a nuclear deal and whole gamut of the decade-long sanctions imposed against Iran was lifted. President Trump administration has clamped sanctions against Iran again and has deployed many warships in Hormuz. This has complicated the problem.

In August 2015, Iranian Foreign Minister Javad Zarif visited New Delhi and met Prime Minister Modi and other ministers. Again, it was reiterated that cooperation on all fronts will be accelerated. During a one-day visit of Mr. Zarif, issues related to Islamic State threat, energy investments, Afghanistan and development of the Chabahar port were discussed. He also stated that India is an important player in West Asia. Prime Minister Modi conveyed India's commitment to work with Iran for development of the Chabahar port that would have far reaching benefit, not only for the people of India and Iran, but also for Afghanistan and the entire the Central Asian region. Mr. Zarif acknowledged India's support during turbulent times. PM Modi visited Iran in 2016 and inked many agreements. Iran has enormous energy reserves, and therefore the relationship between the two countries took a natural way of deepening. India is currently the 5th largest global energy consumer and by 2022 will be the 3rd largest energy consumer leaving Japan and Russia behind. It is also opined by sections of global economic pundits that by 2042, India will be representing 23% of the global GDP. For the sustainability of India's growth saga, sustainable and diverse supply of energy is a must.

Iran is not only important for fulfilling India's energy needs but due to its geographical proximity, it is emerging as India's gateway to Central Asia. In addition, due to the connections between regional terrorist groups in Central Asia and the insurgents in Kashmir and the Punjab, the region's cooperation is seen as instrumental to India's anti-terrorist security. India is also seen by the Central Asian countries as an important gatekeeper of regional terrorism: once the Kazakh President Nazarbayez publicly invited India to join the Shanghai Cooperative Organization (SCO) for the sake of facilitating anti-terrorism.[17] Consequently, in July 2015, India formally joined it. Hence, Central Asia is also involved in the Indian-Pakistani rivalry. In 2004, Uzbekistan was commissioned by the Indian Air Force Mid-Air-Refueling Squadron (MARS) to build three giant IL-78 MKI refuellers. Kazakhstan also signed a military cooperation agreement with India in 2002 for joint production of military hardware such as torpedoes and heavy machine gun barrels.[18] All these gestures have irritated Pakistan. Indeed, India has shown its intention to respond to great power diplomacy in Central Asia by challenging the Big Three as well. For instance, Phunchok Stobdan, former Director of the Indian Cultural Center, once suggested that the US's growing presence in the region "forms a compelling reason for India's reclaiming its geopolitical rights and responsibilities in Central Asia".[19]

V

As far as India's inter-state diplomacy is concerned, the Mandala concept in Kautilya's *Arthashastra* precisely portrays a quasi-balance of power tactic in interactions among states. The Vijigishu, who intends to establish its hegemony over others, should be aware of the motives of the other eleven kings of the Mandala in order to secure peace.[20] The circumstance of friends and foes changes with the existing political and economic situation. When the nation is situated on the circumference, the Vijigishu is the enemy (ari). Next to the ari is the ally (mitra), then the enemy ally (arimitra), one's ally's ally (mitra mitra) then the enemy's ally's ally (arimitra mitra).[21] A smart and inscrutable leader should be required to play the political field with wit and strategy. As can be seen, protection rather than expansion is more important in state governance and the complex mandala concept is easy to ensure in the case of Central Asia but successive Government has failed to do that. India till recently was pursuing its Central Asia policy in a low-profile manner but since the arrival of the Modi Government in 2014, it has scaled up its Central Asia policy and propelled hard ground work to ensure deepening bilateral relations with the region in its first term.

Prime Minister Modi's visit to five countries of Central Asia in July 2015 has indeed been viewed as a major initiative towards bridging the gap between India and Central Asia. Central Asia is extremely important for the promotion of our national interests. Energy security is of utmost importance. Kazakhstan, Turkmenistan and Uzbekistan are endowed with enormous hydrocarbon reserves. Two of these countries Kazakhstan and Turkmenistan are in the Caspian littorals, thereby promising to open the door to other energy-rich Caspian states. Connectivity through the North-South Transport Corridor featured in Modi's speeches in both countries as much as the impending implementation of the two gas pipelines. These are implementable but hinge on the political situation in Pakistan and Afghanistan.[22] Iran could be important facilitator of our interests in Central Asia given the prevailing synergy of interests. Prime Minister Modi has visited entire Central Asia and pledged a lot; now it is the time to implement possible assurances to promote our national interests. It is the need of the hour. India has enormous soft power leverage's in the region and unlike Russia and China, India is always welcome by CAR. PM Modi invited Kyrgyzstan President as chairman of the SCO to participate in his second oath-taking ceremony in May 2019. PM Modi visited Bishkek to participate in SCO Summit and outlined India's deepening interests in Central Asia. The returning of Modi government in power for the second term (2014-19) will act as an accelerator to our relationship with Central Asia. We have to work tirelessly in Central Asia. We have just started working hard to ensure deepening relations with Central Asia. We have synergy with Central Asian Countries. Modi government has started positively and its return to power again in 2019 will of course propel the process of deepening our bilateral relationships. We need to work hard to sustain the process as our bilateral relationship with CAR will be one of the most challenging foreign affairs tasks for the Modi Government.

NOTES

1. Ambassador Ashok Sajjanhar, Distinguished Fellow, *Ananta Centre*, Former Ambassador of India to Kazakhstan, Sweden and Latvia, Vol 4, Issue 6, June 2019.
2. Ibid
3. International Energy Agency, Caspian Oil and Gas: The Supply Potential of Central and Transcaucasia (Paris: OECD Publications, 1998).
4. Shai Feldman (ed.), *After the War in Iraq: Defining the New Strategic Balance* (Brighton; Portland, Oregon: Sussex Academic Press/Jaffee Center for Strategic Studies); Richard Heinberg, *The party's over: oil, war and the fate of industrial societies* (Gabriola Island, B.C.: New Society Publishers, 2003).
5. Barry Buzan, Ole Wæver, Jaap de Wilde, *Security: A New Framework for Analysis* (London: Lynne Rienner Publisher, 1998).
6. Van Ness, *Revolution and Chinese foreign policy; Peking's support for wars of national liberation* (Berkeley: University of California Press, 1971).
7. Charles William Maynes, "America Discovers Central Asia," *Foreign Affairs*, 82, 2 (March/April 2003): 120-33.
8. David Hoffman, "Iran's Drive to Rebuild Seen Posing New Challenges to West," *The Washington Post*, February 2, 1992; Jim Nichol, "Central Asia: Regional Developments and Implications for U.S. Interests," CRS Report for Congress, November 13, 2008.
9. Zbigniew Brzezinski, *The Grand Chessboard: American Primacy and Its Geostrategic Imperatives* (New York: Basic Books, 1997); Mehdi Amineh, *Globalization, Geopolitics and Energy Security in Central Eurasia and the Caspian Region* (The Hague: Clingendael International Energy Program, 2003). Sally Cummings (ed.), *Oil, Transition and Security in Central Asia* (New York: Routledge Curzon, 2003); Robert Legvold, "Greater Power Stakes in Central Asia," in Robert Legvold (ed.), *Thinking Strategically: The Major Powers, Kazakhstan, and the Central Asian Nexus* (Cambridge, MA: MIT Press, 2003).
10. Annete Bohr, "Regionalism in Central Asia: New Geopolitics, Old Regional Order," *International Affairs*, 80, 3 (2004): 485-502; Neil MacFarlane, "The United States and Regionalism in Central Asia," *International Affairs*, 80, 3 (2004): 447-6; Dianne Smith, "Central Asia: A New Great Game?" Research Monograph from Strategic Studies Institute, 1996, p. 20. http://www.strategicstudiesinstitute.army.mil/pdffiles/PUB117.pdf (December 18, 2009).
11. Xu Xiaojie, "The Oil and Gas Links between Central Asia and China: A Geopolitical Perspective," OPEC Review: Energy Economics & Related Issues 23, 1 (1999): 33-54; Ariel Cohen, "U.S. Interests and Central Asia Energy Security," November 15, 2006. http://www.heritage.org/Research/Reports/2006/11/US-Interests-and-Central-Asia-Energy-Security (April 6, 2010); Andrew Monaghan, "Russia's Energy Diplomacy: A Political Idea Lacking a Strategy?" Southeast European and Black Sea Studies 17, 2 (2007): 275-88.
12. Thucydides, *History of the Peloponnesian War* (Chicago: University of Chicago Press, 1989), p. 293.
13. International Energy Outlook 2009. http://www.eia.doe.gov/oiaf/ieo/
14. Shiv Kumar Verma, "Energy Geopolitics and Iran-Pakistan-India Gas Pipeline" *Energy Policy*, 35, 6 (2007): 3280-3301.

15 Scott Moore, "Peril and Promise: A Survey of India's Strategic Relationship with Central Asia," *Central Asian Survey*, 26, 2 (2007): 279-291.
16 Athar Zafar, India-Central Asia: Finding New Synergies for Greater Engagement, Indian Council of World Affairs Policy Brief, New Delhi, 9 July 2015.
17 Rahul Bedi, "India and Central Asia," *Frontline* 19, 19 (2002).
18 Amit Mukherjee, "IAF to get 5th IL-78 refuellers soon," Indiatimes, September 29, 2004.
19 Ibragim Alibekov, "India set to expand presence in Central Asia," Eurasianet, March 12, 2003.
20 Roger Boesche, *The first great political realist: Kautilya and his Arthashastra* (Lanham: Lexington Books, 2002), pp. 77-78.
21 Donald Mackenzie Brown, *The White Umbrella: Indian Political Thought from Manu to Gandhi* (Berkeley: University of California Press, 1953), pp. 59-60.
22 P.L. Dash, When Central Asia Calls, *The Indian Express*, New Delhi, July 27, 2015.

16

Sino-India Bustle for Securing Hydrocarbons in Africa:
Zero-Sum or Win-Win?

Pranav Kumar

Energy Security of a nation can best be described as long term measures to adequately maintain the required supply of energy for at all times and at reasonable price to support its sustained economic, commercial and developmental activities. Man's survival has always depended upon his ability to derive sufficient energy as it is the supply of energy which increases supply of food, improve physical comfort, decide the level of development and expand the quality of life (Loftness 1998: 3). Unlike traditional security, to have sustainable and sustained energy security many dimensions—economic, political, military, social, cultural, environmental—have to be taken into account and various 'levels'—human, state and systemic—have to be factored in (Buzan 1991:146). Energy security ranges from exploration, production, and transportation, to physical security, strategic reserves and even foreign policy (Malakar 2006: 132). Energy security is improved by managing energy demand, increasing domestic energy supply, or increasing the reliability of imported or domestic supplies. Structural change in the economy, transformation in demographic composition, shift in the government policy for the power generation, increasing defence and space related fuel requirements and growing environmental concerns all these call for strenuous demands on the hydrocarbon sector for the supply of India's and China's energy needs. But faced with inadequate energy production the Asian giants' energy security needs are directly linked with the external supply of the hydrocarbons. India and China increasingly see energy security as a national priority and central aspect of their foreign policy. This is mainly driven by the recognition of the countries' increasing oil and gas import dependence and the need to employ a multi-pronged strategy to address its energy security concerns (IEA 2005: 244). Hydrocarbon remains to be the major energy source. Although, the share of oil in world's Total Primary Energy Supply (TPES) in percent term has decreased from 44 percent to 32 percent between 1971 to 2016; share of natural gas has increased from 16 percent to 22 percent during the same period (IEA 2018: 5).

The Asian Giants' Energy Security and Expanding Geopolitical Space

There has been not a single period in modern and industrial history when either European and/or North America have/has not been major force propelling global economic growth and, in turn, determining the pattern of global energy demands. However, one of the most important visible global trends of twenty-first century is the rise of emerging economies from the South or the East. The BRICS countries—Brazil, Russia, India, China, South Africa—have been major source of economic growth in the recent past (Kelly 2015). These countries, unlike the West, have been defying stagnant economic growth post the financial crisis and have been growing way faster than the developed world (Kelly 2015). Rise of their share in global economy has been exponentially transforming global energy consumption trajectory wherein their relative share has been zooming with each passing year. The pattern seems to continue in the foreseeable future. Owing to hydrocarbons' uneven spatial distribution and its persistence centrality in propelling development of major economies, it remains to be one of the most significant strategic commodities shaping the geopolitics of the world since early 1970s. Since then only visible change is that on the place of the West, China and India are leading the demand for hydrocarbons abroad.

China has proved to be the engine that has been pushing global energy demand vigorously. During the two decades following China's opening of its economy in early 1980s, China's economy grew with an averaged 9 percent (Naidu and Martin 2006: 69). Until early 1990s, China was one of the major oil exporters in the East Asia. Since 1993, however, China has been importing oil. Securing energy sources abroad has become one of the major imperatives of China's 'peaceful rise.' During 1993-99 Chinese policy makers realized that production of oil can no longer meet domestic demand. Even in 2016, China alone provided 60.8 percent of Asia's energy production (IEA 2018: xix). But the domestic production does not proved to be sufficient in catering China's ever growing appetite for energy. The Government started to conduct reform to increase competitiveness of the State Owned Enterprises (SOEs) so that they can start to seek oil in foreign markets. Subsequently, under the slogans of "Go global" during 2000-2008, and "Go abroad and buy" (Jian 2011: 6), China has been aggressively pursuing its hydrocarbon diplomacy, mainly with the help of SOEs and track-one channels. China has become the second largest importer of energy (Zweig and Jianhai 2005: 25). The US Department of energy expects that China's imported oil will climb to 9.4 million per day by 2025 (Zahirinejad and Vrushal 2010: 63). China is nearing production of half of the world coal and 29 percent of hydro in 2016 (IEA 2018:5). During 1971-2016, China's share in world's Total Primary Energy Supply (TPES) increased from 7 percent to 22 percent (IEA 2018:6). Although China's dependence IEA's projection predicts that around 2030, it is going to overtake the European Union in gas consumption (IEA 2014a).

Similarly, For India, a country that has been defying trends of global economic meltdown at the large extant and has been growing at a brisk pace; non-other factor would be more pertinent than to support its economic growth with sustained supply of resources-natural and human-at affordable price. Needless to mention that securing constant flow of energy ranks the highest amongst all. Despite the fact that the energy source diversification has been high on India's agenda and her domestic hydrocarbon production bases are expanding, more than eighty per cent of its hydrocarbon energy demand is being fulfilled by the external sources. Thirty percent of India's energy needs are fulfilled by oil and around 80 percent of oil is imported (PTI 2018). The IEA predicts that in order to nourish present growth, India will have to increase its energy consumption by 3.6 percent annually. According to Petroleum Planning and Analysis Cell (PPAC) the oil imports of India are pegged at 219.15 MT for USD 87.725 billion during 2017-18 (PTI 2018). The rate with which India's dependency on eternal sources is increasing, it will be compelled to import 90 percent of its hydrocarbon supply (Hate 2015).

The dependence on imported oil is not going to end in foreseeable future; it may well increase, judging by the Integrated Energy Policy, which projects import dependence in excess of 90 per cent for crude oil, up to 50 per cent for natural gas, and up to 45 per cent for coal (Desai 2013). During the four decades since 1970s, i.e. from 1970-71 to 2010-11, the Compound Annual Growth Rate (CAGR) of production of coal, lignite, crude petroleum, natural gas, and electricity (hydro and nuclear) generation was 5.0 percent, 6.1 percent, 4.3 percent, 9.1 percent, and 4.0 percent respectively. In terms of energy equivalent of all the primary energy sources in 2010-11, the shares of coal and lignite, electricity (hydro and nuclear), and natural gas were 52 percent, 28 percent and 11 percent respectively (GOI 2013: 233).

Domestic annual production of crude oil has been stagnant at around 38 million tonnes in the last four years (GOI 2015: 98). Faced with inadequate energy production India's energy security needs are directly linked with the external supply in the vital energy sectors with special emphasis will remain on hydrocarbons. The vagaries of petroleum supply from the Persian Gulf and over dependence on the region create an atmosphere of insecurity for India and hamper its economic and developmental prospects. Even though the global price of oil has been dwindling of late, the unreliability in the supply pattern of the Persian Gulf emanates from the dynamics of regional geopolitics, internal political instability, use of production as a strategic commodity and the proactive role played by oil cartel OPEC in the region.

In the last few years Indian policy-makers have recognized the fact that increased dependence on the Persian Gulf for oil supply can impede India's vital security interests. India has been keen to diversify her petroleum supply options. The diverse supply patterns would reduce her sense of vulnerability against any supply disruption. In view of an unfavourable demand-supply ratio of hydrocarbons in the country, acquiring equity oil and gas assets overseas has been an important strategy for enhancing energy security for last ten years or so. The government is encouraging state owned companies to purchase oil from foreign sources (Roy-Choudhary 1998: 1671) and to aggressively pursue equity oil and gas opportunities overseas. ONGC Videsh Limited (OVL) has produced about 8.753 MMT of oil and equivalent gas during the year 2011-12 from its assets abroad in Sudan, Vietnam, Venezuela, Russia, Syria, Brazil, South Sudan, and Colombia (GOI: 2013: 239).

Rise of Africa on Global Hydrocarbon Map
Africa's rise on global hydrocarbons map is a parallel and complementary to the skyrocketing external energy demand of India and China. Africa is rich in energy resources. Even the most conservative estimates are to be believed; Africa accounts for 10 per cent of the world's oil reserves; 8 per cent of the natural gas reserves; 5 per cent of the coal reserves; 38 per cent of uranium reserves; and 12 per cent of global technical hydropower potential (Sikhwati 2009). Almost 30 percent of global oil and gas discoveries made over the last five years (2009-2014) were in the continent. Rising output from Nigeria, Angola and a host of smaller producers,

means that sub-Saharan Africa remains an important source of global oil supply. The region emerges also as an important player in gas, as development of the major east coast discoveries off Mozambique and Tanzania accompanies increased production in Nigeria and elsewhere (IEA 2014b). According to International Energy Agency (IEA), Oil production in Africa will exceed 6 million barrels per day (mb/d) in 2020 before slightly falling back to 5.3 mb/d in 2040. The countries that will lead the African production would be Nigeria and Angola. Demand for oil products is supposed to double to 4 mb/d in 2040, and Gas output reaches 230 billion cubic metres (bcm), led by Nigeria, and increasing output from Mozambique, Tanzania and Angola. LNG exports will triple to around 95 billion cubic meter (bcm) (IEA 2014a).

The Gulf of Guinea, an arm of Atlantic Ocean, has a large amount of hydrocarbon energy resources. Eleven African Countries—Ivory Coast, Ghana, Benin, Togo, Nigeria, Cameroon, Gabon, Equatorial Guinea, Democratic Republic of Congo, Republic of Congo and Sao Tome and Principe share its continental shelf. Among these, Nigeria, Gabon and Cameroon are major petroleum producers. Furthermore, Angola which can also be considered to be an extension of the Gulf is the second most important oil producer in Africa. Until very recently the oil discoveries, exploration and production in sub-Saharan Africa (with the exception of Chad and Sudan) has been found in countries located along the Atlantic coast. While prospects for oil in Namibia and South Africa looks promising, and while oil has been found in the waters off Mauritania, most of the major known reserves of any magnitude are concentrated in an area that spans the Atlantic littoral from Nigeria to Angola. Moreover, the crude from the region is of very high quality i.e. light and with low sulfur content. Furthermore most of oil in the region is found and will be extracted from open sea platforms that are offshore, far away from the dire and often troubled mainland of the respective states.

Nigeria is Africa's largest oil producer. The proven oil reserves of the country are approximately 30 billion barrels and it produces approximately 2 million barrel per day of crude oil (Beri 2005: 374). Approximately 65 percent of Nigerian crude oil production is light and sweet, making it particularly suited in the context of growing environmental concerns (Valle 2004: 53). Nigeria has the potential to increase its crude oil production significantly in the next few years as recent deep-water discoveries come on stream. Existing and new producers, such as Angola, Gabon, Equatorial Guinea and São Tomé & Príncipe, are going to continue to develop new oil and gas reserves in the coming years. The Petroleum industry is the principal economic mainstay of Angola (Hughes 2006: 81). Angola has estimated reserves of 1.6 Trillion cubic feet of natural gas (IEA 2006: 133).

The North African country Algeria holds the third-largest amount of proven crude oil reserves in Africa, all of which are located onshore because there has been limited offshore exploration. According to Sonatrach, about two-thirds of Algerian territory remains largely underexplored or unexplored. According to the *Oil & Gas Journal* (OGJ) estimates, released in January 2014, Algeria held an estimated 12.2 billion barrels of proved crude oil reserves (EIA 2014: 5). EIA study also estimates that Algeria contains 707 trillion cubic feet (Tcf) and 5.7 billion barrels of technically recoverable shale gas and oil resources (EIA 2014: 2). The country's all of proved and unexplored oil reserves are held onshore because there has been limited offshore exploration.

West and North Africa has long held the spotlight as a major oil province, but recent discoveries in other areas of the continent have catapulted Africa on the global energy map. Barely appearing on the energy radar until very recently, eastern Africa has become one of the world's hottest spots for oil and natural gas reserves. Beyond Tullow's success in Uganda, the offshore East Africa is attracting attention from various international players. With successes in Mozambique and potential growing in Tanzania, Kenya and Madagascar, East Africa is emerging as a new hydrocarbon province. During past 10 years East Africa, on account of its offshore and onshore discoveries, has emerged as the world's most promising hydrocarbon frontier. 2.3 billion barrels of recoverable oil is discovered in Uganda and Kenya; and more than 50 tcf natural gas in Tanzania (Manson 2015).

Under Shadow of the Red Star

China has a much larger presence in Africa than India, in terms of both acquiring energy deals and government engagement. Chinese oil companies have been investing heavily in the continent. For instance, in Nigeria the Chinese oil giant China's National Offshore Oil Corporation (CNOOC) has owned a 45 percent stake in deepwater block Offshore Mining License (OML) 130 since 2009 (Europetrole 2009). Furthermore, As a part of purchase of Nexen—a Canadian country by CNOOC clinched significant offshore oil reserves in Nigeria. Yet another Chinese company CNPC has purchased shares in Nigeria, buying rights to blocks OPL 298, 471, 721, and 732 from the Nigerian government in 2006. This purchase was followed by a purchase of the rights to blocks OML 64 and OML 66 in 2012. The Chinese oil giant Sinopec also has made inroads in Nigeria, including a deal with Total to pay $2.5 billion for a 20 percent share in block

OML 138 in 2012 (Patel 2012). Almost all of these investments by Chinese companies are in buying shares in blocks, not sole control, so the Chinese often rely on their partners to do most of the actual production work for them, releasing them from the technological demands that come with offshore drilling. While there are a number of onshore fields that Chinese companies have stakes in, most of the oil-rich fields are offshore, so they are not quite as vulnerable to the population of the areas hurting their production (Quigle 2014).

Angola has emerged as one of the major African partners accounting for lion's share. China has made a large amount of diversified oil investments in Angola, spending over $92 billion between 2009 and 2012 in joint ventures and energy acquisition (Quigle 2014). Overall, the Chinese oil companies are operating in nearly 20 African countries in both the upstream and downstream activities (IDE-JETRO 2015). However, the state owned companies are the major actors that China is using for venturing in the continent.

India's Engagements

As part of its international strategy to diversify suppliers, the government's oil exploration and production enterprise, the Oil and National Gas Corporation (ONGC), has ventured into Africa. Nigeria is already India's second largest supplier, with 15 percent of the share. ONGC Videsh, the international arm of the agency, has acquired shares in oil exploration ventures in Libya and Nigeria. It has also made substantial investments in Sudan's hydrocarbon sector and plans to invest in offshore drilling in the Ivory Coast. Reliance Industries, one of India's largest privately held energy companies, is also negotiating energy collaborations for refining with several African countries including Angola and Nigeria. In 2010-2011, India imported 20,726 million USD worth of crude oil from Africa, accounting for 21.6 per cent of India's total crude oil imports (Department of Commerce 2013).

Nigeria, followed by Angola, commanded a major share of this, accounting for 50.85 and 24.5 per cent respectively. These nations are followed by Algeria, Egypt and Libya together contributing around 17.5 per cent of India's oil import. Apart from the import, ONGC Videsh (OVL) has been one of the most active public sector companies in Africa. The company has its exploration projects in Africa—one in Libya, two in Nigeria, one in Egypt and one in JDZ: Nigeria—STP. There are also two producing projects which are in Sudan (one of them is the Greater Nile project). The main countries of interest with confirmed reserves of oil are Angola, Nigeria, Equatorial Guinea, Ghana, Cote d'Ivoire, and Sierra

Leone. The projects in Sudan are the currently the only examples of state-owned companies extracting hydrocarbons. The other public sector companies in Africa are Oil India Limitied (OIL), Bharat Petroleum (BP) and Hindustan Petroleum (HP). Oil India Ltd has interests in three blocks in Libya, two in Egypt and one in Nigeria, Bharat Petro Resources has interests in a block in Mozambique and Hindustan Petroleum has interests in two Egyptian blocks (Deccan Herald 2011). Bharat Petro Resources also announced a major natural gas discovery offshore Mozambique in 2010 (Kulkarni 2010).

Table 1: India's Crude Oil Imports from Africa (2010-11)

S. No.	Country	Values in US$ Million	% Share of Africa	% Share of total import
1	Nigeria	10,536.92	50.85	11.37
2	Angola	5,089.12	24.5	5.49
3	Algeria	1,704.30	8.2	1.84
4	Egypt	983.82	4.75	1.10
5	Libya	961	4.6	1.04
6	Sudan	565.77	3	0.61
7	Congo P Rep	478.65	2.3	0.52
8	Gabon	211.85	1	0.23
9	Cameroon	117.98	0.5	0.13
10	Guinea	76.83	0.3	0.08
	Total - Africa	20,726.62	100	22.4
	Total - Import	92,651.77		

Source: Compiled from Export Import Data Bank, http://commerce.nic.in/eidb/ecntq.asp

Unlike the Chinese case, the Indian private sector has also been making inroad into the oil and gas sector in Africa. Reliance Industries, India's largest private sector player in the energy sector made its first major overseas acquisition through buying a majority stake and management control of Gulf Africa Petroleum Corporation (GAPCO) in 2007 (ENS Economic Bureau 2007). Another private sector company, Essar Energy Overseas Limited has a 50 per cent stake in the Kenya Petroleum Refineries Limited since 2009. Both RIL and Essar have been bidding to acquire assets of British Petroleum in Zambia, Malawi, Botswana, Namibia and Tanzania (Barman 2010).

Zero-Sum Game

The main driver for both Asian giants in Africa is energy. Interestingly, it is against the backdrop of Africa's energy landscape that India and China have started seriously engaging Africa. They have been competing against each other for the African Oil. Nonetheless, India has lost several lucrative oil deals to China and so far India seemingly lacks the obstinate strategic drive that Beijing has skillfully displayed in the African continent (Hate 2015). For instance, Sinopec prevailed over India's state owned ONGC-Videsh Limited (OVL) to acquire Shell Oil's 50 percent stake in Block 18 in Angola, operated by BP-Amoco. To ease out Indian bid China used 'carrot policy,' by extending US$2 billion loan to Angolan government and by partnering in reviving Lobito refinery (IDE-JETRO 2015). Although, both the Asia powers are denying any rivalry for African hydrocarbon, it has been visible in recent forays of India and China in the second largest continent of the world (Rajagopalan 2018).

Win-Win Scenario

Partnership: India and China have also cooperated in hydrocarbon sector. One of the earliest ventures in Africa by India and China was joint venture. In 1997, China National Petroleum Corporation (CNPC) and Oil and Natural Gas Corporation, the State owned companies of India and China respectively, jointly ventured in the Greater Nile Oil Project (GNOPC) alongside Sudan's Supdapet and Malaysia's Petronas (IDE-JETRO 2015). Even though today the venture may not be considered as a great success story as the region has been marred by civil discontent in which Chinese role has also been smelled, it proves that political will and complimentary interest can pave the way for cooperation between perceived competitors (Tiezzi 2015).

Balancing the Energy Order in Africa: Energy sector of Africa has been considered as theatre of the East-West rivalry and indicator of shifting geopolitical and geo-economic focus from the West to the East. Analogous to the 'New Great Game' being played in the other oil rich regions, Africa has also been kept on witnessing a scramble for hydrocarbon resources that involves scores of stakeholders. Earlier it was the colonial powers which were active there. Later, during the cold war, America and other western players started to make inroads there in a big way. During last two decades, however, entry of India and China in the region has compounded the scenario. Like the Gulf of Guinea and other onshore oil rich regions, Asian state-owned oil companies are making forays in the contest for East Africa's energy reserves and are gaining power in export projects that Western explorers used to dominate earlier (Mining Review 2013). China and India have been entering to the region via joint ventures (equity shares). China has forged joint ventures with a number of local state owned companies so that it can remain to be close to policymakers of the country. This has been evident in joint ventures with Nigerian National Petroleum Corporation (Nigeria), Sonangol (Angola),

Sonatrach (Algeria), Sudapet (Sudan). Moreover China and India has been involved in upstream and downstream activities of hydrocarbon rich countries. For instance, China has been involved in hydrocarbon related upstream activities in at least 20 countries and in downstream activities in at least half a dozen countries (Mining Review 2013). Hence, unlike the western model, they have redefined the nature of engagement with the oil producing countries by linking hydrocarbon sector with overall development of the region.

South-South Cooperation: Oil Geopolitics in the region, like other oil rich regions, is closely associated with intervention and interference of external forces; countries, multinational companies, and multilateral international bodies; in the domestic spheres. In this context oil companies have played pivotal role and the French company Elf's intervention in the region is a striking example of this fact. The costs of oil imports include political ties to unstable countries. Prospects of those countries achieving greater political stability simply by acquiring oil wealth are slim, as historical experience amply demonstrates (La Vine 2004:18). More often, oil wealth has triggered power struggles among governmental, socio-political and industrial fractions. Such rivalries, social divisions and developmental distortions can threaten price and supply stability and incur escalating protection cost. As fights over oil revenues become the reason for ratcheting up the level of pre-existing conflict in a society, oil may even become the very rationale for starting wars. This is especially true of economies that are not stable, as is the case of the continent. Petroleum revenues are also a central mechanism for prolonging violent conflict, and only rarely a catalyst for resolution (Fearon 2001).

The West's involvement in Africa has provoked much debate and discussion. The involvement of the western energy hunters has been scrutinized on the ground that whether their energy relationship in the Gulf is based on 'Core-Periphery' model or they are also interested in overall development of the region? Although, China has been proclaiming that her engagement with Africa is based on principles of 'south-south cooperation' and 'all weathered friendship (Kumar 2015: 189),' China's footprints in Africa has also been perceived as asymmetrically skewed in favour of China. China's dubious role has been discerned and deliberated upon in Sudan. India, however, riding on its public sector enterprises, has been more carefully crafting its energy engagement with Africa. Indian and Chinese policy makers have been conscious of the fact that this sort of image may hurt their Energy security and over all prospects in Africa very badly in long term and can loom large on their relations with the continent and elsewhere. India's Energy Security is cardinal to its relation with the region. At any cost it cannot be groomed on the shaky normative grounds of 'Dependency' and 'Neocolonialism'. They must adhere to the framework of "South-South Cooperation".

Securing Energy Sea Lane of Communications (SLOCs): So far as assuring uninterrupted supply of African hydrocarbon to their home is concerned, for both the countries energy security and maritime strategy are irrevocably intertwined (Jacob 137). One facet of energy security though well-known but the implications of which are usually not fully appreciated, is the fact that all most all the hydrocarbon acquired in Africa is transported by sea lanes (Desai 2013). The Sea Lanes of Communication (SLOCs) are channels through which goods, energy and to some extent people are transported from one state to another. The sea-bound transportation of goods and commodities is an essential component of the contemporary world's transnational and international interactions.

The protection of sea lanes has been one of the essential components of energy security of both the countries. As Mahan narrates, 'the necessity of a navy, in the restricted sense, springs from the existence of peaceful shipping' (Mahan 2004: 29). Sea power protected vital commercial flows when other, more peaceful, methods had failed (Blunden 2012: 117). Today, more than 90 percent of intercontinental trade and two thirds of the all hydrocarbon supplies transverse through sea (Kaplan 2010: 7).

Uninterrupted supply of hydrocarbons from Africa to both the countries has been closely linked with the protection of its SLOCs and the effectiveness of navy in the Indian Ocean. China's has been expanding its influence in Indian Ocean and protection of its SLOCs has been main imperative of its 'vertical ambitions' (Raja Mohan, 2013: 110-11). The future projections of emerging patterns of the Sea Lanes of Communications (SLOCs) augur that the region is going to be more significant during the foreseeable future, wherein the Indian Ocean will remain to be important trade route. India, being a major geostrategic player in the region and owing to its geographical location, is bound to face plethora of challenges and is supposed to get scores of opportunities under the backdrop of the undergoing situation and future scenario.

Conclusion

From the perspective of energy security, Africa has emerged as a happy but strenuous hunting ground for both India and China. The two Asian countries have been successful in loosening the western multinational companies' noose on Africa's hydrocarbons. So far as their energy diplomacy in Africa is concerned, they have been anticipated as rivals in the second largest continent. This assumption, nonetheless, is not misplaced as there have been numerous instances in which they found themselves in a zero-sum pay-off matrix. On the contrary, however, there have been occasions, although handful in number, wherein both the countries forged effective cooperative ventures to extract hydrocarbons. Although miles to go, they are learning to calibrate their diplomatic tools in order to balance their acts in Africa in energy sector; by co-operating when it was possible and by competing when necessary. Geopolitics of African hydrocarbons pits the Asian giants in the game of 'prisoners dilemma' wherein strangeness can be detrimental to meaningful cooperation but repeated interaction and an apt assessment of ground realities may induce congruous synergy. The trans-regional international institutional frameworks like BRICS and philosophy of 'South-South Cooperation' can be guiding force in transcending 'zero-sum' situation into a 'win-win' scenario. There has been no big difference when it comes to the normative framework that guides their engagement in Africa. However, when it comes to execution there has always been big mismatch between the strategies adopted by India, a doer, and China, a preacher, in Africa.

REFERENCES

Barman, Arjit (4 August 2010), "RIL, Essar to bid for BP's African Petrol Pumps," *Bussiness Standard*, 22 August 2015, http://www.business-standard.com/article/companies/ril-essar-to-bid-for-bp-s-african-petrol-pumps-110080400092_1.html.

Beri, Ruchita (2005), "Africa's Energy Potential: Prospects for India ", *Strategic Analysis* (New Delhi), Vol. 29, No. 3, July–September, 2005.

Blunden, Margaret (2012), "Geopolitics and the Northern Sea Route," *International Affairs*, Vol. 88 (1), p.117.

Buzan, Barry (1991), *People, States and Fear: An Agenda For International Security Studies in the Post-Cold War Era*, 2e, Hertfordshire, Harvester Wheatsheaf.

Deccan Herald (4 September 2011), "India's Interest Growing in African Oil, Gas Assets," *Deccanherald.com*, 22 August 2015, http://www.deccanherald.com/content/188348/indias-interests-growing-african-oil.html.

Department of Commerce (Government of India) (2012), *Export Import Data Bank*, 3 April 2013, http://commerce.nic.in/eidb/ecntq.asp

Desai, Nitin (17 April 2013), "How to Secure India's Energy," *The Business Standard*, 20 April 2013, http://www.business-standard.com/article/opinion/how-to-secure-india-s-energy-113041700600_1.html.

Europetrole (12 March 2009), "CNOOC Limited Announces Start-up of OML130 in Nigeria," *Europetrole*, 22 August 2015, http://www.euro-petrole.com/cnooc-ltd-announces-start-up-of-oml130-in-nigeria-n-i-2078.

ENS Economic Bureau (4 September 2007), "In First Major Foreign Foray Reliance Buys Gulf Africa Petroleum," *Indianexpress.com*, 22 August 2015, http://archive.indianexpress.com/news/

in-first-major-foreign-foray-reliance-buys-gulf-africa-petroleum-/214536/.
Fearon, James D (2001), "Why Do Some Civil Wars Last So Much Longer than Others?" paper presented to 'Civil Wars and Post-Conflict Transition,' University of California, Irvine, May 18-20, 2001.
Government of India (GOI) (2013), *Economic Survey 2012-13*, New Delhi, Ministry of Finance.
Government of India (GOI) (2015), *Economic Survey 2014-15*, Vol II, New Delhi, Ministry of Finance.
Hate, Vibhuti, "India in Africa: Beyond Oil," Centre for Strategic and International Studies, 22 August 2015, http://csis.org/story/india-africa-moving-beyond-oil.
Hughes, John (2006), "Economy," *Africa South of Sahara 2007*, London, Routledge.
Institute of Developing Economies-Japan External Trade Organization (IDE-JETRO) (2015), *China in Africa*, 22 August 2015, IDE-JETRO, http://www.ide.go.jp/English/Data/Africa_file/Manualreport/cia.html.
International Energy Agency (IEA) (2005), *Energy Policies of IEA countries: 2005 review*, Paris, Organisation for Economic Co-operation and Development (OECD) Publication.
IEA (2006), *World Energy Outlook 2006*, Paris, OECD Publication.
IEA (2014a), "Africa Energy Outlook," *World Energy Outlook 2014*, Paris, OECD Publication.
IEA (2014b), "Executive Summery," *World Energy Outlook* 2014, Paris, OECD Publication.
IEA (2018), World Energy Balance: Overview, Paris, OECD Publication.
Jacob, P. J (2006), "Maritime aspects of Energy Security and the Gulf", in Malakar, S. N. ed.., *India's Energy Security and the Gulf*, Delhi, Academic Excellence, pp.137-38.
Kaplan, Robert D. (2010), *Monsoon: The Indian Ocean and the Future of American Power*, New York, Random House Trade Paperbacks.
Kelly, Evan (21 August 2015), "This Week in Energy: A Dangerous Trend is Emerging," *oilprice.com*, 22 August 2015, http://oilprice.com/Energy/Energy-General/This-Week-In-Energy-A-Dangerous-Global-Trend-Emerging.html
Kumar Pranav (2015), "Dragon's Footprints in Africa: Diplomacy and Dilemmas," *China Yearbook 2014*, New Delhi, Magnum Book Pvt Ltd, pp.189-198.
Kulkarni, S.V. (25 November 2010), "BPCL Announces Major Natural Gas Discoveries in Offshore Mozambique," An official Communication to Secretary, Bombay Stock Exchange Ltd from S.V. Kulkarni, Company Secretary, BPCL, Bharat Petroleum Corporation Ltd., 22 August 2015, http://www.petrowatch.com/BPCL291110.pdf.
La Vine, Victor T. (2004), *Politics in Francophone Africa*, Boulder, Lynne Rienner Publication.
Loftness, Robert L. (1998), *Energy Handbook*, New York, Van Nostrand Reinhold.
Mahan, A.T. (2004), *The Influence of Sea Power upon History, 1660–1783*, Project Gutenberg eBook, release date 26 Nov. 2004 (first pub. 1890).
Malakar, S. N. (2006), *India's Energy Security and the Gulf*, Delhi, Academic Excellence.
Manson, Katrina (12 February 2015), "Falling Crude Price Hits Prospects for East Africa," 22 August 2015, ft.com, http://www.ft.com/cms/s/0/0961f6a2-b13c-11e4-831b-00144feab7de.html#axzz3jbXUAiOV.
Mining Review (18 April 2013), "Asia Makes Inroads in Contest for East African Energy Reserves," 18 April 2013, http://www.miningreview.com/node/22092
Naidu, Sanusha and Martyn Davies (2006), "China Fuels its Future with Africa's Riches", *South African Journal of International Affairs*, Vol. 13, Issue 2, winter /spring, 2006
Patel, Tara (19 November 2012), "Total Sell Nigeria Oil Field to Sinopec for $2.5 Billion,"

Bloomberg.com, 23 August 2015, http://www.bloomberg.com/news/articles/2012-11-19/total-sells-nigeria-oil-field-to-sinopec-for-2-5-billion.

PTI (25 March 2018), "India's oil import bill to jump by 25% in FY18", https://economictimes.indiatimes.com/industry/energy/oil-gas/indias-oil-import-bill-to-jump-by-25-in-fy18/articleshow/63464408.cms.

Quigley, Sam (01 June 2014), "Chinese Oil Acquisition in Nigeria and Angola," The American University in Cairo, 22 August 2015, http://www.aucegypt.edu/huss/pols/khamasin/Pages/article.aspx?eid=14.

Rajagopalan, R.P. (31 July 2018), "India's China Challenge in Africa," *The Diplomat*, https://thediplomat.com/2018/07/indias-china-challenge-in-africa/.

Raja Mohan, C. (2013), "China Eyes the Indian Ocean," *Samudra Mandhan: Sino-Indian Rivalry in the Indo-Pacific*, New Delhi, OUP.

Roy-Choudhary, Rahul (1998), "An Energy Security Policy for India: The Case of Oil and Natural Gas," *Strategic Analysis*, Feb 1998.

Shikwati, James (2009),"Africa as a new frontier", in R. Beri & U.K. Sinha, eds., *Africa and Energy Security: Global Issues, Local Responses*, New Delhi: Academic Foundation, pp.41-42.

Tiezzi, Shannon (13 January 2015), China in South Sudan: Practical Responsibility, *The Diplomat*, 23 August 2015, http://thediplomat.com/2015/01/china-in-south-sudan-practical-responsibility/.

US Energy Information Administration (EIA) (24 July 2014), "Country Analysis Brief Algeria," US EIA, 22 August 2015, http://www.eia.gov/beta/international/analysis_includes/countries_long/Algeria/algeria.pdf.

USA EIA (4 February 2014), "Country Analysis Brief : China," US EIA, 3 March 2015, http://www.eia.gov/countries/analysisbriefs/China/china.pdf

Valle, Vincent (2004), "US Policy Towards the Gulf of Guinea," in Traub-Menz Rudolf et al., eds., *Oil Policy in the Gulf of Guinea: Security and Conflict, Economic Growth and Social Development*, Yaunde, Friedrich Ebert Stiftung.

Zahirinejad, Mahjnaz and Vrushal Ghoble (2010), "Energy Factor in China–Iran Relations," *Journal Peace Studies*, Vol. 17, Issues 2&3 April-September, 2010.

17

Tibetan Struggle for Right to Self-determination and India–China Relation:
A National Security Perspective

Rakhee Viswambharan

Independent India inherited the British policy of keeping Tibet as a buffer zone between China and British India In the post-communist revolution India urged China to maintain Tibet's autonomous status, as it suites India's security interest to minimize China's military presence in the region. However, the invasion of Tibet by People's Liberation Army of China in 1951 put an end to Tibet's status as a buffer zone. It exposed the Indo-China border as undefined and invalidated the agreement between Tibet and British India on border delineation. In 1951 Tibet was forced to sign a 17-point agreement with China and Tibet become part of People's Republic of China. Though, China termed its invasion of Tibet as 'peaceful liberation' gross human rights violations had taken place in Tibet. By the end of 1950's Tibetans rose in an attempt to independence known as 'National Uprising'. The Tibetan system of government was replaced and Dalai Lama and his followers were forced to seek asylum in India. The Tibetans in India formed a government in exile at Dharamsala. India's decision to provide asylum to Dalai Lama and his followers was one of the irritant in Indo–China relations. Ultimately it resulted in the Indo–China war of 1962 and China had annexed a large part of strategically important territory of India. Tibetans are distinct people with their own language and culture. They also form a large majority of the population of Tibet. The UN General Assembly passed a resolution in 1959 in support of the right to self-determination of the people of Tibet. The disintegration of Soviet Union and the formation of a large number of new nation states in Eastern Europe on the basis of right to self-determination of the people once again brought the Tibetan issue before the international and regional organization. As a major stake holder in the Tibetan issue India's stand assumes great significance. Further if the Tibetan struggle for self-determination eventually result in Tibet's autonomous status, it very well serves India's security interest to minimize China's military presence in the region.

I. Tibetan Struggle for Right to Self-determination

The Tibetan struggle for right to self-determination is embedded in the history of Tibetan nationalism and Tibet-China relations. The history of Tibetan nationalism and the Tibet-China relations may be divided into four main periods. (Smith 1996; Goldstein 1989; Grunfeld 1987). The first phase (630-842) is that of the consolidation of the Tibetan state from the beginning of Tibetan history up to the fall of the Tibetan empire in 842.

Tibet was not again politically unified until the mid-13th century when Tibetan Lamas established a political—spiritual relationship known as 'cho-yon' or 'priest-patron' relationship with the Mongol empire. Tibet was a dependent state under the Mongol Yuan (1260-1368) and Manchu Ching (1644-1911) dynasties. Tibet was independent of Chinese influence during the native Chinese Ming dynasty (1368–1644). During the second phase, Tibet was under the direct rule of China for a short span of three years from 1911-14.

In the third phase (1914–50) Tibet experienced modern imperialist pressures and Tibetan nationalism was aroused. Tibetan nationalism was stimulated in the early 20th century by the British imperialist interest in Tibet and Chinese attempt to impose more direct control over Tibet. With the British patronage Tibet managed to achieve de facto independence, however, it failed to gain international recognition to its independence.

In the fourth period (1950 to the present) Tibetan independence was forcibly eliminated. The People's Liberation Army (PLA) marched into Tibet in the 1950 and annexed Tibet through a 'peaceful liberation'. Under the pretext of peaceful liberation China had generally imposed its will on the Tibetan people. Tibet was forced to sign an agreement with China in 1951 known as the '17-Point Agreement on Measures for the Peaceful Liberation of Tibet'. The Chinese consider this agreement as a measure to liberate Tibetan territory from imperialist forces. However it is well known that when the PLA marched into Tibet there were no imperialist forces present in Tibet. Therefore from the Tibetan perspective such 'peaceful liberation' was imposed and promises of autonomy stated in the agreement were not being followed by the Chinese. And the Tibetan national identity comes under intense pressure from China for the 'socialist transformation' of Tibetan society. The Tibetan culture was subjected to assimilationist pressure during the Cultural Revolution (1966–76). However, the Tibetan nationalism survived and grew under the Chinese rule. After 1980, in the period of liberalized Chinese policies in Tibet, Tibetan culture and nationalism revived. During this phase Tibetans gained international support to their plea for right to self-determination (Smith 1996).

The great power game was well visible in Tibet from the beginning of 20th century. In 1904 the British troops entered Tibet and forced it to sign an agreement. This move on the part of Britain was mainly based on then Viceroy Lord Curzon's perception regarding the Russian moves in Central Asia and in particular the Russian interaction with Tibet. However, the British government in London did not approve the invasion of Tibet and the Chinese suzerainty was once again brought into force. The 1907 convention by Russia China and British India approved the Chinese suzerainty over Tibet. However the fall of Manchu dynasty in 1913 once again had given Tibet the de jure independent status. In the 1914 Shimla convention, Tibet attended along with British India and China. (Tibetan Centre for Human Rights & Democracy, Human Rights Situation in Tibet, Annual Report 2009). The final outcome of the convention was the McMohan line which demarcates the border between British India and Tibet. There is difference of opinion regarding the Chinese approval to the final outcome. However, given the weak power position of China at that time it had only limited option but to accept the Shimla convention of 1914. Thus, in the Shimla convention of 1914 the Tibetan plenipotentiary attended it along with China and British India and this clearly shows that Tibet enjoyed independent status to negotiate with others. This status of Tibet continued till the entry of People's Liberation Army (PLA) in 1950–51 and annexed Tibet.

It is important to note that though Tibet was never formally recognized by the League of Nations or the United Nations, Tibet in the period 1913–51 had an independent government, currency, army, judicial and postal systems, and administration. Furthermore, the Tibetan government enjoyed formal bilateral relations with the neighbouring countries of Mongolia, Nepal, India, and Bhutan, and concluded treaties with China and Britain. The Tibetan claim that they have every right to self-determination as China had illegally occupied their territory in the name of 'peaceful liberation of Tibet' in 1951. The China's annexation of Tibet in fact once again altered the geostrategic position in the Himalayan region and also nullified the outcome of Shimla convention of 1914. It is interesting to examine how Tibetan issue forms a significant factor in India–China relations.

II. Tibet and India-China Relations

It appears that there are four major issues which form Tibet as a factor in India-China relations. They are:

 (i) The status of Tibet
 (ii) Tibetan refugees in India
 (iii) The India-China border dispute
 (iv) Common security Concerns

(i) The Status of Tibet

India's position on the status of Tibet has changed from the British policy of recognising the de facto independence of Tibet—'completely Autonomous State'—under ambiguous form of Chinese suzerainty to Tibet as 'autonomous region of China'.

Independent India was not very sympathetic to the Tibetan demand for independence. However, when the PLA entered into Tibet, India did not hesitate to deplore China's invasion of Tibet. (Mehrotra 2000:14). In a note dated October 26, 1950, the Ministry of External Affairs, Government of India, told the Chinese foreign office how it looked at the event:

In the context of world events, invasion by Chinese troops of Tibet cannot but be regarded as deplorable and in the considered judgment of the Government of India, not in the interest of China or peace. This statement clearly shows India's stand on the Tibetan issue in the initial period.[1]

Again, when the PLA entered into Tibet, the Indian Prime Minister, Jawaharlal Nehru stated in the Indian Parliament on 7th December 1950:

It is not right for any country to talk about its sovereignty or suzerainty over an area outside its own immediate range. That is to say, since Tibet is not the same as China, it should ultimately be the wishes of the people of Tibet that should prevail and not any legal or constitutional arguments—the last voice in regard to Tibet should be the voice of the people of Tibet and of nobody else.[2]

Jawaharlal Nehru's statement at the Indian Parliament was significant in many respects. It reflected India's stand on right of the people. It also manifests a clear understanding of the Tibetan question.

In the beginning India had supported the Tibet's claim for self-determination. However, a marked change in India's stand on self-determination was visible after the Indo-China bilateral agreement of 1954, known as Panchasheel.[3] As per the agreement India had accepted China's claim on Tibet. Thus on 29 April 1954, India relented to the Chinese insistence on referring to Tibet as 'Tibet Region of China'. Though India failed to provide any support to the Tibetans right to self-determination when it was taken up at the UN General Assembly in 1958, India had provided political asylum to Dalai Lama and his followers in 1959.

After the 1962 border war, India often merely used 'Tibet' until the 1988 visit of the then Indian Prime Minister, Rajiv Gandhi when the 'Sino–Indian Joint Press Communiqué' referred to Tibet as 'an autonomous region of China'. Again in 2003, Prime Minister Atal Bihari Vajpayee signed a declaration which recognised 'that the Tibet Autonomous Region is part of the territory of the People's Republic of China' (Declaration on Principles for Relations and Comprehensive Cooperation between the People's Republic of China and the Republic of India, 25 June 2003). However, India's acceptance of Tibet as a part of China is conditional upon Tibet's enjoyment of autonomy. China, therefore, demands stronger and more unambiguous statements from New Delhi on China's sovereignty over Tibet, which India has resisted so far.

(ii) Tibetan Refugees in India
India's consistent official Tibetan policy has been to disallow anti-Chinese activities by Tibetan refugees on Indian soil. However, India has allowed the Tibetans to run a government-in-exile, the Central Tibetan Administration. India refuses to bend to Chinese pressure by reducing or suspending its support to Tibetan exiles in India. India will and should continue to support Tibetan refugees because it is in India's national interest. For the foreseeable future, India's material assistance and facilitating role for the Tibetan struggle will continue. This is one of the major irritants in India–China relations. The Chinese complain that such open encouragement and support given by the government of India to the Tibetan in their 'anti-China activities' constitute interference in China's internal affairs and obstruct the progress of India-China relations. It appears that India's gravest threat to China lies in Tibet because of the political asylum that India had provided to over 80,000 Tibetans in India. So long as the exiled community exists, Tibetan nationalism and the demand for self-determination will remain a major apprehension for the communist China. (Suresh R. 2011; 246)

(iii) India–China Border Dispute

The border dispute continues to avoid a resolution ever since India and China have acquired a common border when the PRC occupied the Tibet in 1951. The historical roots of the Sino–Indian border dispute can be traced to the imperial period when the great game between British India, Czarist Russia and Qing China over Tibet and Central Asia. Empires thrived on uncertain borders—frontiers were more preferable to imperial powers—as clearly demarcated borders constrained their own ambitions and strategic exibility. In addition, the inhospitable terrain of the high Himalayas, the absence of sophisticated surveying technologies and existence of a functioning Tibetan state made the delimitation of India's northern border either unnecessary or difficult.

Nevertheless, ultimately in the Shimla convention of 1914, in fact, made the border line between British India and Tibet. However, in the mid-20th century, when two equally nationalistic and territorial states gained control over the Indian and Chinese empires, China was not ready to accept the British proposed McMohan line. This stand of China was well reflected especially after the signing of the 'India–China Agreement on Trade and Intercourse between Tibet Region of China and India' (April 29, 1954) in which India for the first time accepted Tibet as a part of China. On the Indian side Prime Minister, Jawaharlal Nehru at the time of signing of Panchasheel agreement thought that the boundary was no longer an issue, and that the China had accepted the historical status quo.

Jawaharlal Nehru wrote about this to the Chinese Premier, Zhou Enlai in 1958 as the border issue heated up:

> When the Sino–Indian Agreement in regard to the Tibet region of China was concluded, various outstanding problems, including some relating to our border trade, were considered.... No border questions were raised at that time and we were under the impression that there were no border disputes between our respective countries. In fact we thought that the Sino–Indian Agreement, which was happily concluded in 1954, had settled all outstanding problems between our countries.[4]

He had also expressed shock at seeing maps printed in China showing certain 'Indian' areas to be parts of China.

The India-China border problem is embedded on Tibet as China had no border with India except through Tibet and India's border with Tibet was a well-settled border negotiated at the Shimla conference of 1914.[5] Thus it appears that a solution to the Indo-China border problem lays in the implementation of the

Tibetan claim for the right to self-determination and the restoration of Tibet's historical status as a buffer zone between India and China.

Further it appears the communist regime in China is also not very serious about finding an amicable settlement of the border problem due to two important reasons. First, the prevalence of successful democratic system in India poses a challenge to the communist system in China. Any close cooperation and interaction with democratic India would be detrimental to the continuance of the totalitarian system in China. Secondly, the present communist regime in China wanted to keep the border problem unresolved so that they can divert the attention of its own population from the serious domestic issues and also a rationale for its huge defence spending and heavy force deployment along Tibet.

(iv) Security Concerns of India and China

It appears that Tibet is an important factor in security paradigm of both India and China. Since its geopolitical position has wedged it between two great powers, it has to be dependent on either China or India, having no other choice. Tibet has always had a high degree of spiritual identication with India. The Republican Chinese officials way back in 1910 expressed similar assessments when they stated: 'Tibet is a buttress on our national frontiers—the hand, as it were, which protects the face—and its prosperity or otherwise is of the most vital importance to China'.

India has its reciprocal fears arising from Chinese military presence in the Tibetan plateau. The true extent of China's military presence in Tibet cannot be gauged, given the extreme secrecy surrounding information about the People's Liberation Army. The presence of Chinese strategic forces on the Tibetan plateau adds another dimension to India's China threat perception. Again India's security perceptions also centred on the China's management of water resources originating from Tibet, which in fact feed the Indian subcontinent. The historical memory about betrayal and humiliation on account of the 1962 war that continues to casts a shadow over India's perceptions of China.

In essence, the complex of security concerns connected to Tibet underpins the strategic rivalry between the two major Asian players, India and China. Consequently, the China and India have common security concerns that are connected to Tibet. These issues can be well addressed only through mutual trust and confidence building measures. Though there are mechanisms to resolve the border dispute amicably since 1988 through the joint working group (JWG), little progress were reported so far. Meanwhile the external powers exploit the conflicting situation to their advantage through various overt and covert moves.

Concluding Remarks

Tibetans are distinct people with their own language and culture. They also form a large majority of the population of Tibet. The UN General Assembly passed a resolution in 1959 in support of the right to self-determination of the people of Tibet. The disintegration of Soviet Union and the formation of a large number of new nation states in Eastern Europe on the basis of right to self-determination of the people once again brought the Tibetan issue before the international and regional organization. The persistent human rights violations in the Tibetan Autonomous Region in China had aroused the attention of the international community in the era of ICT. As a major stake holder in the Tibetan issue India's stand assumes great significance. Further if the Tibetan struggle for self-determination eventually result in Tibet's autonomous status, it very well serves India's security interest to minimize China's military presence in the region.

NOTES

1. Quoted in L.L. Mehrotra, India's Tibet Policy: An Appraisal and Options, Tibetan Parliamentary and Policy Research Centre, New Delhi, 2000
2. Ibid., p. 14
3. (i) Mutual respect for each other's territorial integrity and sovereignty; (ii) mutual non-aggression; (iii) mutual non-interference in each other's internal affairs; (iv) equality and mutual benefit; and (v) peaceful co-existence.
4. Notes, Memoranda and letters Exchanged and Agreements signed between The Governments of India and China White Paper III, MEA, Government of India, New Delhi
5. Indian Parliament on Issue of Tibet, Lok Sabha Debates 1952-2005, Tibetan Parliamentary and Policy Research Centre, New Delhi, 2006.

REFERENCES

Goldstein, Melwyn C (1989): A History of Modern Tibet, 1913-1951, Munishiram Manoharlal Publishers Pvt Ltd.

Grunfeld, A. Tom (1987): The Making of Modern Tibet, Oxford University Press, Delhi.

Lama, Dalai (1988): Five Point Peace Plan for Tibet, Information Office, Central Tibetan Secretariat, Dharamsala (H.P.), India.

Mehrotra, L.L. (2000): *India's Tibet Policy: An Appraisal and Options*, Tibetan Parliamentary and Policy Research Centre, New Delhi.

Smith. Jr, Warren W (1996): Tibetan Nation A History of Tibetan Nationalism and Sino-Tibetan Relation, Westview Press, Oxford.

Suresh R (2011) Tibetan Right to Self-Determination and Sino Indian Relations, International Journal of South Asian Studies, Vol. 4, No. 2

Tibetan Centre for Human Rights & Democracy (2009): "Human Rights, Situation in Tibet", Annual Report 2009, Dharamsala, Himachal Pradesh.

UN Doc. A/CONF.157/23

Zhao, Suisheng (1996): "The Implication of Demilitarization of Tibet for Sino-Indian Relations and Asian Security", Asian Affairs, Vol. 22, No. 4, Winter.

18

India and Australia:
Closer and Closer

RFI Smith

Introduction

In the big shift of economic and political power back to Asia and the consequent unsettling of established alliances, the prospect of closer relations between India and Australia is tantalizing for Australia. That Prime Minister Modi included Australia in his spectacular round of outreach visits in his first year in office raised high expectations on both sides. But subsequent events have confirmed that there is a long way to go. Turning a multiplicity of hitherto weak ties into robust, mutually rewarding relationships will take persistence, skill and time. Firming up potential agreements, especially on international security and trade and investment, is not as easy as some have hoped. Negotiating such agreements may depend as much on firming up mutual understanding of how to talk to each other as on expecting immediately fruitful negotiations on perceived interests in common. Following Prime Minister Modi's visit, four threshold challenges stood out: identification of a robust range of mutually interesting opportunities; negotiations on an initial set of issues that could lead to substantive results; building up capabilities for more wide-ranging collaboration; and accommodating divergent interests. Although less has been achieved than expected, a positive sign is that interest in the task remains high.

This chapter begins with a summary of the differences in background that hinder closer relationships. It then examines, first, relationships between India and Australia in the Indo-Pacific region and opportunities for strategic convergence, and second, trade, cultural and other initiatives that may help build stronger relationships. It concludes that India and Australia have much to benefit by getting closer to each other. But hoped-for big initiatives are likely to place large demands on two scarce resources: continuing political commitment at the highest level, and the ability of participants on both sides to work across differences of interests, scale and culture.

Differences

The renewed search for productive relationships begins from very different standpoints. Both countries recognize the significance of the rising economic and political power of Asian states. But asymmetries of history, location, perception and aspiration get in the way. India's experience of colonization was of foreign institutions and practices superimposed on local ones. The experience is still raw. Contemporary Australia began as part of the same process of colonization. It started as a set of British settler colonies in which indigenous people were dispossessed and in which recognition of their prior occupancy remains politically contested. While many Australians are proud of the multicultural nature of modern Australia, for many others national identity is enmeshed with their European origins. India occupies a subcontinent with far-reaching geographical and historical links to West, Central, East and South East Asia; Australia occupies a large island continent at the far eastern tip of South East Asia to which it is not only adjacent but also distant (Darwin is closer to Bali than to Melbourne, but New Delhi is further from Melbourne than from London).

With its size, ancient and sophisticated civilization, precolonial significance as an economic and trading power astride the Silk Road and the Indian Ocean, young population and current economic potential, India aspires to great power status. But in the meantime, it needs to handle the immediate problems of soft borders in a troubled South Asian neighborhood. Its internal affairs are complex, demanding and resistant to change. Internationally, it wishes to maintain an independent stance and links with other states in the non-aligned movement in which it played a leading role. It has found it hard to change old positions or commit to new ones. Discussions about foreign policy are subject to competing views. Continued reliance on incremental adjustments to positions adopted first under Prime Minister Nehru has cogent and influential advocates, but so does determination to wring more benefit out of established positions (Hall 2015), advocacy of much bigger changes, and recognition of its ability over the long term to respond to new challenges (Varghese 2013:13).

In comparison, Australia is a small, natural resource–endowed country with a developed economy and a population enriched since 1945 not only by European but also more recently by Asian migration (over 140,000 residents of Australia speak Hindi; 700,000 residents are of Indian origin). It seeks to build up its profile as a middle power (Evans 2012, Andrew Carr) and to be influential in international forums dominated by the great powers. Since the 1950s, its trade links have shifted decisively towards Asia (Harcourt). Indeed, for a quarter of a century, its major trade partners have been in East Asia—China, Japan and Korea. Significantly, trade with India, while growing, is nowhere near as substantial. Despite bruising and inward-looking partisan conflict, it enjoys broad continuity in foreign policy. But the mismatch between its traditional links and the trade patterns that drive its recent economic success is stark. Closer economic integration with Asia, continuing close cultural and security links with the United States and Europe, and adjusting to its developing multicultural and multiracial identity coexist in uneasy accommodation (for a particularly insightful book length discussion, see Wesley 2011).

Even characteristics shared by both India and Australia lead to parallel rather than converging perspectives (Grare). For both, China is the major trading partner (although unlike India, Australia has a favorable trade balance). Both also have significant relationships with the US. But while the prospect of increasingly competitive relationships between China and the US is a source of shared fascination and not a little apprehension, progress towards closer engagement has been slow. Following the collapse of the Soviet Union, India has tended to follow a pragmatic course of interest-based multilateral arrangements. It seeks to maintain strategic autonomy and to resist the emergence in Asia of any one dominant power. A generally closer relationship with the US has nevertheless been characterised by ebbs and flows. Relations with China are pragmatic on trade but testy on borders.

In contrast, Australia continues to rely very substantially for security in Asia on alliance with the US. At the same time, the US looks towards Australia for support and facilities. Australia also actively pursues multilateral as well as bilateral strategies of engagement with Asian states, but not at the expense of the US alliance. Despite its fundamental importance to the economy, trade with China is partitioned off. The significance of power shifts within Asia is acknowledged (Grare), but both sides of politics affirm that no choice between the US and China is necessary (see, for example, Bob Carr). While dissenting voices exist, Malcolm Fraser, a former conservative prime minister, advocated increased independence from the US (Fraser 2014a). Australia's first ambassador to China has suggested a focus on 'security in rather than from Asia' (Fitzgerald); a leading strategic analyst advocates that the US make space for a rising China (White) and a former foreign minister, Gareth Evans, has said that Mr Fraser's book (Fraser 2014b) is a major contribution "to the debate Australia has to have" (Tingle 2014)—official and effective public engagement with the issues they raise has yet to emerge. Indeed Fitzgerald (2015) bluntly cautioned against expecting big shifts from current political leaders: 'they have no foreign policy framework and seem frightened of big ideas'. More recently, Tingle (2018:86) has lamented the ease with which difficult issues are still avoided by political leaders.

Finally, a recent diplomatic history of relationships between India and Australia (Gurry) offers a cautionary tale in which consistent efforts since before independence by committed Australian diplomats were frustrated by diffuse and diverging interests, lack of empathy with Asia by some Australian prime ministers, fluctuating interest in India by others, unwillingness to commit resources to relationship building, adverse impacts of the White Australia Policy and perceptions of continuing racism. While current prospects are much more promising (Jeffrey), the differences in culture through which interests are identified remain daunting (consider the implications, for example, of the contrast between the conjunction of motor cycles, mobile phones and Mahabharata in the lives of newly arrived entrants to the middle class in India and the privileged, secular, hard-working but pleasure-loving lives of upwardly mobile workers in Australia's service industries). Closer relationships between India and Australia still rely on both countries playing a long game.

Indo-Pacific

India and Australia's strategic interests meet most directly in the Indian Ocean. In a sense, they are neighbours (Singh), with India to the north and Australia to the south of an ocean, the significance of which has dramatically re-emerged. The contemporary rise of the ocean as the world's 'busiest and most strategically significant trade corridor' is a potential turning point for both countries (Medcalf: 3). The 'crossroads of the Indian Ocean and the western Pacific' (Medcalf: 3) connects both countries to wider relationships, in 'a very new and yet very old framework' (Kaplan: xii). Significantly, in doing so it focuses attention on the relationships of both countries with China and the US.

Medcalf (2014) and Rumley (2013) outline the rationale for an Indo-Pacific region. It draws its strength less from geography (because of the multiplicity of very different littoral states) than from activities and relationships. In its current incarnation, for which Kaplan provides indispensable background, it has been incorporated in the thinking by defence strategists in Australia, has received bipartisan acceptance by Australian governments and has the potential to support pragmatic policy initiatives by India (Varghese 2013:9). The basis for the region is that (Medcalf: 2):

> The accelerating economic and security connections between the Western Pacific and the Indian ocean region are creating a single strategic system.

This system is about (Medcalf: 2-3):

> ...the arc of trade routes, energy flows, diplomatic bonds and strategic connections between the two oceans. These links in turn emerge especially from the rise of China and India as outward-looking economic and military powers, the expansion of their economic interests, and their strategic and diplomatic imperatives in what each might once have considered its primary maritime zone of interest.

For India, the Indo-Pacific encompasses existing interests in the Indian Ocean, puts it in the company of China and the US and extends its perspectives beyond South Asia (Chacko). For Australia, the Indo-Pacific gives it standing in Asia as a member state (Medcalf), and, unlike Gareth Evans' concept of an 'East Asian Hemisphere' (Evans 1995), gives it reasons to look more closely towards South Asia.

However, the idea of the Indo-Pacific is controversial. By its potential to connect India to tensions between China and the United States, it extends the arena in which contested adjustments to a changing world order are taking place. It lays bare a number of strategic and conceptual sensitivities. For example, it can be seen as a 'manufactured super region' (Pan: 453), a device for building coalitions against China, a token by which Australia can attract attention in India, a means to bind Australia even more tightly to the US, and to put the sea lanes between the Pacific and Indian Oceans at risk of militarisation (Pan, Wilson, Bisley and Phillips, Gordon). It is thus an idea to be used with care. However, using it as a frame of reference directs attention to India and Australia's overlapping security interests in the Indian Ocean, complementary relationships with countries in South East Asia, and potentially shared approaches to wider issues in international affairs. Its greatest value may be to stimulate exploration of otherwise overlooked possibilities (Brewster 2018). However, such exploration depends on political as well as intellectual leadership (Medcalf 2018): 'there is a need for an authentically

Australian public narrative about our future in the Indo-Pacific, and a need for our political class to get serious about that narrative'.

India's Interests

India's interests of particular relevance to Australia begin in the North East Indian Ocean and extend from there into South East Asia. These are a subset of India's interests in the Indian Ocean littoral which extend from the Gulf Region in the west, along the east coast of Africa, and across to South East Asia and Australia. In the North East Ocean, India, despite apprehensions about Myanmar as a possible host to a naval presence by China, has a dominant role. It has also fostered cooperative security arrangements with ASEAN states bordering the Bay of Bengal/Andaman Sea (Brewster 2013:128). From there, as Brewster explains, India's defence facilities in the Andaman and Nicobar Islands potentially project its influence into the South East Asian trade routes and from there into the South China Sea (Brewster 2013:127). The key is the ability to control access to the western end of the Malacca Strait. Echoing an old proverb that 'Whoever is lord of Malacca has his hands on the throat of Venice' (Kaplan 7), Brewster has argued,

> The Indian Ocean is the one area in which India holds a clear military advantage over China and the potential to control the Malacca Strait reinforces that advantage. (Brewster 2013:131)

As traffic through the strait on which China depends continues to increase (one estimate suggests that by 2030, up to 80 per cent of China's oil and 50 per cent of its gas will be imported through the strait; Dupont), the sensitivity of India's role will continue to grow.

However, while India is well-positioned to 'look outward', and has an increasing need to do so, it has hitherto been hesitant about entering into arrangements to formalise such a role. It has tried to position itself in South East Asia as a 'benign security provider to the region as a whole' (Brewster 2013:133), but this aspiration remains unconsolidated, although Mr Modi's recent visits may help. Further, proposals from the US and Japan for multilateral security arrangements involving India for many years did not draw support. While Singapore became India's 'advocate' in South East Asia, strategic relationships did not develop as Singapore would have liked. Similarly, India's relations with Vietnam, which date from the Cold War, did not develop as Vietnam sought. Proposals for closer ties with other South East Asian states, especially Indonesia, and with South Korea for long remained proposals. Moreover, India's potential for leadership too was not accepted by all South East Asian states. India thus found itself building up military relationships bilaterally or with groups of states (including the US, Japan, Singapore and Australia) while also continuing to place a high value on autonomy and restraint.

India's strategic interests in South East Asia are complemented by its 'Look East' economic policies, emphatically restated by Prime Minister Modi. The thinking behind the liberalisation initiatives in the Indian economy in 1991 followed close interest by Indian ministers and advisers in the sources of economic growth in Malaysia and other South East Asian countries (Mukherji). The economic crisis that crystallised policies of liberalisation prompted a drive to expand trade and investment links. India became a 'dialogue partner' of ASEAN in 1995 and it is the institutional vehicle for pursuing economic links in South East Asia. Since 2002, an India-ASEAN summit has taken place each year and India has promoted other sub-regional forums for economic cooperation in the Bay of Bengal and with Indo-China (Brewster: 134). India also promotes ASEAN as a forum for discussions on security and participates in meetings of Ministers of Defence from ASEAN plus Australia, China, Japan, New Zealand, Russia, South Korea and the US. However, ASEAN provides only a limited forum for deliberations on security. Whether an alternative vehicle for such discussions will emerge and what part, if any, India might take in it remain to be seen. In the meantime, India has developed webs of interactions with South East Asian states and the many other states with interests in this region and the wider Indo-Pacific. Also, through active participation in BRICS Summits, India not only extends links beyond the Asia Pacific but facilitates relationships with Russia and China too. The experience gained from these interactions provides a foundation on which to craft more ambitious relationships in the Indo-Pacific Region. The renewed impetus to 'Look East' by the Modi government suggests that in both trade and security, India will seek to do so. But caution seems likely also to continue (Hall 2018).

Australia's Interests

Australia's interests of most relevance to India begin also in South East Asia. But from there, it also looks up towards its trading partners in East Asia and across the Pacific to North America. Despite a long exposure to the Indian Ocean on its western coast, Australia had found the diversity of interests represented by littoral states hard to grapple with (Bisley and Phillips). Until rising trade flows solidified, the definition of the Indo-Pacific, relationships with South Asia in general and India in particular remained fuzzy and easily dissolved (Gurry, Weigold). However, the heightened salience of Indo-Pacific trade routes and maritime security provides a persuasive reason for exploration of potential interests in common. For Australia, as for India, ASEAN and its related forums has provided a vehicle for engagement. However, Australia has been much keener than India to go beyond 'soft security and dialogues' (Grare: 7). In a variety of statements and forums involving a range of stakeholders, including state governments and business groups, Australia has outlined opportunities for closer bilateral cooperation (Cerule Consulting, Grare: 5). In 2008, India and Australia signed a joint security declaration which 'established a framework for the further development of the security relationship' (Grare: 6). Australia also removed the irritant of a ban on uranium sales to India, which recalled the even greater irritant of Australia's reaction to India's nuclear tests. However, a 'quadrilateral security dialogue' initiated earlier by then Secretary of State Colin Powell and involving the US, Japan, India and Australia dissolved (Garnaut, J 2014). In 2013, Australia's Defence White Paper (Grare: 7) reiterated the importance of relationships with India and the then Defence Minister for India made the first visit of such a minister to Australia. The election of the Modi government dramatically revived possibilities for stronger security arrangements.

In July 2014, in a move that linked security in the Indo-Pacific with wider security issues in the Pacific associated with the rise of China, India and Australia agreed to strengthen military ties (since reinforced in 2018 by joint exercises in Australia between the Indian and Australian airforces). The agreement with India took place as Australia was drawing closer to both the US and Japan. These steps sparked renewed interest, as yet resulting in little more than periodic discussions, in a four-way relationship between the US, Japan, India and Australia, with a possible extension to include Indonesia. Following renewed US interest in Asia, governments of both persuasions in Australia agreed to provide improved facilities for the US, for example, facilities for US Marines in northern Australia (Gillard Labor government) and improved military communications (Abbott Liberal National government). US officials and former officials have also been urging Australia to increase expenditure on defence. However, in other areas of the Asia Pacific, uncertainty about US preparedness to come to their assistance, especially during the Trump administration, in the face of rising Chinese assertiveness influenced countries to form their own coalitions. In this context, Japan sought to increase its defence partnerships. It looked to the Philippines, Vietnam, India and Australia. It also moved away from post-1945 pacifism to a policy of 'collective self-defence' in which Japanese forces can be deployed alongside those of allies.

Sensitivities

The moves to closer ties between India and Australia have thus taken place in sensitive circumstances in which the management of relations with China is a major driver. China is concerned about being surrounded by unfriendly neighbours. It has many land borders and maritime neighbours extending from East to South East Asia. However, other powers are concerned about growing Chinese naval strength, territorial claims, an expanded air defence zone, land reclamation, military facilities on existing and newly created islands and other initiatives to project Chinese influence in the South China Sea, loan facilities for small island states in the Pacific, and the wider implications of the ambitious, infrastructure building Belt Road Initiative (One Belt, One Road). They are also trying to extend relationships with China without inhibiting closer ties with current or potential allies. Experiments with overlapping relationships in which consultation and collaboration, including the US, China or neither, take precedence over formal and confrontational alliance building are taking place. However, Chinese comments indicate that the difference between say, a 'consultative security forum' or a 'countervailing coalition' and a 'military alliance' is a matter of interpretation (Garnaut, J 2014; Kerin 2014a). While multi-track strategies or strategies of multi-polarity and multi-alignment continue to be explored (for example, Australia's joint exercises with the US and China [Kerin 2014b] and India's joint exercises with the US and Japan [Aneja]), the extent to which they are sustainable has yet to be determined. In this context, the appreciations that India and Australia make about China and the kinds of responses they make to Chinese assertiveness may be critical to the further development of relations with each other.

Also important will be how adeptly they manage relationships with each other and with other participants with interests in the Indo-Pacific. In addition to ASEAN and related forums, India and Australia participate in other forums where shared interests can be explored. The East Asia Summit is one. Others include the Indian Ocean Rim Association and the Indian Ocean Naval Symposium. While the absence of a single regional institution which spans the whole of Asia is often noted, the more important question may be how to make the best use of those that exist. When former Australian Prime Minister Rudd proposed the creation of a new Asia-Pacific Community, the importance of relationship management was reinforced (Ayson and Taylor). There was little enthusiasm for a new structure but a 'high degree of interest in discussing further how cooperation processes may be enhanced' (Frost). As Ayson and Taylor proposed (Ayson and Taylor: 193),

> The most important *institutions* of regional politics are not the formal organisations that hold regular summits, but the rules and patterns of behavior that operate between the major actors on a daily basis. Such an informal approach would suggest that the basis of Asia's strategic future, including China's role, is not a regional architecture—which seeks to organise and perhaps even to control the actors—but a set of regional bargains that nourish and support their most important strategic relationships. One of these bargains is an effective but informal compact between the United States and China that they will recognise each other's leading role in regional affairs.

From this perspective, there are already enough forums. However, using them creatively to manage competition, promote cooperation and avoid zero sum games is an increasingly sharp challenge.

How effectively India and Australia approach this challenge will be influenced by how they balance internal policy drivers with existing and emerging interests. In different ways, both countries face internal challenges that spill over into how they present themselves to the world. In India, the most prominent challenges are about how to create sustainable economic opportunities that meet the expectations of a restless electorate and enhance its standing in international forums (for a review of India's challenges through the prism of its relations with the European Union, see Winand *et al*, especially pp. 338-358). In Australia, the most prominent challenges are about how to manage a developed economy subject to painful structural change while growing beyond the electoral temptations of fear of 'the other' and to operate more confidently beyond the Anglosphere.

Closer and Closer?

With closer military ties in prospect, questions arise about how far they will extend, whether they will be accompanied by thickening economic and social ties, and whether indeed effective cooperation on security will depend on thicker ties in general (Varghese 2013). The extended gestation period between the identification by security analysts of opportunities for cooperation and recent official announcements is a reminder that analysis alone does not drive policy change. Similarly, the webs of business, institutional and personal contacts between India and Australia that now exist (for example, two-way foreign direct investment, state government business development strategies and offices in India, cultural programs in both countries, Bollywood enthusiasts, student exchanges fostered by universities in both India and Australia, engineering consulting services, participation by Indian civil servants in programs of the Australia and New Zealand School of Government, extensive programs of the Australia India Institute, high-level round table discussions, agreements on vocational education and training, and links between universities and individual scholars) do not guarantee thicker ties. Earlier economic, scholarly and social contacts (for example, Australian economic planners in India in the 1950s, Hindustan Machine Tools investments in Australia in the 1970s, Victorian agricultural scientists in India in the 1970s and the continuing work of Queensland semi-arid tropics scientists with ICRISAT in Hyderabad) were often discontinuous or remained specialised. Similarly, the number of Australian universities offering Hindi language studies declined from six to two. More recent connections such as Indian student enrolments in universities and other institutions of further education have also been troubled. However, the Australia India Institute's network of New Generation Scholars is working on a wide range of contemporary topics (Aii 2018). Furthermore, the Institute published recently an eloquent policy brief on the need for more Australians to learn Hindi (Brown and Barz). Overall, the variety of current links, including those provided by a continuing flow of immigrants from India to Australia and a return of student enrolments, provides a stronger basis than before on which to build connections that link military, economic and soft power.

Realising this potential continues to demand conscious efforts by both countries. Indian interest in doing so is underpinned by Prime Minister Modi's emphasis on the soft power of 5Ts: trade, tourism, talent, technology and tradition (Mattoo). In Mr Modi's nearly 40 international visits, he has not only been enthusiastic about improving bilateral ties with countries in South Asia, participation in forums such as the BRICS Summit in Brazil (Ministry of External Affairs) in 2014, participation in forums of South East Asian countries, and complementing strategic tensions with China with economic common ground (for example, allying with China to urge reform of the international financial order and inviting Chinese investment in India), but has also demonstrated a consistent determination to look outwards.

Modi's visit to Australia in 2014 marked an 'unprecedented level of engagement' (Rajendram). His rapport with Prime Minister Abbott, following an earlier visit to India by Mr Abbott, was strong; his address to a joint sitting of the Australian parliament (delivered in English) was eloquent, witty and warm. In Sydney, Indian community groups greeted him with extraordinary enthusiasm. Business leaders, including the most influential, queued up for introductions. Following the visit, interchanges between the two countries proceeded with enhanced energy and enthusiasm.

Two agreements stood out: a Framework for Security Cooperation, and, following free trade agreements with Japan, China and South Korea, the beginning of negotiations for an agreement between India and Australia. However, neither bore immediate fruit. In India, the news about the Framework for Security Cooperation drew not only favorable comments but also an astringent critique under the title 'In the Making—An Asian NATO?' (*Economic and Political Weekly*: 8). In Australia, satisfaction that Australia is no longer at the periphery of India's vision (Rajendram) was accompanied also by criticism that enthusiasm for security arrangements directly aimed at China was too hawkish. Neither country wants polarisation in Asia. However, as Michael Wesley (2014) observed, avoiding it will require, from Australia's perspective, three things: to maintain regional institutions that include all of the rival great powers and smaller states; to disentangle key bilateral relations with Japan, China, the US and India from each other while making each relationship as strong as possible; and to strive to ensure that rival institutions promoted by the big powers do not encourage regional polarisation (Wesley).

Building trade and investment links through a free trade agreement encountered insurmountable challenges. In India, the liberalisation initiatives of 1991 are still widely criticised, opening up domestic markets is resisted, and the Modi government has moved with caution on further steps towards market-based reform. Market access for foreign firms is especially sensitive. By contrast, despite the reservations about the value of free trade agreements by the Productivity Commission (2015: 62), the Australian government's own in-house source of policy advice, the prospect of such an agreement with India was promoted by the government as a way into a huge and growing market. Two comments by Australian leaders suggested that expectations were overheated: the then Minister for Trade, Andrew Robb (2015),[1] said that India could be 'China all over again' while Prime Minister Abbott, when asked what drove his China policies, replied 'Fear and greed' (Garnaut, J 2015). A focus on prospects for coal and other energy exports and fostering of business contacts mainly through very large companies generated sceptical comments (Sainsbury). Caution was expressed also about the extent to which the two countries' service industries may align. As an experienced Australian manager of engineering services in India observed, his firm was more able to sell India-based services to Australia than to sell Australia-based services to India (Walters: 45). However, the range of educational, cultural and other contacts suggested that whatever the fate of particular trade and investment prospects, organisational links were expanding.

To underpin the task of turning opportunities into tangible results, keeping up momentum and fostering a widening range of links, unofficial as well as official, deserves high priority. The high-level discussions of the 2014 Australia-India Roundtable produced a number of practical suggestions (Lowy Institute). Three continue to stand out:

- Federalise the bilateral relationship, encouraging dynamic states and cities in both countries to connect more with each other.
- Improve business and regulatory environments to enable cross-investments by the private sectors in the two countries, including in the entire energy chain.
- Foster champions for the bilateral relationship among leaders and opinion-makers in both countries, as well as encouraging the further growth of people-people relations (Lowy Institute).

The first recognised the trend for subnational authorities in each country to look outwards and their potential to strengthen a wide range of practical links. It is especially important following the Modi government's federalising initiatives in national policymaking and funding for the states. The second directed attention to the difficulties businesses in both countries have experienced, sometimes substantially, with barriers to foreign investment. The vicissitudes of the Adani Group's proposal for a major new coal mine in Queensland, even without taking into account the merits or otherwise of the business case and funding basis for the proposal, illustrate the range of issues involved. The second priority is also relevant to the argument that greater economic complementarity will help drive improved ties on security (Grare, Earl, Varghese 2013). The third recognised that ultimately the deployment of power, whether hard or soft, depends on strategic relationships between people. Seeding opportunities for specialist dialogues on topics of mutual interest, for example, with national, state, city, business, cultural and educational participants could be a mutually rewarding investment. A program to send Australian students to study in Asia is already under way. For both countries, the size and influence of the Indian diaspora in Australia is a strategic resource. Initiatives by Indian immigrants in Australia and Australian residents and visitors in India are also helpful. A burgeoning of such people-to-people contacts is a good sign that momentum is being maintained.

But further and systematic efforts are essential. The risks of discontinuity are plentiful. Despite Prime Minister Abbott's enthusiasm to follow up Prime Minister Modi's visit, his government summarily archived the Gillard government's Asian

Century White Paper and its implementation plans designed to refocus private and public sector attention on change in Asia (DPMC). In turn, the Asian Century White Paper traversed ground covered by an overlooked report commissioned by the Hawke government in the 1980s (Garnaut, R 1989). Furthermore, since 2015 the Australian government has experienced two changes of Prime Minister. First, in 2015 Malcolm Turnbull replaced Tony Abbott. Although Mr Turnbull visited India, little new resulted (Bisley 2018). Second, in 2018, amid notable tumult about domestic matters within the governing coalition, Scott Morrison replaced Malcolm Turnbull and the long-serving Foreign Minister, Julie Bishop, chose not to remain in the ministry.

In these circumstances, continuity in contact depends on continuing high-quality diplomatic representation. Australian representatives in India have been of exceptional quality. Indian representatives in Australia have also been well regarded. However, the diplomatic services of both countries are spread thinly and timely recommendations from posts depend on receptive political leadership at home. Too often in the past, Australian dispatches have fallen on stony ground (Gurry). Any instability in government compounds this risk.

However, an initiative that bore fruit during the recent instability has set out an ambitious agenda for the future. This was 'An India Economic Strategy to 2035—Navigating from Potential to Delivery' prepared for the Australian government by Mr Peter Varghese and a support team from the Department of Foreign Affairs and Trade (Varghese 2018). The report aimed high. It recommended that Australia should "strive by 2035 to lift India into our top three export markets, to make India the third largest destination in Asia for Australian outward investment, and to bring India into the inner circle of Australia's strategic partnerships, and with people to people ties as close as any in Asia" (Varghese 2018:2). The report set out detailed recommendations designed to engage a wide range of participants and to be pursued over time. Significant recommendations included a focus on services rather than on commodities or manufacturing; on niche rather than mass opportunities; and on opportunities in specific states and regions. Recommendations were supported by substantial analysis, case studies of successful business initiatives, and reference to the economic policies of the Modi government. Running throughout the report was a clear but understated theme: that Australia needed India more than India needed Australia. Accordingly, emerging relationships would need to be different from the commodity-based transactional relationships with East Asia. Initiatives likely to be effective would depend on strong personal links, developed by repeated visits and honed by careful listening to the needs of potential partners in India. Following publication of the report, Australia's High Commissioner to India and other senior officials have led discussions at workshops in India and Australia.

Overall, the report is different in tone and focus from many earlier reports. But as Robin Jeffrey has asked (Jeffrey 2018), 'Is it different this time?' The answer remains to be seen.

Concluding Remarks

India and Australia clearly have a wide range of mutually interesting questions to explore. The good relations between the Modi and Abbott governments provided high-level official support lacking earlier. However, the task of deepening relationships, especially in security and trade, has yet to mature into strings of significant results. While recent instability in the Australian government has not helped, the publication of the Varghese report is a valuable resource for initiatives to improve economic relations. But as the report makes clear, meaningful convergence on specific economic opportunities is likely to depend on much more exploration of questions of mutual interest and potential complementarities. In turn, this will require versatile capabilities and great persistence. A positive sign is that the pool of interest seems to be expanding. But each country will need to become far more aware of what the other can offer and work systematically to turn opportunities into achievements. From the Australian side, this will require a willingness to relate to India on its own terms that many Australians do not appreciate. How tricky this may be is illustrated by recalling that while Mr Modi addressed the Australian parliament in English and a recent Australian prime minister addressed Chinese audiences in Mandarin, the prospect that an Australian leader might be able to address the Indian parliament in Hindi seems remote. Two final questions arise: does this matter, and if so, how might it be remedied? How such questions are answered will tell us something about the depth of any progress being made on the Australian side.

NOTE

1   Quoted in *The Sydney Morning Herald*, 10 January 2015.

REFERENCES

Aneja, Atul (2014). India, U.S., Japan joint naval exercise in Pacific today, *The Hindu*, 24 July

Ayson, R & Taylor, B (2009). Architectural alternatives or alternatives to architecture? in Ron Huisken (ed), *Rising China: Power and Reassurance*, ANU ePress, Canberra Australia, pp. 185-199, Chapter 13

Australia India Institute (2018). New Generation Network Scholars, https://www.aii.unimelb.edu.au/about-us/our-people/new-generation-network-scholars/ (accessed on 12 October 2018)

Brown, T and R Barz (2018). Strategies to Expand Hindi Education in Australia, Australia India Institute, https://www.aii.unimelb.edu.au/publications/strategies-expand-hindi-education-australia/ (accessed on 12 October 2018)

Bisley, N and A Phillips (2012). The Indo-Pacific: What does it actually mean? *East Asia Forum*, 6 October, http://www.eastasiaforum.org/ (accessed on 28 May 2015)

Bisley, N (2018). Australia and India: some way to go yet, https://theconversation.com/australia-and-india-some-way-to-go-yet-76385 (accessed on 12 October 2018)

Brewster, D (2013). India's Defence Strategy and the India-ASEAN Relationship in Ajaya Kumar Das (ed.), India-ASEAN Defence Relations, RSIS Monograph No. 28, Singapore: S. Rajaratnam School of International Studies

Brewster, D (2018). Putting the 'Indo' in Indo-Pacific: How does the Indian Ocean fit into Australia's Indo-Pacific strategy? https://www.policyforum.net/putting-indo-indo-pacific/ (accessed on 12 October 2018)

Carr, Andrew (2015). *Winning the Peace: Australia's Campaign to Change the Asia-Pacific*, Melbourne, Melbourne University Press.

Carr, B (2014). *Diary of a Foreign Minister*, Sydney: NewSouth

Cerule Consulting, India Country Strategy-Australia, http://www.slideshare.net/CeruleConsulting/india-country-strategy-australia (accessed on 14 July 2014)

Chacko, Priya (2014). The rise of the Indo-Pacific: understanding ideational change and continuity in India's foreign policy, *Australian Journal of International Affairs*, 68:4, DOI: 10.1080/10357718.2014.891565

DPMC (Department of Prime Minister and Cabinet) (2014). https://asiancentury.dpmc.gov.au/ (accessed on 14 July 2014)

Dupont, A (2014). China's Maritime Power Trip, *The Australian*, 24 May.

Earl, G (2014). Weight of global expectations rests on Modi's shoulders, *Australian Financial Review*, 1 July

Evans, G (1995). Australia, ASEAN and the East Asian Hemisphere, 2 August, http://www.gevans.org/speeches/old/1995/020895_australia_asean_eahemisphere.pdf (accessed on 19 June 2015)

Evans, G (2012). Idealism and Realism in Australian Foreign Policy, Hedley Bull Lecture University of Sydney, 14 August 2012, http://www.gevans.org/speeches/speech482.html (accessed on 14 July 2014)

FitzGerald, Stephen (2015). An independent foreign policy requires our leaders to take on fear of the US and China, *The Age*, 11 May

Fraser, M (2014a). Foreign Policy in the Asian Century, Fabian Essay, July 2014, http://www.fabian.org.au/files/FabianEssay-MalcolmFraser-July2014.pdf (accessed on 14 July 2014)

Fraser, M (2014b). *Dangerous Allies*, Carlton, Melbourne University Press

Frost, F (2009). Australia's proposal for an 'Asia Pacific Community': issues and prospects, Parliament of Australia, Parliamentary Library, 1 December

Gordon, S (2012). Indian Ocean: Don't militarise the 'great connector', East Asia Forum, 10 April, http://www.eastasiaforum.org/ (accessed on 28 May 2015)

Garnaut, J (2014). Australia and India to strengthen military ties, *The Age*, 2 July

Garnaut, J (2015). A bet each way: our China policy is rational, *The Age*, 22 May

Garnaut, R (1989). *Australia and the Northeast Asian ascendancy: Report to the Prime Minister and the Minister for Foreign Affairs and Trade*, Canberra, Australian Government Publishing Service

Grare, F (2014). The India-Australia strategic relationship: Defining realistic expectations, Carnegie Endowment for International Peace, March 2014, http://carnegieendowment.org/files/india_australia_strat_rel.pdf (accessed on 14 July 2014)

Gurry, M (2015). *Australia and India: Mapping the Journey 1944-2014*, Carlton: Melbourne University Press.

Kaplan, Robert D (2010). *Monsoon: the Indian Ocean & the Battle for Supremacy in the 21st Century*, Collingwood (Vic): Black Inc.

Harcourt, T (2014). Unfinished business: Labor, free trade and structural reform in the Asian century, Fabian Essay, March 2014, http://www.fabian.org.au/files/FabianEssay-TimHarcourt-March2014(web).pdf (accessed on 14 July 2014)

Hall, I (2015). Is a 'Modi doctrine' emerging in Indian foreign policy? *Australian Journal of International Affairs*, 69:3, DOI: 10.1080/10357718.2014.1000263

Hall, I (2018). Modi plays by the "rules" at Shangri-La, *The Interpreter*, Lowy Institute, https://www.lowyinstitute.org/the-interpreter/india-plays-by-the-rules-at-shangri-la (accessed on 12 October 2018)

Jeffrey, R (2018). Australia and India: Is it different this time? *Inside Story*, https://insidestory.org.au/australia-and-india-is-it-different-this-time/ (accessed on 11 October 2018)

Kerin, J (2014a). Dangerous liaisons: Australia's alliances leave China cold, *Australian Financial Review*, 7 July.

Kerin, J (2014b). Australia to host US-China war games, *Australian Financial Review*, 24 July

Lowy Institute (2014). 2014 Australia-India Roundtable—Outcomes Statement http://www.lowyinstitute.org/publications/2014-australia-india-roundtable-outcomes-statement (accessed on 14 July 2014)

Medcalf, R (2014). In Defence of the Indo-Pacific: Australia's new strategic map, *Australian Journal of International Affairs*, DOI: 10.1080/10357718.2014.911814

Medcalf, R (2018). Mapping our Indo Pacific Future, https://www.policyforum.net/mapping-our-indo-pacific-future-rory-medcalfs-speech/ (accessed on 11 October 2018)

Mattoo, A (2014). A doctrine of economic levers, soft power, *The Hindu*, 12 June, http://www.thehindu.com/todays-paper/tp-opinion/a-doctrine-of-economic-levers-soft-power/article6106020.ece (accessed on 14 July 2014)

Ministry of External Affairs (2014). Sixth BRICS Summit—Fortaleza Declaration, http://www.mea.gov.in/bilateral-documents.htm?dtl/23635/Sixth+BRICS+ Summit+Fortaleza+ Declaration (accessed on 24 July 2014)

Mukherji, R (2009). The State, Economic Growth, and Development in India, *India Review*, 8: 1, 81-106.

Pan, Chengxin (2014). The 'Indo-Pacific' and geopolitical anxieties about China's rise in the Asian regional order, *Australian Journal of International Affairs*, 68:4, DOI: 10.1080/10357718.2014.884054

Productivity Commission (2015). *Trade & Assistance Review 2013-14*, Annual Report Series, Canberra, Productivity Commission, June, http://www.pc.gov.au/research/recurring/trade-assistance/2013-14/trade-assistance-review-2013-14.pdf (accessed on 25 June 2015)

Rajendram, D (2014). Modi in Australia: An unprecedented level of engagement, *Lowy Interpreter*, 19 November, http://www.lowyinterpreter.org/post/2014/11/19/Modi-in-Australia-An-unprecedented-level-of-engagement.aspx?COLLCC=2685195111& (accessed on 19 November 2014)

Rumley, D (ed) (2013). *The Indian Ocean Region: Security, Stability and Sustainability in the 21st Century*, Australia India Institute, http://www.aii.unimelb.edu.au/sites/default/files/IOTF_0.pdf (accessed on 14 July 2014)

Sainsbury, M (2015). Australia bets it all on India's coal market, *Crikey*, 19 January.

Singh, Sudhir (ed) (2015). *India in Emerging Asia*, New Delhi, Pentagon Press, p. 18.

Tingle, L (2014). We need to talk about our relationship with the US, *Australian Financial Review*, 30 May.

Tingle, L (2018). Follow the Leader: Democracy and the Rise of the Strongman, *Quarterly Essay*, No 71.

Varghese, P (2013). Our Journey with India, Australia-India Institute Oration, 16 May, http://www.aii.unimelb.edu.au/events/our-journey-india-australia-india-institute-annual-oration (accessed on 19 June 2015).

Varghese, P (2018). An India Economic Strategy to 2035 Navigating from potential to delivery, Department of Foreign Affairs and Trade, https://dfat.gov.au/geo/india/ies/index.html (accessed on 12 October 2015)

Walters, G (2014). Engineering a future in India, in Kanga M and A Mattoo (ed), Hullabaloo: The Fuss About The India-Australia Relationship, Carlton, Australia India Institute, http://aii.unimelb.edu.au/events/buy-now-hullabaloo (accessed on 5 January 2015)

Weigold, A (2013). Australia-India relations in insecure times: Malcolm Fraser's engagement, in Brennan L and A Weigold (eds), *Re-thinking India: Perceptions from Australia*, New Delhi: Readworthy.

Wesley, M (2011). *There Goes the Neighbourhood*, Sydney: NewSouth.

Wesley, M (2014). Face of the Future: Australia has hard strategic choices to make amidst a complex rivalry over leadership and order in the Asia-Pacific, *Australian Financial Review*, 20 November

White, H (2010). *Power Shift: Australia's Future between Washington and Beijing*, Quarterly Essay, September, Collingwood: BlackInc

Wilson, T (2014). The 'Indo-Pacific': absent policy behind meaningless words, *East Asia Forum*, 19 September, http://www.eastasiaforum.org/ (accessed on 28 May 2015)

Winand, P and M Vicziany and P Datar (2015). *The European Union and India: Rhetoric or Meaningful Relationship*, Cheltenham: Edward Elgar.

19

Maritime Dimensions of China's Maritime Silk Route and India's Act East Policy

R S Vasan

The Maritime Environment in the Background

The pre-colonial era witnessed some remarkable engagement amongst nations despite limited connectivity and communication challenges. The centuries old silk and spice routes allowed the countries in different oceans to establish contacts. The initial such exchanges between nations were predominantly over treacherous land as new frontiers over sea routes were being explored. New trade routes were being discovered through the perilous oceans simultaneously by using wind power till the discovery of steam engines. The trade winds or monsoons paved the way for sail ships and dhows to connect continents for promoting trade interests while simultaneously enhancing the people to people contact. The commodities included spices, silk, pottery, horses, precious stones, etc. This in turn enabled cultural assimilation from amongst diverse cultures and religions. The dimensions of trade slowly made way to expansion of imperialist nations and led to establishment of colonies of the West notably in Asia.

The Glorious Past. The example of the setting up of the Sri Vijaya empire and the spread of Hindu influence in Indo-China through both sea and land routes is an example of the influence of the silk and spice routes. Likewise, the adventurous sea journey by the Chinese Admiral Zheng He in the sixth century which took the Chinese fleet and merchandise to many ports in Asia and Africa is again an absorbing tale of the importance of the oceans for trade, commerce and cross cultural exchanges. The Chinese are revisiting their history and are trying to learn the importance of maritime silk routes to peace and prosperity. The spinoff of such expeditions in the past, were always was in the cultural, political and religious domains which led to spread of religion, culture and social practices around the world.

Post-World War Scenario. The end of the World War II ushered in a new era of competitive dynamics of international relations with the sea forces playing a crucial role in providing sea based deterrence and projection of power in far corners of the world. The oceans around the world witnessed the power play by the NATO and the Soviet blocks with seemingly innocuous intention of preventing the third world war. It is ironic that such a measure only led to addition of nuclear arsenal and many near misses that brought the world to the brink of war. With the breakup of the Soviet Union which was least expected, the world order changed to a unipolar one with the US becoming the global super cop with interests around the world. Being the number one economic power with well-oiled military machinery the US was able to project power and intervenes in far off corners of the world to restore order or change the status quo according to the whims and fancies of the only superpower of the world. The recent failed examples in Iraq and Afghanistan even after lengthy stays of the occupational forces and spending of trillions of dollars has not brought peace and stability. On the contrary, the region has been devastated with no sign of lasting peace. Even the enormous loss of tens of thousands of innocent victims of the so called collateral damage has not helped in achieving the desired objectives.

Century of the Seas. The 21st century, designated as the century of the sea, has indeed been extremely challenging thus far in terms of the happenings at sea. There has been string of questions raised about security and stability due to many incidents of significance to a seafarer irrespective of whether he is on a warship or on a merchant ship or a fishing vessel. The maritime environment in the Asia Pacific region which is increasingly being referred to as Indo-Pacific region[1] is undergoing a major transformation. There are great changes in the maritime security landscape of immense importance to the global community. Both China and India are developing maritime power potential which comes with economic prosperity through the oceans[2]. Before examining the Sino Indian maritime equations and its impact in the current century, there is a need to examine some of the important issues that would influence the bilateral, regional and international relations.

One has to examine the indisputable factors that have governed the global maritime domain and the way nations have played out their role based on national interests. These factors have remained constant through the ages. The discussions below while not being exhaustive clearly illustrate that these constants continue to hold sway in the context of politico, military, social and cultural relations between nations irrespective of their geographic location.

Maritime Silk Route (MSR). This is a notable Chinese initiative on the lines of ancient Silk Route to revisit the past and regain the glory of the yester centuries. It was first proposed by Xi Jinping when he visited Southeast Asia in October 2013. Premier Li Keqiang, who also carried out a high-profile visit to the region, announced the setting up of a 3 billion Yuan ($495 million) maritime cooperation fund, part of which would support the plan. This on the face of it appears to be an initiative to promote trade, connectivity and also provide leverages for future contingencies in the Indian Ocean. As subsequent events have demonstrated, this is a 'Win-Win' for China but with minimal advantage to the destination countries many of them are staring at debt traps.

China approached the UN in 2016 to bid for World Heritage Status for Maritime Silk Route. It may be noted that this is the seventh in the prominent list chosen for recognition as world heritage site. Others in the list include ruins of the Nanyue King Palace, the Nanyue King Mausoleum, Guangxiao Monastery, the Light Tower of Huaisheng Mosque, the Ancient Tombs of Muslim Sages and the South Sea God Temple. It is of interest that a Sailor's trading map shown below shows India as the fulcrum for trade routes. Both India and China's combined economy was of the order of more than 55 percent of global GDP in the 14th century and it is only a matter of time before similar position is achieved by these two Asian powers.

A major Belt and Road Forum was conducted for the first time in 2017 and the second edition was concluded on 27th April 2019. India has abstained from the forum expressing serious concerns on the unilateral nature of investments without transparency and more importantly on sovereignty concerns along the China–PoK Economic Corridor.

Response from India's Maritime Neighbours

Maldives: The Government led by Yameen who was totally pro-China and anti-India welcomed and supported the 21st century silk road and assured welcomed Chinese investments in Maldives.

Also in the case of Maldives, with a population of just 3,30,000 people, it attracts more than 3,50,000 Chinese tourists outnumbering the local population annually. China also has investments in Maldives that is a quarter of the Maldives economy.

Maldives under Yameen appeared to be under Chinese spell and was inimical to the interests of India which has been a steadfast friend for decades. Many of the Indian investments were rejected and even two Advanced Light Helicopters given by India for humanitarian aid and Search and Rescue were asked to be taken back to India. Even during Yameen's rule, India readily went to the aid of a thirsty Maldives when there was no water in the archipelago.

The elections last year have restored the old equations between the two countries due to a friendly government in place now. Both Maldives and Sri Lanka are working together with the Indian Maritime agencies through various mechanisms including Dosti a trilateral maritime initiative.

Sri Lanka: This Island country too likewise was willing and it was indicated that the two sides agreed to strengthen defence cooperation and to cooperate in the areas of defence-related science and technology, exchange of military academics, and provide logistic support," It is important to note that Sri Lanka has a Chinese investment of over 50 billion USD with a population of just about 21 million.

As subsequent events have proved, both Sri Lanka and Maldives are deeply in debt and in the case of Sri Lanka, the inability of the new Government of Maitripala Sirisena resulted in handing over of the Hambantota port to Chinese company on lease for 99 years.

The Easter blasts that killed 253 civilians in a terrorist attack by Jihadi terrorists has brought back the memories of the ethnic war that had engulfed the country in violence for over 36 years. This has serious consequences for the future of the small country which is now required to face new forms of threats from the radicalized Muslims who have come under the influence of IS. India will need to help out this country in all respects to see that history does not repeat itself.

Bangladesh and Myanmar who are both land and maritime neighbours have witnessed heavy investments from China in various sectors including defence. The ports of these two neighbours in the Bay of Bengal are in the cross wires of China as it gives it a foothold in the Bay of Bengal. However, both Bangladesh and Myanmar are friendly to India and there have been many collaborative initiatives to enhance the prosperity and development quotient through Security and Growth for All in the Region (SAGAR) which is an important component of foreign policy of Modi Government.

India: From the Indian point of view, the invitation for India (though it was never consulted prior to launching the MSR) was extended just a week after China's naval exercises out of the Sunda Strait in the waters of the eastern Indian Ocean in February 2014.

This was also two weeks after the People's Liberation Army Navy (PLAN) tried to overcome the Malacca Dilemma by carrying out its first-ever drills in the Lombok Straits of the Indian Ocean near Indonesia,

MSR can be assessed to be a bid to reframe China's rise in a non-threatening manner through maritime trade with adequate provisions for Confidence Building Measures (CBMs) entirely by investments close to the ports and harbours, soft loans for improvement of maritime infrastructure and mutual visits. The possibility of expanding naval capabilities through trade, connectivity to strategic outposts in IOR cannot be ruled out with the kind of interest in the protection of energy routes and trade.

Genesis of the MSR

Maritime trade and connectivity through the ages has always been at the centre of international relations. Trade never stopped though the centuries though it may have slowed down during periodic periods of recession. It has only registered constant upward growth except for brief periods in human history. Commercial interests provide leverages by enhanced interaction and interdependence. Such exchanges expand into the politico strategic dimensions that change the balance at times with not too pleasant consequences.

The slant of the US Policy to Asia Pacific indeed is influenced by the growing Asian power equations in that area and the diminishing importance of western economies. Asian powers China and India are expected to overtake US and Japan progressively.[3] This is also due to the fears of a rising China that compels US to try and achieve balance in the region[4]. With the withdrawal from Afghanistan US is expected to lose strategic interest in Middle East also due to its own predicted energy independence due to discovery of Shale oil and gas.

An examination of the conduct of nations in the past centuries clearly illustrates that Commercial interests (and energy interests now) spur nations to different parts of the world to conduct business while shaping their national strategies for engagement in the region. As witnessed by history, the commercial interests do have the potential of transforming the strategy of the host country depending on local conditions and opportunity. The initial commercial interests at times give rise to grand strategies to acquire political, economic and strategic clout through trade and commerce. The classic example of how the British colonized India through the East Indian Company bears testimony to this modus operandi that is available for adoption by others. The setting up of the East India Company in India a predominantly trading company illustrated how trade led to expansionism and setting of the British rule in India that lasted for over 250 years till India got its freedom in August 1947. The story is not very different in other Asian countries where colonial rule was established by the Dutch, Portuguese, British, French and other western colonial powers. The fact that most of such colonies were established through the sea and known trade routes is a telling story of the importance of the oceans which promoted and nurtured ambitions of both great and small powers. The historically recorded Sea voyages/adventures of both China and India as seafaring nations are noteworthy as both nations did not colonise other countries. On the contrary, the connectivity through the oceans was used to promote trade, cultural and religious exchanges that enhanced the peaceful engagements without any major skirmishes at sea.

Sea Lines of Communication are the lifelines of the world. As a form of clean and cost-effective transportation there is no substitute to movement by sea for transporting large volumes of human needs. Without such movement, it has been suggested that, **"Half the world will starve, the other half will freeze"**[5] and many economies will collapse with the onset of Chaos and conflict. The choke points continue to play a pivotal role in both facilitating and regulating the flow of critical goods through them. In the context of the present century, the increased importance of transporting energy goods through the critical straits and choke points cannot be underestimated. Vulnerable as they are, due to the vagaries of regional imbalances/political instability in an area it compels coordinated action to create suitable security architectures both under UN Statutes and also the United Nations Conventions on the Law of the Seas. The safety of the SLOCs and the security of shipping in the choke points is of great importance to nations who are dependent on the sea routes for economy and prosperity. The new MSR has overlapping contours with the SLOCs. Irrespective of how it is nomenclatured, these are routes for providing connectivity between nations from Asia to Africa and in the process, also throw up opportunities for promoting political strategic and economic engagements.

In the context of the South China Sea, the fact that more than 80 percent of the energy goods are imported through the sea routes in the Indian Ocean.[6] They also pass through the South/East China Sea before reaching the eastern destinations brings in acute concerns on the safety of the Sea Lines of Communication (SLOCs). Nations therefore have to initiate measures to safeguard these interests. This explains why China and other navies are sending out their warships to the troubled waters of Somalia where pirates are having a field day in taking over ships and craft to disrupt maritime trade and traffic while instilling fear in the minds of ship owners and the crew. While the disputes in East China Sea (ECS) and South China Sea (SCS) are not new, they seem to be acquiring the potential to destabilize the status quo maintained for decades. The new assertive leadership of Abe in Japan and the increased emphasis on safeguarding national/historical interests is at the core of the problem in the region. The leadership of Xi Jinping a popular leader who is on a mission to set his house in order has certain implications in the region. China will not alter its stance on going to any extent to protect the declared core interests that include sea territories around disputed Islands which are expected to yield high volumes of gas and oil.

While all the involved in the regional dispute are engaged in show of power to assert their sovereignty and ownership claims, two incidents stand out to demonstrate the resolve of those in power in the area. First, China established a province in Sansha (which is also known as Woody Island) under the Hainan province. Second, the Government of Japan bought the Islands in Senkaku which were privately owned by Japanese national. This led to increased protest on both sides and jingoism that has not helped to cool down fraying tempers. The world is watching with bated breath to see if the situation would go out of control due to some miscalculations on any side. The disputes in the region are not entirely due to either historical or sovereignty issues. The assessment is that the disputes have a lot do with the energy security aspirations of the involved nations. China and Japan, just as some of the other East Asian countries are heavily dependent on energy imports, and thus vulnerable to possible intervention and manipulation of the oil prices and interruption of energy products. Any discovery of hydrocarbons/gas in the immediate neighbourhood would help to minimize the energy dependence on imports. The ownership of the disputed Islands or any other territory therefore assumes great significance for the energy thirsty nations in the region. So in the backdrop of discussions above, how does this impact the MSR initiative or how it is relevant at all is a question that needs to be answered? The seaborne interests of China traverse long distances in the Indian Ocean from the energy producing nations and then reach the energy hungry nations after passing through the Malacca Straits. The outposts in countries that have joined the MSR would provide some options for China to use the ports in these countries to provide logistic facilities for out of area operations in IOR.

The very notion of freedom of navigation has been questioned by the aggressive stance of China which has tried to bulldoze its maritime neighbours both in the South China Sea and also the East China Sea. The collision of Vietnamese vessels with Chinese vessels on 05 May 2014 aggravated the situation in the SCS. The claims and counter claims in these areas are not new but with the non-resolution of such disputes, the tension is building up in these areas.

The declaration of ADIZ has complicated the matter even more as now the sea areas and the air envelope in disputed areas is sought to be controlled with the ultimate aim of cementing the ownership claims by physical presence and by such extraordinary proclamation of ADIZ. The declaration of the ADIZ in the East China Sea on November 23, 2013, has escalated the tension in another dimension. In the process of activating the ADIZ, the interception of the Japanese surveillance aircraft by the Chinese Sukhois in the last week of May 2014 can be classified as a near miss as the aircraft closed to less than 50 meters from the Japanese aircraft. Any miscalculation or an unintended manoeuvre would have resulted in an avoidable accident that could propel both the sides to the next level of undesired engagement. It was expected that China would also declare an ADIZ in South China Sea by end of last year. However, this has not yet happened.

The smaller neighbours of China in South China Sea who dispute the exaggerated claims of China and militarization of the SCS are disillusioned with the behaviour of China. A small country Philippines approached the Permanent Court of Arbitration in Hague and was given a favourable verdict which also indicted China. However, this has not made any difference to China's construction of military bases on artificial Islands constructed by environmentally destructive practices of dredging coral and causing irreparable damage to the marine life. The provisions of UNCLOS were blatantly violated by China. The Freedom of Navigation Operations (FONOPS) by USA has not made any difference to the stand of China .

The developments in the Persian Gulf also are not comforting as Iran threatened to block the Straits of Hormuz[7] if the US and the West cross a pre-determined nuclear threshold. While Iran continues to nurture its aspirations to be a nuclear power, the possibility of the situation in the Arabian Peninsula going out of hand with possible impact on the movement of traffic through the world's critical maritime choke points are issues of great concern. However, the recent agreement in April 2015 to allow Iran to use nuclear energy for peaceful purposes under appropriate monitoring by the IAEA has allowed some breathing time though there are other questions of existence being raised by Israel.

Sea-based deterrence (SBD) did not halt with the breakup of the Soviet Union. Resurgence of cold war at regional levels appears inevitable with emphasis on SBD. Mismatch between haves and have-nots of nuclear weapons will see attempts to bridge this gap by weapon programmes, delivery, command and control systems—Iran, North Korea, Pakistan and other aspirants make the list of those who would like to possess nuclear weaponry by hook or crook. The famous quote of ZA Bhutto, "We will eat grass[8] but will make a nuclear bomb," illustrates the point about how the world will have to continue with both the existing and future challenges of nuclearisation. Would the establishment of the MSR help in the Indian Ocean aspirations of China by locating its SBD units (SSBNs) for targeting locations in the West including USA.

While presently, China has a lead in the number of nuclear capable submarines in its inventory, India is joining the club with INS Arihant, a nuclear submarine[9] and follow on submarines that would provide it with the SBD capability. In this context, the dedication of the nuclear submarine Arihant to the nation after its first successful deployment in November 2018 signals the readiness of India to face the nuclear threats in the subcontinent.

The challenges of maintaining an SSBN[10] notwithstanding, the emphasis on Sea-based deterrence will not vanish in the coming decades. With specific reference to the MSR, it is evident that some of the recipient countries in the IOR may be in the cross hair of China for ensuring that there is turn round facility provided in times of need to the units of PLA Navy.

There are some dynamic developments which have the potential to impact in the maritime domain in the present century in the Indian Ocean in particular. The collective and individual responses to these developing situations would determine the shape of maritime safety and security architectures. Some of the important developments with potential for impacting the maritime security dimensions are discussed below in the succeeding paragraphs.

Pivot to Asia

A lot has been said about the possible impact of what the US pivot to Asia would mean to the region and the rest of the world. The analysis for this pivot has been explained as more to do with the rise of China. USA by redeploying its maritime forces in the new areas of interest wants to remain relevant where action is. The turmoil in the South China Sea and the East China Sea has engaged the attention of the countries in this region where almost everyone seems to have a dispute with China.

The recent conflagration in the region with aggressive posturing by North Korea and the joint exercises of South Korea and the USA in the surrounding areas has added to a greater sense of instability and there are fears about the conduct of intransigent North Korea which seems to press on regardless even to the counsel of its mentor China.

With the impending withdrawal from Afghanistan, USA can exercise some flexibility in troop redeployment in other areas of interest if it assessed that their presence is vital and necessary to ensure that regional stability. The revised Maritime Strategy released on 13th March 2015 makes it clear that USA will not withdraw from the Gulf area. On the contrary, there would be a proportionate increase of maritime forces in the region by increasing the numbers to 40 vessels by 2020.[11]

Additional factors in the MSR. In addition to the factors above, the challenges of the 21st century include Proliferation Security Concerns, Environmental concerns, and Traffic density with more vessels which could lead to greater risk of grounding, collision and spillage which exist to a large extent along the MSR. Such accidents unfortunately come with long-term impact on the fragile environment. Piracy seems to be on the rise in different parts as the navies of the world try to contain it in one part or another. Opening up of the Antarctic routes for navigation has its ascendant challenges.

Specific technologies in the recent times include AIS, LRIT, SSAS, VTMS, GPS, and ECDIS,[12] have enhanced the safety of ships and also provide options for contingency planning based on data fusion. Doubtlessly, cutting-edge technological advances enable safe, expeditious and efficient transportation— Advances in propulsion, marine technology, under water and over water surveillance, space-based surveillance, deep sea mining, Tsunami warning systems have transformed the Safety and Security Architecture. Such technological improvements are all pervading and impact the way maritime stakeholders conduct their business. The flip side is that what is available to you is also available to the tech savvy Non-State Actors (Pirates, Terrorists, online fraudsters) a fact that needs to be constantly borne in mind while drawing up security architectures and responses. These factors would need to be taken into account by China when it plans to use the MSR for furthering not just its economic interests but also its strategic posturing.

It is in the context of the facts brought out above, that there is a need to examine the impact of the MSR in shaping the maritime contours in the Indian Ocean. This is particularly so since China is not an Indian Ocean power just as India is not a Pacific power. Yet, both the countries do have enormous interest in the respective regions for economic reasons, global prosperity and stability. The interests stem from the need to access global commons and to use the seas for the common good of the people of the two nations.

There is definitely a sense of competition due to the growing economies of Asia which would like to take centre stage. India is not in a position to challenge China whose growth has been spectacular and has alarmed its neighbours with the military developmental plans. Despite the assurances by China that it is not for any offensive action, the pattern of spending on defence[13] does not bring about a sense of confidence amongst the observers. India and China have no contests in the maritime domain and the only issue apparently is related to resolving the vexed issue of land borders. The perception in India is that China has been overly aggressive with all its neighbours including India when it comes to sorting out the border and sovereignty issues. The concern has shifted to the East China and South China Sea[14] where the occurrences at sea have not reinforced any confidence that the situation would not go out of control due to over indulgence in nationalistic fervour. The diagram below illustrates the number of disputes in which China is involved. The reported disputes numbering 61 in the case of PRC is indicative of the state of flux in the region. The increased military expenditure and the investment in newer technology and weapon systems is adding to the concerns of stability in the region

China has by and large invested heavily in breaching certain technologies to ensure that its maritime anti access-capabilities[15] are fine tuned. The investment in Anti-Satellite technology, Stealth aircraft, Anti-Ship Ballistic Missile (ASBM) and the Cyber war capability has provided considerable teeth to the PLA. As illustrated in the diagram below, it is clear that there is a layered kind of overlapping technologies that would provide China with the capability to take on its adversaries before they even reach the areas of conflict in its backyard. The cyber capability which is being discussed a lot today seems to suggest that they do have an edge and are experimenting with various cyber war options that could tilt the favour one way or the other with the potential adversary including USA. For China, the USA and its actions of recalibration or pivot to Asia poses a serious challenge.

While it faces these challenges in a hostile maritime neighbourhood both in ECS and SCS, through the MSR, it would like to have certain options in the Indian Ocean where again the USA has a dominant maritime presence. The presence of the fifth fleet since the 80s has ensured to a large extent free flow of energy goods from the Straits of Hormuz to the needy markets of the East.

Should India or China challenge the seaborne trade along the SLOCs due to a spillover of the land dispute, and then China would like to be prepared for such a contingency by having some leverage in the Indian Ocean Littorals.

Both China and India are emerging Blue Water Navies if they are already not there. While there is a lot of debate on what constitutes a Blue Water Navy (BWN), the present day definition is as follows: "…A maritime force capable of sustained operation across the deep waters of open oceans. A blue-water navy allows a country to project power far from the home country and usually includes one or more aircraft carriers. Smaller blue-water navies are able to dispatch fewer vessels abroad for shorter periods of time."[16] In present day classification, the classic Blue water Navies include the US, UK and France, whereas the one's in the making are China, India and South Korea.

When one examines the operations undertaken by India, it is clear that since 1971 which is considered the turning point for the navy in India, Indian Navy has demonstrated its potential as a BWN. The details of the operations at Serials a, b and c below have been well covered in the books titled Transition to Triumph (1999), Transition to Eminence (2004) and Transition to Guardianship (2009) by the official historian of Indian Navy, Vice Admiral Hiranandani. Without getting in to the details of the operations, the same are listed to highlight the range of operations which included both the peace time and the activities during hostile environment:

(a) Liberation of Bangladesh in 1971[17]
(b) Prevention of Coup in Maldives in 1988[18]
(c) Deployment of Indian Peace Keeping Force in Sri Lanka[19]
(d) Anti-Piracy Patrols off Somalia (Both India and China have been engaged in anti-piracy patrols since 2008 and have been even cooperating to protect shipping passing through the high risk area)
(e) Evacuation of Indian and Foreign Nationals from Lebanon, Libya and now from Yemen in April 2015.

Historically, both China and India could come under the definition of blue water navies as both ventured out to far corners of the world. So if it was Zheng

He[20] who undertook the voyages in the 14th century and visited many ports in the Indian Ocean, it was the Chola's[21] and Pallavas of the southern Indian dynasties who extended their reach up to South East Asia and beyond. Today, China has commercial and strategic interests in the Indian Ocean just as India has renewed its interests in East Asia by its Look East Policy. India is increasing its engagement with the East Asian nations including China.

The main maritime interest is to protect the ships carrying its energy products and goods. India also possesses the capability to protect its commercial interests in different parts of the world where both China and India are engaged in the hunt for energy resources. The Chinese navy for the first time entered Indian Ocean to protect its interests off the Somali Coast where the scourge of piracy had started affecting all merchant men. The PLA-N has maintained an effective patrol in the areas of interest and it is not usual for either the Chinese or the Indian navy vessels to escort any foreign vessel and to ensure that the SLOCs remain open and secure. This reinforces the belief that the two Asian countries can come together to ward off common threats in the global commons.

While it appears that the concept of "string of pearls" a phrase coined to indicate the extent of strategic inroads in Indian Ocean by PRC[22] has been debated endlessly the perception is that China is slowly establishing its sphere of influence in the immediate neighbourhood of India that is detrimental to the national/maritime interests of India. With the economic clout enjoyed by China coupled with the decision making and political processes that give China an edge over India, PRC has found it easy to make inroads in Sri Lanka, Myanmar, Mauritius, Bangladesh, Seychelles, Pakistan and Maldives. The huge economic investments with soft loans serve as a great incentive for the developing countries in the region. The economic investments in India's immediate maritime neighbourhood have alarmed the Indian establishment even though they concede that China has a major role to play in the economic development of the region.

The assessment is that despite the geo-strategic advantage enjoyed by India, India is slowly conceding its time-tested advantage in the region to the aggressive economic policies of China with long-term strategic dividends in the Indian Ocean Region. While investments in port developments in Pakistan, Sri Lanka, Bangladesh, Myanmar and other investments in Maldives are not designed to create basing facilities for the PLA-Navy, the economic leverages provide a great opportunity for China to use these facilities at a future date for augmenting any naval initiatives depending on the strategic development.

The visit of the Chinese submarines to Colombo on the eve of the visit of Chinese Premier Xi Jinping in September raised the heckles in the Indian establishment. The Mahinda Rajapaksa's Government was seen as pro-China and granting numerous concessions to help China realize its ambitions in the Indian Ocean. However, the change of Government in Sri Lanka consequent to the Presidential election which has brought friendly changes in the Indian neighbourhood. It is from this point of view that the visit of PM Narendra Modi to countries in our maritime neighbourhood takes centre stage. The visit of Modi to Sri Lanka came after 28 years and showed the past policy makers of India and leadership in poor light as they continued to ignore the most important maritime southern neighbour post the visit of Rajiv Gandhi.

In the context of maritime security the security planners would need to work on the two lines of seaward defence peripheries with respect to India The inner periphery passes through Sri Lanka, Maldives and the A&N Islands which houses the Tri Services command. The outer line of maritime defence includes the countries such as Mauritius Seychelles and other Indian Ocean countries. The visit of the Prime Minister to Mauritius and Seychelles is an attempt to ensure that the outer periphery of our seaward defence is not breached by Chinese MSR which could lead to other initiatives using this handle. These visits to these countries which have historic and cultural relations with India offer some advantages for India's initiatives in the Indian Ocean. India has received positive signals about these countries contributing to the Maritime Domain Awareness project of India to have a total picture of the Indian Ocean to be able to thwart off threats emanating from the seas.

Neighbourhood First. The Foreign Policy prescriptions are very clear and lucid as far as the Indian Government is concerned. The message is that if you ignore those who are on the two lines you lose out any advantage that was conferred historically by geography and also by the percentage of Indians who have settled down in these countries of great importance to our maritime security and stability. From the point of view, the maritime neighbourhood extends from the shores of Africa to East Asia through the connecting straits.

This makes it imperative to have good relations with other stakeholders in the Pacific. Therefore the relations with Vietnam, Japan, South Korea and other South East Asian countries also need to have a high priority to ensure that there are leverages available in the Pacific to meet the futuristic strategic developments.

Whether on the MSR or in other areas of interest, the challenges for both the

Indian Navy and the PLA-N are similar due to the nature and scale of maritime developments in the new world. The new era though has a very clear focus on trade and commerce also has brought us back to revisit concerns on safety and security at sea, illegal immigration, environmental degradation, piracy, asymmetric threats, Proliferation and WMD which requires the application of sea-power. The need for greater safe-guards, intelligent use of technology, Rules of Engagement (RoE) and best practices essential to prevent recurrences can hardly be overemphasized. The joining of hands of the major world powers to promote safety, stability, law and order at sea is the need of the hour. The MSR initiative which has trade and connectivity as the central theme cannot be a standalone initiative. It is a package that needs to be handled with care by all the stakeholders.

The areas of engagement along the SLOCs of great importance to all the countries who use the seas obviously allude to anti-piracy, HADR, energy security, coordinated investments for resources, joint exploration and such like. Unlike India, China carries a lot more products using its own shipping fleet. China indeed is very concerned about the piracy attacks and also the vulnerability of its shipping fleet when engaged in trade and commerce in far corners of the world. China is well aware that it would serve its interests if it is part of the global initiatives such as the one witnessed in the Gulf of Aden. The cooperative initiatives of the two big giants of Asia will go a long way in augmenting the regional and global maritime security architecture. However, India somehow does not want to join the MSR initiative as it feels that it would yield strategic space through the trade and connectivity format adopted by China to engage the countries both in Asia and Africa.

There are no doubts any more about the assertion that the 21st century belongs to Asia in general, China and India in particular. This geographic entity is shaping the international landscape as never before. The interplay of major western and eastern powers in economic, strategic, political, military and cultural arenas has witnessed manifold increase due to the changing dynamics of global power play. The revolution in information technology has on one hand shrunk the globe even more and has brought about a paradigm shift in the manner in which nations interact to protect their interests and rights.

The rise of China and India, both Asian powers, is set to change the existing equations and would bring in new changes to the global order. The recent economic report brought out that India has piped Japan to the number three position after US and China. These changes have a far-reaching impact on the military, economic and political developments in the region. The US which continues to take it up on itself to be the guarantor of global security and order is recalibrating to the Indo-Pacific in order to be able to intervene militarily should it be necessary to protect the interests of its allies in the Pacific and its own interests. An increasingly assertive China, which has economic power and a growing modern military, challenges the notion of the only superpower. The fear that any vacuum created by the US would be occupied by China is also a factor that has weighed heavily in the minds of the US policymakers who do not want to surrender the geo-strategic advantage.

The withdrawal from Afghanistan at least theoretically allows for redeployment of certain forces in the areas of interest in the Indo-Pacific. China has been aggressively pursuing its claims for territory in the East China Sea and the South China Sea by quoting historical claims. It has also displayed a tendency to resort to use of force to settle such disputes. This has not gone well with the maritime neighbours in the region who would like to use the presence and friendship of USA to counter the military might of China. The smaller neighbours such as Philippines have even approached the International Court of Justice (ICJ) challenging the Chinese claims. The US has assured its traditional allies that it would uphold the friendship treaties with these countries should there be a need.

The impact of the pivot to Asia can be viewed in two ways. From the American point of view, it would facilitate greater security and stability in a volatile area where claims and counter claims over territory could go out of hand and lead to either localized conflict or escalate to something more bringing in extra-regional players such as the US itself. Some of the recent clashes at sea and certain responses from those involved does not augur well for maritime stability and security in the region under question. From the point of China, the presence of the US is an impediment and China is uncomfortable with the unwanted presence of the only superpower. The recalibration and presence of the US is seen as the inability of the superpower to reconcile to the changed geostrategic landscape and the growth of China in the Indo-Pacific region. The actions and statements of leaders from USA, including from Obama, are perceived as posing hurdles for the maritime military ambitions of China under the guise of peaceful raise. There are legitimate major concerns about the freedom of navigation and the right to safe passage through various SLOCs.

Conclusion. A quick look at the MSR strategy of China and the study of the maritime dimensions in India's neighbourhood brings out that essentially the old silk routes have become the Sea Lines of Communication (SLOCs) connecting oceans and continents sustaining the global economic interests by trade and commerce. The haves and the have nots have used the oceans to bridge the gap by engaging in seaborne trade. The energy dependent countries in Asia such as China, India and Japan have no choice but to use the sea routes to import their energy sources from far corners of the world to sustain the economic growth. China has become the manufacturing hub of the world and again has to use the seas for exporting large quantities of its industrial products for feeding the markets in the West while simultaneously importing oil, gas and other energy resources. The new silk routes therefore have become the indispensable arteries or lifelines of the world which need to be protected. The challenge to these sea routes have come from pirates and VNSAs who interfere in the safe passage of vessels of all sizes and shapes which are engaged in legitimate trade activity. It is evident that there are areas for cooperation in ensuring the free use of the global commons. It is also a foregone conclusion that the MSR would provide those desired advantages to China when more countries decide to join the initiative. India unfortunately, did lose out in the neighbourhood due to lack of good leadership and strategy to engage the neighbours in its traditional areas of influence in the IOR.

Recommendations for Recalibrating the Foreign Policy in the Maritime Domain

China and India will have to initiate measures to face the challenges. This can only be accomplished by coordinated, collaborative efforts to ensure maritime equilibrium. There are areas in which both the counties can easily join hands particularly in the maritime domain without any fear of treading on each other's toes even along the Maritime Silk Routes. Both the countries have a lot to gain by engaging each other in the maritime arena. India will continue to be wary of the Chinese overtures in the Indian Ocean Region though, for the present, it is to do more with the ability of China to invest heavily due to its own growing economy and its intention to develop a powerful maritime power potential.

There is a need to address vulnerability of SLOC and huge volumes of mercantile trade that passes under the watchful eyes of the Indian establishment. Energy Security being of paramount importance to India, there is a need to ensure that it engages with all stakeholder nations in the region to safeguard its interests.

India while not being in the same league as China when it comes to investments, has no choice but to engage its maritime neighbours actively with investments and soft loans. There should be no hesitation to use its soft power in the maritime neighbourhood to obtain long-term benefits. Security and Growth for all in the Region (SAGAR) provides the right kind of platform to engage the neighbours who can be provided the required help to catalyze the process. The Blue economy is another option that opens up opportunities for collaborative efforts particularly in the context of the mandated Sustainable Development Goals (SDG). India can be the facilitator for the small neighbours by offering material and technical help that will lay the foundations for future engagements in many areas of Indian Ocean is the only ocean named after India and it is important that this definition and the import is not lost on policy planners and the leadership.

NOTES

1 https://sldinfo.com/2019/10/the-evolution-of-the-indo-pacific-over-the-next-five-years-implications-for-australian-defense/
2 Geoffrey Till, *Sea power: A Guide for the Twenty-First Century* (Oxon, Routledge, 2013), 20, 203
3 Anil K. Gupta, Haiyan Wang *Getting China and India Right* (San Francisco: Jossey Bass, 2009), 6, 8, 61
4 Shelly Rigger, *Tangled Titans* ed, David L Shambaugh (Maryland: Rowman and Littlefield Publishers Inc 2013), 309
5 Tay Lim Hing , *Maritime Security in Southeast Asia,* ed Kwa Chong Guan, John Kristen Skogan (New York: Routledge, 2007), 201
6 Garver. John W, *China and Iran: Ancient Partners in a Post-Imperial World (*Washington: University of Washington Press, 2006), 246
7 Gibson Bryan R., *Covert Relationship* (California PSI reports 2010), 126
8 Khab Feroze Hassan, *Eating Grass: The Making of the Pakistani Bomb* (California: Stanford, 2012), 87.
9 Verghese Koithara *Managing India's Nuclear Forces* (Washington: Brookings Institute, 2012), 136
10 Ibid.
11 Full document released on 13th March 2015 and accessed by visiting http://www.navy.mil/maritime.
12 As illustrated in Integrated Maritime Policy for the EU, Working Document III on Maritime Surveillance Systems (Joint Research Centre, Ispra), 2
13 Ed SIPRI, Sipri Year Book *Armaments, Disarmament and International Security 2011* (Oxford University Press, 2011), 184, 185,
14 Ibid., 110
15 Ronald O'Rourk, *China Naval Modernization: Implications for U.S. Navy Capabilities* (Washington: CRS Report 2009), 23
16 According to the definition of Defence Security Service of USA
17 Hiranandani GM, *Transition to Triumph* (New Delhi: Lancer 2000), 181, 227, 228
18 Hiranandani GM, *Transition to Eminence* (New Delhi: Lancer 2004), 14, 199, 242
19 Hiranandani GM, *Transition to Guardianship* (New Delhi: Lancer 2009), xxvi, 52, 107
20 Michael M Yamashita, *Zheng He: tracing the epic voyages of China's greatest explorer* (White Star Publishers, 2006) 14, 17
21. Krishna Reddy, *Indian History* (New Delhi: Tata McGraw Hill, 2001), 64,65
22 Ashley J. Tellis, Travis Tanner, Jessica Keough, *Asia Responds To Its Rising Powers: China and India* (Seattle: NBAS, 2011), 110, 111.

20

India–Singapore Bilateral Relation

S. Manivasakan

The year 2015 marks the 50th anniversary of the establishment of India-Singapore bilateral relations. India and Singapore established their bilateral relation when Singapore got Independence in the year 1965. India being distinguished as the rising power, she plays a major role in the platform of the South and Southeast Asian countries. The similarity between the two countries lies in the fact that both are democratic country whilst Singapore a democratic authoritarian country and the difference is also projected through the fact that even though India is often praised as the world's largest democracy (population-wise)[1] it is a developing country while Singapore is already a developed country. The two countries have had experiences under the colonial rule because of which the friendliest of relation in forging a dynamic and multifaceted relationship could be seen.

Singapore first started as a trading settlement in the late 13th century during that time it was known as "Tamasek", people settled there were Malays, Chinese and Orang Laut[2] (early immigrants who inhabited along the coastline of Singapore Island during pre-colonial days).[3] This settlement grew in major importance in the 14th century, the opening of this settlement let to vistas of opportunities, and therefore attracted traders and people who began to settle in the island and thus population began to increase which in turn brought in wealth and development.

India and Singapore have a history of long standing mutual relation which is seen through the relation both countries maintain in the way people have contact with each other. Historically India and Singapore link dates back to the period of the Cholas where they establish a permanent settlement.[4] The modern day relationship between the two countries can be attributed to Sir Thomas Stamford Raffles who landed on the island State of Singapore in the year 1819, which was first established as a trading outpost. The British English East India Company eyeing the need of a base east of Bay of Bengal; the outpost played a major role in controlling the trade in the Malacca region. The camaraderie the two countries share is worth mentioning every time when India-Singapore relation is talked about.

The old and strong bonds the two countries share are boosted further with the improvisation of India's "Look East Policy" under the leadership of Prime Minister Narasimha Rao in 1991. This strategic shift towards Asia led to the beginning of India-Singapore economic partnership. Since then, the relationships between the two countries have grown stronger and more vigorous. The Look East Policy also led Singapore to be a bridge to connect the rest of Asia with India and India regard Singapore as a gateway to Southeast Asia and East Asia. The relationships or bilateral cooperation between the two countries has expanded since then and can be seen through the various MOUs signed and projects being undertaken be it in terms of Defence, Tourism, IT and other sectors.

Political and Defence Relations

Politically the two countries relation started when Singapore got her independence in the year 1965 after experiencing the rule by the British, Japanese, Dutch, Portuguese (in the case of India) and the French under whom India have had the same experience the only difference that India got her Independence earlier in 1947. The reason of the close friendship is because of the fact that since time immemorial there have been close contact between people because of the trade route which takes the people of India to Singapore. For centuries the two countries have maintained commercial, maritime and cultural exchanges as can be seen in the present days where many people of Indian origins are settled in Singapore. However it must be noted that during the post independence period the event of the cold war led to the fall in India-Singapore relations. But the inception of India's Look East Policy brought again various high level interactions between the heads of the two countries. Singapore took a major interest in the economic reforms of India in the 1990s when Prime Minister Goh Chok Tong visited India in 1994 as the Chief Guest at India's Republic Day celebration which was followed by Prime Minister Narasimha Rao visit to Singapore in the same year.[5]

Singapore right after her independence and separation from Malaysia, was in mayhem and the government was left with a handful of things to do from building the nation from scratch to developing its infrastructure. By this time India had settled and had fought as many as three wars; 1947, 1962 and 1965 wars. For Singapore there was also the need to build its defence system and raise its own standing army. It was here that Singapore looked to India for training her army who have had experienced in fighting wars and who at that time had a well-developed standing army. It must also be noted that Singapore was the first country who came to support India in the war with Pakistan in 1965.[6] Moreover Singapore helped India in gaining the dialogue partnership in ASEAN in 1995.[7] Singapore also played a major role in bringing India and ASEAN countries together.[8] India has a close working relation with Singapore in the international platform and a number of regional mechanism bound these two countries together such as ASEAN, ASEAN Regional Forum (ARF), ASEAN+5, East Asia Summit, and in the ASEAN Defence Ministers Meeting (ADMM)-Plus. The visitation to Singapore by the then External Affairs Minister in June 2007 saw the forming of the Joint Ministerial Committee (JMC) with the Foreign Ministers as heads and also the launch of CEO's Forum and the declaration of a Strategic Dialogue.[9]

The relation took a notch up with the signing of Defence Co-operation Agreement in 2003 since then there has been Defence related joint military exercises and training (Bold Kurukshetra exercise between the Indian Army and the Singapore Army, Anti-Submarine Warfare (ASW)-naval training operations) which includes naval and maritime exercises, taken up by both the countries or sometimes with some of the Southeast Asian countries like Indonesia, Malaysia, and Thailand (e.g. the SIMBEX series, the MILAN series). The Defence relation has expanded in the sphere of counter terrorism. Both the countries are affirmed to fight against terrorism of any kind. The two countries Defence Ministers have also renewed the bilateral agreement in 2013 on joint army training and exercises which will be valid for five more years.[10] It must be noted that Singapore is the only country to which India has offered its facilities for training and land exercises.[11] India ranks among the top 10 countries of the world with the highest military expenditure in 2013 (9th place). Singapore on the other hand has got the most advanced military in South East Asia, and the highest military spending in terms of GDP in the Asia-Pacific region.[12]

There have a Number of Bilateral Visits from Singapore to India from the year 1966 where the Prime Minister Lee Kuan Yew first Visited India followed by the visit of Goh Chok Tong in the year 1994. President Sellapan Ramanathan Visited Singapore on January, 2003 followed by the visit of Goh Chok Tong on April, 2003. Deputy Prime Minister and Minister for Finance Lee Hsien Loong

List of Bilateral Visits from Singapore to India

Visiting Delegates	Date of Visit
Senior Minister of State for Defence and Foreign Affairs Dr Mohamad Maliki Bin Osman visited New Delhi	January 16-17, 2018
Minister for Defence Dr Ng Eng Hen and Kalaikunda to attend the second India-Singapore Defence Ministers' Dialogue (DMD) and Emeritus Senior Minister (ESM), Mr. Goh Chok Tong visited New Delhi	December, 2017
Senior Minister of State for Law and Finance Ms. Indranee Rajah to New Delhi	October, 2017
Minister for Foreign Affairs Dr Vivian Balakrishnan visited New Delhi and Guwahati	October 31, 2017-November 1, 2017
Singapore's Deputy Prime Minister (DPM) and Coordinating Minister for Economic and Social Policies Mr. Tharman Shanmugaratnam and Senior Minister of State for Defence and Foreign Affairs Dr Mohamad Maliki Bin Osman	July, 2017
Ministry of Finance Mrs. Tan Ching Yee	April, 2017
Minister of Home Affairs & Minister of Law Mr. K Shanmugam and Minister for Trade & Industry (Industry) Mr. S Iswaran	March, 2017
Prime Minister of Singapore Lee Hsien Loong accompanied by Minister for Trade and Industry Mr. S. Iswaran, acting Minister for Education and Senior of State for Defence Mr. Ong Ye Kung, Senior Minister of State (Defence and Foreign Affairs) Dr. Mohamad Maliki Bin Osman and Members of Parliament	October 3-7, 2016
President Tony Tan Keng Yam	February 8-11, 2015
Emeritus Senior Minister Goh Chok Tong along with Minister in the PMO and Second Minister for Trade and Industry and Home Affairs S Iswaran as well as Minister of State for National Development Desmond Lee	September 7-11, 2014
Minister for Defence Dr. Ng. Eng Hen	August 18-20, 2014
Minister for Foreign Affairs and Minister for Law K. Shanmugam	30th June-4th July 2014
Second Minister for Trade and Industry and Second Minister for Home Affairs S. Iswaran	January 27-29, 2014
Emeritus Senior Minister Goh Chok Tong	December 3-6, 2013
Minister for Defence Dr. Ng. Eng Hen	November 2012
Prime Minister Lee Hsien Loong	July 10-12, 2012
Minister for Foreign Affairs and Minister for Law K. Shanmugam	May 7-10, 2012
Prime Minister Goh Chok Tong	2006
Minister for Education Tharman Shanmugaratnam	September 2005
Prime Minister Goh Chok Tong	July 8-11, 2004
Deputy Prime Minister and Minister for Finance Lee Hsien Loong	January 10-19, 2004
Prime Minister Goh Chok Tong	April 7-9, 2003
President Sellapan Ramanathan	January 2003
Prime Minister Goh Chok Tong	17 January 2000
Prime Minister Goh Chok Tong	1994
Prime Minister Lee Kuan Yew	1966, 1970, 1971

Source: Compiled from High Commission of India, Singapore; Ministry of Foreign Affairs, Government of Singapore; Ministry of External Affairs, Government of India. https://hcisingapore.gov.in, http://www.mfa.gov.sg/, http://www.mea.gov.in/.

had a bilateral Visit to India in the year 2004. Minister of education Tharman Shanmugaratnam paid a visit to India in the year 2005. After the year 2006 when Prime Minister Goh Chok Tong visited India the next Bilateral Visit to India took place in the year 2012 when Minster of Foreign Affairs and Minister of Law K. Shanmugam visited India followed by the Visit of Prime Minister Lee Hsien Loong in the month of July, 2012. The Emeritus Senior Minister Goh Chok Tong paid the next Visit to India on December 3-6, 2013. The Next Imporatant Bilateral Visit was visited by Second Minister for Trade and Industry and Second Minister for Home Affairs S. Iswaran on January 27-29, 2014 and over this period there was a countinous number of Visits that took place over the year by Minister for Foreign Affairs and Minister for Law K. Shanmugam on 30th June-4th July, 2014, Minister for Defence Dr. Ng. Eng Hen on August 18-20, 2014 and Emeritus Senior Minister Goh Chok Tong along with Minister in the PMO and Second Minister for Trade and Industry and Home Affairs S Iswaran as well as Minister of State for National Development Desmond Lee on September 7-11, 2014. In the year 2015 President Tony Tan Keng Yam visited India. Prime Minister of Singapore Lee Hsien Loong accompanied by Minister for Trade and Industry Mr. S. Iswaran, acting Minister for Education and Senior of State for Defence Mr. Ong Ye Kung, Senior Minister of State (Defence and Foreign Affairs) Dr. Mohamad Maliki Bin Osman and Members of Parliament on October 3-7, 2016 where the two PMs had a wide range of Bilateral, Regional and Multilateral issues and reviewed the Bilateral Relationship from time of Joint declaration on strategic partnership since 2015.

Three MoUs on collaboration in the field of technical and vocational education and training and cooperation in industrial property were signed during the Visit. In the year 2017 there was a number Visits from Singapore that included the visit of Minister of Home Affairs & Minister of Law Mr. K Shanmugam to attend Counter terrorism Summit in March, Ministry of Finance Mrs. Tan Ching Yee to hold discussions with Secretary DEA in April, Minister for Trade & Industry Mr. S Iswaran in March, Singapore's Deputy Prime Minister (DPM) and Coordinating Minister for Economic and Social Policies Mr. Tharman Shanmugaratnam to deliver key note address at Delhi Economics Conclave and Senior Minister of State for Defence and Foreign Affairs Dr Mohamad Maliki Bin Osman for Delhi Dialogue in July. The Visit by Minister for Foreign Affairs Dr Vivian Balakrishnan to Delhi and Guwahati during October 31, 2017 – November 1, 2017 marked the Visit for Fifth India-Singapore Joint Ministerial Committee (JMC) meeting and in connection with North East Skills Centre (NESC). Senior Minister of

State for Law and Finance Ms. Indranee Rajah Visited in October to attend Singapore International Arbitration Centre India Conference, Minister for Defence Dr Ng Eng Hen to New Delhi and Kalaikunda to attend the second India-Singapore Defence Ministers' Dialogue (DMD) and to view Joint training of India and Singapore Air Forces and Emeritus Senior Minister (ESM) Mr. Goh Chok Tong visited New Delhi in December 2017. Senior Minister of State for Defence and Foreign Affairs Dr Mohamad Maliki Bin Osman visited New Delhi for participation in Raisina Dialogue on January 16-17, 2018.

List of Bilateral Visits from India to Singapore

Visiting Delegates	Date of Visit
Minister of External Affairs Ms. Sushma Swaraj, Minister for Shipping, Road Transport and Highways and Water Resources, River Development & Ganga Rejuvenation Mr. Nitin Gadkari, Chief Minister of Assam Mr. Sarbananda Sonowal, Secretary (East) Ms. Preeti Saran, and CEO, NITI Aayog Mr. Amitabh Kant.	January 6-7, 2018
Minister of Finance and Corporate Affairs Mr.Arun Jaitley and Finance Minister of Assam Mr. Himanta Biswa Sarma, Minister of Public Health and Engineering of Assam, Mr. Rihon Daimary, Finance Minister of Jammu & Kashmir, Mr. Haseeb Drabu, Minister of Labour and Excise of Kerala, Mr. T.P. Ramakrishnan, and Minister for Tamil development, Tamil Culture and Archaeology of Tamil Nadu Mr. K Pandiarajan	November, 2017
Chief Minister of Maharashtra Devendra Fadnavis	September, 2017
Foreign Secretary Dr. S Jaishankar to deliver S T Lee Lecture co-hosted by Lee Kuan Yew School of Public Policy	July, 2017
Chief Minister of Haryana Mr. Manohar Lal Khattar and Mr. Admiral Sunil Lanba, Chief of the Naval Staff	May, 2017
Minister for Shipping, Road Transport and Highways Mr. Nitin Gadkari for Road Show on India Integrated Transport & Logistics Summit	April, 2017
Minister for Skill Development of Jharkhand Ms. Neera Yadav	Febuary, 2017
Defence Secretary Mr. G Mohan Kumar	January, 2017
Prime Minister Modi Visited Singapore	November 23-24, 2015
Chief Minister of Telangana K. Chandrashekar Rao	August 20-22, 2014
Chief Minister of West Bengal Mamta Banerjee	August 18-22, 2014
External Affairs Minister, Sushma Swaraj	August 15-17, 2014
Ministry of External Affairs Secretary (East) Anil Wadhwa	February 14-15, 2014
Minister of Finance P. Chidambaram	November 21-22, 2013
External Affairs Minister, Salman Khurshid	October 23-24, 2013
External Affairs Minister, Salman Khurshid	July 3-4, 2013
Defence Minister A.K. Antony	June 2013
Minister of Civil Aviation Ajit Singh	April 2-4, 2013

Visiting Delegates	Date of Visit
External Affairs Minister S. M. Krishna	March 8-11, 2012
Prime Minister Dr. Manmohan Singh	November 19-20, 2011
External Affairs Minister S.M. Krishna	May 5, 2011
External Affairs Minister S.M. Krishna	March 2010
Prime Minister Dr. Manmohan Singh visit to Singh to Singapore for 6th India-ASEAN Summit and 3rd East Asia Summit	November 20-21, 2007
External Affairs Minister Pranab Mukherjee	June 19-22, 2007
President Dr. A.P.J. Abdul Kalam	January 31st-3rd February 2006
Prime Minister Atal Bihari Vajpayee	April 7-9, 2002
Prime Minister Atal Bihari Vajpayee	October 2001
President K.R. Narayanan	November 2000
Prime Minister Narasimha Rao	September 1994
President V.V. Giri	September 1971
Deputy Prime Minister Moraji Desai	1969
Prime Minister Indira Gandhi	1968

Source: Compiled from High Commission of India, Singapore; Ministry of Foreign Affairs, Government of Singapore; Ministry of External Affairs, Government of India. https://hcisingapore.gov.in, http://www.mfa.gov.sg/, http://www.mea.gov.in/.

Bilateral Visits from India to Singapore began from the time of Prime Minister Indira Gandhi in the year 1968. Deputy Prime Minister Moraji Desai visited Singapore in the year 1969 and President V.V. Giri visited Singapore in the year 1971. The next Visit from India was in the year 1994 by Prime Minister Narasimha Rao. President K.R. Narayanan Visited Singapore in the year 2000. During the tenure of Prime Minister Atal Bihari Vajpayee there was a number of Visits that took place between India and Singapore in year 2001 and 2002. President Dr. A.P.J. Abdul Kalam had a bilateral Visit to Singapore on January 31, 2006, February 3, 2006. On 2007 External Affairs Minister Pranab Mukherjee visited from June 19-2, 2007. On March 2010, May 2011 and March, 2012 External Affairs Minister S. M. Krishna visited Singapore. In the 2011 Prime Minister Dr. Manmohan Singh paid a visit to Singapore in the year 2011. The number of Visits between India and Singapore slowly grew over the Year 2013, 2014 where there were a number of visits by Minister of Civil Aviation Ajit Singh on April 2-4, 2013, Defence Minister A.K. Antony on June, 2013, External Affairs Minister, Salman Khurshid on July 3-4, 2013, External Affairs Minister, Salman Khurshid on October 23-24, 2013 and Minister of Finance P. Chidambaram on November 21-22, 2013.. In the year 2014 the visits include that of Ministry of External

Affairs Secretary (East) Anil Wadhwa on February 14-15, 2014, External Affairs Minister, Sushma Swaraj on August 15-17, 2014, Chief Minister of West Bengal Mamta Banerjee on August 18-22, 2014 and Chief Minister of Telangana K. Chandrashekar Rao on August 20-22, 2014.

There was a bilateral Visit by Prime Minister Modi Visited Singapore on November 23-24, 2015. In the year 2017 Defence Secretary Mr. G Mohan Kumar for Defence Policy Dialogue on January, Minister for Skill Development of Jharkhand Ms. Neera Yadav Paid a visit to explore cooperation in skill development and IT sector in February, on April Minister for Shipping, Road Transport and Highways Shri Nitin Gadkari for Road Show on India Integrated Transport & Logistics Summit and to launch Masala Bonds, Chief Minister of Haryana Mr. Manohar Lal Khattar for investment promotion and Admiral Sunil Lanba, Chief of the Naval Staff for naval exercise Visited in May and Foreign Secretary Dr. S Jaishankar visited Singapore to deliver S T Lee Lecture co-hosted by Lee Kuan Yew School of Public Policy in July. The Chief Minister of Maharashtra Mr. Devendra Fadnavis visited Singapore in September, 2017 for investment promotion. Minister of Finance and Corporate Affairs Mr. Arun Jaitley Visited Singapore to attend Singapore Fintech Festival and at the Asia Pacific Summit, Finance Minister of Assam Mr. Himanta Biswa Sarma, Minister of Public Health and Engineering of Assam Mr. Rihon Daimary, Finance Minister of Jammu & Kashmir and Mr. Haseeb Drabu, Minister of Labour and Excise of Kerala Mr. T.P. Ramakrishnan, and Minister for Tamil development, Tamil Culture and Archaeology of Tamil Nadu Mr. Pandiarajan visited in November, 2017. In the year 2018 Minister of External Affairs Ms. Sushma Swaraj, Minister for Shipping, Road Transport and Highways and Water Resources, River Development & Ganga Rejuvenation Mr. Nitin Gadkari, Chief Minister of Assam Mr. Sarbananda Sonowal, Secretary (East) Ms. Preeti Saran, and CEO, NITI Aayog Mr. Amitabh Kant with host of other dignitaries from India visited Singapore for Pravasi Bharatiya Divas (PBD) on 6-7 January.

Economic and Commercial Relation

Economic and trade relation plays a major role in the two countries bilateral relation. It was in this area of interest that the relation started off. India and Singapore signed the Comprehensive Economic Cooperation Agreement (CECA) which was the first of its kind for India and also the first for Singapore to have a bilateral economic agreement with a South Asia economy.[13] The CECA was signed in June of 2005, an agreement which covers on trade in investments, goods and services. This initiative took the relation to a whole new level. Since the implementation of this agreement it served as a gateway to more business initiations and avenues for the business communities. Hence, Indian business community has emerged as the leading business community in Singapore.

This later led to the later signing of the Free Trade Agreement (FTA) between the two countries. Among the ASEAN countries Singapore is India's largest trade and investment partner and in the year 2013-2014, it is reported that Singapore is the 7th largest trade partner of India.[14] Because of the strong Indian presence and connectivity Singapore has become a favored destination for Indians to do business hence many Indian corporate offices and banks can be located here such as Indian Overseas Bank, Indian Bank, ICICI, State Bank of India, Bank of India and Axis Bank and UCO Bank are some to mention.[15] The signing of the CECA in the later years led to the enhancement in cooperation related to education, science, technology, relaxation in visa regulations for Indians in the field of Information Technologies.

The recent news on Singapore's government appointing Ambassador-at-large Mr. Gopinath Pillai as Special Envoy to assist Andhra Pradesh to render advice relating to the building of the new capital which included tourism and bringing in capital from foreign companies and also Singapore Companies is also a milestone achieved in the bilateral relations.[16]

Bilateral Agreement between India and Singapore

Agreements	Year
Bilateral Air Services Agreement	1968
Double Taxation Avoidance Agreement	1994
Memorandum of Understanding on Foreign Office Consultations	1994
Executive Programme on Cooperation in the Arts, Heritage, Archives and the Library	2000
Memorandum of Understanding Concerning a Third Country Training Programme	2003
Defence Cooperation Agreement	2003
Comprehensive Economic Cooperation Agreement (CECA)	2005
Protocol amending agreement on avoidance of double taxation and prevention of Fiscal Evasion	2005
Agreement on Mutual Legal Assistance Treaty	2005
Memorandum of Understanding for Army to Army Exercises	2005
Bilateral Agreement for the conduct Joint Military Training and Exercises	2007
Memorandum of Understanding on Cooperation in Vocational Education and Skills Development	2011
Memorandum of Understanding in Management Research and Education: Between the Singapore Management University (SMU) and Indian Institute	

Agreements	Year
of Management Bangalore (IIMB)	2012
Memorandum of Understanding on the establishment of the Nalanda University	2013
India and Singapore are building relations focused on the 5-S plank	2014
Nine bilateral documents were signed/exchanged in areas of defence, maritime security, cyber security, narcotics trafficking, urban planning, civil aviation, and culture and a Joint Statement was issued which outlined areas of cooperation and mutual interest	2015
Revision of Existing DTAA and updated Tax Agreement	2016
The Bilateral Agreement for Navy Cooperation	2017
Revised Comprehensive Economic Cooperation Agreement (CECA)	2018

Source: Compiled from Ministry of External Affairs Annual Reports, Government of India. http://mea.gov.in/annual-reports.htm?57/Annual_Reports

Bilateral agreement has been happening from the year 1968 between India and Singapore. Double Taxation Avoidance Agreement in the year 1994 paved way for many trade and commerce inflows and exports. There was an Executive Programme on Cooperation in the Arts, Heritage, Archives and the Library in the year 2000 and both the countries came into and Memorandam of understanding in the year 2003. There was also a Defence Cooperation Agreement in the same year 2003. Both the countries came into one of the most important agreement the Comprehensive Economic Cooperation Agreement (CECA) in the year 2005 that was further revised in the year 2018. In the year 2005 there were a number of agreements that was signed between India and Singapore in matters of Protocol amending agreement on avoidance of double taxation and prevention of Fiscal Evasion, Agreement on Mutual Legal Assistance Treaty and Memorandum of Understanding for Army to Army Exercises. The most important force the militant force of both the countries agreed upon the Bilateral Agreement for the conduct Joint Military Training and Exercises on 2007. The Memorandum of Understanding on Cooperation in Vocational Education and Skills Development in the year 2011 saw many scopes for exchange educational programs between both the countries. In 2012 Memorandum of Understanding in Management Research and Education—Between the Singapore Management University (SMU) and Indian Institute of Management Bangalore (IIMB) and that Memorandum of Understanding on the establishment of the Nalanda University in 2013 paved way for more number of exchange courses in the educational sector of both countries. India and Singapore are building relations focused on the 5-S plank in 2014 that included Scale up trade investment (5S-I), Speed up connectivity (5S-II), Smart cities (5S-III), Skill development (5S-IV) and State focus (5S-V). In 2015 during the period of Modi there were Nine bilateral documents were signed/exchanged in areas of defence, maritime security, cyber security, narcotics trafficking, urban planning, civil aviation, and culture and a Joint Statement was issued which outlined areas of cooperation and mutual interest. The Revision of Existing DTAA and updated Tax Agreement in the year 2016 saw that there was increase of trade and commerce between India and Singapore. The Bilateral Agreement for Navy Cooperation in the year 2017 was agreed upon with allowing navy ships sailing through disputed SCS or in eastern waters of Andaman Sea to refuel, restock and if needed rearm at Singapore's Changi naval base.

The visit of President Tony Tan Keng Yam in the month of February 2015 which was a reciprocal visit to the External Affairs Minister, Sushma Swaraj's visit to Singapore in the month of August 2014, as a sign to commemorate 50 years of India-Singapore relation shows how close the leaders of these two countries feel about each other. The momentum of the relationship is gaining.

With the NDA government in the present scenario there have been many initiatives taken up by Mr. Narandra Modi, the Prime Minister of India such as the 'Make in India', 'Digital India' and 'Clean India' projects. There have been a number of Bilateral agreements between India and Singapore that have led to inflow and outflow of trade and commerce. Apart from the improvisation of trade and commerce there are also more exchange programs between the two countries in the field of Education. The navy and Military agreement have also been effective in improvising new techniques that can be bought into action. On the whole Singapore's experience in skill development can also be valuable for India and vise-versa.[17]

In general, the large number of Indians settled in Singapore along with the initiatives of both the Government plays a major role in connecting the two countries. So far the relationship has been on a smooth sail though there may be hiccups at times considering the international platform. India should always remember that even though Singapore being a small country it has proven itself to be a nation where countries like India need to engage with. As can be seen in Singapore's support to India becoming a permanent member in the U.N Security Council.[18] Through Singapore, India can forge a deeper relation with the Southeast Asian countries.

NOTES

1. Narlikar, Amrita (2013). India Rising: Responsible to Whom?, *International Affairs*, 89(3), Retrieved from http://onlinelibrary.wiley.com/doi/10.1111/1468-2346.12035/pdf.
2. Lee, Edwin (2008). *Singapore: The unexpected Nation*. Singapore: ISEAS.

3. Orang Laut, Singapore Infopedia. Retrieved from: http://eresources.nlb.gov.sg/infopedia/articles/SIP_551_2005-01-09.html?s=People
4. High Commission of India, Singapore. Retrieved from: https://hcisingapore.gov.in/pages.php?id=68
5. India-Singapore Relations. Retrieved from: http://www.mea.gov.in/Portal/ForeignRelation/Singapore_Dec_2014.pdf
6. Mishra, Rahul. (2010) Locating Singapore in India's Strategic Radar. *Institute of Defence Studies and Analysis.*
7. V. Jayanth (2000, November 9), Strengthening India-Singapore ties, *The Hindu.* Retrieved from : http://www.thehindu.com/2000/11/09/stories/0209000b.htm
8. Ibid
9. India-Singapore Relations, Ministry of External Affairs, Government of India. Retrieved from: http://www.mea.gov.in/
10. India, Singapore Renew Agreement on Joint Army Training (2013, June 3). *The Economic Times.* Retrieved from : http://articles.economictimes.indiatimes.com/2013-06-03/news/39714637_1_indian-army-defence-minister-singapore-air-force.
11. External Affairs Minister's address at the Singapore India Chambers of Commerce and Industry (SICCI). Ministry of External Affairs, Government of India. July 4, 2013. Retrieved from :http://www.mea.gov.in/bilateral-documents.htm?dtl/21908/
12. *SIPRI Yearbook 2014: Armaments, Disarmament and International Security.* (2014). Oxford University Press, United Kingdom.
13. Retrieved from http://www.fta.gov.sg/fta_ceca.asp?hl=6
14. Director General of Commercial Intelligence and Statistics. Ministry of Commerce and Industry, Government of India. Retrieved from http://www.dgciskol.nic.in/
15. Ministry of External Affairs (2014). *India-Singapore Relations.* Government of India. Retrieved from :http://mea.gov.in/portal/foreignrelation/singapore_july2014.pdf
16. Singapore names Special Envoy to Assist A.P. (2015, February 27). *The Hindu,* p. 7.
17. High Commission of India. *India Looking Forward to Embarking Upon a Larger Role in Asia-Pacific, says President.* Singapore, https://www.hcisingapore.gov.in/slide.php?id=23
18. Shekhar, Vibhanshu (2007). India-Singapore Relations: An Overview. *IPCS Special Report,* No. 41.

21

"Friends, Allies and Politics":
Some Musings on India-Latin American Relations

Sabu Thomas

Introduction

Foreign policy, as an instrument of national power, is more or less an art. The game changes with contexts and with different players and systems. This scenario has become more complex as the cold war has given way to different options, instrumentalities and wider choices for the state actors. The most difficult assignment was selection of new friends without damaging existing relations. This was also coincided with the ever-growing importance of economic dimension of foreign policy. Trade and economic relations became a crucial factor in the designing of foreign policies. The result was the emergence of new alliances and relations.

The foreign policy of India is shaped by several factors including its history, culture geography and economy. Preservation of national interest, achievement of world peace and disarmament has been important objectives of India's foreign policy. These objectives are sought to be achieved through some principles, viz. Panchsheel; nonalignment; anti-colonialism anti-imperialism anti-racism and the affirmation of faith in the UN system. Since the end of the Cold War, India emerged as a vibrant actor in the international scenario. In the regional politics, India became an unquestioned actor by virtue of its economy and politics. The country is actively involved in strengthening the regional ties through many regional forums and alliances.

In the international scenario, the Indian position is well established by the Indian presence in economic forums and global groupings. The Indian links with Latin America are also a part of its global strategy to promote international peace and secure national interests. With respect to the Latin American region, its foreign policy was much isolated due to the geographical disadvantages and traditional dependence on United States. By and large, Latin American countries were much absent from mainstream international politics for a long time in history.[1] However, the Indian association with the Latin America can be traced back to the early period of Indian independence. In order to ensure a share in the new global politics, collective voices became a necessity. This culminated in the birth of Non-Alignment Movement. India and Colombia are members of that movement. However, the Indo-Latin America relation is still at its infancy and there are many steps to initiate and complete. The region requires special attention from the policy quarters as there are large potentials and profits both for India and Latin America.[2]

Shared Culture and Shared Concerns

Foreign policy becomes sustainable only in the background of commonalities. If the policy participants are having common concerns and bonds, the relations will become more stable and friendly. In this respect, India and the Latin America have many common issues and concerns. Latin America suffered four hundred years of colonial domination until by the beginning of the twentieth century, the continent was finally free. This story of colonial domination is a common thread that goes with India also. India was under colonial domination for a considerable part of its history. The colonial exploitation and consequent damages to national morality, economy and politics is at the same pitch in both areas. India is not a 'distant', 'strange' land for the Latin Americans in a cultural sense. In many ways India and Latin American countries are natural partners because of their shared understanding of the values of democracy rule of law justice and equality.

The politics of Latin America is more in favor of leftist ideology. It is observed that the majority of the countries in Latin America have leftist governments. However, the regional politics is more pragmatic and admits private sector in the economy to create more wealth.[3] As of present, Latin America can be considered as a land of flourishing democracy. There are regular elections and active political parties, and military coups are of past history. The liberalization wave has already reached the area and India can find many understanding partners in the region.

Trade and commerce make foreign policies more spicy and vibrant. With regard to trade relations, India-Latin America trade relationship can be considered as progressive. Potentials are many. But miles and miles are there to be covered. As of 2010, India and Latin American region traded just $23 billion in goods. It comes to barely one-sixth of the region's trade with China. However, the scenario is very bright since Latin America's trade with India is growing fast.[4] Latin America provides a large market of 600 million population with a combined GDP of US$ 6.9 trillion and a trade turnover of US$ 2.1 trillion. Foreign Direct Investment (FDI) flows into Latin America touched a record high of US$ 166 billion in 2012. In the late 1980s, Latin American countries had a trade-to-GDP ratio roughly equal to the trade-to-GDP ratio of China and two times larger than the trade-to-GDP ratio of India (Lederman, Olarreaga, & Perry, 2009).

A few years back, the economic scenario in the Latin American region was dismal with high inflation, heavy external debt and stagnant economy. But the liberalization process has changed the equations.[6] In the case of external debt, the figure is around 21% of GDP. The high growth rate of the region and the enormous size of the market is a big attraction to Indian investors. Combined with calm politics, the Latin America offers a big business venue.[5] This potential was well realized by China much earlier and they established high-volume trade relations. They have a heavy volume of trade with the area that comes around ten times of Indian trade.

Indian business has strong presence in Latin America. In the Information Technology sector, Indian companies have set up software development centers, business process outsourcing, knowledge process outsourcing and call centers. Indian companies are also active in the agrochemical sector as well as in hydrocarbons and minerals. In the automobile sector, Indian companies have set up assembly plants for automobiles.[7] Latin American region offers a significant and growing market for India's pharmaceutical engineering, textile, handicraft and other exports. It is hoped that the immense endowments of natural resources including hydrocarbons, agricultural land, fresh water minerals and bio-diversity in the area have been increasingly recognized for their potential contribution to India's energy and food security. Understanding the potential of the area, the Commerce Ministry, Government of India started an integrated programme titled "Focus: LAC" in November 1997.[8]

The BRICS Factor

The term BRIC stands for Brazil, Russia, India and China. This term was coined by the Chief Economist of Goldman Sachs in 2001 in a paper titled 'Building

Better Global Economic BRICs' which looked at the growth prospects of the four largest emerging economies that are culturally and geographically disparate. The major finding of the paper was that BRICs have a potential role in changing the global economy. It is visualized as a new economic bloc catering to the emerging markets. South Africa was later introduced into the group, making the term BRICS. The organization emerged in a period when global financial structure was in great trouble due to the financial crisis. The BRICS countries managed to stay stable in the storm of economic crisis. This was a clear signal to the advanced economies. They alone cannot operate the economic structure. Global economy needs an integrated approach to include the lesser powerful actors. Economic blocs like BRICS gained more relevance in this context. BRICS is also a forum for promoting multipolarism in the post–Cold War world.[9]

BRICS countries together account for more than 40% of the global population It is also having nearly 30% of the land mass and a share in world GDP (in PPP terms) that amounts to nearly 25% as of 2010 figures (Finance Ministry, 2012: IX). In the BRICS organization, Brazil plays an important role. Brazil is the major exporter of agricultural products. In the social sphere, the Brazil model of conditional cash transfers proved to be an effective check to poverty in the country. This model was later taken by India to address its poverty issues. Amidst the turbulent waters of global financial crisis, Brazil stood as an unchallenged economy due to its strict regulatory framework and monetary policies. Brazil and India are two giants of their respective regions and they have a unique and important relationship. Brazil and India rank among the largest democracies and economies in the world and share similar development goals.

During the BRICS Summit which took place on October 15-16, 2016 in Goa, India, Prime Minister Narendra Modi and Brazil President Michel Temer met and this was followed by delegation-level deliberations to further strengthen the strategic partnership. The two countries also agreed to explore the early signing of an Investment Cooperation and Facilitation Treaty. It is hoped that the proposed treaty will act as a catalyst to boost trade and economic ties.

In the BRICS, Indian trade with Brazil gave a positive growth in the period 2013-14 with a 20.4% growth. However, the graph is not steady and shows negative trends in certain periods. The conclusion is that the prospects of bilateral trade remaining highly positive, the benefits are yet to be reflected in economic sphere. That demands larger attention for bilateral trade.

Prospects of Partnership

The liberalization of economy is a major propellant in foreign relations. This liberalization process started in India and countries in Latin America at the same time. One result of that policy shift was more international investment opportunities and deeper global economic ties. India and Latin America share a growing young population and price-sensitive consumers. India lacks natural resources whereas Latin America exports them. This relationship has the potential to generate mutual benefits for both the Indian and Latin American economies. It is to be noted that India-LAC bilateral trade during 2017-18 stood at USD 29.33 billion as against USD 24.52 billion in 2016-17.

Latin America is a leading destination for India's exports. It is found that vehicle exports to Latin America from India stands at 3.76 billion. Mexico is the largest market for India's vehicle exports with 2.02 billion. Colombia is one of the top three global markets for Indian motorcycles. On the other hand, India has also become more important to Latin America's exports. India is the third-largest destination of Latin American exports with $22 billion in 2017. Latin America exports more to India than to its traditional partners.

The government of India has expressed growing interest in fostering Latin American connections. There have been frequent high-level visits between the two countries in recent times. In September 2014, Indian Prime Minister Narendra Modi paid a visit to Brazil for the BRICS Summit. During the visit, he met the leaders of twelve South American countries. These meetings opened a new door to the deliberations between India and the region.

In the month of June 2018, President Shri Ram Nath Kovind paid a visit to Cuba and this was the first ever visit by the President of India to Cuba. The visit resulted in MoUs in biotechnology and traditional medicines. India also assured its support for solving the developmental issues in Cuba. In this context, it is to be noted that the Indian trade with Cuba is also showing some positive trends over the years. It is admitted that the trade growth is not steady, but shows great potential.

Table 1: India-Cuba Trade Scenario (Values in Million US$ as on 14 Dec 2018)

Item	2013-14	2014-15	2015-16	2016-17	2017-18
Imports from Cuba	2.40	1.57	1.33	1.31	2.06
Exports to Cuba	35.53	37.32	54.31	41.79	41.80
Bilateral Total Trade	37.93	38.89	55.64	43.10	43.86
Trade Balance	33.13	35.75	52.97	40.48	39.74

Source: Reports of Ministry of Commerce Government of India.

Argentina is another potential partner to India in the Latin American region. The Government of India claims that India-Argentina relations are cordial and encompass political, economic, scientific and technological cooperation. This claim is evidenced with the frequent high-level visits between two countries. Treaties were signed on various sectors of cooperation between the two countries.

Table 2: Indian Trade with Argentina (Up to 2016, in Million US$)

Year	India's Imports	Growth	India's Exports	Growth	Total Trade	Growth
2013	1105	13%	695	21%	1801	-2%
2014	2032	84%	602	-13%	2633	46%
2015	2276	-13%	659	-9%	2935	11%
2016	2186	-4%	596	-9%	2782	5%

The data suggest that there are no steady trends in commercial relations and at times negative growth is expressed. But the volume-wise trade gives a ray of hope for potential growth. It should also be remembered that the general financial scenario in the region during the period was not good and these countries had an overall negative trade trends in the larger global market.

Table 3: Bilateral Trade between India and Chile (in Million US$)

Year	Exports from India to Chile	Imports from Chile by India (FOB)	Total Bilateral trade
2014	619.85	619.85	3191.6
2015	685.76	685.76	2712.74
2016	701.05	701.05	2099.58
2017	776.99	776.99	2519.32

With Chile, another partner to India in Latin America, India maintained a 10.63% exports growth in 2015 and 2.22% in 2016. Between 2016 and 2017, there was an evident increase in bilateral trade between the two partners. It is hoped that this growth rate can be maintained with better policy instruments.

Conclusion

The historical disinterest between India and the Latin American countries is almost over. There is greater understanding between the two, particularly in the era of globalization.[10] The enormous distance between the two areas is not a disadvantage in the new foreign policy paradigm. The economic concerns and trade relations are well rewarding both for India and Latin America. Jorge Heine, who was Ambassador of Chile to India, opines,

At the beginning of the second decade of this new century the appeal that

India is starting to exercise in Latin America is considerable. Its vigorous parliamentary democracy its growing economy its high-tech achievements in combination with its millenarian spiritual traditions make for a heady mix. To make the most of this appeal however requires a much more proactive policy towards the region one that realizes that in this new international order that is emerging by working together India and Latin America have much to gain (Heine, 2011:27).

The end of Cold War and the new international politics demands closer association with likeminded powers. Here are serious issues like climate change, terrorism, natural calamities, human rights etc.[11] These issues can be addressed by global efforts effectively, and the Indo-Latin America collective can contribute to these issues. The problem of combating narcotic trafficking is another problem area in the relations. The grave issue of narcotics can be handled only by the interaction of the actors. The emergence of a turbulent international politics and new global problems demands more and more close collective forums. India and Latin America can be such a potential forum for bringing global order and peaceful human life.

NOTES

1. It is argued that there was an evident reluctance from the part of some Latin American countries to take part in the global politics. This situation is well evidenced by Heine (2011). He says, "The reluctance of some Latin American countries in the not-too-distant past to stand for election as non-permanent members to the UN Security Council (even when according to the rotation principle it was their turn) is a good example of this international shyness. This derives from a feeling that there is little to be gained and much to be lost by engaging global issues on a platform like the Security Council" (Heine 2011:22).
2. See External Affairs Minister's Speech on "India-Latin America & Caribbean: The Way Forward" at the CII India-LAC Conclave Valedictory Session, December 10 2013, http://www.mea.gov.in/SpeechesStatements.htm?dtl/22605/External+Affairs+Ministers+ Speech+ on+ IndiaLatin+ America+amp+Caribbean+The+Way+Forward+at+the+CII+IndiaLAC+Conclave +Valedictory+Session, Accessed on 16-06-2015
3. The non-dogmatic leftism of Latin America was well explained by Ambassador (Retd) R. Viswanathan at his extempore talk at Jadavpur University, Kolkata on 18 April 2015. He observes, "MN Roy was a founder of the Communist Party of Mexico before he came back to found the Communist party of India. He spent over two years in Mexico from 1917 to 1919. He became a communist during his stay in Mexico.... Roy called Mexico as 'the land of his rebirth'. Today the house where he stayed in Mexico City has been converted into a vibrant bar/night club with the name MN Roy". http://www.mea.gov.in/distinguished-lectures-detail.htm?279, Accessed on 22-06-2015.
4. However, presently China's and India's combined share of world exports is 50% larger than LAC's share.
5. Venezuela and Argentina are the exceptions to this statement. However, they also possess

many potentials and they can easily emerge from the problems, many of which are self-created.
6   The stability of the economies of individual countries in the region has been reinforced by the regional integration through Mercosur Andean Community UNASUR and SICA. Mexico is part of NAFTA. In April 2011, another economic grouping, the Pacific (Ocean) Group was formed by Mexico Peru Colombia and Chile with the objective of economic integration. Through these groups, the barriers are being removed for free movement of goods services capital and people, and there is growing intraregional trade and investment. Mercosur has emerged as a formidable trading bloc of the region. The other groups are in various stages of integration. The pace of integration might be slow but regional integration is the clear destination in the long term (see Viswanathan 2011:9).
7   http://www.mea.gov.in/articles-in-indian media.htm?dtl/22142/Fusing+adventure+ with+ diplomacy+Indias+Latin+America+odyssey, Accessed on 18-06-2015.
8   Focus: LAC programme aims at (1) sensitizing the organizations, viz. Export Promotion Councils Chambers of Commerce & Industry EXIM Bank ECGC etc. involved in trade promotion efforts; (2) granting various incentives to Indian exporters and launching of export promotion measures; (3) focussing on the Latin American region with an added emphasis on major trading partners of the region; (4) focussing on the following major product groups for enhancing India's exports to the Latin American region: (a) textiles including ready-made garments carpets and handicrafts, (b) engineering products and computer software, (c) chemical products including drugs/pharmaceuticals (Source: Ministry of Commerce, Government of India).
9   "BRICS is strengthening global multipolarity in the world. This is how it should be. It is important that it does not take us back to the bi-polar world of the Cold War. Fortunately there is no reason for such apprehension. Each of the BRICS members has close economic ties with the West and wishes to promote cooperation with it. BRICS must repose trust in a cooperative approach both with the West and with the rest. BRICS should also endeavour to gain the trust of other developing countries through its developmental activities". See Amb (Retd) Dilip Sinha, Role of India in BRICS, Distinguished Lecture, Visva Bharati West Bengal, April 18 2015, http://www.mea.gov.in/distinguished-lectures-detail.htm?285, Accessed on 23-06-2015.
10 Ambassador R. Viswanathan (2011: 7) observes, "Latin America has undergone a paradigm shift in the last two decades. The region has come out of the past curses of political and economic instability and cycles of booms and busts. A stable and prosperous New Latin America is emerging. The New Latin Americans are looking forward to the future with confidence and optimism. India needs to recognize this new scenario and take strategic steps to engage this region enhance cooperation and promote trade and investment."
11 "India and Colombia are victims of terrorism. India's neighborhood has emerged as the epicenter of world terrorism. Cross-border terrorism continues to impinge on our security. The fight against international terrorism needs a strong commitment from the world community both in the form of actions and multilateral frameworks. India's proposal for a Comprehensive Convention on International Terrorism (CCIT) assumes importance in this regard. We are confident that with the support of countries like Colombia we will be able to ensure its early adoption" (Katju 2011:6).

REFERENCES

Heine, J. (2011), Much to Gain by Working Together in the Emerging International Order. *Indian Foreign Affairs Journal*, 6 (1), 19-27.

Katju, V. (2011), Growing Awareness between India and Latin America. *Indian Foreign Affairs Journal*, 6 (1), 3-6.

Lederman, D., Olarreaga, M., & Perry, G. E. (2009), Latin America's Response to China and India: Overview of Research Findings and Policy Implications. In D. Lederman, M. Olarreaga, & G.E. Perry, *China's and India's Challenge to Latin America Opportunity or Threat?* (pp. 3-39). Washington DC: The World Bank.

Mathur, S., Dasgupta, M., & Sirohi, P. (2013), Trade Policies and Institutions of BRICS. In S. Mathur, & M. Dasgupta, *BRICS: Trade Policies, Institutions and areas of Deepening Cooperation* (pp. 1-158). New Delhi: Centre for WTO Studies, Indian Institute of Foreign Trade.

Ministry of Finance (2012), *The BRICS Report*. New Delhi: Oxford University Press.

Schmid, A.P. (2004), Frameworks for Conceptualising Terrorism. *Terrorism and Political Violence*, 16 (2), 197-221.

Viswanathan, R. (2011), The New Latin America and the Next Steps for India. *Indian Foreign Policy Affairs*, 6 (1), 7-17.

22

Indian Diaspora:
A Reckoning Force, A Lobby Group, and a Friend of NDA–II Government in Stabilizing Relations between India and other Nations

Salu Dsouza

Introduction

Over the years, diaspora communities across the globe are playing pivotal role in the economic development of their host countries and their motherland. The political atmosphere in any country during the time of election as well as crises, it is the diaspora entities come forward to help their host land and the native land. In India, the general election of 2014 and 2019 had the blessings of diaspora communities. Many had come to India and took active part in the political campaigning and canvasing for a particular candidate of a political party. Diaspora is one such entity never allows its home country to be in shambles. Diaspora has a dream and works towards the development of its motherland. All of us leave our homeland for one or the other reason and we are placed in a host country. We have a dream, we long to go back to our motherland, the longing; the desire to go back to homeland, the feeling of belongingness towards our motherland is the notion of diaspora. N. Jayaram who has done research on Indian Diaspora while trying to analyse the behaviour of emigration pattern opines, "The emigration of Indians that began in the second quarter of the 19th century continued into the early decades of the 20th century. The trickle of emigration of Indians to the industrially developed countries, which assumed phenomenal proportions in the post-colonial phase, could be noticed in the 19th century itself." (Jayaram N. 2004, p. 19)

The above observation of Jayaram shows that Indians were always enthusiastic of leaving their home country and go in search of green pasture that they found in various western countries. Many Indians who went to foreign countries were born after the Independence; hence, they are aware of the various democratic principles that govern liberal democratic countries like Canada, USA and UK and conservative democratic countries like China, Cuba, Gulf countries, and few African nations. Though China is a communist country, it says it practices true communism and democracy inside the communist regime. These Indians when they come to India during their holidays are not much perplexed about the Indian system of democratic governance. Indian diaspora had to thank the globalization and the liberalization policies that the Indian democratic administration set in motion in the 1990s where liberal policies towards NRIs and PIOs privileged them as chosen citizens of India that entitled them many concessions. Indian diaspora is pleased with the NDA–II government at the centre headed by Shri Narendra Damodardas Modi, providing able leadership to the ship and stir it into right direction though the opposition wind is not favourable to the present central government due to its excessive criticism.

Indian diaspora, irrespective of its religion, region, and language that it belongs to India, has accepted the Christian Liberal Democratic views of western social set up where multicultural atmosphere is increasingly seen in the daily lives of people. The immigrants in general that are in various countries and Indian diaspora in particular want to have a good life. Bikhu Parekh, who has seen a Multicultural lifestyle in Britain opines, "A multicultural society is characterized by a plurality of cultures. Its members subscribe to different systems of meaning and significance and structure their lives differently. Although some of their values invariable overlap, others do not. Even so far as the former are concerned, they sometimes define and prioritize them differently. Unlike a culturally homogeneous society, members of a multicultural society do not share a common substantive vision of the good life, and disagree about the value to be assigned to different human activities and relationships." (Bikhu Parekh: 2004). This reiterates the multicultural environment that the western countries provide to their genuine immigrants to prosper and the members of Indian diaspora reaping the benefits according to their multi-tasked role in the western society. Indian diaspora has been living outside of India for many years and knows the business tactics in every country.

Role of Indian-American in Influencing the Policies

Indian American population is growing in various cities in the USA. The diaspora communities are very active in social media. There are governors and attorneys of Indian origin in the USA. The corporate houses also controlled by Indian origin people in the USA. The prominent members of Indian diaspora constantly lobby for policies towards India. The pressure groups and the other diaspora communities have become feeding grounds for the foreign policy analysts in the USA. In a study published in Foreign Policy Analysis, Jason Kirk (2008:277) claims: "In 2006, two historical stories converged: one involving the ongoing deepening of the U.S.-India relationship since 1998, the other a general consolidation of organizational capacity within the burgeoning Indian community in the United States. Without the latter, it is unlikely that the bold U.S.-India nuclear agreement would have made it over the requisite congressional hurdles in 2006." Kirk's case study, while being highly interesting, has two major weaknesses that this thesis seeks to address. First, the study included only one personal interview with the Chairman of the U.S.-India Political Action Committee (USINPAC), one of the two leading lobby organizations for the community, and none with other relevant actors. Second and related to this, Kirk's study paid only limited attention to other possible explanations for Congress's strong vote in favour of the controversial agreement.

In 1998, the NDA formed the government with BJP as its largest party. Within weeks of forming the government, to be precise on May 11, 1998, India announced to a stunned world that it had conducted simultaneous tests of three devices. American reaction was angry and swift. It kicked out overnight all the Indian scientists who were working in various US-based laboratories and companies, and imposed a wide range of sanctions on India. Indian diaspora consistently lobbied to lift the sanctions imposed on Indian space technology transfer. Indian Americans have succeeded and India has benefitted. During the election campaign of Donal Trump and Republican nominee, Indian diaspora openly patronized his candidature by donating liberally to Donald Trump's election fund.

Clinton's visit to India, the first visit of a U.S. President since Jimmy Carter, was widely characterized as a success. Interestingly, for the first time, no less than 150 Indian Americans accompanied the U.S. delegation and Clinton's itinerary showcased a "new India"—visiting places such as Hyderabad, "the high-tech city" (Iype 2000). In his address to the Indian Parliament, Clinton "[...] went into an extended critique of India's decision to go nuclear. But the tone was respectful and gave the sense of debate among equals" (Mohan 2006:20). It was interesting to note that, Clinton had stayed five days in India, he stopped only five hours in Pakistan on his way back home. Shri Atal Bihari Vajpayee of the BJP was the Prime Minister of India at that year. He laid the foundation for the modern India's relations with USA only after Indira Gandhi who did that during her tenure.

Those Indians in the Diaspora who went to USA, Canada, UK, Australia, and New Zealand were surprised to see the function of liberal democracy, which had bestowed many rights on their citizens. Certain Indian communities did face occasional racial abuses and discrimination. Tinker Hugh in his book 'Overseas Emigrants from India, Pakistan, and Bangladesh' rightly identified the ethnic complexities that govern people from South Asia in western countries, "With reference to countries where the ethnic relations involving Indians have become complicated, Tinker (1977, pp. 138–139) raises the following questions, '...do the Asian Indians create their own difficulties by their own way of life, and by remaining separate from the host society; or do their troubles arise mainly from excess of chauvinism or racism in the country of their adoption?'" Racial discrimination is a rare occurrence in the present scenario. Few in Indian Diaspora were attacked in South Africa and Australia. Sikhs are targeted by Native Americans due to mistaken identities.

During the key Senate vote that made Vivek Murthy the youngest ever Surgeon General of the US, Indian-Americans there had launched a nationwide campaign calling their Senators to support him. The United States Senate that was scheduled to vote on Tuesday in December 2014 confirmed Murthy, 37 as Surgeon General who was nominated for the position by US President Barack Obama in November 2013. (*Times of India*). Hence, one could see the influence of Indian diaspora in the United States taking the cause of American Indians within America and elsewhere.

NDA–II under Shri Modi with two American Presidents

It was in 2016, the Prime Minister of India, Shri Narendra Damodardas Modi visited the then President of America, Barrack Obama. The visit was a historic moment for Modi, who was once denied the visa to visit the USA when he was the Chief Minister of Gujarat state in India. Modi was given a warm welcome by the president Barrack Obama. They signed few bilateral agreements that would help both America and India economically. Modi had the privilege of addressing the joint session of American Congress, a privilege only the few important world leaders would have once in their lifetime. This showed how much the NDA–II government headed by Shri Modi had already impacted the world leaders in their perspective towards India. The credit for gaining the support of America goes to Shri Narendra Damodardas Modi.

The address of the US Congress by Modi was keenly watched by the Indian Diaspora in the USA. It was reported that many prominent members of the diaspora in USA travelled from different places to Washington DC to hear Modi's address to the joint session of American Congress. Bharat Barai from Chicago had to say about Modi's visit of USA, "I am sure after listening to him, people of this country and Congressmen would realise the importance Modi attaches to the India-US relationship," he said (NDTV on line news portal).

Shri Narendra Modi had in fact won the hearts and minds of the American lawmakers as well as people due to his able administration in India. The Indian diaspora in America too supports the policies of NDA–II government that is headed by Shri Modi. The policies of the present central government towards USA have been strengthening India's relation with the American people.

In his second state visit to USA, Shri Modi met the president of America Donald Trump. Both the leaders emphasized on the strong relations with each country in order to boost the economic ties and cooperation in dealing with global terror. The NDA–II under Shri Modi was fortunate enough to meet two presidents of America and get the best deal from each of them in favour of India. The American Indian community were happy with the outcome of the meetings that Shri Modi had with these two presidents. The credit for signing few agreements with American business persons that boost Indian trade and commerce goes to Shri Modi and his economic policies towards America that has brought two countries closer. The diaspora communities appreciate Indian diaspora from America who admire Modi and the work done by NDA–II ministers. Many had come to India for campaigning in the 2019 general elections in favour of the NDA.

The NDA–III will surely formulate policies in further strengthening of Indo-US relations in order to augment trade and commerce between two nations. However, the recent immigration policies of Donald Trump government in USA were not welcomed by Indian citizens who had the dream of going to USA either for studies or work and settlement. In this condition the availability of visas to Indians in different categories, need to be enhanced, at least highly skilled workers, and genuine students should get preferences from Donald Trump's immigration policies. It would be nice to see how the NDA–III will work with the new president of the USA once the election gets over in 2020.

India and its Neighbourhood: How does Indian Diaspora Looks at its Neighbouring Countries?

Indian diaspora is equally concerned about the various democratic institutions that exist in its neighbouring countries, which play a crucial role in sustaining the democratic system of government. For India, Pakistan is a "dearest" country since its inception in 1947. A stable democratic government of Pakistan can work towards the fulfilment of people's aspirations of Pakistan and have good relations with India, Afghanistan and China. India's concern is the concern of Indian diaspora. Nepal has found it difficult to sustain itself in a democratic institution without any external influence. India is worried about the developments that are taking place in Nepal. Nevertheless, India does not lose its hold on influencing Nepal's political system and tries to wean away from any communist influence that comes from China.

Bhutan is a strong supporter of Indian democracy. However, in the last general elections in Bhutan, India found itself losing hold over Bhutanese political class but eventually the regime had the wisdom to listen to India. Bangladesh is another India's neighbour, needs India's help in many areas. The refugees from Bangladesh who are in India reckoned and non-reckoned, sometime indulge in anti-national activities that has become a headache to Indian law enforcing agencies. The development in Bangladesh is carefully watched by India. The Rohingya refugees who were steadily coming to India had to be stopped at any cost. The NDA–II government was able to deal with the inflow of Rohingya refugees and many were repatriated keeping in line with international laws. The step taken by Shri Modi and his team could get support and appreciation from the government of Bangladesh and Myanmar.

Sri Lankan affair is important to India. Tamil Nadu government and the DMK leaders keep Indian political leaders at Delhi always "informed" about the India-Sri Lanka relations. India was concerned about the civil unrest that brought out the wrath of the people as well as political observers when Maithripala Sirisena dismissed the government of the Prime Minister Ranil Wickremesinghe and brought back the previous president Mahinda Rajapaksa. India was cautious in issuing any statement and closely observing the situation over there. Finally, the president removed Rajapaksa and re-appointed Ranil Wickremesinghe as the prime minister of Sri Lanka. In the April 2019 suicide bomb blast that took away many lives in Colombo, Indian Prime minister Shri Modi while condemning the bomb blasts that took place over there offered immediate assistance in terms of work force that would help the Sri Lankan government in conducting the investigation.

The election in the Maldives helped India in many ways. Though Shri Modi did not visit Maldives during the term of president Yameen for strategic reasons could attend the oath taking ceremony of Ibrahim Mohamed Solih, whose party is close in relation with India. Shri Modi's timely visit to Maldives helped in cementing the bond that India shares with Maldivian people. India wants to keep Maldives and Sri Lanka in good humour to contain Chinese influence in the Indian Ocean. Indian diplomats and policy makers keenly observe the developments in Afghanistan and Myanmar. Indian diaspora is always worried about neighbouring countries of India, especially Pakistan. However, the Balakot air strike that was consented by the NDA–II government was in response to Pulwama attack on Indian security forces had received tremendous appreciation from Indian diaspora who are in different countries. The report shows that the diaspora members had immense faith in Modi led central government of India and the diaspora is convinced about the sincerity of Indian Prime Minister Shri Narendra Damodardas Modi who would never compromise when it comes to security of India.

Look East Policy and its benefits on Indian Diaspora of South East Asia region

The NDA–II government headed by Shri Modi that came into power in May 2014 was determined to change the course of India's foreign policy towards world community. The able and experienced external affairs minister Sushma Swaraj guided the foreign officials to look into the problem faced by Indian diaspora in each country. This had the positive effect in where diaspora once had to struggle in its dreams of business expansion could now do business with ease. Shri Modi, realising this embarked upon the Look East Policy, which eased the economic and strategic relations between India and countries of South East Asia. Indian diaspora is in good number at Malaysia and Singapore. However, in other countries of South East Asia, the diaspora is steadily increasing due to the present policy of the NDA–II government in India. The central government took initiative and signed a series of bilateral business treaties that also eased the visa restrictions and extending the benefit of visa on arrival for few countries of South East Asia made the people of diaspora, students, and business communities to move freely and take advantage of the existing economic policies.

By the virtue of Look East policy of the NDA–II government, India was accorded the status of observer of the ASEAN countries. It is in India's favour that most of the ASEAN countries are one way or the other had troubled relations with China. Shri Modi, understanding the precarious and volatile relations of South East Asian countries, made a point of visiting the most of these countries in order to build support and sign economic agreements. Wherever India had established good relations with ASEAN and other South East Asian countries, Indian diaspora reaped the benefits. The credit for stabilising and enhancing the bilateral relations between India and South East Asian nations goes to Shri Narendra Modi who was able to judge the prevailing global political conditions and took cautious steps in order to win over most of these countries. Hence, Indian diaspora is indebted to NDA–II government that is headed by Shri Narendra Modi.

Among all the South East Asian countries, Vietnam remained as India's closest ally due to China's claim over the sea area that had Vietnamese interest. During the Prime Minister Narendra Modi's visit to Vietnam in September 2016, there were few agreements signed between two countries. It was interesting to see how Shri Narendra Modi would be reacting in the G20 summit in China since he was going to China from his Vietnamese visit. The Indian diaspora in Vietnam though not in large numbers like that of Malaysia or Singapore, had good time with the Prime Minister Modi in a hotel at Hanoi in Vietnam. Overall, the NDA–II government could spread its influence in South East Asia through its Look East Policy that would benefit both India and the other Asian countries.

Conclusion

The visit of previous Australian Prime Minister to India, Ms. Julia Gillard who emphasized on Arts and culture that could be powerful forces for bringing people together and the two countries have pledged to strengthen the bilateral cultural relationship. The recent visit of the present Prime Minister of Australia Tony Abbot Underlined the importance of greater connectivity to support growing commercial and cultural ties, including in the education and tourism sectors.

When we say that migrants who enter into various parts of Australia need to be 'modernized' and assimilate into local culture at the same time preserve the culture of their homeland. The Prime Minister of India visited Australia that was termed as a success by both Australian and Indian media. Mr. Narendra Modi who was in Australia while addressing in the Australian Parliament spoke on people-to-people links that are transforming the relationship. Prime Minister Modi and Prime Minister Abbott welcomed the signing of a Social Security Agreement, which would enhance two-way mobility and lower business costs. Further, they agreed to hold a Festival of India in Australia in 2015 to display the dynamism and diversity of contemporary Indian culture. This will see increasing participation of various Indian diaspora associations and communities in enhancing the bilateral relationship between Australia and India. These relations will definitely help NDA–II led by Modi to have favourable foreign policies towards the west. Even if the NDA–III government would not come to power after 2019 general elections, the policies made by the NDA–II government that was headed by Modi, would help the successive government.

It is true that political parties in India keep on changing but the basic structure of the constitution of India has so far not changed. Indian diaspora loves its motherland and the institution of democracy that India practices. The agenda for development in the era of globalization and liberalization should take everyone into confidence and everyone should have the right to claim the benefits irrespective of their political affiliation. Inclusive growth leads to further sustenance of our democratic institutions. Indian diaspora has strong faith in Indian democracy. They are ever ready in helping less fortunate Indians through various charitable institutions and NGOs. Indian Diaspora is always reliable during the economic crisis that the Indian economy faces time to time. In this juncture, Indian democratic institutions need to be more liberalized with delineation of certain democratic rights to Indian people in general and Indian diaspora in particular.

The foreign policy and the relation that the Modi led government is been establishing with neighbouring countries and rest of the world is unprecedented. India's image has not only made Indians inside India proud and optimistic but also it has seen that members of Indian diaspora could walk keeping their head straight in the host land where Indians are migrants. The host countries have increasingly acknowledged the contribution of Indian diaspora to the growth of their economy. Thanks to the Shri Narendra Modi-led NDA government's robust foreign policy that has won appreciation from the Indian diaspora associations across the world. Indian diaspora would like to see more positive dialogues with the neighbouring countries to make India as a truly regional superpower. The coming days will herald the prosperity not only for India but also for the neighbouring countries who have supported India in every International forums. The NDA–III government if it continues from May 2019, India, and its diaspora would achieve much and there would be economic prosperity within the country and the diaspora members get benefitted when they arrive at their homeland.

REFERENCES

Bhikhu, Parekh (2004), Limits of the Indian Political Imagination. London: Sage Publications.

Jayaram N., (2004), The Indian Diaspora: Dynamics of Migration. New Delhi: Sage Publications.

Kirk, Jason (2008), "Indian Americans and the U.S.-India Nuclear Agreement: Consolidation of an Ethnic Lobby?", Foreign Policy Analysis 4, (3): pp. 275-300.

Iype, George (2000), "PM's cold shoulder upsets NRIs", India Abroad, March 21

Mohan, C. Raja (2006), Impossible Allies: Nuclear India, United States and the Global Order. New Delhi: India Research Press

Neerja Arun & Rakesh Saraswat (2011), Summarizing the History and perspectives of Global Indian Diaspora, Ashok Prakashan Mandir: Ahmedabad

Tinker, Hugh. (1977), The Banyan Tree: Overseas Emigrants from India, Pakistan and Bangladesh. Oxford: Oxford University Press.

http://timesofindia.indiatimes.com/nri/us-canada-news/Indian-Americans-campaign-ahead-of-Senate-vote-on-Vivek-Murthy/articleshow/45519869.cms [Retrieved on 13 April 2019]

https://www.ndtv.com/indians-abroad/indian-americans-keen-about-pm-modis-address-to-us-congress-1415670 [Accessed on 21 April 2019]

23

India-China-US Relations:
Prospects for a Strategic Triangle

Shyna V V

Introduction

The 21st century is witnessing the rises of two home-grown maritime powers against the backdrop of US dominion over the global commons. Their aspirations for great-power status and, above all, their quests for energy security has compelled both Beijing and New Delhi to redirect their gazes from land to the seas. There are mutual convergences and divergences of interests and objectives among the three nations. But the bilateral relationship between all the three countries have grown significantly in the recent years. Among these, the US, the only superpower today, and its strategic interests in Asia must account for the concerns of its two rising powers, China and India. Each has almost 37-38% of the world's population and a great domestic economic transformation of these two countries, thus, has major international implications. But, China's political future remain a big question mark, as China may have undergone increasing economic liberalization, but its polity continues to be marked by a Communist monopoly over political power. Being a democracy, India has an institutionalized political system, and transfer of power between different political parties or alliances is a regular political occurrence.[1]

The last two decades has witnessed a dramatic improvements in Indo-US ties, a reduction of tension in bilateral Indo-China relations and the progression of Sino-US relationship from a strategic partner under the Clinton administration to a strategic competitor under the Bush Government and ambivalence under President Barack Obama.[2] However, the nature of interaction among the Indo-China, Sino-US and Indo-US couplets is currently far from hostile and full of uncertainties at the dawn of the new millennium. The trio is showing a remarkably consistent and restrained reciprocity towards one another. It is unclear what pattern the triangle will evolve into; some speculate about a Indo-US alignment on issues where they share common interests vis-à-vis China. Others emphasise on about India and China, as remerging powers, might join hands to building of a multi-polar world. And some viewed a conflict between India and Pakistan might witness the US and China joining hands against India.[3] Hence, the strategic triangle is an inherently restricted triangle, with the degree of its restriction varying in different situations.

With the economic and military rise of China and India, both countries has become considerably strong regional powers that shift the unipolar position of the US. Considering the fact that the US aims to pursue its balance of power strategy in Asia, it increasingly ties up with India in order to counterbalance China's powerful rise.[4] However, the question is how India will play the game in the changing international power structure: should it go along with the US and contain China? Or, should it play an equiproximity game, maintaining closeness both with the US and China? Thus, the challenge for India is how to boost its relationship with the US that can provide an impetus to its economy and defence capability building without antagonising China. Therefore, the present Government led by Narendra Modi is expected to pursue a more robust and assertive approach and enhance India's influence and prestige on the global stage. Accordingly, the current paper highlights the existing competitive interests between the three countries and tries to find out the ways and means which will strengthen the co-operation. The paper analyses the triangular relationship in reference to three themes: firstly nuclear proliferation, secondly militarization, and thirdly the international political and financial economy. But before going to the triangular aspects, it is necessary to have a look on the bilateral relations between all the three countries.

India-China: Competition or Cooperation?

China and India were the ancient civilizations that together comprise nearly two fifths of humanity. Their entire 4,057-kilometer-long border, one of the longest in the world—remains in dispute without a clearly defined line of control in the Himalayas separating the rival armies. The disputes and tensions between the two countries hold significant implications for international security and Asian power dynamics. China is a big power in East Asia while India is a big power in South Asia and each enjoys advantages and influence in their respective regions. However, the cooperation in the areas include a burgeoning economic relationship, greater dialogue on issues like Afghanistan and counterterrorism, as well as cooperation in multilateral forums, including BRICS and on multilateral issues such as climate change.[5]

China's concerns about the presence of the Dalai Lama and other Tibetan leaders in India, as well as India's concerns about Chinese dam construction on its side of the Brahmaputra river and cyber espionage and cyber security threats led to a conflicting interest between the two countries. As Ashley Tellis rigtly pointed out that, Beijing's and New Delhi's divergent behaviours are shaped by the unique histories governing their formation as modern states, the stark contrasts in their respective political regimes, and their ongoing territorial disputes and geopolitical rivalries.[6] In fact, India fears an encircling by China in South Asia while China fears an encircling in South East Asia and East Asia, by US and its allies, including India. This mistrust led to a geopolitical competition, has been sharpened by China's strategic projects around India including new ports in Sri Lanka and Pakistan and transportation links with Myanmar, Nepal, and Pakistan, as well as China's own major upgrades to military infrastructure in Tibet.[7] These factors make these three countries, an important strategic partners for China and India's relations with these countries will remain an issue for China unless there is an understanding on mutual interests.

As far as the security is concerned, Sino-Pakistan bilateral relationship has been a source of concern, especially its military, missile and nuclear aspects. Delhi viewed China's issuance of stapled visas to Indian citizens from the state of Jammu and Kashmir as a deviation from China's neutrality in the dispute between India and Pakistan and a questioning of Indian sovereignty.[8] The interesting thing is that India wants China to show that India-China relations is a central priority. As long as China allies itself with Pakistan, there will be little hope for improved Sino-Indian relations.

The simmering Sino-Indian tensions threatened to become open conflict in 2013 when Chinese troops stealthily crossed the disputed Himalayan border at night in the Ladakh region. China then embarked on coercive diplomacy and withdrew its troops three weeks later only after India destroyed a defensive line of local fortifications. This episode showed that stoking tensions with Japan, Vietnam, and the Philippines over islands in the South and East China Seas did not prevent an increasingly assertive China from opening yet another front. The fact is that, with its 'peaceful rise' giving way to an increasingly sharp-elbowed approach to its neighbours, China has broadened its 'core interests' and territorial claims while showing a growing readiness to take risks to achieve its goals.[9] But the recent visit of the Xi Jinping to India on September 18, 2014, symbolizes the beginning of a new stage in the development and formulated several agreement between the two countries. It cover a variety of areas including investments into the road and port infrastructure of India, cooperation in space and in nuclear energy, construction of industrial parks in India, joint efforts in combating terrorism, cultural cooperation and a twin cities agreement between Mumbai and Shanghai.[10]

At the economic level, China is one of the most crucial trade partners of India. But the bilateral trade has actually fallen over the last few years from $74 billion in 2011 to about $65 billion in 2013.[11] China's new premier Li Keqiang said, "we are not a threat to each other, nor do we seek to contain each other," and pledged to open China's markets to Indian products to address the trade imbalance and boost commerce to $100 billion a year. While the trade has increased between the two countries becoming a binding factor in improving relations, the ever-widening deficit has become a major stumbling block, especially for India, whose exports were hit by depreciating rupee and also by declining exports of iron ore which previously was the main stay of Indian exports.[12] Anyhow, their bilateral relationship will be characterized more by competition than cooperation because the issues that bind them are also the issues that divide them. Neither power is comfortable with the rise of the other.

India and US: Friendship on Fast Track

In the past decades the Indo-US relationship was like a Stock Exchange, which had its ups and down. The relationships between the two countries were wounded of mismatched obsessions of India's with Pakistan and America's with the erstwhile USSR. After the Pokhran II tests, May 1998 resulted in a review of the relationship and the Clinton visit to Delhi of March 2000 marked the beginning of the thaw. However the more radical decision to admit India into the global nuclear framework was enabled by then US president George Bush in mid-2005 and reached fruition in late 2008.[13] Hence, the US has comprehended India as major partner and both countries agreed to work cooperatively to promote stability, democracy, prosperity and peace throughout the world. It was, however, the offer of the US to "work to achieve full civil nuclear energy cooperation with India, seek agreement from Congress to adjust US laws and policies and work with friends and allies to adjust international regimes to enable full civil nuclear energy cooperation and trade with India." That was the symbolic of the new phase of ties between the two countries.[14] Therefore, the synergy in energy contributed a turning point in the evolution of India's relations with the US. It saw a drastic change in the international community's stance towards India on the nuclear issue.

At the security level, both countries are:

- trying to help Bangladesh to cope with it aggressive, radical Islamic movement and to stop Bangladeshi support to IIGs,
- advising Nepal on how to bring back democracy and to resolve the Maoist movement,
- trying and convince the parties in Sri Lanka to agree to a cease-fire,
- supporting the initiative of Kofi Annan's new initiative on democracy promotion worldwide,
- could undertake practical exercises in anti-narcotic operations and in countering piracy, and
- working jointly to fight global HIV/AIDS in worldwide.

But there are some serious differences of opinion about Iran, Burma, and Pakistan. Even today, the United States is actively trying (for now, unsuccessfully) to force India to support an American initiative to reform the WTO, which, if it should be implemented, would lead to the ruin of hundreds of millions of Indian farmers. Additionally, both countries has divergence over the 'Af-Pak' region and the Middle East, the evolving situation in Asia could well provide the basis for a new bonding. The breakthrough also signalled a significant diplomatic victory for India's stand that it would not dilute its liability law.[15] The nuclear liability issue has remained a stumbling block in Indo-US relations over the past four years. While in opposition, the BJP opposed the nuclear deal and pushed for liability legislation that complicated US companies' ability to invest in civil nuclear projects in India.[16] But President Obama has made a historic visit to India, the first US head of state to attend India's Republic Day and the only sitting US President to visit India twice, has given an opportunity to discuss misgivings over the liability law and also meet foreign governments and the supplier community halfway on the issue.

Inspite of these issue, both share core values and strategic interests including mutual concern about militancy in Pakistan and the rise of China. Therefore, the relationship has success stories. These include robust economic relations, maritime cooperation and a 3-million-strong Indian American diaspora.[17] Besides, The American and Indian militaries has participated in a number of bilateral exercise including Yudh Abhyas, Cope India, Malabar and Vajra Prahar. India conducts more military exercise with the US than with any other country.[18] Thus, PM Modi has referred to the two nations as natural allies. As he noted, "the true power and potential in this relationship is that when the oldest and largest democracies come together, the world will benefit."[19]

As far as the economy is concerned, the bilateral trade between the two countries has increased 60 per cent in the past couple of years to a record $100 billion, but India's exports to the US were still less than 2 per cent of all American imports.[20] The US is India's largest trading partner, but there is immense room for growth. Because China-US trade, for example, is over five times more than Indo-US trade. However, the new Government has promised to open the economy to more private investment, improve the GDP growth rate, create jobs for the rapidly growing youth population, and quicken the pace of India's defense modernization. It will open numerous opportunities for expanded Indo--US cooperation on a range of issues.[21] If India needs US investments and strategic support in Asia where China's futuristic moves are narrowing India's space, the US equally needs the world's largest democracy for its market and for maintaining a fair balance of power in the region.[22]

China-US: Ambivalence Powers

The Sino-US relations has graduated from an environment of hostility to engagement. The two sides welcomed all efforts conducive to peace, stability and development in South Asia. They support the efforts of Afghanistan and Pakistan to fight terrorism, maintain domestic stability and achieve sustainable economic and social development, and support the improvement and growth of relations between India and Pakistan.[23] But there are some differences on issues regarding Taiwan, trade imbalances, China's growing military power, China's global and regional activities, human rights, and domestic and political matters. The state of human rights in China, the situation in Tibet, and the treatment of other minority communities such as Uighur Muslims in Xinjiang remains an important human rights and religious freedom concern for the US.[24] Needless to say, as the relation between the US, the world's great power, and China, the world's rising power is one of the most important yet complicated bilateral relationships in the world today.

China's greatest strategic fear is that an outside power or powers will establish military deployments around China's periphery capable of encroaching on China's territory or meddling in its domestic institutions. At the same time, the US fear, sometimes only indirectly expressed, is of being pushed out of Asia by an exclusionary bloc. If China and the US come to regard each other's trade-pact efforts as elements in a strategy of isolation, the Asia-Pacific region could devolve into competing adversarial power blocs. The key decision facing both Beijing and Washington is whether to move toward a genuine effort at cooperation or fall into a new version of historic patterns of international rivalry.[25]

At the economic level, both countries has expanded substantially over the past three decades. The total Sino-US trade rose from $2 billion in 1979 to $562 billion in 2013 which jumped to $ 87 billion in FY 2018. China is currently the US second-largest trading partner, its third-largest export market, and its biggest source of imports. Besides, China is estimated to be a $350 billion market for US firms (based on US direct and indirect exports to China and sales by US-invested firms in China).[26] By 2018, bilateral trade has gone up to over $ 600 billion. President Trump administration has launched trade war against China in July 2018, alleging gamut of violation of established international norms. It is still prevailing as on August 2019 and expected to sustain till American presidential election in November 2020.

Although China's comprehensive capabilities has been growing rapidly for the past three decades, almost all analysts inside and outside of China agree that there is still a huge gap between China and the US in terms of comprehensive capabilities, particularly when the US is far ahead of China in military and technological realms. China's economy has passed the US economy as the largest one in 2014, but the quality of China's economy still remains a major weakness for Beijing. Thus, it would be a serious mistake for China to challenge the US directly given the wide gap of capabilities between the two.[27]

On 12 November 2014 President Barack Obama sat down with Chinese President Xi Jinping at the Asian Pacific Economic Cooperation (APEC) summit to discuss joint co-operation on a range of international issues. Obama managed to leave Beijing with a guarantee that China would cut greenhouse gas emissions and increase the share of non--fossil fuels in primary energy consumption—a development that was heralded as a diplomatic coup for the US. However, the issue of climate change was not a sensitive issue in the same way that cybersecurity and South China Sea issues are today. In a best case scenario, we could see both sides acknowledging a divergence of opinion on these matters in a joint statement.[28] The important topics might be on the agenda, including progress on a bilateral investment treaty (BIT), military confidence building measures and agreement on what approach to take at December's climate change conference to be held in Paris.[29] However, the 2015 as an important year in Sino-US relations, and making headway both on areas of cooperation and making headway on areas of concern.

Challenges for the Triangle

On the one side US is promoting mutual cooperation, where the mighty and average would work together to reap the benefits of inter-dependence to maintain a peaceful world order. But on the other side, US does not want Asia to be dominated by any single power and, much more, its own exclusion or marginalisation in the Asian geo-strategic architecture.[30] Because there are a number of strategic directions China could take depending on which domestic and external factors emerge as key determinants of Chinese national security policy. And which path China will follow remains unknown, however, and this uncertainty complicates the formulation of an effective policy for managing China's rising power throughout the Asia-Pacific region.

As Asia and its maritime spaces emerge as a major arena of contest between Washington and Beijing, the US and India are drawing closer in their respective policies to the region. It is in this context, India's new triangular dynamic with the US and China added significance and plays out most clearly in the Asia-Pacific.[31] However, a beneficial triangular relationship presupposes, as a minimum, a long-term common goal. India, China, and the US that share a similar long-term vision of prosperity and stability in the Indo-Pacific. Even the Pentagon agrees, viewing India not only as a "regional economic anchor", but also as a "provider of security in the broader Indian Ocean region."[32] But the query is how to cooperate effectively with both US and China without seeming to favour the relationship with one at the cost of the relationship with the other? It will be one of the main concern in the coming decades. Therefore, we can identify the challenges through three important angle-military, nuclear and economy.

Military Confrontation

In regard to militarization, both China and India are increasing their military expenditures in relation to the US. With the Taiwan straits, the Sino-Indian border disputes and recent escalations with the Philippines over the nine-dashed line in the South China Sea amongst others, there is potential for military confrontation in Asia.[33] Besides, China's claims over the entire South China Sea as well as the Spratly and Paracel islands, which sit astride vital sea-lanes through which 25 percent of the world's shipping passes. It is one of the biggest potential flashpoints in the Asia-Pacific region, as it affects virtually all countries in the South China Sea including Vietnam, Malaysia, Taiwan, the Philippines, and Brunei.[34] However, its increasing military re-assertion, many Asian countries seem to seek an alliance with the US to counterbalance China's rise. At the same time, US naval forces are trying to play a major role in a South China Sea contingency, access to the region for US land-based fighter aircraft would complicate Chinese calculations, because of the serious difficulties China would face in establishing air superiority for its naval forces operating in the South China Sea.[35]

Simultaneously, China is closely watching the prospering Indo-US relations with suspicion because it perceives that the expanding multifaceted relationship between India and the US is finally aimed at the containment of China. China doesn't want to see India become a major great power in the world and the relationship with the US is the key to India achieving this objective.[36] One of the eminent strategic analyst S D Muni examined that strategically, the Asian countries are seeking assurance in the heightened US presence in the region and a new strategic balance to be created with greater involvement of Asian powers like India, Australia and Japan. All these countries want to prevent China's domination in the region. But the exceptions, such as Iran and Pakistan who have no problem with a rising and assertive China.[37] Therefore, the question is will India play a balancing game for US. The Indian Government has always upheld that it does not propose to follow an aggressive policy towards China and has declined to be an American proxy or bulwark under any circumstances. But from a geopolitical point of view, if a US policy strategically confines or weakens China in the region, it is unlikely that India would mind, even though it does not want to be directly involved in any anti-China strategy.[38]

Another issue that ties in with this argument is the continuingly unresolved Taiwan question. Taiwan has been an important geostrategic partner for the US throughout the era of the Cold War and the containment of contender states. According to Bruce Cumings, the US geopolitical interests determined the successful development of Taiwan to a considerable extent. Whereas China still claims the 'One-China'-solution, Taiwan is very likely to tie in with other Asian countries to form a closer alliance with the US.[39] In the future it will be interesting to see if China has the ability to balance out military power and a careful rise without making its neighbours too nervous. Taiwan issue has become further tensed by August 2019 and the United States has vowed to protect it. United States has sanctioned sale of modern fighter planes to Taiwan of the tune of $ 7 billion in August 2019, which was fiercely opposed by China. This huge number of fighter planes has been given to Taiwan by the United States after many years.

South China Sea has also emerged as regional flashpoint and if duly managed under the ambit of relevant international laws could be soring United States—China relations in particular. Trump administration has already pledged to protect the norms of international laws of the seas (UNCLOS)

Issue of Nuclear Proliferation

On the one hand, India has upheld that its weapons are deterrent against China but on the other hand Pakistan also maintained that its weapons are a deterrent against India. At the centre of this nuclear climax, if India decides to speed up its nuclear programme whether it is civilian or military, there will be a ripple effect through the region. Consequently, the basic point worth stressing here is that the Indo-US nuclear agreement could prompt Pakistan to go for similar deal with China on the principle that an enemy's enemy is a friend.

The interesting thing is that the US want India's assistance in dealing with a range of dangerous contingencies involving Pakistan. As we know that, Pakistan is already a proliferation risk: Pakistani nuclear scientist A.Q. Khan's unlawful nuclear network, revealed in 2004, shocked the world with its brazen trade of nuclear technology. In fact, many of the nuclear proliferation problems of today are directly linked to the A.Q. Khan network. Parallel with Khan's efforts, China has provided loans and technical assistance to Pakistan for building two atomic power reactors. It has now been revealed that China has signed a US $2.375 billion agreement for supplying two 340 MW power reactors (Chasma-3 and Chasma-4) to Pakistan. Beijing would also loan some 80 percent of the project cost. It is matter of concern for the US. But the Chinese official is arguing that the supply of Chasma-3 and Chasma-4 was included in the earlier agreement of 1985 pertaining to the supply of Chasma-1 and Chasma-2.[40] It will indeed be an uphill task for the new Indian Government to get China to discuss nuclear security matters with India. However, nuclear confrontation is a great concern in the coming decades.

International Economic Competition

The growing economic interests of the three countries is another concern. Indian interests now extend from Aden to Singapore, from the Straits of Hormuz to Malacca and New Delhi will economically integrate with Asia, and work closely with Hanoi and Tokyo and other ASEAN like-minded countries. Consequently, the US wants to assign important strategic role to India from Strait of Hormuz to Strait of Malacca. Because the US is the most powerful military power in this region for its Central Command and Asia-Pacific Command. India is strategically located between these two naval task force. Thus, its location can be beneficial for both the US commands.[41] Moreover the US has vital strategic interests in the world's largest reserves of energy lying in the Middle East, Gulf region and South Asia and India occupies the strategic location linking the Indian and Pacific Oceans.[42] As Harsh V Pant rightly noted that US would like a strong US-India alliance to act as a 'bulwark against the arc of Islamic instability running form the Middle East to Asia and to create much greater balance in Asia.'[43] At the same time, China, in turn, is exploiting the chaos in Afghanistan and Pakistan to extend its influence in the region and into Central Asia.[44] The interesting thing is that China has not categorise India as a threat or challenge even though it considers India as a 'future strategic competitor.' Therefore, managing these interests are significant in the 21st century.

Another aspect is the billions of dollars US corporations are pouring into China. Much of what the largest American supermarket chain, Wal-Mart, sells today—from small appliances to refrigerators—is made in China. Dell, among the largest producers of personal computers, assembles its laptops and desktops in China. The toys for American children are manufactured in China. The more Chinese economy grows and expands, the more resources China will have for military modernization and for 'broadcasting' its power in the world.[45]

Additionally, nearly 70 percent of China's trade is through the Strait of Malacca, the Indian Ocean, and the Suez Canal. The predominance of the US and Indian navies along these sea-lanes of communication (SLOCs) is viewed as a major threat to Chinese security. In recent years United States, India and Japan has further expanded their joint naval exercises in the region and that has further put strategic pressure on China. To protect its long-term economic security interests, China is now laying the groundwork for a naval presence along maritime chokepoints in the South China Sea, the Malacca Straits, the Indian Ocean, and the Strait of Hormuz in the Persian Gulf through acquisition of naval bases in Cambodia, Myanmar, Bangladesh, and Pakistan. India has countered by promoting defense cooperation with Iran, Oman, and Israel in the west while upgrading military ties with Myanmar, Singapore, Maldives, Thailand, Vietnam, Taiwan, the Philippines, Australia, Japan, and the United States in the east. India's new naval doctrine is to influence events around the Indian Ocean and beyond. However, the maritime competition is likely to intensify as Indian and Chinese navies show off their flag in the South China Sea and the Indian Ocean with greater frequency.[46]

Prospects for Strategic Cooperation

The emerging strategic triangle has all three states having their mutual convergences and divergences and also having ongoing strategic partnerships or dialogues amongst them. Each state has partnerships with the other working together on some issues, but finding themselves in disagreement on others without forming any firm or enduring alignment. Hence currently, the strategic triangle is a complex and shifting one, which is highly fluid, as proposed by Harry Harding, the Director, Research and Analysis, Eurasia Group, USA. It means each pair of countries working together on some issues, but finding themselves in disagreements on others, without forming any firm or enduring alignment.[47]

The fluid nature of the India-China-US triangle generates uncertainty, since there are elements of cooperation as well as conflict involving all the three bilateral relationships. The hope for stability lies in mutual accommodation.[48] The three countries share common concerns—including those related to Afghanistan (and even Pakistan), the Middle East and climate change—and this offers the prospect of cooperation, or at least, consultation in the future.[49] In the case of Afghanistan, India worries about stability in its front yard, China is concerned about its economic investments and American fears terrorism. Each has a considerable stake in keeping Afghanistan from becoming a failed state. The three powers have much more in common than not when it comes to stabilizing Afghanistan.[50]

Moreover, the US role in the ongoing global war on terrorism, the Uighur problem in China, and India's counter terrorism initiatives in Kashmir find commonality of purpose. Hence, it is very likely that all three states may work in concert to pursue convergences such as the rising threat of terrorism in near future, other transnational problems, economic inter-dependence and trade benefits, and to curb global developments inimical to their national interests and in furtherance of global peace and prosperity. Similarly, with recent increases in violence in Xinjiang, Beijing is concerned about the flow of militants across national boundaries. On October 31, 2014 Chinese Foreign Ministry Spokesperson Hong Lei told reporters at a press conference that, "China is willing to start cooperating with the international community in striking out against terrorism." Driving this new found willingness to engage with the US on counterterrorism are recent event s in China's far western province Xinjiang.[51]

Further cooperation can be enhanced through trade. Successful initiatives such as the Joint Commission on Commerce and Trade (JCCT) and the Strategic Economic Dialogue (SED) between the US and China will have to be further strengthened to boost economic cooperation. Correspondingly, there is a need for India to increase its trade with both China and the US. The existing forums developed as part of the US-India Economic Dialogue must seek ways to resolve outstanding economic and trade issues and boost trade.[52] Another important area of convergences on the energy and environmental issues as well. Initiatives such as the APEC Energy Security Initiative and Asia-Pacific Partnership on Clean Development and Climate are aimed at collaborative efforts to implement projects that will improve energy security, air pollution, climate change, and efficiency in a variety of energy-intensive sectors.[53]

There is a need for confidence building measures such as a trilateral military and security dialogue and transparency in military matters among all three states. India must maintain transparency and reiterate its adherence to the global non-proliferation norms to dispel Chinese fears about the Indo-US nuclear cooperation. India must also examine the Chinese offer for nuclear cooperation based on its merits. Efforts must be on to promote joint military exercises and exchanges among all three states. Equally, China must maintain transparency about its military modernization and trade issues such as the WTO.[54] The US must also initiate a military and nuclear dialogue besides the ongoing strategic dialogue in the case of US-China. This will in turn lead to stabilizing patterns and prevent a nuclear arms race by China.

In addition to this, the strategic triangle will turn more cooperative if all three states must have equitable representation and play an active role in global and regional forums such as the United Nations Security Council (UNSC), G8 summit, Shanghai Cooperation Organization (SCO), Association of Southeast Asian Nations (ASEAN), ASEAN Regional Forum (ARF), East Asia Summit (EAS) and South Asian Association for Regional Cooperation (SAARC). This will act as a confidence building measure and allay current fears which have manifested due to either restrained participation or exclusion of one of the three states from some of these institutions.[55]

In the case of strategic issues, it is time to include the navies in the on-going Indo-China bilateral military exercises and dialogue, as a confidence building measure. This is especially important given the trend of Chinese submarines conducting longrange patrols into the Indian Ocean and seeking to defend trade routes, even as our own ships venture into the South China Sea. The Indian Ocean has four of the six major maritime chokepoints and serves as a maritime super highway for in-demand energy resources that drive the world's largest economies. Accordingly, the three sides should immediately compare notes on their own Indian Ocean strategies because the secure maritime navigation from Africa and the Middle East to East Asia is vital to energy and resource access. As 40 percentage of the world oil and commerce passes through the Indian Ocean sea-lanes. Almost 68 percent of India's, 80 percent of China's and 25 percent of the US' oil is shipped from the Indian Ocean Region.[56] Recognising mutual interests in the Indian Ocean and in the South China Sea should also be explored, rather than the chess game that is now going on, which adds to the tensions, and where the real beneficiaries are the countries of the region playing-off India and China against each other.[57]

In the aspect of traditional security cooperation, China maintains stable military relationship with the US and India. For instance, China and India joined the RIMPAC naval exercise with the US in 2014 for the first time and held the joint military exercise, 'Hand-In-Hand' in Chengdu in November 2014. And India has also participated in RED FLAG with the US.[58] It's a positive move for trilateral cooperation. However, as the world three largest economies and major players that shape Asia's political and security context, proper management of the trilateral India-China-US relationship has become more important than ever.

Concluding Remarks

Though, the prospects for strategic triangular relationships are looked with some degree of scepticism, the potential benefits of participating in tri-lateral ties are significant for all the three countries in the 21st century. But managing these expanding relations will increasingly be a key challenge for Washington, Beijing and New Delhi. Also the major characteristic of this emerging strategic triangle lies in that it is still in an evolutionary phase and has not assumed a strong and mature form similar to the Sino-Soviet-US strategic triangle during the Cold War. It's a complex and dynamic triangle stands for the linkage of cooperation and conflict and all of them are involved in a hedging strategy. In 2017 Chinese and Indian army remained an eye ball to eye ball situation for almost 70 days for Bhutanese territory Doklam. In April 2018, Chinese president Xi invited PM Modi and had a informal summit at Wuhan and vowed to deescalate. President Xi and PM Modi met 13 times since last five years. President Xi is coming to Varanasi by the end of 2019 for another spell of informal summit with PM Modi.

Despite these level playing field initiatives, China blocked designation of Masood Azhar as global terrorist in the UN in the backdrop of Pulwama terror attack (2019). Strangely in May 2019, China has lifted its and Azhar was declared global terrorist. China has also sided with Pakistan in the backdrop of abrogation of article 370 from Jammu and Kashmir in August 2019. China is a party in Kashmir problem because Pakistan had ceded parts of Kashmir to China illegally in 1960s.

In July 2019, Pakistani PM, Imran Khan visited Washington and President Donald Trump pledged for mediation in Kashmir. But in August 2019 when President Trump met PM Modi for G-7 summit in Paris in August 2019 he towed with Indian line that Kashmir is bilateral issue between India and Pakistan.

Among the three side of a triangle Sin-Indian dyad is sensitive to triangular impacts. India-United States trade relations has gone up phenomenally in recent years and slated to grow. It has started to transcend into strategic domain. The India-US relation has been the facilitator in this triangular regime, and the China-US relation has served as the driving force. As of mutual strategic distrust, China and India could not overcome the conflicts in various spheres and this has created a 'drag' in terms of the development of the triangular cooperation regime. If India, China, and the US can develop strong and amicable economic ties with one another, it will therefore ensure the prosperity of the world as a whole. But because of the geopolitical divergences and territorial disputes, we cannot expect the advent of strategic cooperation in the near future. The most likely possibility is a combination of competition and cooperation.

NOTES

1. Ashutosh Varshney, *A New Triangle: India, China and the US*, available at http://www.india-seminar.com/2006/557/557%20ashutosh%20varshney.htm, accessed on December 11, 2014.
2. Ananya Chatterjee, "India-China-United States: The Post-Cold War Evolution of a Strategic Triangle," *Political Perspective*, Vol. 5, no.3, 2011, pp. 74-95, p.75
3. Sun Xun, "New Nuclear Triangle and China's Role in South Asia," *Regional Centre for Strategic Studies*, Sri Lanka, 2005, p.7
4. Annemarie Detlef, "An Analysis of Contemporary US-China-India Relations," Jul 7 2012, available at http://www.e-ir.info/2012/07/07/an-analysis-of-contemporary-us-china-india-relations/, accessed on December 12, 2014.
5. Tanvi Madan, "The Modi-Xi Summit and China-India Relations," September 16, 2014, available at http://www.brookings.edu/research/opinions/2014/09/16-modi-xi-summit-and-china-india-relations.html, accessed on December 11, 2014.
6. Ashley J. Tellis and Sean Mirski, *Crux of Asia: China, India, and the Emerging Global Order*, Carnegie Endowment for International Peace, 2013, p.4
7. Brahma Chellaney, "An Uneasy Strategic Triangle: the Troubled China India Relationship and

US Asia Policy," *JPRI Occasional Paper*, no.48, January 2014, available at http://www.jpri.org/publications/occasionalpapers/op48.html, accessed on 11 December, 2014.
8. C. Raja Mohan, "India, China and the United States: Asia's Emerging Strategic Triangle," *Strategic Snapshots*, MacArthur Foundation, Loy Institute for International Policy, February 2011,
9. Brahma Chellaney, op.cit.
10. Boris Volkhonsky, "India-China relations: A factor of stability or tension in Asia?" September 24, 2014, available at http://in.rbth.com/blogs/2014/09/24/india-china_relations_a_factor_of_stability_or_tension_in_asia_38523.html, accessed on December 11, 2014.
11. Tanvi Madan, "India-U.S. Relations in 14 Charts and Graphics," Brookings Institution, September 26, 2014, available at http://www.brookings.edu/blogs/up-front/posts/2014/09/26, accessed on January 13, 2015.
12. "India's trade deficit with China rose to $37.8 billion in 2014," *The Economic Times*, 13 January, 2015.
13. India, China, US will be in uneasy strategic triangle, *Business Standard News*, September 2, 2013, available at http://www.business-standard.com/article/news-ians/india-china-us-will-be-in-uneasy-strategic-triangle-113090200647_1.html, accessed on 11 December, 2014.
14. Gopalan Balachandran, "Nuclear Real Politik: The prospects for Indo-US Relations", *Australian Journal of International Affairs*, Vol.61, No.4, 2007, p.546
15. Suhasini Haidar, "N-deal Logjam Cleared: Modi, Obama Agree not to Dilute Liability Law," *The Hindu*, January 27, 2015.
16. Lisa Curtis, "The Quality of the Indo-U.S. Relationship Matters more than the Quantity of Dialogues," August 18, 2014, available at http://www.americanbazaaronline.com/2014/08/18/quality-indo-u-s-relationship-matters-quantity-dialogues/, accessed on January 13, 2015.
17. Michael Kugelman, "It's time for the US to Reset Relations with India," May 18, 2014, available at http://www.latimes.com/opinion/op-ed/la-oe-kugelman-india-election-20140519-story.html, accessed on December 11, 2014.
18. Tanvi Madan, op. cit.
19. "Obama's trip a defining and exciting time in Indo-US Relations: Nominee for US ambassador to India," *The Times of India*, December 3, 2014,
20. Puja Mehra, "Modi's reforms enthuse Obama," *The Hindu*, January 27, 2015.
21. Lisa Curtis, op. cit.
22. Seema Sirohi, "Can Modi Revive the India-US Relationship?" September 29, 2014, available at http://www.aljazeera.com/indepth/opinion/2014/09/can-modi-revive-india-us-relati-201492872246706449.html, accessed on January 13, 2015.
23. B. Raman, "A Balancing Act," *Outlook Magazine*, November 11, 2010, available at http://www.outlookindia.com/article/A-Balancing-Act/267917, accessed on December 12, 2014.
24. Major. Banit Singh Negi, op. cit, p. 70.
25. Henry A. Kissinger, "The Future of US-Chinese Relations," *Foreign Affairs*, March/April 2012,
26. Wayne M. Morrison, "China-U.S. Trade Issues," *Congressional Research Service*, December 5, 2014, available at http://www.fas.org/sgp/crs/row/RL33536.pdf, accessed on December 15, 2014.
27. Dingding Chen, Relax, "China Won't Challenge US Hegemony," *The Diplomat*, January 14, 2015, available at http://thediplomat.com/2015/01/relax-china-wont-challenge-us-hegemony/, accessed on 20 February 2015.

28. Ankit Panda, "5 Predictions for Xi Jinping's US State Visit," *The Diplomat*, February 10, 2015, available at http://thediplomat.com/2015/02/5-predictions-for-xi-jinpings-us-state-visit/, accessed on February 20, 2015.
29. Shannon Tiezzi, "Why 2015 Will Be a Great Year for US-China Relations," *The Diplomat*, February 12, 2015, available at http://thediplomat.com/2015/02/why-2015-will-be-a-great-year-for-us-china-relations/, accessed on February 20, 2015.
30. Snehalata Panda, "Global Energy and Alliances: Challenges for India," *India Quarterly: A Journal of International Affair*, Sage Publication: New Delhi, Vol. 62, No. 92, 2006, pp.92-123.
31. C. Raja Mohan, "India, China and the United States: Asia's Emerging Strategic Triangle," available at http://www.lowyinstitute.org/publications/india-china-and-united-states-asias-emerging-strategic-triangle, accessed on December 12, 2014.
32. Karl D, "US-India Relations: Pivot Problems," Centre for Strategic and International Studies, 2011.
33. Annemarie Detlef, "An Analysis of Contemporary US-China-India Relations," July 7, 2012, available at http://www.e-ir.info/2012/07/07/an-analysis-of-contemporary-us-china-india-relations/, accessed on December 11, 2014.
34. Richard Sokolsky, Angel Rabasa and C. Richard Neu, "The Role of Southeast Asia in U.S. Strategy Toward China," RAND Corporation, 2001, pp.1-2.
35. Ibid, p.72.
36. China's Growing Apprehensions over India-US Strategic Relations, December 1, 2011, available at http://www.turkishweekly.net/op-ed/2915/china-39-s-growing-apprehensions-over-india-us-strategic-relations.html, accessed on 11 December 2014.
37. S D Muni, "Introduction", ed by S.D. Muni and Vivek Chanda, *Asian Strategic Review*, Pentagon Press: New Delhi, 2013, p. 5.
38. Prashant Hosur, "The Indo-US Civilian Nuclear Agreement: What's the big deal?" *International Journal*, Spring, 2010, p.440, pp.435-36.
39. Annemarie Detlef, "An Analysis of Contemporary US-China-India Relations," July 7, 2012, available at http://www.e-ir.info/2012/07/07/an-analysis-of-contemporary-us-china-india-relations/, accessed on 10 December 2014.
40. P.R. Chari, "Nuclear Dealing Wheeling," *Institute of Peace and Conflict Studies*, 10 May 2010, available at http://www.ipcs.org/article/pakistan/nuclear-dealin g-wheeling-3123.html, accessed on 28 October 2014.
41. Tej Pratap Singh, "Indo-US Civil Nuclear Cooperation Agreement: Implications for Asian Security," N.K. Jha, in his ed. *Nuclear Synergy Indo-US Strategic Co-operation and Beyond* (New Delhi: Pentagon Press, 2009), p. 99.
42. Mussarat Jabeen and Ishtiaq Ahmed, "Indo-US Nuclear Cooperation," *South Asian Studies*, Vol. 26, No. 2, July-December 2011, pp. 411-429.
43. Harsh V Pant, *Contemporary Debates in Indian Foreign and Security Policy*, Palgrave Macmillan, 2008, p. 22.
44. Adam Segal, "India-US-China Strategic Triangle," October 25, 2010, http://blogs.cfr.org/asia/2010/10/25/india-u-s-china-strategic-triangle/
45. Ashutosh, op. cit.
46. Mohan Malik, "India-China Relations: Giants Stir, Cooperate and Compete," *Asia-Pacific Centre for Security Studies*, October 2004.

47   Major, op. cit, p.102
48   Mohan Malik, *China and India: Great Power Rivals*, Boulder & London: First Forum Press, 2011, p. 396.
49   Tanvi Madan, op. cit.
50   "The Emerging Strategic Triangle in Indo-Pacific Asia," *The Diplomat*,
51   Kevin Peters, Can China and the US Work Together on Counterterrorism?, *The Diplomat*, December 02, 2014, available at http://thediplomat.com/2014/12/can-china-and-the-us-work-together-on-counterterrorism/, accessed on February 20, 2015.
52   Ibid, p.116
53   Major. Banit Singh Negi, The United States-China-India Relationship: An Analysis of the Emergence of a Strategic Triangle, 2007, p. 69.
54   Major, op.cit, p.113
55   Ibid, p.114
56   Colonel Dan McDaniel, India, "China and the United States in the Indo-Pacific region: coalition, co-existence or clash?" October 2012.
57   Mukul Sanwal, "Reappraising Relations with China: From Strategic Ambiguity to Recognising Mutual Interests," *IDSA Issue Brief*, January 22, 2015.
58   Joint Military Exercise Hand-in-Hand 2014 Begins, Press Information Bureau Government of India, Ministry of Defence, 17 November, 2014, available at http://pib.nic.in/newsite/PrintRelease.aspx?relid=111495, accessed on 10 December 2014.

24

Indo-Pak Relations:
Contemporary Challenges

Sudhir Singh

India and Pakistan came into existence in 1947 after partition. Like India, Pakistan inherited a secular state rule through a bureaucracy led by a civil service elites who were recruited and organised on merit. There is little evidence that Jinnah wanted to effect major changes on many of these fronts.[1] Both it's founding leaders, Jinnah and Liaquat Ali Khan departed within few years after its formation. Muslim League used religion to garner political support and thus created third stake holders popularly known as Mullah. The troika of military, bureaucracy and the Mullah captured the canvass of national building process and instead of egalitarian state they formed a theocratic state which was detrimental for the minorities in particular and welfare state concept in general. General Zia-ul-Haq (1977-1988) military regime further consolidated the power of this troika over the destiny of the country. This troika has become so much powerful that even an elected government has been unable to change the direction which ultimately embarked the country on the path of destruction.

Since inception, different nations have been confronting a turbulent relationship like India and Pakistan. They have fought three and half war since independence.

The post-Pokhran (1998) situation has enhanced Indian status at the global level. This has boosted the sustainable economic developments along with good progress at the strategic level for India. The end of the cold war and post 9/11 situation has further brought Asia as a dominating continent at the global table of governance. In the backdrop of abrogation of article 370 from Kashmir, Pakistan has launched all round diplomatic offensives against India.

In this prevailing situation, it is really turbulent for India to reformulate its Pakistan policy to cope up contemporary challenges? There are many divergences and negligible convergences between both traditional rivals which has made the situation worse. How diplomacy could be used to reduce divergences and increase convergences? It is the focal point of this paper which will be widely debated within its ambit of discussion.

Afghan factors has been important in India-Pakistan relations since many decades but it has become important after 'Operation Enduring Freedom' launched by the United States led NATO forces and wiped out terror infested government from Kabul. Afghanistan-India relations has been traditionally good and have been an apple of discord between India and Pakistan. Pakistan always perceived Afghanistan as its strategic wing to be used as per its prerogative. Since the ouster of the Taliban and Al-Qaeda from Afghanistan in October 2001, India-Afghanistan has reached to new heights of deepening of relationship and it has given unprecedented pain to Pakistan.

Afghani theatre has become violent and within January-July 2015 around 5,000 people have already lost their lives due to terror resurgence. Combined right from 2009 till July 2015, 16,874 people have been killed in terror related violence.[2] Right from January 2015 to July 2015 alone 4,921 people have been killed. According to the UN, at least 32,000 civilians have been killed and another 60,000 wounded in the last decade, when the organisation began compiling the data. Civilian deaths jumped by 11 percent from 2017 with 3,804 people killed, including 927 children, and another 7,189 people wounded. It states the actual situation.[3] United States has started dialogue with the Taliban since October 2018 to resolve Afghan tango and willingness to withdraw NATO army (including US one) before the US presidential election scheduled in November 2020. During his July 2019 Washington visit, Imran Khan assured that Pakistan will support in this exercise and the best evidence is that PM went to White House to meet US president along with its army chief, perhaps maiden time in the history of Pakistan-United States relationship. Peace and stability will prevail in Afghanistan even after deal between Taliban and the United States, it is a matter of future. But old trends vindicate the point that Pakistan remains part of Afghan tango and would not become part of it for solution. Pakistani army never allowed it to happen despite its public posturing. In the midst's of this dialogue, a suicide attack has taken place in a wedding party at a hotel in Kabul in August 2019 and more than 63 people were killed and over 100 became injured. However, Taliban has denied its accountability and the Islamic State has taken the accountability publicly then billion dollar question remains unanswered that how peace will prevail within the anarchic situation. It is providing a template of Afghanistan once Taliban led government will be in power in Kabul. President Donald Trump has however canceled the Afghan peace dialogues just before Afghan presidential elections and that has again left uncertainty on this front.

The Islamic State Afghan affiliate suffered some early setbacks as its leaders were picked by US airstrikes. But it received a major boost when the militant group Islamic Movement of Uzbekistan joined its ranks in 2015. Today, the UN says, its numbers between 2,500 and 4,000 fighters, many from Central Asia, Arab countries, Chechnya, India and Bangladesh, as well as ethnic Uighur's from China.

Within Afghanistan, IS has launched large-scale attacks on minority Shias, who it views as apostates deserving of death. The group said Saturday's attack on the wedding targeted a large Shia gathering, although the celebration was in fact a mixed crowd of Shia and Sunnis, according to the event hall's owner, Hussain Ali. The bombing killed at least 63 people and wounded nearly 200 more.[4] US is intended to deal with the Taliban that it will help them to crush Islamic State but there are wider possibility that disgruntled elements of the Taliban (those who are not happy from the deal with the United States) could join Islamic State and embolden it.

In May 2019 after the general election, BJP in the leadership of Narendra Modi came into power second time in row. The BJP and PM Modi are known for their nationalist temper. Modi invited all SAARC head of the state to participate in his swearing in ceremony on May 26, 2014, but avoided them in 2019 and instead called BIMSTEC leaders.

Before the ouster of Nawaz Sharif from the premier position by the judiciary together met many times. Both PM met at Ufa (Russia) in July 2015, P.M. Modi made a surprising stopover at Lahore in December 2015 to wish Pakistan's PM happy birthday but within weeks it was reciprocated through Pathankot attack in January 2016.

During election process, ruling PTI, PML-N, PPP and other political parties have refrained from their pet rhetoric of anti India megalomania. Sharif promised during election campaign that if elected he will promote cordial relationships with India. His government has released over 350 fishermen in August 2013 as a goodwill gesture. In an interview given to *Telegraph* (London), Prime Minister, Nawaz Sharif asserted that his victory in May 2013 elections as a mandate for peace with India. He further added that" We have been in very unfortunate arm race with India ever since partition and I think we are a very unfortunate country from that point of view". He stressed that trust deficit should end and both countries must settle all outstanding issues through dialogue and remain with peace and development.[5] It was repeated during 2018 general election campaign and all three mainstreaming parties (PML-N, PPP, PTI) avoided jingoistic attacks on India. PM Imran Khan also retreated many times before and after as PM wished to promote cordial relations with India.

I must return back to the focal issue now. What are the basic irritants between both traditional rivals of South Asia? It kept on changing but more or less it has been sustainable. When Benazir Bhutto's PPP took over in 1988 and became first women Prime Minister of Pakistan, the Pakistani army took three assurances from her, where she agreed not to intervene in them. Kashmir, Afghanistan and Nuclear issue were the three arenas and it remained no go areas even today for the civilian regimes which is sustainable since 2008.

Terror has remained an instrument of Pakistan's foreign policy and since early 1980s Pakistan has extended support to cross border terror activities in India. Pakistani army believes that through promoting terror in a concealed way they will keep India on tense situation, preventing its economic growth and secure strategic depth in Afghanistan. But in return things have not turned upto the expectations of the army. It has pushed Pakistan on the path of destruction. Its economy is crumbling. Imran Khan stressed during election campaign that he will better do suicide than obtaining foreign debt but his government has taken 13th bailout package from IMF, other agencies and countries. Since the assassination of former PM Benazir Bhutto in December 2007, Pakistan has lost over 90,000 thousand people both civilian and the military in combating terror menace. It has derailed the contours of development. Its economy has been considered as the weakest growth rate in South Asia and perhaps in entire Asia. Pakistan was at par with South Korea in the pace of economic development in 1960s. Today Pakistani economy is leading from the bottom. Military never perceived this reality and even defended this prevailing destruction mode. But military has been successful to ensure its own dominance over the system and manipulated its political processes.

In May 2011 Osama Bin Laden was killed at Abbottabad by special action of the United States commando forces, just few hundred meters away from prestigious Kabul military academy, which is also not far away from Islamabad. The Pakistani commission which was constituted for its investigation has revealed many things which proved the allegation that OBL had protection from the army. It has also been revealed by the commission that OBL was in Pakistan since ouster from Afghanistan.

Afghanistan remains a hot spot not only between Pakistan and India or United States and Pakistan but entire globe has its genuine stakes in Afghanistan. It is producing over 80% of the global drugs. Drug trafficking has threatened the societies across the globe in general but adjoining to Afghanistan it has leased unprecedented devastation to the younger generation. In the backdrop of NATO withdrawal Pakistan is trying its level best to maximise its interests. President Donald Trump administration wishes that US led NATO left over forces must withdraw from Afghanistan before 2020 presidential election. One must remember that whenever there was stability in Afghanistan, it has had thorny relations with Pakistan. Afghanistan was the first country to oppose Pakistani demand of plebiscite in Kashmir in the United Nations.

The issue of Pakhtunistan is raking high with the stability in Afghanistan. Pakistan feel worried in this situation therefore intended to keep Afghanistan as its satellite country. Despite many rounds of talks held at different foreign locations between Taliban and the USA since last one year, no tangible progress has been noticed till date. PM Imran Khan visited Washington in July 2019 and had a meeting with US president Donald Trump and both agreed that US and NATO forces will be withdrawn from Afghanistan by September 2019. Withdrawal of US troops from Afghanistan was one of the electoral pledges of president Trump in 2016 election. PM Imran Khan was very happy after his US trip and stated that it seems that he has won another world cup. The question is very complicated. According to leading Pakistani columnist, Khurram Husain:[6]

> "For Pakistan, the biggest fear is that there might be a repeat of 1990 all over again. The fear is that once they are gone, the Americans will forget all about this region (their foreign policy already lays limited stakes in South Asia beyond Afghanistan), and Pakistan will once again be left to face the consequences all on its own. The other side of this fear is what happens if the Americans are not able to get all that they want out of the process currently under way. Trump's smile has saddled Pakistan with a steep ask, and nobody here wants to know what his frown might look like if things don't work out as expected."

However Chief of Pakistani army, General Bajwa also accompanied Imran Khan in his Washington trip to assure US that both military and civilian establishment are on the same page on Afghanistan issue but given the prevailing nature of Pakistani army it seems unlikely that they will allow a peaceful Afghanistan. In August 2019, PTI government extended second term to General Bajwa and he will in the helms of affairs till November 2022. In this situation there is a possibility of another serious round of civil war among various stake holders within Afghanistan and of course, Pakistani army will try to consolidate its own puppet as they did in 1994 for Taliban. This will be another delicate challenge for India, Iran, Central Asia, Russia and China given the interconnectivity of their security architecture with terror and its interlinkage with Afghanistan-Pakistan zone.

It is significant that Pakistan has facilitated this process. But thinking of Pakistani establishments may change once the US led NATO forces will be withdrawn from Afghanistan. In post-Pulwama (February 2019) and Balakot, Pakistan threatened that if India is hostile then Afghan peace process supported by her will be derailed, which was strongly opposed by Afghanistan. This argument Pakistan can again repeat in the backdrop of abrogation of article 370 from Kashmir.

In August 2019, Modi government has scrapped special status of Kashmir while removing article 370. Pakistan adopted all brands of propaganda to catch the fish from the troubled waters but hardly any exclusive support was offered to it. Chinese which is all weathered friend of Pakistan despite visits of high-profile Pakistani leaders were guarded when they suggested to settle the problem on the basis of existing bilateral framework of resolving disputes.

After Pakistani foreign minister Beijing visit in August 2019 in the backdrop of scrapping of article 370, joint statement stressed "China recognises that the Kashmir dispute must be properly resolved "based on the UN Charter, relevant UN Security Council resolutions and bilateral agreement".[7]

According to eminent strategic thinker Pervez Hood-boy, Pakistan status at the global stage has reduced a lot

> "Third, patrons have their own interests. To call a friendship higher than the Himalayas, deeper than the oceans, and stronger than steel may be good poetry. But patrons act after a cold calculation of losses and gains. China's silence on Kashmir and its climb-down in May at the United Nations on Masood Azhar's blacklisting shows just how carefully it weighs things. Saudi Arabia, on which Pakistan pins its hopes, went along with India."[8]

The editorial comment of the prestigious Pakistani daily 'Dawn' comments vindicated Pakistan's isolation on this issue.

> "The crisis in India-held Kashmir could trigger global consequences, yet the world has not responded to Pakistan's urgent exhortations with the level of robustness as situation warrants. Instead of full-throated condemnation, there is a language of equivocation.
>
> Indeed, some countries, most notably US and UAE, have even gone along with India's brazenly false assertion that stripping Kashmir, an internationally recognised disputed territory, of its special status is an "internal matter". Saudi Arabia's bland reaction thus far avoids expressing any opinion whatsoever."[9]

Despite Pakistan's all round mobilization and British Member of Parliament protest, United Arab Emirates has conferred its highest national award to PM Modi. Pakistani diplomacy has been frustrated after it. It is vindicated with the following statement of Pakistani foreign minister Shah Mehmood Qureshi:[10]

> "International relations are above religious sentiments. The UAE and India have a history of relations in connection with investment. However, I will soon have a meeting with the UAE foreign minister to inform him about the prevailing situation in India-held Kashmir," he said while responding to media queries regarding the grant of the UAE's highest civilian award to Indian Prime Minister Narendra Modi."

This statement also vindicates that Pakistan's appeal even within the Muslim world has reduced to bare minimum and these countries are also not taking interest in Pakistani version of the Kashmir saga.

> "It's a game-changer in Indian politics... It's not like a third party can get India to walk back its decision. The deed is done," says the usually strong India critic, Michael Kugelman, at the Asia Program in Woodrow Wilson Centre in Washington DC.[11]
>
> In the last five days, Pakistan Prime Minister Imran Khan has lost the "Great Game on Kashmir". As the NYT wrote in a column on Friday, "Pakistan runs out of options on Kashmir".[12]

Kashmir has been core issue between India and Pakistan and also remains an unfinished agenda of partition. It has been provided sustainable legitimacy for the illegitimate hegemony of the Pakistani army over the decision-making process of Pakistan. Kashmir has been an apple of discord between both countries and for many experts core issue of distrust. Pakistan has been claiming over Kashmir because of its religious and geographical proximities. It is also an open secret that despite many wars and cross border terrors in Kashmir, Pakistan was not able to snatch Kashmir from India. This has helped the Pakistani military to remain as the most important and powerful institutions of the country. In May 2014, COAS, Raheel Sharif had stated that the Kashmir is jaguar vein of Pakistan, this sentiment was retreated again by PM Nawaz Sharif in August 2016 and in post removal of article 370, Imran Khan is singing the Kashmir saga. Both military and civilian establishment played victim cards on Kashmir when their particular position was threatened within Pakistani power structure. Due to Kashmir the army availed lion share in the resource s less than Pakistan economy. This process has helped the militaries of the country and thus negated fundamental freedom and human rights. Abrogation of article 370 by India in August 2019 has snatched this point from Pakistan. It will also be detrimental for the sustainable hegemony of the military because now questions will be raised from different quarters that military could not protect core interests of Pakistan.

Aisha Siddiqa, an eminent military expert of Pakistan has however opined in her famous book 'Pakistan Military Inc' that even if India will hand over Kashmir to Pakistan in a silver plate, there is hardly any guarantee that animosity between both rivals will end. For the time being both countries must sustain the dialogue process on Kashmir till its final resolution and in the meantime cooperate on the areas where there are hardly any divergences like trade and commerce.

Cross border terror in India has been supported by Pakistan. Pakistan has understood the reality that even after 3-1/2 war they could not gain the desired results therefore adopted the tactics of thousands cuts propelled for the first time by Z.A. Bhutto. After Ajmal Kasab, few terrorists from Pakistan have been caught alive in Kashmir, which vindicates that Pakistan has tacit understanding with the terror groups based there.

Till date the master mind of Mumbai attack, Hafiz Sayeed and Pulwama attack, Masood Azhar are enjoying full freedom and spreading hatred against India despite their designation by the United Nations as international terrorists. Dawood Ibrahim is also rooming in Pakistan. Pakistan must understand that sustainability of its support to the terror groups has been proved detrimental for the stability of the country. Just before PM Imran Khan July 2019 Washington visit, Pakistan arrested Hafiz Sayeed and Masood Azhar was placed under house arrest. It was only for the lip services. Both have been arrested many times by the agencies previously too but no prosecution has taken place despite India's sustainable request for their role in terror attacks from Mumbai to Pulwama.

Pakistani army will never reconcile cordial relations with India. It could hamper its monopoly over the system which it has been availing since independence.

According to Wilkie Boris "The people in charge-bureaucrat's on the one side, army officer on the other—were at great pains in protecting and dominating the state field against adversaries from in and outside the official borders. Internally, they had to confine their effort to some 'core' state; secular and most essential rules inside narrowly drawn boundaries, they had to prepare for war, since Pakistan's territorial status (if we include—as we must—following official ideology-Jammu & Kashmir) was not clearly determined. More importantly, external and internal matters were mixed right from the start, giving the army a key state building role."[13]

Economic cooperation on India–China module could be emulated by India and Pakistan also. India has already extended MFN status to Pakistan long back in 1995 but despite WTO requirements, Pakistan has not reciprocated it till date. By 2015 India and Pakistan bilateral trade projected to reach $10 billion but it has the capability to cross $35 billion as per new World Bank estimates if proper will power will be applied. Unfortunately, it remains only $3.7 billion in fy 2018-19. In post abrogation of article 370 by India, Pakistan suspended trade with India. It has hampered Pakistani business houses and common man together. According to Dawn, leading Pakistani English Daily "Solidarity with Kashmiris may be the common rhetoric among all businessmen. But when it comes to business interests, especially of small-scale firms that may be unable to shift vendors or absorb extra costs, commercial interests may supplant patriotism. Those who have the scale and the availability of alternate avenues can afford nationalistic sentiments."[14]

Army has been always powerful in Pakistan. In the words of former army chief, General Jehangir Karamat, "Whenever there is a breakdown in...stability, as has happened frequently in Pakistan, the military translate its potential into the will to dominate, and we have military intervention flowed by military rule."[15] Since independence and out of 72 years of history, Pakistani army has ruled for 32 years and when it was not ruling it was shaping the policies related to core issues of foreign policies like Kashmir, Afghanistan, United States, China and Nuclear etc. when civilian regime is ruled over by Pakistan leading to empirical experience which vindicated that more anti Indian megalomania prevailed in the Pakistani system in comparison with the periods directly ruled by the army.

Post-Balakot Challenges

Terror has been sustainable integral fulcrum of Pakistan's foreign policy. Pakistan supports all terror related activities in India right from north east to Kashmir.

Kashmir as per Pakistani perception remained an unfinished agenda of partition. Due to majority of the Muslims, Pakistan believes that Kashmir is its natural territory. Despite all round efforts including terror, Pakistan could not snatch Kashmir from India since last 72 years but it has dismantled the growth of the country and undermined democratic institutions. Abrogation of article 370 by Modi government has further reduced the importance of Kashmir in bilateral relations.

In February 2019, suicide terror attacks killed 40 para military soldiers in Pulwama, Kashmir. It created huge public demand to teach Pakistan a lesson. PM Modi assured the nation that it will be revenged soon and finally on 26th February early morning, Indian Air Force bombarded terror organisation HUGI training centre at Balakot, Pakhtunwah province. It was the maiden attack on Pakistani soil after 1971 war. This early morning air force attack on training centre had eliminated over 250 terrorists. Next day Air force plane intruded in Pakistani space and crashed but pilot Abhinandan was caught by the Pakistani army. He was released within days.

United States NSA, John Bolton had stated that India has the right to retaliate and US support India in its fight against terrorism. According to Munir Akram, Pakistan's representative in the United Nations General Assembly:

> "Pakistan is near if not in the eye of the brewing Sino-US storm. Neutrality is not an option for Pakistan. The US has already chosen India as its strategic partner to counter China across the 'Indo-Pacific' and South Asia. The announced US South Asia policy is based on Indian domination of the subcontinent. Notwithstanding India's trade squabbles with Donald Trump, the US establishment is committed to building up India militarily to counter China.
>
> On the other hand, strategic partnership with China is the bedrock of Pakistan's security and foreign policy. The Indo-US alliance will compel further intensification of the Pakistan-China partnership. Pakistan is the biggest impediment to Indian hegemony over South Asia and the success of the Indo-US grand strategy. Ergo, they will try to remove or neutralise this 'impediment'."[16]

Saudi Arabia, Iran and all other important Muslim countries also supported India. Despite Pakistan's strong resistance, Indian foreign minister, Sushma Swaraj delivered key note address in OIC (Organisation of Islamic Countries) India demanded handover of terror mastermind, Masood Azhar which was refuted by Pakistan. China also played almost neutral stand and advised both parties to resolve the dispute through dialogue. China however blocked designation of Azhar as global terrorist at the UN despite global support for it. It was 4th veto in row since last few years to save Azhar. But in May 2019, China lifted its veto (technical objections) and came under huge global diplomatic pressure mobilised by India and Azhar was declared global terrorist by the UN. It was one of the most significant diplomatic victory of India over Pakistan in recent years. Through this international community has accepted that Pakistan is the nursery of the terror networks.

Despite open hostility, Pakistan could not threat to use its nuclear devices and through this episode, India has successfully exposed Pakistani physiological edge that its nukes are big deterrent.

Kamran Akhtar, Director General Arms Control and Disarmament, Ministry of Foreign Affairs—told journalists at an interaction hosted by the Islamabad Policy Institute (IPI) that deterrence worked despite dangerous escalation witnessed in the last week of February 2019. Akhtar also indirectly accepted the fact that deterrence was not worked as per the established perceptions.

He said deterrence was largely a misunderstood concept and "some have come to believe that even a stone cannot be hurled at us". It by no means implied that India could now do nothing against Pakistan, he maintained while explaining how the Indian Air Force intruded into Pakistani airspace despite knowing that Pakistan possessed nukes. He cautioned that the misunderstood concept of deterrence could undermine public confidence and work against deterrence from psychological and political point of view:

> "If Indians are trying to sell this narrative that deterrence failed then it is an irresponsible and dangerous narrative, which could undermine strategic stability and lead to escalation for India would be responsible."[17]

Concluding Observations

Jinnah was the founder of Pakistan even though he was advocating for peaceful relations between both countries. On his final flight from Delhi he conveyed this message to the new Indian government

> "I bid farewell to the citizens of Delhi, amongst them I have many friends of all communities and I earnestly appeal to everyone to live in this great and historic city with peace. The past must be buried and let us start afresh as two independent sovereign states of Hindustan (India) and Pakistan. I wish Hindustan prosperity and peace."[18]

Jinnah died 13 months after partition. Mullah-military alliance took over the levers of power in the absence of able second tier leadership. Due to this prevailing situation, Pakistan has perceived India as their existential enemy from its existence. In recent years, Pakistan has witnessed killings of thousands of innocent citizens. This has triggered a smaller debate in Pakistan that its western border is more dangerous than its eastern border for national security. According to BBC, defense analyst Talat Masood "Pakistan army for the first time has admitted that the real threat is emanating internally and along the western borders and not from India, which was previously considered as number one enemy of the state.[19]

Through emulating China-India model, Pakistan could earn the financial leverage to eradicate its fundamental problems. Pakistan is confronting its biggest ever financial crisis since independence and its foreign reserves has gone down to the bare minimum of $7 billion as July 2019. But again, all powerful army has prevented it to release. There is a fear in Pakistan that due to huge in size India will be the ultimate beneficiary. But question remains that Pakistan has already accorded MFN status to China, which is superior economy than India. Pakistan can learn some lessons from this experience. It is an era of globalisation and despite being rhetoric, it is clear that every country has to cooperate with each other in order to sustain their developmental processes.

Pakistan could not ensure sustainable development without ensuring peace with India. Being a nuclear power both countries are aware of the consequences of conflicts. As pointed out by E. Sridharan "Explicit nuclearization with a demonstrated missile capability has assured Pakistan's security in a way that reduces the sensitivity to relative gains in the military sphere... Pakistan is more secure vis-à-vis a possible Indian military threat than ever before... Therefore, it has less to fear and much to gain from greater economic engagement with India."[20]

It is also true with lesser sense for India. It is well perceived by the Modi led BJP government. The fact remains that despite its hawkish posture, the BJP government has the capacity to deal with Pakistan properly.

India has emerged as an Asian power and aspiration for global power. India must shed its anger and engage with Pakistan at the lower level and must prove that she is a responsible country. PM Modi has pledged to ensure India's aspirations of $5 trillion economy by 2024. Through this process India cannot only sustain its developmental process but also convince the global communities that despite all odds it is also abided by reconciliation and international norms in South Asia. Relations with Pakistan was significant challenge for Modi-1 and it will be again a delicate challenge during Modi-2 (2019-2024).

France and Germany fought many bitter wars and they fought both World Wars from different poles and lost huge number of their populace. But they have learnt a good lesson from their bitter experiences. The youth of France and Germany have played a vital role to bridge the gaps between the two countries. Both countries exchanged six million youth, who got education in each other's country. The Elyse Treaty of 1963 brought the two rivals closer for progress and prosperity. Both are cooperating in a massive way under the framework of the EU. India and Pakistan share not only common border but common fate as well therefore they must forget the past and cooperate.

India and Pakistan are neighbors and they must live with peace and stability. Cordial relations with each other will lead to win-win situation for both. This will act as a facilitator of global peace for all. Of course, Pakistan will not reciprocate Indian gestures but India must sustain its soft efforts for durability of peace and tranquility between both countries.

NOTES

1. Iqbal, Rana Saleem (ed), The Quaid on Civil Servants: Speeches and Statements, October 1947 to August 1948, National Documental Centre, Islamabad, 2007.
2. 2014 among deadliest years in AF with 10 k civilian casualties, The Times of India, New Delhi, August 9, 2015.
3. Afghanistan civilian deaths hit record high in 2018: UN, Aljazeera, 24 February 2019.
4. The rise of the militant Islamic State affiliate in Afghanistan, AP, August 19, 2019.
5. Blame Game between India, Pak has to stop, *The Indian Express*, New Delhi, August 24, 2013.
6. Khurram Husain, Trump's Smile, *Dawn*, Karachi, 1 August 2019.
7. Naveed Siddiqui, China to 'Uphold justice for Pakistan on Kashmir Issue, *Dawn*, Karachi, August 9, 2019.
8. Pervez Hoodbhoy, Client and Patrons, *Dawn*, Karachi, July 6, 2019.
9. A Tepid Response, Editorial, *Dawn*, Karachi, August 9, 2019.
10. Shakeel Ahmed, FM moves to paper over UAE award for Modi, *Dawn*, Karachi, August 26, 2019.
11. Manish Pandaya, Modi's 370 removal a game-changer, Pak isolated: U.S. experts, Print, New Delhi, August 11, 2019.
12. Ibid.
13. Boris, Wilke, 'State Formation and the Military in Pakistan; Reflections on the Armed Forces, their State and some of their Competitors, Working Paper, No.2, Research Unit of Wars, Armament and Development, University of Hamburg, 2001, p. 26.
14. Fatima S Attarwala, Patriotism vs Commercial Interests, Dawn, Karachi, August 19, 2019.
15. Nawaz, Shuja, Crossed Swords, Its Army, and the Wars Within, Oxford University Press, Oxford, 2008, pp. xxvii-xxviii.
16. Munir Akram, Pakistan and Sino-US Cold War, *Dawn*, Karachi, June 9, 2019.

17 Deterrence didn't fail during stand-off with India, *Dawn*, Karachi, June 1, 2019.
18 Mohammad Ali Jinnah (1989) Quaid-i-Azam Mohammad Ali Jinnah; Speeches and Statements 1947-48, Islamabad, Government of Pakistan, Ministry of Information and Broadcasting, Directorate of Films and Publications, p. 39.
19 *Dawn*, Karachi, January 9, 2013.
20 Sridharan E, 'Improving Indo-Pakistan relations; International Relations Theory, Nuclear Deterrence and possibilities for economic cooperation, Contemporary South Asia, Vol. 14, No. 3, September 2005, p. 322.

25

India–Taiwan Relations:
Looking towards the Future

Sumit Kumar

The post-Cold War has witnessed a profound shift in India's policy towards Taiwan. This is evident from the fact while the two sides have not only established unofficial diplomatic-cum-economic ties with each other, New Delhi and Taipei have also developed cooperation in the fields of education, science & technology, agro-agricultural, automobile and others. Sure, the coming of the BJP-led government in India and the DPP government in Taiwan has further strengthened the ties between them. This is evident from the fact that the total trade volume between the two countries rose to $6.3 billion in 2017.[1]

However, these positive developments notwithstanding, the relationship continues to face some inherent problems. Of course, managing China is a major problem. Though both the countries consider China as a common security threat, they do not want to jeopardy their bilateral ties with China. It is in this context that the present tries to examine India's interests in Taiwan. It also intends to analyses areas of cooperation between the two countries. The Chapter also deals with the challenges both the countries are facing in deepening their bilateral ties and finally recommends some policy prescriptions for enhancing cooperation between India and the Taiwan. However, proceeding further, it would appropriate to examine the question of Taiwan's identity as an independent country in international relations.

The Status of Taiwan: An Overview

Taiwan, officially the Republic of China (ROC), claims as a sovereign state in East Asia.[2] The Republic of China, originally based in mainland China, now governs the island of Taiwan, which makes up over 99% of its territory as well as Penghu, Kinmen, Matsu and other minor islands. Neighbouring states include the People's Republic of China to the west, Japan to the east and northeast, and the Philippines to the south. Taipei is the seat of the central government. New Taipei, encompassing the metropolitan area surrounding Taipei proper, is the most populous city.

Historically, Taiwan, formerly known as "Formosa", was mainly inhabited by Taiwanese aborigines until the Dutch and Spanish settlement during the Age of Discovery in the 17th century, when Han Chinese began immigrating to the island.[3] In 1662, the pro-Mingloyalist Koxinga expelled the Dutch and established the first Han Chinese polity on the island, the Kingdom of Tungning. The Qing Dynasty of China later defeated the kingdom of Tungning and annexed Taiwan.[4] When Taiwan was ceded to Japan in 1895, the majority of Taiwan's inhabitants were Han Chinese either by ancestry or by assimilation. The Republic of China (ROC) was established in China in 1912 and after Japan's surrender in 1945, the ROC assumed the control of Taiwan.[5]

The Chinese-Taiwanese Conflict began in 1949, after the Chinese Communist Party, led by Mao Tse-tung, overthrew the nationalist government of the Republic of China (ROC). It was during this time that President Chiang Kai-sheck of the ROC and his political party, the Kuomintang (KMT), was forced to flee with soldiers and civilians loyal to them to the Chinese island of Taiwan and re-establish the Chinese nationalist government. In 1950, the Chinese Communist Party established the People's Republic of China (PRC) and invaded Taiwan with the aim of unifying all of China under its rule. However, the Chinese Communist Party failed completely in achieving its goal, as the US came to the rescue of the ROC by sending its naval forces and. Since then, both countries have existed in a state of neither complete independence nor integration, of neither war nor peace. The PRC claims that the ROC ceased to exist in 1949 and that Taiwan is a province of "one China." In fact, the PRC also asserts itself to be the sole legal representation of China and claims as its 23rd providence to under its sovereignty, denying the status and existence of ROC as a sovereign state. The PRC has threatened the use of military force as a response to any formal declaration of Taiwanese independence, or if it deems peaceful reunification no longer possible. The ROC also does not recognise the PRC. In fact, the ROC continues to treat itself as a lawful Government of entire China. For it, Taiwan, a Chinese territory under the two declarations, legitimately belonged to the ROC. The Taiwan crisis took an ugly turn in August 1958 when the People's Liberation Army (PLA) bombed the Taiwanese islands of Kinmen and Matsu.

Not surprisingly, the immediate reaction of the world community to the crisis was divided. As the Cold War was in full swing and the world was virtually divided between two power blocks-the US and the Soviet Union, countries took their stands on the issue in the light of the fact that which block they belonged to. This became more glaring when the Korean War and other Cold War compulsions led the US to refuse to recongised the PRC as an independent country, continuing to recongise ROC in order to prevent ROC from becoming a communist follower. The US and its allied countries also helped ROC in retaining its seat in the United Nations Security Council (UNSC). On the other hand, the Soviet Union took no time in switching over its recognition from the ROC to PRC.

However, in 1971, the ROC received a big blow when the UN General Assembly passed Resolution 2758 restoring all its rights to the People's Republic of China. The resolution also recognises the representatives of its Government as the only legitimate representatives of China to the United Nations. Consequently, ROC lost its seat to the PRC in the Security Council. This in turn made it clear that the United Nation. In 1979, the US also recognised the People' Republic of China as an independent country. And, most countries also switched recognition to the PRC. These developments indeed went against the ROC' maintain its position as an independent state and get international recognition as the representative of mainland China. Not only this, the KMT Government came under scathing criticism of western countries that there was no democracy in Taiwan. This was evident from the fact that the KMP Government had put in place martial law. There was controlled media and there was no opposition. At the same time, some dissenting voices against the Government also started being raised. Thus, the KMT Government realised that fact that if it continued to ignore the ground reality, public resentment would further increase against it, and China could use the internal crisis of Taiwan as a pretext to remove the KMP Government, annexing ROC with PRC. It was against this background that Taiwan began to witness a democratisation process in late 1980s and 1990s. The beginning of the democratisation process was indeed an important development in the sense that people genuinely got an opportunity to participate freely in the political process in the country, realising their natural right to freedom and equality. This, in turn, soon led to the formational of other parties. For instance, 1986, the

Democratic Progressive Party was established as the first opposition party to the KMT. The DPP fundamentally was formed by those Taiwanese people who seek for complete independence from mainland China. In turn, the legitimacy of Taiwan's bid for international recognition as a sovereign entity was considerably boosted in the eyes of Western popular opinion by its rapid democratization under the presidency of Lee Tenghui.[6]

In the meantime, Taiwan also began to register high growth rates, becoming one of the Asian Tigers in Asia. Today, Taiwan is ranked as the 19th largest economy in the world in terms of purchasing (PPP), and as 18th in terms of gross domestic product (GDP). The economy of Taiwan has also been ranked the highest in Asia for 2015 Global Entrepreneurship Index (GEI) for specific strengths.[7] Certainly, Taiwan's robust and growing economy started receiving the attention of the rest of the world, with countries expressing their desire to establish economic ties with Taiwan. This is evident from the fact that Taiwan enjoys a special status in the International economic order by getting the membership of most of the International economic organisations including the World Trade Organisation (WTO), Asia-Pacific Economic Cooperation (APEC), Asian Development Bank (ADB) and others. At the same time, Taiwan has close economic ties with the United States, Japan, European and Asian Countries. By the end of July, 2015, Taiwan's foreign exchange reserves have increased to US$ 421.96 billion.[8]

Taiwan has also assumed added significance in international politics in view of its strategic significance. As most of other countries fell that a rising China would attempt to change the balance of power in its favour at least first in East Asia, these counties are of the opinion that as long as Taiwan remains independent of Beijing, much of China's increased capability and resources will be absorbed and digested by the Taiwan issue, which will effectively prevent Beijing from inflicting security threat to other neighbouring countries.[9] At the same time, a war over Taiwan would affect all states in the region and many beyond. Even in the absence of conflict, Taiwan has an important role to play in ensuring sea-lanes in its backyard.

These economic, strategic and other factors have, therefore, scaled up Taiwan's stature in international politics. Thus, despite the fact that only 21 UN member states and the Holy See currently maintain official diplomatic with the ROC, one may estimate the increasing importance of Taiwan in the world from the fact that it has unofficial ties with most other states via its representative.[10]

India's Policy towards India

Historically, India has close ties with Republic of China. However, following the establishment of People's Republic of China in the Mainland, India under the leadership of Prime Minister Jawaharlal Nehru decided to establish diplomatic relations with the PRC, parting with the ROC. Nehru informed Indian Parliament in March 1950 that the PRC had been recognised because "it is a question of recognising a major event in history," and because it controlled 'practically the entire mainland of China." Moreover, its Government was stable and unlikely "to be supplanted or pushed away by any force." He informed the Parliament that the recognition of the PRC and the exchange of diplomatic missions had only happened after all the facts had been carefully ascertained.[11] The successive Indian Governments also maintained the consistency in India's stand on the issue of China-Taiwan relations.

But, in the 1990s the Narsimha Rao Government reoriented India's policy towards Taiwan. More to the point, In the 1990s India faced some serious domestic and foreign policy challenges. For instance, domestically, India had to deal with one of the worst economic crises in the post-independent era. In fact, it did not have sufficient foreign reservoirs to buy oil even for a month. Externally, India needed to adapt to a new international order which emerged following the end of the Cold War. In turn, India lost its time-tested friend—the Soviet Union, which had not only provided security cover to India, but also financial and defence assistance during Cold War time. China started flexing its political military power against India by developing close ties with India's neighbours. On the other hand, its lack of interest or oversight had resulted in complete cut off between India and China's neighbours in East Asia, despite the fact that India has historically close cultural and economic ties with these countries of East Asia. Thus, these and other factors forced India to make fundamental changes in its foreign policy orientation towards East Asia. It was in this context that the P.V. Narsimha Rao Government focused on reviving India's historical ties with East Asia Countries by initiating the Look East policy.

Of course, Taiwan figured pre-eminently in India's look east policy for various reasons. First, Taiwan's economic muscle, particularly its huge foreign exchange reserves was the main attraction for India. Second, having emerged as a major economic giant in the world, China stared modernising its military and asserting its position in the Indian Ocean. At the same time, Beijing initiated the policy of string of Pearls aimed at encircling India by winning over the South Asian neighbours. China's move forced the Indian strategists to search for options helping

India in pushing back China from this region. Given its strategic location and acrimonious relations with China, Taiwan was viewed a much valued country by India to forge close ties with in order to contain Beijing.

Consequently, a delegation led by Inder Kumar Gujral visited Taiwan in 1992 with the purpose of inviting the business community of Taiwan to invest in India. The delegation met the President, Prime Minister, legislators and top-ranking officials.[12] Subsequently, India and Taiwan established 'unofficial' relations in 1995 with the establishment of the India-Taipei Association (ITA) in Taipei to promote interactions between India and Taiwan, including business, tourism and cultural and people-to-people exchanges. The ITA also serves as a de facto Indian embassy, authorised to issue visas and provide other consular services.[13] In the same year, Taiwan opened the Taipei Economic and Cultural Centre (TECC) in New Delhi.[14]

When the Democratic Progressive Party under the leadership of Chen Shi-bian was voted into power, the prospects of improving ties between India and Taiwan increased in view of the fact that the DPP had fought the election on the slogan of anti-China and pro-independence. True to the expectations, the new regime of Chen Shi-bian appeared interested in cementing the ties between the two countries. This facilitated interactions between people to people. Following the 2001 earthquake in Gujarat, the Taiwanese Government had offered a million dollar relief package and Taiwanese Vice-President Annette Lu expressed her desire to visit India. However, the Indian Government refused to give her a visa and instead, Parris H. Chang, Deputy Secretary General of Taiwan's National Security Council (NSC) came to India, bringing the relief material.[15]

On October 17, 2002, the directors of the ITA and the TECC signed the Agreement on Promotion and Protection of Investment. In 2002, Vincent Chen spent three months at the Institute for Defence Studies and Analyses (IDSA) in New Delhi as a Visiting Fellow. He was probably the first Taiwanese scholar to spend that much time in India. K. Santhanam, the then Director General of the IDSA, visited Taiwan. In 2004, Taiwan began offering the Taiwan Scholarship and Mandarin Scholarship (National Huayu Enrichment Scholarship) to Indian students and the Faculty of Social Science at the University of Delhi and Taiwan's National Chengchi University (NCCU) also signed an MOU in 2007.[16] Furthermore, China Airlines started a direct flight between New Delhi and Taipei in 2003, establishing direct air contact between Taiwan and India. Although the DPP government started with low-key contacts, Taiwan soon began making further efforts in the direction of strategic cooperation with India.[17] In an unexpected move, George Fernandes, former Defence Minister of India, visited Taiwan twice in his personal capacity—first in 2004 and again in 2006—at the invitation of the Taiwan Think Tank.[18] His visit was first such visit by any senior most Indian politician since the independence of India. His focus on "China is India's No. 1 enemy" was seen very encouraging by the DPP Government.[19]

The DPP Government moved to explore the possibility of security cooperation with India. With this hope, the DPP Government sent several mid-level military officers to India during 2000-08 as a part of its delegations. In fact, *United Daily News* (UDN) quoted an unnamed military official as saying "The military cooperation is limited to exchange of military intelligence." UDN military reporter Lu Tehyun wrote that "Taiwan has sent a military attache to its trade office in New Delhi and an Indian Air Force officer ... visited Taiwan at the invitation of Taiwan Air Force Commander-in-Chief Chen Chaomin."[20]

In 2006, the Taiwan-India Cooperation Council (TICC), a private organisation was established in Taipei, with Democratic Progressive Party (DPP) Chairman Yu Shyikun elected as its first chairman. The Council aims to act as a bridge to promote economic exchanges and broader cooperation on bilateral interests between Taiwan and India. At the occasion, Yu further said:

> India is seen as having the best potential among the four golden BRIC[21]— Brazil, Russia, India and China countries. Besides, Taiwan and India's collaboration in software and hardware and India's overall economic takeoff will provide even more opportunities for Taiwan-India economic and trade cooperation.[22]

Yu emphasised the fact that the idea to promote closer Taiwan-India exchanges is in line with the Indian government's "Look East policy," which overlaps with Taiwan's "Go South Policy." On the other hand, Brigadier Arun Sahgal, the deputy director of India's United Service Institution, attended the council's founding ceremony. He said the council provides a channel for India to reach out to East Asia, a policy the Indian government has been working toward in recent years. Arun Sahgal categorically stated:

> "India's 'Look East Policy' engages mostly with Southeast Asia, but India is looking for much greater engagement with East Asia. It is in this context that our relationship with Taiwan is extremely important. We would like to use our new-found confidence and new-found economic development model to engage to a much greater degree with Taiwan."[23]

In 2007, the ITA and the TECC signed an MOU on behalf of India's Department of Science and Technology (DST) under the Ministry of Science and Technology and Taiwan's NSC. As per the MOU, the DST and the NSC hold annual meetings alternately in New Delhi and Taipei, which are attended by four to five representatives from each side. The main purpose of the annual meeting is to invite research proposals into begin with, Taiwan Scholarship was provided by Ministry of Education (MOE), Ministry of Economy Affairs (MOEA), and the National Science Council (NSC).[24]

India-Taiwan Ties under the KMT Government

When the KMT Government came to power in 2008, there was a growing concern in sections of Taiwanese experts that India-Taiwan ties would not receive the same priority in the foreign policy of the President Ma Ying-jeou Government, given the fact that the KMP party carries strong inclination towards mainland China. However, the act of President Ma Ying-jeou Government did not collaborate this apprehension. For instance,, Ma Ying-jeou, then as the Presidential candidate of the KMP party, had already visited New Delhi to diversify Taiwanese cooperation with Indian businesses. Apart from the reported meetings with certain mainstream political and business leaders, Ma Ying-jeou addressed a gathering at Indian Council for World Affairs at New Delhi on June 12, making it a KMT event after six decades at the same venue. While emphasising expanding relations with India, which he said are "old friends, exploring new opportunities," a major portion of his speech consisted, surprisingly, of tensions in Taiwan Straits—displaying internal political differences on a range of issues between the KMT and DPP.[25]

India and Taiwan signed the Double Taxation Avoidance Agreement in 2011 and the Customs Cooperation Agreement. This agreement clearly reflected the growing synergy between India and Taiwan, especially in the economic area. In particular, the DTA aims at establishing the taxing rights over permanent establishments in each country, while reduced withholding taxes on dividends and interest should promote a rise in the flow of capital investment. At the same time, a Customs Cooperation Agreement between the two sides was also signed on the same occasion which came into effect on August 1, 2011.[26] The Ministry of Economic Affairs of Taiwan Government established the India Task Force in 2010.[27] There are five sub-groups of this Task Force: Economic Cooperation, Industrial Cooperation, Trade Cooperation, Education Cooperation and Economic Cooperation Agreement (ECA). These sub-groups hold separate meetings with Government agencies. The Task Force has made two recommendations: the Government of Taiwan should encourage private sector companies to invest in India and the Government should send more delegations to India. Indian Federation of Indian Chambers of Commerce and Industry (FICCI) and the Taiwan External Trade Development Council (TAITRA) signed the Carnet Protocol in 2013.[28] The Chung-hua Institution of Economic Research (CIER) and the Indian Council of Research on International Economic Relations (ICRIER) conducted a joint feasibility study on a FTA/ECA. The Bureau of Foreign Trade and the office of Trade Negotiation in Taiwan supervised this study.[29]

The most significant evidence of Taiwan-India relations warming up was provided when ROC President Ma Ying-jeou made a stopover in Mumbai en route to Africa in early April, an event that went almost unnoticed by India's media. The visit, part of a phenomenon called "refueling diplomacy," is historic because India had never allowed a serving ROC president to land on Indian soil. The ROC Ministry of Foreign Affairs described Ma's stopover as a "sign of improving ties" with India, even though New Delhi itself barely remarked on the event.[30]

India's decision to green light Ma's stopover indicates that the country is slowly but surely asserting an independent position in foreign affairs, demonstrating an unprecedented nonchalance towards mainland China, which generally reacts by kicking up a stink whenever it finds Taiwan getting too close to any nation. Of course, the present state of tranquility in the Taiwan Strait, characterised by growing trade and direct air links between the two sides, contributed to India's decision to allow Ma to land in Mumbai. India, of course, does not need mainland China's prior approval to permit visits by foreign heads of state on its soil. In addition to allowing Ma's stopover, New Delhi has been taking some "bold initiatives," to quote Indian experts, by encouraging its companies to explore for oil and gas in the disputed South China Sea with Vietnam. This is a sign of India's growing assertiveness in foreign affairs where it has, in the past, played a low-key role. At the same time, another sign of this can be seen in the island's move to open a representative office in Chennai, bringing the total on the subcontinent to two. There is no question that strengthening bilateral ties have necessitated this development.[31]

India-Taiwan bilateral trade has also grown from the 1995 levels when the bilateral trade was reportedly around $700 million. The trade volume between India-Taiwan has risen from $700 million in 1995 to $6 billion in 2013. More than 70 Taiwanese firms had invested in India by the end of 2013.[32] Bilateral business and other forms of cooperation are more evident in the IT sector. Companies such as Acer, Asus, D-link and HTC are major Taiwanese brands recognized in India. Taiwanese companies such as Hon Hai, Compal and Wintek are suppliers to multinationals such as Nokia and Motorola in India.[33] Taiwan also has an enclave on a 500 acre area in Sri City, Andhra Pradesh (property development underway for "Taiwan Formosa Industrial Park"; an exclusive zone for Taiwanese manufacturing companies in India. The park entails a total investment of around 50 million USD and over 70 companies are expected to set shop in the SEZ. In terms of institutional arrangements, one of the main agencies for promoting the India–Taiwan economic partnership is the Taiwan External Trade Development Council (TAITRA), which is a non-profit trade promotion organization under Taiwan's Ministry of Economic Affairs (MOEA). The Taiwanese construction giant, Continental Engineering Corporation (CEC) and steel giant China Steel Corporation (CSC) have business operations in India. Taiwan keeps track of India's naval build-up, and China's naval activities in the Indian Ocean.[34]

The TECC set up a new office in Chennai in 2012. The China Trust Bank opened its second branch in Sriperumbudur, Tamil Nadu. The TECC assisted and facilitated the entry of Taiwan's steel giant China Steel Corporation (CSC) into India. Initially, China Steel invested $178 million in Gujarat where it has since begun operations. The Vice-Minister of MOEA visited India in September 2013 to attend the seventh EMMA Expo held in Chennai, from 5-7 September 2013. The delegation was supposed to have economic dialogue with India's commerce ministry.[35]

The educational and academic communications between Taiwan and India have been developed smoothly in the last several years. MoU on acknowledgement of each other's university degrees was signed between Foundation for International Cooperation in Higher Education of Taiwan (FICHET) and Association of Indian Universities (AIU) in 2010, which has resulted in close and frequent academic exchange and cooperation between the two sides.[36] Now Indian students have opportunities to study in Taiwan through Taiwan Scholarships and Huayu Enrichment Scholarships provided by the Government of Taiwan. To encourage enrolment of Indian students, Taiwanese universities and colleges also provide scholarships to attract outstanding Indian students. In an average there are around 600 Indian students studying in Taiwan every year. Taiwan and India's academic cooperation is developing in fast paces. The Ministry of Education, the Government of Taiwan, established the first Taiwan Education Program (TEP) in the OP Jindal Global University in the Indian state of Haryana in 2011. Later the TEP was established in Amity University in Uttar Pradesh in 2011 in the

Jamia Millia Islamia in Delhi in 2013 and in the China Studies Centre, IIT Madras in 2013. The Taiwan Education Programme, funded by The Ministry of Education, the Government of Taiwan, works under the supervision of the National Tsing Hua University (NTHU). The aim of this joint Programme of India and Taiwan is to promote learning of Mandarin Chinese language and culture among Indian students in higher education and to facilitate greater understanding and cooperation. In so doing, while Taiwan provides teachers and teaching material, the Indian universities provide them with free accommodation and some other facilities. At the same time, in 2009, The National Tsing Hua University signed MOUs with the University of Delhi, IIT Delhi, IIT Madras, the IISC Bangalore, and. Jawaharlal Nehru University, New Delhi and the IIT Kharagpur signed and National Chiao Tung University of Taiwan signed an MOU for student exchange in 2012. These MOUs have increased mobility and interactions between Indian and Taiwanese student and teachers.[37]

The Modi Government's Policy toward Taiwan

With a new Union Government in New Delhi under the leadership of Narendra Modi, it is hoped that India would pursue a proactive foreign policy towards Taiwan. In fact, Taiwan extended its congratulations on the BJP's poll victory and on Narendra Modi to take over as prime minister and said bilateral ties are expected to be strengthened to create a win-win situation. In a letter of congratulations, the Taipei Economic and Cultural Centre in India said the Indian Lok Sabha election "went smoothly and peacefully, bearing testimony to the democratic quality and vitality of the people of India."[38] True to the expectation, Taiwan has indeed assumed an important place in Prime Minister Narendra Modi's vision of "Act-East Policy."

When Bennet Chen, deputy director general in Taiwan's economic affairs ministry's Department of Investment Services visited India in September 2014 with a 21-member delegation of automobile parts manufacturers and traders. He said:

> "In response to Prime Minister Narendra Modi's vision of 'Come and Make in India' inviting manufacturers from across the world to invest in India and help boost India's industrial growth, Taiwanese automobile manufacturers are looking forward to exploring the possibilities of business cooperation for the Taiwanese auto parts and automobile electronics makers in India."[39]

He also asserted that expanding cooperation in trade and investments highlighted the potential for further cooperation between the two countries in the manufacturing sector. Chen added that apart from the automobile sector, Taiwan looked towards India for cooperation in information technology enabled services (ITES), textiles, infrastructure development, construction and engineering.[40] Furthering Prime Minister Narendra Modi's call to foreign companies to "make in India," the India Electronics and Semiconductor Association (IESA) and Taipei Computer Association (TCA) signed a memorandum of understanding to promote local manufacturing in the field of semiconductors and electronics.[41] A pact signed between the two sides in December 2017 institutionalizing cooperation in areas, including engineering, product manufacturing, and research and development, should further boost their engagement in this field.

In 2014, the India Electronics and Semiconductor Association and Taipei Computer Association on signed a memorandum to promote local manufacturing in the field of semiconductors and electronics. In August 2015, Hon Hai Precision Industry Co, known abroad as Foxconn, one of the largest hardware manufacturers in the world, announced an investment of US$5 billion in India. China Steel has also proposed to make a US$180 million investment in India. CPC Corp, Taiwan, has proposed a US$6 billion investment in India, which would surely boost the Make in India program in the petrochemical industry. The first Taiwan Expo was held in at the Pragati Maidan, New Delhi, from May 17 to May 19, 2018. A total of 130 Taiwanese exhibitors showcased their latest technologies, products and services in the exhibition area, with products ranging from the information and communication technology, electric vehicles, auto parts and fasteners to medical devices, health and personal care, textiles, food and beverage and home products.

Challenges

However, it is also true that unless both the sides seriously address the structural constraints hampering improvement the bilateral ties, India and Taiwan may not be able to garner the economic and other benefits they hope for. For instance, while it is true that people-to-people interaction between India and Taiwan has considerably increased over the period, yet systematic efforts have hardly be taken to increase the understanding of India among Taiwanese people. This evident from the fact that the general perceptions of Taiwanese about India is this that India is not conducive economic destiny believing India does not have good infrastructure facilities like road, electricity, proper law and order which are essential for doing smooth business. The Taiwanese business community also has the strong feeling that the Indian bureaucracy is an instrument supportive for doing business in India. They believe that unless the Indian Government takes initiatives to ease the bureaucratic hurdles in order to attract foreign investment, it would not very difficult for them to invest in India.

China is another factor that has overshadowed Taiwan's economic relations with other countries. It has emerged as Taiwan's number one trading partner and investment destination, accounting for 23.07% of total trade and 19.07% of Taiwan's imports in 2016. China is the biggest and the closest market available to the Taiwanese entrepreneurs, and is capable of satiating their appetite. At the same time, it has the advantage of nearness, shared language, culture, customs and traditions where personal connections are easy to build. In comparison, India is a distant country, with an unfamiliar civilisation and language, and where personal connections and bonds are difficult to cultivate. Besides, Taiwanese entrepreneurs are more inclined to trade with the developed world rather than with the developing economies. China's export-friendly policies have been a major attraction for them. Taiwanese companies doing business in China is, in general, export-oriented; they use China to gain access to the markets of the developed world. In the case of India, they are convinced that India does not provide better, or equal, options for export.

Taiwanese companies also face stiff competition from Japan and South Korea because of India's CEPA with Japan and South Korea, and it's FTA with ASEAN. India's CEPA with South Korea and Japan, and its FTA with SEAN are major causes of worry for such Taiwanese companies as petrochemical and steel industries. With lower import tariffs on relevant products from Japan, South Korea and some ASEAN countries, which will eventually come down to zero over a period of time, some Taiwanese products have lost their competitiveness in the Indian market. This phenomenon has not only hurt the competitiveness of Taiwanese products in the Indian market, but may also discourage Taiwanese investment in India. For Instance, China Steel Corporation (CSC) indicated that the plan for the first phase of production and sales of electrical steel coils by its branch 'China Steel Corporation India Private Limited' in the state of Gujarat calls for its raw material 'cold rolled steel coils' to be supplied CSC. However, India's import tariff of 7.5 percent on cold rolled steel coils from Taiwan is excessive, and higher than the 2.5 per cent on imports from Japan and South Korea. This will significantly increase procurement costs for CSC's branch in Gujarat, seriously impacting its competitiveness and ultimately affecting the feasibility of subsequent expansion of investment in India.[42]

Another problem that India-Taiwan relations are facing is the displeasure of

Taiwanese over the fact that India does not recognise Taiwan as independent of mainland China. Thus, India's policy to deny visa to Taiwanese people to the places where Chinese people are not allowed is not seen by Taiwanese in good light. The Taiwanese business community has also expressed its reservation over the fact that Taiwanese companies like the Chinese companies, have to undergo a longer review process in India, and are not given a one-time banking clearance to bring in capital.[43] KMT Government's inclination towards PRC is also viewed as a factor which hampers the consolidation of the relationship between India and Taiwan. Consequently, India does not receive the same priority from the KMT Government as it had during the DPP Government.

The China First Policy also works as a barrier in India-Taiwan ties. For instance, this policy allows Taiwan to join any those international organisations in which statehood is not a criterion, and only if China is already a member of the organisation in question. For example, China allowed Taiwan to join the WTO only after it had joined it first. This policy is not limited to international organisations. When Taiwan succeeded in having a direct flight between New Delhi and Taipei in 2002, China asserted its China First Policy by starting direct flights between New Delhi and Beijing on April 1, 2002, four days before the flight between New Delhi and Taipei was scheduled to be inaugurated.[44]

Conclusion

These impediments notwithstanding, the prospect of India-Taiwan relations will be determined by the extent the two sides show their commitment towards cementing their improving bilateral ties. Undoubtedly, New Delhi and Taipei have their own reasons for forging close ties with each other. First, China's assertive behaviour certainly concerns India and Taiwan. As China has emerged as an economic and military power can be felt in Southeast Asia, it would be surprising if it further uses military might to annex Taiwan and bullies all other powers like the US, Japan and India to stand off this part of the region. This fact, China has already reflected its ambition of doing so by asserting that the South China belongs to China. Therefore, both the countries need to work together to push China to regulate itself. In so doing, India and Taiwan should closely work with Japan and the US-the two countries which also have similar threat perceptions from the rising China. Second, close bilateral ties would help both the sides in accelerating its economic growing. As India has an expertise in software, and our companies are looking for markets abroad, if we can marry this with Taiwanese expertise in hardware this venture would be beneficial to both sides. Third, India can have a better understanding of China's strategic behaviour by developing security ties with Taiwan. At the same time, Taiwan has seen India as an emerging region power which can work as counter-balancer to the rising China. Fourth, India and Taiwan can also engage in information sharing and cooperation to resist China's cyber-attacks. India should also understand that stability of the Taiwan Strait and South China Sea is very important for its trade interests, and it should promote a peaceful solution to regional disputes and safeguard freedom of navigation.

In the light of these common objectives, India and Taiwan need to take some concrete initiates to deepen their ties. For instance, as Taiwan has better understanding of People's Republic of China and it is also ready to host Indian military students at its National Defence University (NDU), India should utilise this opportunity to study the functioning of the Chinese military establishment. India should also promote joint bilateral military exercises, seminars and other important military engagements with Taiwan. As Taiwan expects India to allow its ships to make port visits for freshwater and fuel replenishment, India should develop naval cooperation with Taiwan at the highest level. As there is a demand of Taiwanese business community for a free trade agreement, India should address this issue in order to further facilitate trade and commerce.

At the same time, further efforts should be taken by both the sides to institutionalise their ties. This in turn would help the two sides in expanding cooperation in different areas. In so doing, a Task-Force could be constituted, either jointly or separately, by the two countries to identify possible institutional linkages and potential areas of functional cooperation between the ministries and departments on both sides. The expertise of the private sector could also be utilised to carry out more specialised sector-based studies to identify competition and complementarities within the economies.

While it is true that dialogues are held at different levels between the two sides, yet there is need for acceleration in this process. For instance, while there are interactions between think-tanks of India and Taiwan, there is need to encourage MoUs between key research institutes in India and Taiwan that have an active component of scheduled annual exchanges. It is imperative that India and Taiwan should focus on multi-level academic exchange programs (faculty exchanges, semester abroad programs with Universities, reciprocal research faculty visits, etc.) with a host of institutions across India (beyond a Delhi-centric or Taipei-centric focus) to attract domain experts (those specifically dealing with the subject matter) and allow more eclectic policy inputs to emerge.

As there is no much interaction between the people-to-people level between the two sides, there is huge lack of misgivings and misunderstandings about each other, damaging the bilateral ties. India and Taiwan should take steps to address this issue. As Buddhism is the religion of the majority of Taiwanese people and India is the home land of this religion, India should promote religion tourism to improve contacts between the people of the two sides. This step would also add to the India's economic prosperity. High-ranking officials of the two sides should visit each other and hold meetings. These visits would play a pivotal role in cementing the ties between India and Taiwan in the sense that the two sides have ironed out their misperceptions about each other.

To conclude, while it is true that India-Taiwan relations are determined and constrained by India's acceptance of "one China policy," this does not deter New Delhi to seek close security and economic ties with Taiwan. Thus, India should take bold initiatives to reach out to Taiwan, without wittingly angering China. At the same time, India should also assert its right to decide what type of relations it wish to have with Taiwan, if China dictates India not to directly deal with Taiwan.

NOTES

1. "ROC Says Taiwan, India to Strengthen Bilateral Economic Relations; Congratulates Modi," http://zeenews.india.com/business/news/economy/roc-says-taiwan-india-to-strengthen-bilateral-economic-relations-congratulates-modi_100024.html.
2. Christopher J. Carolan, "The Republic Of Taiwan: A Legal-Historical Justification for a Taiwanese Declaration of Independence," http://www.nyulawreview.org/sites/default/files/pdf/NYULawReview-75-2-Carolan.pdf
3. "Ministry of Taiwan," http://taiwanvisanoc.com/
4. "Taiwan," http://heyevent.com/venue/cebbl6tg2agika
5. "Taiwan," International Chamber For Service Industry (ICSI), http://www.icsiindia.in
6. Chris Rahman, Defending Taiwan, And Why It Matters, Naval War College Review, Autumn 2001, Vol. 54, No. 4, pp. 70-97.
7. Economy of Taiwan, https://en.wikipedia.org/wiki/Economy_of_Taiwan
8. Pan Chi-i and Lauren Hung, "Taiwan's Foreign Exchange Reserves Increase," August, 6, 2015, Focus Taiwan New Channel, http://focustaiwan.tw/news/aeco/201508060049.aspx
9. Wu Xinbo, The Taiwan Issue and U.S.–Asia/Pacific Security Strategy, *American Foreign Policy Interests*, 24, 2002, p. 2311.
10. Foreign relations of Taiwan, https://en.wikipedia.org/wiki/Foreign_relations_of_Taiwan
11. K.P. Mishra, 'India's Policy of Recognition of States and Governments', The American Journal of International Law, Vol. 55, No. 2, April 1961, p. 401, cited in Prashant Prashant Kumar Singh, Transforming *India-Taiwan Relations New Perspectives* (New Delhi: Institute for Defence and Security Analysis, Series No. 35 April 2014), p. 47.
12. 'The India-Taipei Association: A Mission Extraordinaire', Interview with Ambassador Vinod C. Khanna, Indian Foreign Affairs Journal, 5 (2), April 2010, pp. 240-251.

13. *Manesh SV,* "Good Vistas for Taiwan-India Ties," Taiwan Info, June 06, 2006, http://taiwaninfo.nat.gov.tw/ct.asp?xItem=21893&CtNode=103&htx_TRCategory=&mp=4
14. The Taipei Economic and Cultural Centre (TECC) in New Delhi, http://www.roc-taiwan.org/IN/ct.asp?xItem=481336&CtNode=5053&mp=277&xp1=
15. Prashant Kumar Singh, Transforming *India-Taiwan Relations New Perspectives* (New Delhi: Institute for Defence and Security Analysis, Series No. 35 April 2014), P. 92.
16. Ibid, p. 91.
17. Ibid, p. 92.
18. Walter C. Ladwig, III "Looking East 2: East Asia and Australasia/Oceania," in David Scott, ed., *Handbook of India's International Relations* (New Delhi: Routledge, 2011), p. 145.
19. Singh, n. 15, p. 95.
20. "Taiwan, India Develop Military Ties," Inside China Today, January 2, 2002, http://www.freerepublic.com.
21. BRICS became BRICS when South Africa jointed this grouping in 2010. There are five counties in BRICS (Brazil, Russia, India, China and South Africa).
22. Chang Yun-ping, "Council Established to Boost Taiwan-India Exchanges," Taipei Times, February, 12, 2006, http://www.taipeitimes.com/News/taiwan/archives/2006/02/12/2003292656
23. Ibid.
24. Annual Report 2006-2007: International Science & Technology Cooperation, Ministry of Science and Technology, Government of India.
25. "What do Growing India-Taiwan Ties Mean," Rediff. Com, June 14, 2007.
26. Mary Swire "Taiwan-India DTA Comes Into Effect" August 23, 2011, http://www.tax-news.com
27. MOEA Calls for Closer Taiwan-India Trade Ties, Taiwan Today, July 8, 2012, http://taiwantoday.tw/ct.asp?xItem=194466&ctNode=421
28. "India-Taiwan Protocol," the Federation of Indian Chambers of Commerce and Industry (FICCI), March 13, 2013, http://www.ficci.com/ficci-in-news-page.asp?nid=6989
29. Namrata Hasija, "Time India Stopped Looking at Taiwan through Chinese Prism Spotlight,) July 11, 2014 http://southasiamonitor.org/detail.php?type=sl&nid=8534
30. Manik Mehta, India's Changing Attitude toward Taiwan, 06/17/2012, Taiwan Today, http://taiwantoday.tw/ct.asp?xitem=192274&CtNode=423
31. Ibid.
32. *Rupakjyoti Borah,* "Taiwan-India Relations Need an Extra Push," June 10, 2015 http://www.geopoliticalmonitor.com/taiwan-india-relations-need-an-extra-push/
33. Joe Thomas Karackattu, *The Economic Partnership Between India and Taiwan in a Post-ECFA Ecosystem (*New Delhi: Springer, 2013).
34. Ibid.
35. "150-Strong Taiwan Trade Team to Visit India," *The Business Standard* (New Delhi), 3 September 2013
36. Taiwan, India Sign Education Agreement, Taipei Economic and Cultural Central in India, http://www.roc-taiwan.org/IN/ct.asp?xItem=481336&CtNode=5053&mp=277&xp1=
37. Ibid.
38. Taiwan Congratulates BJP and Modi, *Indian Express* (New Delhi), May 21, 2014.
39. "Taiwan-based Auto Parts Traders to Visit Delhi," *Business Standards*, September 4, 2014.

40 Ibid.
41 IESA, TCA sign MoU for make-in-India push, *The Economic Times* (New Delhi), September 12, 2014.
42 P. 106
43 Singh, n. 16, p. 107.
44 Prakash Nanda, Rediscovering Asia: Evolution of India's Look-east Policy (New Delhi: Lancer Publishers, 2003), p. 570.

26

The US Policy Towards Asia Pacific and India's Maritime Security

Suresh R.

The post-Cold War International Scenario

A glimpse into the history of international politics shows that there were various methods adopted by nation states to protect and promote their national interests. During the 19th century and early 20th century it was the policy of imperialism and colonialism. However, with the end of Second World War and the establishment of the United Nations Organization marked the end to the policy of colonialism as a means to promote national interests. The Cold War period witnessed the dominance of power politics in international politics. In fact, international politics had become synonym with military power and its predominance. It was known as the period of political realism and the consequent role of military power. The realists focus was on the role of states in international politics, and how the behaviour of states is motivated by power considerations. However, without the use of military power, either conventional or nuclear weapons, the Cold War has ended. This development poses a major question regarding the dependence of military power as the sole means to protection and promotion the national interests.

The unexpected disappearance of discipline enforced by the super power rivalry and competitions on nation sates prompted at least one incident of violation of sovereignty and territorial integrity of a nation in the international system. The enthusiasm shown by the international community of nations under the collective security principle to nip in the very bud the revival of use of force to endanger the sovereignty and territorial integrity of nation was also a warning to all decision makers of nation states, especially the dictators who adopt war as an instrument of foreign policy. Again, the challenge posed to national security by the non-state actors such as international terrorist groups was also effectively addressed by multilateral efforts. These new challenges to national security once again demonstrate the imperatives of multilateral efforts to wipe out threats to national security.

Further, the end of Cold War marked the beginning of accelerated pace of globalization. The post-Cold War period also witness some major alterations in the national security threat perception of nation states. The non-traditional threat to the security of nation states have become more grave, numerous and imminent than the traditional threat that emanates solely from other nation states. Among these threats international terrorism is the serious and looming. A viable solution to this tribulation can be found only through collective efforts of all, developed and developing, militarily strong and weak nations.

It is the responsibility of the government to frame policies to ensure security. While framing the policies both domestic and external, the security of the people should be the sole criterion. It appears that in the post-Cold War period the threat to security of the people emanates mostly from non-state actors. This new situation demands a multilateral effort with the cooperation of all nations both developed and developing, militarily powerful and weak nations. However, it is very difficult for the decision makers to take up this new course of action based on drastic amendments in the existing security policies.

In the changed international situation India has to revisit its external policy. Commensurate with changes in the international situation the defence policy also need reorientation. The futility of arms race and competitions are well reflected towards the end of cold war. Moreover the vertical and horizontal nuclear weapon proliferation makes the conventional arms built up as a means for the survival of international arms business establishments. In the post-Cold War deeply interdependent world, war as an instrument of foreign policy has lost its relevance. However, a minimal force is required to wage limited war and to deter any military adventure from state or non-state actors across the land or maritime borders.

The US Policy in the Asia Pacific

The Asia Pacific region is important in international politics because two-third of the world's population lives in the region. The maximum number of conflicts since the 1990s has been witnessed in this region though some of them are very old. The Asia Pacific region also accounts for more than 20 per cent of the land on the globe. It is in this changed context of security threat, the rebalancing policy of the US towards the Asia Pacific region need to be analysed.

The rebalancing policy in the Asia Pacific region by the US is not disengagement and then re-engagement in Asia. Instead, it is a matter of emphasis and priority, building on an elaborate foundation of US-Asia relations that was already in place. The US has had powerful national interests in the Asia-Pacific region since World War II and was deeply engaged in the region—militarily, economically, and diplomatically—throughout the Cold War. The post-Cold War administrations of Presidents Bill Clinton and George W. Bush were actively engaged in Asia. The defence report of Feb 2006 clearly stated the US intention in the Asia pacific region. The US aims with the active support of major players in the region including Russia, China and India the defeat of terrorist networks and to prevent the proliferation of weapons of mass destruction by state as well as non-state actor. The report specifically stated that it was the US aim to encourage China to play a constructive peaceful role in Asia pacific region to serve as a partner in addressing common security challenges including terrorism, proliferation, narcotics and piracy.

During Barrack Obama administration period the policy toward the Asia-Pacific region has gone through two distinct phases. When the policy was first rolled out in 2011-12, much of the emphasis was placed on military initiatives in the region. However, due to opposition from dominant players in the region the Obama administration adjusted its approach in late 2012, playing down the significance of military initiatives, emphasizing economic and diplomatic elements, and calling for closer U.S. engagement with China.

The policy of rebalancing in Asia pacific has been driven by a much broader set of strategic, economic, and political considerations. The rebalance is a region-wide, multidimensional policy initiative. In regional terms, the shift includes a stronger emphasis on Southeast Asia and South Asia to complement traditionally strong US attention to East Asia. In policy terms, the rebalance entails three sets of initiatives—security, economic, and diplomatic elements.

The fundamental goals of the new US policy are to broaden areas of cooperation beneficial to the US with regional states and institutions; strengthen relations with American allies and partners, including great powers such as China and India as well as important regional powers such as Indonesia; and develop regional norms and rules compatible with the international security, economic, and political order supported by the US. Thus rebalancing matters not only with regards to military presence, but also as "an effort that harnesses all elements of US power—military, political, trade and investment, development and our values". The Secretary of State Kerry put forth President Obama's four principles of growth—"strong growth, fair growth, smart growth, and just growth"—at his visit in Asia, highlighting the aim for development in the rebalancing strategy.

A major change that has been effected by the present Donald Trump administration in its Asia Pacific policy is that of giving a new shape the US strategic initiative in the region. Though Trump administration had abandoned the 'Pivot to Asia" initiated by Obama, it continues to emphasis the strategic significance of Asia Pacific region. Instead of announcing a comprehensive policy declaration the Trump administration follows an issue based approach in the region. This has been well reflected in the US policy on the North Korean nuclear and missile technology proliferation issue. The Trump administration was successful in altering the behaviour the North Korean dictator Kim Jong-un and leading to a pacific settlement of the issue through deliberations.

Again, in the realm of trade, Trump administration had also announced withdrawal of the US from the Trans-Pacific Partnership (TPP) immediately after taking office and claimed to replace it with multiple bilateral trade agreements. As a follow up of this policy he had addressed the US-China trade deficit issue. The ongoing trade war between US and China appears to be an after effect of this new initiative. Thus in stark contrast to Obama's broad "internationalism," Trump advocates "America First". It appears that the US Asia-Pacific policy under the Trump administration prioritizes the interests of the US over those of its allies. It also reflected the US initiative to address the issues through bilateral interactions on a case by case basis.

Perceptions on the US Policy in Asia Pacific

There are divergent perceptions regarding the US policy towards the Asia pacific region. With regard to the rationale of the rebalancing policy and the more recent 'America first' policy, it is viewed that these policies aimed at containment of China, the growing great power in the global scenario. Another perspective is that such an initiative aims at harnessing maximum benefits from growing strategic, economic and military importance of the Asia Pacific region. This region possesses abundant human and other resources. It is also the most significant sea borne international trade route. All these factors appear to have influenced the rebalancing policy as well as the more recent 'America first' policy. However, the containment of communism in China seems to be of lesser role in these policy initiatives. Though the US–China relation is conditioned by lack of mutual trust, the ongoing globalisation process has tied them together in balancing the economic interests. Despite the ongoing trade war between US and China the volume of trade interaction between these two global economic powers is the testimony to this perspective.

The US policy of protecting the interest of its strong supporters in the Asia pacific region also appears to have prompted for such an initiative. Thus the rebalancing policy and the more recent 'America first' policy also appears to have aims at the protection of various interests including the security interests of Japan, South Korea, Vietnam, and Philippians against any China supported offensive measures. The maintenance of power equilibrium in the region is sine quo non, especially in the context of an unresolved South China Sea dispute exist in the region. None of the Asian countries could singlehandedly meet the military power of China. Therefore the US presence in the region not only helps to maintain power balance in Asia but also pre-empt any aggressive move on the part of non democratic countries in the region.

The US presence in the region is also advantageous to India as long as it help to ensure the protection and promotion of democratic regimes in the region, especially in the context of democratic transitions that takes place in the neighbouring countries. India cannot and should not afford to spend more on arms race and militarisation of the region mainly on two counts. Firstly, the human security issues confronted by India are multifarious and any further delay in addressing these problems like poverty and infrastructure development in the so far neglected area would jeopardise the internal security situation. Secondly, the possession of nuclear weapon by its immediate neighbour having an unstable regime, not only pose a direct threat to its national security but also necessitate the external power presence inevitable to maintain some kind of discipline among the players in the region.

Another major threat that India has confronted in the post-Cold War period is cross border terrorism. A solution to this problem is possible only with the involvement of external powers, especially the US. Similarly, it is the anti-terrorism moves in the immediate aftermath of the 9/11 in 2001 which brought together the world's largest democracy and powerful democracy to a common platform. Since one of the major components of the rebalancing policy of the US is anti-terrorism measures there is ample scope for collaboration and joint action between India and the US against the menace of international terrorism.

However, one of the major security predicaments in the region is that any closer interaction between India and the US will be viewed by China as part of a move towards containment of China. And any close China and the US interaction would be viewed by India as move against its national interest. Though there is balance of interests of these three major players of the Asia Pacific region, India, China and the US, at the bilateral level they lack mutual trust. In the absence of mutual trust any minor issue may aggravate to a major national security issue. In such a scenario it would be interesting to look into India's maritime security concerns.

India's Maritime Security Concerns in the post-Cold War Period

The maritime security is very important to India's military, economic, energy, environment, and human security. India has a coast line of 7516 km and an exclusive economic zone (EEZ) of 2 million sq km. The significance of the maritime domain has long been recognized. The famous words of Alfred Tyler Mahan testifies this "whosoever control Indian Ocean dominates Asia. This Ocean is important in the seven seas, in the twenty first century the destiny of the world will be determined in its waters."

India occupies a central position in the Indian Ocean region, a fact that exercises an increasingly profound influence on India's security environment. Writing in the 1940s, K.M. Pannikar, noted the importance of the Ocean to India that "while to other countries the Indian Ocean is only one of the important oceanic areas, to India it is a vital sea. Her lifelines are concentrated in that area, her freedom is dependent on the freedom of that water surface. No industrial development, no commercial growth, no stable political structure is possible for her unless her shores are protected." In tune with the above observations the first Prime Minister of India, Jawaharlal Nehru observed "History has shown that whatever power controls the Indian Ocean has, in the first instance, India's sea borne trade at her mercy and, in the second, India's very independence itself..." The significance of the Indian Ocean to India has also been emphasized in the Annual Report (2004-2005) of India's Defense Ministry, which noted that "India is strategically located vis-a-vis both continental Asia as well as the Indian Ocean Region."

Again the Indian Maritime Doctrine asserts: "All major powers of this century will seek a toehold in the Indian Ocean Region. Thus, Japan, the EU, and China, and a reinvigorated Russia can be expected to show presence in these waters either independently or through politico-security arrangements." There is, moreover, "an increasing tendency of extra regional powers of military intervention in [IO] littoral countries to contain what they see as a conflict situation." Thus the Indian Ocean and its littoral and hinterland area have a direct bearing in safeguarding India's maritime security interests which is closely connected to national security.

India's Maritime Security Policy in the post-Cold War Period

India's maritime security policy also underwent a sea change in the post-Cold War period. The policy of exclusive engagement and elimination of outside powers has given place to overt engagement with extra regional powers. This has been well reflected in India's joint military exercises along with the US, Japan, France, and Australia. India no longer considers the external power presence as a threat to its security. Rather it considers a joint effort is required to wipe out the major threat to India and international community posed by terrorism. It is not possible for any single nation whatsoever powerful to address the menace of international terrorism singlehandedly. India began to realize the importance of major amendments in framing its security policy objectives and pursuing it through increased naval power and active collaboration with extra regional as well as intra-regional powers. This policy shift in India's stand is visible in the maritime doctrine as well as in the Navy's vision document published by the Indian Navy.

It essentially encompasses:

(i) Shaping a favorable maritime environment in the IOR for operations in peace as well as during conflict.
(ii) Preventing incursions by powers inimical to India's national interests by actively engaging countries in the IOR littoral, and rendering speedy and quality assistance in fields of interest to them.
(iii) Engaging extra-regional powers and regional navies in mutually beneficial activities to ensure the security of India's maritime interests.
(iv) Projecting the Indian Navy as a professional, credible force and the primary tool for maritime cooperation.

India has also ear marked the area which falls within its immediate concern. "India's growing international stature gives it strategic relevance in the area ranging from the Persian Gulf to the Strait of Malacca...." India's post-Cold War India's maritime policy had stated: "India has exploited the fluidities of the emerging world order to forge new links through a combination of diplomatic repositioning, economic resurgence and military firmness."

It appears that India has adopted a three pronged strategy to protect and promote its national interests. Firstly through diplomatic means, India has pursued a policy of cooperation with all major players in the Indian Ocean, including extra regional powers. This policy would help India to increase further its international stature. The Indo US civilian nuclear agreement can also be viewed as an attempt to do away with nuclear isolation. The process of globalization has also accelerated better and cordial interaction with outside powers as the movement of people as well as commodities would further cement relation between nations.

India has developed a friendly and cordial relation not only by bilateral exchange with nations but also strengthened the bilateral cooperation through interactions in regional organizations, such as ASEAN, EAS, SCO, BRICS, ASEM, IBSA, APTA, and IOR ARC. India is vigorously pursuing the objective to become a developed nation by 2020. This requires the Indian economy to maintain an annual average growth rate of 8 per cent per annum.

India has adopted "Look East" followed by 'Act East Policy' in pursuance of this objective. Now the look east policy and act east policy are a vital part of India's foreign policy. More than an external economic policy or a political slogan, the look east policy and act east policy show a strategic shift in India's vision of the world and its place in the evolving global economy. It was also a manifestation of India's belief that developments in East Asia are of direct consequence to its security and development. Therefore India actively engaged in creating a bond of friendship and cooperation with East Asia that has a strong economic foundation and a cooperative paradigm of positive inter-connectedness of security interests. India becomes a member of the ARF in 1996 and considers it as an experiment in fashioning a pluralistic, cooperative security order reflective of the diversity of the Asia Pacific region. India has also successfully clinched a free trade agreement with the ASEAN which had come into force on 1 January 2010. India is also a member of the East Asia Summit (EAS) which includes the ASEAN members and India, China, Japan, Republic of Korea, Australia, and New Zealand. It focuses on energy, environment, climate change, and sustainable development. The look east policy of India has included not only vigorous interaction with ASEAN but also improved relation with China. The ultimate objective, it appears, is to evolve an Asian Economic Community on the lines of EU.

India has also pursued a policy of strengthening its economic and military power. It appears that in order to increase the national power India had not only declared itself as a nuclear weapon power but also augmented its non-nuclear defense capabilities manifold. India is the largest importer of weapons as per the

SIPRI reports. Again the maritime doctrine of India focuses mainly on building blue water navy. India's role in ensuring the security of Indian Ocean region has been recognized by major players in the region mainly because of the major shift in its external policy through a pragmatic approach. As a result India was not hesitant to cooperate with any regional and extra regional powers. India has undertaken several innovative steps towards economic resurgence of the country. India's initiative to interact with nations at the bilateral and multilateral levels through various regional groupings appears to be based on this policy initiative. The existence of non-traditional threat to India's security also demands multilateral approach towards security with the involvement of regional and extra regional countries. The NDA II government led by Prime Minister Narendra Modi, had taken several initiative to improve India's relation with neighbouring countries and also with major powers through bilateral and multilateral engagements. The initiative to strengthen the economic and military power and also special focus on the maritime security of India are policies in the right direction.

Conclusion

Thus a closer look into the divergent approach followed by the US in the Asia Pacific region and India's post-Cold War maritime security policy shows convergence of interests. However, with regard to the means to be applied for the achievement of these objectives there is divergence. The US as a global power has all means to achieve its stated objectives, including use of coercive power, however, India as a functional democratic developing country having a hostile border with non-democratic nuclear weapon neighbours have only limited options to achieve its objectives. In such a situation, it appears that, the external power presence, especially the US presence in the Asia Pacific region is advantageous to India.

27

Contemporary Indo-Bhutanese Relations:
Issues of Concern for the Modi Government

Unnikrishnan G.

Introduction

The bilateral relations between the Himalayan Kingdom of Bhutan and the Republic of India have been traditionally close. The basis for the bilateral relations between India and Bhutan is formed by the Indo-Bhutan Treaty of 1949, which provides for, among others, "perpetual peace and friendship, free trade and commerce and equal justice to each other's citizens."[1] The Article 2 in this Treaty, in principle, calls for Bhutan to seek India's advice in external matters, while India pledges non-interference in Bhutan's internal affairs[2]. This treaty was updated and signed in 2007 during the visit to India of His Majesty Jigme Khesar Wangchuk of Bhutan and in it the provision requiring Thimbu to seek New Delhi's guidance in foreign policy was replaced with a broader sense of sovereignty for Bhutan[3]. Moreover India is Bhutan's largest trading partner and India's economy significantly relies on Bhutan for hydroelectric power besides other socio-political and economic overlaps. Recently Indo–Bhutan relations got a further momentum with the Prime Minister of India, Narendra Modi's maiden foreign visit to the Bhutan. Although there are no big agreements concluded, but the Modi's short visit marked his high regard for the South Asian neighbourhood over the extended international community.

Historical Background

The geo-political scene in the entire Himalayan region and in the Indian subcontinent underwent great change following the formation of the People's Republic of China in 1949 and the takeover of Tibet by People's Liberation Army in 1950. These events, plus the presence of Chinese troops near Bhutan's border, the annexation of Bhutanese enclaves in Tibet and the Chinese claims all led Bhutan to re-evaluate its traditional policy of isolation and the need to develop its lines of communications with India became an urgent necessity (Kohli 1993: 63-64). Consequently, Bhutan was more inclined to develop relations with India and the process of socio-economic development began thereafter with Indian assistance. For India's own security too, the stability of Himalayan states falling with its strategic interest was a crucial factor to consider (Hasrat 1980: 112). With border tensions between India and China escalating into military conflict in 1962, India could not afford Bhutan to be a weak buffer state.

Based on this backdrop, Indo-Bhutan relations began to take on concrete form following the state visit made by the third King of Bhutan, His Majesty Wang Chuk to India, and by Prime Minister Jawaharlal Nehru of India to Bhutan between 1954 and 1961 (Kohli 1993:88-90). Besides emphasizing India's recognition of Bhutan's independence and sovereignty in his public statement in Paro, Nehru's visit in 1958 was also significant with discussions initiated for development co-operation between the two countries. Formal bilateral relations between Bhutan and India were established in January 1968 with the appointment of a Special Officer of the Government of India to Bhutan (Verma 1988: 78-80). The India House (Embassy of India in Bhutan) was inaugurated on May 14, 1968 and Resident Representatives were exchanged in 1971. Ambassadorial level relations began with the upgrading of residents to embassies in 1978. In addition to this, India is Bhutan's most important economic and trading partner, accounting for nearly 60 percent of Bhutan's exports and 75 percent of its imports, as well as being a vital donor of economic aid to the country.

Geo-political Importance of Bhutan

The kingdom of Bhutan is often described as being physically small with limited economic scope and military might. Inspite of these limitations Bhutan has earned the reputation of being a peaceful country where the development of threats from militancy, terrorism and economic disparity within itself has virtually been absent. In this sense, Bhutan has been more fortunate than many of its neighbours in the South Asian region. Moreover at first glance, the Kingdom of Bhutan would not seem to be a country that would factor heavily in the calculus of regional powers. But this land locked Himalayan country has now become increasingly important strategically to both New Delhi and Beijing, and the main reason for this importance is, Bhutan's geographical location (Parmanand 1998: 125-128). Recently it finds itself caught up in a discreet but high stakes diplomatic battle between India and China and the main factor which induces this diplomatic battle is the issue of territory (ibid 130).

The three main territorial areas of Bhutan are the Jakarlung and Pasamlung valleys on the Bhutan-Chinese north-central border, and the Doklam Plateau in Eastern Bhutan. While the first two territories of the north are of interest to China due to their proximity to Tibet and Doklam Plateau is strategically significant to India (Yadav 1996: 148). The Doklam Plateau lies immediately east of Indian defences in Sikkim. The Chinese occupation of Doklam would turn the flank of Indian defences completely and it gave Chinese the commanding view of the Chumbi Valley and the Siliguri Corridor. The Siliguri Corridor (described by some analysts as a 'Chickens Neck') is a narrow stretch of land that connects India's North Eastern states to the rest of India. If the Chinese were to gain possession of the Doklam Plateau, in the event of hostilities, it would have the ability to essentially 'cut-off' India's land access to 40 million citizens in its north-east territories (ibid 168). Moreover there are reports of grave concern to India, like the activities of insurgent groups from north-eastern India which have taken sanctuary along Bhutan's treacherous border with the Indian state of Assam and also the Chinese army's activities in north and north-west Bhutan (Rizal 2013: 12). Apart from all the above factors, Bhutan also plays a significant role in ensuring energy security to the region through the provision of hydro electric power.

Issues of Concern for the Modi Government

While India and Bhutan share an extraordinary warm friendship, issues such as the growing Chinese influence in Bhutan, the liberalization policies in India and its implications for Bhutan and the illegal presence of militants using Bhutan as a base against India are the most important issues which demands greater concern from the Modi Government.

(a) The China Factor

The anxieties about China's intentions is a factor in India's relations with its neighbours now, the same is the case of Indo-Bhutanese relations also. Though neighbours Bhutan and China have not yet established diplomatic relations, and Bhutan is Chinas only neighbour which does not have diplomatic relations with the People's Republic of China (Kumar 2010: 243-252). Even trade and economic contacts between the two countries are very small and their common border remains closed. This fact must be understood in the larger context of Chinese suzerainty claims on Bhutan till the recent past, border conflicts ranging from cartographic to geographical intrusion, integration of Tibet to the 'mother land ' and the China-India relation factor (Bisht 2012: 14-18). The two countries have long standing differences on the delineation of their common border, which follows the watershed of the Chumbi Valley in the north-west and the crest of the Great Himalayan range in the north.

But the situation is changing since 1970's and thereafter China-Bhutan relation entered a period of normalisation (Mathou 2003: 174-188). In 1971, Bhutan joined the United Nations and voted in favour of giving to the People Republic of China, the Chinese seat in the UN. In 1974, China along with few other countries invited to the coronation of King Jigme wangchuk[4]. It was a unique opportunity for Bhutan to assert its personality on the international scene. The Chinese delegation's visit to Thimbu was described by Bhutanese News Agency as a 'new page in the friendly contacts between the two countries' (Ying 2012: 8-10). The Chinese congratulatory message emphasised the 'desire of the Bhutanese government in developing its economy and safeguarding its national independence'. The invitation of a Chinese delegation in Thimbu was a clear message showing that Bhutan was ready to normalise its relations with China. Also Bhutanese table tennis teams visited China in 1977 and 1979.

In addition to this, Bhutan shown support to China in defeating anti-China drafts at the UNCHR conference, maintaining the 'One China' policy, voting against the drafts on Taiwan's participations in the United Nations and opposing Taiwan's bid to host the 2002 Asian Games (ibid 10). The surprise meeting of the then Prime Ministers of Bhutan and China, Jigme Thinley and Wen Jiabao respectively, on the side-lines of an international summit in Brazil in 2012, regarding border dispute is the another remarkable event. Bhutan's Prime Minister described the visit as of great historic significance, as it marks the first meeting between the heads of the two governments. He further asserted that Bhutan must firmly stick to the 'One China Policy' and has strong desire to strengthen understanding and friendship with China (Gopilal 2012: 22-24).

In short Chinas pragmatic foreign policy in contemporary times with the smaller South Asian countries indicates that China fully takes into account the geographical and economic importance of Bhutan. China fully knows Bhutan could hold the key to China's legitimacy claims regarding Tibet and act as the last milestone in discrediting and demoralising India in its own backyard (Singh 2013: 19-22). Moreover China's continued motivation in engaging Bhutan relates to the strategic benefits its geography can deliver. So like Nepal, China will employ a mix of persuasion and coercion with Bhutan as well as reminding the repercussions of siding with India. With Pakistan, Nepal, Sri Lanka, and even Bangladesh offering China more leverage in South Asia now against India than ever before, Bhutan also could play a critical role for China; firstly in furthering its strategic depth against India's north eastern periphery, secondly in restraining its Tibetan dilemma from spilling over into Bhutan and lastly in stopping Bhutan from being guided by Indian concerns alone (ibid 26-28).

This does not mean that China expect a lean from Bhutan to the Chinese side overnightly. But it aims at neutralising Bhutan in the wake of any political or military conflict with India and use it as a base to further trade and commerce in Tibet and rest of South Asia. China also induces Bhutan to look up to her as an effective and reliable counterbalance to contain the inevitable Indian domination. Moreover, Bhutan's transition from monarchy to parliamentary democracy saw the revision of the 1949 treaty with India in 2007 and this is a welcome sign for China. The next would be the Indian military presence there. As recent developments suggest, it could be a matter of time that Bhutan moves to balance its tilt towards India (Bisht 2012: 26-27).

(b) India's Liberalization Policies and its Impact on Bhutan
The second important issue of grave concern to Modi government is the issue of India's growing liberalization policies and its impact on Bhutan. Until 1990's, Bhutan has enjoyed more or less protected status in its trade relations with India. With the economic liberalization on the rise in India, Bhutan is facing a gradual loss of this earlier status, and unless Bhutanese industries are able to remain competitive they could lose their market share in the increasingly open market in India. Bhutan has already felt the impact of the reform in India's subsidy policies that has resulted in a gradual phasing out of subsidies and a decrease in India's budget assistance to Bhutan (Yadav 1996: 210-212). Bhutan will also have to face the effects that would be brought on by India gradually moving towards privatizing its power, petroleum and other traditional public sectors. At the same time China looks for more economic, tourism, hydroelectricity and infrastructure related co-operation and resource exploitation within Bhutan; areas where it has a decisive

edge. China probably believes that with the rise of economic and other related interaction involving financial stakes, other benefits will naturally occur (Krishnan 2012).

(c) Anti-India Elements and Bhutan
The third issue of great concern to the Modi government is the illicit establishment of camps by the United Liberation Front of Assam (ULFA), National Democratic Front of Bodos (NDFB) and the Kamtapuri Liberation Organization (KLO) in the dense jungles of South-East Bhutan.[5] The unwanted but continued presence of the above militants on the Bhutanese soil has not only posed potential threat to the friendly relations between Bhutan and India but also created problems for commercial activities of the business sector and affected implementation of development programmes in the country.[6]

The militants started infiltrating into Bhutanese forest after the Indian Army launched operations against the ULFA militants in 1990-91. It was easy for the militants to take advantage of the 266 Kilo meter porous and open Assam-Bhutan border since military posts at that time were mainly concentrated along the north bordering China and the Bhutanese government was largely occupied with the rise of the problems in the southern Bhutan. The presence of the militants inside the country came to the government's attention only in the mid-1990's and since then Bhutanese government repeatedly urged the militants to leave the country peacefully. But Inspite of the Bhutanese government's effort, militants had no real intention of leaving Bhutan until their own objectives had been fulfilled.

Recent Developments in India-Bhutan Relations

The year 2017 can be marked as the testing time for India-Bhutan ties. The Dokhlam dispute, the pivotal issue pushed India-Bhutan relation in to a high pressure. The Dokhlam is a long disputed area between China and Bhutan. The place spread over less than a 100 sq km is located at the tri-junction between India, China and Bhutan. The Dokhlam issue started in June 2017 when the Chinese were trying to construct a road in the area, and Indian troops in aid of their Bhutanese counterparts objected to the construction and had resulted in a two month stand-off between PLA Army and Indian army. The dispute later resolved through diplomatic efforts between India and China and correspondingly between Bhutan and China. However the Dokhlam dispute reaffirmed Bhutan's special security relationship with India. In addition to this on December 2018 the Bhutan's Foreign Minister made it clear that "India remains the cornerstone of Bhutan's foreign policy."⁸ Another issue that India and Bhutan to be sort out is the BBIN (Bangladesh-Bhutan-India-Nepal) project. Though a promising initiative as far as India and Bhutan is concerned it remains in the pipeline. The Bhutan parliament shelved the BBIN Motor Vehicle Agreement over some differences. However In December 2018 Indian Prime Minister held wide ranging talks with his Bhutanese counterpart Lotay Tshering and announced that India will contribute Rs 4,500 crore in Bhutan's 12th five-year plan. Along with this both the countries have decided to elevate their long held hydro power cooperation to new heights.

Conclusion and Recommendations

In short, India still maintains an advantage over China in Bhutan case as it has a deep and long standing relationship with Bhutan. This naturally gave India a wide array of diplomatic options. Firstly and most importantly India must ensure that Bhutan will not go the Nepal way, where the perceived creation of dependency on New Delhi and interference by it had caused resentment against India. It pushed Kathmandu closer to China, which is now the biggest foreign investor in Nepal overtaking India[7]. The act of Modi to select Bhutan as the first country for his foreign trip is a welcome sign and he must continue this momentum. It also shows his high concern for the immediate neighbourhood and its geographical and strategic significance.

As Bhutan is on its way to democratization, the number and variety of stakeholders in that country are increasing and India must prop up its foreign policy with consultations across the sectors, particularly the emerging business community. Trust factor is another element which has been an area of strength between both the countries. Efforts should specifically be made from the Indian side to sustain it. There is also a need to focus on technological up gradation. Given that 50 percent of the Bhutanese population is young and economically Bhutan seems to be opening up and a new generation of Bhutanese youth also seem to be emerging. Thus the key to contemporary Indo-Bhutan relations would depend on the engagement and experiences of this age group.

Finally, the public diplomacy or keeping people at the centre of the bilateral relations is another option for India. Since India-Bhutan share a 699-km-long border, interaction across borders should be institutionalised, through frequent border haats. Even while patrolling the area, good contacts with the locals is important. Further, a lot of Bhutanese students are now coming to India for education and more scholarships should be given to them. New Delhi should also make an effort to reach out to the people of Bhutan. A lackadaisical attitude on the part of New Delhi could be detrimental to the relations of both the countries in the long run.

NOTES

1. As quoted on the website of the Indian Embassy in Bhutan at http:www.eoithimpu.org/(viewed on 15 November 2014).
2. Ibid.
3. India-Bhutan Friendship Treaty 2007, Ministry of External Affairs, Government of India. http/mea.gov.in/images/pdf/india-bhutan-treaty-07.pdf (viewed on 18 November 2014).
4. The only representatives allowed to attend the crowning ceremony were those of Bangladesh, China, India, Sikkim, the Soviet Union and the United States.
5. The ULFA, Fighting for the independence of Assam, NDFB, fighting for an independent State of Bodoland and KLO, fighting for an independent State of Kamtapur.
6. Trade routes of at least twelve of twenty districts in Bhutan have to pass through the Indian Territory in Assam.
7. China is the largest FDI source for Nepal, overtakes India now, The Hindu, 26 January 2014.
8. India Remains the Cornerstone of Our Foreign policy: Bhutan Foreign Minister, Interview, *The Hindu*, 4 December 2018.

REFERENCES

Bisht, Medha (2010). "Sino-Bhutan Boundary Negotiations: Complexities of the 'Package Deal'." IDSA Comment: 19 January 2010. Viewed on 30 November 2014 (http://www. Idsa.in/idsacomments/sino-bhutan boundary negotiations-mbisht-190110)

Bisht, Medha (2012). "Chinese Inroads in to Bhutan: Diplomatic Gimmick or Strategic Reality?" IDSA Strategic Comment: 14 August 2012. Viewed on 2 December 2014 (http//www.idsa.in/idsa comments/Chinese inroads in to Bhutan-mbisht-140812)

Gopilal, Acharya (2012). "When the small Dragon meets the Big One". IPA Journal: 30 July 2012. Viewed on 8 December 2014 (http:/ipa journal. Com /2012/07/30/ when-the-small-dragon-met-the-big-one)

Hasrat, B.J. (1980). History of Bhutan: Land of Peaceful Dragon (Thimpu: Education Department, Royal Government of Bhutan)

Kohli, Manorama (1993). From Dependency to Interdependence: A Study of Indo-Bhutan Relations (New Delhi: Vikas Publishing House)

Krishnan, Ananth (2012). "China's rail network to touch India's border". The Hindu, 18 January 2012.

Kumar, Pranav (2010). Sino-Bhutanese Relations: Under the Shadow of India-Bhutan Friendship (New Delhi: Pragati Publications)

Mathou, Thierry (2003). "Bhutan-China Relations: Towards a New Step in Himalayan Politics". Paper presented at the International seminar on Bhutanese studies, Thimphu, Centre for Bhutan studies, 20-23 August 2003

Parmanand (1998), The Politics of Bhutan (New Delhi: Pragati Publications)

Rizal, Govinda (2013), "China sets up Three Camps; PLA's Patrol inside Bhutan", 29 June, Bhutan News Service, viewed on 12 November 2014 (http://www. Bhutannewsservice.com/main-news/china-sets-up-three-camps-plas-petrol-inside-bhutan)

Sing, Teshu (2013), "India, China and the Nathula understanding Beijing's Larger Strategy towards the Region". IPCS Issue Brief: 9 August 2013. Viewed on 18 December 2014 (http://www.ipcs.org/pd.f-file/ issue/ IB204-CRP-Teshu-Nathula-pdf)

Verma, Ravi (1988), India's Role in the Emergence of Contemporary Bhutan (New Delhi: Capital Publishing House),

Yadav, Lal (1996), Indo-Bhutan Relations and China intervention (New Delhi: Anmol Publications)

Ying, Fu (2012), "It is time for China and Bhutan to Develop bridges of Friendship and Cooperation". Kuensel online: 9 August 2012. Viewed on 5 December 2014 (http:/www. Kuensel online. Com/2011/?p=35042).

28

Sustainable India-Australia Partnership Calls for Rationalization of their Expectations vis-à-vis Preferences

Y. Yagama Reddy

Premise of Expectations of India and Australia

The multidisciplinary students, specialized in their respective fields concerning the Indian Ocean region, generally entertain fond hopes over the potentials of partnership, simply the prospects of sustained bilateral relations. The geological history, in the first instance, unravelled the semblance between the Indian peninsula and the Australian continent in their geological formations and mineral wealth owing to super-continent connection. India and Australia, thanks to their historical legacy as the British colonies and geographical proximity as the Indian Ocean littorals, have certain shared values and linkages as, for instance, democratic system of governance, English language, accountancy and jurisprudence as well as climatic pattern and crop structure. As logical corollary, there are discernible advantages on a win-win basis for both these Indian Ocean littoral states. Evidently, the set of commonalties and complementarities had become conducive to promoting the bilateral relations from the beginning of 19th century. But historiography amply portrays the India-Australia relations as having witnessed longer periods of estrangement intercepted by accidental and brief spells of cordiality. The common denominators between them and their complementary features were found to be consequences in steering the bilateral partnership. Thus, India-Australia bilateral relationship is replete with the envisioned prospects and failure of expectations testifying to invidious preferences.

Unequivocal Contribution of Indians to the Australian Economy in 19th Century

Aboriginal Australia had never evolved any economic system based on agriculture, livestock and mineral wealth; as a logical corollary, the newly settled Britishers endured food shortages coupled with famine conditions that forced the British Australia depend on the food supplies from India. Rice was imported from Calcutta by sending 'Sydney Cove' in 1792, a few years after the colonization of Australia in 1788 (*Asia Link* and University of Melbourne 2008). As the farming undertaken by the convicts deported from Britain was proved to be a futile exercise, Australia's farming became virtually dependent on the itinerant Indians from the early 19th century. Besides largely engaged as labourers in pastoral and sugar industries as well as household servants, the Indian indentured labourers, especially the camel drivers, were instrumental for keeping the transport and communication lines open from the coastal cities to the interior parts in early 18th century and later on for developing the telegraph (1870-72) and other construction projects like Central Australian Railway (1870-1929) and Transcontinental Railway from Augusta to Kolgoorlie (1912-1917) (*Australian Encyclopedia* 1958: 156). Having gained thorough exposure to different facets of India during his extensive travel in India much before he became the Prime Minister of Australia (1903-04, 1905-08, 1909-10), Alfred Deakin had reportedly observed in his book, *Irrigated India* (1893), that "the future relations of India and Australia possess immeasurable potencies. Their geographical proximity cannot but exercise a very real and reciprocal influence upon the forces of national life in each" (ASSCFADT 1990).

Australia's White Policy Aberrations

But the observations of Geoffrey Blainey and Alfred Deakin were proved to be a myth in the context of discrimination against Indians who, although declared as the British subjects, were victimized on account of the restrictions on the immigrants all through the period of 19th century. Australians, who were proud of being identified as the European 'cultural outpost' at the tail-end of Asia, had a very thin memory of the remarkable contribution of the Indian community to the economic development in Australia in the 19th century. The newly formed Federated State of Australia (1901) had only reinforced the restrictions through its White Policy of 1901. India's wartime help so impressed Australia as to reward

Indians through the Hughes' Reciprocity Resolution of 1918 and the four Imperial Conferences between 1917 and 1923. Nonetheless, the privileges became obliterated, and the State legislations discriminated against Indians, who, for practical purposes, remained victims of the White Policy weirdness (Palfreeman 1967: 19-42). The Indian population had thus hardly witnessed any growth during the period from 1901 (7760) to 1947 (7500), and this does not even qualify for comparison of its growth over a period of 40 years since 1861 (2500) (Hugo 2004: 229-298). Though the Indian Prime Minister Jawaharlal Nehru strongly felt that the demographic composition was essentially a policy of the nation concerned, Indians became critical of the offensive White Australia Policy and its aberrations, despite the Commonwealth connection between India and Australia.

Envisioned Prospects of Australia-India Partnership

In the midst of Indian misconceptions and resentment over the Australian White Policy, there were well-expressed intentions for strengthening the future relations as, for instance, by Betram Stevens, the Premier of New South Wales and H V Evatt, the Australian External Affairs Minister, and instances indicative of the spirit of cooperation at regional and global levels, besides keeping up close and cordial relations. On the eve of opening of the official mission in New Delhi in 1944, Stevens favoured *"close commercial links with India in view of the implicit benefits of trade (for Australia) and of employment opportunities that would improve the living standards of life in India"* (ASSCFADT 1990: 10). Evatt in his message on the eve of independence to India emphasized, *"the mutuality of interests and a sense of belonging to a shared region"* based on their *"geographical proximity and common interests in the affairs of Indian Ocean and Southeast Asia..."* (Gurry 1996: 5). His successors, Spercy Spender (1949-51) and R G Casey (1951-63) too envisioned fruitful Australia-India partnership. Newly independent India led by Nehru enjoyed close and sympathetic relations with Australia under the Labour Government of Prime Minister, Joseph Benedict Chiefly. Besides developing a good perception of India's non-aligned policy, Australia also collaborated with India on the issue of Indonesia's independence (1947-49).

Ideological Divergence eclipsed Benevolence and Support

It was a great incongruity that these colonial cousins began drifting apart along the Cold War ideological equations. The repulsive behaviour in their bilateral relationship was perpetuated due in large part to their differential estimates of security risks and differential methods of ensuring security in the context of Cold

War. While India was wedded to the policy of Non-alignment, Australia's responses were determined by its alliance with the Western bloc. To Nehru, SEATO was an anti-thesis of Panch Sheel; however, the Australian Prime Minister Menzies considered security in the area as a collective concept that called for Australia's participation in SEATO, ANZUS and ANZAM (Greenwood and Harper 1963: 342-345). Their arguments were much "deeper than the differences" to the extent of enduring divergence on matters irrelevant to their bilateral relationship and eclipsing the Australian gesture towards India in the form of food-aid in 1950s and 1960s under the Colombo Plan, benevolent assistance on the eve of 1962 Chinese aggression on India and refusal to concede the Pakistan's demand for military assistance during the 1965 Indo-Pak war. The proposal of Australian Prime Minister John Gorton that India was to evince real interest in playing a role in Southeast Asia received only lukewarm response from the visiting Indian Prime Minister Indira Gandhi in May 1968 (*A R* 1968: 834-837). India, having wedded to non-aligned policy, was neither mindful of Australia's negligence of India, nor mainly interested to promote relations with Australia. Further, there was a mismatch between the importance attached to India by Australia and the insignificant view of Australia in India's global interests (Neale 1968: 67). All said and done, Australia was the first Western bloc country to recognize the newly liberated Bangladesh through the Indo-Pak War of 1971 (*AR* 1972: 10645-46).

Poverty of Knowledge-Indifference-Nonchalance

The lacklustre relationship, due in large part to 'lack of knowledge of Australia' in India and an 'ignorance or neglect of India' in Australia, made the people of both the countries develop exotic impressions of each other. Deplorably, Indians were ignorant of Australia's geographical location and the human geography of the Aborigines, leave alone that of the linkages between India and Australia. On their part, Australians have gained a scanty knowledge of India that it was once a British domain. This was nothing but 'the poverty of communication links', as commented by the Indian Minister for Information & Broadcasting, I.K. Gujral, on 7 November 1972, at the meeting of the Consultative Committee of the Colombo Plan (*IFR* 1972: 7-9). The former Australian Prime Minister, Gough Whitlam, during his visit to India in June 1973, lamented "the inability of India and Australia in forging the much expected 'very close relationship' is as an anomalous... though shared common values in democracy and democratic institutions, links in the commonwealth and their belonging to the geographical region of the Indian Ocean" (*AR* 1973: 11392). Bruce Grant who was then the Australian High

Commissioner recollected Whitlam's observation that "India, a great democracy, had been neglected by previous Australian Prime Ministers because of its 'neutrality' in the Cold War" (Grant 2014).

The Labour government of Gough Whitlam attached much importance to improving the relations with India even at the cost of its traditional alliance with the US, and its official reaction was pretty mild in the face of the Conservative Party's intense opposition to India's nuclear tests of May 1974. The succeeding Malcolm Fraser's government got the Whitlam's Asia-oriented policy reverted to the old dictum of alliance with the US and favoured the continuation of the US bases in the Indian Ocean by subscribing to the 'concept of balance' as opposed to the 'Indian Ocean Zone of Peace' championed by India and other Indian Ocean littoral states. The US withdrawal from Southeast Asia and India's enhanced naval capabilities had further widened the gulf for over two decades until late 1980s. Australia was used to look at India as 'a key player' in South Asian politics, a 'champion' of non-aligned movement, and a 'critic' of the US and a 'proxy' or simply an 'ally' of the Soviet Union during the Cold War period. That "Australia has mostly been the suitor and India the reluctant bride" bears testimony to their nonchalant attitude (Gordon 2007).

Post-Cold War New Economic Order and Bonhomie

The much needed rapprochement between the Indian Ocean littorals was facilitated by the initiatives of the Indian Prime Minister Rajiv Gandhi and his Australian counterpart Bob Hawke. The post–Cold War imperatives of globalization propelled the oft-demurred nations to embark on strategies for reinforcing the bilateral relationship through a series of initiatives like India's Look East Policy (1992) complemented by Australia's Look West Strategy (1994), establishment of Australia-India Council (1992), India Today Festival (1994), DFAT's study of India's Economy at the Mid-night Hour (*EAAU* 1994), and launching of Australia-India New Horizons Campaign (*DFAT* 1996) that had won the bipartisan support. Australia, probably taking India's eventual response for granted, has repeatedly exemplified the commonalities (based on geology, mineral wealth, geography and climate) and the essential complementarities in their economies in pursuit of promoting "developmental cooperation with India on a sounder basis" and identifying the avenues of cooperation in commerce and trade, transfer of scientific and technical know-how, and investment. It was most probably the Cold War political adrift between these two nations that overshadowed the unequivocal scientific fact all through the four decades until the recession of Cold War. Post-Cold-War–related security issues and bilateral trade prospects have brought these two Indian Ocean littorals closer through certain common denominators. In pursuit of "expanding the awareness and understanding" of each other *(IDSA NR* 1991: 566), it was Australia that had taken the lead to rediscover the basic linkages (cricket, Commonwealth, accountancy, legal system and English language owing to British colonial legacy), while India was found lagging far behind Australia.

Of much relevance to the present context is the observation of Australia India Institute (n.d.) in its Submission to the *White Paper on Australia in the Asian Century* that "strategically, both countries need to work to develop stable and cooperative security architecture for the Asia-Pacific region, and there is a greater urgency for Canberra and New Delhi to coordinate their policies on critical global issues". India has been looked upon to provide security to the sea lanes of communications (SLOCs), particularly to the commercial ships from non-conventional threats like sea piracy, in the corridor spanning the Indian Ocean–Malacca Strait–South China Sea. In retrospect, the Dibbs Report (1987) and the Senate Standing Committee Report (1990) dispelled the apprehensions over India's blue water capabilities. India and Australia have "common security interests" linked with Southeast Asia and "immense potentials for building strong economic and defence ties". ASEAN looks upon India to work closely with ASEAN in combating international terrorism and other forms of trans-national crime.

Australia's Reaction to India's Nuclear Tests incompatible to Claims of Shared Values

That the Australian mindset had for long been Pacific-oriented was well evident: For instance, the former Prime Minister Paul Keating was opposed to India's inclusion in APEC; the famous 1989 Garnaut Report as well as the 1997 *White Paper* had no mention of India in them. Further, Australia and India have for long adopted an approach of "rubbing each other up the wrong way on practically every issue on which their interests touched" (Wesley 2012). For all the eloquent appreciation of India's economic reforms and self-reliant security mechanism, Australia scorned the India's nuclear tests of May 1998 in the form of a series of sanctions, besides its unsuccessful diplomatic manoeuvres at the ARF meeting in Manila (July 1998) towards the end of indicting India. The diplomatic chill between these two nations manifested in a setback to the burgeoning bilateral relationship after decades of stagnation. Unlike the short-sighted official policy, Australian public, nonetheless, showed a better grasp of India's nuclear imperatives

(*The Hindu* 1998: 12). While quoting this statement in his *Foreword* to *AII's submission to the White Paper on "Australia in the Asian Century"*, Professor Amitabh Mattoo, Director of Australia India Institute (AII) remarked that

> ...while New Delhi and Canberra may know each other, they still do not have a nuanced understanding of each other. This needs to change if the two countries are to work with each other and in the interests of the region. Australia cannot afford to have a purely mercantilist approach towards India. Indeed, the Australia-India relationship cannot realize its full potential without a more comprehensive Australian knowledge of India. (Mattoo, n.d.)

This gets an oblique support from the statement of the then Deputy Prime Minister and Minister for Education, Julia Gillard in September 2009 that the Australian Government "is committed to building a greater understanding between our two peoples and Australians' understanding of India, its culture, its history and place in the world." In the context of India's role being increasingly sought after by all the regional powers in this region and the Indo-US blossoming relationship, Australia didn't like to find itself lagging behind in forging security and strategic partnership with India. The India-Australia relationship was aptly described by Peter Varghese, Australian High Commissioner to India, in his lecture at the Observer Research Foundation, New Delhi, on 3 May 2012 that "ours was a friendly yet largely undeveloped relationship, punctuated by phases, usually short-lived, when we rediscovered each other" (Varghese 2012). Varghese further observed that India with high moral tone of its foreign policy and Australia being strategically an anxious nation inhabited different universes. While underscoring the need for Australians to come to terms with a dynamic and resurgent India, Kama Maclean, Editor of *Journal of South Asian Studies*, was critical of the Australians' hypothesis that 'English is enough' to get by in India and their failure to appreciate India's glorious historical, political and social complexities (Maclean 2012).

India's Expectations and Impediments

Australia expects India's significant role in the emerging power balance in the region, but with an element of doubt over the latter's capacity. Australia's attachment to the mechanics of multi-lateralism and unilateral assumption of middle power role is something India loathes. Democratic India, Wesley (2012) laments, "will almost certainly disappoint such expectations.... India has a sense of status that is not matched by its capacity to shape events beyond South Asia; its influence will be rhetorical and potential rather than actual". Even as Australia's unilateral assumption of custodian of Southeast Asia's security concerns and its military engagement in East Timor had incurred the wrath of ASEAN, India expected Australia to accept India's greater role in ASEAN and cooperate with India.

For all its eloquent appreciation of India and its economic reforms, Australia abhorred bureaucratic hassles which remained a major hurdle in the flow of Australian investments into India and the growth of trade, and hence Australians showed nothing but a profound concern for the snail pace of India-Australia relations. The much expected closer Indo-Australian relationship has always faced confrontation between an impatient Australia and a non-committal India. Indians' belated decisions in the eleventh hour have always frustrated the impatience of Australians who have been used to the line of thinking up initiatives and executing them in short order (Wesley 2012).

But, there was perceptible change noticed in the Australia's *2003 White Paper* and the Foreign Minister Alexander Downer considered the emerging India vitally important to Australia's national interest. For all his China's inclination, Kevin Rudd belatedly included India along with the US, China, Japan and Indonesia. If his foreign minister Stephen Smith strongly supported India's bid to join APEC, so did his Indian counterpart Pranab Mukherjee favour the inclusion of Australia as an observer in SAARC. Considerable improvement in the political and security relationship over a decade no doubt reflects a convergence of strategic perspectives, and this would have been a prelude for the visiting Australian Prime Minister Kevin Rudd in 2009 to share with the audience in New Delhi that India and Australia were "natural partners" destined to become "strategic partners". His visit paved the way to take the relationship to the level of a strategic partnership. They are also "natural maritime partners" to attain an increased level of naval cooperation (Bishop 2011) as well as to become "active participants in the provision of maritime security through the entire Indo-Pacific littoral" (Sheridan 2013).

But Australia is neither a major power that is inherently important to India nor a small and useful "gateway" state, such as Singapore (Brewster 2014). Appreciably, having realized the importance of India to Australia's national prosperity and regional security, Howard had restored the post-Pokhran mired bilateral relations and renewed sense of purpose into the strategic relationship through the bold decision of selling Australian uranium to India for its civilian nuclear power needs, and Australia entering into a security arrangement—the Quadrilateral Initiative—with India, the United States and Japan. But what was diplomatically unpalatable was the reversal of decision to sell uranium to India by his successor Kevin Rudd. The ban on uranium sales, as per the joint research paper by the Lowy Institute (Australia), the Observer Research Foundation (India) and the Heritage Foundation (USA), was identified as a key impediment to a closer security relationship between Australia and India. Furthermore, unforgivable snub to India was Rudd's announcement of Australia's withdrawal from the Quadrilateral Initiative in the presence of the visiting Chinese Foreign Minister. Equally surprising was Rudd's unilateral decision to withdraw from the four-power naval exercises which had Australia, Japan, Indonesia and India participating, without any prior consultation with India or any others. A series of violent attacks on Indian students in Australia in 2009-10 triggered diplomatic discomfort to India. A research by Lowy Institute for International Policy observed that 61 per cent of the respondents viewed the attacks on Indian students as a reminiscent of the continuation of the White Australia policy (Sugden 2013). In fact, Australian disdain over nuclear testing, violence against the Indian students and uranium ban set the Indian minds against Australia.

Being distrustful of rising China, both these Indian Ocean littorals have a common focus convergence in their strategic concerns: India needs to build stronger diplomatic, military and commercial linkages with the countries to its southeast, while Australia realizes a new the strategic importance of the Indian Ocean. Though both are apprehensive of China's insatiable interests and hefty actions, both have differential expectations and preferences. For all his explicit inclination to China, Prime Minister Rudd expected India and Australia to provide a bridge to the Asia Pacific Community idea, and lobbied successfully to have India included in the G20 meeting held in Pittsburgh in September 2009 (Drysdale 2008). "Through shared membership of multilateral institutions including the G20 and the East Asia Summit", Bishop and Medcalf justifiably argued, "Australia and India (are) natural partners to work together to resolve the issues facing the region" (Bishop 2011; Medcalf 2013). Australia has of late pursued a skillful diplomacy as evident from the announcement of its Prime Minister Julia Gillard that India would be ranked in the same category of strategic importance for Australia as the United States, Japan, China, South Korea and Indonesia (Jain 2012). It was in 2011 that Gillard's Labour Party government tipped over the hoary ban on uranium sale to India for its use in peaceful nuclear programmes, besides the decision to conclude a civilian nuclear-energy cooperation agreement on the eve of Gillard's visit to India on 15-17 October 2012.

In pursuit of understanding the imbalance between these oft-demurred nations, a comprehensive survey of Indian public opinion on key foreign policy issues and critical challenges of governance was conducted in 2012 by the Lowy

Institute for International Policy and the Australia-India Institute with 1233 adults across the length and breadth of India representing different strata of society. Interestingly, the Indians ranked Australia in the top four nations, next to the US, Japan and Singapore, besides being appreciative of Australian values. Even as being critical of attacks on Indian students, a strong positive perception of Australia among Indians was discernible: Australia a safe country and a good place to live and to get work (50%) and a country with welcoming people (51-71%); Australia a good supplier of energy and other resources (60%), agricultural produce (57%); Australia well-disposed to India (50%); both countries having similar national security interests (59%) and qualified to be good security partners in the Indian Ocean (56%); and Australia known for excellence in science (61%) and in tertiary education, besides being considered as a preferred tourist destination. All said and done, according to the *Anholt-GfK Roper Nations Brands Index* (2010), Australia's reputation in India as a welcoming country fell dramatically from 5th place in 2008 to 49th in 2010 (Bishop 2011). Similarly, according to the study carried out by Australian Council for Educational Research, there was a decline of 71 per cent (2012) in Indian students in Australia from 120,000 (2009) as against a meagre of 20,512 in 2004. Of much significance is the rapidly growing Indian community of nearly 450,000 in Australia (India World Forum 2011).

For all the tall claims and rhetoric of commonalities, there is a lack of complementarity between the two economies (Gurry 1996: 75) manifesting in a weak trading relationship. Yet, there has been phenomenal growth in the bilateral trade from $3.3 billion in 2000 to over $20 billion in 2011. Australia is India's sixth largest trading partner and India is Australia's fifth largest. India has its rank among the Australia's export destinations improved from twelfth to fourth over a short span (2003-04 to 2009-10), and the Indian investment in Australia has witnessed impressive growth and vice versa (http:// www.dfat.gov.au/ fta/aifta/).

Modi's Visit Transcending India's Sluggish Attitude

The need of the hour is to develop mutual understanding and adaptability in pursuit of obliterating the troubled history due, in large part, to mismatched personalities and lack of commitment. The divergence was persisted on account of lack of reciprocity in the visits of heads of state or heads of government of India. Every Australian Prime Minister starting with Robert G Menzies—save Harold Holt, John McEwen, John Gorton, William McMahon and Paul Keating—visited India, while only four Indian Prime Ministers (Indira Gandhi, Morarji Desai, Rajiv Gandhi and Narendra Modi) did visit Australia, including the visits on the occasions of Commonwealth Heads of Government Meetings (CHOGM). Glaringly, none of the seven Indian Prime Ministers paid a state visit to the Down Under in the last 28 years, since Rajiv Gandhi's visit in October 1986, while seven Australian Prime Ministers paid official visits to India since the government of Bob Hawke in 1989. Never in the past had the Indian Prime Minister missed participating in CHOGM. Contrary to this tradition, the Indian Vice-President attended the last CHOGM in September 2011 at Perth, and this simply speaks of India's symbolic importance attached to Australia and India's apathy towards Australia as well. Remarkably, close on the heels of the visit of Australia Prime Minister Abbott in September 2014, Modi reciprocated the visit in just a couple of months; furthermore, he became the first ever Indian Prime Minister to address the Australian parliament. Unlike the Congress party's rhetorical attachment to nonalignment, the Modi Government is likely to have greater ideological freedom to develop closer security relationships with Australia and other middle powers in the Indian Ocean and Asia-Pacific regions. Accordingly, Modi in Canberra avowed that "Australia will not be at the periphery of our vision, but at the center of our thoughts", and thus, Modi's visit has paved the way for a new chapter in bilateral ties. Certainly, it was for the first time that Australian and Indian Prime Ministers underscored the growing depth of the Australia-India strategic partnership and building on converging interests, shared values and common democratic institutions as well as harnessing the potential of the economic relationship, especially in priority areas such as resources, education, skills, agriculture, infrastructure, investments, financial services and health (Gupta 2014). Modi's visit has set the tone for the future of the relationship through strengthening people-to-people links to enhance mutual understanding and thereby to improve the relationship to the level of strategic partnership. In pursuit of enhancing India's global diplomacy, Modi strongly believed that subnational governments have a pivotal role in the foreign affairs. Modi during his visit to Australia in November 2014 called upon the India Community to contribute to his vision of a 'new India' and for his 'Make in India' initiative (Jain and Maini 2014). India-Australia relations need to transcend the three 'Cs' and embark on the strategies for deepening trade, security, cultural, educational, and services ties that together provide considerable ballast to the bilateral relationship.

Indo-Australian Convergence of Security Interests and Partnership in Indo-Pacific

Canberra's bipartisan consensus on the Indo-Pacific puts emphasis on Australia's re-embracing the Indo-Pacific as the defining geographic expression of defence strategy. At the side of bipartisan compromise was the bureaucratic manoeuvre to make the Indo-Pacific continuity rather a good idea accomplished by Labour and Liberal strategies (Dobell 2015). "The greater reality of this Indo-Pacific logic of geography transcends domestic political considerations within Australia" (Gelber 2012: 19), and the dictates of strategic geography "makes the 'Indo-Pacific' concept an increasingly influential framework" (Scott 2013: 19). Given India's intention for a more active role in Indo-Pacific security in concert with the other major regional power of Australia, both India and Australia asserted themselves towards greater peace and security in the Indo-Pacific, as testified by India-Australia Security Framework (agreed in November 2014 by the Indian Prime Minister Modi and his Australian counterpart Abbott), as a natural corollary of India's Strategic Pivot to the Indo-Pacific entailing the active revival of the US-Japan-India-Australia Strategic 'Quadrilateral.' As well as some unique complementarities, Australia and India have the benefits of their strategic geography entailing substantial capabilities. That "Australia and India share a common view on the importance of the Indo-Pacific region," was the viewpoint of Australian Foreign Minister Julie Bishop during her visit to India on 12-13 April 2015 (DFAT 2015). It was later in early September 2015 that the Australian Minister for Defence Kevin Andrews linked the growth and deepening India and Australia relations to the shared history, coupled with our shared democratic values and a strong interest in a secure Indo-Pacific region (Andrews 2015). The significant complementarities between Australia and India, according to Ms Harinder Sidhu, Australian High Commissioner to India, are expected to become an Indo-Pacific model *per se*. India's strategic orientation towards the Indo-Pacific entails India's role as a key regional partner alongside Australia's traditional partners (Brewster 2016: 10). Indo-Pacific is viewed as an acknowledgement of India's future role, and it is also asserted that "it widens the understanding of the emerging power structure" (Dobell 2015). For all of India's obsession with the disgruntled neighbours in South Asia, Australia has been cognizant of its future closely linked with South Asia and the Indo-Pacific region that represents the confluence rather than centre of gravity of Australia's economic and strategic interests.

Modi typically stands up for FOIIP Policy

Even as firmly holding the Indian Ocean as the "key to India's future" testifying to the importance of the IOR for strengthening India's relationships and promoting collective security through forums, India's Prime Minister Modi placed Indo-Pacific "at the heart of India's engagement with the world" (Roy-Chaudhury 2018), the position of which is based on "India's geographical, historical and civilizational links with the region" (Roy-Chaudhury 2018A). The spirit and purpose of India's 'free, open, inclusive' Indo-Pacific (FOIIP) policy was quintessentially announced by Modi in his keynote address at the Shangri-La dialogue of the International Institute for Strategic Studies (IISS) in Singapore on 1 June 2018. While vouching for the importance of partnerships on the basis of shared values and interests, Modi was in affirmative of "India's vision to balance between major powers, trilateral and multilateral organizations to ensure its own growth in harmony" (Sarkar 2018). Given the fact that the "Acting East is no longer just an option but an imperative for Indian foreign policy" (Pant 2016 A), India is thus well on its way to pursuing a proactive strategy of an action-oriented and inclusive approach in the Indo-Pacific region. India and Australia membership in a gamut of multilateral bodies is not diplomatic tactic, and instead provides a critical platform for strategic economic cooperation between India, China, Japan, Southeast Asia and Australasia.

Concluding Remarks

Despite its two-millennium-long contacts with the Southeast Asian region abutting on the Australian continent, it is ironical that until and after the British colonization of Australia in the late 18th century, India was totally ignorant of the geography of the vast continent inhabited far and wide by the Aborigines who have a degree of ethno-linguistic semblance with some tribal communities in the peninsular India. The great distance between Australia and England, as Blainey interpreted in his "Tyranny of Distance" (1966), made Australia to become an economic satellite of India in the late eighteenth century, besides being a colony of England (Blainey 1966, 2001). Similarly, Alfred Deakin was fully convinced of the prospects of Australia-India bilateral relationship. But, the infirmities of White policy had further impeded people-to-people contacts, and as a consequence Australia and India were swayed by the exotic impressions that had only perpetuated their ignorance and the state of hibernation.

It is a great paradox that Australia and India which forged partnership during both the World Wars could not share a uniform vision during the peace time thereafter. There was apparent India's reluctance towards the Australian-proposed Five Power Defence Arrangements in the context of India's penchant for the Soviet Union through the Treaty of Friendship and Cooperation (1971) and contempt for Australia's alliance with the US. Australia found no enthusiasm in the expansion of relations with India which too regarded Australia as an ally of the US thereby considering it irrelevant to its interests. It was simply the attitude of 'indifference' that eventually manifested in 'drift and discord' attitude exemplifying the state of impercipience and nonchalance. Though 'commonalities and complementarities' have become the catchphrase for Canberra, in fact, there had been such efforts made long back by the Australian Prime Ministers (Deakin, Hughes, Chiefley and Whitlam) and the External Affairs Ministers (Evatt, Spender and Casey) who had envisioned the potential prospects of India-Australia cooperation and partnership. The climatic semblance was identified as early as 1879 during the interaction between Sir Henry Blandford (Director of Indian Meteorological Service) and Charles Todd (South Australian meteorologist), and so was the super-continent connection between India, Australia and Antarctica brought to light by Dubey (Director General of Geological Survey of India) in 1953. In the face of disengagement, all that 'extraordinary potential based on so many commonalities', the 'mantra' of shared experiences and 'English is enough' to get by in India would be of no consequence, and simply unproductive. These basic linkages have scarcely served to bring them closer, at the most to bring transient reconciliation of omissions and commissions.

India needs to remind itself of its indifference to Australia's proposal in 1968 for India's active role in the Southeast Asian affairs and its refusal to join the Australia's proposed FPDA in 1971 as well as its predicament of having remained as mute spectator of the 1998 financial crisis that worst-hit the ASEAN economies. India's 'betwixt and between' position on account of its implicit inclination to the Soviet Union almost shattered the well-spirited age-old contacts with Southeast Asia. It was simply India's longing for identity contrary to the past. Both these Commonwealth nations have a troubled history of relations; both are termed as being hypocritical in their interests and priorities with scant regard to the other. Both have bitterness of discontented objectives: India's Look East Policy is yet to build up significant economic linkages and power-projections in the Pacific, including its unfulfilled ambition of becoming a member of APEC, and Australia has been equally worried of its feeble grip over the affairs of Indian Ocean. Certainly, India has been unfortunately displaying a nonchalant attitude in matters of deriving benefit out of Australia's forthcoming fascination for India. India has been critical of Australia's inclination to China, but unable to reconcile to the need of adopting action-oriented approach. This speaks of "less about acts of commission than about acts of omission and avoidance of decision-making", laments the former Indian Foreign Secretary Shyam Saran who further points out, "there is a continuing reluctance to acknowledge that the post-Independence framework can no longer meet the domestic and external challenges that confront India today" (Saran 2012).

Despite their abiding interest in the maintenance of a stable strategic balance in the Indo-Pacific, Australia and India suffer from lack of symmetry in the modus operandi due to exigencies of geography and geo-strategy. If India is obsessed with the disgruntled neighbours in South Asia, Australia is relatively secure in its southern ocean. Further, it is highly uncertain of their alignment: India's position in the event of a confrontation of China with the US and its allies in the Pacific as much as Australia's ambivalence in the context of a Sino-Indian confrontation. Australia is equally worried of a predicament in the event of a confrontation between its economic partner (China) and strategic ally (the US). Further, as pointed out by Frederic Grare, Director of South Asia Program at the Washington-based Carnegie Endowment for International Peace, these two Indian Ocean littorals "want to prevent the emergence of a China-dominated regional order. (But) neither country views the other as a potential security provider in the face of China's rise; (as) India and Australia enjoy strong ties to Washington, they have few incentives to look for alternative partnerships" (Grare 2014). As a corollary, Australia is figured in the calculus of India's foreign policy priorities as a third-tier partner among a large group of nations of limited strategic significance to India. Implicitly, the observation of Bonnor that "neither country is central to the other's strategic planning, yet both are influential in regions about which the other wants a deeper understanding" (Bonnor 2001:17) is an attestation of "little understanding that each is a crucial element in the other's security" (Brewster 2014) testifying to old rhythm that their impercipience stemmed from mutual ignorance and negligence.

It is largely believed that the upsurge in the Indians' settlement would continue, and this trend would have its impact on the spread of social networks which in turn would facilitate the pursuit of strengthening India-Australia partnership. Furthermore, the spirit of bonhomie in their bilateral relationship depends more on the political will than on any other parameter for the integration of these two communities in the spirit of accommodating the interests and appreciating the attitudes of each other. Australia-India relations hold great promise: rapidly growing trade, major economic complementarities, shared democratic values, common security concerns such as terrorism, and potentially convergent attitudes on how to address uncertainties in their shared wider region, the most profound of which is China's rise. The deep complementarity between our two economies serves as a stimulant in shaping the future of the Australian and Indian partnership in Asia. India and Australia are on the cusp of a historic opportunity for sharing a new, much more important relationship in the future than they have shared in the past. Of much significance is the prowess of Narendra Modi, as evident from his SAAGAR and FOIIP policy pursuits testifying to the proven ability of India for enhancing economic cooperation and its institutional synergies for deepening defence and security cooperation in Asia. The much expected closer Indo-Australian relationship, which has for long faced confrontation between an impatient Australia and a non-committal India, has of late received the much needed impetus through proactive strategies conforming to the impressions he has created in his speech to the Australian Parliament in November 2014 and thus set the stage for a new chapter in bilateral ties.

REFERENCES

Andrews, Kevin (01 September 2015), "India is a key partner in Indo-Pacific region," *The Hindu*; http://www. thehindu.com/opinion/op-ed/india-is-a-key-partner-in-indopacific-region/article7600487.ece (Accessed on 09 January 2017).

Asia Link and University of Melbourne (16 July 2008), "High Commissioner's Address at Asia Link;" https://asialink. unimelb. edu.au/high-commissioners-address-at-asia-link (Accessed on 26 August 2009).

A R *(Asian Recorder)* (1968), 14(30), 22-28 July.

A R (1972), 18(10), 4-10 March.

AR (1973), 9(17), 16-22 July.

ASSCFADT (Australian Senate Standing Committee of Foreign Affairs, Defence and Trade) (1990), *Australia-India Relations: Trade and Security,* Canberra, Australia Government Publishing Service.

Australia-India Institute (n.d.), Submission to White Paper on *Australia in the Asian Century,* Australia-India Institute, Victoria, The University of Melbourne, *Australian Encyclopedia* (1958), Vol. 3: 156.

Bishop, Julie (2011), "Charting the future of Australia-India relations", *Australian Polity,* Vol. 2, No. 3. http:// australianpolity.com/australian-polity/charting-the-future-of-australia-india-relations (Accessed on 22 December 2012).

Blainey, Geoffrey (1966), *The Tyranny of Distance: How Distance Shaped Australia's History*, Melbourne, Sun Books.

Blainey, Geoffrey (2001), *The Tyranny of Distance: How Distance Shaped Australia's History*, Melbourne, Pan Macmillan, p. 413.

Bonnor, J (2001), *Australia–India Security Relations: Common Interests or Common Disinterests?* Working Paper No. 67, Canberra, Australian Defence Studies Centre.

Brewster, David (2014), "Australia-India Strategic Relations: The Odd Couple of the Indian Ocean?" *Future Directions International*, Dalkeith (Australia).

Brewster, David (10 August 2016), "The Indo-Pacific Century: New Concept, New Challenges," *Asia & the Pacific Policy Society Policy Forum.*

DFAT (Department of Foreign Affairs and Trade) (1996), *Australia-India New Horizons: Towards a Strengthened Partnership; http://www.dfat.gov.au/media/speeches foreign/ 1996/india_ci.html*

DFAT (13 April 2015), *The Indo-Pacific Oration: Australian Minister for Foreign Affairs, The Hon Julie Bishop MP*, Speech at Observer Research Foundation, New Delhi; https:// foreignminister.gov.au/speeches/Pages/2015/jb_sp_150413.aspx?w=tb1CaGpkPX%2FlS0K%

2Bg9ZKEg% 3D%3D (Accessed on 04 February 2016).

Dobell, Graeme (10 August 2015), "India and the Indo-Pacific," *Australian Strategic Policy Institute's The Strategist*; https://www.aspistrategist.org.au/india-and-the-indo-pacific-2/printni/21938/ (Accessed on 09 January 2017).

Drysdale, Peter (5 June 2008), "Where does Australia really want regional architecture to go?" *East Asia Forum*, http://www.eastasiaforum.org/2008/06/05/where-does-australia-really-want-regional-architecture-to-go/ (Accessed on 12 August 2013).

E A A U (East Asia Analytical Unit) (1994), *India's Economy at the Mid-night Hour: Australia's India Strategy*, Canberra, Department of Foreign Affairs and Trade.

Gelber, H., 2012, "Australia's Geo-Political Strategy and the Defence Budget," *Quadrant*, Vol. 56, No. 6, pp. 11–19.

Gordon, S (2007), *Widening Horizons: Australia's New Relationship with India*, Canberra, The Australian Strategic Policy Institute Ltd.

Grant, Bruce (28 October 2014), "He imagined a different Australia", *Indian Express,* http://indianexpress.com/article/opinion/columns/he-imagined-a-different-australia/

Grare, Frederic (2014), *The India-Australia Strategic Relationship: Defining Realistic Expectations*, Washington, Carnegie Endowment for International Peace.

Greenwood, Gardon and Harper, Norman (eds.) (1963), *Australia in World Affairs, 1950-1960* (Vol. 2), Melbourne.

Gupta, Sourabh (24 November 2014), "A new vision for Australia-India relations", *East Asia Forum*, http://www.eastasiaforum.org/2014/11/24/a-new-vision-for-australia-india-relations/ (Accessed on 26 November 2014).

Gurry, Meg (1993), "A Tale of Missed Opportunities: Australia's Relations with India since 1947," Marika Vicziany (ed.), *Australia-India Economic Relations: Past, Present and Future*, Nedlands, Indian Ocean Centre for Peace Studies, the University of Western Australia.

Gurry, Meg (1996), *India: Australia's Neglected Neighbour? 1947-1996*, Brisbane, Centre for the Study of Australia-Asia Relations, Griffith University, p. 105.

Hugo, Graeme (2004), "Recent Population Movements between India and Australia: Trends and Implications", in D. Gopal and Dennis Rumley (eds.), *India and Australia: Issues and Opportunities*, New Delhi, Author Press.

IDSA NR (IDSA News Review on Southeast Asia) (1991), 23 (10), October.

IFR (Indian & Foreign Review) (15 November 1972), 10 (3).

India World Forum (July 2011), "India Australia Relations and Strategic Partnership", *foreign relationsofindia.blogspot.in*, http://foreignrelationsofindia.blogspot.in/2011/07/india-australia-relations-and-strategic.html (Accessed 13 August 2013).

Jain, Purnendra (23 October 2012), "Australia plays catch up in India", *East Asia Forum*; http://www.eastasiaforum.org/2012/10/23/australia-plays-catch-up-in-india/ (Accessed on 26 July 2013).

Jain, Purnendra and Maini, Tridivesh Singh (8 December 2014), "Modi's new Diplomatic Instruments for a New India", *East Asia Forum*; http://www.eastasiaforum.org/2014/12/08/modis-new-diplomatic-instruments-for-a-new-india/ (Accessed on 13 December 2014).

Maclean, Kama (9 March 2012), "Australia–India relations and the Economy of Ideas", *East Asia Forum;* http://www.eastasiaforum.org/2012/03/09/australia-india-relations-and-the-economy-of-ideas/ (Accessed on 17 August 2013).

Mattoo, Amitabh (n.d.), "Foreword to AII's submission to the White Paper on Australia in the

Asian Century", *Australia-India Institute*, Victoria, The University of Melbourne.

Medcalf, Rory (25 January 2013), "Australia and India: Common Goals, Budding Partnership", *thediplomat.com*, http://thediplomat.com/flashpoints-blog/2013/01/25/ australia-and-india-common-goals-budding-partnership/ (Accessed on 17 August 2014).

Neale, R.G. (1968), "Australia's Changing Relations with India", Millar, J.D.B. (ed.), *India, Japan, and Australia: Partners in Asia?* Canberra, Australian National University.

Palfreeman, A. C. (1967), *The Administration of the White Australia Policy*, Melbourne, Melbourne University Press.

Pant, Harsha V. (6 August 2015), "India, Japan and Australia: Asia's new Geopolitics", *DNA Analysis*; http://www.dnaindia.com/analysis/column-asia-s-new-geopolitics-2111445 (Accessed on 02 May 2016).

Saran, Shyam (20 June 2012), "A Season of Missed Opportunities", *Business Standard*, https://www.business-standard.com/article/opinion/shyam-saran-a-season-of-missed-opportunities-112062000062_1.html (Accessed on 26 July 2013).

Saran, Shyam (15 August 2012), "India's next tryst with Destiny", *Business Standard*.

Sarkar, Mrittika (16 June 2018), "India's Foreign Policy for Indo-Pacific through the Shangri La Dialogue," *Oriental View*; https://orientalreview.org/2018/06/16/indias-foreign-policy-for-indo-pacific-through-the-shangri-la-dialogue/ (Accessed on 11 September 2018).

Scott, David, 2013, "Australia's embrace of the 'Indo-Pacific': new term, new region, and new strategy?" *International Relations of the Asia-Pacific*, pp. 1-24 (Accessed on 30 December 2103).

Sheridan, Greg (20 March 2013), "Australia and India 'could lead region'", *The Australian;* http://www.theaustralian. com.au/national-affairs/policy/australia-and-india-could-lead-region/story-fn59nm2j-1226601040340# (Consulted on 18 June 2013).

Sugden, Joanna (17 April 2013), "Australia's Reputation Still Poor in India", *India Realtime*; http://blogs.wsj.com/ indiarealtime/2013/04/17/australias-reputation-still-poor-in-india/ (Accessed on 26 August 2013).

The Hindu (30 September 1998).

Varghese, Peter (2012), "Australia-India Strategic Partnership in an Asian Century", *Observer Research Foundation (ORF) Discourse*, Vol. 5, Issue 16.

Wesley, Michael (February 2012), "The Elephant in the Room: Australia–India Relations", *themonthly.com.au*, No.75, http://www.themonthly.com.au/australia-india-relations-elephant-room-michael-wesley-4522 (Accessed on 13 August 2012).

Index

Act East Policy, 78, 111-13, 120, 143, 148-49, 162, 164, 169, 172, 175-76, 343, 358
Admiral Harris Jr., former U.S. Navy officer, 163
Afghan Jihad, 196
Afghan National Army (ANA), 4, 86
Afghan Taliban, 87
Afghanistan, 4, 7, 14, 88, 90, 94, 321, 323, 327
Africa's rise on global hydrocarbons map, 215
Air Defence Identification Zone (ADIZ), 79, 164, 259
Akram, Munir, 328
Alibaba, 113
Al-Qaeda, 3, 104, 183, 184, 192, 320
Al-Qaeda in Iraq (AQI), 185
Anholt-GfK Roper Nations Brands Index, 378
Anti-access, area denial (A2/AD), 164
Anti-Ship Ballistic Missile (ASBM), 262
Anti-Submarine Warfare (ASW), 165
Arab Spring, 187
Argentina, 287
ASEAN Defence Ministers Meeting (ADMM)-Plus, 272
ASEAN Regional Forum (ARF), 272, 313
ASEAN+5, 272
ASEAN-India Car Rally, 157
ASEAN-India Centre (AIC), 157
ASEAN-India Commemorative Summit, 157, 159
ASEAN-India Eminent Persons Lecture Series, 160
ASEAN-India Network of Think Tanks, 160
ASEAN-India Regional Diaspora Summit, 159
Asian Development Bank (ADB), 336
Asian Migration, 236
Asian Pacific Economic Cooperation, 307, 336
Asia-Pacific, 97-98, 100
Association of Indian Universities (AIU), 342
Association of Southeast Asian Nations (ASEAN), 77, 241, 242, 272, 298, 310, 313, 376
Australia, 236, 241, 311, 371, 375-76
    Lack of Knowledge of, 372
    White Paper on Asian Century, 374
Australia's
    Interests, 240
    Look West Strategy, 373
    Reaction to India's Nuclear Tests, 374
Australia-India Council, 373
Australia-India New Horizons Campaign, 373
Azhar, Maulana Masood, 90

Bahrain, 35, 36
Barack Obama, 302
Barack Obama's two-day visit to India, 55
Barrack Obama administration, 353
Bay of Bengal Initiative for Multi-Sectoral Technical and Economic Co-Operation (BIMSTEC), 16, 27, 76, 149, 151
Beijing Miteno Communication Technology, 113
Better Story, 157
Bharat Petroleum (BP), 219
Bhutan, 296, 362, 364, 366
    Anti-India Elements and Bhutan, 365
Bhutan, Geo-political Importance, 361
Bhutto, Benazir, 94, 322
Bilateral Economic Ties, 114
Blainey, Geoffrey, 370
Blue Economy Workshop, 160
Blue Water Navy (BWN), 263
Bolton, John, 328
Boris, Wilkie, 327
Brazil, Russia, India and China (BRIC), 284
Brewster, 239
BRICS, 107, 108, 143, 213, 244, 285, 303
Brig Arun Sahgal, 339
Brunei, 309
Business and Investment Meet and Expo, 160
Business Council Meeting, 160
ByteDance, 113

Caliphate, 194, 198
Central Asia, 324
Century of the Seas, 253
Chabahar, 8-9
Chang, Parris H., 338
Chaulia, Sreeram, 48
Chen, Bennet, 343
Chile, 287
China, 9, 18, 24, 28, 72-74, 76, 81, 91, 100, 104, 138, 149, 165, 207, 213-14, 218, 221, 228, 231, 236, 241-42, 254, 258, 262, 264, 266, 268, 301, 303-5, 309, 324, 327, 345, 383
China First Policy, 346
China National Petroleum Corporation (CNPC), 220
China Steel Corporation (CSC), 342, 345
China, Tibet Region of, 230
China's
    nine-dash line, 76
    Security interests in Nepal, 22
    Trade, 311
China's National Offshore Oil Corporation (CNOOC), 217

China-Bhutan Relation, 363
China-India Model, 330
China-Indian Tensions, 303
China-Pakistan Bilateral Relationship, 303
China-Russian
  Cooperation, 108
  Economic Ties, 109
China-Soviet-US strategic triangle, 314
China-US
  Trade, 307
  Ambivalence Powers, 306
Chinese Cooperation Port of Gwadar, 9
Chinese-Taiwanese Conflict, 334
Christian Liberal Democratic, 292
Chung-hua Institution of Economic Research (CIER), 341
Civil Nuclear Agreement, 53
Civil Nuclear Deal, 56
Clinton's visited India, 293
Cohen, Stephen P., 47
Cold War, 2, 5, 12, 47, 98, 288, 309, 335, 337, 352, 371
Commonwealth Heads of Government Meetings (CHOGM), 379
Communications Compatibility and Security Agreement (COMCASA), 144, 150
Comprehensive Economic Cooperation Agreement (CECA), 279
Comprehensive Economic Partnership Agreement (CEPA), 116
Confidence Building Measures (CBMs), 256
Confronted by Weaker Adversaries in Iraq and Syria, 192
Confucius, 73
Connect Central Asia, 204
Connectivity Summit, 160
Continental Engineering Corporation (CEC), 342
Cope India, 306
Council of Scientific and Industrial Research, 37
Cross border terror in India, 326
Crude Oil, 215

Dailyhunt, 113
Dalai Lama, 303
Deakin, Alfred, 370, 381
Defence Procurement Procedure (DPP), 168, 171
Demobilization, 131
Dharma-Dhamma Conference, 160
Diaspora Linkages, India's Foreign Policy, 67
Distributed Denial of Service (DDOS), 77
Djibouti, 80
Donald Trump administration, 354
Drawing Business Report (DBR), 145
Drug Trafficking and Terrorism, 5
Durand Line, 86
Durrani, Mahmud Ali, 92

East Asia Summit (EAS), 272, 313, 359
East China Sea, 259
East–West Silk Road Project, 10
Economic and Social Benefit of Diaspora, 66

Economic Relationship with Potential Adversaries, 147
Employment, 40
Energy Security, 212
Energy, 38
European trade, 82
Ex Malabar-16, 172

Fernandes, George, 339
Filling the Void in Afghanistan, 51
Film Festival, 160
FOIIP Policy, 380
Foreign Direct Investment (FDI), 52, 168, 284
Foreign Investment Promotion Board (FIPB), 171
Formed Police Units (FPUs), 126
Formosa, 334
Foundation for International Cooperation in Higher Education of Taiwan (FICHET), 342
France, 331
Free Syrian Army (FSA), 187
Freedom of Navigation Operations (FONOPS), 259
Freedom of Navigation, 83
Future Strategic Competitor, 311

G7, 315
G8, 313
G20, 298
  Political Rock Star, 151
GCC, 40, 64
Gandhi, Indira, visited US, 47
Gen Bajwa, 324
Gen Jehangir Karamat, 327
Gen Zia-ul-Haq, 3
Germany, 331
GGC, 68
Ghani, Ashraf, President of Afghanistan, 89, 92
  visited Islamabad, 91
Gillani, Yousuf Raza, Former Prime Minister of Pakistan, 93
Gillard, Julia, 298, 375
Global and Strategic Partnership, 173
Global Entrepreneurship Index (GEI), 336
Global SME Summit, 160
Global War on Terror (GWoT), 188
Gorbachev, Mikhail, 101
Gough Whitlam, 373
Grand Chessboard, 207
Great Game II, 207
Greater Emphasis on National Power, 145
Greater Nile Oil Project (GNOPC), 220
Gujral, Inder Kumar,
  visited Taiwan, 338
Gulf Africa Petroleum Corporation (GAPCO), 219
Gulf Crisis, 37
Gulf Remittances, 41
Gulf, 38, 42, 70

Hackathon and Startup Festival, 160
Haitian National Police (HNP), 135
Haqqani network, 51
Harkat-ul-Ansar, 88

Index

Harkat-ul-Mujahideen, 88
Hillary, Clinton, , 82
Hindustan Machine Tools, 244
Hindustan Petroleum (HP), 219
Hiramatsu, Kenji, 163
Howdy Modi-Trumph Show, 58
Humanitarian Assistance and Disaster Relief, 167
Husain, Khurram, 323

ICT Expo, 160
Identity Politics in the Middle East, 191
Imran Khan–led PTI government, 7
Imran Khan–led PTI, 2
India, 6, 10, 14, 18, 25, 29, 32, 35, 48, 63, 74-75, 78, 84, 127-28, 130, 136, 165, 214, 232, 240-41, 256, 268, 301, 308, 324, 331, 358-59, 382
    and its Neighbourhood, 296
    Electronics and Semiconductor Association, 344
    Today Festival, 373
    Tibetan Refugees in, 230
India's Crude Oil Imports from Africa, 219
India's Department of Science and Technology (DST), 339
India's
    Engagement with Afghanistan, 88
    Foreign Policy, 63
    Liberalization Policies, 364
    Look East Policy, 373
    Maritime Security Policy, 357
    Maritime Security, 356
    Policy Initiative, 68
    Recalibrating its Relation with Nepal, 24
    Relation with Nepal and Maldives, 150
    Soft Power, 156
India-ASEAN
    Friendship Park, 160
    Students Exchange Programmes, 157
India-Australia, 237, 248, 369
India-Bhutan Relations, 365
India-Chile
    Bilateral Trade between, 287
India-China
    Border Dispute, 231
    Competition or Cooperation, 302
    Militarization, 308
    Relations, 229
    Security Concerns, 232
India-China-US, 308, 312
India-Cuba Trade, 286
India-Japan
    Global Partnership between, 173
    Relations, 144, 162
    Strategic Relations, 175
    Strategic Ties, 169
India-Iran, 11
India-Japan-US
    Foreign Ministerial level (trilateral) meeting, 171
India-Korea Centre for Research and Innovation Cooperation (IKCRI), 117
India-LAC bilateral trade, 286
Indian Business, 284

Indian Contribution to Individual Police Officers, 136
Indian Contribution to UN Police, 127
Indian Council for Cultural Relations (ICCR), 157
Indian Council of Research on International Economic Relations (ICRIER), 341
Indian Diaspora, 64, 70, 292, 296, 299
Indian Federation of Indian Chambers of Commerce and Industry (FICCI), 341
Indian Maritime Doctrine, 356
Indian Navy, 167
Indian Ocean Littorals, 377
Indian Ocean Naval Symposium (IONS), 167, 242
Indian Ocean Region (IOR), 166
Indian Ocean Regional Association (IORA), 167, 259
Indian Ocean Zone of Peace, 373
Indian Ocean, 83
Indian Trade with Argentina, 287
Indian Workers in Gulf, 65
Indians in the Diaspora, 294
India-Russia Relations, 147
India–Singapore Relations
    Political and Defence, 271-73
India-Singapore, 270
India-Taipei Association (ITA), 338
India-Taiwan
    Bilateral Trade, 341
    Challenges, 344-46
    Relations, 348
    Ties, 340
India-US
    Bilateral Relations, 13
    Friendship on Fast Track, 304
Indigenously Designed Developed and Manufactured (IDDM), 171
Individual Police Officers (IPOs), 126
Indo-Australian Convergence of Security Interests, 379
Indo-Bhutan Treaty, 360
Indo-China Relations, 301
Indo-Pacific quadrilateral dialogue (Quad), 82
Indo-Pak Relation, Projecting a Lakshman Rekha, 146
Indo-US Relations Developed into a Global Strategic Partnership, 150
Indo-US Trade, 306
Influx of Refugees, 197
INS Arihant, 165
INS Chakra, 165
INS Vikramaditya, 165
INS Vikrant, 165
INS Viraat, 165
Intensifying Recruitment in Cyberspace, 192
International Court of Justice (ICJ), 267
International Economic Competition, 310
Iran, 3, 4, 10, 12, 208, 324, 328
Iran–India Relationships, 5
ISIS, Ideological Predilection, 186
Islamabad Policy Institute (IPI), 329
Islamic State in Iraq (ISI), 185
Islamic State in Iraq and al-Sham (ISIS), 184, 187, 190-91, 193-95, 198
    Causes of Rapid Rise of, 186

Islamic State Looming Threat, 87
Islamic State, 186
    Implications of Rise, 193

Jamaat al-Tawhid wal-Jihad (JTJ), 185
Japan, 311
Japan's 'Partnership for Quality Infrastructure', 176
Japan's Shin Maywa Industries, 168
Japan-India Maritime Exercise (JIMEX), 167
Jayaram, N., 291
Jinnah, 329
Joint Commission on Commerce and Trade, 313
Joint Working Group (JWG), 69

Kamtapuri Liberation Organization (KLO), 365
Karakoram Highway, 9
Kashmir, 325, 327
Kashyap, Ajay, 130
Kautilya's, 2, 7
    Arthashastra, 208
Kennedy, John F, 46
Kerry, John, 171
Khan, A.Q., 310
Khan, Imran, 93, 326
    visited Washington, 315, 323
Khurshid, Salman, Indian Foreign Minister, 277
    visited Tehran, 6
Kim Hyun Chong, 113
Kim Jong-un, 354
Kishida, Fumio, 171
Kissinger, Henry, 73
Korea International Trade Association (KITA), 114
Korea Trade Investment Promotion Agency (KOTRA), 116-17
Korean Manufacturing Investment Destinations, 116
Kovind, Ram Nath, President of India, 286
Kundu, Sanjay, 130
Kuomintang (KMT), 334
    Government, 340, 346
Kuwait Institute of Scientific Research (KISR), 37
Kuwait, 39
Kwon Oh Joon, 119
Kyrgyzstan, Manas Airbase of, 103

Labour and Liberal Strategies, 380
Lashkar-e-Taiba (LeT), 51, 88
Latin America, 286, 287
    Politics of, 283
Leonard, Mark, 64
Li Keqiang, 304
Liberalization, 286
Look East Policy, 32, 112, 148, 297, 337

Majlis Shura al-Mujahedin (MSM), 185
Make in India, 113-14, 120, 168, 170, 174, 176
MakeMyTrip, 113
Malabar Exercise, 172
Malaysia, 309
Maldives, 254, 297, 311
Maritime Silk Route (MSR), 254, 256-57, 261-62, 268

Marshall Plan, 74
Materialisation, Caliphate Dream, 189
Medcalf, 237, 238
Media.net, 113
Mekong-Ganga Co-operation, 149
Menzies, Robert G, 378
Mid-Air-Refueling Squadron (MARS), 208
Milan Vaishnav, 60
MILAN, 167
Military Assistance Programme (MAP), 47
Minimum Referral Wage (MRW), 70
Ministry of Defence's
    Acquisition, Technology & Logistics Agency, 171
Mirat-ul-Akhbar, 1
Mission-wise Contribution of India to UN Police, 129
Modi and Indo-US Relations, 49
Modi, Narendra, Prime Minister of India, 49-50. 53, 59, 75, 84, 90, 94, 112, 114, 117, 118, 120, 141, 143-44, 159, 164, 173, 203, 294-95, 297, 299, 302, 314
    Doctrine, 141, 152
    Government, 143, 324, 362, 364
        Policy toward Taiwan, 343
    Mission in United States, 52
    visited Nepal, 16, 25, 26
    visited Australia, 244
    visited Vietnam, 81, 298
    visited Transcending India's Sluggish Attitude, 378
    visited Japan, 173-74
    Multi-lateral Engagements, 151
    visited US, 52
Mohan, Raja, 13, 90
Moon Jae-In, South Korean President, 113
Murthy, Vivek, 294
Muscat, Sultan Qaboos University, 43
Music Festival, 160
Myanmar, 311

Narsimha Rao Government, 337
National Children's Science Congress, 160
National Defence University (NDU), 347
National Defense Programme Guidelines, 170
National Democratic Front of Bodos (NDFB), 365
National Missile Defense (NMD), 102
National Register of Citizens, 59
NATO, 87, 105, 253
    Bombing on Yugoslavia, 102
    Forces, 4, 86, 88, 95, 189, 320, 323, 324
Naval Communications "North West Cape", 100
NDA II, 136
    Modi's Foreign Policy, 48
Nehru, Pandit Jawaharlal, 1, 229
Neighbourhood First, 265
Nepal, 17, 18, 20, 24, 28
Nepal, Elections, 18
    Indo-China Concerns, 21
Nepal's Economy, 22
Nepal's New Leverage, 27
Net Security Provider, 166
New Development Bank (NDB), 108

New Great Game, 220
New Southern Policy, 120
New World Order in 21st Century, 102
Nigeria, 216, 218
Nigerian National Petroleum Corporation, 220
Non-Alignment to Re-alignment, 147
Non-combatant Evacuation Operations (NEO), 167
North East Skills Centre (NESC), 274
NRIs, Participation of, 148
Nuclear Proliferation, 310
Nye, Joseph S., 74, 154
    Bound to Lead, 154
    The Paradox of American Power, 154
    Soft Power, 154
    Power in Global Information Age, 154
    Future of Power, 154

Obama Doctrine (Pivot to Asia Policy), 167
Obama Visit, a Sign of Progress, 54
Oil & Gas Journal (OGJ), 217
Oil and National Gas Corporation (ONGC), 218
Oil and Natural Gas Corporation, 220
Oil India Limitied (OIL), 219
Oli, K.P., 18
    visited India, 28
One Belt, One Road (OBOR), 23, 74, 151, 242
One China Policy, 348, 363
One-China-solution, 309
ONGC-Videsh Limited (OVL), 218, 220
OP Jindal Global University, 342
Operation Enduring Freedom, 87, 88, 203, 320
Organisation of Islamic Countries (OIC), 328

Pakistan, 5, 92, 327, 330, 331
Pakistan's Inter-Services Intelligence Agency, 88
Pakistani Army, 94, 324, 326
Pak-occupied Kashmir (POK), 74
Pannikar, K.M., 356
Pant, Harsh V, 311
Pay.tm, 113
Peaceful solution of Korean Peninsula, 105
Peacekeeping CIVPOL (Civilian Police) Training Centre, 138
People's Liberation Army (PLA), 226-27, 229, 361
People's Liberation Army Navy (PLAN), 79, 164, 260, 264
People's Republic of China, 226, 230, 264, 334
Permanent Court of Arbitration (PCA), 76
Philippines, 309, 311
Police Contributing Countries (PCCs), 126
Polisia Nasional de Timor-Leste (PNTL), 134
Political Economy of ISIS Rise, 190
Post-Balakot Challenges, 327
post-Cold War, 353, 355
    International Scenario, 351
    New Economic Order, 373
Post-Conflict Reconstruction, 125
post-Pulwama, 324
Powell, Colin, 241
Prasad, Ravi Shankar, Law Minister, 68
Pravasi Bharatiya Divas, 67

President Obama, 55, 172
President Xi, 107
President Yeltsin, 101
Prof Amitabh Mattoo, 375
Public-Private Partnerships (PPP), 112
Pye, Lucian, 73

Qatar Fertiliser Company (QAFCO), 35
Qatar Petrochemical Company (QAPCO), 35
Qatar, 35, 39
QUAD 2.0, 83, 167
Qureshi, Shah Mehmood, Pakistani Foreign Minister, 325

Rajasthan State Industrial Development and Investment Corporation (RIICO), 119
Ramayana Festival, 160
Rao, PV Narasimha, 111
Recruitment, 132
Republic of China (ROC), 334
Republic of Korea (ROK), 114
Robb, Andrew, 245
Rouhani, Hassan,
    visited New Delhi, 14
Rudd, Kevin, 376
Russia, 97, 98, 100, 103, 207, 324
Russia–China, 101, 102, 106, 107
    Strategic Co-operation, 100

S. Jaishankar, Indian External Affairs Minister, 204
Safety of Migrant Workers, 197
SAR aircrafts, 175
Saran, Samir, 112
Saudi Arabia, 2, 39, 40, 328
Sawang, Gautam, 130
Sayeed, Hafiz, 326
Sea Lanes of Communication (SLOCs), 169, 222, 257, 263, 264, 266, 268, 311
Sea-based deterrence (SBD), 260
Search-and-Rescue (SAR), 174
Second Persian Gulf, 206
Security and Growth for All in the Region (SAGAR), 255, 268
Self-Defence Forces (SDF), 169
Shanghai Cooperation Organization (SCO), 104, 208, 313
Shangri-La, 75
Shared Culture and Shared Concerns, 283
Shared Values, Common Destiny, 159
Sharif, Nawaz, 322
Shi'ite-Sunni divide, 192
Shinzo Abe, 82, 144, 164, 168
    visited India, 173
Siddiqa, Aisha, 326
Silk Road Economic Belt (SREB), 166
Silk World Order, 107, 108
Singapore, 270, 311
Singh, Dr. Manmohan, the then Prime Minister of India, 67, 142
Sistan-Balochistan province, 8
Soft Power of 5Ts, 244

Soft Security and Dialogues, 241
South Asian Association for Regional Cooperation (SAARC), 149, 313
South China Sea, 76, 78, 79, 81, 99, 166, 259, 308, 309, 310
South Korea–India Bilateral Trade, 115
South Korean Small and Medium Enterprises, 114
South Korean Trade Promotion Agency, 119
Soviet-China Relations, 101
Special Strategic and Global Partnership, 173
Sri Lanka, 255, 296
Standing Police Capacity (SPC), 126
State Owned Enterprises (SOEs), 214
Stevens, Betram, 371
Strategic Economic Dialogue (SED), 313
Sushma Swaraj also visited Nepal, 25
Swaraj, Sushma, the then Union External Affairs Minister, 16, 25, 148, 171, 277, 280, 297, 328
Syrian jihad, 189

Taipei Computer Association, 344
Taipei Economic and Cultural Centre (TECC), 338
Taiwan, 309, 311, 336
    Go South Policy, 339
    Status, 334
Taiwan Education Program (TEP), 342
Taiwan External Trade Development Council (TAITRA), 341-42
Taiwan's Ministry of Economic Affairs (MOEA), 342
Taiwan's National Chengchi University (NCCU), 338
Taiwan-India Cooperation Council (TICC), 339
Taliban, 3, 94, 104, 320
    Rule in Afghanistan, 87
Tehrik-e-Taliban Pakistan, 4
Tellis, Ashley J, 49, 303
Tencent, 113
Terminal High Altitude Area Defense (THAAD), 113
Terror, 322, 327
Terrorists' Homecoming, 196
Textiles Event, 160
Thailand, 311
Theatre Missile Defense (TMD), 102-3
Tibet Status, 229
Tibet, 226, 232
Tibetan Struggle for Right to Self-determination, 227
Ties between the US and India, 54
Tony Tan Keng Yam, 280
Trade and commerce, 283
Trade Facilitation Agreement (TFA), 53
Training, 134
Transit Transport Agreement (TTA), 24
Trans-Pacific Partnership (TPP), 354
Triggering Causes, 187
Trump, Donald, 57, 150, 293, 323
Tyranny of Distance, 381

UN Charter, 98
UN General Assembly, 233
UN Peacekeeping Operations, 125-28, 130
UNCLOS, 79, 176, 259, 310
UNDPKO, 134-35

United Arab Emirates (UAE), 34, 39-40
    Indian Schools in, 42
United Daily News (UDN), 339
United Liberation Front of Assam (ULFA), 365
United Nations Assistance Mission in Afghanistan (UNAMA), 129
United Nations General Assembly (UNGA), 53
United Nations Interim Administration in Kosovo (UNMIK), 132
United Nations Mission in Bosnia-Herzegovina (UNMIBH), 132
United Nations Mission in
    Liberia, 130, 133
    Sierra Leone, 135
    South Sudan, 130, 135
    Timor-Leste, 134
    Côte d'Ivoire, 135
United Nations Organization Mission Democratic Republic of Congo (MONUC), 130
United Nations Police (UN Police), 125
United Nations Security Council, 104, 313, 335
United Nations Special Committee on Palestine (UNSCOP), 124, 127
United Nations Transitional Authority in Cambodia, 128
United Nations Truce Supervision Organization (UNTSO), 124, 127
United States (US), 7, 48, 51, 75, 80, 108, 165, 207, 236, 242, 266, 293, 295, 305, 308, 311, 327, 355
    AFRICOM, 80
    and NATO, 104
    Export-Import Bank, 56
    Overseas Private Investment Corporation, 56
    Pivot to Asia, 260
    Policy in Asia Pacific, 352, 354
    Trade and Development Agency, 56
US-Asia relations, 353
US-India, 46
    Perceptions, 47
    Political Action Committee, 293
    Partnership to Advance Clean Energy, 54
US-Japan-India-Australia,
    Strategic Quadrilateral, 380

Vajpayee, Atal Bihari, the then Prime Minister of India, 67, 141, 230, 294
Vasudhaiva Kutumbakam, 152
Vice Admiral Hiranandani, senior Indian Navy officer, 263
Vietnam, 309, 311
Visas, 52
Vladimir Putin, Russian President, 106-7

WANA, 34
West Asia, 4, 6, 9, 32-33, 43-44, 58, 64, 91, 166
World Bank's Doing Business index, 50
World Trade Organisation (WTO), 53, 305, 313, 336

Xi Jinping, 265, 307

Yu Shyikun, 339

Zardari, Asif Ali, Non-State Actors, 88
Zarif, Javad, visited New Delhi, 91, 207